North Carolina
JOURNEYS

A Journey Through
North America

Gibbs Smith, Publisher
Salt Lake City

NC STATE UNIVERSITY

This series is dedicated to Burt and Pauline Beers
for their dedication to history and social studies education,
but most importantly for their dedication to North Carolina's students.

Published by
Gibbs Smith, Publisher
P.O. Box 667
Layton, UT 84041
800-748-5439
www.NCJourneys.com

Cover Design: John Vehar, Jeremy C. Munns

Designed in the United States
Printed and bound in China
ISBN 978-1-4236-0228-6

13 12 11 10 09 08 07   10 9 8 7 6 5 4 3 2 1

Gibbs Smith, Publisher wishes to thank all the contributors
to the second and third editions of this series.

Gibbs Smith, Publisher

Julie Dumont Rabinowitz
Managing Editor

Christopher Harlos, Ph.D.
Editor

John Vehar
Lead Designer

**Michelle Brown, Alan Connell,
Robert Jones, Jeremy C. Munns**
Designers

Janis J. Hansen
Photo Editor

Lynn P. Roundtree, Wendy Knight
Photo Researchers

Content Specialists

Writers

Alvis Dunn, Ph.D.
Latin America
Guilford College

Stephen Middleton, Ph.D.
United States History
North Carolina State University

Linda Scher
Raleigh, North Carolina

Area Specialists

Joel Cline
Meteorology, National Weather Service
Raleigh, North Carolina

Charles R. Ewen, Ph.D.
Anthropology
East Carolina University

Clifford E. Griffin, Ph.D.
Latin America and the Caribbean
North Carolina State University

Steve Martinez
Chicano Studies
University of New Mexico

Douglas C. Wilms, Ph.D.
Geography
East Carolina University

Tom Parker
Consultant
Bard College

James A Wood, Ph.D.
Latin American History
NC A&T State University

Curriculum Specialists

Mary Vann Eslinger
Social Studies Consultant
Morehead City, North Carolina

Jacqueline Boykin
Social Studies Consultant
Williamston, North Carolina

Consulting Teachers

Gloria E. Arriagada
Wiley Elementary School
Raleigh, North Carolina

Judy Craig
Claremont, North Carolina

Pat Brooks Ellington
New Hanover County Public Schools

Rose H. Cooper
Carthage, North Carolina

Ann Hamzé
C. M. Eppes Middle School
Greenville, North Carolina

Wanda Dale Henries
Hardin Park Elementary School
Boone, North Carolina

Patsy Hill
High Point, North Carolina

Pamela S. Myrick
Greensboro, North Carolina

Rhonda V. O'Janpa
South Topsail Elementary School
Hampstead, North Carolina

Sharon S. Pearson
High Point, North Carolina

Linda Weeks Peterson
Raleigh, North Carolina

Constance Schwarz
Hampstead, North Carolina

Sue Trent
Charlotte, North Carolina

Laurie Walsh
Bend, Oregon

Cathleen T. Wilson
Bradley Creek Elementary School
Wilmington, North Carolina

Michele Lynn Woodson
Southern Middle School
Burlington, North Carolina

Susan D. Zárate
Wake County Public Schools
Raleigh, North Carolina

Cathie A. McIntyre
Durham Public Schools
Durham, North Carolina

NC State University

Humanities Extension/Publications

James W. Clark, Ph.D.
Director & Professor of English

Burton F. Beers, Ph.D.
Editor Emeritus
Humanities Publications & Professor
of History

Regina Higgins, Ph.D.
Editor
Humanities Publications

James Alchediak
Chief Videographer & Lecturer in
Communications

Pamela H. Ellis
Administrative Assistant

Lisa Morgan
Bookkeeper

Zachary H. Jackson
Editorial Assistant

Pallavi Talwar
Editorial Assistant

Frances Higgins
Editorial Assistant

Editorial Support

Bryan Smithey
Copy Editor
Warrenton, North Carolina

Contents

North America

Unit **4** Our Nation Today

316

v

Unit 5 Canada

434

Skill Lessons

Eyewitness to History

A Journey to...

Portraits

Carolina Connections

Go to the Source

Maps

Civil War Battles, 1861–1865

A Journey Across North America

Brendan Johnson, a fifth grader, lives in Wilmington, North Carolina. His dad, Jim, is a long-haul truck driver. Jim drives hundreds of miles to bring goods from one place to another. He owns his truck. It has beds for sleeping, a microwave, a TV, and even a small refrigerator in the cab. When Jim is on the road, he can live in the cab of his truck.

This past summer Brendan went with his dad on a long trip. This trip was special. Brendan got to see many different parts of North America. He told his grandparents in Goldsboro, North Carolina, that he would e-mail them each day about the places they visited. Here's what he wrote them about his trip.

Interstate 40 in North Carolina

The cab of Jim Johnson's truck

June 15, 8:00 A.M.

We're leaving now because we have to be in Laredo, Texas, on June 20. We'll deliver recycled paper and pick up a load of engine parts. Dad says that he usually makes the trip in about two days. But we're going to take five days so we can visit some places along the way.

We'll leave Wilmington on Interstate 40. We learned in school last year that you can drive on Interstate 40 all the way to California. Dad says that we're going to drive mainly on interstate highways. They were built to handle large trucks like ours. We can make better time on interstates, too. There are no stoplights, and the highways all connect with one another. We're getting on Interstate 95 in Benson. Then we'll drive south and west to Atlanta, Georgia.

2:30 P.M.

We stopped in Fayetteville to see the new Airborne and Special Operations Museum. My favorite part is the "ranger" who looks like he's parachuting into enemy territory. Cool!

Tonight we'll sleep in the truck in Atlanta. Tomorrow we're going to go to an Atlanta Braves baseball game. The stadium's on Hank Aaron Drive, a street named after the baseball player who hit more home runs than anybody for more than 30 years. I hope I get to see somebody hit a homer tomorrow. Or maybe I'll catch a foul ball!

Virginia

North Carolina

Fayetteville

South Carolina

Atlanta

Wilmington

Georgia

ATLANTIC OCEAN

Airborne and Special Operations Museum

June 16, 11:00 A.M.

Dad says Atlanta's the "crossroads of the South." That means a lot of roads connect here. He told me that the city used to be a railway center. Now it's a big center for highway traffic and airplanes.

We left I-95 in South Carolina and headed west on I-20 to the city. These numbers can be confusing. But Dad explained that the north-south interstates have odd numbers. The east-west ones have even numbers. So, you always know which way you are heading if you know your evens and odds.

This afternoon, we're going to the Atlanta Zoo. They have giant pandas, the only ones in the Southeast. Then we're off to Turner Field for the game!

The Atlanta Zoo

A Journey Across North America

Civil Rights Memorial in Montgomery, Alabama

June 17, 7:00 P.M.

I didn't catch a foul ball, but it was great to see the game. We slept in Atlanta. Then early this morning we headed west on I-20 to Birmingham, Alabama.

Dad told me that Alabama is where many of the first struggles for civil rights took place. He said that in Montgomery, the bus boycott made many people realize that African Americans were being treated unfairly. Martin Luther King, Jr., led the boycott there, and then became a national leader in the civil rights movement.

I saw the civil rights memorial in Montgomery. It's a round black table with the names of people who have died carved in it. Water flows over the table. Dad says the flowing water is to show that justice should flow as freely as the water does.

Next, we headed south on I-65. Suddenly the land is really flat! At Mobile we turned west, right along the coast on the Gulf of Mexico. Pascagoula was the first town we saw in Mississippi.

June 18, 6:00 P.M.

Driving along the coast in Mississippi and Louisiana, we saw a lot of the destruction from Hurricane Katrina. It was a huge storm in August 2005. Dad says that it will take years for the people to rebuild. He told me that it looks very different now from the way it was before the storm.

We visited the French Quarter of New Orleans. This part of the city was not terribly damaged by the floods from Katrina, unlike other areas. We ate dinner and had beignets (ben · YAYZ), fried dough sprinkled with powdered sugar, for dessert. Yum!

New Orleans is where the Mississippi River meets the ocean. Ships use the Mississippi like a road to the Midwest.

New Orleans after Hurricane Katrina

Oil well in Texas

June 19, 12:00 P.M.

We traveled through the flat "Cajun" country of southwest Louisiana. As we got closer to Houston on I-10, I saw oil wells. Texas has a lot of oil, and Dad says there's a lot of Texas, too!

We visited Mission Control at the Johnson Space Center. There were really cool exhibits, with astronaut's space suits and the rockets that took them to the moon. I asked Dad if he thought I could be an astronaut. He said if I keep reading a lot and study math, social studies, and science, I might really be one some day.

June 19, 7:00 P.M.

We're in San Antonio! Visited the Alamo, which stands right in the middle of downtown. In 1836, Texas volunteers fought the army of the Mexican general Santa Anna here. It's strange to imagine the city as it was then, just a very small town. Now San Antonio is big and modern. But Texans like to remember their past, too.

The Alamo (above) and the Paseo del Rio (right) in San Antonio, Texas

8:30 P.M.

Lots of streets here have Spanish names. There's a winding path along the river that's called the Paseo del Rio. This means the River Walk. You have to walk down steps to get to the path, since it's below street level. Strolling musicians play and sing in Spanish, too.

Tomorrow, we're heading southwest on I-35 to Laredo. We're going to meet Juan Cansinos. He's a truck driver from Mexico. He'll have the engine parts for us that we need to take north. We're going eat lunch together.

A woman working in a factory in Tijuana, Mexico

June 20, 10:00 A.M.

After we dropped off the recycled paper, we met Señor Cansinos. He's brought the engine parts we're hauling to Guelph, in Canada. The parts are from a factory in Monterrey, Mexico. Factories in Mexico do a lot of assembly work, putting together parts made in other countries. These parts have a long way to go. Guelph is about 1,650 miles from here, "as the crow flies," Dad says.

Señor Cansinos drives on the Pan-American Highway. It starts way up in Alaska. It runs south, all the way down the west coast of Canada, the United States, and Mexico, then through Central America, down the west coast of South America, and ends at the very tip of Argentina. Señor Cansinos mostly travels it within Mexico and a few miles into California on short runs. Someday, though, he'd like to travel the entire highway from end to end. Dad says that it would be fun for them to drive it together.

3:00 P.M.

We spent a long lunch with Señor Cansinos today, eating empanadas (a kind of turnover filled with chicken and vegetables). We talked about life on the road. Señor Cansinos said our visit was a treat because he's got a long haul ahead. So do we. Dad says we can't stop at many places until we deliver the load. We have to be in Guelph by June 24.

Oklahoma

● Little Rock

Arkansas

● Dallas

Mississippi

Louisiana

Texas

● Austin

● San Antonio

● Laredo

Gulf of Mexico

empanadas

June 21 10:30 P.M.

Now I know what Dad meant when he said there was a lot of Texas. This is our fourth day in the state, and we haven't even been all the way across!

We drove through two big cities today—Austin, which is the state's capital, and Dallas. Austin's state capitol is huge! Dad said it took 15,000 railroad cars to haul all the granite just to build the outside.

Dallas is a modern city, but we found some old-fashioned fun, too—a rodeo! We ate a plate of Texas barbecue (it was beef, not pork!) and took our seats in the grandstand. What a show! Everyone whooped and cheered when the rider stayed on a wildly bucking horse or roped a calf. Dad said rodeos started when cowboys competed to see who was best at the kind of work you'd do on a ranch. Now it's a big show as well as a competition.

Stayed up late. Now I'm tired.

The Texas state capitol in Austin (above)
and a rodeo in Dallas (right)

June 22

Been on the road a week. We have traveled more than 2,100 miles!

We're coming up on Little Rock, the capital of Arkansas. I've noticed that all the capitals we've driven through are right in the middle of their states. I looked at the United States map and that seems to be the way it is in a lot of states. Dad says it's because people want to feel that the capital is near everyone in the state, not just the people in one area. That's one reason why North Carolinians chose Raleigh as the capital.

Little Rock, Arkansas

The Mississippi at St. Louis, Missouri

June 23, 9:30 A.M.

We're going north on I-55, driving through Missouri. The Ozark Plateau is a real change. Lots more hills and even some mountains along the way.

When we came to St. Louis, I remembered what the Mississippi looked like in New Orleans. Here, the banks of the Mississippi are right in the city. I can see the river from the highway. It's much smaller and narrower here than in New Orleans.

Dad says that rivers—especially the Mississippi—were the first great highways. People and freight traveled all over the country by river and canals before railroads and highways made it easier to travel over the land.

2:00 P.M.

Driving north on I-55 through Illinois, I saw cornfields spread out on all sides for miles and miles. I wondered out loud who they thought was going to eat all the corn growing here. Dad smiled and told me that cattle will eat a lot of it.

While we were talking, I asked him about something that I was curious about. I had figured that as we drove north, it would get a little cooler. But Illinois is as hot as Arkansas, which is a lot farther south. How could that be?

Dad explained that because most of the Midwest is far from the water it has cold winters and hot summers. The summer in Illinois might just be as hot as some days in Arkansas or Louisiana, but the winters will be much colder.

Corn in Illinois

6:00 P.M.

Chicago is awesome! We went to the Shedd Aquarium. It's the largest indoor aquarium in the whole world. Saw dolphins, seals, and really tiny sea horses. We could even go down to a place where we could see whales and dolphins playing underwater!

Then we rode to the top of the Sears Tower. It's taller than the Empire State Building in New York City!

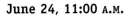

The Shedd Aquarium (left) in Chicago (above)

June 24, 11:00 A.M.

This morning we made our way east on I-94 across Michigan. It's the only mainland state that's in two parts. There's the Upper Peninsula and the Lower Peninsula. On the map, the Lower Peninsula looks like a big, left-hand mitten.

Detroit is a port city. It's the busiest one on the Great Lakes. It's also where they make a lot of cars and trucks. That's why Detroit is called "the Motor City" or "Motown," Dad says.

From the road I could see fruit farms with cherry trees and grapevines. But the fruit wasn't ready to pick yet.

The Ford assembly line (left) in Detroit (below)

4:30 P.M.

We crossed the Ambassador Bridge. When we reached the other side, we were in Canada! We had to stop at the border and show our passports because we were entering another country. Passports have your picture and prove you are a citizen of the United States. By the end of the afternoon, we had pulled into Guelph. Right now, they are unloading the engine parts from Mexico. Dad says he's pleased with the time we made. We're right on schedule!

June 25

In Guelph, we took on a load of rolled paper. Dad says that Canada's forests produce a lot of paper and paper products. We're taking this paper to Richmond, Virginia. It's another long haul, but we have a few days. We can even stop in Washington, D.C.

In the meantime, we visited Toronto, the provincial capital of Ontario (Canada has provinces instead of states). The CN Tower is even taller than the Sears Tower! But some people say it doesn't really count as a building, because it's really a television and radio antenna. You can go up inside it, though. And the floor of the observation deck is glass, so you can see right down to the bottom!

Dad says the Great Lakes are a road, too, connecting the Atlantic Ocean with cities in the middle of the continent.

Guelph City Hall in Guelph, Ontario

Niagara Falls

Canadian coins

10:30 A.M.

This morning we crossed back into the United States. I saw Niagara Falls up close! You can go on a boat to see the falls from the river. Everybody has to wear raincoats. The water crashes down so hard that a mist rises up. It's like it's raining all the time.

Toronto, Ontario and the CN Tower

Gettysburg, Pennsylvania

CANADA

Ontario

Guelph •
• Toronto
Niagara Falls •
New York

• Buffalo

Corning •

Scranton •

Pennsylvania

Ohio

Gettysburg •

Civil War Confederate canteen

3:30 P.M.

Drove through Buffalo. They have a Pierce Arrow museum, with really neat classic cars. Cars sure have changed in a hundred years!

It was 80°F in Buffalo this afternoon, but in the winter it's freezing cold. Way colder than North Carolina! It can snow up to 2 feet during one storm!

Corning, New York. We went to the Corning Museum of Glass. Really fun! I wore safety glasses and worked with a blow torch to make a glass bead! The glass looked like thick goo when it was hot. It was really hard to make the bead round.

On some of the mountains we passed, I saw what looked like green roads cut through the trees down the sides. I asked Dad about them, and he said they were ski slopes. They look strange in the summer!

June 26

Headed south into Pennsylvania. The name, Dad told me, means "Penn's woods." Mr. Penn sure had a lot of them! We drove along the edge of the Allegheny National Forest. "Penn's woods" were everywhere. Mountains and creeks, too.

Scranton, Pennsylvania, was our next stop. Years ago, Dad says, the coal fields here fueled many of the trains that ran coast to coast. We went down into an old coal mine. It was dark! Miners wear special lamps on their hats so they can see.

Next, we headed south on I-81. Then we drove east to Gettysburg, where the North and the South fought one of the bloodiest battles of the Civil War. The place is beautiful—green with rolling hills. It's hard to imagine it as a battlefield where many people died. This is also where Lincoln made his famous speech that we call the Gettysburg Address.

Pierce Arrow Museum, Buffalo, New York

The Washington Monument

June 27

Arrived in Washington, D.C., this morning. We are traveling all around the city by the Metro. It's the subway. I've never traveled by subway before, so I had to learn how to do it. First you buy your ticket. Then you put the ticket in a machine and walk through the gate. Make sure to take your ticket when the machine zips it back to you 'cause you need the ticket to leave the Metro. The trains roar through the tunnels!

The Washington Monument is the tallest building in Washington, D.C. We rode the elevator to the top (555 feet up) and could see the White House, the Capitol Building, the Lincoln Memorial, and the long Reflecting Pool.

The Metro (left) and the White House (below)

11:30 A.M.

The White House is where the president lives and works. I've seen it lots of times on TV. But it's fun to see it right in front of you!

The House of Representatives and the Senate meet in the Capitol Building, on the opposite end of Pennsylvania Avenue from the White House. Across from the Capitol is the Supreme Court Building, where the justices decide important cases. So all three branches of the federal government have their headquarters very close to one another.

Vietnam Veterans Memorial

9:30 P.M.

As the sun started to go down, we visited the Vietnam Veterans Memorial. Some people call it "the Wall." It's made of black granite in the shape of a long, wide V. On the wall are the names of all the Americans who died in Vietnam. There are more than 58,000 names. Dad and I found the name of his cousin. We put paper over it and rubbed black crayon over the letters.

I saw lots of flowers placed under names along the wall. People were standing in front of the wall and gently touching the names. Some were crying. When I looked at the names on the wall, I could see my own face reflected in the black granite.

Pennsylvania

Gettysburg •

Washington, D.C. ★

Maryland

Virginia

• Richmond

*ATLANTIC
OCEAN*

**North
Carolina**

*National Air
and Space
Museum*

• Wilmington

Richmond, Virginia

June 28

We began the day in National Geographic Society's Explorers Hall. There were photos from all over the world to see, and fun stuff about geography to do. My favorite part was the huge globe that looks like it's floating in the air. Cool!

Do you remember last summer, when we all went to Kitty Hawk, North Carolina? The place where the Wright brothers first flew their plane, the Wright Flyer? Today, we visited the National Air and Space Museum and saw the real Wright Flyer! Even though it flew for only about 12 seconds, it started a whole new way to travel— air travel. When we get home, Dad and I are going to make our own model of the Flyer.

11:30 A.M.

Now we're headed south on I-95. We're almost back to the highway we started out on. In Richmond, Virginia, we'll deliver the rolled paper we got in Canada.

Richmond is the capital of Virginia. It was the capital of the Confederate States in the Civil War. We're going to see the Museum of the Confederacy.

6:00 P.M.

We delivered the rolled paper and toured Richmond. We saw many Confederate memorials. Richmond has a great art museum. We saw Roman statues and some awesome African masks!

Now we're on our way home. We'll be there late tonight. I'm looking forward to sleeping in my own bed again, but it's been great being with Dad on the road.

Dad says that the more you travel, the more you want to learn about the places you visit and the things you see.

He said I was a born traveler. Maybe I am!

*Reading Social Studies Materials
and Increasing Social Studies Vocabulary*

Being a Historian

What Is History?

Have you ever read a story about something that happened long ago or far away? When you read this book, you are learning about what happened a long time ago or how people live in other places. We are also learning about where we live—our country, the United States of America, and our continent, North America.

When we read stories about what happened a long time ago, we are learning about the past. The past is everything that has happened up until this very moment. *History* is the story of the past. It is the story of what people thought, how they lived, and what choices they made.

What Makes History Happen? History did not have to turn out one way. Things happened because people made choices. They chose how to solve problems and how to treat each other. We study history to learn why people made certain choices.

History is not always peaceful. Sometimes people worked well together. Sometimes they fought or did terrible things to each other. We can look back and see what poor choices people made. We can learn from those mistakes. We can also learn from the good decisions people made.

We can see how our lives are different from the lives of people in the past. We can also learn how we are the same. When we study history, we begin to learn who we are.

Think Like a Historian

Historians are people who study history. They help us understand why things happened the way they did. Historians are detectives of history. They ask questions and look for *evidence,* or proof, of what happened long ago.

When we study history we can ask the same questions historians do:

- What happened?
- When did it happen?
- Who took part in it?

- Why did it happen?
- Where did it happen?
- How did it change things?

Let's learn about some of the types of evidence we can use to learn about the past.

Primary and Secondary Sources

There are two types of evidence historians can use to learn about the past. These are primary sources and secondary sources.

Primary Sources Sources made by people who were there at the time are called *primary sources.* Let's say your great-grandfather kept a diary during World War II when he was in the navy. He wrote in it every day. His diary might tell us what it was like to be on a ship at sea. It would be a primary source. There are many types of primary sources.

Artifacts are things that have been made or used by people in the past, like an arrowhead. Artifacts tell us what materials people had. We might also learn about how they used the item. This tells us something about their lives.

Documents and photographs are also primary sources. Documents are paper records like letters, birth certificates, a newspaper story, or even a map. Documents can tell us what someone saw or did in the past. Photos and pictures drawn at the time show us what people and places looked like.

Historic sites can be primary sources because they are places where history happened. Another primary source is an *oral history.* Oral history is someone's personal history told aloud. When you listen to someone tell you a story about his or her life, that is an oral history.

When Brendan visited the Alamo, he visited a historic site. He learned what life used to be like there.

Secondary Sources You can probably guess what a secondary source is. *Secondary* *sources* are things written, said, or made by someone who was not there at the time. For example, a book written today about the Revolutionary War is a secondary source. It is a second-hand account of the events that took place. Books are just one type of secondary source.

Movies or TV shows about history can also be secondary sources. A painting by a person who was not at the event is a secondary source, too.

We can learn a lot from secondary sources. They add to stories of the past. Sometimes they use information that was discovered long after the event happened.

Primary or Secondary Sources?

On a separate piece of paper, number from one to five. Put a "P" if the item is a primary source. Put an "S" if it is a secondary source.

1. _____ A letter written by our first president
2. _____ A modern copy of an old rifle
3. _____ A rock painting made 6,000 years ago
4. _____ A photograph taken during a battle
5. _____ A movie made today about the first airplane flight

Is this nineteenth century iron a primary or secondary source?

skill

*Reading Social Studies Materials
and Increasing Social Studies Vocabulary*

Introducing Geography's Five Themes

When we read stories about places close to home or far away, we are studying geography. What is geography?

Geography means "earth description." A person who studies the earth, the people who live on the earth, and how people use and change the earth is a **geographer**.

We use geography when we explore a new or faraway place, when we use a map or a globe, or when we talk about the weather. Geography helps us move about in the world, value the earth and its resources, and understand people from other places.

Brendan and his dad learned a lot about the places they visited on their trip. They learned a lot about the geography of North America, too. Brendan's e-mails to his grandparents organized the information they learned so we could learn, too.

We can also organize this information using the Five Themes of Geography. The five themes are **Location, Place, Human-Environmental Interaction, Movement,** and **Region.**

Location answers the question "Where is this place?" What is the location of New Orleans, one of the cities Brendan visited? We will learn how to describe location in two different ways in Chapter 2.

Place answers the question "What is this place like?" What, for example, is the climate of Illinois (one of the states Brendan visited)? Knowing about climate or elevation helps us describe the physical characteristics of places. Brendan learned about the human characteristics of places by visiting a rodeo in Texas and the civil rights monument in Alabama.

Human-Environmental Interaction asks two questions: "How have people's lives been shaped by the place?" and "How has the place been changed by humans?" In Atlanta, for example, how have people changed the environment by building ballparks and highways? How does the environment there affect the ways in which people live?

Movement asks the questions "How do people, goods, and ideas move from one place to another?" and "How has the movement of people, goods, and ideas affected a place?" We might ask, "How has the Mississippi River moved people, goods, and ideas? How has this movement affected our country?"

Region asks the question "How is this place similar to, and different from, other places?" How is the Southeast similar to and different from the Midwest?

You will use these Five Themes as you study North America. Enjoy your trip!

Unit 1

North America is amazing. The plains of Canada, the cities of the United States, the mountains of Mexico, and the jungles and islands of Central America and the Caribbean are all part of it.

People from everywhere on earth have come to live in North America, including Native Americans, Europeans, Africans, and Asians.

Geography helps us make sense of North America. You will study location, place, human-environmental interaction, movement, regions, history, cultures, governments, and economies. This book is about where you live.

North America from space

North America as Home Place

19

Where in the World?

Have you ever been lost? Did you ever find a great picnic spot in the woods and then have trouble finding it again? Today, technology can help us find our way. It can help us when we are lost. It can help us find our picnic spot.

This technology, called Global Positioning Systems (GPS), was invented by the United States armed forces about 25 years ago. It was created to help pilots, soldiers, and sailors in their vehicles, planes, and ships find their exact location anywhere in the world. Today, people everywhere on earth use GPS to track where they are.

We use it in airplanes, boats, and cars. Many people who hike, fish, hunt, or bike use it, too. Meteorologists use it to forecast the weather. It is important to know your location.

This satellite sends signals to the GPS receiver.

This skier in Vail, Colorado, has his GPS receiver on his shoulder.

Chapter Preview

LESSON 1
Finding North America Using Relative Location
Relative location helps us know what North America is near.

LESSON 2
Finding North America Using Absolute Location
Absolute location uses an imaginary grid. It helps us find North America.

Jerry
03-Dec-98   Total Vertical Feet 17,506, Total Miles 34.3
Peak Speed 124.8 mph, Elapsed Time 1.72 hrs

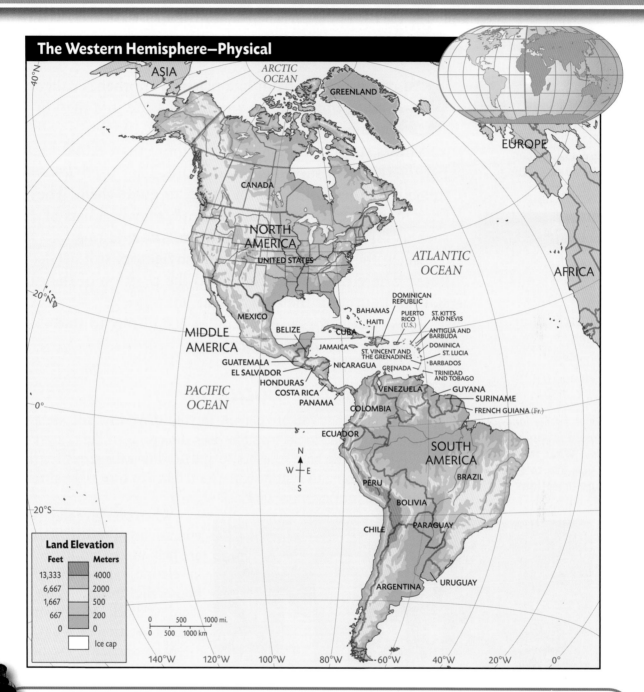

The Western Hemisphere—Physical

ASIA
ARCTIC OCEAN
GREENLAND
EUROPE
CANADA
NORTH AMERICA
UNITED STATES
ATLANTIC OCEAN
AFRICA
MEXICO
MIDDLE AMERICA
BELIZE
BAHAMAS
DOMINICAN REPUBLIC
HAITI
CUBA
PUERTO RICO (U.S.)
ST. KITTS AND NEVIS
ANTIGUA AND BARBUDA
JAMAICA
ST. VINCENT AND THE GRENADINES
DOMINICA
ST. LUCIA
BARBADOS
GUATEMALA
EL SALVADOR
HONDURAS
NICARAGUA
GRENADA
TRINIDAD AND TOBAGO
COSTA RICA
PANAMA
VENEZUELA
GUYANA
SURINAME
FRENCH GUIANA (Fr.)
PACIFIC OCEAN
COLOMBIA
ECUADOR
SOUTH AMERICA
BRAZIL
PERU
BOLIVIA
PARAGUAY
CHILE
ARGENTINA
URUGUAY

40°N
20°N
0°
20°S

140°W 120°W 100°W 80°W 60°W 40°W 20°W 0°

N
W — E
S

Land Elevation

Feet	Meters
13,333	4000
6,667	2000
1,667	500
667	200
0	0
Ice cap	

0   500   1000 mi.
0   500   1000 km

Navigating with Lighthouses

Sailors have used the lighthouses along North Carolina's coast to guide their way for more than 200 years.

The waters off the Outer Banks are nicknamed "the Graveyard of the Atlantic." Hundreds of shipwrecks have happened there. To help ships navigate, the United States government supported the building of two lighthouses in 1794.

It's not just the shining light that helps sailors know where they are. The time between the flashes of the light lets a sailor know which light he or she is near. So does the color of the light. Each Outer Banks lighthouse is painted in a unique style. They are easier to tell apart during the day. This helps sailors navigate, too.

CAROLINA CONNECTION

Getting safely from one place to another is called *navigation.* When you find a store in a mall or walk home from school, you are navigating.

Sailors started using navigation more than 5,000 years ago. Early navigators stayed close to shore. They used *landmarks,* things that they could see on shore, to guide them. They did not have maps like we do today. Instead, they had lists of directions such as "north," "south," "between," and "along."

When they could not see land, navigators still needed to know where they were. They used the position of the sun or the stars to figure out their own position.

These navigators used a tool of geography to find their way. We call this tool *relative location.*

Using Relative Location

Imagine that you are playing in your driveway. You see a girl riding her bike. She looks lost. She asks directions to the nearest store. You tell her to ride past your house and go down the street for three more blocks. She'll come to a stop sign. You tell her to turn right at the stop sign and ride for one more block.

Sometimes simple land-marks make it easy to find your way. **What landmarks would you use to give someone directions to your school?**

When you give these directions, you are using relative location. You are helping the girl locate the store in relation to other things—your house, the street, the stop sign, and the next block. Most people use this kind of location each day.

We use relative location when we describe a place in relation to other places. When we say "Yanceyville is located in Caswell County, south of the Virginia state line," we are using relative location. This is like saying that "Middle America is between the United States and South America."

Finding North America

We all know we live on the earth. But just where on the earth is North America? We live on the continent of North America. *Continents* are huge land areas with oceans or seas on many sides. There are seven continents: North America, South America, Africa, Australia, Antarctica, and Europe and Asia. You can see them on the map below.

Most continents are divided into *countries.* A country is a land area under the control of one government. Look at the map on page 21. Our country is the United States of America. The country north of us is Canada. The country south of us is Mexico.

Our country is divided into states. North Carolina is one of the 50 states in the United States. States are divided into counties. Within each county there are towns and cities.

North America's Relative Location

Now, using the tool of relative location, let's locate North America. There are two continents named America. North America is north of South America.

The top of North America borders the Arctic Ocean near the North Pole. It runs south and meets South America at a narrow piece of land called an *isthmus.* The Atlantic Ocean is on the East Coast of North America. The Pacific Ocean is on the West Coast.

WORDS THAT SHOW RELATIVE LOCATION

north	along	between	next to
south	around	close	on
east	away	far	over
west	before	in	past
right	behind	in front of	through
left	beside	near	under

Customs

Orienteering is an activity that can be enjoyed as a walk in the woods or as a competitive sport. Orienteers use a very detailed map and a compass to find points in the landscape. They follow courses that have been laid out for the game. Teams must locate a number of specific sites, marked by flags, before they reach the finish line.

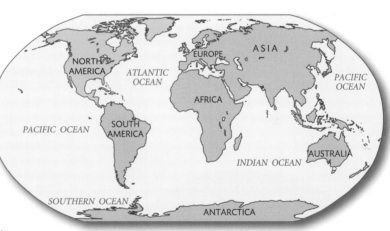

Use relative location to describe the location of North America in relation to the other continents.

LESSON ① REVIEW

Fact Follow-Up
1. What is a landmark?
2. What is a continent?
3. What is a country?
4. How would you use relative location to tell a classmate where to find North America on a map?

Talk About It
1. Think of how you would tell a classmate to reach the school playground from your classroom. How far would you tell your classmate to walk? How many turns would he or she take?
2. Now think of how you would use relative location to tell a classmate where to live.

What do we do if relative location cannot help us? Imagine that you are one of the early navigators. You are on a large ship in the middle of the ocean. You must figure out where you are and how long it will take you to reach land. Those early navigators relied on landmarks and the sun and stars to guide them.

Absolute Location

Today, sailors, airplane pilots, and many others use something else to tell them exactly where they are. They use an imaginary grid system called latitude and longitude. When we use latitude and longitude, we are establishing the *absolute location* of a place.

GPS systems use computers, receivers, and satellites to tell you your absolute location using this imaginary grid. In space, 24 satellites circle the earth all day and night. They send signals to the computer in the GPS receivers. The receiver tells the person his or her exact location on the earth's surface using latitude and longitude.

Parallels of Latitude

Lines of *latitude* are imaginary lines. They are circles that go east to west around the globe. You can see them on this map.

The Equator

The *Equator* is the longest line of latitude. It rings the earth at its middle. The Equator is given the latitude measurement of 0°. The symbol "°" means *degree.* A degree is the unit we use to measure the latitude and longitude.

All the other lines of latitude are called *parallels.* All points on the same line are the same distance from the Equator. The parallels tell us the distance from the Equator. They are measured in degrees, too. Each degree is equal to about 70 miles (113 km).

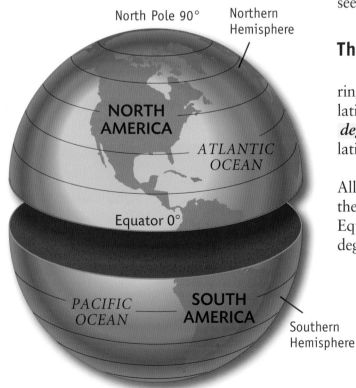

North Pole 90°
Northern Hemisphere
NORTH AMERICA
ATLANTIC OCEAN
Equator 0°
PACIFIC OCEAN
SOUTH AMERICA
Southern Hemisphere
South Pole 90°

The world can be split in half along imaginary lines to create the hemispheres. **What line separates the Northern and the Southern Hemispheres?**

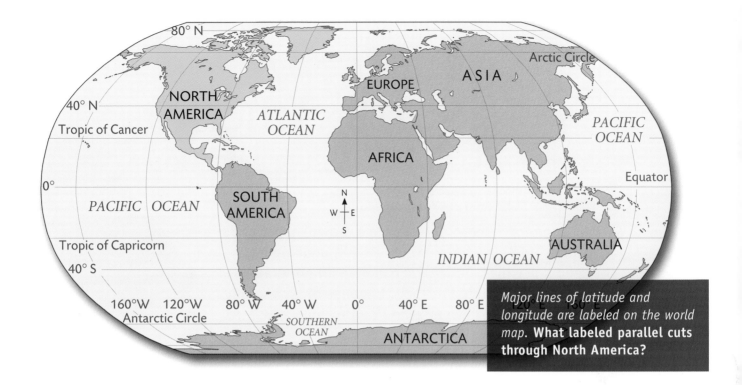

Major lines of latitude and longitude are labeled on the world map. **What labeled parallel cuts through North America?**

Hemispheres

The Equator divides the earth in half. We call the halves of the earth hemispheres. The half of the earth from the Equator to the North Pole is the *Northern Hemisphere.*

The half of the earth from the Equator to the South Pole is the *Southern Hemisphere.* There are 90 degrees of latitude between the Equator and the North Pole and 90 degrees between the Equator and the South Pole.

Using Latitude

Remember that the Equator is 0°. This means that the farther away, either north or south, you go from the Equator, the higher the number of degrees the latitude will be. So the parallels running through North Carolina have higher degrees than those in South Carolina. South Carolina is closer to the Equator. So parallels there have lower degrees than those running through North Carolina.

Panama City, Panama, is at 10°N. The "N" means north of the Equator and in the Northern Hemisphere. The low number means that Panama City is closer to the Equator. Locations in the Southern hemisphere use an "S".

This farmer is using a GPS device to map out where he will pant seeds. **Why might a farmer want to know the absolute location of his crops?**

EYEWITNESS TO HISTORY

Mapping
North America
Using Absolute Location

Cartographers —mapmakers—have drawn maps for as long as people have been exploring. Mapmaking has changed since then. Today, we can measure degrees of latitude and longitude precisely. Because of technology, cartographers also have new and better tools to use. Today's maps are very accurate.

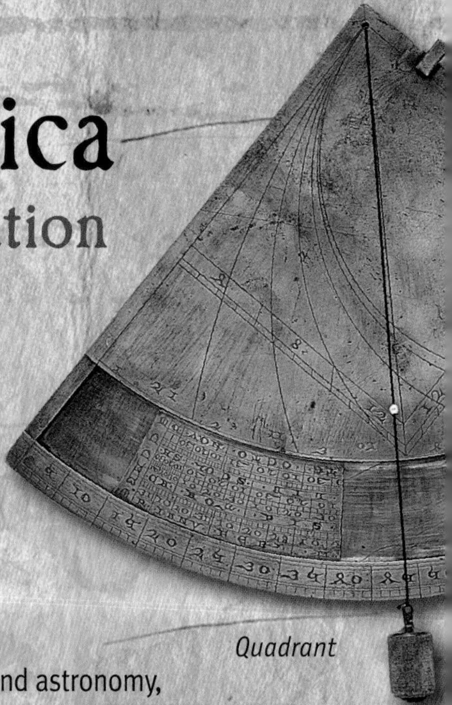

Quadrant

Explorers used mathematics and astronomy, the study of the position of the stars and planets, to draw maps. Special tools called the astrolabe, quadrant, and sextant measured the height of the sun and stars in the sky. Explorers used these measurements to figure distance. Early maps had only latitude. Longitude was added to maps about 400 years ago.

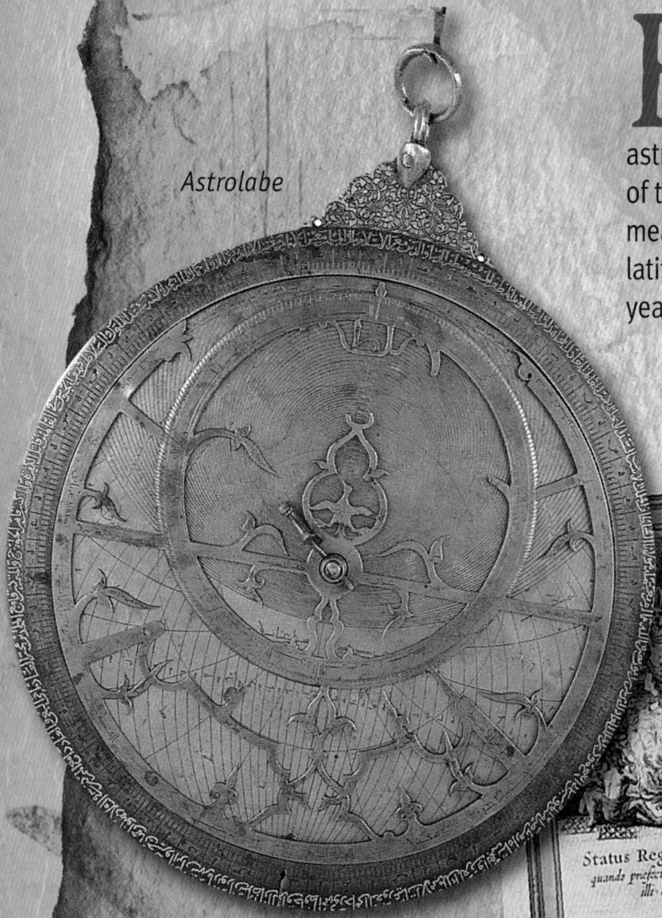

Astrolabe

1636 map of Virginia

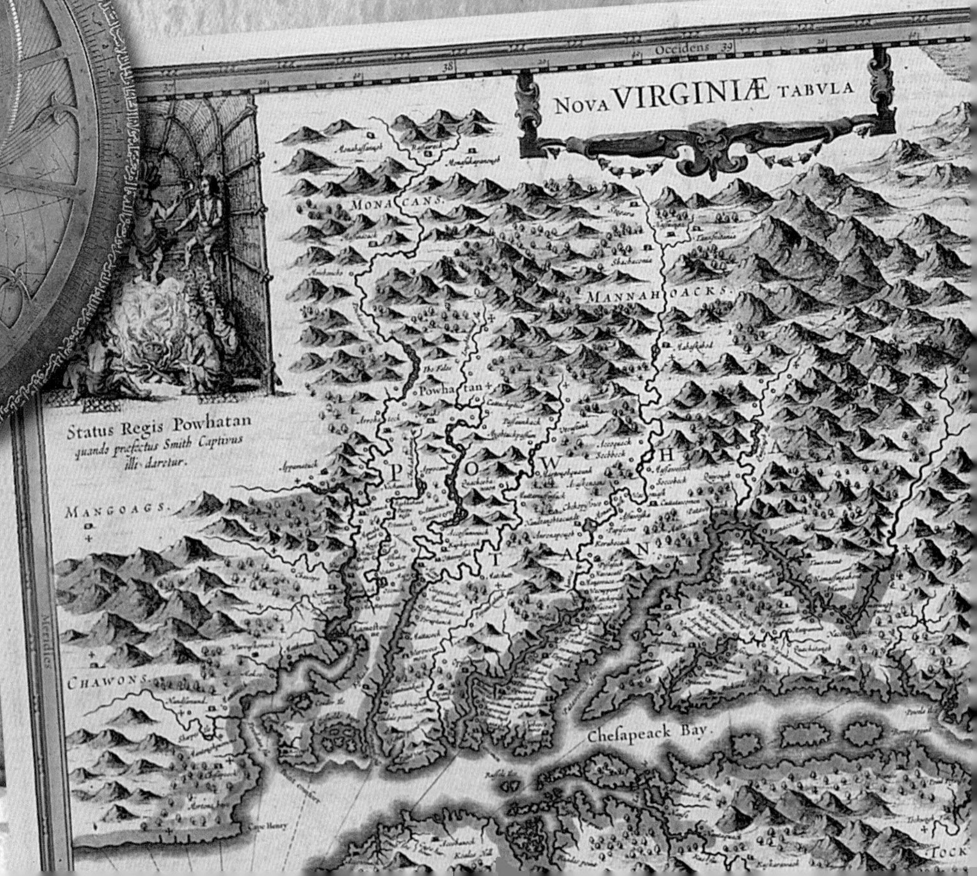
Occidens
Nova VIRGINIÆ TABVLA
MONACANS
MANNAHOACKS
Powhatan
Status Regis Powhatan quando præfectus Smith Captivus illi daretur.
MANGOAGS.
CHAWONS
Chesapeack Bay

Royal Greenwich Observatory

In 1884, mapmakers around the world agreed to make the meridian of the Royal Greenwich Observatory in Greenwich, England, the prime meridian. Before this, each mapmaker had placed the 0° line of longitude in his own country. In 1913, the International Map of the World project set standards for maps all over the world. For example, roads would be red on all maps.

Cartographer at work

Infrared map of the United States

In July 1986, the United States, Canada, and Mexico cooperated in the National Geodetic Survey. New measurements of latitude and longitude were made. These were so precise that the absolute location of some places in North America moved as much as 330 feet (99 meters). There were changes of more than 660 feet (198 m) in Alaska, Puerto Rico, and the Virgin Islands. But, most significantly, Hawaii's coordinates changed about 1,300 feet (390 m). Satellite photography and other technology continues to improve mapmaking.

Amerigo Vespucci
1451–1512

Amerigo Vespucci (ah·MAY·rih·go VES·poo·chi) was born in Florence, Italy. He was a trader, explorer, and mapmaker. Vespucci sailed on two trips to explore the coasts of North and South America. On his second trip, he discovered that the land of South America was much, much larger than people in Europe thought it was. Many Europeans thought that the land was the continent of Asia. But Vespucci decided that this land was not Asia. Instead, he believed that it was part of a new continent.

A few years after his trip, a new world map was drawn. It showed the new continents. The mapmaker named these new continents "America" after Vespucci's first name, Amerigo.

Because of his special skills and his discovery, the government of Spain created a new job just for Vespucci. They called him the pilot major. This meant that he was the chief of navigation. His job was to train new navigators to sail the ocean.

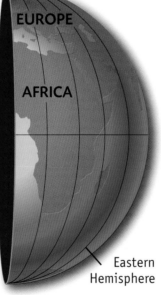

Meridians of Longitude

Knowing how far a place is from the Equator gives us only half the information we need to find its absolute location. Lines of longitude give us the other information.

Imagine you are peeling an orange. Once you have all of the peel off, you can see lines that run from the center of the top of the orange to the center of the bottom. These lines divide the orange into sections.

Lines of ***longitude*** look almost the same as the lines on your orange. These lines are called ***meridians.*** They are measured in degrees, just like lines of latitude. But they are not drawn parallel to the Equator. Instead, each meridian line runs north to south from the North Pole to the South Pole.

The Prime Meridian

The ***prime meridian*** is the starting point for measuring longitude. It is assigned the longitude of 0° and is located at Greenwich, England.

Like the Equator, the prime meridian also splits the earth in half. Look at the drawing of the earth. If you cut the earth in half along the prime meridian, you would have two hemispheres.

The half, or hemisphere, west of the prime meridian is the **Western Hemisphere.** High Point, North Carolina, is located in the Western Hemisphere. Its longitude is 80°W. The "W" means west. It means that High Point is west of the prime meridian.

The hemisphere east of the prime meridian is the ***Eastern Hemisphere.*** Locations there are written with longitude in degrees east. East is written as "E."

Time Zones

Longitude is important in another way. It is used to set the time zones around the world. For every 15 degrees of longitude, time changes by one hour. When it is 8:00 A.M. in North Carolina, it is 7:00 A.M. in Chicago, Illinois, 6:00 A.M. in Denver, Colorado, and 5:00 A.M. in San Francisco.

Using the Grid

There is an imaginary grid all over the surface of the earth. It is made up of the parallels of latitude and the meridians of longitude. With this grid we can locate any spot on the earth's surface.

To write a place's location, first note its latitude. Then note its longitude. Look at this map. The point where 30°N and 90°W intersect is New Orleans, Louisiana. We write the city's position as 30°N, 90°W.

North America's Absolute Location

Use your map-reading skills of absolute location to locate North America. Greenland, a mostly ice-covered island with few people, is often included as part of North America. This map shows the most northern, southern, eastern, and western points of North America.

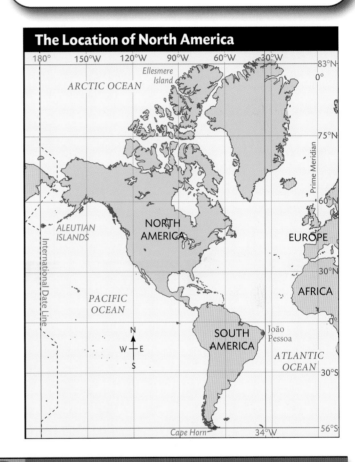

The Location of North America

LESSON 2 REVIEW

Fact Follow-Up
1. How is absolute location different from relative location?
2. What kind of jobs require that absolute location be used?
3. What is the International Date Line?

Talk About It
1. What are some uses for absolute location?
2. When is using relative location more appropriate than using absolute location?
3. Why do we need time zones?

Where in the World?

Accessing a Variety of Sources; Gathering, Synthesizing, and Reporting Information

Using Geography's Themes: Location

Location is the first of the Five Themes of Geography. You will practice using this theme by applying it in your own community. Then you will apply the same theme to North America.

Describing Your Hometown/City with Location

Start a graphic organizer that looks like the one below. Name this organizer "My Hometown." Leave enough space in each category to record several pieces of data.

My Hometown	
Geography's Themes	**Data**
1. Location	
a) Relative	
b) Absolute	
2. Place	

Theme number two, Place, will be studied next. Leave room for the other three themes of geography. Now that you have begun, what information will you need to describe the relative location of your town? A North Carolina road map or the map of North Carolina on 691 may help.

Here are some possibilities (you may include others not shown on a map): direction and distance from one or two other cities; distance from one of the state's borders; distance from the ocean, river, or mountains; and direction and distance from some famous landmark or historic site.

Would you give the same information to everyone? Or are there several ways to describe the relative location of your town or city?

For absolute location, study the map. Find as closely as you can the latitude and longitude of your town or city.

In telling someone where you live, are you more likely to use relative location or absolute location? Why?

Keep your organizer in your notebook. You will use it again.

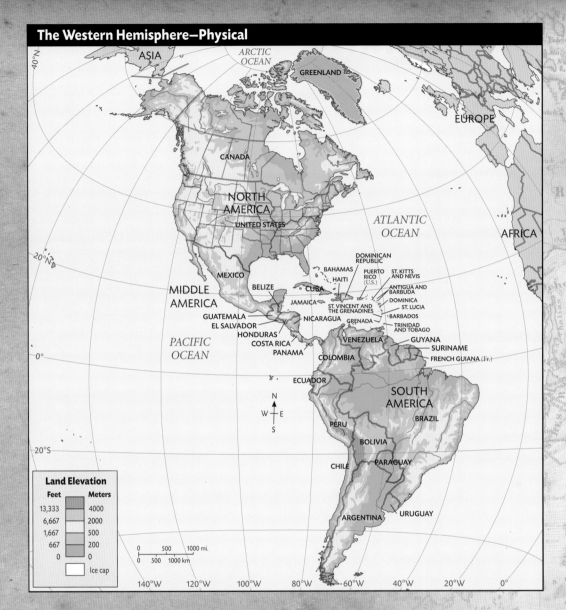

Describing Three Cities in North America Using Geography's Themes

Prepare three more blank graphic organizers. Title these "A City in Canada," "A City in the United States," and "A City in Middle America." Use the map on page 35 to choose each city. Using the map, find their absolute locations. Record the data for each city.

Next, refer again to the map to determine how to describe the relative location of each city. Where are they located? What are some nearby cities? In which direction are they located from your cities? Are your cities on the east or west coast of the continent? Are they near large lakes, bays, or rivers?

Does the map tell you anything else you can add about relative location?

Keep these organizers in your notebook next to the one on "My Hometown." You will need them again.

Use the index in this book to see if you can find the three cities you have chosen. Does the textbook give you any more information about the three cities?

Lessons Learned

LESSON 1
Finding North America Using Relative Location
Relative location is the way we mostly use to describe where a place is found. When you give directions using landmarks near the place, you are giving its relative location.

LESSON 2
Finding North America Using Absolute Location
Absolute location is a more exact way of describing where a place is located. The coordinates of longitude and latitude are a place's absolute location.

Talk About It

1. Suppose ways of determining absolute location had not yet been discovered. What would happen to ships on the ocean? to planes in the sky?
2. How would a map be helpful if you were driving from your home to New York City?
3. Why do hurricane trackers use absolute location in televised weather forecasts and reports?
4. Why is relative location used in weather alerts to describe the location of tornados?
5. If you had a map describing the location of buried treasure, would you prefer to have it give you the relative or the absolute location?

Mastering Mapwork

LOCATION

Use the map on 691 to answer these questions:
1. Locate the North Carolina cities lying nearest 78°W.
2. Find Wilmington and describe its relative location.
3. Locate the three North Carolina cities lying nearest 36°N.
4. Locate the Neuse River. Which three cities lie on the banks of this river?
5. Which North Carolina city lies nearest the intersection of 36°N and 80°W?
6. Describe the location of Cape Hatteras relative to Elizabeth City.
7. Describe the location of Greensboro relative to High Point.

Becoming Better Readers

Previewing
One of the most important reading skills is hardly reading at all! It's called previewing. When you preview you read the parts that jump out at you on each page like headings and pictures. Another way to preview a book is to look at the Table of Contents. Find the Table of Contents in your book. (Hint: It is always in the front.) Preview the chapters. What chapter do you think will be the most interesting?

Go to the Source

Reading Historic Maps

Study the map of the Western Hemisphere below. Compare it to the map of North America on page 681 in the Atlas to help you answer the questions. This map, called America, *was drawn by the cartographer Ortelius in 1570.*

Questions

1. What two continents did Ortelius draw on the map? Do they look like any continents you have seen? Explain.
2. Why is the drawing of Ortelius' map of North America different from the maps of North America today?

North America: A Place of Variety

Scientists use technologies like GPS not just to find the location of things but also to measure the changes in those places over time.

For example, it is difficult to measure the height of a mountain precisely. But GPS allows scientists to measure the heights of the world's tallest mountains. This information tells us how those mountains have changed over the years.

The height of Mount Rainier in Washington State was recalculated in 1999 using GPS. The mountain's new height is 14,411.05 feet (4,323.32 m). That is 12.6 inches (32 cm) taller than the U.S. Geological Survey had calculated using traditional methods in 1956.

CAROLINA
CONNECTION

Beach Erosion

Every day, the waves hitting the shore slightly change North Carolina's coastlines. Strong currents and wind from storms and hurricanes can quickly change coastlines. Sometimes, especially after big storms, new channels are created between the ocean and the bays.

People living along the Outer Banks have tried to stop erosion by building jetties and sand dunes. Jetties are long rock walls that keep the waves from wearing away the beach. Usually, though, the erosion just continues. Some people think that the government should not try to stop beach erosion because it is expensive. What do you think?

Chapter Preview

LESSON 1
Features of North America
North America is shaped by forces working both from inside the earth and on the earth's surface.

LESSON 2
Climate of North America
North America has several climate regions.

LESSON 3
Vegetation of North America
North America has different kinds of vegetation because of its different climates and soil types.

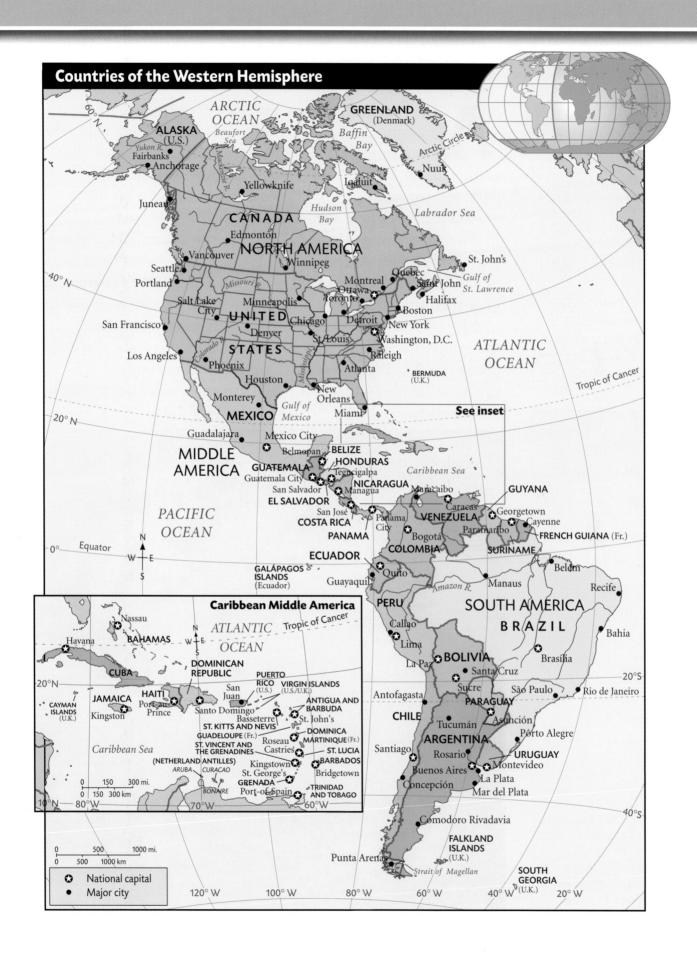

Countries of the Western Hemisphere

ARCTIC OCEAN

GREENLAND (Denmark)

ALASKA (U.S.)

Beaufort Sea

Baffin Bay

Fairbanks
Anchorage
Juneau
Yellowknife
Iqaluit
Nuuk

Arctic Circle

60° N

CANADA

Hudson Bay

Labrador Sea

Edmonton

NORTH AMERICA

Vancouver
Seattle
Portland
Winnipeg
St. John's

40° N

Salt Lake City
Minneapolis
Montreal
Quebec
Saint John
Gulf of St. Lawrence

San Francisco
Missouri R.
UNITED
Chicago
Ottawa
Toronto
Halifax
Boston
Detroit
New York

Denver
STATES
St. Louis
Washington, D.C.
ATLANTIC OCEAN

Los Angeles
Colorado R.
Phoenix
Raleigh
Atlanta

Houston
Mississippi R.
BERMUDA (U.K.)

Tropic of Cancer

Monterey
New Orleans
Gulf of Mexico
Miami

20° N

MEXICO
See inset

Guadalajara
Mexico City
BELIZE

MIDDLE AMERICA
Belmopan
HONDURAS
Caribbean Sea
GUYANA

GUATEMALA
Guatemala City
Tegucigalpa
NICARAGUA
Maracaibo
Caracas
Georgetown

San Salvador
Managua
VENEZUELA
Cayenne

EL SALVADOR
San José
Panama City
Paramaribo
FRENCH GUIANA (Fr.)

PACIFIC OCEAN
COSTA RICA
PANAMA
Bogotá
SURINAME

Equator
ECUADOR
COLOMBIA
Belém

0°
GALÁPAGOS ISLANDS (Ecuador)
Quito
Guayaquil
Amazon R.
Manaus
Recife

N
W E
S

PERU
SOUTH AMERICA
BRAZIL

Callao
Lima
Bahia

BOLIVIA
Brasília

La Paz
Santa Cruz

20° S

Sucre
São Paulo
Rio de Janeiro

Antofagasta
PARAGUAY

CHILE
Tucumán
Asunción
Pôrto Alegre

ARGENTINA
URUGUAY

Santiago
Rosario
Montevideo
La Plata

Buenos Aires
Concepción
Mar del Plata

40° S

Comodoro Rivadavia

FALKLAND ISLANDS (U.K.)

Punta Arenas
Strait of Magellan
SOUTH GEORGIA (U.K.)

Caribbean Middle America

Nassau

ATLANTIC OCEAN
Tropic of Cancer

N
W E
S

Havana
BAHAMAS

CUBA
DOMINICAN REPUBLIC

20° N
PUERTO RICO (U.S.)
VIRGIN ISLANDS (U.S./U.K.)

JAMAICA
HAITI
San Juan
ANTIGUA AND BARBUDA

CAYMAN ISLANDS (U.K.)
Kingston
Port-au-Prince
Santo Domingo
Basseterre
St. John's

ST. KITTS AND NEVIS
DOMINICA

Caribbean Sea
GUADELOUPE (Fr.)
Roseau
MARTINIQUE (Fr.)

ST. VINCENT AND THE GRENADINES
Castries
ST. LUCIA

(NETHERLAND ANTILLES)
Kingstown
BARBADOS

ARUBA
CURAÇAO
St. George's
Bridgetown

BONAIRE
GRENADA
TRINIDAD AND TOBAGO

Port-of-Spain

10° N
80° W
70° W
60° W

0   150   300 mi.
0   150   300 km

0   500   1000 mi.
0   500   1000 km

⊛ National capital
• Major city

120° W   100° W   80° W   60° W   40° W   20° W

KEY IDEAS

- North America looks the way it does because continents were formed through the movement of huge plates of rock.

- Movement continues to change the surface of the earth.

- Landforms also have been changed over millions of years by wind, water, and glacial erosion.

KEY TERMS

deltas
erosion
fault lines
fossils
glaciers
landform
lava
plate tectonics

A few years ago in the northwestern United States, a volcano exploded with terrible force. Lava rose from deep in the earth. It created so much pressure that an entire side of Mount St. Helens was blown away. Forests were flattened for miles around. Streams were filled with hot ash and mud. This volcano is still active today.

The theory of *plate tectonics* says the continents of the earth move around on large plates of rock. These plates float on a bed of *lava,* which is hot liquid rock under the earth's surface. The movement of these huge rock plates is very slow.

Most of the time we do not feel this movement. But sometimes the people who live above these pushing and pulling plates can feel the movement. We call this movement an earthquake. Buildings and roads are sometimes destroyed by earthquakes.

On May 18, 1980, Mount St. Helens erupted near Amboy, Washington. It is now a National Volcanic Monument. **What causes volcanoes to erupt?**

Forming North America

Earthquakes and erupting volcanoes are only two kinds of changes on the earth. The continents themselves have been moving slowly over time. Look at the maps on the right. Over millions of years, the plates that the continents sit on have moved. This caused the Mid-Atlantic Ridge to push through the ocean floor. It split the Americas from Europe and Africa.

The continents are still moving apart along the Mid-Atlantic Ridge. They move about 2 inches (5.1 centimeters) a year. North America is still changing wherever the great rock plates meet. Along the West Coast, these collisions have broken the earth's crust. These breaks are called *fault lines.*

If you visit California you can see one such break in the earth. The San Andreas Fault line runs near Los Angeles and San Francisco. Both of these cities have suffered severe earthquakes. Mount St. Helens is located farther north on the same fault line.

Plate movement also created many landforms. A *landform* is a shape on the earth's surface, such as a mountain. Plates pressing together lifted rock high into the air. This formed tall mountain ranges, such as the Rocky Mountains in North America. Plates pulling apart formed some of the great valleys.

The San Andreas Fault is the line running to the right of the mountains. **What is a fault line?**

Creating Continents

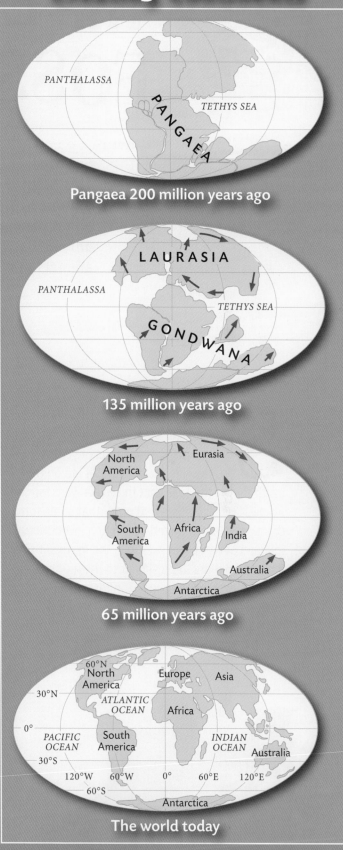

Pangaea 200 million years ago

135 million years ago

65 million years ago

The world today

Scientists believe the earth's landmasses gradually split apart into the continents that exist today. **Draw a map showing how you imagine the earth to look 65 million years in the future.**

North America: A Place of Variety

THE LIVING FOSSIL RECORD

Scientists study the animals and plants of the past. This helps them learn more about the natural history of the earth. When they study fossils, scientists learn about the earth's landforms, climate, vegetation, and animal life. *Fossils* are the remains of plants or animals that lived long ago, preserved in rock.

Modern slit shell

Scientists often find in fossils proof that animals and plants that no longer exist did live many thousands of years ago. Fossils give us a picture of life on the earth during the time that the rocks were formed. Sometimes, scientists find proof that some forms of life have not changed very much, even through millions of years. For example, the fossil slit shell (below) appears to be similar to the modern slit shell (above), even though the fossil shell is many millions of years older.

Fossil worm

Fossil slit shell

Chapter 3

The Burgess shale deposits in British Columbia, Canada, are rich in fossils. They contain images of fossilized animals that are related to animals living today. Crabs and spiders have a common ancestor found in the shale deposits. Clams and oysters are also distantly related to creatures found there.

Modern velvet worm

Living history can be found in Costa Rica's rain forests. Velvet worms there are holdovers from worms that first evolved about 515 million years ago. They have remained almost exactly the same since then. They look similar to the fossil worms pictured below.

Velvet worm fossil in rock

Water and Wind

Forces at work on the earth's surface also change landforms. Water, wind, and ice change the shape of the land. They create and destroy landforms. One way these forces work is through *erosion.* Erosion is the slow wearing away of rocks and soil over time because of water, wind, or ice.

Ocean waves, rivers, and rainwater erode rock and soil. Streams carry pebbles that rub and grind away more rock. Water erosion has created such dramatic landforms as the Natural Bridge in Virginia and the Grand Canyon in Arizona.

Wind changes the landscape. Soil can be blown away if it is not held in place by plants. Many years ago, farmers plowed the grasslands of the Great Plains. The soil provided rich farmland. Then the area was hit by a long period without rain. The winds blew soil away in great dust storms. The rich top soil was lost.

Glaciers Shape the Land

Glaciers are huge sheets of compacted ice. They crush or move whatever is in their path. These slowly flowing rivers of ice erode and move large sections of land.

Most of earth's glaciers are at the poles today. **What is a glacier?**

During the last Ice Age, glaciers covered much of North America. The glaciers scooped out millions of tons of dirt and rock, scraping the surface of the earth.

These glaciers acted like giant road graders. They scraped down the middle of North America from the Arctic Circle in Canada south beyond the Great Lakes (see map below). Today, a thin layer of soil covers much of the rocky ground there.

When the ice melted, the landforms in much of North America had completely changed.

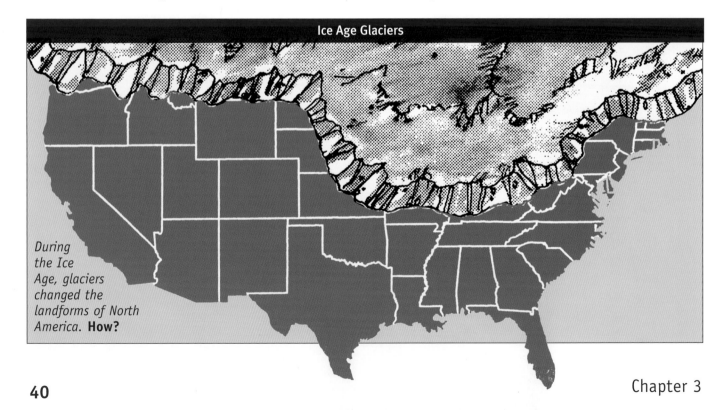

Ice Age Glaciers

During the Ice Age, glaciers changed the landforms of North America. **How?**

Erosion Changes Mountains

Imagine you are looking at North America from far out in space. You would see high mountain ranges running south from Canada all the way to South America. These mountains rise up like a sharp spine along the western edge of North America.

From space you could also see lower, rounded mountains along the east coast of North America. Millions of years ago, these lower mountains were high and sharp like those out west. But they are much older than the western ranges.

Over a long time, erosion has worn them down to lower mountains with rounder peaks. These eastern mountains are the Appalachians (ap·ah·LAY·chuns) of Canada and the United States.

Rivers

Streams and rivers change the land in two ways. They erode rock and soil. They also move *sediment*. Sediment is mud and soil particles small enough for river water to carry.

Sediment settles down on the bottom of the riverbed. It builds up over time. When it does this at the mouth of a river, it creates a delta. *Deltas* are flat plains of sediment. They create more land where the river flows into a larger body of water.

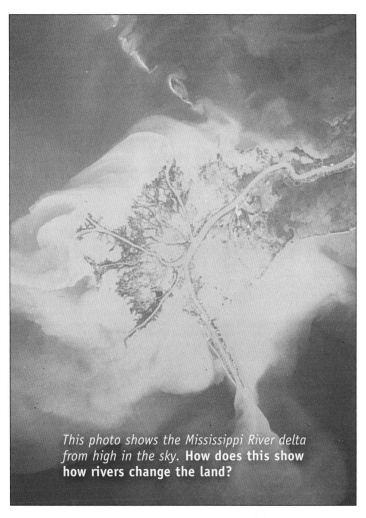

This photo shows the Mississippi River delta from high in the sky. **How does this show how rivers change the land?**

Huge rivers drain North America. They deposit huge amounts of sediment. The Mississippi River carries more than 500 million tons of sediment a year. As more and more sediment is deposited in the delta, the shape of the shoreline there changes.

LESSON 1 REVIEW

Fact Follow-Up
1. Describe major landforms of the Americas.
2. In what ways has nature changed the way land appears in the central parts of the Americas? in the West? in the East?

Talk About It
1. How did the movement of large plates of rock affect the way the Americas were formed?
2. How does water change landforms?
3. How did glaciers change the land?

North America: A Place of Variety

A man from North Carolina left home in late August. He took a trip to northern Canada. When he left Raleigh, the sun was hot. People were wearing shorts and had on their air conditioners. He flew to an airport north of the Arctic Circle. The plane had to land on a slippery runway during an ice storm.

Weather and Climate

You might say, "What's the big difference between the Arctic Circle and North Carolina. North Carolina has ice storms, too."

When we talk like this about the difference between such places as North Carolina and the Arctic Circle, we are talking about the difference between weather and climate.

Weather is the day-to-day change in temperature and rainfall. Here in our state, when the temperature drops, it gets cooler. You might decide to wear a heavy coat to school. On other days, the hot temperature in North Carolina may be similar to that of a place near the Equator.

Climate is the weather pattern of a place over a long period of time. Climate includes both temperature and the amount of rainfall a place receives.

The climates of North Carolina and the Equator are very different. Climate is affected by the tilt of the earth, latitude, nearness to water, and height above sea level.

Beaches in North Carolina (above) and Mexico (below) look alike and share similar weather. **Does that mean they have the same climate? Explain.**

The Four Seasons

The types of weather found in a place during the four seasons tells us what kind of climate the place has. As you know, the four seasons are spring, summer, autumn, and winter. Over a year's time, the changes in the tilt of the earth affect the temperature of areas on the earth. This gives us seasons.

The Tilt of the Earth

Imagine a candy apple on a stick. Now imagine that the earth is the apple. The *axis* of the earth would be the stick. The axis is an imaginary straight line that passes through the center of the earth from the North Pole to the South Pole.

The earth is is tilted to one side. It orbits the sun in one year. As it orbits, every spot on the earth's surface is tilted both away from and back toward the sun.

This tilt causes some areas of the earth's surface to receive more direct sunlight than other areas. Those places are hotter. In other places, the sun's rays do not beat down from directly overhead. The sun's rays spread out and lessen the heat. Those places are cooler all year.

Between March and September, the earth tilts so that more and more sun hits the Northern Hemisphere. More sunlight in the north eventually brings summer. Meanwhile, the Southern Hemisphere's sunlight is becoming more spread out. This is when the Southern Hemisphere has winter.

July in North Carolina, in the Northern Hemisphere, brings the hot days of summer. July in Argentina, in the Southern Hemisphere, brings the cooler days of winter.

What would YOU do?

The Western Hemisphere offers many different types of places to live. Imagine that you are one of the first settlers in the hemisphere. You can pick any place for your family to live. Where would you decide to live? Why?

The amount of direct sunlight that strikes different places on the earth changes depending on the season of the year. The arrows pointing to the earth represent the direct sunlight of summer. **Which hemisphere is receiving more direct sunlight on December 21? on June 21?**

Vernal equinox (March 21)

Summer solstice (June 21)

Winter solstice (December 21)

Autumnal equinox (September 21)

North America: A Place of Variety

Seasons at the Equator and Poles

The tilt of the earth hardly affects the Equator, because it continually receives direct sunlight. Seasons on the Equator are not hot or cold but may be either rainy or dry.

At the poles, the sunlight lasts longer when that part of the earth is leaning toward the sun. The sun never sets at the North Pole during the summer. During those same months, the South Pole is dark. The sun never rises. Even during the long days of polar summer, the temperature remains cool. The sun's rays are indirect.

Islands in the Caribbean Sea, such as Martinique, are not far from the Equator. **How does the tilt of the earth affect climate in such places?**

Latitude and Climate

As you have read, the earth's tilt causes sunlight to fall unevenly across the earth. In general, the tilt of the earth is the greatest factor that determines a region's climate. The farther away we move from the Equator and the low latitudes, the cooler the climate.

The Tropical Latitudes

Look at the map on page 45. There are two special lines of latitude. *The Tropic of Cancer* is at 23.5°N. *The Tropic of Capricorn* is at 23.5°S. These mark the tropical latitudes. They are also called the *Tropics.* In this region, temperatures stay hot all year.

There are two climate types in the Tropics. The area closest to the Equator that is hot and mostly wet all year is the *Tropical Rainforest* climate. Many of the world's rain forests can be found here. Plants stay green and leafy all year long.

The other tropical climate has both rainy and dry seasons. It is the *Tropical Savanna* climate. Southern Mexico has this climate.

WORD ORIGINS

The **Tropics** are parts of the earth that lie between two imaginary lines north and south of the Equator. The northern boundary of the Tropics is the **Tropic of Cancer.** The southern boundary is the **Tropic of Capricorn.**

The word *cancer* in Latin means "crab." *Capricorn* comes from two Latin words: *caper,* meaning "goat," and *cornu,* meaning "horn." Early mapmakers named the two lines after Cancer and Capricorn, the star groups that were directly overhead in the north and south.

Chapter 3

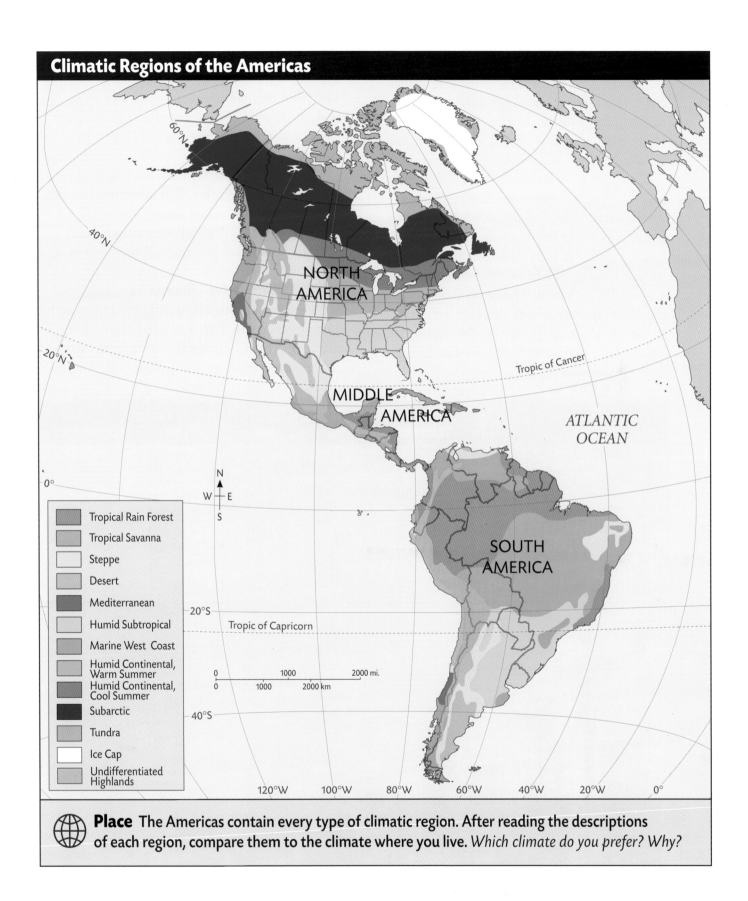

Tropic of Cancer

ATLANTIC OCEAN

NORTH AMERICA

MIDDLE AMERICA

SOUTH AMERICA

60°N
40°N
20°N
0°
20°S
40°S

Tropic of Capricorn

120°W 100°W 80°W 60°W 40°W 20°W 0°

N
W E
S

0   1000   2000 mi.
0   1000   2000 km

Legend:
- Tropical Rain Forest
- Tropical Savanna
- Steppe
- Desert
- Mediterranean
- Humid Subtropical
- Marine West Coast
- Humid Continental, Warm Summer
- Humid Continental, Cool Summer
- Subarctic
- Tundra
- Ice Cap
- Undifferentiated Highlands

Place The Americas contain every type of climatic region. After reading the descriptions of each region, compare them to the climate where you live. *Which climate do you prefer? Why?*

North America: A Place of Variety

The Temperate Latitudes

As the map shows, the middle latitudes are called *temperate.* They range from 23.5° to 66.5° in both the Northern and Southern Hemispheres. Places with temperate climates are cooler than the Tropics. Temperatures and rainfall vary greatly here. Thus, there are several types of temperate climates.

The temperate *Mediterranean* climate features hot and dry summers and mild and rainy winters. It is named after the Mediterranean Sea between southern Europe and northern Africa. The areas that surround the Mediterranean have this type of climate. In North America, places on the southern Pacific Coast, such as Southern California, have this climate.

Another climate with mild and rainy winters is the *Marine West Coast* climate. This climate's summers are cool and rainy. Southwestern Canada and the northwestern United States along the Pacific Ocean have this climate.

The *humid subtropical* climate also has mild and rainy winters. The summers are hot, too. But it has a humid spring and summer. The southeastern United States enjoys this climate. It is good for raising crops nearly all year long.

The *continental* climates have cold and snowy winters. But one continental climate has a short, cool summer. The other has a long, hot summer. Much of central and eastern North America experiences the continental climates.

Climate Types				
TROPICS	**TEMPERATE**	**DRY**	**POLAR**	**ELEVATION**
Tropical Rain Forest Tropical Savanna	Mediterranean Humid Subtropical Marine West Coast Humid Continental (warm summer) Humid Continental (cool summer)	Desert (arid) Steppe	Subarctic Tundra	Ice Cap Undifferentiated Highlands

Seattle, Washington, is on the Puget Sound. It's in a Marine West Coast climate region. **What are the characteristics of that climate?**

Northern Mexico has two kinds of dry climates. What are they? **Which do you think is pictured?**

Dry Climates

Look at the temperate latitudes on the map on page 45. You can see *dry* climate regions near the border with the tropical latitudes. Much of the country of Mexico near 23.5°N is dry. There are two kinds of dry climates: *desert* and *steppe.* Deserts can be found in North America. They receive less than 10 inches of rain per year. They are sometimes called *arid* climates.

Steppe climates are not as dry as deserts. They are sometimes called semiarid regions, meaning partially dry. Some parts of the western United States have steppe climates. They get between 10 and 20 inches (25.4 and 50.8 cm) of rainfall per year.

Customs

Cultures often have traditions that relate to their climate. In the dry southwestern United States, many Native Americans dance to pray for rain. The Hopi Indians did a snake dance. One dancer clutched a rattlesnake in his teeth. Another dancer calmed the snake with a feathered stick. After the dance, the snakes were carried in four directions and set free in the desert. The Hopi believe that the snakes return to the underworld with prayers for the rain god.

The Poles

There are two cold climates at the poles. The first is *subarctic.* It covers most of northern Canada and nearly all of Alaska. Subarctic climates are warm enough for trees to grow.

Weak sunlight produces a climate at the poles called *tundra.* From the latitudes of 66.5° to the North and South Poles, water stays frozen. Temperatures here are low all year. Far northern Canada and Alaska have this climate.

Elevation and Climate

If you have hiked to the top of a mountain, you know that the air gets cooler the higher up you go. When you climb up 3,000 feet (900 m) above sea level, you are in a cooler climate. *Elevation* is a place's height above sea level. All climates are changed by elevation, no matter the latitude.

The *highlands* climate changes with elevation and the direction of the wind. The Rocky Mountains and the mountain ranges of Middle America have the highlands climate.

Although many parts of the Rockies are in temperate climates, their peaks are capped with snow all year. The temperature there rarely goes above freezing. In the same way, the mountains of Middle America are cool, even though most of Middle America is in the Tropics.

The Rain Shadow Effect

Mountains can block some rain from falling. This creates a drier climate on the other side of the peaks. This is called the *rain shadow effect* (see illustration, page 49). Rainfall in highland areas varies a lot. The wind blows rain clouds over the mountain. But mountain peaks block some of the rain. It does not reach the side of the mountain that is away from the wind. The side away from the wind may be drier because of this.

In North America, the wind blows from the Pacific Ocean toward the east. The coasts of Washington and Oregon receive heavy rainfall. But places east of the Cascade Mountains in Washington and Oregon receive little rain. This is because of the rain shadow effect.

The Rocky Mountains have a highlands climate. Elevation's effect on temperature is shown by high peaks where snow never melts. **How else do mountains affect climate conditions?**

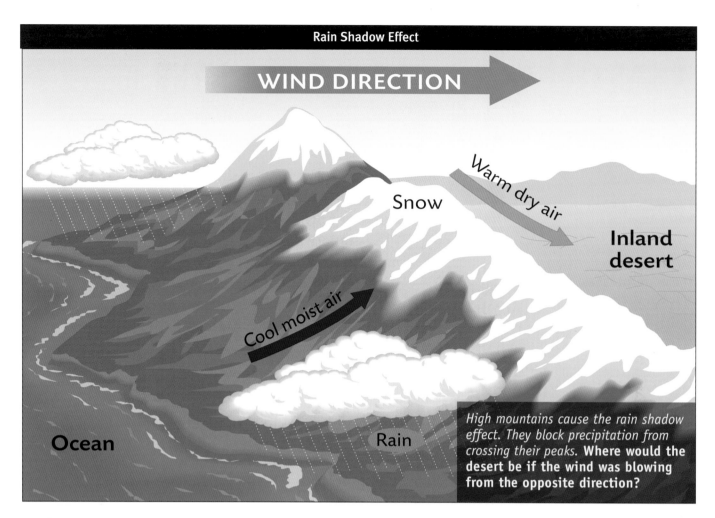

WIND DIRECTION

Cool moist air

Snow

Warm dry air

Inland desert

Ocean

Rain

High mountains cause the rain shadow effect. They block precipitation from crossing their peaks. **Where would the desert be if the wind was blowing from the opposite direction?**

Climate and Nearness to Water

Like elevation, nearness to the sea can also affect a place's climate. Generally, places that are closer to oceans have milder winters and cooler summers than areas further inland. They also have more *precipitation.* Precipitation is rain, snow, hail, and sleet.

Why is this so? Oceans release stored heat in winter.

They cool the air during the summer. Oceans also release a lot of moisture into the air. It falls as rain or snow.

However, mountains along the coast change this pattern. When the wind blows from the mainland toward the ocean, the air hits the mountains. The elevation of the mountains cools the air. This causes precipitation. Therefore, the air that crosses over the mountains is drier. The coast then has a drier climate.

LESSON 2 REVIEW

Fact Follow-Up
1. Explain the difference between weather and climate.
2. Explain why the seasons change.
3. Describe the climates of North America. In what climate is Mexico? North Carolina?

Talk About It
1. How does latitude affect climate?
2. Explain the effects of elevation and nearness to the sea on climate.
3. How does the rain shadow effect change climate patterns?

KEY IDEAS

- Varied climates in North America allow many different types of vegetation to grow.

- There are four main types of vegetation: forest, grasslands, desert, and tundra.

KEY TERMS

culture

deciduous forests

desert

dry temperate grasslands

evergreen forests

forest

grasslands

human characteristics

humid temperate
   grasslands

physical characteristics

place

tropical grasslands

tropical rain forests

tundra

vegetation

Like climate, the types of plants growing in North America vary greatly. Just as there are climate regions, there are regions of *vegetation* or plant life. Climate affects which plants can grow in a place. The vegetation map closely matches the climate map.

There are four broad types of vegetation—*forest, grasslands, desert,* and *tundra.* Forest and grasslands can be found in highland, temperate, and tropical climates. Desert vegetation is found in dry climates. Tundra is mainly found in tundra climate zones.

Forest

Forests are found in almost every climate except tundra. The types of forests change according to the climate.

Tropical rain forests are found near the Equator. About one third of Costa Rica is covered by tropical rain forests. Tall broad-leaved trees never lose their leaves. They form a high canopy over the forest floor. Very little sunlight reaches the ground.

Deciduous forests are in temperate climates. Deciduous trees like maples, birches, and oaks shed their leaves each autumn. Many of the deciduous tree forests in North America have been cleared for farmland.

In the autumn, some trees change color and lose their leaves. **What kind of trees have leaves that change to beautiful colors during the fall, like these in North Carolina?**

Evergreen forests of pine, fir, and spruce keep their green, needle-like leaves all year. These forests provide much of the world's supply of lumber and paper. Evergreen forests include conifers—cone-bearing trees.

Evergreen forests also grow well in humid temperate and dry temperate climates. Large stands of needle-leaved trees live in the humid southeastern United States and southern Mexico, as well as the dry western United States.

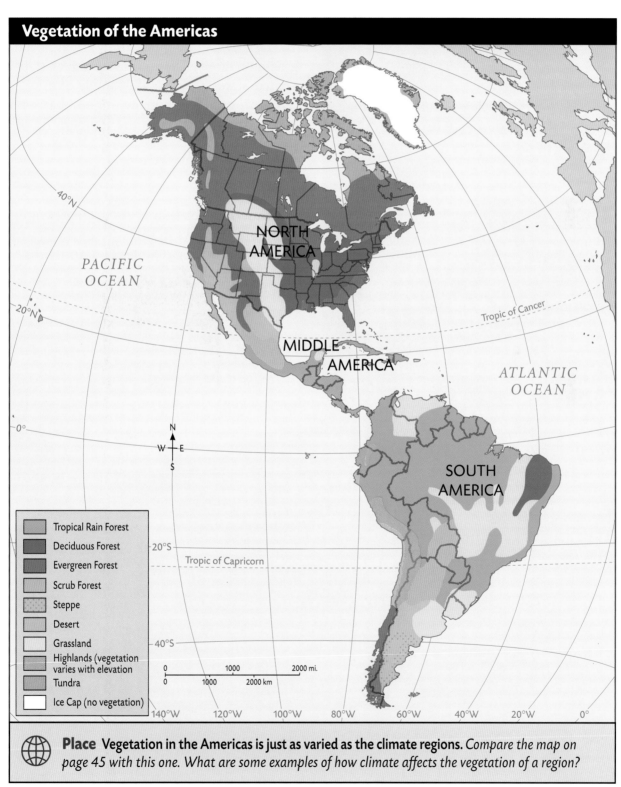

Vegetation of the Americas

Legend:
- Tropical Rain Forest
- Deciduous Forest
- Evergreen Forest
- Scrub Forest
- Steppe
- Desert
- Grassland
- Highlands (vegetation varies with elevation)
- Tundra
- Ice Cap (no vegetation)

Place Vegetation in the Americas is just as varied as the climate regions. *Compare the map on page 45 with this one. What are some examples of how climate affects the vegetation of a region?*

North America: A Place of Variety

Grasslands

Types of grasslands also change according to the climate. *Humid temperate grasslands* grow on flat or rolling plains. These are fertile areas good for raising grain. These grasslands are found in the wheat-growing areas of the United States and Canada.

Dry temperate grasslands are important grazing regions. The prairies of the western United States are a good example of this. *Tropical grasslands* grow in humid areas of North America, such as the southern tip of Florida.

Desert

Desert vegetation of cactus plants and scrub brush grows in such dry regions as the southwestern United States and northern Mexico. Desert plants have long roots and thin leaves to adapt to a hot and dry environment.

Tundra

Plants of the polar regions grow on the treeless plain called tundra. Plants growing on the tundra adapt to the cold to survive. Tiny wild flowers grow quickly from short roots during the brief polar summers. Mosses and algae (AL·gee) cling to rocks where they absorb moisture.

Tundra plants poke through the ground only during the short summers. **What characteristics of these plants help them survive the harsh cold?**

Cattle graze on the grasslands of the prairie in Oklahoma. **Would you like to live on the prairie?**

Vegetation			
FOREST	**GRASSLANDS**	**DESERT**	**TUNDRA**
Tropical Rain Forest Deciduous Forest Evergreen Forest	Humid Temperate Grasslands Dry Temperate Grasslands Tropical Grasslands	Desert	Tundra

AMERICAN PORTRAIT

John James Audubon
1785–1851

John James Audubon was born on the Caribbean island now known as Haiti. He was raised in France. Growing up, he was interested in birds, nature, drawing, and music. He came to America when he was eighteen.

He first lived near Philadelphia, Pennsylvania. There he hunted, studied, and drew birds. He married Lucy Bakewell and they moved to western Kentucky.

Audubon was a talented artist. He painted and drew pictures of hundreds of birds. He set a goal to draw every kind of bird in America. When he was forty-one, he published a set of four books called *Birds of America*. Many people today believe this is still the best picture book ever made.

Audubon drew his birds in their natural habitat. He was the first naturalist to do this. A naturalist is a person who studies nature. His drawings include detailed pictures of trees and plants.

Over the years, Audubon wrote and drew pictures for several more books about the birds and animals of North America. The National Audubon Society was named in his honor.

LESSON 3 REVIEW

Fact Follow-Up
1. What are the major vegetation types found in the Americas?
2. What are the different types of forests? Where are they?
3. What vegetation is in North Carolina?

Talk About It
1. How is desert vegetation similar to tundra vegetation?
2. What type of vegetation is found near your home? How does your climate affect it?
3. Why are grasslands important?

North America: A Place of Variety

Accessing a Variety of Sources; Gathering,
Synthesizing, and Reporting Information

Using Geography's Themes: Place

My Hometown	
Geography's Themes	**Data**
1. Location	
a) Relative	[completed]
b) Absolute	[completed]
2. Place	
a) Physical Characteristics	
b) Human Characteristics	

Place is geography's second theme. To describe a place, geographers gather two kinds of information or data.

One kind describes *physical characteristics*. What are the natural features—the landforms—of the place? What other features are there? Ocean beaches or rivers? Is it a place where there is a lot of rain or snow?

The second kind deals with *human characteristics,* including culture. *Culture* covers every part of a group of people's way of life.

What do people talk about when they return from a trip? Almost no one mentions latitude and longitude. Instead, they tell us about sunny beaches, good ski trails, neat museums, tasty food, or interesting people.

They are describing both physical and human characteristics. These are the things that make a place worth remembering.

Describing Your Hometown

Write "Place" on the second line of your graphic organizer, "My Hometown." Your graphic organizer should now look like the chart in the next column. Be sure to make room for both physical and human characteristics.

Data for Line 2a

Think of three or four physical characteristics that identify your community. Here are some suggestions.

- Landforms. What is the shape of the land? flat? hilly? mountainous?
- Climate. Are summers long and hot? Do snow and ice come almost every winter? Or are winters chilly without much snow or ice?

Data for Line 2b

- People. How large is your community? What is the racial and ethnic makeup— White? African American? Hispanic? Native American? a mixture? Are there any people from India? Southwest Asia? Middle America? South America? East Asia? Europe?
- Religion. Can you estimate how many places of worship are in your community? How many are Protestant? Catholic? Jewish? Muslim? Hindu? Other?

- Food. What are the special foods prepared by restaurants? Do these restaurants tell you what people in your community like to eat?
- Economic activity. What kind of farms or businesses are in your community?

Describing Three Cities in North America

Pull the three graphic organizers for cities in North America from your notebook. To help fill in data, use the questions that you answered for the organizer on "My Hometown."

Look at line 2a—physical characteristics—for "My Home Town." You described the land and the climate. You may have described what kinds of trees and plants grow there. You could describe all of these things without looking in any book. You live there.

To describe the three cities that you picked, you should study the maps on pages 21, 35, 45, and 51. On those maps, find the areas close to your three cities. Use the map keys to identify elevation, climate, and vegetation. Refer to the text to help you describe in detail each of these characteristics.

Line 2b—human characteristics—should be filled out with information on the people living in the area around your three cities before Europeans arrived. Chapters 2 and 3 do not provide you with this information. You will need to fill out these lines after reading the next chapter.

Chapter 4 will help you learn about people in North America. Remember to save your graphic organizers. You will use them again.

The North Carolina places of the Blue Ridge Parkway, Charlotte, and Elizabeth City show the variety of physical characteristics that help define the theme of place.

Lessons Learned

LESSON 1
Geographic Features of North America

Almost every kind of landform can be found in North America—from high mountains to low coastal plains. This variety is the result of the movement of great plates of rock within the earth and changes by the forces of nature. Wind and water work on the surface of the earth. The landforms are still changing, because these great forces inside and outside the earth are still at work.

LESSON 2
Climate of North America

The earth's tilt brings changes in the seasons. In the higher northern and southern latitudes—near the North and South Poles—the sun's rays are never direct, so that even summers are short and cold. The changing direction of the sun's rays is a major factor in determining the climate in any part of the world.

LESSON 3
Vegetation of North America

North America is home to four broad types of vegetation—forest, grasslands, desert, and tundra. Climate is a major factor in determining which of these types will grow.

Talk About It

1. Why is it summer in North Carolina when it is winter in the south of South America?
2. Which has most influenced the physical geography of South America: plate tectonics or erosion? Explain.
3. Imagine that you enjoy winter sports. Should you persuade your family to move to the higher or lower latitudes? Explain.

Mastering Mapwork

PLACE

Use the map on page 35 to answer these questions:

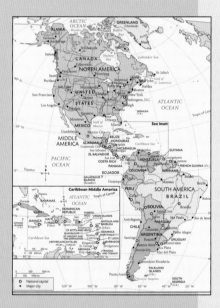

1. Locate San Francisco, California, on the map. Describe its physical characteristics of place.
2. Locate Winnipeg, Canada (Winnipeg lies near 50°N and east of 100°W). Describe its physical characteristics of place.
3. Locate Mexico City (near 20°N and 100°W). Describe its physical and cultural characteristics of place.
4. Locate New Orleans. What physical characteristics of place would you expect to see in New Orleans?

Becoming Better Readers

Using What You Know

We learned that good readers make connections between what they already know and new information. Name one thing that you knew about the geography of the United States before you read the chapter. Connect what you knew to one thing you learned from reading the chapter.

Go to the Source

Analyzing Photographs

This is a photograph of North America taken by a satellite. The maps on pages 21, 45, and 51 will help you answer the questions below.

Questions

1. Looking at this photo, what landform do you think can be found where there is white on the land (other than the clouds)?
2. What do the brown areas on the image tell us about the vegetation and the climate?
3. Where are the high areas of elevation located on North America?
4. Why do you think the northern part of the continent is a darker shade of green and brown?

2

*H*aving passed into the center of the city we were received by the lord Moctezuma II (MOCK·teh·ZOO·mah), with about two hundred chiefs, all dressed in a kind of livery [uniform], very rich according to their custom. They approached in two processions [parade lines] near the walls of the street (which is very broad, and straight and beautiful). There were large houses, smaller dwelling places, and temples.

—*from a letter by explorer Hernán Cortés to the Spanish monarch describing his first sight of Tenochtitlán, the Aztec capital.*

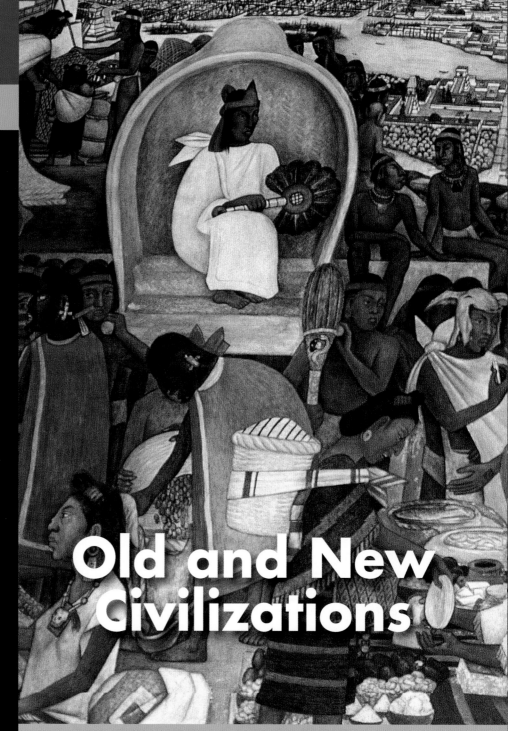

Old and New Civilizations

Timeline of Events

	1400		1500		1600	
					1734–1781	1781–1854
	Chapter 4	**Chapter 5**	**Chapter 6**	**Chapter 7**
	• The first settlers probably came from Asia. • The Aztec and Maya built large civilizations. • The first Americans had many different ways of life.	• Spain explores North America. • The French and other Europeans explore North America. • England founded colonies along the Atlantic coast.	• American democracy grows out of British traditions. • The colonies declare their independence from Great Britain. • The United States wins the War of Independence.	• The Constitution is written and a new government is formed. • Many Americans begin to move west. • The U.S. wins the Mexican-American War.

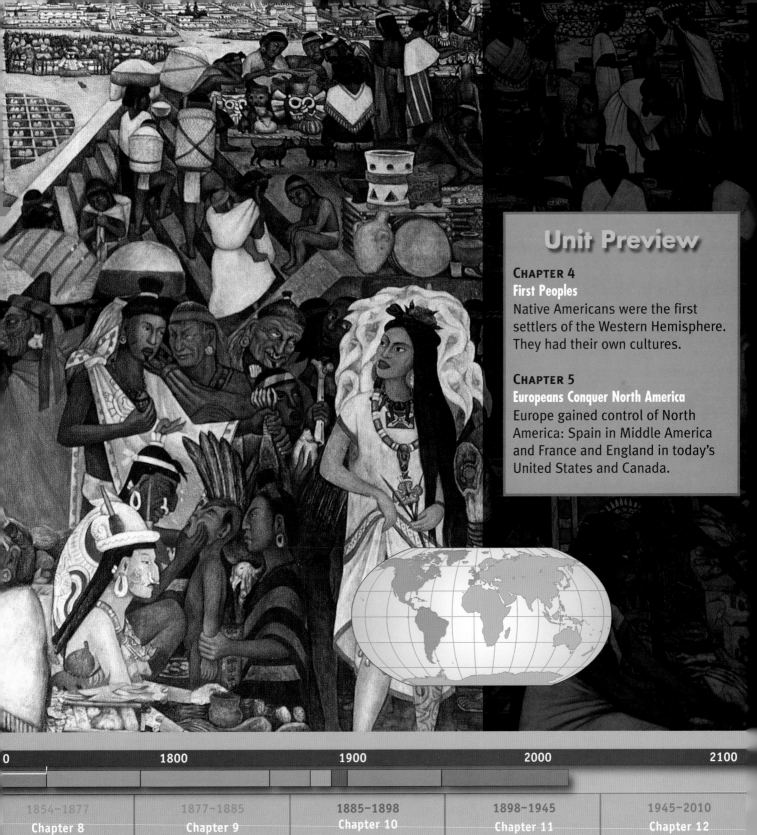

0	1800	1900	2000	2100

1854–1877	1877–1885	1885–1898	1898–1945	1945–2010
Chapter 8	Chapter 9	Chapter 10	Chapter 11	Chapter 12
• Disagreements over slavery lead to war. • The Civil War lasts more than four years. • The Emancipation Proclamation frees the slaves. • Reconstruction brings political and social changes to the South.	• Better roads and canals make transportation easier. • East and West are united by the Transcontinental railroad. • The United States becomes a nation of big businesses.	• Early immigrants to the United States arrive with hopes for a better life. • Immigrants settle all over the country. • More immigrants come from Asia, South America, and Africa.	• The United States begins to play a greater role in world affairs. • World War I and the Depression bring changes. • World War II makes the United States into a world leader.	• The Cold War is the American-Soviet rivalry. • The civil rights movement ends segregation. • The late twentieth century is a time of change.

First Peoples

Time Line of Events

4000 B.C.
Maize (corn) is first grown in what is now Mexico

1500 B.C.
Olmec Civilization begins

18000 B.C.　　8000 B.C.　　4000 B.C.　　1500 B.C.

18,000 B.C.
People cross the land bridge from Asia

8000 B.C.
People reach the tip of South America

The Spanish explorers who first saw the Aztec city of Tenochtitlán (tay·noh·chit·lahn) gazed at it in wonder. There were tall, brightly painted pyramids. The city was surrounded by sparkling water and green fields. The Spanish had never seen a city as large or rich.

The explorers were stunned. They had no idea how the Aztecs had reached the land now called Mexico or how they had built Tenochtitlán.

We now know much more about early Native Americans. To find out about them, we must go back in time thousands of years.

Tenochtitlán, the Aztec capital

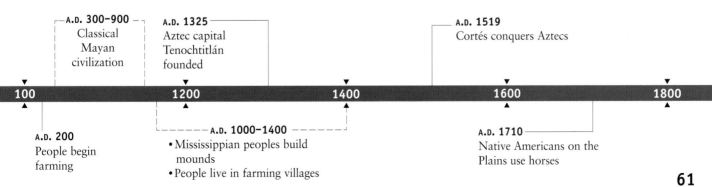

A.D. 300–900
Classical Mayan civilization

A.D. 1325
Aztec capital Tenochtitlán founded

A.D. 1519
Cortés conquers Aztecs

| 100 | 1200 | 1400 | 1600 | 1800 |

A.D. 200
People begin farming

A.D. 1000–1400
• Mississippian peoples build mounds
• People live in farming villages

A.D. 1710
Native Americans on the Plains use horses

61

KEY IDEAS

- The first settlers in the Americas probably arrived about 20,000 years ago from Asia.

- Many walked to the Americas on a land bridge.

- These first settlers are now called Native Americans.

- They built advanced civilizations.

KEY TERMS

Aztecs
Beringia
hunting and gathering
Ice Age
Maya
Native Americans

Many scholars believe that hunters from northern Asia crossed a land bridge to the northwestern tip of North America. This was more than 20,000 years before the Aztecs built Tenochtitlán.

These people were following animals. They hunted these animals for food. From there, they moved south in search of game. The crossing to the New World took many hundreds of years.

A Land Bridge

The land bridge appeared during a period called the Ice Age. During the *Ice Age,* the earth's temperature dropped a few degrees. The earth grew colder for a long time. The water at the poles froze.

The Ice Age

Do you remember reading about glaciers in Chapter 3? Fields of packed snow and ice covered the poles. These became glaciers. Glaciers spread southward from the North Pole and covered much of North America.

At one point, a lot of the earth's water had been frozen into ice. This made ocean levels drop about 300 feet (90 m). New land was uncovered as oceans pulled away from the shores.

The first people in North America walked from Asia to Alaska. Today, the land bridge is under a body of water called the Bering Strait. **How long did it take them to settle the Americas?**

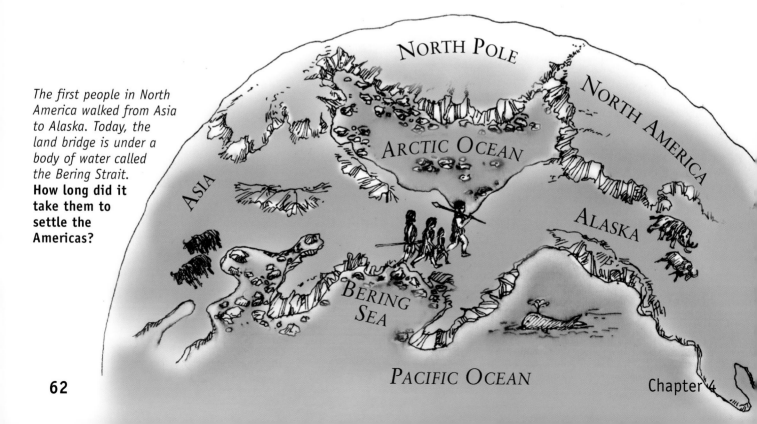

Beringia

Some of the land that was uncovered connected the continents of Asia and North America. Today, scientists call the land that appeared *Beringia* (beh·REN·gee·ah). This bridge of land remained above water for several thousand years. It was located where today's eastern tip of Russia almost touches the western tip of Alaska. The Bering Strait, a narrow waterway, flows between the two nations and continents now.

Over time, the earth's temperatures warmed again and the great ice fields shrank. Ocean waters rose and covered the land bridge. The waters of the Bering Strait again divided Asia and North America. On the other side of the continent, the broad Atlantic Ocean separated the Americas from Europe and Africa to the east.

The First Americans

The first Americans never knew they were crossing a bridge to a new continent. The land bridge was bigger than North Carolina.

These people slowly moved south over many, many years. They spread across North and South America. They may have reached the tip of South America about 10,000 years ago.

Some people may have traveled by boat. They probably followed the Pacific Coast of North and South America.

These first Americans are now usually called *Native Americans.* People in Canada call them First Nations. That is because Native Americans built their own civilizations and cultures. Each tribe, or group, was its own nation.

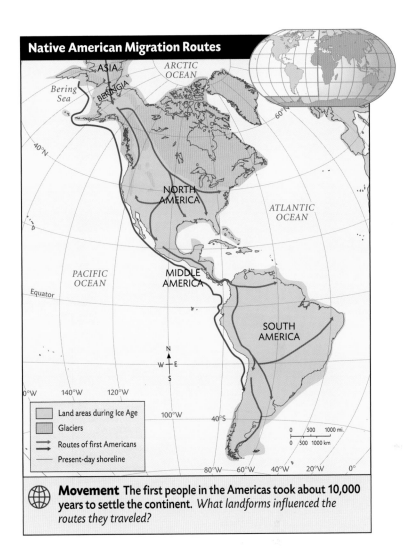

Native American Migration Routes

Land areas during Ice Age
Glaciers
Routes of first Americans
Present-day shoreline

Movement The first people in the Americas took about 10,000 years to settle the continent. *What landforms influenced the routes they traveled?*

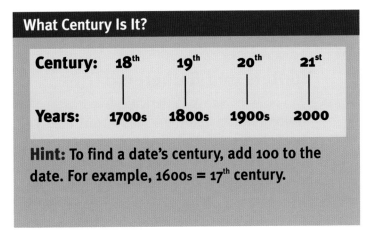

What Century Is It?

Century:	18th	19th	20th	21st
Years:	1700s	1800s	1900s	2000

Hint: To find a date's century, add 100 to the date. For example, 1600s = 17th century.

The Temple at Palenque, Mexico, shows how skilled the Maya were at building. **How did farming allow the Maya to build temples and other structures?**

Hunters and Gatherers

The first Native Americans lived by **hunting and gathering.** This means that people hunted or gathered everything they needed to live. They killed game or caught fish. They ate wild berries, plants, fruits, and nuts. They ate the food fresh and dried some of it to eat during the winter.

Everyone in a hunting and gathering society had to search for food. Most societies, sometimes called tribes, had to move with the seasons. When the ripe wild plants and fruits ran out in one place, they needed to find a new place with more food.

They also followed animal herds. The first Americans were following herds when they crossed the land bridge. They were probably following herds as they spread out across North America.

Farming

Life changed when Native Americans learned how to farm. They grew maize (corn), squash, and beans. Farmers could grow larger amounts of food. They also could raise crops year after year in the same area. This was important.

Often, farmers grew more than their families needed. The extra food meant that more people could settle in one place. It also meant that people could do many different things.

Chapter 4

Early Civilizations

Europeans knew nothing about the people and cultures of North America. This is why the Spanish were surprised when they saw Tenochtitlán.

By this time, Native Americans had built large communities almost everywhere in North and South America. Two of the greatest Native American civilizations developed in the southern part of North America. These two cultures were the last in a long line of peoples that started with the Olmecs, Zapotecs, and Mixtecs around 4000 B.C.

The Maya and Aztecs

These peoples were the *Maya* and the *Aztecs*. The Maya lived in Mexico's Yucatán Peninsula and areas to the south beginning about 1800 B.C. The Aztec capital, Tenochtitlán, stood where Mexico City is today. Their civilization lasted from A.D. 1345 to 1521. The Aztec were successful because they learned how to farm and use their natural resources. They used this knowledge to improve their lives.

The Maya organized thousands of people to cut and move huge stones. With these they built great buildings and tall pyramids. Their study of the moon and stars helped them make calendars.

You will read later that the Spanish were able to take control of the Aztecs. Native Americans could not match the Europeans in battle. They did not have guns or horses. But their civilizations were still great. For example, Tenochtitlán was larger than any other city in the world when the Spanish arrived.

In many ways, the Aztec civilization was not far behind Europe. One historian wrote that with only "a few years development, it is not difficult to imagine Aztec . . . sailors and soldiers setting sail to explore Asia or Europe."

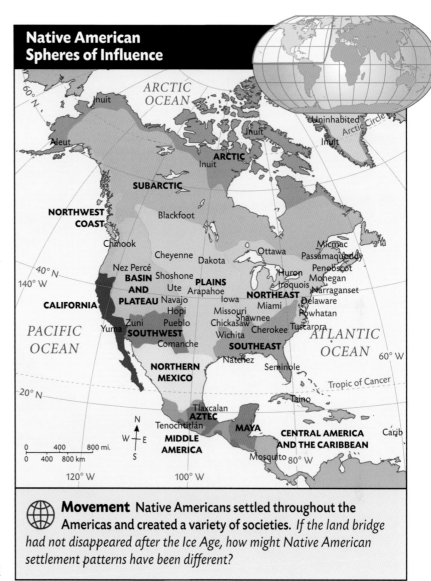

Native American Spheres of Influence

Movement Native Americans settled throughout the Americas and created a variety of societies. *If the land bridge had not disappeared after the Ice Age, how might Native American settlement patterns have been different?*

What would YOU do?

Imagine what it was like when people began to be successful farmers. People had extra food at harvest time. They could store and share the food. Therefore, some people did not have work on the farm.

If you were living then, would you want to raise crops? Or would you want to become a sculptor? a weaver? a priest? an astronomer? Maybe you would want to design the new pyramids. How would you contribute to the community?

Native American Mathematicians

Mathematicians played an important role in Native American civilizations. The Maya and the Aztecs developed counting systems. These helped them keep track of goods being made and traded. They used mathematics to plan and construct buildings, temples, and houses. Calendars told them when to sow and harvest crops and when to hold religious holidays.

The ancient Aztecs used dots and pictures, called glyphs, to represent numbers. The number 1 was shown by a dot. A flag represented the number 20, a feather was 400, and an incense pouch symbolized the number 8,000.

The Maya invented a calendar. It was more accurate than the one brought to the Americas by European settlers. The Maya used the calendar to figure out when religious holidays should be. The calendars helped them know when to plant crops.

The Maya studied the stars and planets. They used their knowledge to make their calendar.

Native Americans used math to design and build huge temples. The Temple of the Moon was one of the tallest structures built by humans in North America until the mid-1800s.

Mayan temple at Chichén Itzá on the Yucatán Peninsula

LESSON 1 REVIEW

Fact Follow-Up

1. About how many years did it take Native Americans to travel from the northwestern tip of North America to the southern tip of South America?
2. How do scientists explain the appearance and disappearance of a land bridge between Asia and North America?
3. Name some feats of Native Americans.

Talk About It

1. The Native American settlements along North America's Pacific coast and the Aztec civilizations were the most heavily populated centers in the Western Hemisphere by the 1400s. How was food found for so many people?
2. The Aztec civilization is described as "advanced" for its time. Why was farming essential to the Aztecs?

When Europeans sailed into the Caribbean, they met Native Americans living on almost every island. Europeans soon learned that Native Americans lived all over North America.

Adapting to the Environment

About 2,000 different Native American groups lived in the Western Hemisphere. Each lived its own special way. Each had its own religious beliefs, tools, language, food, clothing, and type of housing.

The ancestors of these first settlers were probably much alike when they arrived in North America. As they spread out they developed different ways of life.

You can probably guess why this happened. North America has large lakes, high mountains, huge open plains, great rivers, dry deserts, and many climates. This means that Native Americans moved into lands with different environments. An *environment* is the surrounding in which people, animals, and plants live.

The Coastal Native Americans of the Pacific Northwest are an example of how the environment changed the way people lived. The Pacific Northwest was a place with a lot of food. People there could live differently from the ways of their ancestors. No longer did they have to move all the time in search of animals to hunt or wild berries to gather.

Large numbers of Native Americans in the Northwest could settle in one place. Unlike their ancestors, they did not live for a few days or weeks in tents or huts. They built log houses in villages. There they and their children stayed all their lives.

Other groups moved into different environments. To survive, they developed different ways of living.

KEY IDEAS

- The Native Americans of the United States and Canada created many different societies.

- People adapted to different environments.

- Most Native Americans hunted for game. Not all tribes farmed.

KEY TERMS

adobe
environment
harpoons
igloos
Inuit
irrigation
kayaks
pueblos

This drawing shows how Native Americans used their environment to live. **What things do you see in the picture that show how these people adapted to their environment?**

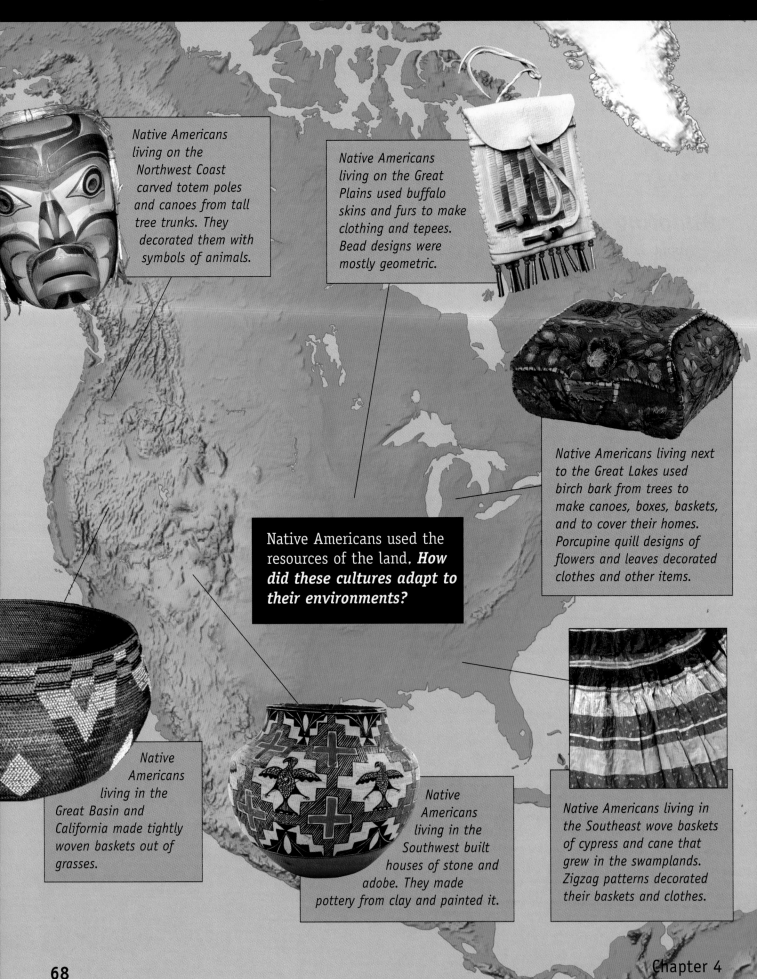

Native Americans living on the Northwest Coast carved totem poles and canoes from tall tree trunks. They decorated them with symbols of animals.

Native Americans living on the Great Plains used buffalo skins and furs to make clothing and tepees. Bead designs were mostly geometric.

Native Americans living next to the Great Lakes used birch bark from trees to make canoes, boxes, baskets, and to cover their homes. Porcupine quill designs of flowers and leaves decorated clothes and other items.

Native Americans used the resources of the land. *How did these cultures adapt to their environments?*

Native Americans living in the Great Basin and California made tightly woven baskets out of grasses.

Native Americans living in the Southwest built houses of stone and adobe. They made pottery from clay and painted it.

Native Americans living in the Southeast wove baskets of cypress and cane that grew in the swamplands. Zigzag patterns decorated their baskets and clothes.

Peoples of the Far North

The people of the far north probably were the last Native Americans to arrive in the Western Hemisphere. They have often been called Eskimos. But the people in today's Canada prefer the name **Inuit** (IN·you·it), a word meaning "the people." Native Americans in northern Alaska are called the Aleuts. The Inuit and Aleuts are distantly related.

The Inuit and Aleuts both learned how to live in a harsh environment. In the far north, summers are so short that only a few inches of the ground thaws. This means that there are few, if any, plants to eat.

The Inuit learned to survive in the cold, icy environment. They hunted and fished. They made spears to hunt with called **harpoons.** Animal bones were used to make knives and needles. They sewed animal skins for clothing and for covering **kayaks.** Kayaks are light boats that are similar to canoes.

The Inuit made snowshoes. Snowshoes look almost like tennis rackets. They make walking through deep snow easier.

On hunting trips the Inuit built temporary shelters called **igloos.** These were made of blocks cut from snow. Packed earth, stone, and driftwood were used to make year-round homes.

Everyone in an Inuit community learned how to cooperate. Hunters had to work together to stalk and kill animals. The Inuit believed that no one should go hungry as long as someone had food. Inuit religious beliefs stressed living in harmony with nature and one another.

The Inuit made temporary shelters out of snow on their hunting trips. **What were these called?**

Peoples of the Northwest

There were two groups of Native Americans living in what is today's northwestern United States. These groups were the Coastal and the Plateau. Coastal peoples lived in villages along the Pacific Coast. Plateau people lived east of the Cascade Mountains in eastern Washington and Oregon. There were many tribes that made up each group of people.

The Coastal people lived in an area with a mild climate. Food could easily be found in the ocean and rivers. Foods like clams and salmon were important. The Coastal people have a saying, "When the tide is out, the table is set." What do you think that means?

They used wood to build homes, cradles, and canoes. Some tribes, like the Makah, used canoes to hunt whales.

In the east, the Plateau peoples lived in a drier climate. They did not have many trees, so they could not use much wood for building. They could not eat seafood from the ocean. Instead, they were hunter-gatherers. They followed animals in the summer months. Salmon were an important food source. Salmon were also important in their culture.

In the winter, the Plateau peoples lived in longhouses. These were made of wooden poles covered with woven mats. A fire in the center kept it warm. Mats on the floor were used for sitting and sleeping.

Peoples of California and the Great Basin

Native Americans in today's California were not farmers in the way we think of today. But they cared for their environment. They trimmed bushes and trees to grow wood for arrows.

They took care of plants to make sure that they would have enough food. They ate seeds, roots, leaves, and fruit. Many tribes ate acorns. Women pounded the hard nuts with stones. They washed the bitter taste away with water.

Native people cared for the grasses that the women used to weave baskets. They were used to carry and store food. The Pomo made watertight baskets for cooking acorn mush.

Some tribes in California had as many as 2,000 people living in a community. Their basic house had a round frame covered with grass. There was a cooking fire in the center and a skylight in the roof.

Native Americans on the coasts used the resources of the sea. These Makah people are going whaling.
Why was finding food usually easier for the Coastal peoples?

Chapter 4

Great Basin

Water and food were often hard to find in the desert between the Rockies and the Sierra Nevada mountain ranges. This area is called the Great Basin. Most of the area was too dry for farming. So most people ate seeds and nuts. For example, the Paiute and Shoshone gathered the nuts from the piñon (PIN·yon) tree.

These people killed deer, antelope, and rabbits whenever they could. Native Americans here had to stay on the move to find food. Their homes had to move with them. They made tents out of a few wooden poles and covered them with grass.

The Ute used the desert resources to hunt and gather food. They also borrowed many ideas from people in the Southwest and Plains.

Photographing Native Peoples

Not long after the camera was invented, a few early photographers came west to take pictures of native peoples. Sometimes they took pictures of native people in a studio and dressed them in fancy clothing or costumes. What do you think about the way these Paiutes are dressed? Do you think they wore clothes like these everyday?

This photograph of a Paiute family was taken in the early 1900's. **What kinds of foods did the Paiute gather?**

Peoples of the Southwest

The areas of today's southwestern United States and northern Mexico have a dry, hot climate. The steppe climate is almost like a desert. Many different tribes lived here. They had different ways of living, too.

Ancient Peoples

Prehistoric Native Americans developed in different parts of the region. They traded goods and ideas with one another. They traded turquoise and cotton. They also traded with other Native American groups. They got seashells from the Pacific Ocean and buffalo hides from the plains.

The Anasazi The Anasazi (ahn·ah·SAH·zee) were farmers. They used rain to water their crops. They built trails and roads and sent signals to communicate with other communities.

The Anasazi found protected places on the walls of cliffs. There they built their houses. They reached their houses by climbing long ladders. If the ladders were pulled up, enemies had trouble attacking the village.

This photograph shows ancient Anasazi dwelling in Mesa Verde, Colorado. **Why did the Anasazi build their homes on cliffs?**

Chapter 4

The Hohokam Some people learned how to farm even though there was little rain. Water flowed through the Southwest in rivers. So people learned how to bring water from the river to their crops. *Irrigation* is bringing plants water using ditches or canals. The Hohokam people were the first to irrigate crops in the Southwest. These farmers grew beans, squash, and corn.

The Mogollon The Mogollon (MUH·gee·own) lived in the mountains of the Southwest. They hunted animals in the mountains and grew corn. The mountains had lots of wild berries and nuts, so they did not have to grow as much of their food as the Hohokam or Anasazi. They made beautiful pottery.

All of these chiefdoms, and some others, thrived for hundreds of years. Then the people went away. Historians still do not know why these peoples left their homes. The Anasazi and the Hohokam are the ancestors of some of the Native Americans who met the Spanish.

Making Flour

People made flour by using grinding stones called manos and metates. The manos were small stones people held in their hands. They pushed the manos on larger, flatter stones, called metates. In between the two stones were seeds. As they pushed the mano over the metate, the seeds were crushed into flour.

The Hohokam built canals to bring water to their crops. **How did this allow them to farm in a desert environment?**

The Peoples Who Met the Spanish

When the Spanish explored the Southwest, they discovered many tribes. Each had found ways to adapt to the environment. These people are the ancestors of Native Americans living in today's United States.

Athabascan Tribes Some of the tribes moved a great deal. These are the Athabascan tribes (ath·ah·BASS·kan). At different times of the year, tribes like the Apache (ah·PATCH·ee) moved to places where they knew there would be fresh water and plants for their animals. They were also warriors. The Apache fought with other groups for rights to the land.

Some groups, like the Navajo (NAH·vah·hoh), herded animals. The Navajo raised sheep. Women wove blankets with wool from the sheep. It was dyed beautiful colors. Other Navajo made silver jewelry. Silver and many gemstones are resources found in the Southwest. Navajo art is famous around the world today. They are one of the largest groups of Native Americans in the United States.

The Pueblo Peoples If you visit Colorado, Arizona, or New Mexico today, you may see very old buildings that are similar to modern apartment buildings. These are *pueblos.* They were large enough to hold the people of an entire village.

Pueblos were built of stone or *adobe* bricks. Adobe is made by mixing mud and straw and baking the bricks in the sun. For each roof, heavy logs were laid across the walls. Ladders were used to get from one level to the next.

This home style gave these Native Americans the name they are known by today. When the Spanish arrived, they called both the buildings and the natives by the same name, *pueblo.* Pueblo is the Spanish word for "village." The Zuni, Hopi, and Chociti as well as many other tribes are pueblos. They all grew corn, beans, and squash. These peoples live today. They have different customs and languages.

Desert Farming People Many of these peoples are descendants of the Hohokam. Some tribes, like the Pima, have lived near the desert rivers for hundreds of years. They grew corn to eat and cotton to make cloth. They hunted and gathered wild plants.

Plateau Tribes Most of the plateau tribes used to be hunters and gatherers. They had to move around a lot to find food. The Havasupai (hah·vah·SOO·pie) lived at the bottom of the Grand Canyon. There they were able do some farming. They still live in the Grand Canyon today.

LESSON 2 REVIEW

Fact Follow-Up
1. How did the peoples of the far north adapt to their environment?
2. How did the peoples of California and the Northwest adapt to their environment?
3. What is a pueblo?
4. What were the main crops of the peoples of the Southwest?

Talk About It
1. What are some of the differences between the people of the far north and the people of the Southwest?
2. Consider the environment of the Southwest. What might have happened there that made the ancient people leave their homes?

In the 1500s, the Europeans were exploring much of what is now the United States and Canada. They did not find civilizations the size of the Aztec. One historian called the native cultures of that time "a continent of small villages."

The Mississippian Peoples

About 600 years before the Europeans came, there were many Native American cities along the Mississippi River. The Mississippian peoples lived here. They had an amazing culture.

Mississippian farmers grew corn, beans, squash, pumpkins, and other crops. There was plenty of food, so most people did not have to grow their own. They lived in small towns or cities along the river. Craftspeople made copper into fine jewelry.

These people built large mounds and pyramids of earth. Sometimes the hills were made in the shapes of animals. Other mounds were used to bury people. Sometimes palaces or temples were built on them. No one knows for sure why they were built.

KEY IDEAS

- The Mississippian peoples built great societies.

- Native Americans of the Great Plains and eastern North America adapted to many different environments.

- Buffalo were important to the peoples of the Great Plains.

- The horse changed the lives of Native Americans.

KEY TERMS

human-environmental interaction
tepee
wattle and daub

The Mississippian city historians now call Cahokia was located on the eastern side of the Mississippi River where St. Louis, Missouri is today. It became one of the largest cities in the world. **Why could people live in cities?**

Work and Trade

In the Mississippian cities, everyone worked. Men built houses and buildings, hunted, fished, and made tools. Women watched the children, did most of the gardening, made clothing from animal skins, cooked meals, and made pottery. People traded goods in the marketplace.

Mississippians traded with other groups far to the north and south. They got mica from the Appalachian Mountains, sea shells from the Gulf of Mexico, and copper from the Great Lakes area. Trading trips took many weeks by boat or on foot. People from other tribes also came to Mississippian cities to trade their goods.

After a few hundred years, the people left Cahokia and the other communities. Why this happened is a mystery. No one knows for sure what happened to the mound builders.

Peoples of the Great Plains

The Great Plains are a broad stretch of grasslands between the Rocky Mountains and the Mississippi River. It was home to many Native Americans. Some tribes were hunter-gatherers. Others farmed for part of the year and hunted during the rest of the year.

For example, the Caddo, Osage, and Wichita tribes were farmers. Many rivers flowed through this land. The Caddo and Wichita lived in villages in the river valleys. Crops like corn, beans, and squash grew well there. The Osage lived in western Missouri.

The Caddo hunted deer and also traded with other tribes. They made baskets and tools. They made cloth from plant fibers. The Wichita and Osage grew corn and other crops, but they also hunted buffalo. Women stayed in villages to raise food. Men went out to hunt. The buffalo was the most important animal to the Wichita, Osage, and many of the hunting tribes of the plains.

Making Things From Buffalo

The buffalo gave people almost everything they needed to survive. Here are some of the ways people used it.

Parts and Uses

1. **Hides and furs** were used for robes, blankets, *tepee* covers, rugs, and shields.

2. **Horns** were used for spoons and headdresses.

3. **Hair** was used for rope.

4. **Bones** were used for arrowheads and sewing needles.

5. **Meat and bone marrow** were eaten.

6. **Tails** were used as flyswatters.

7. **Sinews** were used for thread and twine.

8. **Tongues** were made into brushes.

Chapter 4

Horses Changed the Native Americans' Way of Life

- Native Americans became better hunters. They no longer had to hunt on foot. Now they could ride horses to find buffalo. They could get closer to the buffalo and chase them farther and faster.
- Horses could carry more than dogs could.
- Warriors could ride horses into battle.

- Native Americans went back to being mostly hunters. It was a more dependable way to get food than farming. Crops might do better or worse from one year to the next, but hunting was a sure way to get food if you had a horse.

The Buffalo

The buffalo grazed in huge herds on the thick grass of the plains. Native Americans learned that buffalo could supply most of their needs. The meat was their main food. Buffalo hides became clothing.

Buffalo did not stay in one place. The plains people followed the herds. Tepees were taken down. Women packed up what the family owned. An entire village would move wherever the buffalo led them.

Women did most of the moving. They carried whatever they could. The rest was packed on sleds pulled by dogs.

Hunting and moving camp became easier when horses came to the Great Plains. For thousands of years, there were no horses in North America. The Spanish brought horses to Mexico in the 1500s.

As the Spanish explored the Southwest, Native Americans saw the horses. They told stories of "big dogs" that could carry heavy loads. Other Native American tribes sent people to visit tribes that had horses. These visitors learned how to ride and brought some horses back home. Many tribes became highly skilled hunters using horses. They worked in well-organized teams.

Peoples of the Southeast

Some of the Native American tribes in what is now the Southeastern United States were the Muscogee, the Choctaw, and the Chickasaw.

The Muscogee peoples were probably descended from the Mississippian Peoples. There were many smaller tribes that made up the Muscogee. They lived in villages in river valleys in today's states of Tennessee, Georgia, and Alabama. These groups were called the Creeks by English settlers because they lived near the rivers. The Seminoles are related to the Muscogee. They moved to Florida in the 1600s.

The Chickasaw and Choctaw were enemies. They lived where Tennessee is now.

The Choctaw are descendants of the Mississippian Peoples. The Chickasaw might be. But some historians think the Chickasaw might have moved to the area from someplace else.

All of these groups lived similarly. They wore clothes made from animal skins. They hunted deer, turkey, and bears and caught fish. They grew corn, squash, and beans.

They did not live in tepees. Instead, they lived in huts made with *wattle and daub.* Wooden poles were covered with vines and grasses. Then the people covered the vines and grasses with mud plaster.

There was a lot of clay in the Southeast. The Native Americans who lived here were the first to use clay to make pottery.

The Algonquian peoples lived longhouses like this. **In what season did they live in these types of shelters?**

Chapter 4

Peoples of the Eastern Woodlands

The Eastern Woodlands stretch from Quebec, Canada, to the Gulf of Mexico. These lands were home to many Native American groups.

These peoples hunted many different animals. Along rivers and the ocean shore, they fished and gathered shellfish. They chopped down trees in the forest to clear areas for farming. There women tended crops of corn, squash, beans, and tobacco.

The environment provided enough food for many people. It is estimated that about 500,000 people lived in the Eastern Woodlands when the Spanish arrived in North America.

The Algonquian Tribes

The Algonquian (al·GONG·kwee·ehn) peoples lived across today's midwestern and northeastern United States and eastern Canada. Most Algonquians lived by hunting and fishing. A number of tribes grew corn, beans, and squash. The Ojibwe (ob·JIB·way) also grew wild rice.

Many Peoples There were many Algonquian peoples in New England. They included the Mohegan (moh·HEE·gan), Pequot (PEE·quot), Narragansett, Wampanoag (wahm·PAN·oh·ahg), and Massachusett. The Micmac tribes lived in northern Maine and eastern Canada.

The Ojibwe/Chippewa, Ottawa, and Cree lived where Minnesota, Wisconsin, Michigan, Ontario, and the Canadian prairie provinces are now. The Powhatan, Nanticoke (NAN·tuh·coke), and Lenape (leh·NAH·pay) tribes are also part of the Algonquian peoples. They live in the Mid-Atlantic and southeastern United States.

Algonquian Life These tribes usually lived in villages with a few hundred people. In the summer, people would move to places where food was plentiful. They lived in temporary shelters made of wood and grass mats. At the winter village, people lived in longhouses. They were about about 80 feet (24 m) long and 25 feet (7.5 m) wide. They were made of poles and covered with bark. Several families lived in one home.

Algonquian people living near the ocean also hunted whales, porpoises, walruses, and seals. The women and children gathered shellfish and crabs.

Many Algonquian tribes gathered wild berries and nuts. In the fall, tribes split into small groups and moved to the forest. There they hunted beaver, caribou, moose, and deer.

The Tuscarora

The Tuscarora Native Americans are one of the Six Nations of the Iroquois. Their tribe was centered in northeastern North Carolina. In 1701, there were 15 major Tuscarora towns there. More and more Europeans arrived. They took the Tuscarora's lands. Some Tuscarora villages were raided. The Native Americans suffered.

The chief of one Tuscarora village was a close friend of the Blount family. He called himself Tom Blount. In 1711, the Tuscarora War started. Chief Blount did not allow his people to take sides. Because of his loyalty to the settlers, he was given 56,000 acres on the Roanoke River in Bertie to live on as a reservation.

WOMEN IN NATIVE AMERICAN SOCIETIES

At the North Carolina Museum of History in Raleigh, a female mannequin stands in a glass case. She is dressed beautifully in special clothing made from leather. It is decorated with shells, beads, and bells. Her clothing is copied from clothing found on the remains of a woman. She was a member of the Saura people. They lived on North Carolina's Dan River in the 1600s.

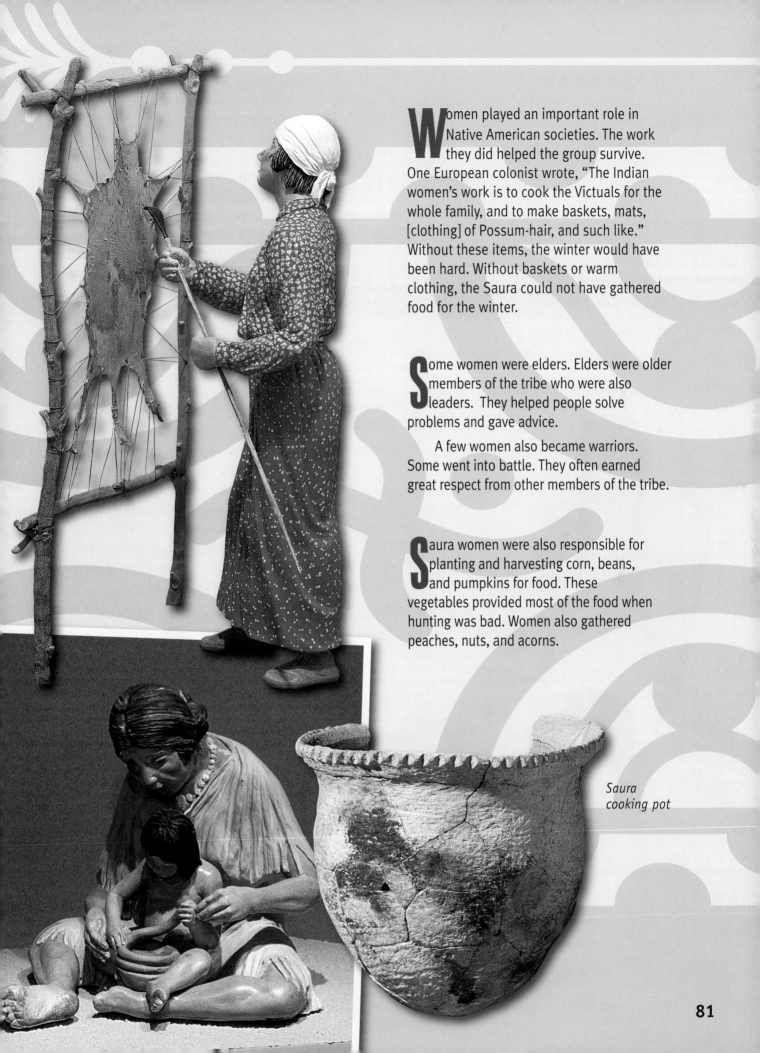

Women played an important role in Native American societies. The work they did helped the group survive. One European colonist wrote, "The Indian women's work is to cook the Victuals for the whole family, and to make baskets, mats, [clothing] of Possum-hair, and such like." Without these items, the winter would have been hard. Without baskets or warm clothing, the Saura could not have gathered food for the winter.

Some women were elders. Elders were older members of the tribe who were also leaders. They helped people solve problems and gave advice.

A few women also became warriors. Some went into battle. They often earned great respect from other members of the tribe.

Saura women were also responsible for planting and harvesting corn, beans, and pumpkins for food. These vegetables provided most of the food when hunting was bad. Women also gathered peaches, nuts, and acorns.

Saura cooking pot

The Iroquois

The Iroquois (EAR·a·quoy) were one of the largest groups in the East. They were enemies of the Algonquian peoples. Both groups competed for resources.

Many different groups living in the East were Iroquois. The Mohawk, Oneida (o·NYE·dah), Onondaga, Seneca, and Cayuga (kye·YOO·gah) were Iroquois groups centered in what is now New York state.

Some of the tribes of the Southeast were related to the Iroquois. The Cherokees had moved south from New England hundreds of years before the Europeans came. Later the Tuscarora became part of the Iroquois League.

In the Northeast, the Iroquois peoples lived in large villages. They also lived in longhouses.

Iroquois women had a lot of power. They could help choose their leaders. Iroquois law recognized their importance. Anyone guilty of killing a woman owed her family 20 strings of wampum. Wampum was Iroquois money. For killing a man, the fine was only 10 strings.

The Iroquois peoples and the Algonquian did not get along. Their relationship grew worse after the Europeans arrived.

Changes for Native Americans

The Europeans, as you will read in Chapter 5, began to use North America's resources in the 1500s. They explored, trapped animals for fur, and fished for many years before any colonies were founded.

Sometimes the Europeans were friendly to the Native Americans. Sometimes they were not. But their arrival brought changes to Native American ways of life.

Fur trapping became important for many tribes. They traded furs to Europeans for things that native people had never seen before. Guns, iron axes, knives, and metal pots were all items they could use.

Word Origins

Some words we use today are from Native American languages. **Hickory, moccasin, moose, succotash, toboggan, tomahawk,** and **woodchuck** come from the Algonquian language. The Algonquian lived in what is now the northeastern United States.

These men are catching eels. **Can you see the special trap they made?**

Trade with Europeans changed many things for native peoples. **What were some of the things native people traded?**

Native peoples became trading partners with the newcomers. The Algonquian partnered with the French. The Iroquois partnered with the British. But these partnerships did not help the natives get along.

In the early 1600s fighting broke out. Battles among the Native Americans lasted for about 100 years. Many were killed. Sometimes European settlers got involved.

Once the Europeans arrived, life for the Native American peoples of North America would never be the same.

LESSON ③ REVIEW

Fact Follow-Up
1. Pick any three groups of Native Americans living in North America in the 1400s. Describe the ways in which their lives were similar and different.
2. The accomplishments of the Native Americans called the Mississippian Peoples are thought by scientists to have been similar to those of the Aztecs. Why?

Talk About It
1. The lives of these Native Americans were not all alike. Why?
2. Imagine that you could pick as your home a settlement of any one of the Native American groups described in Lessons 2 and 3. Which one would you pick? Why?
3. What can we learn today from these cultures about how to use the environment?

First Peoples

skill

Accessing a Variety of Sources; Gathering, Synthesizing, and Reporting Information

Using Geography's Themes: Human-Environmental Interaction

Human-Environmental Interaction is geography's third theme. You can practice this theme if you ask and then find answers to these questions:

- How does the environment of a place affect what people do?
- How do people use the environment?
- How do they change the environment?
- Why do people change the environment?

In this chapter you have read about the first Americans. Those in the far north lived in a world of long winters and cold temperatures. Native Americans along both coasts lived where fish and game provided plenty to eat. In southern Mexico, nature provided less food for hunters. Native Americans learned how to increase their food supplies by farming.

Different environments affect the ways people live. But some people find ways of changing their environments. Interaction is a word that refers to ways the environment affects people and how people change the environment.

Pull out your graphic organizers to practice using this theme.

My Hometown	
Geography's Themes	**Data**
1. Location	
a) Relative	[completed]
b) Absolute	[completed]
2. Place	
a) Physical Characteristics	[completed]
b) Human Characteristics	[completed]
3. Human-Environmental Interaction	
a) How Environment Affects People	
b) How People Use Their Environment	
c) How People Change Their Environment	

Describing Your Hometown: Human-Environmental Interaction

Write Human-Environmental Interaction in the space below Place. This will be number 3. Below that add: 3a: How Environment Affects People, 3b: How People Use Their Environment, and 3c: How People Change Their Environment. Your graphic organizer should now look like the one to the left.

Before you begin to write, review what you have already written about your community. Think about the ways in which climate influences the way people live.

1. Does your community's climate affect the clothes that you wear or the games that you play?

2. What are two ways people in your community use the land? Would your answer be different if you lived near Carowinds or near a golf course in Southern Pines?

3. What inventions used by people in your community have changed the environment in some way?

Describing Three Cities in North America

Here you will practice using the Human-Environmental Interaction theme to describe three points in the Americas a long time ago. You have been reading about the first settlers in the Americas. They lived differently from the way people live today in your community.

Add to your graphic organizers for the Western Hemisphere all the items that you listed for theme number 3 on your community.

Choose the parts of this chapter that discuss places in the Western Hemisphere nearest the cities that you selected, when you completed the first two themes.

3a: Are the environments in each place the same or different? Did different environments present people with different needs for shelter?

3b: How did people in each place use their environments? For example, did the environments permit everyone to fish?

3c: How much did people in each place change their environment? How did the changes affect their lives?

Read carefully before you begin to write! Remember to use the index to help you learn more about human-environmental interaction in areas near the three cities you have chosen. Are there other resources you can use?

Lessons Learned

LESSON 1
Building Civilizations in North America
The first settlers in North America probably crossed a land bridge from Asia more than 20,000 years ago. These first settlers came in small groups of hunters and gatherers. They learned how to farm the land. The Maya and Aztecs built great civilizations.

LESSON 2
Native Americans of the North and West
The Native Americans of today's United States and Canada adapted to many environments. The people of the far north, the Pacific Northwest, California and the Great Basin, and the Southwest had many different cultures and ways of life.

LESSON 3
Native Americans of the Plains and East
The Mississippian Peoples and tribes of the Great Plains and Eastern Woodlands created many different societies. Buffalo and horses were important on the Great Plains.

Talk About It

1. Imagine that you could go back through time to visit Native Americans either shortly after they arrived in the Americas about 20,000 years ago or shortly before Europeans arrived about 500 years ago. Which time would you choose? Why?
2. Learning how to farm has been described as a key discovery. The text says that it made possible the development of the Mayan and Aztec civilizations. In what ways was it of such importance?
3. Before Europeans arrived, many Native American groups had learned to farm. Native Americans along the northwest Pacific Coast, however, showed little interest in farming. Why might they have been different from others?

Mastering Mapwork

HUMAN-ENVIRONMENTAL INTERACTION
Use the map on pages 63 and 65 to answer these questions:

1. One migration route went southeast and then south along 120°W. What physical environment was at the end of this migration route?
2. Describe how these first Americans interacted with their physical environment.
3. Do you think the people who settled in North America affected the environment very much, or were they more affected by the environment? Explain your answer.

Becoming Better Readers

Making Predictions
After previewing a chapter, good readers make predictions. A prediction is a guess based on the information you have. Use what you learned in this chapter to make a prediction about what you will learn in the next chapter. Quickly preview Chapter 5. What do you predict you will learn by reading the next chapter?

Go to the Source

Understanding Legends

Many Native American societies told legends. Legends are stories that are passed down from parents to children over and over again. Read the legend below. Then answer the questions using the information from the legend.

The Legend of the Spider Symbol

One day, an Osage chief was hunting in the forest. He came upon the tracks of a huge deer. He became excited and began to talk to the deer. "Deer, please let me find you. You will be a symbol of great strength to my people."

The chief began to follow the deer tracks. His eyes were on the ground as he ran faster and faster, trying to catch the deer. Suddenly, he ran right into a spider's web that had been strung between two trees across the path. The web was very sticky, and this made the chief angry. He tried to kill the spider that was sitting on the edge of the web. The spider jumped away just in time.

The spider began to talk to the chief. "Why are you running through the woods with your eyes on the ground?" the spider asked. "Because I am trying to catch a great deer that will be a symbol of strength to my people," the chief answered.

"I can be a symbol of strength for your people," said the spider. The chief laughed and said, "How can you be a symbol of strength? You are so small, I didn't even see you as I ran by looking for the great deer."

"Look at me," answered the spider. "I am patient. I watch and I wait. All things I need come to me. If your people learn this, they will be strong indeed."

The chief understood, and the spider became a symbol of his people.

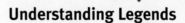

Questions
1. What lesson did the spider teach the Osage chief?
2. Why did the chief think that the deer would be a symbol of great strength for his people?
3. What can people today learn from this legend?
4. What does this legend tell us about how the Osage people live?

Spanish coin showing Ferdinand and Isabella

Chapter Preview

LESSON 1
The Spanish in North America
Spain explored and settled much of North America.

LESSON 2
Europeans Come to North America
The French and other Europeans began to explore and settle in North America. They came for different reasons.

LESSON 3
Early English Colonies
England founded colonies in today's Virginia and New England.

LESSON 4
The Later English Colonies
The English colonies in America were founded for different purposes.

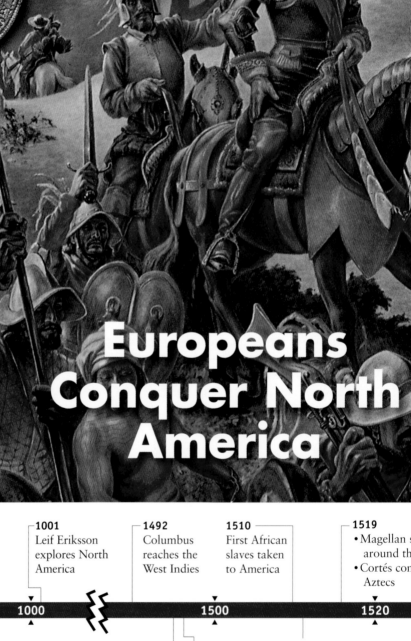

Europeans Conquer North America

Timeline of Events

1001
Leif Eriksson explores North America

1492
Columbus reaches the West Indies

1510
First African slaves taken to America

1519
• Magellan sails around the world
• Cortés conquers Aztecs

1000   1500   1520

1493
Columbus founds Hispaniola

1497
Cabot discovers Newfoundland

1513
• de León explores Florida
• Balboa reaches Pacific Ocean

1528
de Vaca explores the Southwest

For a long time, North America was a place of mystery to people other than American Indians. Then explorers, traders, and missionaries came here. Most of the explorers came from Spain, France, and England. They claimed land in the New World and hoped to find great treasures to take back to their home countries.

This painting shows one artist's view of this time period. **How would you describe what is happening in the painting? What does it say about different cultures meeting?**

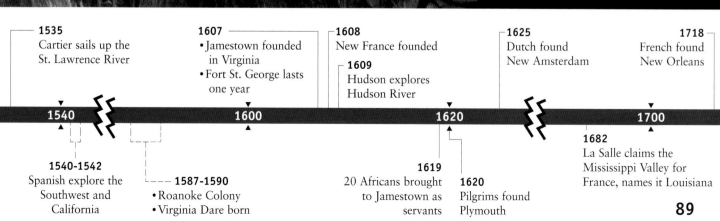

1535
Cartier sails up the St. Lawrence River

1607
• Jamestown founded in Virginia
• Fort St. George lasts one year

1608
New France founded

1609
Hudson explores Hudson River

1625
Dutch found New Amsterdam

1718
French found New Orleans

1540

1600

1620

1700

1540-1542
Spanish explore the Southwest and California

1587-1590
• Roanoke Colony
• Virginia Dare born

1619
20 Africans brought to Jamestown as servants

1620
Pilgrims found Plymouth

1682
La Salle claims the Mississippi Valley for France, names it Louisiana

LESSON ① The Spanish in North America

KEY IDEAS

- Spain began the European conquest of the Americas.

- Spain looked for gold, first in the Caribbean, then on the mainland.

- Spain set up plantations. They brought enslaved Africans to work on them.

- Spain explored much of what is now the southern and western United States.

KEY TERMS

conquistadors
convert
Hispaniola
Indians
plantation
slavery

PEOPLE TO KNOW

King Ferdinand and Queen Isabella of Spain
Christopher Columbus
Hernán Cortés
Juan Ponce de Leon
Cabeza da Vaca
Francisco Coronado
Hernando de Soto
Juan Rodríguez Cabrillo
Bartolomé de Las Casas

Europeans had been trading with people in Asia for many years. They got rugs, silk, gems, and spices from the lands there. But they had to travel a long way to get the things they wanted. The trip to Asia by land was long and full of danger. Explorers wanted to find a shorter route.

Columbus and the New World

One of the first explorers who looked for a shorter route to Asia was Christopher Columbus. King Ferdinand and Queen Isabella of Spain agreed to pay for his journey. In the spring of 1493, they had their people prepare a celebration. Columbus had returned to Spain with news that he had found an ocean route to the Asia and claimed the new land for Spain.

Columbus came to Spain's royal court with gold, island spices, and six people he had taken from the far away land. He called the people Indians, because he believed he had reached the Asian islands named the East Indies. But he had really landed on the edge of two great continents— North and South America. The people living there were not the "Indians" of Asia. They were Native Americans who lived on islands in the Caribbean Sea.

Hispanolia

Columbus gave King Ferdinand and Queen Isabella a plan to settle the islands in what was called the New World. He went back to the islands in 1493 and founded the first permanent colony in the Americas. It was on the island of *Hispaniola.* Haiti and the Dominican Republic are located there now (see map, page 104).

The Spanish had three goals. First, they wanted gold from the islands. Second, they wanted to introduce the Native Americans to Christianity. Third, they wanted to set up colonies using Native American workers.

Soon after Columbus returned, other explorers from Spain began sailing west. They wanted to find the gold that the native people wore. Not long after, ships loaded with gold and silver sailed back to Spain. These riches made Spain one of the greatest powers in Europe for many years. This was also the beginning of Europe's takeover of the Americas. Almost all of North and South America would fall under Spanish, Portuguese, French, and English rule.

Spain in the Caribbean

Ships full of explorers and Catholic priests began sailing for other Caribbean Islands, such as Cuba and Puerto Rico. The priests wanted to change, or *convert,* the Native Americans' religion to Christianity.

The Spanish quickly mined all the gold on the islands. So to make money, they turned to a plantation system of agriculture.

Plantations

A *plantation* is a large land area where people usually grow a single crop. Most are located on rich soils in the tropical regions of the world.

The Spanish raised sugarcane on plantations. The Caribbean's soil and climate were perfect for this crop. Sugar sold for high prices in Europe. It was easily shipped to market from Caribbean ports.

Slavery

The Spanish set up the plantations and oversaw the work. They forced the Native Americans on the islands to work on the plantations without pay. Forced work without pay is *slavery.*

Almost all the Native Americans in the Caribbean died from diseases brought by the Europeans or from forced labor. So Spanish ships brought enslaved Africans to the plantations. The Africans replaced the Native Americans.

Europeans also made money from selling slaves. Enslaved Africans had hard lives. They were forced to do tough work. They were not treated well. But even though they lost their freedom, they kept much of their African heritage alive.

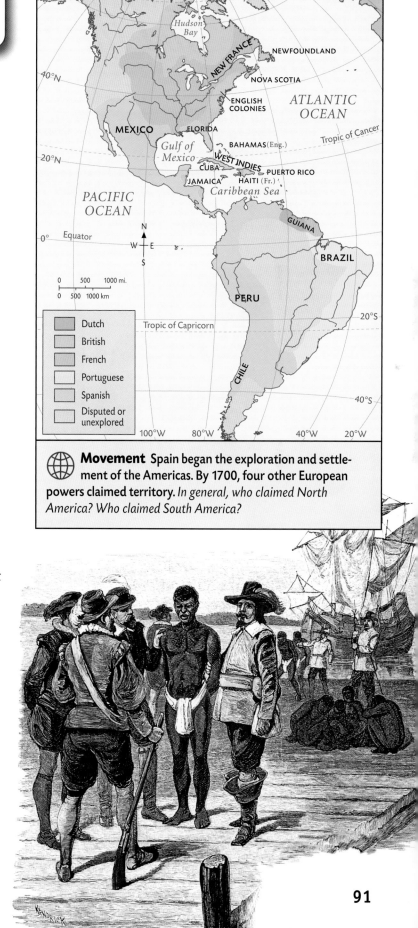

European Claims in the Americas, 1700

Dutch
British
French
Portuguese
Spanish
Disputed or unexplored

Movement Spain began the exploration and settlement of the Americas. By 1700, four other European powers claimed territory. *In general, who claimed North America? Who claimed South America?*

Bartolomé de Las Casas and the Black Legend

Catholic priests did much more than help spread the Catholic faith. Some of them worried about the welfare of the Native Americans. They saw that the plantations were unfair and cruel to the Native Americans. Some of the priests tried to help them.

Las Casas

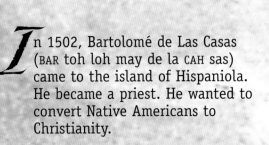

*I*n 1502, Bartolomé de Las Casas (BAR toh loh may de la CAH sas) came to the island of Hispaniola. He became a priest. He wanted to convert Native Americans to Christianity.

*L*as Casas was shocked by what he saw. He watched the Spanish destroy a Carib (a Native American island tribe) village. He saw Native Americans on the mainland beaten because they could not understand Spanish. This made las Casas upset. He wrote a book, *A Very Brief Account of the Destruction of the Indies*. He described the cruel way many Spanish colonists treated Native Americans. Las Casas angrily told the Spanish *conquistadors* that finding gold was their only goal. He thought that there were more important things than just finding gold.

Page from Las Casas' *Destruction of the Indies*

*L*as Casas' writings became the basis for the Black Legend. This legend turned many Europeans against the Spanish treatment of Native Americans. It finally made the Spanish rulers understand that they should stop enslaving Native Americans.

Spanish explorer Hernán Cortés conquered Tenochtitlán. **Who helped Cortés seize the city?**

Spain on the Mainland

The Spanish still hoped to find gold and silver. They began to explore the mainland of North and South America. The Spanish conquerors were called *conquistadors.*

Native Americans told the Spanish of great cities and cultures in other places in the Americas. These stories described amazing treasures. The idea of riches made many Spanish want to find these places. They wanted to take the treasures for themselves and Spain.

The Spanish *conquistador* Hernán Cortés and others heard these stories. By 1519, Cortés was on the mainland of Middle America making his way to Tenochtitlán, the great Aztec city. He soon seized the city with the help of several thousand Native American enemies of the Aztecs. Other *conquistadors* explored what is now Central America.

Spanish conquistadors brought horses to the Americas. **What did the Spanish hope to find?**

Chapter 5

One of these explorers was Vasco Núñez de Balboa. He founded the settlement of Santa María la Antigua del Darién in today's Panama. This was the first permanent European settlement on the mainland of the Americas. Then Balboa crossed Isthmus of Panama to the Pacific Ocean. An isthmus is a narrow strip of land (see map, page 91). He was the first European to reach the Pacific from the New World. He claimed the ocean for Spain.

New Spain

The Spanish claimed all the land they explored. They named their territory New Spain. You will learn more about New Spain in the lands that became Mexico and the nations of Central America and the Caribbean in Units 6 and 7.

Spain and Portugal each claimed part of South America. Portugal took the territory that is now modern Brazil. Spain claimed all of the remaining land except for a small strip along the Caribbean coast claimed by France, England, and the Netherlands.

Balboa claimed the Pacific Ocean for Spain. **What did Spain call their territory?**

A Journey to FLORIDA

Founding Florida

Juan Ponce de León (wan · pons · de · lay · OHN) was a Spanish *conquistador*. He sailed with Christopher Columbus on his second voyage to the New World.

A popular story is that Ponce de León was searching for the Fountain of Youth when he discovered Florida. De León did discover Florida in 1513. But he was not looking for the fountain of youth. He wanted the journey to bring himself a new feeling of rebirth. He was

looking for glory and honor. The story of the Fountain of Youth seems to have come from a book written several years after de León's death.

Some Native Americans in the Caribbean told the Spanish of a large, rich island to the north. De León was searching for gold and more land to claim for Spain. He sailed north and landed somewhere on the northeast coast of today's state of Florida. He claimed it for Spain.

De León named the land *La Florida*, meaning flowery. This

was either because of the flowers blooming there or because he landed during *"Pascua Florida."* That means Flowery Passover, or the Easter season, in Spanish.

Saint Augustine, Florida, is the oldest city in the United States founded by Europeans. The area was first visited by de León. But Pedro Menendez de Aviles built the first settlement there in 1565.

The Spanish sold Florida to the United States in 1821. Pascua Florida Day, April 2, is a state holiday in Florida today.

Europeans Conquer North America

Cabeza de Vaca and other men pretended they were medicine men and could cure sick people. **What did the Spanish want to learn from the Native Americans?**

Exploring the American Southwest

Many Spanish men were excited about exploring New Spain. They wanted to find gold. They set sail on long ocean voyages to explore the land Cortés had made famous.

Cities of Gold

About 20 years after Cortés, more than 500 Spanish explorers sailed in five ships from Spain to the New World. Three of the ships were lost at sea. The others landed in Florida. Some sailed back to Spain. The rest decided to explore.

Many got sick. They had trouble finding food. The Native Americans were unfriendly. The Spaniards decided to build boats and sail to Mexico. The men knew other Spanish people were living there.

Their small boats could not make the journey. Some men died at sea. Others made it to an island off the coast of Texas. Native Americans made the men their slaves. Most of the men died.

But one man, Cabeza de Vaca, pretended to be a medicine man. He rattled a gourd and made the sign of the cross. Many of the sick got well. The Native Americans gave him freedom to visit other tribes.

De Vaca and three others, including an African slave named Estevan (ehs·STAY·vahn), headed for Mexico. Along the way they met other Native Americans. The Native Americans told them wild stories of the Seven Cities of Cibola. They said the cities were made of gold.

De Vaca and his men finally made it to Mexico. They told the Spanish leaders about their journey. It had been eight years since they had left Spain. The leaders were surprised that the men had made it. But they also wanted to learn more about the cities of gold.

Spain in the Southwest

The leader of New Spain sent Estevan and a priest named Fray Marcos de Niza to find the golden cities. When Estevan got to a Zuni village, he was killed by the Native Americans there. De Niza went back to tell the leader of New Spain about Estevan's death.

When he got back, he met with New Spain's leader, Viceroy Mendoza. But instead, de Niza told Mendoza that he had climbed to the top of a hill and seen a golden city with high buildings and turquoise doors. The viceroy decided to send another man, Francisco Coronado, to look for the gold.

New Mexico

Coronado gathered an army of men to search for gold. There were hundreds of Spanish, plus more than 1,000 Native Americans and African slaves.

Coronado led a smaller group of men ahead of the main army. After many days of travel, they ran out of food. They were half starved when they got to a Zuni village in what is now New Mexico. The Zunis threatened the army. They tried to kill Coronado's interpreter. So Coronado ordered an attack.

In less than an hour the Zuni were forced to flee. The hungry Spanish ate all the food. The beans and corn were better than gold! Coronado soon learned that the Zunis did not have cities of gold. He wrote to the viceroy to tell him.

Arizona

Coronado sent two groups of his men to explore Arizona. Pedro de Tovar was helped by Native American guides. They took a small group of men to the Hopi villages. At first, the Hopi were not friendly. But Tovar attacked the Hopi and forced them to give up.

The Hopi told Tovar about a great river and rich Native Americans to the west. Tovar hurried back to the Zuni villages. He shared this news with Coronado.

Coronado was excited. He sent another group of men back to the Hopi village to find out if the Hopi were telling the truth. Hopi guides led the men to the Grand Canyon. They were the first Europeans to see this natural wonder. But they did not find any gold. So they returned to the Zuni village where Coronado was staying.

Coronado traveled to what is now Texas and Kansas before he returned to Mexico. He never found gold, but he did learn a great deal about the lands of the Southwest.

California

Several explorers sailed up the coast of California. They were led by Juan Rodríguez Cabrillo. They were looking for a water route to connect to the Atlantic Ocean. They also wanted to find the golden city of Cibola they had been told about. Instead, they learned that California was not an island. In 1542, Cabrillo arrived at "a very good enclosed port." That port is known today as San Diego Bay. Spain claimed California, too.

Coronado explored the Southwest looking for gold.
What were the areas claimed by Spain?

Explorers and Priests

Hernando de Soto explored America from Florida all the way to what is now Arkansas. He was the first European to see the Mississippi River.

Over the next 150 years, other explorers and Catholic priests traveled around the Southwest. The explorers wanted gold. They claimed the lands they explored for Spain. They did not find gold, but they did find silver.

The priests wanted to bring Christianity to the Native Americans in the region. They also claimed a lot of land for Spain and created settlements in what is now New Mexico and southern Arizona.

Spanish Rule

You will read in the next two lessons about the colonies in eastern North America. The Spanish ruled the southwest during the time that these colonies were settled. When the 13 colonies formed the United States, Spain still ruled the southwest. This region would not become part of the United States until the 1840s and 1850s. Spain ruled for about 300 years. Its influence still can be seen in the southwestern United States today.

Spain's Territory

By 1550, Spain's land in the New World extended from southern South America into North America, including what is now the southwestern United States and Florida. Spain's territory in North America would at times form the southern and western borders of the English colonies. To guard their new lands, the Spanish leaders built fortresses throughout the Caribbean and Gulf of Mexico.

Spanish priests and Native American workers built the San Xavier del Bac mission near Tucson, Arizona, more than 200 years ago. **What did the priests want to do?**

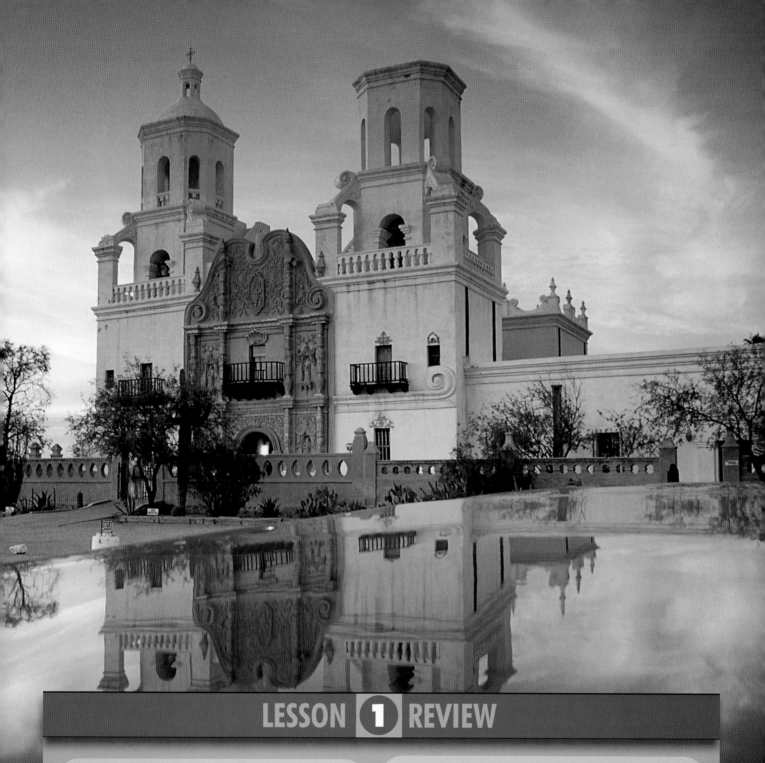

LESSON 1 REVIEW

Fact Follow-Up

1. Why did Columbus call Native Americans "Indians"?
2. What was the location of the first permanent Spanish colony in the Americas?
3. Describe the relative location of the Spanish colonies in the Americas.

Talk About It

1. Why did the Spanish develop plantations in the Americas?
2. What do you think the Native Americans meant when they told stories of riches to the Spanish?
3. Why do you think some Native American tribes helped the Spanish explorers and others did not?

Europeans Conquer North America

KEY IDEAS

- The Vikings were the first Europeans to set foot on North America, but they did not stay.

- Many Native Americans died from European diseases.

- The French, English, and Dutch began competing with Spain for land in the Americas.

- France began its North American settlement in Canada.

- The English founded Roanoke in today's North Carolina.

KEY TERMS

missionaries
Northwest Passage
Spanish Armada

PEOPLE TO KNOW

Leif Eriksson
John Cabot
Henry Hudson
Queen Elizabeth I
Sir Walter Raleigh
John White

Christopher Columbus was not the first European to see North America. Almost 500 years earlier, a small group of Norsemen, or Vikings, came. They lived for a time in what is now Newfoundland, Canada.

But Christopher Columbus' discovery set off a new wave of exploration. Soon many European nations were sending explorers, missionaries, fishermen, and traders to the New World. They wanted riches, glory, and land, too.

The Vikings

In Europe the Vikings told stories, called sagas, about a man named Leif Eriksson. About 1,000 years ago, Eriksson sailed from Greenland. He and his crew found a lovely bay on the coast of North America. The land there had rolling hills with meadows, forests, and lakes. The tides were amazing.

The Vikings decided to stay. The streams were full of salmon. There was plenty of timber. The Vikings found wild grapes in the forest, so they called the new land Vinland, or Vine Land. Early the next summer Eriksson returned to Greenland with lumber and grapes.

The stories of the new land made others want to come. A small number of Vikings spent several summers exploring. They built a few other settlements. The Vikings brought back lumber, furs, and other things that could be sold in Greenland and Europe. But the Vikings did not get along with Native Americans. They returned to Greenland.

For hundreds of years, most people did not believe that the saga of Leif Eriksson was based on fact. But in 1960, proof that Vikings lived in North America was found at L'Anse aux Meadows (lanz oh MED·ohz) in Newfoundland, Canada. Helge and Anne Stine Ingstad discovered Viking artifacts.

The Viking sagas are the first European descriptions of North America. Europeans would not return to the New World for five centuries.

According the the Viking sagas, Leif Eriksson lived in North America for a time.
Why did the Vikings leave?

Looking for Asia

Soon after Columbus returned to Spain, the English explorer John Cabot sailed west. He also thought that Asia could be reached by crossing the Atlantic. His route took him near the Gulf of St. Lawrence and Newfoundland in what is now Canada. Cabot's trip proved that North America was a very large continent.

To reach Asia, explorers believed that they could find a *Northwest Passage.* This was a waterway that they hoped would link the Atlantic and Pacific Oceans. We know today this passage does not exist. But explorers from Spain, England, France, and the Netherlands searched for this waterway for many years. During their searches, explorers claimed large parts of North America for their nations.

Spain is Challenged

England's ruler, Queen Elizabeth I, let English sea captains raid Spanish ships. Spain's ships were loaded with treasure from the New World. Spain was upset by the loss of gold and silver from the raids.

Also, Spain's king did not believe Elizabeth I should be Queen of England. Therefore, King Phillip of Spain ordered the Spanish Armada to sail to England and invade the country. The armada was a force of 130 ships and 25,000 men. The invasion failed. English forces and a fierce storm drove the armada away. Spain no longer controlled the Atlantic.

Because of this, Spain's hold in the Americas weakened. The English, Dutch, and French seized several Caribbean islands. Other European powers now could establish colonies in North America.

Native Americans

Native Americans lived all over North America when the Europeans began claiming their land. But the Native Americans lost more than just control over their land. Millions died from diseases brought by the Europeans.

This Native American medicine man hopes to cure his patient. **Why did many Native Americans die?**

Native Americans had never been exposed to these illnesses, like small pox. Their bodies could not fight these new diseases.

In places like the Caribbean, there were few Native Americans left. They could not defend their lands. This helped Europeans take control of new territory. Other Native Americans died fighting the Europeans or from forced labor.

Native Americans were losing lands where their ancestors had lived for thousands of years. Yet, wherever large numbers of them remained, they continued to fight to keep their way of life.

The Native Americans on the mainland where the French and English settled sometimes helped the newcomers. Sometimes they fought them. But within 300 years of the first European settlements, the Native Americans' traditional ways of life would be changed forever.

Jacques Cartier explored the St. Lawrence river. **Where did the French build settlements?**

New France

The French arrived in North America in the early 1500s. They came to fish the North Atlantic. In 1535, a French explorer named Jacques Cartier began to explore the area near the St. Lawrence River (see map, page 104). He first met the Native American Micmacs near where Newfoundland is today.

The Fur Trade

When Cartier met the Micmacs, he saw the furs many of them wore. Back in Europe, furs were popular. Wealthy people liked to wear them during the cold winters. Soon more than a thousand French ships a year sailed to North America. They traded with the Micmacs and other Native Americans for ermine, mink, and beaver furs.

The French built trading posts. Quebec and Montreal are two cities that were founded in the 1600s. They were built in places that were good for trading furs. Catholic *missionaries* came to convert Native Americans to Christianity.

Some settlers came, too. In 1604, French colonists built a settlement at Port Royal, Acadia. This colony covered parts of today's state of Maine and the Canadian provinces of New Brunswick and Nova Scotia.

All of these settlements became part of New France. You will learn more about these French explorers and New France in Unit 5.

These beaded moccasins were made by the Micmacs. **What did the Micmacs trade with Cartier?**

French Settlements

French explorers, fur traders, and missionaries soon moved west. They explored the area around the Great Lakes. In 1682, Rene-Robert LaSalle led a small group of explorers. They paddled down the Mississippi River to the Gulf of Mexico. France claimed this huge territory and called it Louisiana in honor of French King Louis XIV.

The French government tried to encourage some of its people to settle on farmland along the St. Lawrence River in what is now Canada. Some French settlers came. But fur trading was the way most people made a living in New France.

French forts and trading posts were slowly built near the Great Lakes and along the Mississippi. Many of today's great American cities, such as Detroit and St. Louis, began as French trading posts. In 1718, the French started a trading post at New Orleans, near the southern end of the Mississippi River. This tiny village soon became a great seaport.

The Dutch and Swedes

The Dutch were also interested in getting rich in the New World. In 1609, the Netherlands hired the English explorer Henry Hudson to find the Northwest Passage. Instead, he discovered what we now call the Hudson River and the Hudson Bay (see map, page 104). He claimed the land along the river for the Netherlands.

The Dutch built trading posts and plantations in the Americas. Many of the Dutch settlements were abandoned after several years.

The Swedes also built a colony. New Sweden was located in today's state of Delaware. The Dutch later conquered it. But the Swedish colonists stayed. Some of the settlers brought a style of log house to the New World. This style became the famous log cabin of American pioneers.

The Swedes founded what is today's Delaware. **What did they bring with them to the New World?**

The English

England saw that France and Spain were getting rich from their colonies in North America. The English wanted riches, too. They also believed settlers would convert the Native Americans to Christianity.

Sir Walter Raleigh

Sir Walter Raleigh was a favorite of Queen Elizabeth I of England. He wanted to build a colony in the New World.

In 1583, Raleigh's half-brother, Humphrey Gilbert, sailed to Newfoundland to start a colony. He claimed St. John's, Newfoundland, for the queen. Only a few fishermen were there. Gilbert died in a shipwreck on his trip home. Because of Gilbert's death, the new colony would not be settled until 1610.

The next year, Raleigh sent a small group of men to Roanoke (ROH·uh·nohk) Island on

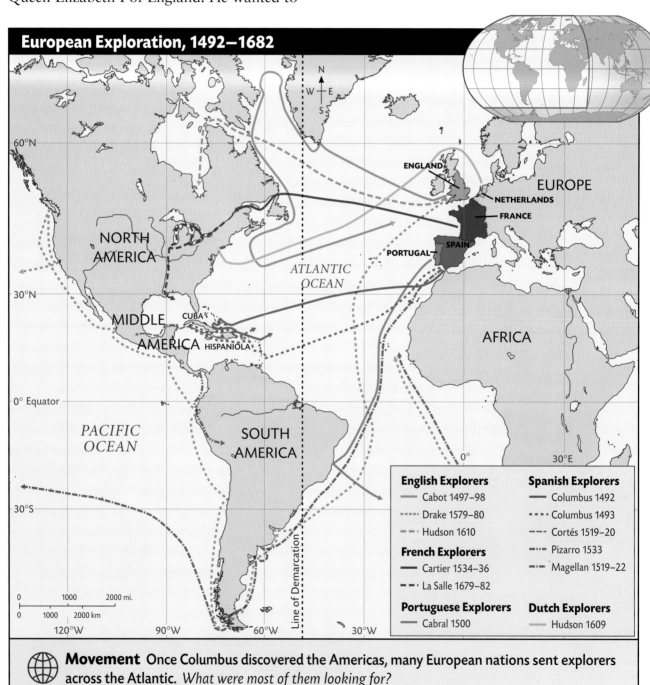

European Exploration, 1492–1682

ENGLAND
EUROPE
NETHERLANDS
FRANCE
SPAIN
PORTUGAL

NORTH AMERICA

ATLANTIC OCEAN

MIDDLE AMERICA
CUBA
HISPANIOLA

AFRICA

PACIFIC OCEAN

SOUTH AMERICA

0°   30°E

Line of Demarcation

English Explorers	Spanish Explorers
Cabot 1497–98	Columbus 1492
Drake 1579–80	Columbus 1493
Hudson 1610	Cortés 1519–20
French Explorers	Pizarro 1533
Cartier 1534–36	Magellan 1519–22
La Salle 1679–82	
Portuguese Explorers	**Dutch Explorers**
Cabral 1500	Hudson 1609

0 1000 2000 mi.
0 1000 2000 km
120°W   90°W   60°W   30°W

Movement Once Columbus discovered the Americas, many European nations sent explorers across the Atlantic. *What were most of them looking for?*

the coast of today's North Carolina. He wanted know if it would be a good place for a colony. The men returned with a good report. Raleigh called the new land "Virginia" to honor the queen.

Raleigh sent 108 men there to build a colony a year later. The colonists landed but returned to England after only a few months. Their supplies had run out. Raleigh decided to try again. He sent men, women, and children to found Roanoke in 1587.

The Lost Colony

Roanoke was the first English colony in North America. The first English child in the New World, Virginia Dare, was born there. John White was Roanoke's governor. Once the colony was settled, White returned to England for more supplies and people.

Because of England's war with Spain, White could not return to Roanoke until 1590. When he came back, the settlement was gone. Only the word CROATOAN was carved into a tree. Stormy weather and problems with the ships made it impossible to go to Croatoan. White could not find any of the colonists.

We still do not know what happened to the settlers of Roanoke. It is called the Lost Colony. Many historians believe that the settlers moved away and started new lives with the Native Americans.

Russia

The Russians discovered Alaska. They did not found a colony there until about 50 years later, in 1784. Russian Orthodox Christian priests went to Alaska to convert the Native Americans. Other Russians went to trade fur.

Russian explorers and settlers built trading posts in Alaska, the Aleutian Islands, and what became Oregon Territory. They went as far south as northern California. The colony was never very profitable. So Russia sold Alaska to the United States for $7,200,000 in 1867.

Colonial Beaufort

Beaufort is on the North Carolina coast. One of the oldest settlements in the state was laid out in 1713 on the site of a Native American village. The town was named for Henry Somerset, Duke of Beaufort. It became a port for trading with the Caribbean islands.

In 1747, ongoing fighting between the British and the Spanish was brought to our shores. Beaufort was captured by Spanish soldiers. After three days, the soldiers were driven off by a group of local militia.

CAROLINA CONNECTION

LESSON 2 REVIEW

Fact Follow-Up
1. Why did Europeans want to find the Northwest Passage?
2. What happened to the Native Americans after the Europeans arrived?
3. Describe the relative location of the French colonies in the Americas.
4. How did the French colonies make money?

Talk About It
1. Why do you think people did not believe the Viking sagas about Vinland were true?
2. How and why did England challenge Spain in the Americas?
3. What were the resources that the New World had that the Europeans wanted? Why do you think they wanted them?

LESSON ③ Early English Colonies

KEY IDEAS

- Fort St. George failed.

- Jamestown was founded to make its investors wealthy. It became a success.

- The colonies of Plymouth and Massachusetts Bay were founded for religious freedom.

- Other New England colonies were founded by settlers from Massachusetts.

KEY TERMS

cash crop
indentured servants
Pilgrims
Puritans
toleration

PEOPLE TO KNOW

King James I
George Popham
John Smith
William Bradford
Pocahontas
Squanto
Samoset
John Winthrop
Anne Hutchinson
Roger Williams
Thomas Hooker

King James I of England wanted to stop France and Spain from controlling of all of North America. He wanted England to have the New World's riches, too.

After Roanoke, others in England saw that much money could be made from North America's resources. But starting colonies was expensive. Ships and supplies needed to be bought.

Therefore, merchants and large landowners formed special partnerships to raise money, called companies. In return for his investment, each partner in the company would get a portion of the colony's profits once the colony was successful in America.

The Royal Charter

King James I gave permission, called a charter, to start colonies in Virginia. The charter set up two companies to do this. Look at the map on page 115. The Virginia Company of London was given the land in the south, between 34° and 41°N. The Virginia Company of Plymouth was given the land in the north, from 38° to 45°N.

Each company founded a colony in its own territory. The Company of London built its colony at Jamestown, Virginia. The Company of Plymouth built its colony at present-day Popham Beach, Maine.

Fort St. George

Explorers and fishermen had been sailing off the coast of today's Maine for many years. In 1607, the Company of Plymouth sent 100 men on the *Gift of God* and the *Mary and John* to build a colony there.

At the mouth of today's Kennebec River, the men landed and built Fort St. George. Their leader was George Popham. Sir Walter Raleigh's nephew, Raleigh Gilbert, was second-in-command.

The colonists included a minister, doctor, shipwrights (shipbuilders), soldiers, farmers, carpenters, and a cooper (barrelmaker). The men planned to send fur and timber back to England. They wanted to find gold and the Northwest Passage.

But life in the New World was harder than they had imagined. The men arrived too late to plant crops. They did not expect the winter to be so long and cold. Popham died. Gilbert was not a good leader.

The Native Americans there, the Wabanaki, would not trade furs with the settlers. Two years earlier, explorers had captured four Wabanaki and possibly one man from another tribe and took them to England. As a result, the Wabanaki did not trust the English.

The colonists did have one success. They built the first English ship in North America, the *Virginia*. They sailed home on it in 1608. The men abandoned the colony. Fort St. George's ruins were not found until 1994.

The English colony of Jamestown succeeded because the settlers began growing tobacco. **Why did the colony almost fail?**

Jamestown, Virginia

The colony founded in 1607 by the Virginia Company of London was more successful. But it, too, almost did not make it.

Three small ships landed on the shores of the Chesapeake Bay in today's Virginia. There they built Jamestown, named after King James I. The settlers had a hard trip. More than 40 of 144 men died on the journey. More problems faced the colonists in the New World.

The men wanted to find gold. So they did not plant crops or build good shelters. They did not make friends with the Native Americans. They settled in an area with insects that spread diseases. During the winter, many men died.

John Smith

In 1608, John Smith took control. He was a soldier. He issued a command to the settlers: If you don't work, you don't eat. Smith made the men plant crops. He improved the relationships with the Native Americans.

When Smith was injured in an accident in 1609, the colony returned to its old habits.

Many died from starvation and disease.

Yet Jamestown survived. More English settlers came. People from Poland and Germany joined the colony. Tobacco became its *cash crop.* Cash crops could be sold to Europeans for a profit. Tobacco became popular in Europe.

England finally had created a successful colony on the Atlantic coast.

John Smith took control of Jamestown. **What did he do there?**

Europeans Conquer North America

Pocahontas
1595–1617

Pocahontas is one of the best known Native Americans. Stories have been told about her for almost 400 years. She was a favorite daughter of the great Chief Powhatan of the Algonquian people in present-day Virginia. Her name meant "full of mischief."

In late 1607, John Smith and others were attacked by members of Powhatan's tribe. They killed the other Englishmen, but took Smith back to Powhatan. Smith believed he was going to be killed by the tribe, but Pocahontas saved him. The young girl probably saved the lives of many colonists by bringing them food when they were starving.

Years after John Smith was set free, Pocahontas was captured by the English. They wanted some corn, so they took her prisoner and used her to trade for the corn. They took Pocahontas to their settlement at Henrico. There she learned English and dressed as an English girl. She was converted to Christianity and given the name of Rebecca.

When Chief Powhatan learned of this, he was very angry. Some stories say that, to calm the chief's anger, a young Englishman named John Rolfe married Pocahontas. They had a baby boy named Thomas.

The family sailed to England. There Pocahontas met Queen Anne. She also met an old friend, Captain John Smith.

Pocahontas never saw her Virginia home again. Shortly before a planned trip back to Virginia, Pocahontas died at the age of 22. There are many descendants of Pocahontas. They are proud of their ancestor who tried to create friendship between the Native Americans and the white people in Virginia.

Pocahontas

Pocahontas saving John Smith

Indentured Servants

Jamestown's successful tobacco farms created new challenges. Tobacco farming needed many workers. So farmers brought *indentured servants.* These people agreed to work in exchange for free passage to America. They received food, clothing, and shelter from the farmer.

After working from seven to 14 years, they became free. Sometimes they were given land or money to start a new life.

Africans are Enslaved

Most Africans, as you read in Lesson 1, were brought to America as slaves. Men and women from Africa arrived in Jamestown in 1619.

The first to come were not slaves. They were indentured servants. Like indentured servants from Europe, they worked for several years and were freed. Anthony Johnson was an African settler. He started life in Jamestown as an indentured servant. When he was finished with his contract, he bought his own land and hired servants.

Slavery did not happen all at once. It first began with people deciding to keep Africans as indentured servants for life. Farmers and merchants realized that this would cost them less money. The first document that describes an African being kept a servant for life is from 1640. But within 20 years, Africans were being brought to the colony as slaves. Slavery spread to the other English colonies.

This is a contract for an indentured servant. **What was the difference between an indentured servant and a slave?**

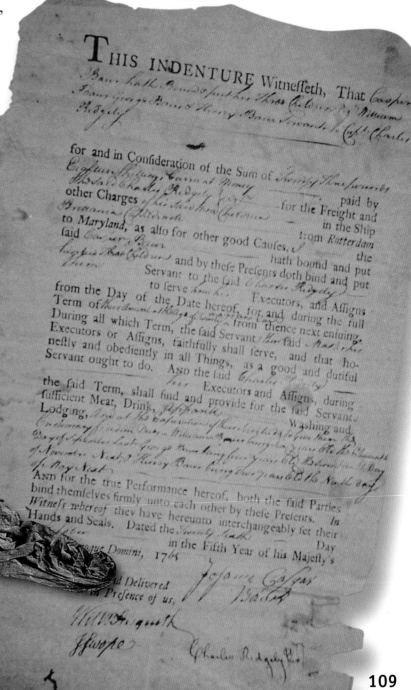

Tobacco was the cash crop of the Jamestown settlement. **What is a cash crop?**

The English who settled Plymouth Plantation came to North America for religious freedom. **Who helped them survive?**

Massachusetts

In 1614, John Smith returned to the New World. He sailed along the coasts of Maine and Massachusetts. He named this area New England.

A few years later, English settlers sailed to New England. These people came for religious freedom and a desire for a better life. They were *Pilgrims* and *Puritans.*

In England both of these groups were persecuted, or caused to suffer, because of their faith. They were treated this way because they did not join the Church of England. They thought the New World would be a place where they could worship in peace.

Both groups settled in today's Massachusetts. These colonies led to the founding of other colonies in New England.

Plymouth

The Pilgrims came first. In 1620 men, women, and children sailed on a small ship called the *Mayflower*. They founded the Plymouth Colony in December when they landed. William Bradford became their leader.

By the end of the first winter, almost half of the settlers had died from accidents or illnesses. The colony survived with a lot of help from the Native Americans.

Massachusetts Bay

The Puritans settled the Massachusetts Bay Colony. Their leader was John Winthrop. He got his idea for the colony from the Bible. He wanted to create what the Bible called a "city upon a hill." This meant a Christian colony that would be a model for the world.

Puritan settlers brought their families, livestock, equipment, and supplies in 1630.

They had a religious mission and plenty of food and supplies. The Puritans were successful, but ran a strict colony. They did not allow religious freedom in Massachusetts Bay. There were many rules.

A new charter was given to the colony in 1691. This gave Massachusetts Bay's government control over the colonies in Plymouth and what is now Maine.

The Pilgrims wanted to give thanks for surviving the first, harsh winter in their new home. They invited their Native American neighbors to a harvest feast. The custom of gathering together to give thanks developed into our Thanksgiving. Many families celebrate this holiday in November with a big turkey dinner.

A Journey to THE COLONIES

Life in the Massachusetts Colonies

During the Protestant Reformation many of Europe's Christians broke away from the Catholic Church. England formed its own church. It was headed by the king or queen. Everyone in England had to belong to this newly formed Church of England.

But some people, including Pilgrims and Puritans, believed that this new church was too much like the Catholic Church they had left. They wanted to worship in their own way. Both of these religious groups founded colonies in Massachusetts.

The Pilgrims

The Pilgrims settled in Plymouth. They were not prepared for the conditions there. William Bradford wrote about starvation and bad weather. Many died the first winter.

Bradford described how two Native Americans who spoke English helped the Pilgrims. Squanto had been taken to England a few years earlier. Samoset had learned English from fishermen.

The seal of Massachusetts Bay Colony.

During the next year, Native Americans traded with the Pilgrims. They showed them where to fish and how to grow crops. The Native American leader, Massasoit, and the colonists signed a peace treaty. Both sides promised to live in peace and support the other if attacked.

The Pilgrims survived. They invited the Native Americans to join them in a celebration that is now called Thanksgiving.

The Puritans

John Winthrop and about 900 Puritan colonists settled at the mouth of the Charles River. They created the Massachusetts Bay Colony where Boston is today.

Life in the colony was challenging. The Puritans believed in hard work. Everyone worked from sunrise to sunset. There was little free time. Everyone had to go to church on Sunday. Dancing was frowned upon. Plays were banned. There were laws against stylish clothing. Punishments for crimes were harsh.

Yet the Puritans made time for celebrations. They gathered with friends at weddings, house-raisings, town meetings, and other events.

The Puritans developed the purest type of democratic government in America. This was the town meeting.

At a town meeting, every male church member had the right to speak. Decisions were made by voting. In some towns, men who owned property but were not church members could also vote. Many New England towns are still governed by town meetings today.

Squanto
1585–1622

Squanto's real name was Tisquantum. He was nicknamed "Squanto" by the English.

It is believed that Squanto was one of the five young Native American men captured near Fort St. George in Maine. He was taken to England. There he learned to speak English.

He was treated well, but he always wanted to go back to his own village, Patuxet, on Cape Cod. Captain John Smith took Squanto back to Cape Cod, but Squanto was soon kidnapped by another Englishman, John Hunt.

Hunt sold Squanto into slavery in Spain. A Spanish priest helped Squanto escape to England. Later, he returned home to Patuxet. But his village was empty. Everyone had died from a disease brought by the Europeans.

Squanto walked westward for days. Finally, he came to the village of a chief named Massasoit. The chief became his leader. Massasoit made Squanto the interpreter for the pilgrims and the Wampanoags.

The Pilgrims had come from England. They settled in Squanto's old village, but they now called it Plymouth. Squanto was kind to the Pilgrims and helped them survive in the New World. He showed them how to fertilize their crops and where the best places for fishing were.

Other New England Colonies

The leaders of Massachusetts did not allow disagreement in religious matters. The strict religious life there caused some settlers to leave. They formed their own colonies.

Rhode Island and Connecticut

Anne Hutchinson was a Puritan who came to Massachusetts from England. Her beliefs differed from the ideas held by most Puritan leaders, yet many people wanted to hear her teachings about the Bible. She held meetings at her home. The colony's leaders demanded that she stop the meetings. When Hutchinson did not give up her Bible classes, she was taken to court. The court ruled that she was disruptive. It ordered her to leave the colony. Some people believe that Hutchinson was punished because she was a woman. But she was not the only one driven from Massachusetts.

Roger Williams was also a Puritan. He criticized the colony for its law that required people to go to church. He believed going to church was a personal choice. Williams also criticized Massachusetts because it took land from the Native Americans without paying for it. Massachusetts sent him away.

Williams bought land to start his own colony from the Native Americans. Anne Hutchinson joined him. They founded the colony of Rhode Island.

Rhode Island differed from Massachusetts in three ways. First, it separated the church from the government. Second, it allowed people to decide their own faith. Third, it gave the vote to all white men.

Settlers who disliked Massachusetts moved to Rhode Island. Jews, Catholics, and Quakers also came to the colony. Rhode Island became known for its toleration of other viewpoints. This meant that people were able to follow their own beliefs.

Connecticut was founded for similar reasons. Thomas Hooker was its leader. He

This ship is anchored in Portsmouth Harbor, New Hampshire. **New Hampshire's settlements were protected by which colony?**

wanted the people to have more say in running the government. The people who agreed joined him to start a new colony. They founded a town called Hartford. After they formed other towns, they wrote a new constitution, or set of rules for their government.

New Hampshire

The first settlers of New Hampshire arrived on the coast in 1623. They farmed, fished, and built a trading post. Over the next few years, a few other small settlements were started. Dover, Portsmouth, Exeter, and Hampton were the only permanent towns in New Hampshire until 1673.

Until the late 1670s, New Hampshire's towns were protected by Massachusetts. New Hampshire then became a royal colony. But its government still could not protect its people. Massachusetts protected New Hampshire until 1741.

The colonies did not get along well. For example, the Massachusett's government gave away land in New Hampshire. However, often that land was the same piece that New Hampshire's government had already given someone else.

In 1741, New Hampshire became independent. It gained more territory and appointed its own royal governor.

LESSON 3 REVIEW

Fact Follow-Up

1. Why did England decide to establish colonies in North America?
2. What was the difference between indentured servants and slaves?
3. The Virginia colony and the Massachusetts Bay colony were founded for different reasons. What were the reasons?
4. Who established the Rhode Island and Connecticut colonies?

Talk About It

1. Compare the leadership of John Smith in the Virginia colony and John Winthrop in the Massachusetts Bay Colony.
2. Why were the Puritans of the Massachusetts Bay Colony as strict as they were?
3. Compare the reasons for founding the Connecticut and Rhode Island colonies.
4. Describe the relationships between Massachusetts Bay and the other colonies?

The English founded colonies for two reasons. First, people wanted religious freedom. Second, people wanted to become wealthy. Each colony was founded and run separately from the others.

Maryland

Maryland was founded for religious freedom. George Calvert worked in the government of King Charles I. Calvert converted to Catholicism. Like Puritans, Catholics were persecuted in England. Calvert asked the king for land in America. He called it Maryland.

Calvert would not live to see this new colony. His son became Lord Baltimore of Maryland. Maryland welcomed Catholics and people with other religions. To keep peace, the government passed a law of religious tolerance. This allowed people of any religion to live there. Maryland's settlers got help from Virginia and local Native Americans. They grew tobacco and traded for fur.

The Carolinas

The Carolina colony was very large. It covered what are now the states of North Carolina, South Carolina, and Georgia. It was owned by a group of eight noblemen called *Lords Proprietors.* A proprietor is a person who owns property.

The nobles received the land from King Charles II in 1663. Some settlers were already there. They had come to the land when it was part of Virginia. Some Virginians moved south to settle in the new colony. Other settlers came from England, France, Germany, and Switzerland.

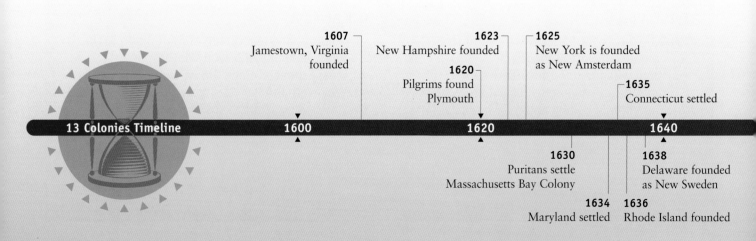

13 Colonies Timeline

1607 Jamestown, Virginia founded

1623 New Hampshire founded

1620 Pilgrims found Plymouth

1625 New York is founded as New Amsterdam

1635 Connecticut settled

1600

1620

1640

1630 Puritans settle Massachusetts Bay Colony

1638 Delaware founded as New Sweden

1634 Maryland settled

1636 Rhode Island founded

Soon there were more African slaves than European settlers.

Two different ways of life developed in the Carolina colony. In the northern part of the colony, tobacco was an important cash crop. Settlers also made a living producing turpentine, pitch, and tar for shipbuilding.

Rice and indigo were the important cash crops in the southern part of the colony. Settlers there created large plantations to grow these crops. They depended on slave labor more than settlers in the northern part of the colony.

By 1712 the Lords Proprietors had divided the colony into North and South Carolina. The two colonies had separate royal governments by 1729.

New York and New Jersey

At the mouth of the Hudson River, the Dutch founded the city of New Amsterdam. The Dutch were mainly traders. They competed with the English.

By the 1650s, England had declared war on the Netherlands. As a result, England took over New Amsterdam. King Charles II gave the land to his brother, the Duke of York. It was renamed New York.

New York was a huge territory. The Duke of York decided that he could not manage such a large area. He divided the colony. He gave some of the land to his friends, Lord Berkeley and Sir George Carteret. This land became the colony of New Jersey.

1663
Carolina founded

What would YOU do?

Imagine that you live in a country that does not let your family practice your religion. Your parents have decided to move to a new country.

You will have to leave behind everything that you know and make a long and dangerous journey. It will be difficult but also full of opportunity. Your parents have given you the choice to stay in your country with your grandparents or go with them. What would you do?

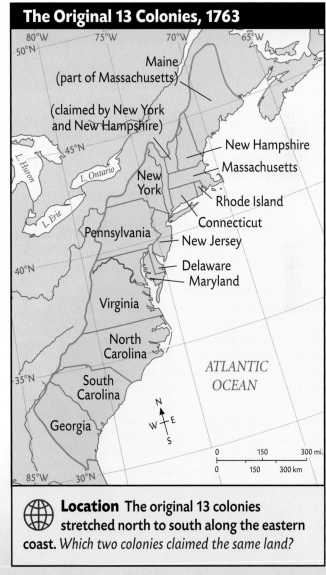

The Original 13 Colonies, 1763

Location The original 13 colonies stretched north to south along the eastern coast. *Which two colonies claimed the same land?*

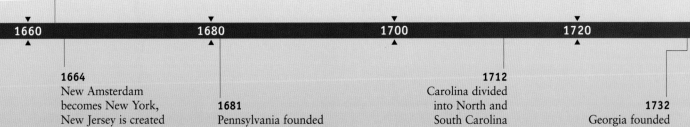

1660

1680

1700

1720

1664
New Amsterdam becomes New York, New Jersey is created

1681
Pennsylvania founded

1712
Carolina divided into North and South Carolina

1732
Georgia founded

115

Pennsylvania and Delaware

In the 1680s, religious differences still divided England's people. William Penn was a Quaker. He wanted to be free to follow his faith. So he founded Pennsylvania.

Penn was well educated. His father was a personal friend of the king and an officer in the Royal Navy. Penn could have followed in his father's footsteps. But he did not.

Penn surprised everyone by becoming a Quaker. Quakers believe that all people were equal in the sight of God. They believed Christians did not need the Church of England, its ministers, and religious ceremonies for worship. Quakers refused to pay taxes to the church. They also would not serve in the military.

Like other Quakers, Penn was criticized. His father and others demanded that he change his beliefs. He refused. Instead, he went to America and founded Pennsylvania.

WORD ORIGINS

Philadelphia

Pennsylvania's capital was Philadelphia. The city became famous. Its name was translated from a Greek word meaning "brotherly love." This is how Philadelphia got its nickname, "the city of brotherly love."

The word Pennsylvania means "Penn's Woods." Pennsylvania quickly became a *haven,* or safe place for many religions. Penn and other Quakers opposed slavery. They also wanted fair treatment of Native Americans.

Pennsylvania took over the land south of New York and New Jersey. New Sweden had been founded there. The settlers of New Sweden wanted their own government. Penn granted them self-rule. They formed the colony of Delaware.

Georgia

Georgia was the last of the 13 colonies. It was carved out of South Carolina.

James Oglethorpe was a reformer. He wanted to improve the life of others. He had helped poor people at home. They had been put in jail because they could not pay their debts. Oglethorpe believed that the poor could

Peter Cooper painted this view of the harbor of colonial Philadelphia. **What does the name "Philadelphia" mean?**

start a new life in America. He wanted to found a new colony to help them.

Spain controlled Florida to the south of the Carolinas. To get the king's support, Oglethorpe told the king that Georgia could help defend the other colonies against an attack from Spain or another enemy.

Georgia was unique in other ways. From the start, Oglethorpe and other leaders adopted strict rules to make its poor settlers work. They made selling rum illegal. They also opposed slavery at first. They thought that poor Europeans needed to learn good work habits. But slavery did come to the colony.

Colonial Profits

The leaders of England thought that their American colonies could make them rich in two ways. First, the colonies would send England crops and goods they did not have in Europe. Second, settlers in America would buy clothing and other goods from English merchants. The government would tax this trade.

England had founded colonies on several islands in the Caribbean. These included Saint Kitts, Barbados, and Jamaica. These islands became important to England's economy. Sugar was grown on plantations there.

Europeans were now drinking tea, coffee, and cocoa. They wanted sugar to sweeten these drinks and other foods.

The Southern American colonies traded tobacco, cotton, and rice. The Northern colonies traded lumber, naval stores, and furs. The 13 colonies did not make as much money as those in the Caribbean.

Triangular Trade

England developed a trading system called triangular trade. This described the trade between the Caribbean plantations, New England, and the west coast of Africa. Look at the map on page 104. Find Africa, New England, and the Caribbean. You can see that these places form the points of a triangle. That is why the system was called triangular trade.

Slaves captured in Africa were brought to the Caribbean. They were sold to the sugar plantation owners. There sugar from the Caribbean was shipped to New England and made into rum. That rum was shipped to Africa and traded for slaves.

Later, cotton became an important crop. It was shipped to England and made into cloth. The cloth was sold back to the colonists in America. England grew wealthy from this system. Many colonists did, too.

LESSON ④ REVIEW

Fact Follow-Up

1. Why were the Pennsylvania and Maryland colonies established?
2. Describe the two ways of life that developed in the Carolina colony.
3. Who founded the colony of New York?
4. What were William Penn's dreams for the Pennsylvania colony?

Talk About It

1. Compare the reasons for founding the Carolina colony and the colonies of Pennsylvania and Maryland.
2. How did New Amsterdam become New York?
3. Why did James Oglethorpe found the Georgia colony?

skill

Accessing a Variety of Sources; Gathering, Synthesizing, and Reporting Information

Using Geography's Themes: Movement

Movement is the fourth theme of geography. Movement is everywhere in nature. Rivers flow. Snow falls. Birds fly.

Geographers use the theme of movement to study how people, goods, and ideas get from one place to another.

This chapter describes the movement of people to North America. It tells us about the changes that they made.

Let's work on our graphic organizer. You will soon see that you already know quite a lot about movement.

Describing Your Home Town/City

Write "4. Movement" in the bottom space. Add below it "4a) People," "4b) Goods," "4c) Ideas."

Your organizer should now look like the table at below. Let's complete this section.

My Home Town	
Geography's Themes	**Data**
1. Location	
a) *Relative*	[completed]
b) *Absolute*	[completed]
2. Place	
a) *Physical Characteristics*	[completed]
b) *Human Characteristics*	[completed]
3. Human-Environmental Interaction	
a) *How Environment Affects People*	[completed]
b) *How People Use Their Environment*	[completed]
c) *How People Change Their Environment*	[completed]
4. Movement	
a) *People*	
b) *Goods*	
c) *Ideas*	

4a. Ask yourself these questions: Has your family moved? Has anyone in your family moved? Have any new people moved into or out of your community? Have those moves affected the lives of your family? Have they changed the community?

4b. What kinds of things (crops or other products) leave and come into your community? How is this movement of goods important?

4c. How do ideas come into your community? Do they come from school textbooks, the Internet, ideas from your teachers, TV, or newspapers? Do people in your community send ideas to other parts of the United States or the world? Has movement of ideas affected life in your community? Might ideas from your community have affected others?

Describing Three Cities in North America

Use information from this chapter in your graphic organizer on places in North America. Put it under Movement. This means that you will be looking at the ways that movement affected life in North America.

Locate the parts of this chapter that describe what happened nearest the cities that you picked. Review these pages. Also, use the maps on pages 91, 104, and 115 to help answer these questions.

4a. From what part of Europe did the people who first settled near each of your cities come? Did Africans also reach these points? Did the coming of these people change the places? Or did people quickly move on without leaving much change?

4b. What goods did the newcomers bring? What did they take away? How did this movement of goods affect lives in the areas that you selected?

4c. Did the newcomers bring ideas that were different? What were those ideas? How did these ideas affect life in the cities that you chose. What ideas did the newcomers learn from the Native Americans? How did this exchange affect life in those places?

It may not be easy to find all the information you need to complete your charts on your cities. You may want to use other such sources as the Internet, encyclopedias, atlases, and other media center materials.

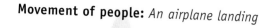

Movement of people: *An airplane landing*

Movement of goods: *Trucks and truckers delivering products*

Movement of ideas: *Students using the Internet to research school projects*

CHAPTER 5 REVIEW

Lessons Learned

LESSON 1
The Spanish in North America
Spain began the conquest of the Americas. They were looking for gold. They set up plantations and brought enslaved Africans to work on them. They explored much of North America.

LESSON 2
Europeans Come to North America
The Vikings were the first Europeans to visit America. Many Native Americans died from European diseases. The French, English, and Dutch competed with Spain for land.

LESSON 3
Early English Colonies
Fort St. George failed. Jamestown was the first successful English colony. Plymouth and Massachusetts Bay were founded for religious freedom. Connecticut and Rhode Island were founded by settlers from Massachusetts.

LESSON 4
The Later English Colonies
Religious tolerance was important in Maryland and Pennsylvania. The Lords Proprietors founded North and South Carolina. The Dutch founded New York. Georgia was founded to help people who could not pay their debts. Trade was important to the settlers.

Talk About It

1. Compare ways of life in Spanish and French colonies in the New World.
2. If you had lived in the Massachusetts Bay Colony, how would your life have been different from the life of someone living in Pennsylvania?
3. Were any of the English colonists well prepared for their lives in the New World? Explain.
4. Were the Puritans wise not to tolerate dissent? Explain.
5. If you had lived in the Carolina colony, would you have chosen to live in the northern or the southern area? Explain why.
6. Compare the religious beliefs of the Quakers in Pennsylvania and the Puritans in Massachusetts.
7. Compare the reasons for founding the Georgia colony and the Carolina colony.

Mastering Mapwork

MOVEMENT
Use the map on page 104 to answer these questions:

1. Which English explorer moved farthest north in his explorations?
2. Which English explorer moved farthest south and west?
3. In what directions did the explorer, Henry Hudson move?
4. Which explorer moved down the middle of what is now the United States, and for which country did he explore?
5. Which country was most active in exploring in the sixteenth century?

Becoming Better Readers

Learning New Words
Good readers are continually learning new words and expanding their vocabularies. This chapter had lots of new Key Terms. Choose one of your new words like *convert* or *toleration* and use it a conversation. Write how you used the word you chose in your conversation.

Go to the Source

Comparing Points of View

Compare the journal entry and painting about the first Thanksgiving. Then answer the questions below with specific reference to the sources.

Our harvest being gotten in, our governour sent . . men on fowling [hunting birds], that so we might. . . rejoyce together, . . . they foure in one day killed as much fowle, [to last] almost a weeke, at which time . . . many of the Indians coming amongst us, and . . . their great king Massasoyt, with some nintie men, whom for three dayes we entertained and feasted, and they went out and killed five Deere, which we brought to the Plantation . . . And although it was not always so plentifull, . . . by the goodness of God, we are so farre from want, that we often wish you partakers of our plentie.

—Edward Winslow

Questions
1. Whose point of view do you think the painting and Thanksgiving quote shows? How were they similar?
2. Edward Winslow's account says there were 52 Pilgrims at the feast. What evidence supports that there were more Indians (Native Americans) than Pilgrims at the feast?
3. Based on the text, how long did the people feast together?
4. What does Edward Winslow's written account tell you about his opinion of the Thanksgiving feast?
5. What do you think Winslow meant when he said the Pilgrims were "farre from want?"

Europeans Conquer North America

121

The History of the United States

In 1776, the United States was born. The founders of our country gave it a Latin motto, "E Pluribus Unum." These words mean "Out of Many, One." The leaders meant that 13 different colonies were joining together to create one strong nation. Many people with different backgrounds would become citizens of one new nation.

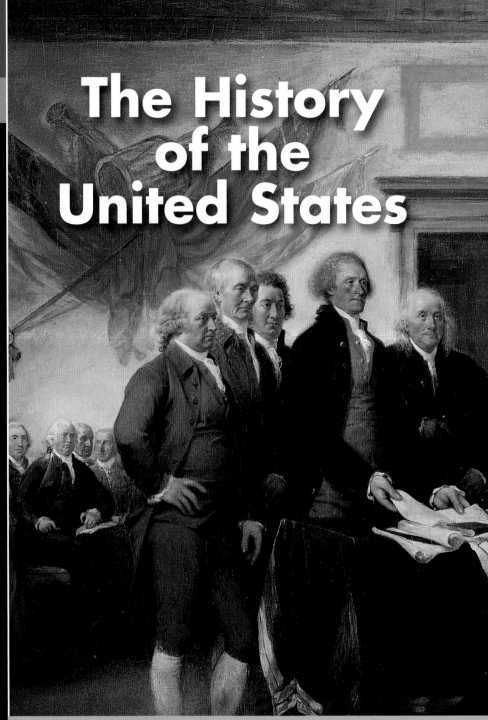

Signing of the Declaration of Independence *by John Trumbull*

Timeline of Events

1400	1500	1600	
1400–1492	1492–1733		
Chapter 4	**Chapter 5**	**Chapter 6**	**Chapter 7**
• The first settlers probably came from Asia.	• Spain explores North America.	• American democracy grows out of British traditions.	• The Constitution is written and a new government is formed.
• The Aztec and Maya built large civilizations.	• The French and other Europeans explore North America.	• The colonies declare their independence from Great Britain.	• Many Americans begin to move west.
• The first Americans had many different ways of life.	• England founded colonies along the Atlantic coast.	• The United States wins the War of Independence.	• The U.S. wins the Mexican-American War.

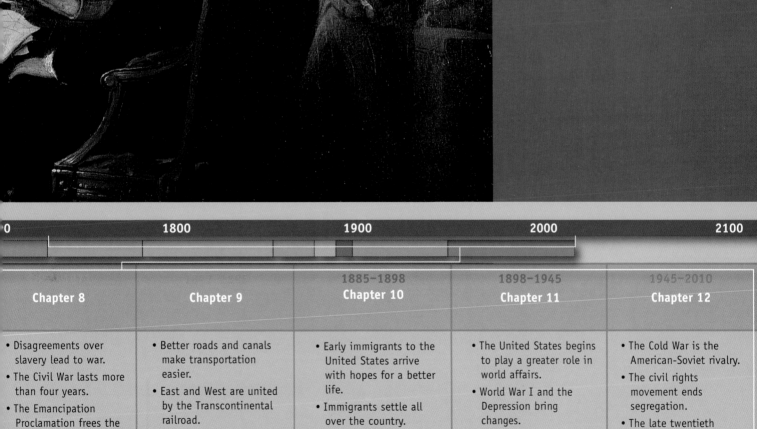

0	1800	1900	2000	2100

		1885–1898	1898–1945	1945–2010
Chapter 8	**Chapter 9**	**Chapter 10**	**Chapter 11**	**Chapter 12**
• Disagreements over slavery lead to war. • The Civil War lasts more than four years. • The Emancipation Proclamation frees the slaves. • Reconstruction brings political and social changes to the South.	• Better roads and canals make transportation easier. • East and West are united by the Transcontinental railroad. • The United States becomes a nation of big businesses.	• Early immigrants to the United States arrive with hopes for a better life. • Immigrants settle all over the country. • More immigrants come from Asia, South America, and Africa.	• The United States begins to play a greater role in world affairs. • World War I and the Depression bring changes. • World War II makes the United States into a world leader.	• The Cold War is the American-Soviet rivalry. • The civil rights movement ends segregation. • The late twentieth century is a time of change.

The Birth of a New Nation

Chapter Preview

LESSON 1
The Roots of Democratic Government
American democracy grew out of British traditions. Each colony developed in its own way.

LESSON 2
The Colonies Choose Freedom
After struggling against unfair taxes, the colonies declared their independence from Great Britain.

LESSON 3
The War of Independence
George Washington led the Continental Army against the British forces and won independence.

Timeline of Events

1619
Virginia's first governor appointed

1639
Fundamental Orders of Connecticut written

1707
Great Britain formed by Act of Union

1600

1700

1620
Mayflower Compact created by the Plymouth colonists

1649
Maryland passes Religious Toleration Act

1743
United Colonies of New England formed

New leaders were emerging in the 13 American colonies. Many of these people had lived only in America. They loved their homes and were loyal to their colonial governments. George Washington was one such person.

When he was a young man, Washington was in the British military. He took a message from Virginia's governor to the commander of the French forces on the frontier. Washington brought the commander's reply back to Williamsburg, the capital of Virginia.

That answer started the French and Indian War. In this war the British colonists fought the French and Native Americans for control of much of North America. It led to the the birth of a new country, the United States of America.

British General Charles Cornwallis surrendering to George Washington at Yorktown in Virginia

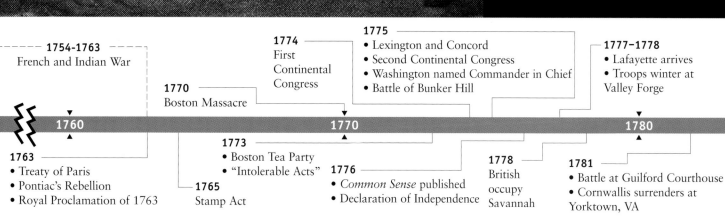

1754-1763
French and Indian War

1763
- Treaty of Paris
- Pontiac's Rebellion
- Royal Proclamation of 1763

1760

1765
Stamp Act

1770
Boston Massacre

1773
- Boston Tea Party
- "Intolerable Acts"

1774
First Continental Congress

1776
- *Common Sense* published
- Declaration of Independence

1775
- Lexington and Concord
- Second Continental Congress
- Washington named Commander in Chief
- Battle of Bunker Hill

1770

1778
British occupy Savannah

1777-1778
- Lafayette arrives
- Troops winter at Valley Forge

1781
- Battle at Guilford Courthouse
- Cornwallis surrenders at Yorktown, VA

1780

LESSON **1** Our Democratic Roots

KEY IDEAS

- American democracy grew out of British traditions.

- Each colony developed its own system of representative government.

- The colonies experimented with forming alliances.

- The French and Indian War increased the King's involvement in the colonies.

KEY TERMS

alliances
allies
assemblies
consent
defeat
democratic
French and Indian War
House of Burgesses
legislature
Mayflower Compact
monarchy
Parliament
Religious Toleration Act
representatives
subjects
Treaty of Paris (1763)

England was governed by a *monarchy.* A monarchy is a system of government headed by a king or queen. He or she holds most or all of the power. The king or queen rules the people. They are called the *subjects.*

In the seventeenth and eighteenth centuries, however, the power of England's monarchy was growing more limited. The government was becoming more democratic.

What is a Democracy?

A *democratic* government is a political system. In a democracy, the people of a country create their own government. They rule themselves. The town meeting in Massachusetts Bay is an example of this.

In many democracies there are too many people to make decisions all together in a large group. So *representatives* are elected by a vote of the people. The representatives work in a *legislature* where they make the laws. Legislatures are also called *assemblies.* Representatives are supposed to represent the wishes of the people who voted for them.

Democratic Traditions

England had a king. But, it also had *Parliament,* a two-part legislature. Parliament is made up of the House of Lords and the House of Commons. Representatives in the House of Commons were elected by the votes of property-owning men.

While the English were colonizing North America, the king was slowly losing powers. Parliament, especially the House of Commons, was gaining power. For example, the king could not tax his subjects without the approval of both houses of Parliament. American colonists brought these democratic traditions with them when they crossed the Atlantic. Soon, the colonies developed their own types of representative democracy.

England Becomes Great Britain

It was also at this time that England became part of the kingdom of Great Britain. The Act of Union was passed in 1707 by the parliaments of England and Scotland. This united England, Wales, and Scotland into one nation. The 13 English colonies in North America became the 13 British colonies.

Virginia's House of Burgesses

Those first settlers who founded Jamestown always had a government. It was the Virginia Company of London. The company decided where to build the colony. It sent supplies and settlers to Jamestown. But the company knew that it would be hard to manage the colony from far away in London. They created a council to run it.

Virginia took another step toward self-government in 1619. The company appointed a governor and allowed settlers who owned land to elect people to advise him. This assembly was called the *House of Burgesses.* It helped the governor make laws for the colony.

Only white men who owned property could vote. But Virginia had shown that the people should have a voice in running the colony.

Early Democracy in Massachusetts

In the north, Plymouth's settlers also formed a government at the start of the colony. It was based upon *consent,* or agreement by the people. The consent allowed their representatives to make laws for them.

They did this because some of the people who founded Plymouth did not follow the religion of the Pilgrims. The Pilgrims called them Strangers. To avoid conflicts between these groups, the leaders agreed to form a government before the Mayflower landed. They called their agreement the *Mayflower Compact.* The Mayflower Compact is the oldest American document that creates a government based upon the consent, or agreement, of the people to be governed. Both the Pilgrims and the Strangers agreed to obey the colony's laws.

This is the reconstruction of the capitol building in Williamsburg, where Virginia's assembly met. **What was the name of Virginia's assembly?**

Who Could Vote in Colonial Virginia?

Yes

White men with property

No

Women

Men who did not own property

Native Americans

Slaves

As Plymouth grew larger, it was no longer possible for the colony to function as a direct democracy. As in Virginia, representatives were elected to an assembly.

In the Massachusetts Bay Colony, only people who invested money in the Massachusetts Bay Company could vote. This caused hard feelings. Therefore, the government changed the rule to allow church members to vote for the governor.

Later on, the colony let church members vote for representatives to their assembly. As you read in Chapter 5, the religious focus of the colony drove away other settlers. These new colonies also created democratic institutions.

Colonial Laws

In Connecticut, Thomas Hooker helped set up a government based upon the consent of the people. In 1639, Hooker and other settlers wrote the Fundamental Orders of Connecticut. This was the first constitution of the colony. It gave all property owners the right to vote. The Orders also limited the powers of the governor.

Other colonies began representative governments shortly after forming. In Maryland, Lord Baltimore created a council to advise the governor. He also let settlers elect an assembly. The assembly passed the *Religious Toleration Act.* This gave freedom to most religions. Freedom of religion later became a key part of our government.

Uniting the Colonies

After several years, the colonies began to try making *alliances*—agreements between the colonies to help one another. These alliances were the first steps toward bringing the colonies together.

Hats like this one protected settlers from the sun in seventeenth-century America. **Who could vote in the Massachusetts Bay Colony?**

The Mayflower Compact was the first American document establishing a government based on the consent of the people. **Why was the Compact signed on board ship?**

Chapter 6

United Colonies of New England

Massachusetts Bay, Plymouth, New Haven (later part of Connecticut) and Connecticut formed the United Colonies of New England in 1643. Their main goal was to protect the colonies from Native American attacks. The United Colonies wrote a constitution showing their firm friendship among the colonies. They agreed to help one another, to exchange advice, and to promote safety and welfare for all.

The agreement faded over time and ended in 1684. Even though it did not last, it was an important first step toward forming what would become the United States.

The French and Indian War

Both France and Great Britain claimed North America. Unlike the British, the French had come to the New World to trade. France's network of trading posts extended from the southwest (present-day New Orleans) to the northeast (present-day Quebec, Canada). With these posts, France planned to control trade in North America. They also wanted to stop British colonists from settling west of the Appalachian Mountains (see map, page 131).

North American Rivals

Because of trade, the French had good relationships with many Native American tribes. Native Americans were called Indians by the colonists. Some Indians had become partners, or **allies**, with the French. They, too, wanted to keep the British from moving west.

Britain thought the lands in the west were valuable. In addition to trade with the Native Americans, they expected to dig minerals like copper and iron from the earth. They also wanted to catch fish from streams and rivers and cut timber from the forest. For France and Britain, North America's natural resources were worth risking war.

The map on this powderhorn shows fighting in the French and Indian War. **Who fought on which side in that war?**

The Battle on Snowshoes was fought in New York in March of 1758. Robert Roger's Rangers fought the French and Native Americans but lost the battle. **Why did the French want to stop the British?**

War Breaks Out

Back in Europe, the two countries had been bitter rivals for more than 100 years. Finally, in 1754, the *French and Indian War* started in America. In this war, the French and their Indian allies fought the British.

Major George Washington of Virginia was a young man. He was sent west into the Ohio River Valley where many English people had settled. Washington demanded that the French leave the area, but the French refused. They believed the territory was theirs. A short time later, Washington marched back with a few troops from Virginia. The French, with their Indian allies, had the forces to *defeat,* or beat, Washington.

At that point, Britain joined the fight. Britain ordered General Edward "Bulldog" Braddock to return to the Ohio River region with his troops. The French and the Indians defeated Braddock in this battle.

This fight over land then spread into a larger war in both Europe and North America during the 1750s. For a few years, France won most of the fighting in America. Then William Pitt became the prime minister of Great Britain. He had the British government pay for the war in America instead of just the colonies. This gave the British troops more support. Soon, the British were winning more battles than the French.

Treaty of Paris

After a few more years of fighting, Britain won the war. France agreed to the *Treaty of Paris* in 1763. A treaty is an agreement to end a war. France had to turn land in America over to Britain and Spain. Britain got full control of the lands from the Atlantic Ocean to the Mississippi River, including Canada. Spain had Florida and the lands west of the Mississippi all the way to the Pacific Ocean (see the map, page 131).

This painting by F. Watteau, shows the death of French General Louis-Joseph, Marquis de Montcalm, in 1759 in Quebec City during the French and Indian War.

Which future general fought the French in the Ohio River Valley?

Chapter 6

Colonial Self-Government

The colonists liked being British. They also liked having their freedom. The king was far away. The colonists thought he did not understand what life in the colonies was like.

Colonists wanted to elect their representatives and be governed by their own colony. They did not want a government other than their own assembly to tax them. Colonists had formed alliances to protect themselves. The citizens of these 13 colonies were most loyal to the government of the colony they lived in, and worked to strengthen it.

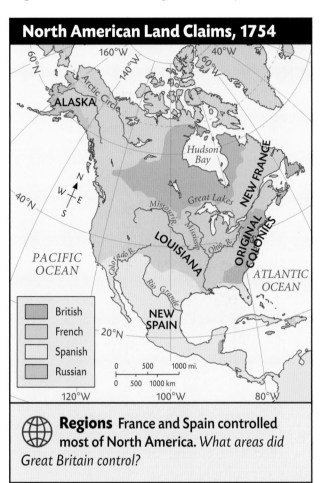

Regions France and Spain controlled most of North America. *What areas did Great Britain control?*

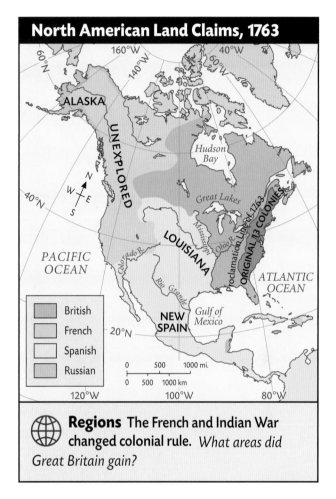

Regions The French and Indian War changed colonial rule. *What areas did Great Britain gain?*

LESSON ❶ REVIEW

Fact Follow-Up
1. How was the British government becoming more democratic?
2. How did representative government develop in Massachusetts and Virginia?
3. What was the importance of the Mayflower Compact?

Talk About It
1. Which colony was most democratic? Why?
2. Why was the French and Indian War fought?
3. How and why did colonial ideas about self-government form?
4. What were the results of the French and Indian War?

After the French and Indian War, the American settlers were more confident. The French had blocked colonial settlement in the west. Conflicts with French settlers had led to the war. Now France was defeated. The settlers looked west with plans for the future.

New Troubles for Britain

Many American settlers now saw themselves on the same level as their rulers in Great Britain. Some settlers believed that Britain had become more wealthy and powerful because of the colonies. The system of trade with the colonies made Britain's economy strong.

Making the Colonies Pay

British leaders in London were worried about the American colonists. Some thought that the Americans had not paid their fair share during the French and Indian War. The Americans, one London official wrote, talked about rights and privileges, but really did not want to pay their fair share to protect themselves.

Some London officials were more critical. One called Americans dirty and cowardly dogs. Others accused Americans of smuggling, which is sneaking things into a country that are against the law. They said Americans smuggled goods into the colonies without paying taxes during the French and Indian War.

British leaders in America shared many of these views. Francis Bernard, the royal governor of Massachusetts, was worried about the colonists' new ideas. Bernard warned King George III that Britain must act if it wanted to keep control of the colonies.

King George Acts

King George III and his advisors took Bernard's warning seriously. The king ruled a huge empire. He wanted to keep control over his subjects. The king looked for a way to make the colonists pay for the war, but he was not sure what would be best to do.

Something happened in 1763 that gave King George III an idea. A Native American tribal chief named Pontiac *rebelled,* or rose up, against Britain's colonies. The king believed that this was a good reason to ask for more support from the colonies.

Troubles on the Frontier

Pontiac and other Native American leaders had been allies of France during the French and Indian War. When France and Great Britain made peace in 1763, they ignored the Native American's claims. In fact, France gave Britain some lands that belonged to the Native Americans. This angered leaders like Pontiac.

Native Americans were losing land that they had lived on for centuries. Colonists moved into western territory. They settled on the land that France had given Britain.

Pontiac organized an alliance of almost all of the Native Americans on the western frontier. Their war plan had each tribe attack and destroy the nearest British fort. Then they attacked nearby settlements.

The plan did great damage and caused many deaths on the frontier. Some settlements were destroyed. British forces coming to help were attacked. About a year passed before the British controlled the frontier again. In 1766, Pontiac had to ask for peace.

The Royal Proclamation

The fighting in the west gave King George III a reason to change his policies. The new law, he said, would protect the colonists.

A *royal proclamation* —a law made by the king—was made in 1763. It banned colonists from crossing over the Appalachian

King George III ruled a vast empire. **Which Native American chief rose up against the king in 1763?**

Mountains into the West. It also demanded that the settlers who were already there return east. Britain drew an imaginary line along the mountains (see map, page 131). West of the line would be Native American land. To enforce this, the king sent 10,000 more troops.

The Path to War

Many settlers did not agree with this policy. George Washington said he would not give up his land. Others joined him. In the end, the settlers ignored the proclamation. This response was the first sign of the *resistance,* or refusal to cooperate, during the 1760s.

These are playing cards from the colonies. Cards were made of paper, so they were taxed by the Stamp Act.

Stamps such as this one (top) had to be attached to all printed documents in the colonies. This sketch (bottom) shows Bostonians burning Stamp Act papers. **Why did the British government require the colonists to buy stamps?**

The Stamp Act Crisis

Back in Great Britain, George Grenville was the secretary of the treasury. He believed that the colonies needed to pay more of the costs of running a large empire. He wanted them to pay for their own protection. He asked Parliament to pass a law to raise money from the colonies.

Parliament passed the *Stamp Act* in 1765. This put a *tax,* or government fee, on all paper products. Newspapers, wills, and marriage certificates were some of the taxed items.

No Taxation Without Representation

In the Virginia House of Burgesses, Patrick Henry made five proposals. One said that colonists should only pay taxes passed by their own representatives. Colonists did not have any elected representatives in Parliament. The slogan "no taxation without representation" became a popular cry in the colonies.

Nine colonies sent representatives to New York to meet at the Stamp Act Congress. They agreed that they were loyal to the king, but they did not approve of the stamp tax. It was a law that representatives of the colonies did not help make.

The Stamp Act Congress asked colonists not to buy British goods until the act was *repealed,* or undone. British merchants lost money. So Parliament repealed the act. Parliament, however, did not agree to stop taxing the colonies.

Unrest in Boston

King George sent troops to the colonies to help keep control. The British troops made the settlers angrier.

In March of 1770, some colonists in Boston were bothering and throwing rocks at British soldiers. The soldiers lost control and shot at several people. Five colonists died, including Crispus Attucks, a runaway slave working in Boston. Colonists called the incident the *Boston Massacre.*

Chapter 6

After the Boston Tea Party the British passed laws the colonists called the Intolerable Acts. **Why did the colonists find the British actions "intolerable?"**

Over the next two years, conditions grew worse. Colonists in Rhode Island burned a British ship, the HMS *Gaspée* in 1772 and wounded a British officer.

After the Boston Tea Party in 1773, Parliament passed laws to punish Boston. The British closed the harbor and sent the members of the Massachusetts assembly home. This made the colonies angry. They called the laws Intolerable Acts. Bostonians thought the other colonies needed to know what was happening there. Two of them, Samuel Adams and John Adams, who were also cousins, set up Committees of Correspondence. They wrote letters to the other colonies about the events there. Massachusetts was suffering under the Intolerable Acts.

The First Continental Congress

The correspondence committees in the other colonies thought about what they should do to help Massachusetts. All British colonies from New England to the Carolinas (but not Georgia) sent representatives to the

First Continental Congress. It met in Philadelphia in September 1774.

The Continental Congress agreed to stop all trade with Britain. The colonies would also set up and train a *militia* (mih·LIH·shuh), an army of citizens set up during a crisis. Congress wanted Parliament to repeal the Intolerable Acts. The delegates agreed to meet the next year.

Fighting Breaks Out

Things grew worse in the spring of 1775. British soldiers were ordered to capture colonial leaders and take all weapons in towns near Boston. Fighting broke out at Lexington and Concord. British soldiers *retreated,* or went back, to Boston.

In June, fighting again broke out on Breed's Hill near Boston. This is called the Battle of Bunker Hill today.

Choosing Independence

Now that things had turned violent, the colonists were in trouble. They needed to make choices about their future.

The Birth of a New Nation

Colonial Protests in Boston

Parliament passed the Stamp Act in 1765. It taxed colonial paper goods. Colonists, led by Patrick Henry in Virginia and Samuel Adams in Massachusetts, protested. They called it "taxation without representation." Parliament passed more taxes on items used every day by colonists—tea, paper, and glass. Americans began refusing to buy British goods.

Revenue stamp

British troops firing on colonists, The Boston Massacre

As protests spread, British troops were sent to Boston. In March of 1770, protests against the Redcoats led to violence. The British soldiers lost control and fired upon the protesters, killing five colonists. This became known as the Boston Massacre. Samuel Adams and his cousin, John Adams, set up Committees of Correspondence in the colonies.

Boston leaders organized the Boston Tea Party in 1773. Late one night, Bostonians dressed as Native Americans boarded British ships docked in Boston Harbor. They dumped chests of taxed tea overboard. Parliament then closed the Massachusetts assembly and the harbor. It forced people to let British soldiers stay in their homes. Colonists called these laws the Intolerable Acts.

The Committees of Correspondence set up the First Continental Congress in September 1774. They talked about how to deal with the Intolerable Acts. They voted to stop all trade with Britain until the Intolerable Acts were repealed. These conflicts led to war in April 1775. The British and colonists clashed at Lexington and Concord. British and Americans again fought each other in June at the Battle of Bunker Hill.

The Birth of a New Nation

AMERICAN PORTRAIT

Benjamin Franklin
1706–1790

Benjamin Franklin was a printer, writer, businessman, inventor, leader, and patriot. Any one of these skills would have made him famous. Put them all together, and he was known all over the world.

Franklin the Writer

Franklin loved to write. He bought a newspaper and called it the *Pennsylvania Gazette*. He wrote many funny stories. He also wrote and printed a book called *Poor Richard's Almanac*. An almanac is a book about the weather, ocean tides, and the movement of the sun, stars, and moon for each year. Farmers used the almanac to learn when to plant crops. The almanac also had jokes, stories, and good advice.

Before long, people in every colony were reading his almanac. People in Europe were reading it, too. It made Franklin rich and famous. He did not have to work for money anymore. Now he could spend time on his hobbies.

Franklin the Inventor

Benjamin Franklin loved to do experiments. His most famous experiment was with electricity. He tied a metal key onto a kite, then flew the kite during a storm. When lightning struck the key, it made a spark! Franklin proved that lightning was electricity.

We still use some of Franklin's inventions today. One is the lightning rod. Lightning rods help keep homes safe from fire. The lightning hits the metal rods instead of the house. Another invention we still use is bifocal lenses. Before bifocals, people who could not see things that were close or far away had to switch between two pairs of glasses. Franklin had a lens maker cut his lenses in half and put them in the same frame. The near lenses were on the bottom, and the far lenses were on the top.

Franklin the Citizen

Benjamin Franklin believed that by working together, people could do great things for their communities. Here are some of his best ideas:

- He started the first lending library. People who could not afford to buy books could borrow them.
- He started a volunteer fire company and fire insurance. They were the first in America.
- He helped start the Pennsylvania Hospital, the first public hospital in America. It took care of people who could not afford doctors.
- We also owe him thanks for street paving, street lighting, street cleaning, the University of Pennsylvania, and a plan for uniting the colonies.

The Second Continental Congress

The *Second Continental Congress* met in Philadelphia in May 1776. The members prepared for war. They chose George Washington to lead the *Continental Army.* This was the army of all 13 colonies.

The colonists also chose someone to speak for them in Europe. They picked Benjamin Franklin from Pennsylvania. He went to France and other countries asking for help.

Congress also sent the king a letter. They wrote that they were still loyal to him. They again asked Parliament to repeal the Intolerable Acts. The king said the colonies were rebelling against their government. Things grew worse.

A writer, Thomas Paine, had come to live in the colonies at this time. He wrote about these issues to help settlers think about their loyalty to the king. His pamphlet, *Common Sense*, quickly sold many copies.

Paine wrote that the colonists had been patient long enough. Britain was too far away to solve the colonies' problems. Living under a government led by a king was not best for the colonies. *Common Sense* made many colonists change their minds. They began to think more seriously about being free from Britain. They wanted independence.

The Declaration of Independence

The Continental Congress asked Thomas Jefferson and a few other men to write the *Declaration of Independence.* This would tell the king why the colonies were breaking away. Jefferson wrote: "We hold these truths to be self-evident [seen by all], that all men are created equal, that they are endowed [gifted] by their Creator with certain unalienable [cannot be taken away] Rights, that among these are Life, Liberty and the pursuit of Happiness." Jefferson listed the ways that the British had not let the colonists have these rights.

He ended by saying that the colonies had a right to create a new government. This government would protect the rights of all people. The Declaration was adopted on July 4, 1776, *Independence Day.* The American Revolution had begun.

Thomas Paine's pamphlet, Common Sense, *sold many copies.* **How did the pamphlet change the minds of many colonists?**

LESSON 2 REVIEW

Fact Follow-Up
1. What was the result of the troubles on the frontier?
2. Why were the Stamp Act and the Intolerable Acts important?
3. What decisions were made by the First Continental Congress?
4. What decisions were made by the Second Continental Congress?

Talk About It
1. What was meant by the phrase "no taxation without representation"?
2. Do you agree or disagree with the arguments of the pamphlet Common Sense?
3. If you had been living in Britain at the time, how would you have felt about the Declaration of Independence? Explain.

The Birth of a New Nation

KEY IDEAS

- Britain had more resources to fight the war and was expected to win.

- The Continental Congress appointed George Washington to lead the Continental Army.

- The Continental Army was made up of regular people, not professional soldiers.

- France and Spain became allies of the new United States and helped win the war.

KEY TERMS

Loyalists
mercenaries
minutemen
Patriots
surrendered
Treaty of Paris (1783)

PEOPLE TO KNOW

Ethan Allen
Benedict Arnold
William Dawes
Francis Marion
Dr. Samuel Prescott
Paul Revere   ·
Nathaniel Greene
Phillis Wheatley

After the Second Continental Congress issued the Declaration of Independence, Great Britain refused to allow the colonies to break away. Britain thought it would win any fight with the colonists.

Britain had many more resources than the colonies. In 1775, the population of Great Britain was more than 10 million people. In America, there were only 2.5 million colonists and slightly more than 500,000 African American slaves.

The British wanted to show a mighty military force to scare the colonists into staying part of Great Britain. There were more than 48,000 soldiers in the Royal Army. Britain sent thousands of these trained soldiers to America. It also hired Hessian (HESH·en) *mercenaries,* soldiers who fight for money. The Hessians were German soldiers.

The American Forces

Congress chose George Washington from Virginia to be the commander of the Continental Army. He had experience because he had fought in the French and Indian War. By picking a leader from a southern state, Congress hoped to get more support from the South for the war. They did this because, up to that point, most of the major conflicts with Britain had been in Massachusetts in the North.

Congress also created a Continental Navy. The colonies had eight armed ships. Congress chose Commodore Esek Hopkins to lead it. Hopkins was from Rhode Island. He had spent most of his career at sea. He had also fought in the French and Indian War.

The Continental Army was not as well trained as the British army. It was made up of citizen-soldiers called *minutemen.* They wore everyday clothes and carried hunting rifles. These men would show up with only a "minute's warning" when fighting broke out.

Even though they were not well trained, the minutemen were confident and enthusiastic. This helped them be successful early in the war.

WORD ORIGINS

Revolution comes from the Latin word revolvere, "to revolve." One revolution of the earth is a complete turning around the sun. A social revolution means a complete change in society or government.

Major Battles of the American Revolution

Maine
(Part of MA)

NH

Fort Ticonderoga
(1775)

Bennington
(1777)

Lexington
(1775)

Bunker Hill
(1775)

Saratoga
(1777)

Concord
(1775)

Boston

MA

CT

New York

Rhode Island

Newtown
(1779)

West
Point

White Plains (1776)

Pennsylvania

Princeton (1777)

Monmouth Courthouse (1778)

Fort Wyoming
Massacre (1778)

Trenton (1776)

Valley Forge

Germantown (1777)

Philadelphia

Brandywine
(1777)

New
Jersey

Maryland

Delaware

Lafayette
1781

ATLANTIC
OCEAN

Virginia

Ohio R.

Richmond

Yorktown
(1781)

Guilford Court
House
(1781)

NC

Moore's
Creek Bridge
(1776)

Cowpens (1781)
Kings Mountain
(1780)

South
Carolina

Wilmington

Georgia

Charleston
(1776, 1780)

Savannah
(1778)

L. Huron

L. Ontario

L. Michigan

L. Erie

Proclamation Line of 1763

Cornwallis - 1781

Cornwallis - 1781

0   100   200 mi.
0   100   200 km

	Original 13 colonies
→	American or French movement
→	British movement
★	American or French victory
★	British victory
★	Indecisive battle
■	Fort

🌐 **Place** The 13 colonies created a new country through the Revolutionary War. *What are some things that made the 13 colonies a region?*

Battle of Guilford Courthouse
The Battle of Guilford Courthouse in March 1781, was one of the bloodiest battles of the American Revolution. The British won the battle but took heavy losses—more than a quarter of their troops. They failed to destroy the American force led by Nathanael Greene.

Although defeated, Greene won his goal to weaken the British army. Cornwallis moved on to Virginia, where he finally surrendered to Washington at Yorktown seven months later.

Greensboro is named for Nathanael Greene.

The Birth of a New Nation

Lexington and Concord

While the Congresses were meeting, violence broke out, as you read in Lesson 2. When King George III heard of the minutemen, he ordered 700 soldiers in Boston to go to Concord. The kings wanted the leaders arrested. He also wanted all of their guns taken.

When the colonists in Boston heard of this, they asked Paul Revere, William Dawes, and Dr. Samuel Prescott to ride to Lexington and Concord. They warned the minutemen that the British were coming. The American leaders were not captured.

The minutemen embarrassed the British. Colonists met British troops in Lexington. At Concord, about 400 minutemen forced the British to retreat. Minutemen continued to attack the Redcoats as they retreated to

The minutemen first fought at Lexington and Concord. **How did they get their nickname?**

Boston. These battles helped many colonists support independence. These Americans called themselves *Patriots.*

The War Heats Up

Patriots captured Fort Ticonderoga (TIE·kahn·der·ROH·gah) in Canada in May 1775. Benedict Arnold, an officer in the Connecticut militia, had suggested the attack. He wanted to take British weapons and supplies. Connecticut told Ethan Allen of Vermont (which was not its own colony at the time) to command the mission.

Allen led a group of men called the Green Mountain Boys. They joined Arnold and took the fort by surprise. The colonists took 60 cannons from the fort. But the Americans still faced many more challenges.

In June, fighting again broke out near Boston. The Americans lost the Battle of Bunker Hill because they ran out of gunpowder. Still, they felt strong because they had killed more than 1,000 redcoats, the name they called British soldiers because they wore red coats.

What would YOU do?

Imagine being eleven years old during the time of the American Revolution. You are not old enough to fight, but you can help the Patriots' cause by delivering messages or supplies. Would you risk arrest by the British to help win the war?

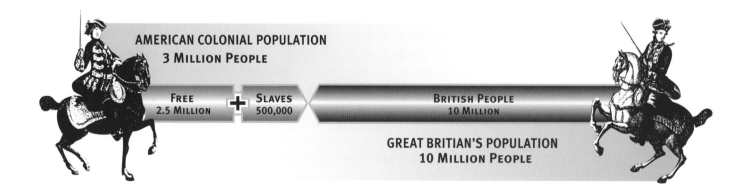

AMERICAN COLONIAL POPULATION
3 MILLION PEOPLE

FREE
2.5 MILLION + SLAVES
500,000

BRITISH PEOPLE
10 MILLION

GREAT BRITIAN'S POPULATION
10 MILLION PEOPLE

Tough Times

Over the next year, the British won several battles. They controlled New York. Washington was worried.

There had never been a regular army in the colonies. Instead, each colony had a small militia for emergencies. Once an emergency ended, the men went home. Washington's men had signed up to fight for only one year. He needed them to stay and fight. He worried that too many of them would go home. The Patriots needed to win a big battle so the men would want to stay.

Battle of Trenton

Washington came up with a bold plan to help raise the spirits of his troops and the nation. He heard that the British were planning to attack Philadelphia. As soon as the Delaware River froze, the Redcoats were going to march across it to the city. Washington needed to strike first.

On Christmas morning 1776, Washington's army marched to the Delaware River. There they got onto boats. That afternoon it began to snow and sleet. It was very cold. Washington was in one of the first boats. He led the troops as they crossed the river with all of their weapons. It took all night to get everyone across.

Then, the Americans marched south. The plan was to attack the Hessian forces in Trenton. Because it was Christmas and the weather was so bad, the Hessians did not think the Americans would attack. They were wrong.

Washington's plan worked. His troops surprised the Hessians and won the battle in less than two hours. The British were shocked. The Americans were hopeful that they could win the war.

Valley Forge

When General Washington took command of the army, he thought the soldiers were hard to control and poorly trained. They were also poorly funded. The Continental Congress was not really a government. It could not raise taxes. It depended upon the former colonies to provide money. But the money did not always come.

One of the lowest points for the Continental Army came in 1777. The Patriots marched to Valley Forge, in Pennsylvania, to spend the winter. The Continental Congress did not have enough money to purchase proper supplies. The weather was terribly cold. Washington's army slept in huts. They were poorly clothed and fed.

Many of the men became sick. Some died from lack of food or disease. When people learned of their troubles, some came to help, including Washington's wife, Martha.

Washington and his men crossed the Delaware River before the Battle of Trenton. **Were the Hessians expecting them?**

Many Challenges

The United States did not have any allies at first. France was not sure if the colonies and Britain would settle their differences. After the Americans defeated a British force in Saratoga, New York, France thought the Americans could win. France joined the war. France brought Spanish forces to help America, too. Their help arrived in the spring of 1778.

France's aid was a key factor in winning the war. They sent money, supplies, troops, and ships.

The new country had other problems, though. Many Americans still wanted to stay a part of Britain instead of breaking away. The troubles in Massachusetts had not changed their minds. Thomas Paine's *Common Sense* had led more people to support the Patriots, but a few still were against independence. The British called them *Loyalists.* The Patriots called them Tories, or traitors. Many were forced to flee to Canada.

Even with all of its advantages, Britain did not beat the Americans. Britain had expected the fighting to end quickly, but it was wrong. The war lasted five years. Britain had more soldiers than the Americans and also won many more battles. But the Americans learned that they had advantages, too.

Because they were fighting on their homeland, the Americans knew where to launch surprise attacks against the British. The Americans then quickly retreated back into the forest or to their homes. They had learned how to fight this way from the Native Americans. In North Carolina and South Carolina, some Americans became famous for their quick strikes and retreats against the British army.

AMERICAN PORTRAIT

Phillis Wheatley
1753–1784

Phillis Wheatley went from being a slave to being a poet. She was the first African American to publish a book of poems.

When Phillis Wheatley was eight years old, she was brought to Boston as a slave. Phillis was not her real name. Most slaves did not get to keep their real names. Once they got to America, they were given new names. Phillis was the name of the slave ship that brought her to America. Her last name, Wheatley, was from the man who bought her. His name was John Wheatley.

It did not take long for Phillis to learn English. She was very smart. She learned to read the Bible well. The Wheatleys saw how smart the little girl was.

Phillis' first poem was published when she was only fourteen. Later, she published a book of poems. Mr. Wheatley freed her that same year.

People began to know Phillis Wheatley's name. She traveled to Great Britain to talk about her book. She helped many people see that African Americans should be treated better. She even sent George Washington a letter with a poem in it. She called him the "great chief." Washington wrote back to her. He said she was a good poet and that he would like to meet her someday.

The War in the South

The Continental Army was a new creation. Most of the soldiers had never been tested in war. Many had been indentured servants or were poor teenagers. It took time to train them. Some panicked in the heat of battle. Others quit because they did not want to follow the military's rules. Because of these things, Washington worried that the Americans would be badly defeated.

Near the end of the war, Britain tried to capture the South. It was the most valuable region because of its cash crops of tobacco, rice, and indigo. The British also believed that more Loyalists lived there. Loyalists could support and supply British troops and keep land safely in British hands.

When the British captured Charleston in 1780, Patriot troops pulled out of South Carolina. Frances Marion stayed. He created a small force of men, and he trained them in the fighting skills the Native Americans had used in the French and Indian War.

Living off the land, Marion and his men made many small surprise attacks on British troops. They captured small groups of British soldiers, hurt supply lines, and rescued American prisoners.

After each attack, Marion withdrew his men to the swamps where it was hard for the British to track them. A British leader gave Marion his nickname when he said that it was impossible to catch the "swamp fox."

Near the end of the war, Marion and American General Nathanael Greene joined forces. In 1781, they forced the British to retreat to North Carolina. After suffering heavy losses there at the Battle of Guilford Courthouse, Lord Cornwallis moved his forces to Virginia. There at Yorktown, the Patriots, with French help, defeated Cornwallis' army. Cornwallis **surrendered**, or gave up. This ended the fighting.

Thomas Marion was known as the "swamp fox."

Benjamin Franklin travelled to Paris to help negotiate the Treaty of Paris. In the treaty, the British officially recognized the United States of America as independent. **Why did the British think they would win the war?**

The War Ends

The war dragged on until 1781, when George Washington forced British General Charles Cornwallis to surrender at Yorktown in Virginia. Britain and the United States signed the *Treaty of Paris* in 1783, ending the war.

LESSON 3 REVIEW

Fact Follow-Up

1. How were the mercenaries and the minutemen different?
2. What happened at the Battle of Lexington and Concord?
3. What were the differences between the "Patriots" and the "Loyalists"?
4. What were some challenges faced by the Continental Army?

Talk About It

1. Compare the advantages of the British and the Americans in the war.
2. How was the alliance with the French important in winning the war?
3. How did Native American fighting tactics help the Continental Army during the war?

Applying Decision-Making and
Problem-Solving Techniques to World Issues

A Question of Loyalty

What does it mean to make a promise? or to be loyal? These were questions British colonists in North America had to answer when the American Revolution began. Towns and even families were split between the Patriots and Loyalists. In 1776, about two fifths of the colonists supported the Patriots. One fifth supported the Loyalists. The rest were undecided.

Colonists had to choose between loyalty to Britain and loyalty to a new government that had not yet been formed. As the armies began to fight, men and women up and down the Atlantic Coast were forced to choose.

For some, the choice was very hard. Scottish Highlanders in North Carolina had just moved to the colonies. They had fought against the British in Scotland. Very independent, they did not like the way the British ruled the Scots there. The British wanted the Highlanders to move to the colonies. They gave land in America to those who would swear that they would be loyal to the king. So the Highlanders took an oath of loyalty to the king and got land in the backcountry of North Carolina. They settled there.

March of the Highlanders

Virginia

North Carolina

Cross Creek

South Carolina

Wilmington

ATLANTIC OCEAN

0   30   60 mi.
0   30   60 km

80°W   78°W   76°W

36°N

34°N

Early in 1776, the royal governor of North Carolina sent General Donald MacDonald to ask the Highlanders to support the British. The British wanted the Highlanders to march from Cross Creek (present-day Fayetteville) to Wilmington. There, they were to meet a fleet of British ships waiting in the harbor. Together they would take North Carolina's most important port, Wilmington. The Highlanders and the British navy would keep the colony for the British and prevent the southern colonies from uniting with Virginia and Massachusetts. If General MacDonald was successful, the British would win a great victory.

What should the Highlanders do? To whom should they be loyal?

Lessons Learned

LESSON 1
Our Democratic Roots
American democracy grew out of English traditions. Each colony had its own system of representative government and made its own laws. The colonies experimented with forming alliances. The French and Indian War increased the direct involvement of the king in the colonies.

LESSON 2
The Colonies Choose Freedom
The British government wanted the colonies to pay for the cost of the French and Indian War. They taxed the colonists. The colonies told the British government that "taxation without representation" was unfair. The colonies united in their stand against the British. They declared themselves independent in 1776.

LESSON 3
The War of Independence
Britain had more resources than the American colonies to fight the war. The Continental Congress appointed George Washington to lead the Continental Army. France and Spain became allies of the new United States and helped America win the war.

Talk About It

1. Why did democracy take root in the British colonies in North America?
2. Should the colonists have insisted that they were equal to people living in Great Britain? Explain your answer.
3. Britain insisted that the colonists pay taxes for their own defense. Was the British point of view fair? Explain your answer.
4. What do you think was the most important reason for the American Revolution? Explain why.
5. Why were the Americans able to win the war?

Mastering Mapwork

LOCATION
Use the map on page 131 to answer these questions:

1. Describe the location of Lake Ontario relative to the Proclamation Line of 1763.
2. What two battles noted on the map were fought in North Carolina?
3. Describe the location of Yorktown relative to Richmond.
4. Describe the location of three 1775 battle sites relative to Boston.

Becoming Better Readers

Making Mental Pictures
Good readers "see" the story in their heads as they read. It's like going to the movies in your head every time you open a book. Picturing the story or information in your head helps you make the connections needed to understand. We call this reading strategy making mental pictures. Go back to page 129 and read again about the French and Indian War. Picture what it would have been like to fight during this war. Would you have like to been a part of this war? Why or why not?

Go to the Source

Understanding a Political Cartoon

Benjamin Franklin created this political cartoon "Join or Die," during the French and Indian War. He had proposed that the colonies join together to better defend themselves against the French. This was called The Albany Plan of Union. Study the political cartoon below. Answer the questions using information from the cartoon.

Questions

1. Based on the text and cartoon, what do you think "Join or Die" means?
2. What do the letters and pieces of the snake stand for?
3. A common myth is that a severed snake will join itself back together. Why is it significant that the snake in the cartoon is severed?
4. Based on the message of the cartoon, do you think Franklin was loyal to the colonies or Great Britain? Why?

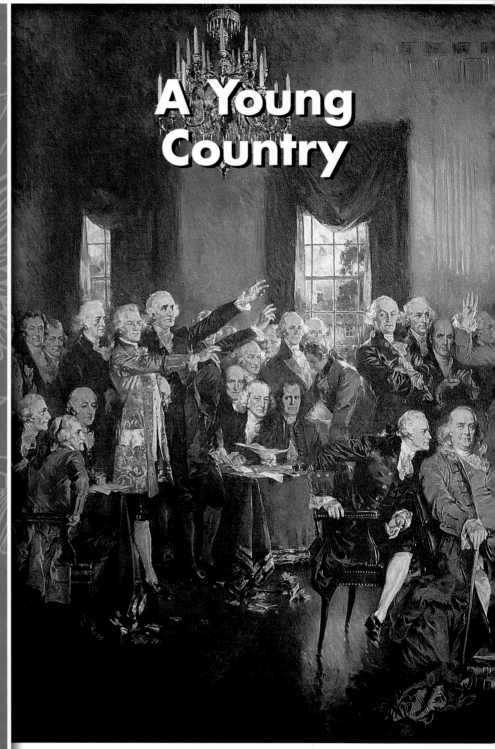

A Young Country

Chapter Preview

LESSON 1
A New Form of Government
At the Constitutional Convention, the states created a new plan for an American government.

LESSON 2
Building the Foundations
The early days of the American government set a pattern that has lasted through today.

LESSON 3
Moving West
Many Americans move to the western territories for new opportunities.

1777
Articles of Confederation drafted by Second Continental Congress

1788
The Constitution goes into effect after New Hampshire ratifies it

1791
Bill of Rights ratified

Timeline of Events

1770   1780   1790

1781
Articles of Confederation ratified

1787
• Constitutional Convention meets in Philadelphia
• Congress sends Constitution to States for ratification

1789
• Washington elected first U.S. president and takes office
• The new government under the Constitution begins

July 4, 1826, was the fiftieth anniversary of the signing of the Declaration of Independence. On that day, just hours before the death of his close friend John Adams, Thomas Jefferson died. He had served his state and nation in many ways. He was the author of the Declaration of Independence and the Virginia Statute for Religious Freedom. He was the third president of the United States and the founder of the University of Virginia.

Jefferson was also a historian, philosopher, architect, and inventor. He invented a special plow and a swivel chair, among other things. His home, Monticello, in Virginia, is a showplace for his brilliant mind.

During his lifetime, Jefferson worked to create a government that would best preserve the freedom of individuals.

U.S. Constitution, 1787 by Howard Chandler Christy.

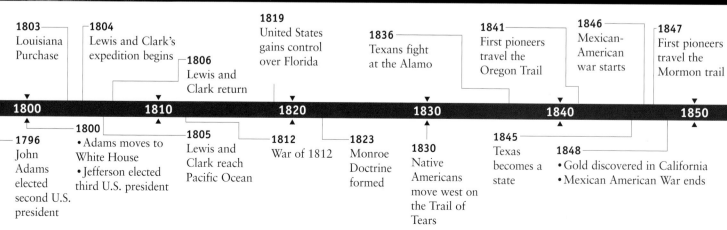

1803
Louisiana Purchase

1804
Lewis and Clark's expedition begins

1806
Lewis and Clark return

1819
United States gains control over Florida

1836
Texans fight at the Alamo

1841
First pioneers travel the Oregon Trail

1846
Mexican-American war starts

1847
First pioneers travel the Mormon trail

1800 — **1810** — **1820** — **1830** — **1840** — **1850**

1796
John Adams elected second U.S. president

1800
• Adams moves to White House
• Jefferson elected third U.S. president

1805
Lewis and Clark reach Pacific Ocean

1812
War of 1812

1823
Monroe Doctrine formed

1830
Native Americans move west on the Trail of Tears

1845
Texas becomes a state

1848
• Gold discovered in California
• Mexican American War ends

LESSON (1) A New Form of Government

KEY IDEAS

- The Articles of Confederation created strong states but a weak national government.

- The states decided to create a new form of government at the Constitutional Convention.

- The Constitution is a flexible document. It can be changed.

KEY TERMS

abolish
amendments
Articles of Confederation
Bill of Rights
compromise
Constitutional Convention
delegates
executive
faction
federalism
Great Compromise
judiciary
ratify
Three-Fifths Compromise
veto

PEOPLE TO KNOW

James Madison
Alexander Hamilton
William Patterson
Roger Sherman

After independence, the United States had to decide on a plan of government. Each state wrote its own constitution. The Second Continental Congress formed a committee to write a plan of government for the nation. The majority of people wanted strong states and a weak national government. They wrote the *Articles of Confederation* to create that form of government.

The Articles of Confederation

The Articles formed a bond among states. The states united to defend themselves and to work for their general good. But the new government under the Articles faced challenges. It could not control trade, raise an army, or collect taxes.

Problems quickly occurred under the Articles. The states disagreed about who could use their ports. Each state made its own money, and this caused confusion when people from one state tried to pay people in other states. There was no national army to stop revolts or protect the country. James Madison of Virginia and many others wanted a stronger national government to solve these problems.

Madison, George Washington, Benjamin Franklin, and Alexander Hamilton of New York went to Philadelphia in May 1787. They joined 51 other *delegates,* or representatives, from 12 states (Rhode Island did not send anyone). Their goal was to fix the Articles of Confederation.

The Constitutional Convention

Even though the summer was hot that year in Philadelphia, the windows stayed shut in the Convention's meeting room. Guards were posted at the doors. The delegates did not want anyone to listen to the meetings. These were important talks.

Delegates debated whether to keep the Articles or to drop them and write a new constitution. Their meeting became known as the *Constitutional Convention.*

Making Compromises

Delegates at the Constitutional Convention were in two groups. One group, led by Madison and others, wanted a strong national government. Another group, led by Alexander Hamilton and William Patterson, wanted to keep the Articles and make them stronger.

WORD ORIGINS

In addition to being a democracy, the United States is also a republic. **Republic** comes from two Latin words *res*, meaning "rule," and *publica*, meaning "the people." Together these words mean "rule by the people." The United States is a republic because citizens choose its leaders in elections.

The Virginia Plan

The Madison group presented the Virginia Plan. This called for getting rid of the Articles. The delegates would make plans for a new government instead. It would have an *executive* (a person to carry out the laws), a legislature, and a *judiciary*, or court system. The Articles only had a legislature.

The large states supported the Virginia Plan. Under it, a state would elect representatives based upon its size. Large states would be able to elect more representatives to Congress. They could control the laws that were passed.

The New Jersey Plan

William Patterson proposed the New Jersey Plan. He wanted to make the Articles stronger. His plan created an executive office. It also gave more powers to Congress.

But Patterson wanted to keep the states strong. Under his plan they could *veto,* or reject, laws that they did not like. The New Jersey Plan would keep the Articles because it gave the states equal representation. It did not matter how small or large a state was. Smaller states supported the New Jersey Plan.

There were other problems to decide. States that allowed slavery did not want a government that would *abolish,* or do away with, slavery. To keep the convention from failing, the delegates had to *compromise,* or make a deal. Each side had to give up a little in order to get most of what they wanted.

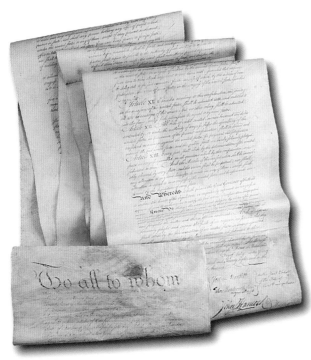

The Articles of Confederation formed a bond among states. **What were the problems of government under the Articles?**

James Madison served as a delegate at the Constitutional Convention. **What kind of national government did Madison support?**

A Young Country

Great Compromise

Roger Sherman represented Connecticut at the convention. He proposed the *Great Compromise.* To balance representation, Sherman suggested that Congress have two houses, or sections. This was like Parliament in Great Britain.

One house would have an equal number of representatives from every state, no matter the size of the state's population. This pleased the small states. In the other house, representation would be based upon the population of each state. This pleased the large states.

Compromises Over Slavery

The Constitutional Convention also faced the problem of how to deal with slavery. The delegates were afraid the Constitution might not be adopted because the states did not agree on whether it should be allowed.

Authors of the Constitution

North Carolina at first refused to accept the new Constitution. William Blount of Bertie County, Richard Dobbs Spaight of New Bern, and Hugh Williamson of Edenton were three of North Carolina's representatives at the Constitutional Convention. They signed the Constitution. Then they worked to get it approved at the 1788 state convention in Hillsborough. Delegates voted against the Constitution because it lacked a Bill of Rights. In Fayetteville the next year, North Carolina accepted the Constitution after delegates were promised that a Bill of Rights would be added. North Carolina was the twelfth state to join the United States.

William Blount

States that allowed slavery wanted to count the number of slaves as part of the total population of the state. Larger populations would allow them to elect more representatives to Congress. The states that did not allow slavery, or that were in the process of ending slavery, did not want to count slaves for this purpose.

The compromise allowed slaveholding states to count three fifths of the people who were slaves for the purpose of representation in Congress. But they would count all the free people. This agreement became known as the *Three-Fifths Compromise.* Citizens of slaveholding states would pay taxes on three fifths of enslaved people as well as on land they owned.

The convention made a few more deals over slavery. The Fugitive Slave Compromise allowed slaveholders to hunt down slaves who were fugitives, people who had escaped and run away. The runaways would be returned to slavery.

They also agreed to the Slave Trade Compromise. The Constitution stated that a law ending the slave trade could not be passed by Congress for 20 years, which would be 1807. This, they thought, would prevent a strong Congress from ending the slave trade right away. This would delay the larger conflict over slavery for a few years.

Federalism

The biggest problem the convention had was not slavery. The delegates at the Constitutional Convention had to settle the issue of whether they would have strong states or a strong national government. They solved this problem by making the states and national government strong in different areas.

This system of sharing of powers between government is called *federalism.* The national government would have certain powers, such as the ability to make rules about trade and to raise taxes and an army.

There would also be an executive—the president—and a court system.

Under the Constitution, the states would have their own governments. States could conduct their own business. But they could not use a power that belonged to the national government. The national government, in turn, could not use a power that belonged to the states. When it was not clear if a power belonged to the states or to Congress or to the president, the Supreme Court would decide who had that power. The Supreme Court would be the highest court in the nation.

Adopting the Constitution

The convention finished its work in September. The problems did not end, however. Two *factions,* or groups, formed. One group supported the Constitution. They were called Federalists. Federalists wanted Americans to approve, or *ratify,* the Constitution.

The other group, Antifederalists, asked the country to reject the Constitution. The Antifederalists objected because the Constitution did not include a Bill of Rights. They wanted a guarantee that citizens had certain rights that the government could not take away.

Ratification

The Constitution could not take effect until nine states had ratified it. People in each state met in their own conventions. Some states, like North Carolina, would not ratify the Constitution without a Bill of Rights. The Federalists promised that a Bill of Rights would be adopted during the first meeting of Congress.

New Hampshire became the ninth state to ratify the Constitution on June 21, 1788. Then the leaders prepared for the new government under the Constitution. On March 4, 1789, the government under the Constitution began to work.

The delegates to the Constitutional Convention sign their approval to the Constitution. **Which group approved of the Constitution? Which group disapproved?**

The Bill of Rights

The new Congress met as part of this new government. There, James Madison proposed the guarantees of freedom that became the Bill of Rights. The *Bill of Rights* is the first ten *amendments,* or changes, to the Constitution.

Once the Bill of Rights was adopted by Congress, it had to be ratified by three-fourths of the states to go into effect. In 1791, all ten amendments became part of the Constitution when Virginia ratified them.

The First Amendment guarantees freedom of speech, freedom of the press, and the freedom to assemble, or gather. It also says that the government will not create a state church. Other amendments say that an American is not required to house or feed soldiers in peacetime. An American who is arrested has a right to a speedy trial, to have a jury hear the case, and to have a lawyer. You can read the Bill of Rights in the appendix.

Our Flexible Constitution

The Bill of Rights was not the only change made to the Constitution. The Founding Fathers, the men who wrote the Constitution, wanted it to be a flexible document. The amendment clause, or section, in the Constitution allows the rules to be changed. You will read about many of these changes.

Benjamin Franklin understood that it was important for the Constitution to be able to change in the future. When the convention was almost done meeting, he looked at a half-sun painted in gold on the back of George Washington's chair. He wondered if it was a rising or setting sun. With hope for the nation's future, he finally decided that the sun was rising.

George Washington's "rising sun" chair was made in 1779 and is on display at Independence Hall in Philadelphia. **What did Benjamin Franklin think about the chair? Why?**

LESSON 1 REVIEW

Fact Follow-Up
1. What were the strengths and weaknesses of the Articles of Confederation?
2. Compare the Virginia and New Jersey Plans.
3. What was the Great Compromise?
4. What is federalism?
5. Who were the Antifederalists?

Talk About It
1. Why were compromises made over slavery during the Constitutional Convention?
2. Compare beliefs of the Federalists and Antifederalists.
3. Why is the Constitution described as a flexible document?

George Washington is called the "Father of our Country." He led the Continental Army during the Revolutionary War and was president of the Constitutional Convention. After the convention, he planned to return to his farm, Mount Vernon, in Virginia. But other American leaders did not want him to retire. They thought that he was the one person who could lead the newly formed country.

New Nation, New Problems

James Madison compared leading the new nation to being lost in a wilderness without a footstep to follow. The new nation was on its own. It faced many problems.

Problems at Home

The Continental Congress and the states had borrowed money to pay for the war. They had given certificates to soldiers, promising that they could later trade them in for money. But, as you read in Lesson 1, under the Articles of Confederation, Congress could not raise money with taxes. Without money, Congress could not pay the war debts or the soldiers.

There were also political problems. Under the Articles, each state was like a nation. They made decisions about trade, taxes, and other matters on their own. With the new Constitution, the states had to work together. They needed a leader to guide them.

Problems with France and Great Britain

The United States also faced challenges from Europe. Britain did not believe the United States would survive. Great Britain kept troops in the western territory. Britain gave Native Americans guns to attack the Americans, too.

Britain also was fighting France again. France looked to the United States for help because France had helped the Americans during the Revolution. France learned that the new United States of America was trading with Britain. So French ships stopped American trading ships and stole their goods. Britain did the same whenever they found merchant ships going to France.

The United States was in a difficult position. Choosing the right person to be the new president was important. Many Americans believed that Washington was the only person who could guide the country during these difficult years.

KEY IDEAS

- President Washington was our first president.

- The nation doubled in size under President Jefferson.

- The War of 1812 and the Monroe Doctrine were important turning points in early foreign affairs of the United States.

KEY TERMS

Louisiana Purchase
Monroe Doctrine
neutral
precedents
War Hawks
War of 1812

PEOPLE TO KNOW

Abigail Adams
Meriwether Lewis
William Clark
Sacagawea
York
James Monroe

George Washington was the first president of the United States. **Who told Washington that he had the character to be president?**

Washington: Our First President

The idea of becoming president worried Washington. It was not that he did not want to serve. Like many leaders at the time, he believed the survival of the nation was still at stake.

Many people told Washington that his country needed him again. Abigail Adams, John Adams' wife, told Washington that he had the character needed to lead the country. Washington finally agreed be the candidate for president in the first election. No one ran against him. He became president in April of 1789.

What would YOU do

The Congress is trying to decide what to call the new president. People have many different ideas, and each one believes that his is the best. How would you organize a discussion of each possible title? What would you do to work toward a decision?

Getting Started

Washington knew that the nation's problems could be solved, but he also realized that the work would be hard.

As the first president of the United States, Washington set many **precedents.** Precedents are examples for others to follow. He picked leaders to make up his cabinet, or group of advisors. They helped him do the nation's business at home and build relationships with other countries.

One of the first issues that concerned the president and Congress was what Americans and people around the world should call him. He was not a king, but some people in the Senate wanted to give him an important title. Some suggested "His Majesty the President." Washington liked "His High Mightiness." After talking over many high-sounding titles, Congress decided to call him the president of the United States.

Washington brought his good reputation and sense of honor to the office. He also brought a new sense of cooperation. Few Americans trusted a king, because they had just broken away from Britain's king. But many people trusted Washington. They expected their leader to do only good.

Solving Problems

Washington chose smart people he trusted to give him advice in his cabinet.

The Economy Alexander Hamilton ran the treasury and developed the new nation's economy. He suggested that the country create a national bank and issue savings bonds to raise money. People could open

Alexander Hamilton was the first Secretary of the Treasury. **What did Hamilton suggest be done to raise money?**

John Adams served as Washington's vice president and then was elected president himself. **What country did Adams negotiate with to avoid war?**

savings accounts at the bank and borrow money. Congress wrote laws to set up the bank and allowed the treasury to make bonds.

Foreign Affairs Relationships with other countries were also a problem. Washington chose Thomas Jefferson to help with foreign affairs. The United States could not tell other countries what to do. The government had to negotiate with the leaders of foreign nations.

Jefferson had a lot of experience dealing with other nations. He had served as the new nation's ambassador to France. But Washington did not always agree with him. Jefferson wanted the nation to support France in its war against Great Britain.

Washington decided to be *neutral,* to not take sides. He did not side with either France or Britain. The president believed that the United States was still young. It did not have the money or soldiers to get into another war.

His decision kept the nation out of war.

After leading the nation for two four-year terms, Washington retired. His vice president, John Adams, was elected to be our second president.

Adams as President

Like others who founded the United States, John Adams had done a lot for his country. He had helped build a strong colonial government in Massachusetts. He wrote his name in bold letters on the Declaration of Independence. This showed his strong support of the American Revolution.

In fact, the British government called Adams the most dangerous of the American rebels. This showed his importance to the Revolution.

Adams had served his country at home and in Europe. After the new government took effect, he was elected to be Washington's vice president.

American Portrait

Abigail Smith Adams
1744–1818

Abigail Smith was born in Weymouth, Massachusetts. She was the wife of one president, John Adams. She was also the mother of another president, her son, John Quincy Adams.

Abigail Adams was also a gifted and clever person. She wrote nearly 2,000 letters that described society and politics.

She believed that women could best help the nation by being educated and independent thinking wives and mothers. Women did not hold political office or work outside the home at that time.

Although she did not openly support voting rights for women, she did fight for their legal right to divorce and to own property.

Abigail Adams often gave her husband and son advice. She shared her point of view with them. In this way, she helped them be strong leaders who stood up for what they believed.

She was both the wife of the first vice president and the second first lady of the United States. In these roles, Abigail Adams helped Martha Washington set the standard for future first ladies of the United States.

Challenges

When he was elected president, Adams faced crisis after crisis. The French had their own revolution. They, too, had a new government. It made demands on the United States.

Like Washington, Adams thought war would be dangerous for the young nation. He started talks with France to settle their problems. These helped avoid war, but the talks made him unpopular with the friends of France in America. He lost the election to Thomas Jefferson when he ran for a second term as president.

"Honest and Wise Men"

On November 1, 1800, just before that election, Adams arrived in the new capital city of Washington, D.C.. He was moving into the new, still unfinished, White House. On his second evening there he wrote to his wife, Abigail.

Before I end my letter, I pray Heaven to bestow [give] the best of Blessings on this House and all that shall hereafter inhabit [live in] it. May none but honest and wise Men ever rule under this roof.

Jefferson as President

When Thomas Jefferson was elected our third president in 1800, he called it a "revolution." He thought of it this way because both presidents before him were members of the Federalist Party. The Federalists were also the majority in Congress.

That changed with the election of 1800. The new president and Congress were in the hands of the Democratic-Republican Party (today's Democratic Party). This type of peaceful change in government was unique in the world.

Many Accomplishments

Jefferson was a rare person. He grew up in a hardworking family in Virginia. His father wanted him to get an education, so Jefferson went to college. Everyone who knew him saw that he had many talents. He became a lawyer and went on to found the University of Virginia.

Jefferson represented Virginia at the Second Continental Congress. He had a special gift for words, and so was chosen to write the Declaration of Independence. A political party was developed around his ideas.

New Ideas

Jefferson came to office promising change. His ideas about how the government should be run were different from many Federalists. He thought that the United States should remain a small nation of mostly farmers. He believed that government and the armed forces should be small.

To show that he was different from other presidents, Jefferson walked to the Capitol for his inauguration. He wore simple clothing. When a senator visiting the White House saw him from a distance, he thought that Jefferson was one of the servants.

The Louisiana Purchase

Once he was president, Jefferson changed some of his views. American farmers between the Appalachian Mountains and the Mississippi River used the Mississippi as a highway. It carried farm goods, fur, and timber to the port at New Orleans, near the Gulf of Mexico (see map, page 166).

In 1803, the city of New Orleans was owned by France. France also claimed the Mississippi River and the territory west of it. Jefferson sent representatives to France. He wanted to buy New Orleans for the United States. France decided to sell all of its land, called the Louisiana Territory. It needed money to pay for its wars in Europe.

The *Louisiana Purchase* doubled the size of the nation (see map, page 166). The United States now stretched from the Atlantic Ocean to the western edge of present-day Montana. Jefferson appointed a group of about 50 people to explore the territory. They were led by Meriwether Lewis and William Clark.

The Louisiana Purchase was the key that made westward expansion possible. **What might have happened if France had kept the Louisiana Territory?**

UNDER MY WINGS EVERY THING PROSPERS

Lewis and Clark

Before the size of United States territory doubled with the Louisiana Purchase in 1803, President Thomas Jefferson had already planned to explore the area. Meriwether Lewis and William Clark (below) led the team of explorers called the Corps of Discovery. They started at St. Louis on the Mississippi and Missouri Rivers. They then traveled to the Pacific Coast. Their journals give an early picture of the region's landforms, animals, and plants.

Aaron Arrowsmith's 1802 map used by Lewis and Clark

One purpose of the journey was to discover a water route across the continent. They crossed half of the present-day United States from May 1804 to September 1806 by boat and on foot. The explorers discovered that the Rocky Mountains "present a formidable [strong] barrier." The mountains prevent the rivers of the West from forming a water route to the Pacific Coast.

The Corps of Discovery took this keelboat and smaller boats on their journey.

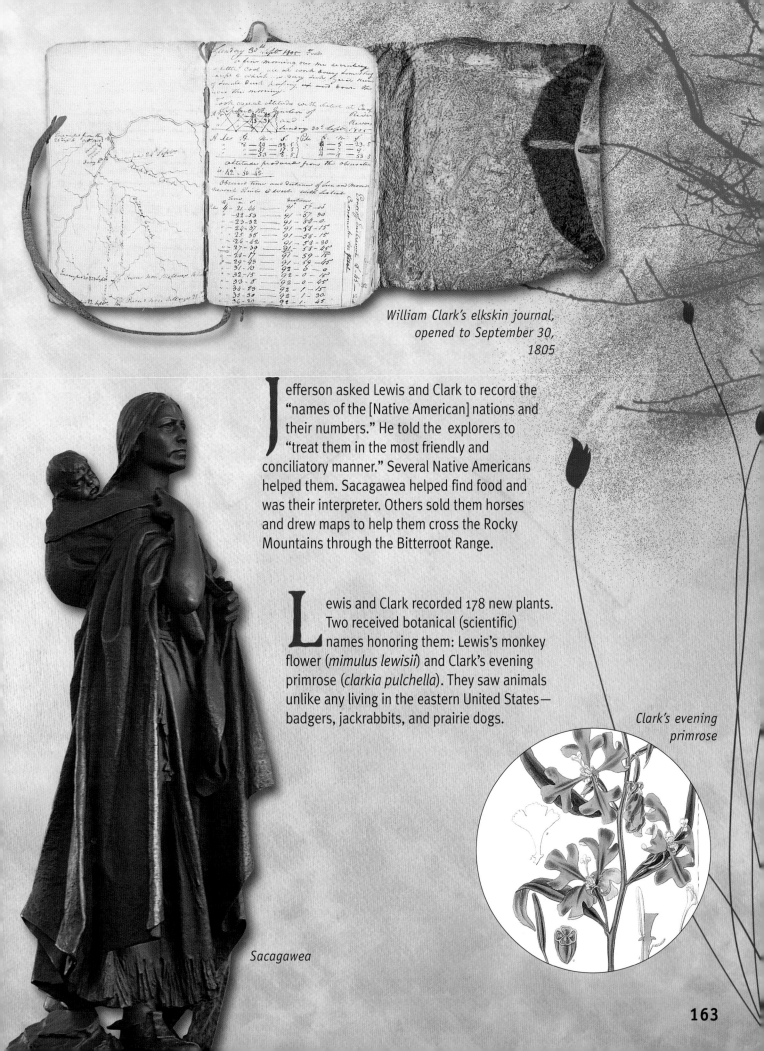

William Clark's elkskin journal, opened to September 30, 1805

Jefferson asked Lewis and Clark to record the "names of the [Native American] nations and their numbers." He told the explorers to "treat them in the most friendly and conciliatory manner." Several Native Americans helped them. Sacagawea helped find food and was their interpreter. Others sold them horses and drew maps to help them cross the Rocky Mountains through the Bitterroot Range.

Lewis and Clark recorded 178 new plants. Two received botanical (scientific) names honoring them: Lewis's monkey flower (*mimulus lewisii*) and Clark's evening primrose (*clarkia pulchella*). They saw animals unlike any living in the eastern United States— badgers, jackrabbits, and prairie dogs.

Sacagawea

Clark's evening primrose

163

Lewis and Clark

In 1804, the Lewis and Clark expedition set off. Their goals were to meet and identify the Native Americans who lived in the territory and to find an all-water route to the Pacific Ocean. A Shoshone woman named Sacagawea (sah·KAH·guh·WEE·ah) helped guide them. Lewis and Clark needed her to translate Native American languages. They also believed that having a woman with them would let Native Americans know that they were on a peaceful mission. York, William Clark's slave, also went with them.

The expedition reached its goal in November 1805. Lewis wrote in his journal that there was great joy in their camp because they finally could see the Pacific Ocean. A few years after the journey, Clark freed York because of the great help he had provided.

The War of 1812

France had agreed to sell the Louisiana Territory to the United States partly to have money to continue its war with the British. These conflicts continued. The United States could no longer stay neutral.

In 1810, France had agreed to stop its attacks on American merchant ships. The United States agreed to trade with France.

Some members of Congress were called *War Hawks,* because they called for war against Britain. They encouraged President James Madison to ask Congress to declare war. Under pressure, Madison sent a request to declare war on Britain to Congress. This began the War of 1812. It ended two years later. The United States was at peace, and the nation grew stronger.

Two Great Men

John Adams and Thomas Jefferson were the only presidents to sign the Declaration of Independence. They both died on its fiftieth anniversary, July 4, 1826. Adams' dying words were "Thomas Jefferson survives." He did not know that his friend Jefferson had passed on only a few hours earlier.

The British bombed Fort McHenry outside of Baltimore, Maryland, during the War of 1812. This inspired Francis Scott Key to write the poem "The Star Spangled Banner". **What song did this poem become?**

The Monroe Doctrine

The United States hoped that avoiding conflicts in Europe would make it even stronger. The United States did not want European nations to help Spain win back its colonies in the Americas. President James Monroe gave a speech to explain that the United States did not want European governments interfering with the new independent nations in the Americas.

This policy became known as the *Monroe Doctrine.* President Monroe worried that if a European nation had colonies in the Americas, a war in Europe might draw the United States into the conflict.

Customs

Americans have honored some presidents by printing their pictures on paper money. Many of the presidents we see there are from the earliest days of the nation. George Washington's picture is on the one dollar bill. You can see Jefferson on the two dollar bill and Alexander Hamilton on the ten dollar bill. Abraham Lincoln appears on the five dollar bill, and Andrew Jackson on the twenty.

James Monroe was president from 1817–1825. **What did the policy named after him state?**

LESSON 2 REVIEW

Fact Follow-Up
1. Describe problems the United States faced in 1789.
2. What precedents did George Washington set as our first president?
3. What was the Louisiana Purchase, and why was it important?
4. Why was the War of 1812 fought?

Talk About It
1. Compare the leadership of George Washington, John Adams, and Thomas Jefferson as president.
2. If you could have met one of these presidents, which one would you have chosen? Explain why.
3. Was the Monroe Doctrine important?

LESSON ③ Moving West

- The expansion of the territory of the United States led many people to move west.

- The government forced Native Americans to relocate.

- War with Mexico added more land to the nation.

KEY TERMS

Manifest Destiny
migrate
Mormons
National Road
Oregon Trail
Trail of Tears

Following the War of 1812, the United States entered a new era. Americans started to think about developing the country. They built the *National Road,* the first highway that connected the East and West.

The road started in Baltimore, Maryland, and ran all the way to Dayton, Ohio. It helped farmers and trappers carry their goods more easily to ports and markets in the East.

The United Kingdom, as the nation of Great Britain and Ireland was now called, gave the United States more land in the treaty that ended the War of 1812. As America grew, many people began to move, or *migrate,* west.

Manifest Destiny

Many Americans thought that it was the United States' destiny, or fate, as a nation to expand westward from the Atlantic to Pacific Oceans. This belief was later called *Manifest Destiny.*

As part of Manifest Destiny, America's mission was to expand and spread democracy and freedom. The United States did expand west. But as

Territorial Growth of the United States

Region This map shows how the United States added land over time to become the size it is today. It began with the Louisiana Purchase. *Why was that an important region?*

you will see in this lesson and in Chapter 8, many challenges still lay ahead. The move westward did not always bring freedom for everyone.

A Growing Nation

The United States first gained territory to the south. Spain had control over Florida. In 1819, the United States signed a treaty with Spain for Florida. In return for the land, the United States agreed to give up its claims on Texas.

Adding Florida was good for the United States, but it was bad for the Native Americans. Settlers wanted to farm the lands in the south. But those lands had been promised to Native Americans in many treaties, or agreements between the governments and the tribes.

Indian Removal

In the southeast, the Cherokee tried to stop the United States from making them leave their homes. They organized the Cherokee Nation and wrote a constitution. They challenged the taking of their land in court.

The United States Supreme Court ruled that the states could not take away Native American lands. But President Andrew Jackson refused to enforce the court's decision. The Cherokee and four other tribes were forced to move. They left the area starting in 1830.

The relocation of the Cherokee brought starvation and death along the way. The Native Americans called their journey the *Trail of Tears* because of their suffering. They were forced to move to what was called Indian Territory, now Oklahoma, in the West.

Population Changes for the Five Tribes		
	At Time of Removal (1830–1840)	By 1860
Cherokee	20,042	13,821
Choctaw	18,963	13,666
Chickasaw	5,224	4,260
Creek	24,162	13,550
Seminole	4,883	2,253

The Cherokee and other Native Americans were forced to move from their homelands to the newly created Indian Territory. **Why are their journeys known as the Trail of Tears?**

Western Settlement

Ever since the first colony was founded, Americans had lived in the East. Many Americans believed more opportunities existed for them in the "West."

To the first settlers along the Atlantic coast, the "West" was the land on the eastern slopes of the Appalachian Mountains. Then it became the land between the Appalachians and the Mississippi. As the United States expanded to fill the continent between the Atlantic and Pacific Oceans, the American vision of where the "West" was also changed.

The Oregon Trail

Oregon was one of the first places west of the Mississippi where many people settled. They saw moving to the Oregon Territory (see map, below) as an opportunity to improve their lives. As more people went west, the route to the territory became known as the *Oregon Trail.*

Trails to the West, 1840s

Movement Americans traveled on several routes to the western territories. *Why are there different routes? What landforms may have influenced the direction of the trails?*

Missionaries Other Americans wanted to go to Oregon to spread Christianity. Missionaries were some of the first Americans to go there. Marcus and Narcissa Whitman, for example, went to convert Native Americans to Christianity. Dr. Whitman provided medical care, too. His wife ran a school for Native Americans.

They made many sacrifices to get to Oregon. They rose early, ate strange foods, and slept outdoors. Narcissa described their hardships in letters to her mother. Though they were frequently hungry, she said she did not regret going west.

Many Go West Thousands of Americans migrated to the territory during the 1840s and 1850s. A wagon train of settlers used the trail to reach Oregon in 1842. During the great migration of 1843, more than a thousand people and livestock followed the trail west. In just two years, more than 5,000 made the trip.

By the 1850s, thousands of families took the trail to make new homes in the West. The Oregon Trail continued to be the main route to move west until railroads were built.

Estimated Number of Travelers on the Oregon Trail					
Year	Travelers	Year	Travelers	Year	Travelers
1841	100	1846	1,000	1851	10,000
1842	200	1847	2,000	1852	70,000
1843	1,000	1848	5,000	1853	35,000
1844	2,000	1849	40,000		
1845	5,000	1850	65,000		

This chart shows how many people traveled the Oregon Trail between 1841 and 1853. **What events affected the numbers of people going west?**

The Mormon Trail

Religious groups also moved west. Joseph Smith, a farmer from New York, founded the Church of Jesus Christ of Latter-day Saints in 1830 (also called the Mormon church). Mormon missionaries converted thousands of people in the United States, Canada, and Great Britain. Some people in Illinois did not agree with their teachings. An angry mob killed Smith. Church members, called *Mormons,* moved to other states. Brigham Young became their new leader.

Brigham Young had read about Utah. He thought that it would be a good place for Mormons to live without being persecuted for their beliefs. During the 1840s, more than 15,000 Mormons moved there. Mormons migrated from other areas. By 1860, more than 40,000 of them had relocated to Utah. Their new home was made a territory of the United States. Utah became a state in 1896.

Texas and War with Mexico

Expansion to the West also brought conflict between the United States and Mexico. Mexico had been independent since 1821. Americans had been living in the territory of Texas since the 1820s. The large territory, however, belonged to Mexico.

At first, the Mexican government sold the American settlers land. As the number of settlers grew, Mexico decided to stop settlement from the United States.

In 1834, General Antonio Lopez de Santa Anna became the ruler in Mexico. Americans living in Texas wanted to break away, but Mexico defeated them in a battle at the Alamo in 1836. Later, Sam Houston, an American living in Texas, defeated the Mexican army and captured Santa Anna. Texas became an independent state.

Texas remained independent for almost ten years. Many Americans living there wanted to join the United States. Texas became the twenty-eighth state in the Union in 1845. Some people in the United States were not satisfied with gaining just Texas. They wanted more land from Mexico.

When James K. Polk became president, he tried to buy the land. Mexico refused. Polk decided to take it by force. He led the nation into the Mexican-American War in 1846. When the war ended in 1848, the lands of the United States extended to the Pacific Ocean. The states of New Mexico, Arizona, Nevada, Utah, Colorado, and California came from this territory.

An Expanding Union

Between independence in 1776 and 1850, the United States grew from a loose nation of 13 former British colonies to a large democratic nation made up of former colonies of Britain, France, and Spain. By 1850, there were 31 states and five territories in the Union (see map, page 166). Its peoples had increased from slightly under 4 million in 1790 to more than 23 million in 1850. This rapid growth was good for our country, but it also caused tensions to increase.

When General Sam Houston captured Santa Anna, the war with Mexico ended. **What was the result of the war?**

California Gold Rush

In January 1848, James Marshall discovered gold at Sutter's Mill in California's Sacramento Valley. By early May, boats filled with people were heading up the Sacramento River to look for gold. During the summer, the news of gold had spread up and down the West Coast, the East Coast, and Mexico. Newspapers were filled with stories of the men. Some had become rich overnight by picking gold out of California's rivers and soil. During the winter of 1849, people left their homes and families to strike it rich in California. The gold seekers were called Forty-niners.

Forty-niners panning for gold in California (above), and a gold nugget (right)

By 1852, almost 275,000 miners had reached California. They all needed food, housing, banks, mining equipment, and clothing. They also had a lot of gold to spend.

Businesses sprang up overnight. Prices soared in the mining towns. Boots sold for $20 a pair, eggs for 50 cents each, and potatoes for $1 a pound. Some frontier mining settlements would rise quickly and then disappear when the gold ran out. Others became towns.

When the gold ran out or the mines were taken over by larger mining companies, many Forty-niners returned to their homes in the East. However, the Forty-niners had made important contributions to the nation. They had pioneered new trails west and opened up more territory for settlement. Many stayed in California and other western territories. They brought their families to live with them.

LESSON ③ REVIEW

Fact Follow-Up
1. What was the Trail of Tears, and how did it get its name?
2. What was the Gold Rush?
3. What was the Mexican War fought over?
4. By 1850, how many states were there in the United States?

Talk About It
1. How did the definition of the term "the West" change between 1790 and 1850?
1. Should the United States have gone to war with Mexico in 1846? Why or why not?
3. Compare the Oregon and the Mormon Trails.

Heading West

Has your family ever moved? Have you ever packed a suitcase for a trip? How did you decide what to pack and what to leave behind? Have you ever made a mistake and packed the wrong things? Making a mistake in packing is not usually a problem today.

But when the United States was being settled, packing wisely often meant the difference between life and death on the ocean voyage from Europe or on the wagon train headed west.

As more and more people crossed the Atlantic or traveled west, they learned from the experiences of the first travelers. Still, there were many burials at sea, and the trails west were marked with the graves of those who died on the journey. Those trails were also marked by abandoned wagons, pieces of furniture, and the skeletons of animals left behind as the pioneers had to lighten their loads.

The leaders of wagon trains, or groups of wagons traveling together, learned that there were three things needed for the journey: wood to build fires, grass to feed the animals, and water for drinking, cooking, and for the livestock. The Oregon Trail and the Mormon Trail were laid out with these things in mind. No wagon train could go more than two or three days without these important items.

The travelers in wagon trains packed their own belongings. They chose what to bring with them and what to leave behind. They made their choices based on their own lives and the new lives they were planning in the West.

Space in the wagon was limited. Every item added to the burden of the oxen drawing the wagon. What were the most important items for these people to take with them?

People already living along these trails helped people who traveled in the wagon trains. Their aid often meant the difference between success and failure for Americans headed west.

Covered wagon on the Oregon Trail near Scotts Bluff, Nebraska

Lessons Learned

LESSON 1
A New Form of Government
The new states wrote the Articles of Confederation. This created strong states but a weak national government. The states decided to create a new government at the Constitutional Convention. Many compromises were made over representation and slavery. Some states would not ratify the Constitution without a Bill of Rights. The Constitution can be changed.

LESSON 2
Building the Foundations
President Washington was our first president. He set many precedents for presidents to follow. The Louisiana Purchase doubled the size of the country. Lewis and Clark explored the new territory. The War of 1812 and the Monroe Doctrine were important turning points in the nation's early foreign affairs.

LESSON 3
Moving West
The expansion of the United States' territory led many people to move west. Many followed the Oregon and Mormon Trails. The government forced Native Americans to relocate to lands in the West. Texas joined the United States. War with Mexico added more land to the nation.

Talk About It

1. Of all Thomas Jefferson's accomplishments, which do you think was most important? Explain why.
2. George Washington is often called the "Father of our Country." Do you think this title is an accurate one? Explain.
3. Of all the compromises at the Constitutional Convention, which do you think was more important: the Great Compromise or the compromises over slavery? Explain your answer.
4. Why did George Washington and John Adams think the United States should remain neutral (not take sides) from the wars in Europe?
5. Given what he believed about the national government, should Thomas Jefferson have purchased the Louisiana Territory? Explain.

Mastering Mapwork

LOCATION
Use the map on page 166 to answer these questions:

1. Describe the location of lands gained by treaty with Great Britain in 1783 relative to the 13 original colonies.
2. What bodies of water lay to the east, west, and southwest of lands gained from a treaty with Spain in 1819?
3. In 1860, which state shown on this map had been most recently admitted to the Union?
4. What land did the United States gain from the Treaty with Mexico? What is it's relative location?

Becoming Better Readers

Developing Vocabulary
Social studies books, as well as other nonfiction books, are filled with lots of new words. Good readers use lots of strategies for learning new words. Good readers also play games with new words to help them build their vocabularies. Review the Key Terms in the three lessons in this chapter. Use the Key Terms to make three lists of Events in a Young Country, Actions of a Young Country, and Things or People in a Young Country. Grouping words together will help you remember their meanings.

Go to the Source

Analyzing Budgets

Pioneers moving west had to make sure they brought enough supplies for the journey. The following estimate of an outfit, for one year, for three persons, with ox teams, is copied from "The Emigrants Guide to California" by Joseph E. Ware. Read the budget below and answer the questions using information from the document.

Four yoke of oxen, $50 each	$200.00
One wagon, cover, &c	$100.00
Three rifles, $20	$60.00
Three pair pistols, $20	$45.00
Five barrels flour, 1080 lbs	$20.00
Bacon, 600 lbs	$30.00
Coffee, 100 lbs	$8.00
Tea, 5 lbs	$2.75
Sugar, 150 lbs	$ 7.00
Rice, 75 lbs	$3.75
Fruit, dried, 50 lbs	$3.00
Salt, pepper, &c., 50 lbs	$3.00
Salteratus, 10 lbs	$1.00
Lead, 30 lbs	$1.20
Powder, 25 lbs	$5.50
Tools, &c., 25 lbs	$7.50
Mining tools, 36 lbs	$12.00
Tent, 30 lbs	$5.00
Bedding, 45 lbs	$22.50
Cooking utensils, 30 lbs	$4.00
Lard, 50 lbs	$2.50
Private baggage 150 lbs	....
Matches	$1.00
One mule	$50.00
Candles and soap	$5.30
Total 2,583 lbs	$600.00

Questions
1. What would be the cost of four yoke of oxen?
2. Which items weighed 50 pounds?
3. According to this excerpt, what does the term "outfit" mean?
4. How would the total weight change if you had 150 pounds of rice?

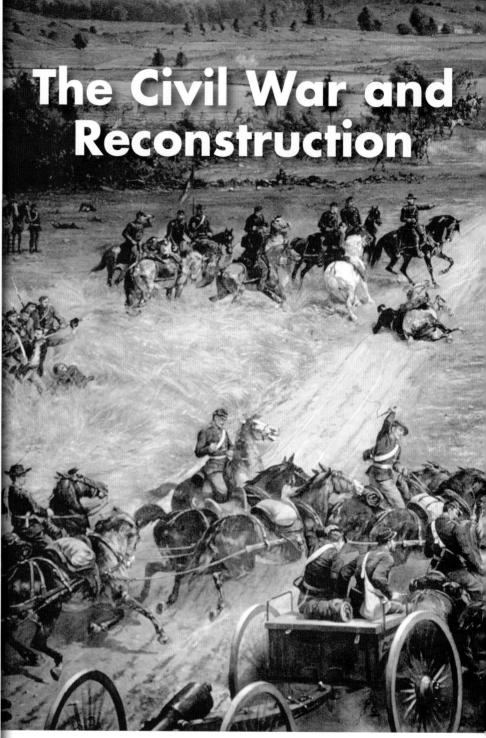

The Civil War and Reconstruction

Chapter Preview

LESSON 1
Heading Toward Civil War
As the nation grew, the disagreements over slavery became more difficult to solve.

LESSON 2
The Civil War
Although both sides believed the war would be short, its destruction lasted more than four years.

LESSON 3
The Reconstruction Period
Reconstruction brought many political and social changes to the South.

Timeline of Events

1800   1810   1820

1820
Missouri Compromise keeps an equal number of slave and free states

1807
Congress bans the importation of new slaves into the United States

Two great men were generals in the Civil War. Ulysses S. Grant led the Union army. Robert E. Lee led the Confederate army. But they were very different. Lee was considered a Southern gentleman. Grant seemed to be more of a businessman than a soldier.

But there were also similarities between the two men. Both graduated from the United States Military Academy at West Point. Both fought in the Mexican-American War. Both were outstanding military leaders who greatly respected each other.

The Union victory at the bloody Battle of Gettysburg forced Lee to retreat. But the two leaders' armies would continue fighting for two more years.

Battle of Gettysburg

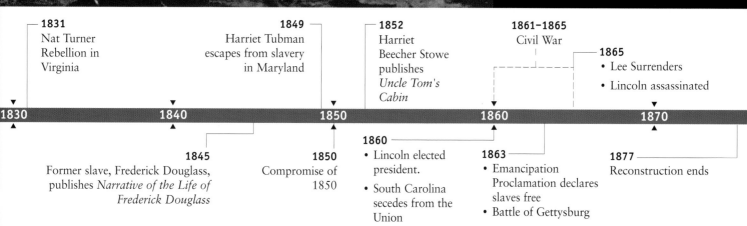

1831
Nat Turner Rebellion in Virginia

1849
Harriet Tubman escapes from slavery in Maryland

1852
Harriet Beecher Stowe publishes *Uncle Tom's Cabin*

1861–1865
Civil War

1865
• Lee Surrenders
• Lincoln assassinated

1830 — 1840 — 1850 — 1860 — 1870

1845
Former slave, Frederick Douglass, publishes *Narrative of the Life of Frederick Douglass*

1850
Compromise of 1850

1860
• Lincoln elected president.
• South Carolina secedes from the Union

1863
• Emancipation Proclamation declares slaves free
• Battle of Gettysburg

1877
Reconstruction ends

As the nation gained more territory in the West and added new states, slavery became more and more of problem. Slaveholders moving to the new land wanted to take their slaves with them. The owners did not want to free their workers. Others wanted the new lands to remain free from slavery.

As you have read, the United States purchased the Louisiana Territory from France in 1803. Slavery had already existed in many parts of the territory. When Louisiana became a state in 1812, it allowed slavery. This did not cause a political debate. Ten years later, slavery became a political issue. The national debate over slavery arose when Missouri wanted to become a state.

Slavery in America

Congress outlawed bringing new slaves into the country in 1807. But slavery still grew.

Slavery had developed everywhere in the colonies, both in the North and in the South. But the regions were different. The North developed factories. The South developed agriculture. After the War of 1812, the differences became even greater.

The North grew into a region with large cities, industries, and networks of canals and railroads. Its population also grew faster than the South's. Immigrants from Europe looked for jobs in cities in the North. The North had turned away from slavery. Many states began to ban it.

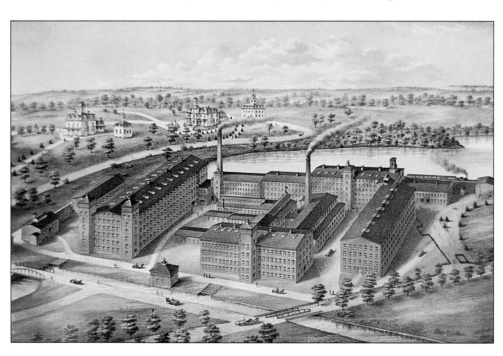

Slavery Expands

The South's economy depended on large plantations. These grew cotton, tobacco, and rice. Enslaved people tended these crops.

Cotton was a key cash crop. Northern factories bought a lot of it to make *textiles,* or cloth. But it took a great deal of work to produce cotton for the factories.

Before cotton could be made into cloth, it had to be cleaned of seeds. Slaves spent many hours slowly picking seeds out of the cotton fibers by hand. This limited the amount of cotton that plantation owners could grow and sell. If slaves could clean it faster, owners could grow and sell more.

In 1793, Eli Whitney from Connecticut patented the cotton gin. This machine was a quicker way to clean the seeds out of cotton. Before the cotton gin, a person could only clean about 5 pounds of cotton a week. With the cotton gin, a person could clean 50 pounds a day. More money could be made.

This expanded slavery in the cotton growing states of the South. More land was planted in cotton. More slaves were bought to grow, pick, and clean it, too.

The South relied on slavery more than ever. The differences between the North and South grew and soon led to conflict.

A Cruel System

It is impossible to know the exact number of Africans taken against their will as slaves to the Americas. We do know that millions of men, women, and children were sold as slaves in America. Many of them died in the *Middle Passage.* This was the long ocean trip from Africa to America. Some were taken to the Caribbean first. Then they were sold to owners in the United States.

Most Africans ended up in the South, in places like North Carolina. Slave owners fought to keep slavery. But many enslaved Africans fought to free themselves.

The North built industry (opposite left) while the South relied on farming (above).
How did these differences bring the regions into conflict?

The Civil War and Reconstruction

Meetings and newspapers drew abolitionists together in the fight against slavery. **Who was the publisher of *The Liberator*?**

Slaves Revolt

Nat Turner was an African American preacher. He led a revolt in Virginia. Turner believed that slavery was wrong. He said that his religious beliefs let him use violence to end slavery. In 1830, some of his followers fought to end slavery in Virginia. Turner was caught and hanged for leading the revolt. Because slave owners had weapons and more power, slaves could not win a revolt.

Tensions Rise

Slavery also caused tensions between the North and South. Few people in the South spoke out against slavery. Many more did so in the North. This caused debate in Congress. The first debate came in 1819 when the Missouri territory asked to be made a state.

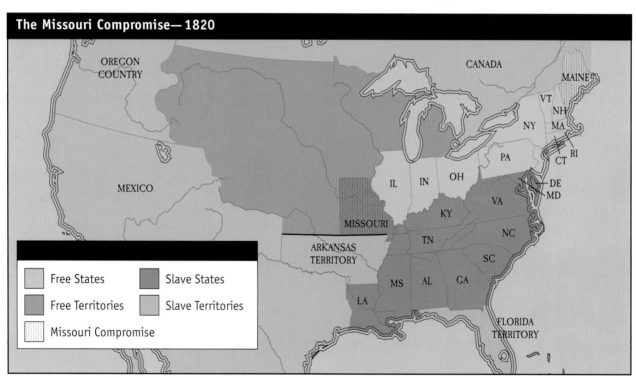

The Missouri Compromise—1820

☐ Free States	☐ Slave States
☐ Free Territories	☐ Slave Territories
☐ Missouri Compromise	

This map shows the free and slave states and territories after the Missouri Compromise. The Missouri Compromise drew a line to limit the spread of slavery. **Why did Congress agree to admit Missouri and Maine to the United States at the same time?**

Compromises Over Slavery

When Missouri applied for statehood, there were an equal number of free and slave states in the Union. Missouri wanted to come into the Union as a slave state. Leaders in the North were worried. With one more slave state, they thought the South might gain control of Congress.

Missouri, as a slave state, would give the South two more votes in the Senate and at least one more vote in the House of Representatives. Northern leaders feared that when major issues came up in Congress, the South would outvote them.

A Journey to THE SOUTH

The Underground Railroad

The Underground Railroad was one of the most important protests against slavery. It was not really "underground" nor a "railroad." Instead, it was a loose network of escape routes. They started in the South and crisscrossed the North. Many routes ended in Canada. Some escape routes led to western territories, Mexico, and the Caribbean. The peak of the railroad's use was from 1830 to 1865.

The Underground Railroad secretly resisted slavery. It helped runaways gain freedom. Abolitionists helped large numbers of men and women to freedom. Newspapers wrote about the Underground Railroad. This made Northern whites more aware of the evils of slavery. More people wanted to end slavery.

People from many ethnic and religious groups, such as free African Americans or Quakers, helped people escape from slavery. Harriet Tubman, a former slave, and Levi Coffin, a Cincinnati Quaker, were two famous rescuers.

Escaping was dangerous. Most slave owners believed the railroad stole their property. They offered rewards for returned slaves. Slave catchers tracked runaways for the money.

Escaped slaves traveled by night to avoid getting caught. They used the North Star to guide them. Usually they looked for farms,

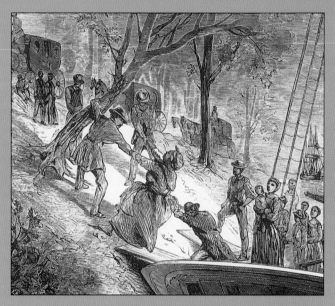
Enslaved people risked their lives to escape.

where free African Americans could hide them. These were called stations. When possible, "conductors" met them when they crossed into free states. Runaways could quickly escape to Canada from the Great Lake ports of Detroit, Michigan; Sandusky, Ohio; Erie, Pennsylvania; and Buffalo, New York.

Historians estimate that Underground Railroad conductors assisted thousands of people. But the exact number of runaways will never be known because of its secrecy. The heroes of the Underground Railroad were not the abolitionists. They were the runaway slaves who risked their lives to be free.

Harriet Tubman (left) was a former slave who led many others to freedom. **What was the name of the escape route she traveled?**

Missouri Compromise

Congress ended the debate with the *Missouri Compromise.* They agreed to bring Missouri into the Union as a slave state. But to balance it, Maine would enter as a free state. It had been part of Massachusetts.

Congress also made a new policy. Slavery would be allowed in lands south and southwest of Missouri. But it would not be allowed in the area north of Missouri. This kept the number of slave and free states even. There were now 12 free and 12 slave states in the Union.

Abolition

Americans argued over slavery. This started the abolitionist movement. People who believed slavery was wrong were called *abolitionists.* They wanted to abolish, or end, slavery.

Abolitionists held meetings, wrote in newspapers, and asked the federal government to end slavery. William Lloyd Garrison was a white reporter in the North. He published an abolitionist newspaper called *The Liberator.*

What would YOU do?

You are a bookseller in the South. Some of your customers want to read Harriet Beecher Stowe's *Uncle Tom's Cabin.* Others threaten to stop buying books from you if the book appears in your store. Would you order the book and place it in the window? Would you refuse to order it in order to avoid trouble?

The Underground Railroad

Other abolitionists helped African Americans escape from slavery. The path to freedom became known as the *Underground Railroad.* It was not a real railroad. Its name came from the secret places where runaway slaves stopped for food and shelter on their journey to freedom.

Harriet Tubman escaped slavery using the Underground Railroad. She was called Moses because she rescued other African American slaves. She said that her train never ran off the tracks and she never lost a passenger.

Frederick Douglass was one of the most famous people who led slaves to freedom. After he escaped slavery he became a writer and speaker. Because of the work of Tubman and Douglass, thousands of slaves used the Underground Railroad to travel to freedom.

An Important Book

In 1852, a young white woman living in Ohio helped conflict over slavery grow. Harriet Beecher Stowe was a gifted writer. Her sister told her to write about how horrible slavery was. Harriet listened to her sister and wrote *Uncle Tom's Cabin.* Her book was a best-seller in the North and around the world. She became famous.

Stowe told the story of how slavery was cruel. She pointed out that slaveholders could beat or even kill a slave. Slaveholders criticized her book, saying that she had wrongly described slavery. Stowe later met President Lincoln. He said to her, "So you are the little woman who started this big war."

This mural shows John Brown leading a slave rebellion in Harpers Ferry, Virginia. **What happened to Brown and his followers?**

Problems Get Worse

The slavery debate rose up again when California wanted to join the Union as a free state. The Missouri Compromise had not solved this problem.

The Compromise of 1850

Congress came up with the Compromise of 1850 to settle the conflict. California was admitted as a free state and the Fugitive Slave Act was passed.

The Fugitive Slave Act

The fugitive slave law allowed federal marshals (government police) to capture runaway slaves. It treated the runaways as if they were criminals. The law also created special courts. The courts reviewed requests from slaveholders who wanted to take accused runaways in free states back to slave states.

Congress set up these courts because they did not trust the courts in free states. The courts in free states might not allow a fugitive slave to be turned over to his owner if the owner was going to keep that person enslaved. The fugitive slave law also did not allow a judge to take the word of a runaway African American slave.

Sometimes free African Americans were stolen. Slaveholders lied to the courts, saying that the person they had captured was a runaway. These free people were forced to be slaves.

Also, the Compromise of 1850 let people in a territory decide for themselves whether they wanted their state to be free or allow slavery. Four years later, the debate about slave and free states came up yet again. But it turned bloody.

The Conflict Turns Violent

Kansas applied to enter the Union. Congress passed the Kansas-Nebraska Act. It said people living there could vote on whether they wanted Kansas to be a slave state or a free state. People who wanted slavery and those against it both rushed to Kansas. A civil war broke out there. Because many people were killed, the area became known as *Bleeding Kansas.*

John Brown decided to use force to end slavery. Brown, a white abolitionist, led a slave rebellion in Harpers Ferry, Virginia. He wanted to steal guns from the federal armory and give them to slaves. He and his followers were caught and hanged for treason. Some were killed in the fighting at Harpers Ferry. But Brown had made it clear that slavery could no longer be accepted in the United States.

The Civil War and Reconstruction

Dred Scott

The Supreme Court, in the 1857 case of *Dred Scott* v. *Sanford,* put an end to the compromises in Congress. Dred Scott, a slave, had been taken by his master from Missouri to the free state of Illinois and then on to Wisconsin Territory. He had lived there for several years. Abolitionists believed that because Scott had lived in a state and territory where slavery was illegal, this made him a free man. They helped Scott sue, or challenge in court, for his freedom.

Scott's case made it to the Supreme Court. The justices voted six to two that Scott was still the property of his owner. They wrote that the Fifth Amendment to the Constitution made the Missouri Compromise and the other compromises illegal. The Fifth Amendment says that no person can be deprived of "life, liberty, or property without the due process of law." Because Scott was considered the property of his owner, Congress did not have the power to pass any law that would take that property away. He was returned to his owner.

State's Rights

There were other issues that divided the states besides slavery. One was called "state's rights." The national government had placed a tax on goods imported, or brought to the United States from other countries. Northerners liked this tax. It made the imported things cost more to buy than the things they made in their factories.

Southerners thought this tax was unfair. Because there were few factories in the South, they had to buy many imported goods. They did not want to pay more for them. Senator John Calhoun from South Carolina spoke out about this. He said that South Carolina did not have to follow this law. Southerners believed that it was a state's right to disagree with the national government. In the same way, they also thought that it was a state's right to decide if it wanted slavery.

These disagreements were deep. There did not seem to be an easy way to solve the nation's problems peacefully. All of the ways the nation had tried to fix the problem had not worked. The South feared that as more free states were admitted to the Union, they would outvote the South. There might be a vote to end slavery. The South feared losing its way of life. The time for compromising had ended.

Dred Scott sued his owner to become free. **What did the Supreme Court decide?**

LESSON 1 REVIEW

Fact Follow-Up
1. Describe how the North and the South developed differently.
2. What did the abolitionists believe?
3. Compare the Missouri Compromise and the Compromise of 1850.
4. What was the Underground Railroad?

Talk About It
1. Why did admitting new states to the Union increase the controversy over slavery?
2. How did John Brown make it clear that slavery could no longer be accepted in the United States?
3. What does the idea of state's rights mean?

LESSON 2 The Civil War

Abraham Lincoln won the election of 1860. He led the new Republican Party. The Republicans were anti-slavery.

Lincoln's name was not on the ballot in ten Southern states. This did not make much difference in the election. There were more people in the North, and they outvoted the people in the South.

Southerners believed that the national government was now in the hands of anti-slavery leaders. Lincoln had promised to stop the spread of slavery. But Southerners did not believe the new president when he said that the national government would not change slavery where it existed in the South.

Secession

South Carolina seceded first. Its leaders voted to break away from the Union in December 1860. Six more states joined them in February 1861. These were Mississippi, Florida, Alabama, Georgia, Louisiana, and Texas. They formed the *Confederate States of America.* They elected Jefferson Davis to be their president.

In April, four more states joined the Confederacy. These were Arkansas, Tennessee, North Carolina, and Virginia.

Some slaveholding states did not *secede,* or leave the Union. These were Missouri, Kentucky, Maryland, and Delaware. Virginia was so divided that secession actually split the state. The western part of the state did not secede. It became its own state, West Virginia.

President Lincoln wanted to keep control of the Union government's property in the South. He tried to send supplies to Fort Sumter, the Union fort in Charleston, South Carolina. The Confederate army tried to stop that from happening. Therefore, they attacked Fort Sumter in April 1861. This was the start of the Civil War.

After Confederates took over Fort Sumter, they flew this flag. **Why did the Southern states secede?**

KEY IDEAS

- The Southern states did not trust Lincoln, so they left the Union.

- Both sides thought that the war would be short.

- Part of the Union's strategy was to blockade Southern ports, cut off supplies, and divide the Confederacy.

- President Lincoln issued the Emancipation Proclamation, freeing all of the slaves in the Confederate states.

- More than 600,000 men died in the Civil War.

KEY TERMS

Anaconda Plan
blockade
Confederate States of America
Emancipation Proclamation
Gettysburg Address
Massachusetts Fifty-fourth
secede
Sherman's March
Thirteenth Amendment

PEOPLE TO KNOW

Abraham Lincoln
Jefferson Davis
General William T. Sherman
General Joseph E. Jonhston
General Robert E. Lee
General Ulysses S. Grant
Clara Barton

Women
in the Civil War

During the Civil War, most women in both the South and the North had at least one male family member fighting in the war. These women faced the war bravely and helped their side in every way that they could.

Women near the battle sites on both sides often had to hide what little food, livestock, and valuables they had from enemy raiders. They learned how to shoot guns and armed themselves for self-defense.

In the North, women worked in the textile and weapons factories in jobs that had been done by men. They also had to run the farms. Southern women also had to take on the hard work of farming and running plantations. They often had small harvests. Meat disappeared from many tables. Families lived on diets of greens, field peas, or even just tomatoes. Starvation threatened many Southern families.

Doll used to smuggle medicine to Southerners

Nurse Clara Barton was called "the angel of the battlefield." She later founded The American Red Cross

Northern and Southern women set up hospitals and aid societies. They proved that the war was something they fought, too. They held fairs, raffles, concerts, and plays to raise money to buy expensive cloth, thread, and needles. In Charlottesville, Virginia, ladies met every day to sew uniforms. "Our needles are now our weapons," one woman stated.

Sarah Blalock fought dressed as a man.

Confederate spy Rose Greenhow, with her daughter

Many women on both sides served in the armies as nurses and laundresses. Other women, such as Rose O'Neal Greenhow and Sarah Lane Thompson, were spies. Perhaps as many as 400 women from the North and South disguised themselves as men and served as soldiers during the war.

Abraham Lincoln
1809–1865

Abraham Lincoln described his early life: *I was born Feb. 12, 1809, in Hardin County, Kentucky. . . . My mother . . . died in my tenth year . . . My father . . . removed from Kentucky to . . . Indiana, in my eighth year. . . . It was a wild region, with many bears and other wild animals. . . . There I grew up. . . . when I came of age I did not know much. Still somehow, I could read, write, and cipher [do math].*

Lincoln had fewer than two years of school. He learned by studying every book he could find. He spent so much time reading that neighbors thought he was lazy.

When Lincoln was twenty-one, his family moved to Illinois. There he became a lawyer and was active in politics. He married Mary Todd. They had four sons, but only one lived past childhood. Lincoln was well-known in Illinois. He served one term in Congress. He often spoke against slavery.

In 1860, Lincoln was elected president (the first from the Republican Party).

Lincoln signed the Pacific Railway Acts—starting the building of a railroad to the Pacific, and the Homestead Act—opening the West to settlers.

Lincoln wrote wonderful speeches that comforted and brought hope to a nation divided by war. His words inspire people today. Lincoln is often ranked as America's greatest president.

A Long War

Both sides thought the war would be short. Southerners believed they would win because they thought the Union did not have their fighting spirit. Northerners believed their factories and larger population meant they would win.

Early Southern Successes

In 1861, it looked like the Confederacy would win. They had an experienced leader in General Robert E. Lee. They won an early victory at the Battle of Bull Run (the Confederates called it the Battle of Manassas Junction) in 1861. In the following year the Confederates continued to win key battles. They kept the Union army out of Richmond, Virginia, the Confederate capital.

This political cartoon shows the Union's Anaconda Plan. **What did the plan do?**

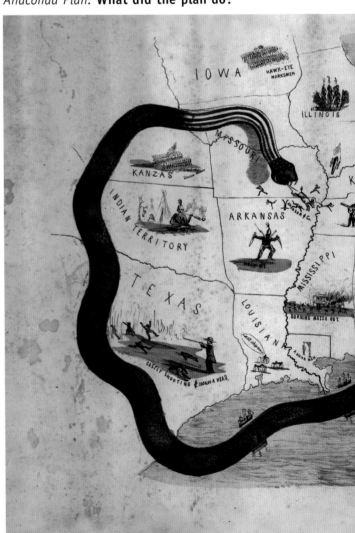

The Anaconda Plan

The Union developed a plan to pressure the South into surrendering. They placed a *blockade* on southern ports. Naval blockades cut off supplies and any help sent by other countries to the South.

The Union also fought to control rivers and ports along the Mississippi River. They did this to divide the South. They thought this would bring a speedy end to the war. Newspaper publishers called the strategy the *Anaconda Plan.* An anaconda is a powerful South American snake that can squeeze to death whatever it grabs.

The Confederacy tried to defeat the blockade by building ironclads, warships made of iron. When the Union navy fired upon the Confederate ironclads, their cannon balls bounced off them. The Union then made its own ironclads. So the war was also fought on the sea. The South was never able to defeat the Union blockade.

AMERICAN PORTRAIT

Jefferson Davis
1808–1889

Jefferson Davis, the only president of the Confederate States of America, was born in Kentucky. He graduated from the U.S. Military Academy at West Point and then served in the army for several years.

He married Sarah Knox Taylor, the daughter of future president Zachary Taylor. Sarah died shortly after their wedding and a sad Davis moved to his cotton plantation in Mississippi. A few years later, he became active in politics and married Varina Howell.

Davis fought again in the Mexican War. Afterwards, he became a United States Senator. The slavery debate was growing. Davis supported slavery and states' rights. He did not want the South to secede, but he wanted the national government to have less power. When Mississippi seceded, Davis left the Senate.

Two weeks later, Davis became president of the Confederacy. Southerners loved him, but he could not lead the South to victory. He could not raise enough money for supplies, convince other nations to recognize his country, or get local leaders to support his decisions.

The South lost the war. Union soldiers captured Davis and charged him with treason. He went to prison for two years. After he was released, he traveled and wrote histories of the Civil War. Davis spent his last years at Beauvoir, his home in Biloxi, Mississippi.

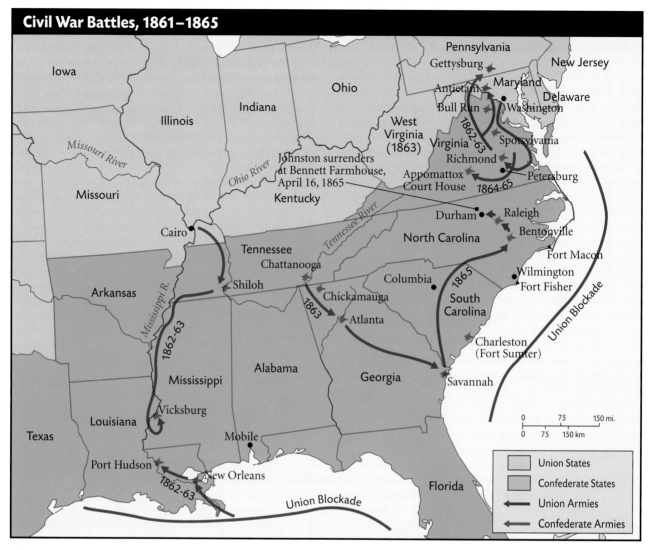

Civil War Battles, 1861–1865

The Civil War was fought mostly in the South. **Why do you think this was so?**

A Nation Divided— the Civil War

North
Name: Union
Nickname: Yankees
Color: Blue
Number of States: 23

South
Name: Confederacy
Nickname: Rebels
Color: Gray
Number of States: 11

President:
Abraham Lincoln

General:
Ulysses S. Grant

President:
Jefferson Davis

General:
Robert E. Lee

The Emancipation Proclamation

The war took another turn in the Union's favor in 1863. When the war first started, Lincoln had not promised to end slavery in the South. To show to the rest of the world that supporting the Union was important, Lincoln issued the Emancipation Proclamation. This freed all slaves in the Confederacy.

The proclamation did not end slavery in Southern states that were loyal to the Union. It would have allowed any state that returned to the Union to keep slavery, too. However, by the end of the war, Slavery could not continue. The proclamation had grown into the *Thirteenth Amendment.* This change to the Constitution would end slavery in America.

The Emancipation Proclamation changed the war in another way. The proclamation allowed African American soldiers to join the Union army. African American abolitionists like Frederick Douglass recruited African American soldiers for the war. The most famous of these troops were those of the *Massachusetts Fifty-fourth.*

Customs

Memorial Day is celebrated on the last weekend of May. It used to be called Decoration Day. After the Civil War, families gathered at cemeteries on that day each year. They decorated the graves of war veterans with flowers. We still honor those who have sacrificed for our country on Memorial Day with parades and services. The holiday also marks the unofficial beginning of summer.

By the time the war was over, more than 200,000 African American men had served in the Union army.

Lincoln also showed that he was committed to freedom in 1863. He gave the *Gettysburg Address,* a speech that dedicated a cemetery in Pennsylvania to honor the men who lost their lives there in a fierce battle. Lincoln reminded everyone that the Founding Fathers, the men who wrote the Constitution, had formed a nation based upon liberty and equality. He described the Civil War as a test to see if such a nation would last. He closed by saying that the United States was governed for the people and by the people. It must not perish (die).

The End of the War

The Union began to make progress on the battlefield when Lincoln put General Ulysses S. Grant in charge of the army. Grant was a strong leader. He had won control of the Mississippi River and a key battle at Vicksburg.

Sherman's March

In 1864, Grant ordered the Union army to destroy the Confederate army and the Southern farms and towns that supplied that army's food and shelter. General William T. Sherman led Union troops into the South. This began *Sherman's March.*

Sherman went to Atlanta, Georgia, then turned east toward the port of Savannah. Along the way his army burned plantations and cities and destroyed railroads. They took supplies, food, and equipment from the Confederate army.

Surrender

The Civil War came to an end in 1865 when Grant invaded Virginia. As Union troops took over Petersburg and Richmond, the war ended.

General Lee surrendered to General Grant at Appomattox Courthouse on April 19, 1865. Nine days later, General Joseph E. Johnston met Sherman at the Bennett Farmhouse, located near Durham, North

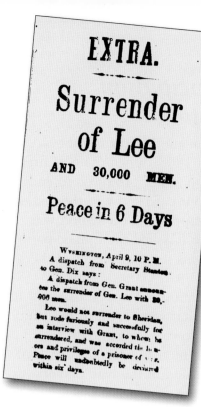

EXTRA.

Surrender of Lee

AND 30,000 MEN.

Peace in 6 Days

WASHINGTON, April 9, 10 P. M.
A dispatch from Secretary Stanton to Gen. Dix says:

A dispatch from Gen. Grant announces the surrender of Gen. Lee with 30,000 men.

Lee would not surrender to Sheridan, but rode furiously and successfully for an interview with Grant, to whom he surrendered, and was accorded the honors and privileges of a prisoner of war. Peace will undoubtedly be declared within six days.

Robert E. Lee surrendered to Grant at Appomatox Courthouse. **Where did Joseph Johnston surrender to William Sherman?**

Carolina, to negotiate the surrender. Jefferson Davis did not surrender immediately. He escaped to Georgia. He was later captured.

More than 600,000 men died in the Civil War. The once wealthy South was in shambles. Cities, farms, and railroads were gone. The Union army stayed in the South to restore order.

WORD ORIGINS

The word **confederacy** comes from the Latin *foedorare*, meaning "to join together." Federal comes from the same Latin word.

LESSON 2 REVIEW

Fact Follow-Up
1. What was the Anaconda Plan?
2. How did the Emancipation Proclamation change the war?
3. What was the purpose of Sherman's March?
4. Who commanded the Union and Confederate armies when the Civil War ended?

Talk About It
1. Why did the Confederate states withdraw from the Union?
2. Why did Lincoln describe the Civil War as a war to save the Union?
3. Should General Joseph E. Johnston have surrendered to General Sherman at the Bennett Farmhouse? Explain.

LESSON ③ The Reconstruction Period

Lincoln had looked forward to the day when the war would be over. That would be a time "to bind up the nation's wounds." In his second inaugural address he spoke about the nation coming back together. His famous words were, "with malice toward none, with charity for all."

Lincoln's plan for restoring the nation and rebuilding the South was called *Reconstruction.* He would not punish the South. Instead, he would bring the nation back together quickly.

Lincoln's Plan

Lincoln called his plan of Reconstruction the Ten Percent Plan. He gave a *pardon,* or forgiveness, to all Southerners. To be pardoned, they had to swear loyalty to the Union and support the freedom of former slaves. Leaders of the Confederacy were not pardoned immediately.

When 10 percent of the state's voters had taken the oath, Lincoln said the state could return to the Union. His plan did not call for civil rights for African Americans, such as giving them the right to vote.

Many Republicans in Congress called the Ten Percent Plan too easy on the South.

Lincoln's plans for Reconstruction ended when he was *assassinated,* or murdered. An actor, John Wilkes Booth, shot the president on April 14, 1865. Lincoln's vice president, Andrew Johnson, tried to carry on some of Lincoln's plans for Reconstruction. He faced many challenges from Congress, however.

Johnson was from Tennessee. He had remained loyal to the Union. Like Lincoln, Johnson wanted to bring the South back into the Union quickly.

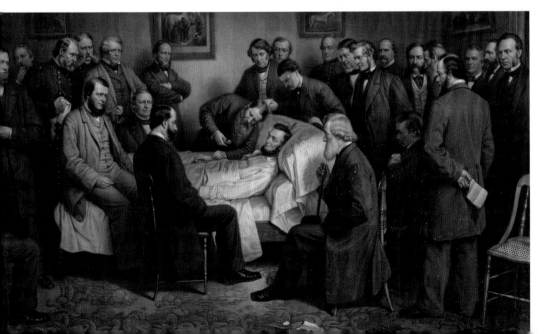

KEY IDEAS

- President Lincoln wanted to bring the nation back together peacefully. These plans ended when he was assassinated.

- The plan for reuniting the nation and rebuilding the South was called Reconstruction.

- African Americans gained many new rights. But soon limits were placed on their freedom.

KEY TERMS

assassinated
carpetbaggers
Freedmen's Bureau
Jim Crow laws
Ku Klux Klan
literacy tests
pardon
poll taxes
polls
Reconstruction
scalawags
segregated
separate but equal
sharecropping

PEOPLE TO KNOW

John Wilkes Booth
Andrew Johnson
George Henry White
Rutherford B. Hayes

Lincoln was assassinated shortly after the end of the war. **What was Lincoln's Ten Percent Plan?**

191

Congress Takes Over

Unlike Presidents Lincoln and Johnson, Congress treated the Confederacy as a nation that was conquered in war. They created standards to bring Southern states back into the Union.

They did not allow ex-Confederate leaders to vote or run for political office. They required the states to ratify the Fourteenth Amendment to the Constitution. This amendment defined a citizen as a person who was born in the United States. This made African Americans citizens. Congress later required the states to accept the Fifteenth Amendment, which prevented the states from using color to deny a person the vote.

Congress also made the army the temporary government in the South. The army supervised elections that were open to African American men as well as loyal white men. Many white Southerners did not participate in state or national elections.

People called *carpetbaggers* came from the North. They used the situation in the South to make money. Some entered state government. Southern Republicans called *scalawags* also entered politics. These people were loyal to the Union. They did not want former Confederates to control state government.

New Freedoms

In every Southern state African Americans were in the majority. They elected African American men to state and national offices.

Some African Americans held law degrees and others were trained in the ministry. Some were also teachers and businessmen. These individuals ran for political office in the South.

Joseph Hayne Rainey and Blanche Kelso Bruce were the first African Americans to be elected to the United States Senate during this period. Many African Americans served in state legislatures and in local governments. Representative George Henry White, a North Carolina lawyer, was the last African American to serve in Congress during this period.

Carpetbags (left) were used for travel because they were lightweight, durable, and inexpensive. Later, the term referred to Northerners (above) who moved to the South to make money during Reconstruction after the Civil War. **Why did Southerners resent the carpetbaggers?**

Chapter 8

African American men and white men who were loyal to the Union could vote in the South during Reconstruction. **What amendment protected African American men's right to vote?**

Freedmen's Bureau

Before President Lincoln was murdered, he joined Congress in creating the *Freedmen's Bureau.* The bureau provided food, shelter, and medical care to freed slaves in the South. It helped African Americans find jobs. The bureau also helped needy whites, and it provided medical care for more than a million people. One Southerner was amazed to see the Union, which had once fired upon them, feed their poor.

The Freedmen's Bureau also set up schools and hired teachers for African American children. By 1869, more than 600,000 African American children attended these schools. Most of their teachers were women volunteers from the North.

African American parents were determined to help their children get an education. Many African American parents made great sacrifices so their children could go to school. But children were not the only ones eager to read and write. African American adults went to school for the first time, and they also were eager to learn. These classrooms later became part of the public schools in the South.

The Civil War and Reconstruction

Many former slaves became sharecroppers. **Why was it hard for sharecroppers to make a profit?**

The Nation Changes

Reconstruction brought economic changes throughout the nation. In the North and West, railroad networks were extended. The steel industry grew larger. More people moved west. The mining industry expanded. Instead of running small farms and shops, Americans took jobs in factories. The United States entered the modern era.

Changes in the South

There were also economic changes in the South. The national government had finally abolished slavery. Now, a new way of getting the work done needed to be created.

Sharecropping became common. In this system, a landowner rented a family part of his land. Each family raised crops on the land for part of its profits. The owner also supplied seeds and equipment. The family had to pay the owner back for these out of his own profits. Sharecroppers rarely made any money.

Both whites and African Americans became sharecroppers. The practice prevented many African Americans from getting out of poverty. A successful season for them was just being able have food and shelter for their families.

Poor whites and blacks who owned farms also owed money. They got supplies and equipment on credit from a merchant. Credit means the store lets a person buy something now, but waits to be paid until the buyer has money.

At harvest time, small farmers paid what they owed from the money they got from selling their crops. But this was not always enough. Sometimes, storekeepers took advantage of them. In the end, many small farmers had to sell their land and become sharecroppers.

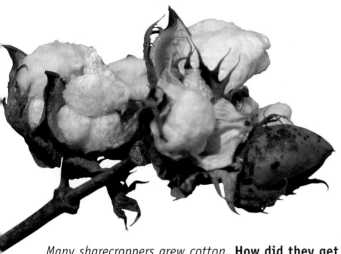

Many sharecroppers grew cotton. **How did they get money for seeds and equipment?**

Limits on Freedom

Many white Southerners were against Reconstruction's changes. They wanted to end African American participation in government as soon as possible. Some whites created hate groups to scare the African Americans and the people who helped them.

The most well known of these was the secret society called the KKK, or *Ku Klux Klan.* Its members dressed in white robes with hoods that hid their faces. They went to African American communities and burned crosses, homes, and businesses.

But these threats did not always keep African Americans away from the *polls,* or voting places. So the Klan also used violence. They killed thousands of African American men, women, and children. They also attacked white friends of African Americans.

Reconstruction came to an end in 1876. President Rutherford B. Hayes, a Republican from Ohio, agreed to remove federal troops from the South. No more would be done to help former slaves start new lives as free people.

More Struggles

When Reconstruction was over, whites in the South took away the vote from African Americans. They found ways to get around other federal laws, too.

Southern states created *poll taxes.* Voters had to pay a fee to vote. Since just whites

George Henry White represented North Carolina in Congress from 1897 to 1901. He was a Republican. **What did states do to stop African Americans from voting?**

worked at polling places, they made only African Americans pay the poll tax. Whites did not have to pay.

The states also created *literacy tests.* These laws required African American voters to read and explain parts of the Constitution. As slaves, African Americans could not go to school, and many could not read. They stayed away from the polls, knowing that they would not be allowed to vote. Poor white people who could not read or write did not have these problems.

Finally, the states created a *segregated* society. Laws separated people of different races. African Americans and whites were forced to attend different schools, eat in different places, play in separate parks, be buried in separate cemeteries, and drink from different water fountains. When visiting a doctor or dentist, African Americans and whites sat in separate waiting rooms. These restrictions were called *Jim Crow laws.*

The Civil War and Reconstruction

After Reconstruction, many African Americans moved from North Carolina to the North and Midwest.
Why do you think they moved?

Separate but Equal

The national government approved of these laws. In 1896, the United States Supreme Court said that segregation did not take away African American rights under the Constitution. The court said that, so long as African Americans had a place to go, it did not matter if they were separated from whites.

The court called this idea *seperate but equal.* However, everyone knew that separation was not equal. Public schools for African American children, for example, did not receive the same money as those for whites. They did not have good school books, nice buildings, or even enough desks.

The rights African Americans gained during Reconstruction were short-lived. Though slavery was gone, it would take more than a hundred years to fix what happened in the South after Reconstruction.

LESSON ③ REVIEW

Fact Follow-Up
1. What was Abraham Lincoln's plan for Reconstruction?
2. Describe the congressional plans for Reconstruction.
3. What was sharecropping, and how did it affect African Americans?
4. How did Southern states create a segregated society after Reconstruction ended?

Talk About It
1. If you had been a Republican in Congress, would you have favored Lincoln's Ten Percent Plan or the congressional plan for Reconstruction? Explain.
2. Why did Republicans in Congress oppose President Lincoln's plan for Reconstruction?
3. Was "separate but equal" really equal?

*Accessing a Variety of Sources; Gathering,
Synthesizing, and Reporting Information*

Causes and Effects

Fort Sumter is located on an island just off the coast of Charleston, South Carolina. United States troops were serving there. Because the fort is located on an island, the navy's ships would land there to unload food, uniforms, guns, and ammunition. These are the supplies that any fort needs.

In April 1861, when President Abraham Lincoln tried to send supplies to the fort, South Carolina had already seceded from the United States. It and ten other states formed the Confederate States of America. Confederate troops fired cannons to keep the United States forces from landing. The Civil War had begun.

The events leading up to this event go far back in our history. When we study both the causes and the results of these events, we can see a pattern of compromises. Beginning with the birth of our country, these compromises continued until just before the war began.

Here is a sample of a causes and consequences chart.

You will notice that the Great Compromise, the first event, happened in 1787, as you read in Chapter 7. The Civil War did not begin until 1861. What other event (or compromise) of the Constitutional Convention might have been one of the causes of the Civil War? Search Chapter 7 for other compromises or events to include on the chart.

In this chapter you have read about many compromises. What were the causes behind these compromises? What were their results? Finally, why did the compromises end in war in April 1861?

Graphic Organizer		
Causes	**Event(s)**	**Consequences/Results**
	Great Compromise, 1787	

Lessons Learned

LESSON 1
Heading Toward Civil War
The problem of slavery grew larger as more states were added to the nation. Abolitionists helped slaves escape and asked the government to end slavery.

LESSON 2
The Civil War
President Lincoln wanted to keep the Union together. Southern states did not trust him as president, so they seceded. The war lasted more than four years and more than 600,000 men died. Lincoln issued the Emancipation Proclamation, freeing all of the slaves in the Confederate states.

LESSON 3
The Reconstruction Period
President Lincoln's assassination ended his plan to bring the nation back together peacefully. Republicans in Congress controlled Reconstruction, the plan for reuniting the nation and rebuilding the South. Reconstruction brought many political and economic changes to the South. African Americans gained many new rights under Reconstruction. When Reconstruction ended, most of the rights were taken away by the governments of Southern states.

Talk About It

1. After the War of 1812, why did the North turn away from slavery and the South rely on slavery more than before?
2. If you could have met Harriet Tubman or Harriet Beecher Stowe, which would you have chosen to talk with? Explain why.
3. What advantages did the Union and the Confederacy have at the beginning of the war?
4. Compare life in the North and in the South at the end of Reconstruction.

Mastering Mapwork

MOVEMENT
Use the map on page 188 to answer these questions:

1. What was the most northerly movement of the Confederate armies?
2. In what directions did Union armies move to capture the Mississippi River?
3. Trace the movement of the Union army from Chattanooga on the Tennessee River to Savannah, noting major battles fought along the way.
4. In what direction did the Union army move as it marched from Bentonville to Bennett Farmhouse in North Carolina?

Becoming Better Readers

Increasing Vocabulary
To help learn new words and increase their vocabulary, good readers use many different strategies to learn new words. One strategy is called R2C2 or read, recite, cover, check. To learn a new word, begin by reading the word along with its definition. Then say it out loud or recite it. Cover the word up and see if you can say the word and its definition. Finally, check to see if you were right. Try this strategy using the words from Lesson 3 on page 191.

Go to the Source

Comparing Eyewitness Accounts

The passages below were written by people who were at the Battle of Gettysburg, Pennsylvania, in 1863. Read their stories and answer the questions using information from the documents.

As the afternoon wore away the churches and warehouses . . . were filled with wounded. Then the court house, as well as the . . . school house . . . received the injured soldiers, until those places [were full], . . . when private homes were utilized. . . .

With Miss Julia Culp. . . I went into the court house with buckets of water and passed from one to another of the wounded. . . . Some of them were so frightfully wounded that a lady could not go near them. These I gave water to, while she cared for those who were not so severely wounded. Quite a number of our townspeople were there doing everything they could . . . as the wounded were carried in.

This, my first sight of a great battlefield, with all its . . . suffering and death—made a deep and lasting impression on my young mind, stamping war on my memory as too horrible to even think about. . . .

—Daniel Skelly of Gettysburg,
sixteen years old

After a while the artillery wagons began to go back . . . . Then came the order: 'Women and children to the cellars; the rebels will shell the town. . . .' Our cellar was a good one and furnished a refuge for many besides our own family.

The noise above our heads, the rattling of musketry, the screeching of shells, and the unearthly yells, added to the cries of the children, were enough to shake the stoutest heart.

. . . The firing ceased and we came up from the cellar. They had begun bringing wounded and injured into town. The Catholic and Presbyterian churches . . . were [used] as hospitals. . . . From that time on we had no rest for weeks.

While the battle lasted . . . I went back and forth between my home and the hospitals without fear. The soldiers called me brave, but I am afraid the truth was that I did not know enough to be afraid and if I had known enough, I had no time to think of the risk I ran, for my heart and hands were full.

[The soldiers] bore their suffering . . . with . . . matchless courage. Their patience was marvelous. I never heard a murmur. Truly, we shall not look upon their like again.

—Sally Myer, twenty-one year-old
schoolteacher

Questions

1. How are both accounts of the Battle of Gettysburg similar?
2. What is the overall mood or tone of each account?
3. What do these two accounts tell you about the Battle of Gettysburg?
4. Are these accounts of the Battle of Gettysburg accurate? How do you know?

Chapter Preview

LESSON 1
Transportation: Roads and Waterways
Travel by road was slow. Better roads and canals made transportation easier.

LESSON 2
Railroads
When the transcontinental railroad was built, the East and West were united in transportation and communication.

LESSON 3
An Agricultural and Industrial Giant
By the end of the nineteenth century, the United States was a nation of big businesses.

Timeline of Events

1798
Eli Whitney invents interchangeable parts

1817
Erie Canal project begins

1857
George Pullman invents Pullman Sleeping Car for trains

1862
Homestead Act grants free family farms to settlers

1800   1820   1840   1860   1862   186

1806
Building the National Road begins

1807
Robert Fulton's steamboat makes first trip

1837
Telegraph invented

1860
Pony Express makes first run

1861
Transcontinental telegraph line completed

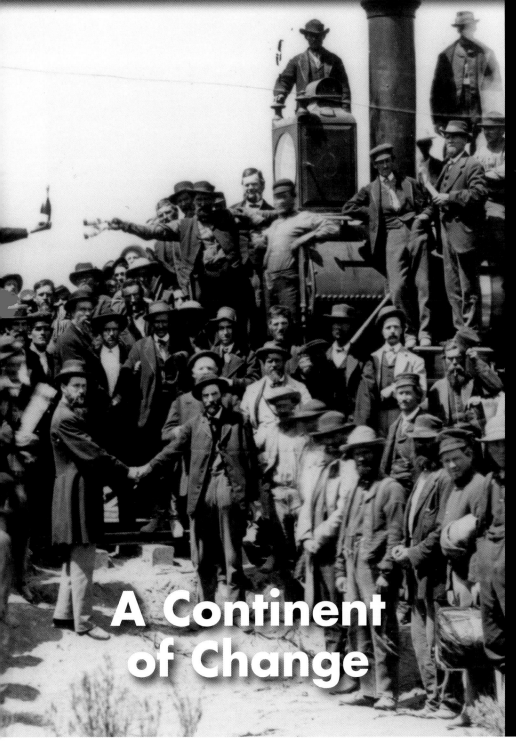

A Continent of Change

Even before the Civil War, the United States was divided. California was a whole continent away from Washington, D.C. People who needed to travel to and from this state had two choices. They could make a dangerous trip by boat all the way around South America. Or, they could journey more than 2,000 miles (3,220 km) overland. They had to cross mountains, deserts, and lands belonging to Native Americans.

Many people thought that the country needed a railroad to the Pacific. It took six years to build. On May 10, 1869, at Promontory Summit, Utah, the dream became reality. A golden spike was hammered into the tracks. The transcontinental railroad was complete. This was the greatest engineering achievement of the nineteenth century.

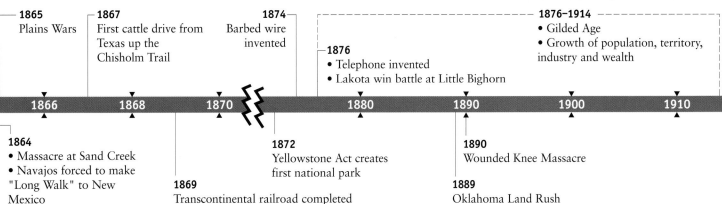

1865
Plains Wars

1867
First cattle drive from Texas up the Chisholm Trail

1874
Barbed wire invented

1876
• Telephone invented
• Lakota win battle at Little Bighorn

1876–1914
• Gilded Age
• Growth of population, territory, industry and wealth

| 1866 | 1868 | 1870 | 1880 | 1890 | 1900 | 1910 |

1864
• Massacre at Sand Creek
• Navajos forced to make "Long Walk" to New Mexico

1869
Transcontinental railroad completed

1872
Yellowstone Act creates first national park

1889
Oklahoma Land Rush

1890
Wounded Knee Massacre

KEY IDEAS

- Early roads in America were difficult to travel.

- Shipping goods by roads was expensive.

- The development of canals and steamboats made water travel faster, easier, and cheaper.

KEY TERMS

Erie Canal
Industrial Revolution
livestock
plank roads
toll
Wilderness Road

PEOPLE TO KNOW

Daniel Boone
Robert Fulton

This wilderness road was the main route used by settlers to reach Kentucky for more than 50 years. **Why were roads becoming more important in early America?**

In 1801, first lady Abigail Adams traveled in a horse-drawn carriage from Washington, D.C., to her home in Massachusetts. The roads in most places were almost like trails.

At one point, the driver lost his way in the forest. Mrs. Adams wrote her husband, the president, that she was badly bruised. She had been tossed about as the carriage rode over rough ground. In the nation's early years, only dirt roads, and in some cases trails, connected cities. Some cities and towns did have a few paved streets. They were usually paved with cobblestones or bricks.

Before the American Revolution, it was not important to have roads between cities. The colonies were located along the Atlantic Coast. They used boats on rivers or the ocean to get from city to city. As people moved west, dirt roads connected cities and towns. Roads were not paved until automobiles were widely used in the 1920s.

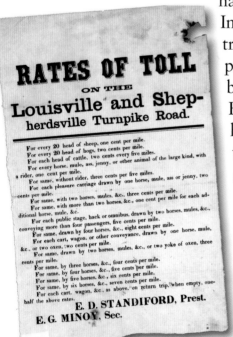

RATES OF TOLL
ON THE
Louisville and Shep-herdsville Turnpike Road.

For every 20 head of sheep, one cent per mile.
For every 20 head of hogs, two cents per mile.
For each head of cattle, two cents every five miles.
For every horse, mule, ass, jenny, or other animal of the large kind, with a rider, one cent per mile.
For same, without rider, three cents per five miles.
For each pleasure carriage drawn by one horse, mule, ass or jenny, two cents per mile.
For same, with two horses, mules, &c., three cents per mile.
For same, with more than two horses, &c., one cent per mile for each additional horse, mule, &c.
For each public stage, hack or omnibus, drawn by two horses, mules, &c., conveying more than four passengers, five cents per mile.
For same, drawn by four horses, &c., eight cents per mile.
For each cart, wagon, or other conveyance, drawn by one horse, mule, &c., or two oxen, two cents per mile.
For same, drawn by two horses, mules, &c., or two yoke of oxen, three cents per mile.
For same, by three horses, &c., four cents per mile.
For same, by four horses, &c., five cents per mile.
For same, by five horses, &c., six cents per mile.
For same, by six horses, &c., seven cents per mile.
For each cart, wagon, &c., as above, on return trip, when empty, one-half the above rates.
E. D. STANDIFORD, Prest.
E. G. MINOY, Sec.

This sign shows how much people had to pay to travel on a turnpike in Kentucky. **Look closely. How much did a person have to pay to transport 20 sheep?**

Early Roads

The settlers had cut trails west before the Revolutionary War. British General Edward Braddock and George Washington cut trails to the Ohio Valley at the start of the French and Indian War. Pioneers like Daniel Boone also cut trails west.

Boone lived in a valley in western North Carolina during the 1760s. He spent months alone in the land that would become the state of Kentucky. The trail he followed became known as the *Wilderness Road.* These trails were the first roads Americans used to go west.

Road Improvements

Even with roads and trails, Americans did not like traveling over land. When it rained, their horse-drawn wagons could get stuck in mud.

To solve this problem, *plank roads,* or roads made from wooden boards, were built. Where heavy wagons traveled, boards were placed close together. Dirt was packed around them. Plank roads kept wagons from sinking into the ground.

But the ride did not improve much for travelers. With only a few bridges built, going by wagon was not always possible. Traveling over bumpy roads was uncomfortable and hard.

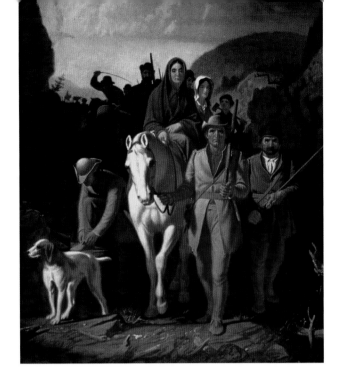

Daniel Boone led people along the Wilderness Road.
Why were early roads difficult to travel?

Toll Roads

Private companies also built roads to connect cities and towns. During the 1790s, a Pennsylvania company built the Lancaster Turnpike. This linked the cities of Philadelphia and Lancaster. Its builders put down gravel for the foundation and topped it off with smooth stones. Later, the turnpike was extended from Philadelphia to Pittsburgh, near the Ohio River.

This type of road did not change travelers' minds. The ride was still rough. Also, they often had to pay money, called a *toll,* to travel on these roads. The roads cost a lot of money to build and fix, so toll roads did not really make much money. Most people who shipped goods or traveled long distances would rather travel by water.

Plank roads (above) were common in the 1850s, but the planks needed replacing after only a few years. Toll roads were not popular, either (right).
Why was wagon travel difficult?

A Continent of Change

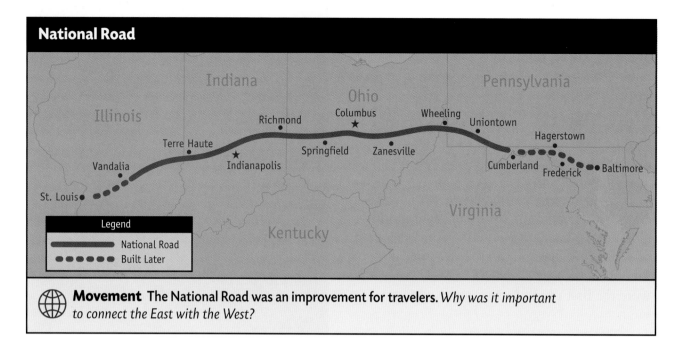

National Road

Legend
— National Road
•••• Built Later

🌐 **Movement** The National Road was an improvement for travelers. *Why was it important to connect the East with the West?*

The National Road

Settlers going west traveled rough roads and trails. It was dangerous for humans and their animals. The government wanted to make it safer. So Congress set aside money in 1806 to build the National Road. This connected the East and West, starting in Baltimore, Maryland.

The National Road was made from crushed rock. This was a smoother surface for walking or riding. Better roads meant that people could get anywhere along the way more easily. Many made the trip to Ohio, Illinois, and Indiana.

Shipping Goods

Unlike travelers in carriages and wagons, farmers usually used dirt roads and trails. Farmers could drive, or lead, their **livestock,** or animals they raised on the farm, through the woods and over roads and trails to market. They could also drive them across shallow rivers.

Merchants who had goods to move were not so lucky. It cost a lot of money to carry large and bulky crates and barrels over the roads. Using boats on rivers and streams was better. Merchants and some farmers found it easier to float their items downstream to get them to market. Large rivers, like the Ohio and Mississippi, were the main waterways for shipping goods. Shallow rivers and streams were also used.

Once they reached the end of the river, stagecoaches or freight wagons would take the people or goods the rest of the way. Travelers on stagecoaches could only take a few things with them in a trunk. People could get off or on at any town along the way. Stages also carried the mail.

Freight wagons carried goods. Freight is any large amount of something that needs to be moved from one place to another. Many supplies were sent across the prairie by wagon. Drivers stopped in towns to sell things or to pick up more things to sell in other places.

River Transportation

Using rivers to transport goods also had problems. Floating downstream with the river's current was easy. But going upstream, against the current, was difficult and slow.

Going upstream required muscle. People used paddles or poles to push the boat or raft. Others tied ropes to the raft or barge and tied the other end to a person or animal on the river bank. The people or animals would pull the raft upstream. It was hard work. So inventors looked for a better way to move people and things.

Chapter 9

Samuel Clemens
1835–1910

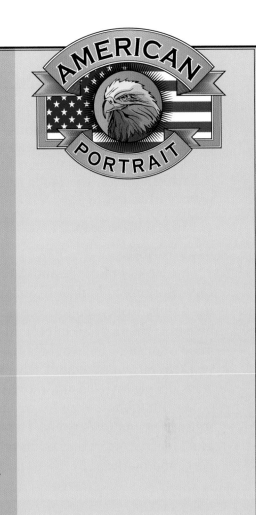

Mark Twain is one of America's greatest writers. His name was really Samuel Clemens. He was born in Florida, Missouri.

When he was four, Clemens' father moved the family to Hannibal, 30 miles (48.3 km) away. Clemens remembered his boyhood in Hannibal for the rest of his life. Those memories became a big part of his writing.

Clemens grew up around slaves. His father owned one slave. After moving to Hannibal, Clemens spent a few months a year on his Uncle John's farm. His uncle owned several slaves. Clemens loved going to the slaves' cabins and listening to their music and stories. He loved the stories of one slave, a man people called "Uncle Dan." Some of the stories were funny, while others were sad. Clemens loved the way Uncle Dan talked.

Becoming a Writer

Clemens' boyhood ended when he was a teenager. His father died. Clemens went to work to support the family. First, he worked at his brother's newspaper. He helped set the type in the printing presses. He enjoyed reading the exciting stories. He loved writing and began to print his own stories in the paper.

As he grew up, Samuel Clemens lived an exciting life. For a few years, he was a riverboat pilot on the Mississippi. When the Civil War began, he was a soldier in Missouri. After two weeks he left the war and went west. He lived in Nevada, California, and even Hawaii. All along the way he wrote for magazines and newspapers. People across America loved his writing. Clemens made them both laugh and think about the problems of society.

Clemen married and had children. His family lived in New York and Connecticut. They rarely made it back to Missouri.

Worldwide Fame

When he wrote, Clemens used a pen name. The name he chose was "Mark Twain," a riverboat term. To see how deep the water was when a riverboat moved upriver, a sailor would throw a rope overboard. The rope had marks on it to measure the water's depth. If the water was 12 feet (3.6m) deep, the sailor would shout, "by the mark twain." This meant it was deep enough for the boat. Many people knew Samuel Clemens only by the name Mark Twain.

Mark Twain traveled throughout America and Europe giving talks. People loved his stories. These stories found their way into his books. Many of them are still read today. His most famous books are *The Adventures of Tom Sawyer* and *The Adventures of Huckleberry Finn*. Though the books are fiction, many of the characters in the books were people Clemens knew as a boy.

Samuel Clemens wrote under the pen name Mark Twain.

Steamboats

Inventors in Europe and America had been working to build a steam engine since the 1700s. Robert Fulton was an American inventor. He made an important improvement in the way steam engines worked. His work completely changed the ways people traveled and moved their goods.

By 1820, more than 60 steamboats traveled the nation's rivers. They moved grain, corn, cotton, and other produce to ports and markets. By 1840, farmers were transporting by river more than 500,000 tons of produce a year.

The steamboat changed the way people traveled. This new technology was part of the **Industrial Revolution.** During this time, new inventions changed the ways in which goods were made and moved.

Canals

It was also cheaper for governments to invest in waterways rather than roads. In areas without rivers, state governments built waterways, called canals.

New York State built the **Erie Canal.** It connected the Hudson River with Lake Erie. People could travel by boat from New York City to Albany, and on to Buffalo. Irishmen, local farm boys, and prisoners built the canal. Three men working with horses or oxen could dig a mile of canal in one year. At 363 miles (584 km) long, work was hard and slow.

United States Canals, 1890

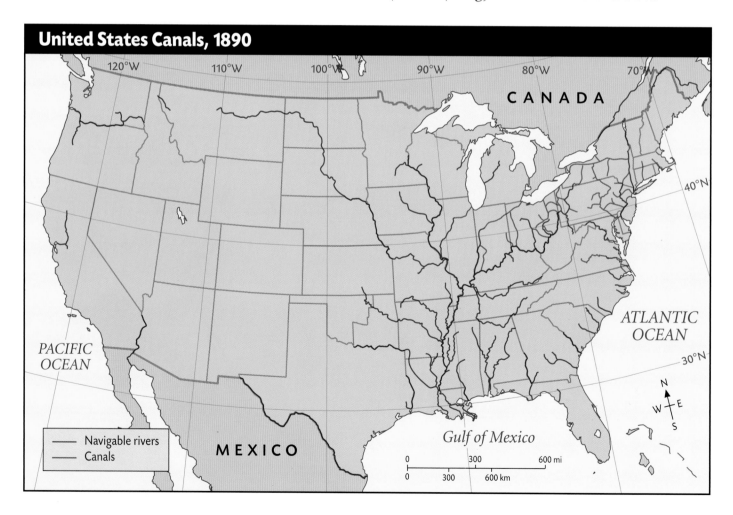

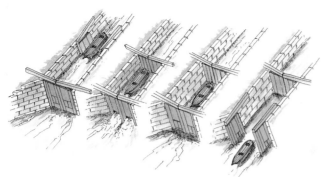

Locks allowed boats to be lowered as the elevation decreased. **How did this work?**

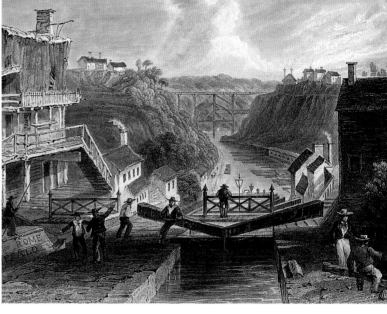

The Erie Canal linked the Midwest to the cities of the Northeast. **What city grew into an important commercial center because of the Erie Canal?**

Inland Shipping

Before the canal opened, grain and other products from the Midwest were often shipped down the Mississippi River to the port of New Orleans. From there they went to eastern and world markets. The Erie Canal opened up a new shipping route.

Farmers could now grow crops and get them to market in the East more easily. New York grew into an important trading center. The Midwest and Northeast were closely linked once canals were built.

Because of the success of the Erie Canal, leaders in other states began their own canal projects. Most of these were built in the Northeast and Northwest (see map, page 206). By 1840, there were more than 3,000 miles of canals built in America.

The building of canals continued for ten more years. But after 1850, few were built. New railroads became a better way of traveling and moving goods.

Dismal Swamp Canal

In May 1763, George Washington made his first visit to the Great Dismal Swamp. He suggested that it be drained and a north-south canal be dug there. This would connect the waters of the Chesapeake Bay in Virginia to the Albemarle Sound in North Carolina.

The digging of the canal began in 1793. It was all done by hand. Most of the labor was done by slaves hired from nearby landowners. It took approximately 12 years of hard work to complete the 22-mile (35.4-km)-long waterway.

CAROLINA CONNECTION

LESSON 1 REVIEW

Fact Follow-Up

1. What were some problems of traveling on land before the 1830s and 1840s?

2. What was the first federal highway in the United States, and what areas did it connect?

3. How did the building of canals make travel by water easier?

Talk About It

1. Which do you think was more important: the National Road or the Erie Canal? Explain why.

2. Explain which area of the United States benefited most from transportation improvements.

3. How might have the development of steamboats benefited people living in the West?

LESSON ② Railroads

KEY IDEAS

- The first trains were slow and ran short distances.

- Improvements in train engines and tracks made railroad travel faster and cheaper than canals.

- The transcontinental railroad connected the East and the West.

- Rail travel ended the way Native Americans lived in the West.

KEY TERMS

hub
transcontinental railroad

PEOPLE TO KNOW

Peter Cooper

When canal workers first saw railroad trains, they laughed. Samuel Hopkins Adams, a famous American writer, told a story about his grandfather and the new trains.

When Grandfather Adams saw an early train, he thought it looked silly. The engine looked like a teapot on wheels. Black smoke poured out of its smokestack. Hot steam hissed from the engine. Yet Grandfather Adams wanted to know how one ran, so he decided to take a ride.

The trip was an unhappy one. The train went so slowly, a person on horseback rode faster than the train for about a half-mile. Then it began to snow. The engine's wheels slipped as the train started up a little hill. The train's conductor asked the passengers to step off the cars and help push. Then a piece of hot ash from the smokestack hurt Grandfather Adams' eye.

Railroads, Grandfather Adams said, would never replace canals. Of course, he was wrong. Railroads soon brought major changes to the nation's transportation system.

A Network of Trains

Carts on tracks were introduced in England in the seventeenth century to help miners move loaded carts more easily. These were called wagon ways. In the early 1800s, inventors had the idea of using the steam engine to move the cart. This led to the invention of the first railroads and trains.

The building of the Baltimore and Ohio Railroad (usually called the

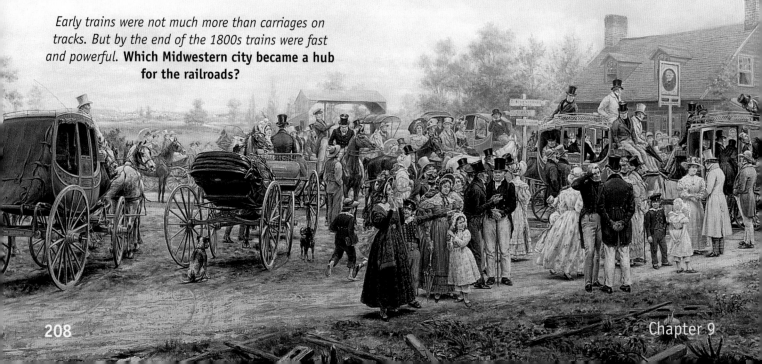

Early trains were not much more than carriages on tracks. But by the end of the 1800s trains were fast and powerful. **Which Midwestern city became a hub for the railroads?**

The building of the Baltimore and Ohio Railroad (usually called the B&O) started on July 4, 1827. The B&O offered canals serious competition.

At first, horses pulled the railroad cars over a few miles of track that connected Baltimore with a nearby town. In 1830, Peter Cooper, an inventor, introduced his small steam engine, the "Tom Thumb." Many improvements were made to this early train.

Building a Network

Within 20 years, there were several train trips every day. They carried passengers and freight between Baltimore, Maryland, and St. Louis, Missouri.

Soon the United States had many more railroads than canals. The federal government had given rail companies more than 200 charters, or permits to use the land for railroads. These companies opened more than 1,000 miles (1,610 km) of track.

By 1860, more than 30,000 miles (48,300 km) of tracks were in use. The North had a bigger and better railroad network than the South. This helped them move supplies and soldiers in the Civil War.

Faster and Better Travel

Some said that railroads multiplied because an iron pony (Cooper's "Tom Thumb") had become an iron horse. Steam

The officers of the Raleigh and Gaston Railroad stand on one of the line's locomotives. **Which railroad line first began to compete with canals?**

engines had quickly grown larger and more powerful. They could pull a long line of heavily loaded freight cars. Passenger trains could take people farther and more quickly than people had traveled before.

Steel rails replaced those made of iron, making them stronger and longer lasting. Tracks running for hundreds of miles replaced the short lines of the early years. By the end of the 1800s, railroads formed major links uniting a large nation. Chicago had become a *hub,* or connecting center, for more than ten railroad companies.

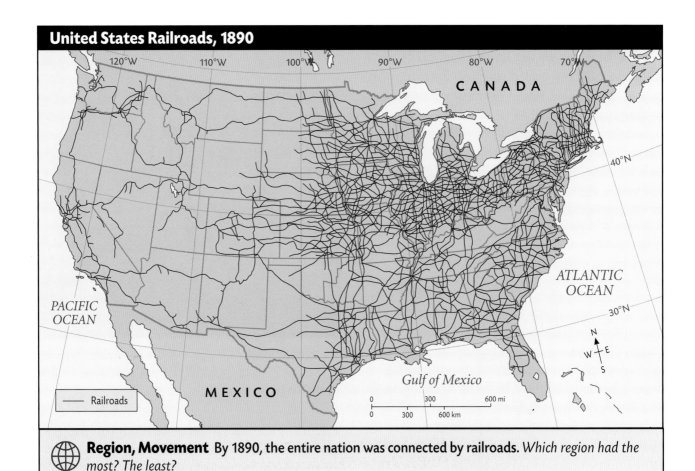

United States Railroads, 1890

CANADA

PACIFIC OCEAN

ATLANTIC OCEAN

MEXICO

Gulf of Mexico

— Railroads

0   300   600 mi
0   300   600 km

Region, Movement By 1890, the entire nation was connected by railroads. *Which region had the most? The least?*

Transcontinental Railroads

As you have read, Americans from the East rushed to California in the 1840s. Gold had been discovered there. Still more headed toward the Pacific Northwest and the Rocky Mountains as news spread that gold and silver could be found in those regions.

To reach the mines, some Americans sailed around the southern tip of South America. Thousands more made their way by horse or wagon across the flat grasslands called the Great Plains. Overland travel to the far western regions of the United States cost a lot of money. It was slow and tiring.

In 1860, railroad lines did not reach much beyond the Mississippi River. A few stagecoach lines had opened. Anyone with $200 for transportation could take a bumpy ride in one of these horse-drawn vehicles from Missouri to California. The trip took about three weeks.

East Meets West

People began to talk about building a *transcontinental railroad.* This would be a rail line connecting the East and West coasts of America.

People in the West wanted railroads to link to the East. Building them would be expensive. Private railroad companies did not have the money to do the job. But Congress and President Lincoln supported the project. The Railroad Act created two railroad companies to do the job.

One—the Central Pacific—started laying track in California. It headed east. The other—the Union Pacific—laid its first rails in Omaha, Nebraska. It headed west. The Central Pacific faced huge challenges. Its tracks had to be built through high, steep mountains. In its first four years of work, the company constructed only 100 miles of rails.

The Union Pacific put down track on flat ground. Its crews could sometimes make 3 miles (4.8 km) a day. On May 10, 1869, the first transcontinental rail line was finished. East and West met at Promontory Summit. Before 1900, four more transcontinental lines connected the East and West.

Customs

Railroads changed the way Americans tell time. Before 1883, many cities and towns kept their own time. When it was 12:00 noon in Chicago, it was 11:27 A.M. in Omaha and 11:56 A.M. in St. Louis. Railroads could not make train schedules. So the major railroad companies met. They created standards for time in four zones across the United States. We still use these zones, Eastern, Central, Mountain, and Pacific, today.

Singing Work Songs

Workers doing difficult, dangerous, or boring work often sang songs as they labored. The songs helped groups of workers stay aware of where everybody was and what they were doing so no one would get hurt. Other songs were a way to communicate information.

Workers hauling barges on the Erie Canal sang this song to pass the time.

I got a mule, her name is Sal,
Fifteen miles on the Erie Canal.
She's a good worker and a good old pal,
  Fifteen miles on the Erie Canal.
We've haul'd some barges in our day,
  Fill'd with lumber, coal and hay,
And we know ev'ry inch of the way
From Albany to Buffalo.
Low bridge, ev'rybody down! Low
  bridge, for we're going through a
  town.

You have probably heard this work song, "I've Been Workin' on the Railroad."

I've been working on the railroad
All the live long day,
I've been working on the railroad
just to pass the time away.

railroad spike

LESSON 2 REVIEW

Fact Follow-Up

1. What were some difficulties of early rail travel?

2. What cities did the B&O Railroad eventually connect?

3. How did gold seekers travel to the West?

4. What two companies built the first transcontinental railroad?

Talk About It

1. If given the opportunity to travel by steamboat or railroad during this time period, which would you have chosen? Explain why.

2. The government of the United States helped finance the building of the transcontinental railroads. Should it have done so? Explain your answer.

LESSON ③ An Agricultural and Industrial Giant

KEY IDEAS

- At first, people thought that the Great Plains were nothing but desert. Later, cattlemen and farmers found it was good land.

- Railroads encouraged people to move west into the area that is now North Dakota, South Dakota, Nebraska, Kansas, Texas, and Oklahoma.

- Farming, the cattle industry, and the growth of the railroads changed the lives of Native Americans.

- After the Civil War, the United States became a nation of big businesses.

KEY TERMS

brand
mass production
reservations

PEOPLE TO KNOW

Alexander Graham Bell
Andrew Carnegie
Red Cloud
James B. Duke
Crazy Horse
Samuel F.B. Morse
George Pullman

The United States sent some men in the early 1800s to explore what are now parts of Kansas and Colorado. The expedition reported finding only miles of wind-blown sand. No grass or trees grew there.

Another expedition went to present-day Nebraska and Oklahoma. It found only tall grass. This group called the area the "Great American Desert." It recommended that the government not encourage settlement in the region. It should be left to Native Americans, who lived by hunting buffalo.

You have already read, however, that in the mid-1800s some Americans did settle in the West. Some were searching for gold and silver. Others traveled across the Great Plains—the region that had been called the Great American Desert—to reach Utah or Oregon.

For quite a few years, no one showed any interest in trying to establish farms or build cities on the plains. But these old ideas about the plains disappeared. Railroads began to push westward, bringing people with them.

Cattle branding dates back to ancient times. **Why is it necessary?**

The Cattle Frontier

Cattlemen from Texas were the first to discover what the Great Plains had to offer. In the mid-1800s, people raising herds of longhorn cattle in Texas began moving north. The grasslands of the Great Plains were excellent for raising thousands of animals.

Americans had learned about raising large herds of cattle from Mexicans living in Texas. Cattle were raised for beef. They could be turned loose in the great open grasslands. There they found plenty to eat and drink.

Cattlemen did not worry if animals belonging to different owners got mixed up. Each owner had a **brand,** or special mark. Cowboys burned brands into each animal's skin.

At roundup time, the cowboys sorted the cattle. The brands let them know who owned each animal. Since young calves stayed with their mothers, cowboys knew who owned them, too.

Cattle Drives

The cattle industry on the plains did not grow much at first. Owners had no way of shipping the cattle to the growing American population in the East. That changed, however, with the railroads. A steer could be sold in Texas for around $5. That same steer could be sold at a railroad terminal for $30 to $50.

It was hard work to drive the cattle from Texas to the railroad. Cowboys were on their horses for long hours day after day. They pushed the herd hundred of miles. But the profits could make a cattleman wealthy. As a result, the cattle industry spread northward. It went from Texas across the Great Plains to the Canadian border.

The cattle business turned towns such as Abilene, Kansas, into booming cities. In 1867, Abilene had no more than a dozen small houses. Three years later, 300,000 cattle were shipped from the cattle yards beside the railroad. Abilene was a business center.

Cattle sales provided much of Abilene's wealth. Still more money came from the cowboys who stayed in town to spend their hard-earned pay.

Ranching Changes

The production of cattle for beef remains an important industry in the West today. Raising cattle on open grasslands and driving them long distances to market, however, disappeared in the 1870s and 1880s.

Two years of extremely cold winters and hot summers dried pasture grass. This killed millions of cattle. Many cattlemen lost their fortunes. Some had to leave the business. At about the same time, farmers came and claimed the land and water that cattlemen had been using.

Faced with these changes, cattlemen bought land, called ranches. They built fences around their ranches with a new invention. Barbed wire had small, painful spikes. It kept cattle on the owner's ranch and out of farmers' lands.

Cattle changed the economy and the lifestyles of the West. **How did ranching change in the 1870s and 1880s?**

The Cheyenne lived on the Great Plains. As settlers moved west, the Cheyenne and other plains indians faced great challenges. A group of Cheyenne and Arapaho were victim of the Sand Creek Massacre. **What happened there?**

The Indian Wars

Historians call the series of conflicts in the 1800s between the United States government and the Native American peoples the Indian Wars. During this time, the government made many treaties with different tribes. But then the government would go back on its word.

Over and over again, promises to the Native Americans were broken. On January 31, 1876, the government ordered all remaining Native Americans to move onto reservations. Native Americans struggled to protect their lands and their ways of life.

As you read in Chapter 4, Native Americans were (and still are) diverse peoples. They each have their own histories and cultures. Many tribes, like the Utes of the Great Basin in Utah and the Nez Perces of Idaho, fought the whites. But the Sioux of the Northern Plains and the Apache of the Southwest were some of the fiercest warriors. Strong chiefs, such as Red Cloud and Crazy Horse, led these tribes. The Sioux were skilled at fighting on horseback. The Apaches were skilled at fighting in the deserts and canyons where they lived.

In 1864, one of the more terrible attacks took place. It was called the Sand Creek Massacre. The Cheyenne and Arapaho Indians were living on land at Sand Creek in southeastern Colorado. They had been told by the national government that they would be safe there. A local militia attacked a Native American village. Soldiers killed about 150 men, women, and children.

Sometimes the Native Americans won, like at the Battle of Little Bighorn. But the government would always fight back. Its policy was to break up "tribal relationships" and bring "Indians to the white man's ways, peaceably if they will, or forcibly if they must." Under this policy, for example, more than 150 Native Americans were massacred at Wounded Knee in 1890.

The Indian Wars are a complex story in American history. Depending on whom they were fighting, Native Americans and whites sometimes fought alongside each other. Native American tribes often fought other tribes.

Overall, though, the Indian Wars were about the conquering of Native American peoples by the United States government. It was also about the taking and settling of their land by whites. The wars ended when the tribes were forced to live on reservations.

> *I am tired of fighting. Our chiefs are killed. . . .It is cold, and we have no blankets. The little children are freezing to death. My people, some of them, have run away to the hills, and have no blankets, no food. . . .I want to have time to look for my children, and see how many of them I can find. Maybe I shall find them among the dead. Hear me, my chiefs! I am tired. My heart is sick and sad. From where the sun now stands I will fight no more forever.*
>
> —Chief Joseph of the Nez Perce

Chief Joseph

Farmers Head West

The Homestead Act gave free land in the West to people who would live on it for five years. A homesteader had to be the head of a family and at least twenty-one years of age. People from Europe, farmers from the East who did not own land, single women, and former slaves signed up to homestead.

Homesteading

It cost only the $18 fee to get the land. But the real payments were the hard work and sacrifice required to keep the land. Homesteaders had to build homes, live on the land, and farm for five years before they could own it.

Farmers competed with ranchers for land. Higher grain prices made more people want to try farming on the Great Plains. They claimed land in North and South Dakota, Nebraska, Kansas, Texas, and Oklahoma.

Railroad companies encouraged farmers to head west. Sometimes they hired men to visit farmers in the Midwest and East. The men told farmers that they might do better on the Great Plains. Some railroads even got European farmers to emigrate to the United States. Bringing farm families to live near their rail lines meant new customers for the trains.

New Inventions

The Great Plains also could be opened to farmers because important improvements had been made to farmers' tools. Big plows with steel tips were very important. It took four to six horses to pull them, but they were needed to break through the deep roots of the prairie grasses.

Other machines, called reapers, cut grain so that it could be piled on wagons. Threshing machines separated the grain from the chaff. Steam engines mounted on wheels could be used as tractors to pull this machinery from place to place. These engines also ran the threshing machines.

All of these machines cost money, but farmers needed the equipment. Western farms had become much too big to be operated by intensive hand labor. They were now food-producing factories. These farms fed the people who lived in eastern cities.

Fighting for a Way of Life

Western settlement brought great changes to the lives of Native Americans. Native Americans on the plains had lived chiefly by hunting buffalo and other game for thousands of years. They did little to change the environment. As eastern lands were settled, many tribes were forced to move farther and farther west.

These settlers, however, did change the environment. Whites killed thousands of buffalo for sport. Land was given to the settlers. Train tracks criss-crossed the plains. Native Americans could no longer follow the buffalo. They could not stay on the lands where their ancestors had lived.

Owners of railroads advertised land to encourage westward settlement along the rail lines. **How else did railroad owners persuade people to move west?**

Chapter 9

Native American baskets are an art form that served a practical function. **What changed the lives of Native Americans?**

This Native American family posed in front of their home on a reservation near Tejon, California, in 1890. **What created the reservations?**

Reservations

The United States set aside land called Indian *reservations.* The government forced Native Americans to live on the reservations. Many reservations were on land that was not good for farming. Many tribes fought back. Bloody battles were fought between the U.S. Army and Native Americans. Sometimes, women and children were killed in the fighting.

In one struggle, Colonel Kit Carson forced the Navajo far from their homeland. Soldiers and enimies of the Navajos, the Utes, burned Navajo fields and homes. They killed and stole Navajo livestock. Finally, the Navajos decided that going to the reservation was the only way to survive.

The Navajos, with some other tribes, walked 300 miles to the reservation. About 200 people died of cold and starvation. Many more people died after they arrived. The land was poor. They could not raise crops. Four years later, the government allowed the people to return to their homeland.

Whites tried to destroy Native American culture and way of life. Children were forced to go to new schools. They were not allowed to speak their own language.

Luckily, Native American traditions have survived. But many Native Americans still live on reservations.

The End of the Frontier

The United States Census for 1890 noted the nation had been settled from the Atlantic to the Pacific. The western frontier was gone.

COMMUNICATING ACROSS A CONTINENT

As America expanded toward the Pacific, people in the East needed faster and better ways to keep in touch with those in the West. American inventions would change the lives of people all over the world.

Medallion commemorating Pony Express riders

In 1860, a letter took three weeks to get from New York to San Francisco. That year the Pony Express mail service was founded. Mail was carried all day and night by a series of lightweight riders on horseback. Special saddle bags were quickly moved to fresh horses at changing stations. It took about ten days to cover the almost 2,000 miles between St. Joseph, Missouri, and Sacramento, California. The route was dangerous, but only one mail delivery was ever lost.

Samuel F. B. Morse completed his first telegraph in 1843. An operator, using a telegraph key, translated messages into Morse Code. The code is made of patterns of long and short electrical pulses. The pulses stand for letters of the alphabet or numbers. The code was translated back into letters by an operator at the message's destination.

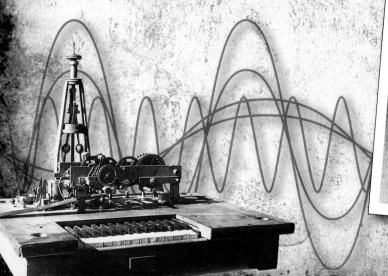

1855 telegraph

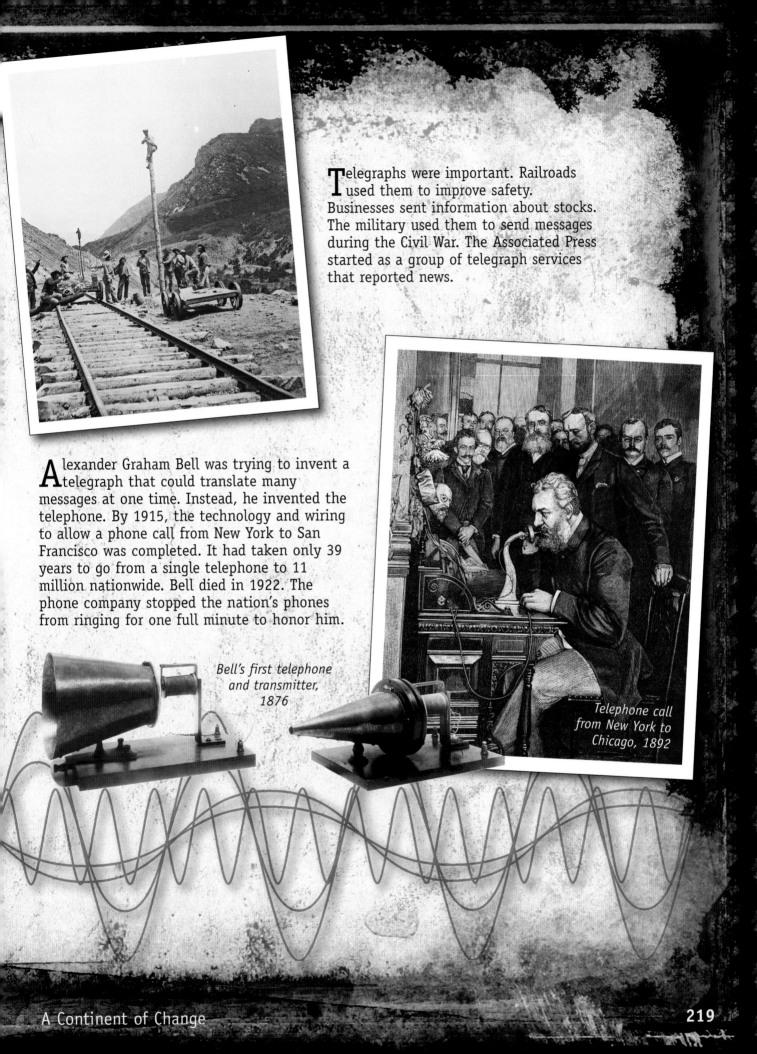

Telegraphs were important. Railroads used them to improve safety. Businesses sent information about stocks. The military used them to send messages during the Civil War. The Associated Press started as a group of telegraph services that reported news.

Alexander Graham Bell was trying to invent a telegraph that could translate many messages at one time. Instead, he invented the telephone. By 1915, the technology and wiring to allow a phone call from New York to San Francisco was completed. It had taken only 39 years to go from a single telephone to 11 million nationwide. Bell died in 1922. The phone company stopped the nation's phones from ringing for one full minute to honor him.

Bell's first telephone and transmitter, 1876

Telephone call from New York to Chicago, 1892

Making an Industrial Nation

Before the Civil War, modern industry had arrived in the United States. You have read how Eli Whitney patented the cotton gin. In 1798, he made other improvements that had important effects.

Mass Production

Until that time, most items were made by hand by skilled workers. Even parts for the few machines that were used were all made by hand. Parts made by hand did not always fit together well.

Whitney realized that by using a special format, workers with little skill could use machines to make parts that were the same in all ways. He first used the new system to make muskets (a kind of gun). He invented other machines to replace hand tools.

Working Together

Railroads Needed:

Steel for train tracks, wheels, cars, and bridges

Coal for fuel to run the trains

Steel Companies Needed:

Railroads to bring iron ore, coal, and limestone; to take steel products to their customers

Coal to run their furnaces

Coal Companies Needed:

Steel companies to buy the coal

Railroads to help take coal to markets in the cities and mills

These inventions led to the American system of manufacturing called *mass production.* This system made it easier and cheaper to use machines to do the work of many people.

Factories

Textile mills in New England used machines that had been invented in England. Other factories manufactured iron and steel. These changes were part of the Industrial Revolution.

In the 35 years after the Civil War, the United States became an industrial giant. Factories made many different products. Big cities sprang up around them.

Steel manufacturing led the way. In the mid-1860s, American factories made only 2,000 tons of steel a year. Forty years later, they made 7 million tons. A big market had developed for steel. It was much stronger than iron. It was also cheaper than it had been. Making steel from iron had been difficult and expensive. Inventors, however, had learned how to make steel more quickly and cheaply.

New Inventions

Other inventions helped build new industries. Meat packers used to packed fresh beef into barrels with a lot of salt to preserve the meat. With refrigeration beef could be handled differently. Meatpacking companies were built in Chicago. Cattle raised on the Great Plains were shipped to Chicago as live animals. They were then killed and cut into sides of beef. After being cooled in refrigerated rooms, the sides were loaded into refrigerated railroad cars. The fresh meat was shipped to markets in eastern cities.

Some inventions improved things that were already in use. For example, passengers on long train trips could not sleep comfortably on regular seats. This prompted George Pullman to invent sleeping cars. These cars were divided into small beds where passengers could sleep. The railroads liked these so much that a large company was created to build them.

Carnegie's steel making plant in Pittsburgh was the largest in the country.
How did Andrew Carnegie (right) make his business even bigger?

Taller buildings were built in cities. People in the buildings had a hard time climbing so many stairs. This led to the invention of elevators. Another company was created.

Big Business

The boom also caused businesses to grow in size. In Pittsburgh, for example, Andrew Carnegie built the largest steel making plant in the United States. The company sold more steel rails to the nation's railroads than any other. But he did not want to stop with this success. Carnegie knew that any one of the other steel makers might find ways of taking some of his customers.

So Carnegie began to buy companies that supplied his raw materials—mining companies, rail lines, and ships that carried iron ore. Soon he controlled all of the companies that supplied his factory. In this way, he could keep those other steel companies from hurting his business. By doing this Carnegie did more than protect his factory. He turned a big business into a giant one.

Other businessmen used different ways to protect their companies from competition. The results, however, were the same. The United States became the home of many giant businesses.

A Continent of Change

The South developed textile manufacturing into one of its leading industries. **Why was the South a likely place for textile manufacturing?**

Industry in the South

Most of this new industry was located in the nation's Northeast. Some industries did grow in the South.

In the late 1800s, that part of the country still suffered from the effects of the Civil War. Some Southerners saw industry as a way of getting rid of poverty. They thought it would be helpful to link the South's resources to manufacturing.

Textiles and Tobacco   Since the South grew cotton, textile manufacturing was a good fit. Several factories were built. Another cotton-based industry was created. The American Cotton Oil Trust crushed cottonseed to get the oil. Cottonseed oil was used in soap, as a substitute for butter, and in cosmetic products. The cottonseed meal that remained could be used as fertilizer and cattle feed.

Both industries provided badly needed jobs. But they did not match the growth of business in the North. In 1880, the entire South produced fewer textile products than the state of Massachusetts alone.

James B. Duke from Durham, North Carolina, however, became one of the nation's most successful business leaders. He built a giant cigarette manufacturing business. His factories were located mainly in North Carolina and Virginia. Later, Duke built a large electrical power company. His success led the way for future changes in the South's economy.

LESSON 3 REVIEW

Fact Follow-Up

1. What was the cattle frontier, and what caused it to develop?
2. What practices and inventions brought farmers to the Great Plains?
3. Why were Native Americans moved to reservations during this period?
4. For what is Alexander Graham Bell remembered?

Talk About It

1. Which of the inventions described in this lesson do you think was most important? Explain why.
2. Why did businessmen such as Andrew Carnegie want to protect their businesses from competition?
3. What are some positive and negative results of the changes described in this lesson?

A Continent of Change

Analyzing, Interpreting, Creating, and Using Resources and Materials

Gathering Data from Maps

Study these maps.

The first map shows where the population of the United States lived in 1870. Compare that map with the one on page 206. That map shows canals and rivers in 1890. You can see that the nation's water transportation network did not extend much beyond the Mississippi River.

On the 1870 map, you can see how the population of the United States grew and moved westward. What present-day states were being settled?

Compare the map on page 225 with the map below and the map on page 210. Is there a connection between the change in transportation and the growth of population? Had railways changed the relationship of people to the environment?

Look also at the map on page 683. What natural features kept the transportation network from extending farther? What features aided the construction of transportation?

In this chapter you have learned about changes in transportation and communications during the nineteenth century. The expansion of railroads was a major change. Study the map of population

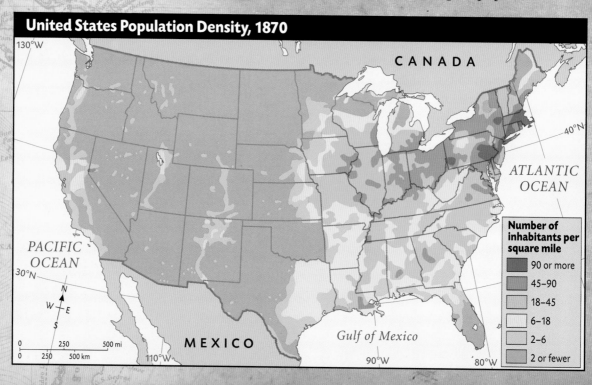

United States Population Density, 1870

PACIFIC OCEAN

ATLANTIC OCEAN

CANADA

MEXICO

Gulf of Mexico

Number of inhabitants per square mile
- 90 or more
- 45–90
- 18–45
- 6–18
- 2–6
- 2 or fewer

0   250   500 mi
0   250   500 km

Graphic Organizer

Information	1870	1890
Number of populated states		
Chief method of transportation		
Physical barriers to movement		
Physical features that helped movement		
Other		

density. What can you observe about how building railroads may influence the population west of the Mississippi? What information from Chapter 9 will help you answer this question?

Record your observations on a graphic organizer. Make a table with two headings, like the one above. Complete the table by writing what you observed from the maps and from reading Chapter 9. You can add more categories, too.

Follow-Up

Think about adding the year 1950 to your chart. Would you have different conclusions about population growth west of the Mississippi? Suppose you were to add the year 2000? What new forms of transportation might affect this?

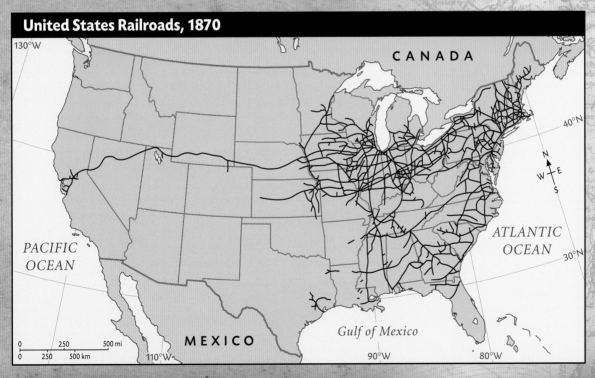

United States Railroads, 1870

CHAPTER 9 REVIEW

Lessons Learned

LESSON 1
Transportation: Roads and Waterways
Early roads in America were difficult to travel. Shipping goods was expensive. The development of canals and steamboats made water travel faster, easier, and cheaper. The Industrial Revolution brought new inventions that improved transportation and manufacturing.

LESSON 2
Railroads
The first trains were slow and ran short distances. Improvements in train engines and tracks made railroad travel faster and cheaper than canals. The transcontinental railroad connected the East and the West.

LESSON 3
An Agricultural and Industrial Giant
The United States found that the Great Plains, once thought to be nothing but desert, was good for farming and ranching. The ways Native Americans had lived in the West ended. By the late 1800s, the United States was a nation of big businesses. Telegraphs and telephones helped people across the United States communicate with each other.

Talk About It

1. Which development in transportation—steamboats or canals—do you think was more important? Explain your answer.
2. Which inventor do you think changed American life more: Samuel F. B. Morse or Alexander Graham Bell? Explain your answer.
3. What were the Indian Wars? What was their result?
4. Explain why there was such a rush of inventions in the late nineteenth century.
5. How did businesses, such as the one built by Andrew Carnegie, grow into huge companies? Was this a good thing?

Mastering Mapwork

Regions
Use the maps on page 206 and 210 to answer the following questions.

1. Which political region had most rail lines?
2. Which city in which state was the largest railroad hub?
3. Through what political regions did the transcontinental rail lines pass?
4. Describe the railroad systems of the South, Northeast, Midwest, and West.
5. Which region of the country had the poorest transportation system?

Becoming Better Readers

Pacing Yourself
Good readers pace themselves as they read. Not all reading should be done at the same speed. Some reading, like previewing, can be done quickly. When the reading becomes difficult or has a lot of new terms or ideas, good readers slow down. When good readers come to something they don't understand, they stop and reread the section. This chapter presented lots of new people, terms, and ideas about the big changes in the United States in the 1800s. How did you pace yourself while reading this chapter? If you had difficulty reading the chapter, go back and try pacing yourself.

Go to the Source

Comparing a Photograph to a Painting

Compare the photograph below with the painting. Both show a homestead in Nebraska in the late 1800s. Then answer the questions below.

Questions

1. Create a Venn-Diagram showing similiarities and differences between the painting and the photograph.
2. Which picture shows the best interpretation of what life was like?
3. What would be a good title for the photograph? Why?

Many Different People

Timeline of Events

1763
Jewish people build first American Synagogue in Rhode Island

1819
First national legislation on immigration passed

1825
First group of Norwegian immigrants arrive

1848
Germans emigrate

1750   1800   1850

1815
First great wave of immigration

1820
U.S. population is 9.6 million

1846
Irish emigrate because of potato famine

Today, a walk through a supermarket shows that Americans enjoy many foods from other countries. Italy offers spaghetti, lasagna, and a variety of pastas. China offers egg rolls and stir-fries. Germany offers sauerkraut and many kinds of sausages. Mexico offers tacos and enchiladas.

There are more and more restaurants in North Carolina that serve the popular foods from France, India, Thailand, and Vietnam. Newcomers bring foods from their heritage. Music, customs, and art from other lands also enrich our diverse society.

At the turn of the century, thousands of immigrants came to the United States.

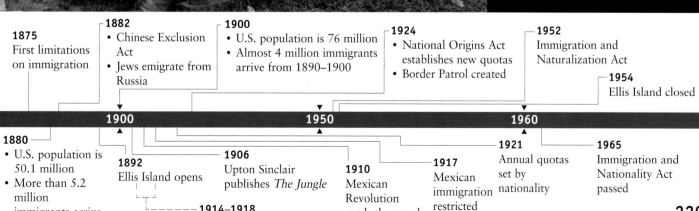

1875
First limitations on immigration

1880
• U.S. population is 50.1 million
• More than 5.2 million immigrants arrive from 1880–1890

1882
• Chinese Exclusion Act
• Jews emigrate from Russia

1892
Ellis Island opens

1900
• U.S. population is 76 million
• Almost 4 million immigrants arrive from 1890–1900

1906
Upton Sinclair publishes *The Jungle*

1914–1918
World War I halts immigration to the U.S.

1910
Mexican Revolution sends thousands to U.S.

1917
Mexican immigration restricted

1921
Annual quotas set by nationality

1924
• National Origins Act establishes new quotas
• Border Patrol created

1952
Immigration and Naturalization Act

1954
Ellis Island closed

1965
Immigration and Nationality Act passed

1900   **1950**   **1960**

KEY IDEAS

- British, Scotch-Irish, Irish, and German immigrants were the first to come to the colonies that became the United States.

- Immigrants come to the United States seeking freedom and opportunity.

KEY TERMS

diversity
emigrated
immigrants

In 1782, a French traveler asked, "What then is an American?"

He thought about all the *immigrants* he had met. Immigrants are people who come to live in the United States.

The visitor answered his own question. He wrote, Americans are "English, Scots, Irish, French, Dutch, Germans, and Swedes." Even that early in our history, Americans were something new. We were, and still are, a nation of great variety.

Early Immigrants

As a young nation, the United States was British in culture, lifestyle, and government. This was because British immigrants laid most of the foundations of our country.

As you have learned, Africans were brought to America as slaves. They also influenced our culture, including American music, foods, and language. By the 1720s, immigrants were arriving from other European countries. Until about 1880, most of these newcomers came from northwestern European countries. They left places like Ireland, Germany, Sweden, and Norway. They emigrated, or left their country and came to the United States.

Immigrants from the British Isles

Many Scotch-Irish first settled in central Pennsylvania and in the Shenandoah Valley of Virginia. The Scotch-Irish were Scots who had lived in Ireland for many years. Now they were coming to America.

They usually came to the colonies to improve their lives. Many of them settled on the frontier, west of the populated area of the colonies. There they looked for cheap or free land. By 1750, the Scotch-Irish had moved into western Pennsylvania. They then moved south into the "back country." Many settled in the Piedmont and Mountains regions of the Carolinas.

Irish immigrants came to America for freedom and to escape hardships in Ireland. A disease wiped out Ireland's potato crops for several years. Many people starved. This was called the potato famine.

The potato famine forced thousands of Irish to leave. They made new homes in such cities as New Orleans, New York, and Boston. The Irish worked on some of our nation's large construction projects. They helped build the Erie Canal.

Many Irish laid railroad tracks. Irish settlers in Savannah built the first railroads in Georgia. In New Orleans, they built dams to protect the city from floods. This was dangerous work. Many lost their lives.

Others Emigrate

Many early immigrants came from Germany. Today tourists visit Lancaster, Pennsylvania, and neighboring towns. There they find descendants of the German Amish people.

The Amish came for religious freedom. They kept many of the traditions of their German ancestors. Many dress in plain clothing, ride in horse-drawn buggies, farm the land with simple tools, and worship in small churches.

Some Germans introduced Protestant religions to their communities. These include the Lutheran and Moravian faiths. Other German religious groups, such as the Mennonites, built farms on the fertile soil of Maryland, Virginia, Georgia, and the Carolinas. In 1710, German-Swiss settled New Bern, North Carolina.

A few European Jews also *emigrated,* or left their homeland, to America. They settled in such colonial cities as Boston and New York. Jewish settlers built a synagogue in Rhode Island, the first one in the colonies.

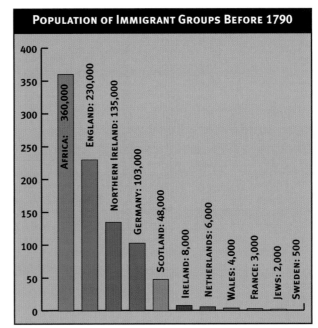

POPULATION OF IMMIGRANT GROUPS BEFORE 1790

AFRICA: 360,000
ENGLAND: 230,000
NORTHERN IRELAND: 135,000
GERMANY: 103,000
SCOTLAND: 48,000
IRELAND: 8,000
NETHERLANDS: 6,000
WALES: 4,000
FRANCE: 3,000
JEWS: 2,000
SWEDEN: 500

This shows the population of different nationalities around the time the Constitution was written. **Which group was the largest?**

Word Origins

The word **immigrant** refers to people who move permanently to a country that is not their native land. The word immigrant comes from a Latin phrase meaning "to go in."

Homesick in America

Henriette, called Jette, came with her husband, Bernhard Bruns, from Germany. About five years later, three of their four children got sick and died. The couple had more children, but two more children also got sick and died.

Like Jette, many immigrant women were lonely and homesick. Their work was hard. They had to have a big breakfast ready for the family before sunrise. Then they spent the rest of the day taking care of children, keeping up the house, cooking, working in the fields, and tending the garden.

In a letter, Jette wrote to her brother about her struggle to learn to speak English:

Today I was alone all day long with my little ones. And I thought that I would write you a lot. I talked with you in my thoughts all morning. But here comes an American on horseback, and I have to try to speak English with him. He is waiting for Bruns, who will not return until this evening. I have progressed with my English speaking so far that I can understand ... a few common little sentences. . . . I must really learn more, for it annoys me when I stand there like a blockhead and cannot answer. . . .

A Land of Diversity

For a time, life in American colonies was much like that of Great Britain. But even before the Revolutionary War, America had many people from different backgrounds. This made America different from other places in the world.

In 1750, one European visitor to New York City noted that it was made up of "different nations, different languages, and different religions." That *diversity,* or variety, increased as immigrants continued to arrive.

Between 1830 and 1850, more than 2.5 million newcomers came to the United States. They moved to eastern cities. They settled new lands in the West.

Arrivals from Southern and Eastern Europe

Immigrants arriving later in the 1880s came from southern and eastern Europe. Their homes had been in Poland, Russia, Greece, Italy, and many places in southeastern Europe. They brought many different languages. They also brought different religions. They were Roman Catholics, Orthodox Christians, and Jewsish people. Their cultures were different from the "old" immigrants: the English, Irish, Scots, and Germans from northern Europe.

Why Immigrants Came

Many immigrants saw coming to America as special. Families often had to save money for a long time to be able to pay for tickets. Mary Antin, a Jewish immigrant from Russia in the early 1900s, was excited about coming to the United States. She wrote in her novel *The Promised Land*, "So at last I was going to America . . . Really, really going at last!"

As you read in Chapter 5, religious persecution had caused many Europeans to come to America. Starting in the 1600s, Puritans, Catholics, and Quakers fled persecution in England. Mary Antin also belonged to a group persecuted because of its religion.

Jewish Immigrants Jews living in Russia and Eastern Europe were forced to live in segregated areas. They were often violently attacked. Both the Russian government and Russian Orthodox Church approved of this. Sometimes the government ordered its troops into Jewish villages to destroy property and beat the people.

Eastern European Jews fled to the United States. Life here, however, was not trouble-free. They suffered from discrimination. Their traditions and their religion seemed to be so different to some Americans.

Italian immigrants wait to be processed at Ellis Island, New York. **How many immigrants came to the United States between 1830 and 1850?**

Chapter 10

Yet Russian Jews continued to come. Most, like Mary Antin, found that life in the United States offered many more opportunities than their old life did.

Economic Opportunties and Freedom You have already read how the economy of the United States grew in the late 1800s. Railroads opened hundreds of thousands of acres of the West for farming and raising livestock. Huge industries, such as coal and iron mining, steel manufacturing, petroleum refineries, and food processing, created thousands of new jobs. The work was hard and often dangerous. Wages for unskilled workers were low. Living conditions in industrial cities were poor.

Yet when poor Europeans heard about jobs in America, they wanted to come. By the 1890s and early 1900s, as many as 1 million immigrants a year came to the United States.

Freedom in America   Europeans also came to the United States to live in a free society. During the late 1800s and early 1900s, many European countries, such as Russia and Germany, did not have governments that protected their rights.

In Austria, some people were forced to serve in the army for as many as 10 or 12 years. In Russia, some had to serve in the army for as long as 25 years. Many men were forced to serve for life.

To get out of the army, some soldiers hurt themselves by cutting off a finger or a toe. America did not force people to serve in the military. These people saw America as a place where they might have freedom.

What would YOU do?

Imagine that you are a person in another country trying to decide whether or not to move to the United States. Going to a new country might mean a better life for you and your family. But leaving will also mean that you will have to learn a new language. You will have to find your way in an unfamiliar country and leave your friends and relatives. What would you do?

Like many colonists two centuries before, this Jewish family came to America for religious freedom. **What else brought people to this country?**

LESSON ❶ REVIEW

Fact Follow-Up
1. What does the word "immigrate" mean?
2. Which areas of the world sent the most immigrants to North America before the 1850s?
3. After 1880, from what areas of the world did most immigrants come?
4. What religious differences were there between the "old" immigrants and the "new" immigrants who arrived after 1880?

Talk About It
1. Why did many immigrants move from the settled eastern areas to the West?
2. Of all the reasons why immigrants came to this country, which do you think was the most important one? Explain why.
3. Why did Jette Bruns feel badly because she could not speak English?
4. How did immigration make America more diverse?

Many Different People

KEY IDEAS

- Immigrants settled all over the United States. Some nationalities settled together in certain areas.

- Europeans were the largest group of immigrants. In recent years, the number of European immigrants has decreased. The numbers of Asian and Hispanic immigrants have increased.

- Immigrants did not have an easy life when they arrived in America.

- African Americans migrated from the rural South to Northern cities.

KEY TERMS

Ellis Island
Harlem
neighborhoods
prejudices
racism
sweatshops
tenement houses

Upton Sinclair's novel *The Jungle* describes life in the meatpacking plants of Chicago. Sinclair, as well as other writers, wanted to draw attention to the poor conditions and treatment of workers in factory jobs.

The men who did these jobs were mostly unskilled. They earned, Sinclair wrote, "for the most part, eighteen and a half cents an hour." Sinclair's point was that these men were not paid enough to feed their families.

Many immigrants understood what Sinclair was writing about. They started their new lives in America by doing the hard jobs other workers did not want.

Immigration After the Civil War

From the founding of the colonies until the twentieth century, most immigrants came of their own desire. Most were from Europe, but many came from other areas, such as Asia, Middle America, and South America. As you have read, people from Africa were brought against their will to be slaves.

In the 25 years after the Civil War alone, more than 10 million immigrants came to the United States. From 1890 to 1914, another 15 million immigrants arrived.

Ellis Island in New York became the port where most people from Europe entered America. The Statue of Liberty was built there to welcome them to a new life.

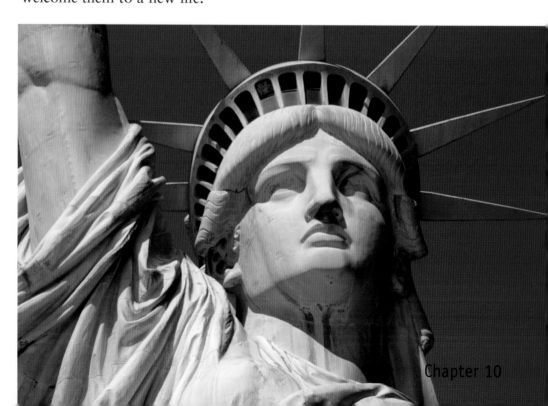

In 1886, France gave The United States the Statue of Liberty. **What do you think she symbolizes?**

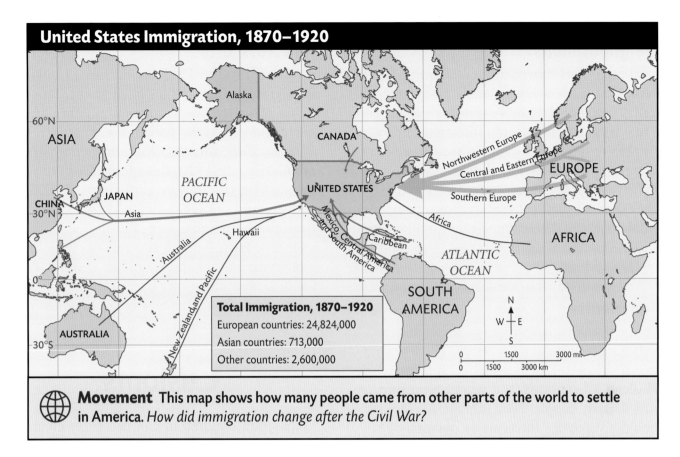

United States Immigration, 1870–1920

Total Immigration, 1870–1920
European countries: 24,824,000
Asian countries: 713,000
Other countries: 2,600,000

Movement This map shows how many people came from other parts of the world to settle in America. *How did immigration change after the Civil War?*

Where Did They Settle?

European immigrants made new homes in many places in America. They worked at many different jobs.

The South had relied upon slave labor until 1865. Many European workers did not believe there were jobs for them in the South. The former slaves were there to do the work.

Instead, northern Europeans looked to settle in the North, Midwest, and West. In the Midwest, they settled in towns near railway stations. There they started businesses and farms. Many settled in Wisconsin, Minnesota, and places in the Great Plains.

Immigrants Move to Cities

Many newcomers moved to cities. They became factory workers in Philadelphia, New York, Chicago, and Boston. As the Industrial Revolution took off, American cities grew larger than ever before.

Cities like Chicago had big changes. They went from a farming-based economy and culture to a factory-based economy and culture. Only about half a million people lived in Chicago during the 1880s. By 1910, Chicago had more than 2 million residents.

Working in America

Many immigrants to cities were single men looking for work. They were mostly unskilled. They did not have a special trade to set up a shop, as a tailor or blacksmith might. Without special skills, they had to take whatever work they could get.

In the workplace, people born in America and immigrant groups were often treated differently. Those who were born here often had skilled and professional jobs. They might have worked as clerks and engineers, and in other specialties.

Immigrants got the jobs the native-born Americans did not take. The jobs were often dangerous or unhealthy. Jobs in factories had poor quality air to breathe. Both men and women worked in small factories called *sweatshops.* They and their children sometimes worked up to 16 hours a day. The conditions were terrible.

Many Different People

Neighborhoods

Immigrants moved into communities that reminded them of home. These places were called *neighborhoods.* People there spoke the same language and shared the same culture.

Many single men came to the United States, got jobs, and saved their money. When they had enough to pay for passage, they sent for their sweethearts from their home country. These immigrant families often lived in crowded apartment buildings called *tenement houses.*

Tenements

Living in tenement houses brought more suffering to immigrant families. There was much sickness. Diseases such as smallpox, cholera, tuberculosis, and scarlet fever hurt or killed many people. Poor immigrants often could not pay for medicine or doctors.

According to one report, in 1900 alone almost 400,000 of the 1.7 million people living in Chicago were poor. It would take a few more years before people started to try to fix these problems.

New York City

From 1900 to 1915, more than 15 million immigrants came to the United States. This figure was the same as the total number of newcomers from the previous 40 years.

New York City also had a huge immigrant population. In 1910, three fourths of the people living there were immigrants. The majority did not speak English. They came from southern and eastern Europe—countries including Italy, Poland, and Russia. They had a different culture and language. Dealing with life here was sometimes hard. Living near people from home made it easier to adjust to living in new country.

Customs

Immigrant children in crowded cities created their own version of baseball during the early 1900s: stickball. Instead of a bat and baseball, kids played with an old broom handle and a cheap, pink rubber ball. Bases might be lampposts and home plate could have been a sewer cover. Other street ball games were stoop-ball and seven-up.

This family sewed clothing to earn money. They are in their tenement. **What percentage of New Yorkers were immigrants in 1910?**

Immigrant Neighborhoods

In 1890, foreign-born residents of the Greater New York area numbered more than 1 million. In Manhattan, home to the region's largest immigrant population, more than 40 percent of residents had been born outside of the United States.

Life was more dangerous and crowded for newly arrived immigrants in the Lower East Side than in the country they had left. People lived on top of one another in crowded, multi-story apartment buildings called tenements instead of side by side in villages. Time was measured by a clock, not by the sun in the sky. This created many problems for immigrant families. Most children of the Lower East Side adjusted to their new life a lot faster than their parents.

Immigrant children learned English at school. They ventured into other parts of the city. They translated documents for their parents and acted as interpreters when government officials came around. Some even taught their parents at night the lessons they had learned in class that day.

For these immigrants, New York City was supposed to be the great "melting pot." Speaking dozens of languages and eating and dressing differently, the immigrants were expected to quickly become just like other Americans. Their children helped them adjust to this new life in America. At the same time, the immigrants were changing America: the music we listen to, the food we eat, the words in our language. Immigrants have kept many of their own traditions, adopted new ones, and added their own traditions to the culture of the United States.

Coming Home to Ellis Island

An important place for immigrants can still be found on an island near the Statue of Liberty— the Ellis Island Immigration Station. Ellis Island opened in 1892 to serve the thousands of immigrants coming from Europe. When it closed in 1954, more than 12 million people had passed through its halls.

Ellis Island (left) was a confusing, noisy place filled with voices speaking many languages. Children became tired from waiting in long lines, the standing, and the noise. After many hours, children and their parents would be put on a ferry boat that would take them to New York City.

Immigrant Room, Ellis Island

Once they reached Ellis Island, immigrants had numbered tags tied to their coats (below). Then they were asked such questions as "What kind of work do you do?" and "Can you read and write?" They were examined by doctors. Those who had medical problems were sent back to Europe or held until they were healthy.

COMPAGNIE GÉNÉRALE TRANSATLANTIQUE
INSPECTION CARD
(Immigrants and Steerage Passengers)

Port of departure HAVRE
Name of ship, LA LORRAINE   Date of departure FEB 22 1913
Name of Immigrant Abud Bahia Last residence Alexandria

People came through Ellis Island for many reasons. But for almost all of them, the reason for emigrating was that they wanted a better life. "They used to tell us that the streets in the United States were paved with gold," said one woman. "When I was a little girl I thought that all Americans were millionaires."

Immigrant mother and child

Many Different People

African Americans dance in a Harlem nightclub in 1934. **Where is Harlem?**

African Americans Move North

Not all new city dwellers came from Europe. During the early 1900s, thousands of African Americans moved from the South to northern cities. By 1910, approximately 72,000 blacks had migrated to Illinois alone.

Many African American families left the farms of the South during World War I to work in northern factories making materials for the war. They also migrated to New York, making *Harlem,* a community in Manhattan, famous throughout the world.

Harlem Culture

In the early part of the twentieth century, Harlem was a center of African American culture. During these years many of our nation's famous black writers, such as Langston Hughes and James Weldon Johnson, lived or worked in Harlem.

But life for blacks was also hard. African Americans worked in many of the jobs that whites did not want. Over time, Harlem lost many of its businesses. It became a poorer community.

Still Separate

In other northern cities, blacks lived in some of our nation's poorest neighborhoods. They lived separately from whites.

No Jim Crow laws existed in the North to segregate blacks and whites. Still, people in northern cities made it difficult for blacks to live anywhere other than African American neighborhoods.

Whether forced by law or by culture, African Americans lived apart from whites in almost every city in the United States.

Asian Immigrants

Asian Americans had been brought to the United States by railroad companies which needed workers to build railroads.

Chinese immigrants first built railroad tracks for the Central Railroad Company in California. They linked the cities of Sacramento, Marysville, and San Jose.

When railroad companies decided to build transcontinental railroads, some considered hiring Chinese workers. Discrimination against Asians occurred in these large projects. Many were victims of *racism,* the belief that one race is superior to another.

Railroad Workers

Some railroad company leaders said that Asians were physically too small to do the heavy work on the railroad. A Central Pacific Company official reminded them that the Chinese had built the Great Wall in China. The Chinese were hired.

Many Chinese workers helped lay the tracks that linked America from coast to coast. They made about $28 a month. They did one of the most dangerous jobs in America at the time.

For example, to open railroad tracks through mountains, tunnels needed to be made. Chinese workers were lowered in baskets down the mountainside. They drilled holes in which to place the explosives. The blast would blow away part of the mountainside.

Many Chinese workers died while laying these railway lines. Without the efforts of the Chinese railroad workers, western settlement might have been delayed for many years.

These Japanese immigrants are arriving in San Francisco in 1920. **What is racism?**

Many Chinese immigrants built the first transcontinental railroad. **Why were immigrants often given dangerous jobs?**

Many Different People

The United States Grows

The surge of immigration had a dramatic effect on the growth of the United States. You read in Chapter 9 that railroads made transportation to the West easier. With better transportation, immigrants were able to settle in the West.

As the western territories grew in population, new states entered the Union (see map, page 367). In 1889 alone, North Dakota, South Dakota, Montana, and Washington joined the Union. Only one year later Idaho and Wyoming followed.

Six more states would be added to total today's 50 states. By World War I, the United States' population had doubled to more than 90 million people.

The pattern of immigration has changed in our nation. Newcomers to America are no longer primarily from Europe. The United States still welcomes more immigrants than any country in the world.

Mixed Reactions to Immigrants

New Americans had hard lives at first. Many of them did not speak English. They lived in poorly kept buildings. Sometimes they were laughed at because of their names or the way they talked. Young children had difficulties adjusting because of their clothing. American children teased them.

Many Americans distrusted certain groups of people, such as those from Ireland and Germany. Most Irish immigrants were Catholics. Many Americans were *prejudiced,*

This immigrant mother and daughter lived in a New York City tenement in 1911.
How did Americans react to immigrants?

These women are sewing jackets by hand in New York in 1908. **What types of jobs did immigrants do?**

or had negative ideas, about the Roman Catholic Church. People born in America, whose families had immigrated earlier, sometimes attacked Irish Catholics. They burned their churches and schools.

Some Americans complained about immigrant workers. They accused them of working for low pay and driving down wages. They were against newcomers. Even though immigrants did the jobs native-born Americans did not want, anti-immigration activists urged Congress to place limits on immigration.

More Trouble for Immigrants

Anti-immigration activists targeted Asians in California, where most Chinese entered the country. In 1882, Congress passed a law to stop Chinese people from entering. The law worked. The number of Chinese Americans decreased for many years. Chinese immigrants could not become candidates for American citizenship until 1943.

Congress also placed restrictions on other Asian immigrants. In 1905, it restricted Japanese immigration. Once these restrictions were lifted, many more Asians came to make new homes in the United States. By 2000, almost 12 million Asians lived here. Asian peoples include those from Korea, the Philippines, Thailand, Cambodia, Vietnam, Laos, Japan, and China. The Hmong are people from Vietnam and Laos.

LESSON 2 REVIEW

Fact Follow-Up
1. What was Ellis Island?
2. Why were neighborhoods important to immigrants?
3. What were sweatshops?
4. What important job did many Chinese immigrants do?

Talk About It
1. Why did few immigrants settle in the southern United States during this period?
2. How did the national network of railroads influence where immigrants settled?
3. Why did people want to restrict immigration?

Many Different People

LESSON ③ Immigration Patterns

KEY IDEAS

- In the twentieth century, new immigrants came from Asia, Middle America, South America, and Africa.

- New immigration laws make it easier for citizens to bring families to the United States.

- Many Hispanics from Mexico have come to the United States in the past decades.

KEY TERMS

braceros
deported
Hispanic
naturalized
quotas

During the twentieth century, the types of people who emigrated to America changed. These immigrants came from all over Asia, Middle America, South America, and Africa.

When the century opened, the United States was uneasy about their entry. Therefore, Congress first placed barriers on the number of people hoping to become Americans.

This political cartoon shows politicians making immigrants into voters through naturalization. **What does naturalization mean?**

Limiting Immigration

The anti-immigration feelings from the late 1800s continued in the 1900s. Some Americans did not welcome different religions or other cultures. As you read in Lesson 2, Congress passed laws to limit immigration to the United States.

Quotas

Congress passed more laws to restrict immigration. *Quotas* are set limits. Quotas were set for each country. During the 1920s, Congress limited immigration to a total of 164,000 people a year.

Around this time, the United States began to allow immigrants to come into the country if they had nowhere else to go due to war in their home country.

This law mainly allowed Europeans to come. During World War II more than 400,000 whites from Europe entered the United States. But the national government did not welcome others, such as Jews, Palestinians, and South Asians. They were also homeless because of war.

In 1952, Congress passed another law that set quotas on immigrants. The law limited the number of Asians to 2,990, Europeans to 149,667, and Africans to 1,400. Congress wanted to make it difficult for nonwhites to enter the United States.

Naturalization

The Immigration Act of 1965 did away with some of these laws. Congress considered whether an immigrant already had a relative living in the United States.

But some quotas still existed. People in different regions of the world still had limits. For example, a limited number of Europeans could immigrate to the United States every year. The same applied to people in other sections of the world.

The law also made it easier for a naturalized citizen, to bring a spouse, unmarried children, and parents into the country. *Naturalized* citizens are people who were not born here.

Group quotas did not affect people seeking to immigrate with families already here. Congress required only that the immigrant living here first become a citizen.

This policy brought many more immigrants hoping to become naturalized citizens to the United States. The law was intended to make the system more equal for people coming from all parts of the world. Today, many people come to the United States to escape war and persecution.

President Lyndon B. Johnson speaks before signing the Immigration Act of 1965. **What did the immigration law do?**

Immigration Continues

Many of our new residents and citizens come from Asia, Middle America, and South America. By 2000, more than 11 million Asians lived in the United States.

Today, many Asian Americans live in North Carolina. The Research Triangle Park and major universities attract immigrants. Some seek advanced university degrees. Others work in technical, medical, and scientific fields.

People who leave their native land come with hopes for a better life. Those with skills or a good education can do well here.

Many immigrants, however, come with little skill or education. These people usually enter the service industry. Some work as migrant farm workers, planting and harvesting crops. These jobs pay very little.

Like other American immigrants, they hope for a better life for themselves and their families. They work hard, sometimes at more than one job. They want their children to have a better life.

Hispanic Americans

The term *Hispanic* refers to individuals whose ancestors are from the Spanish-speaking nations of Middle and South America. They come from a mixed culture. This culture began to form in the 1500s, soon after Columbus landed in today's Bahamas.

These cultures include Spanish and other European nationalities, Native Americans, and Africans. Some migrated early in our history to territories that became the United States. Their descendants are Hispanics. Many Hispanic families have lived in what is now the United States for hundreds of years.

CAROLINA CONNECTION

Immigrants to North Carolina

North Carolina is home to many of the world's nationalities. A large number are from Latin America.

The Latino Initiative is an educational program to help increase understanding about immigrants from Latin America. It is run by the University of North Carolina's Center for International Understanding.

The program helps school principals, police chiefs, business owners, and social-service workers. They get a sense of why people migrate to the United States.

The highlight of the program is a weeklong visit to Mexico. When they get back to North Carolina, they use what they have learned to reach out to Hispanic immigrants in their area.

Today, immigrants from all over the world live and work in the United States. This doctor is from India. These engineers in an automobile factory are from Mexico. **What does Hispanic mean?**

Mexican Americans   Mexican Americans make up the oldest Hispanic culture living in the United States. You have read about Spain's exploration and rule of the Southwest and Florida in the 1500s.

Since that time, Spanish settlements have expanded. They covered Mexico during the 1500s; Texas during the 1600s; and California during the 1700s. After the anexation of Texas and the Mexican War, these lands were added to the United States.

The Mexican American population in the United States grew slowly at first. It was estimated at only about half a million in 1900. Their numbers slowed when Congress placed restrictions on their entry. Then, Congress created the Border Patrol. The goal was to stop illegal immigration from Mexico.

During the Great Depression the federal government *deported,* or sent back home, more than 500,000 Mexican immigrants. Many people accused Mexicans of taking away their jobs.

Temporary Workers

Mexican workers continued arrive. Companies, construction firms, and farmers in the Southwest needed cheap labor. So they asked Congress to let Mexican *braceros,* or temporary workers, come into the country.

Today, in many parts of the country, farmers and businesses still hire workers from Mexico.

Mexican Immigrants Today

With better relations with Mexico, today the national government is seeking ways to help illegal residents from Mexico become legal residents or naturalized citizens.

Word Origins

The word *bracero* is used to refer to temporary laborers admitted legally into the United States to help with seasonal crop harvests. In Spanish, *brazo* means "arms," so literally *bracero* means "one who uses his arms."

Many farmers depend on hiring migrant farm workers to pick their crops.
Where do many of the workers come from?

Many Different People

The Roldans own an Hispanic grocery store and restaurant in Raleigh, North Carolina. **How many Mexican Americans were in the United States in 2000?**

According to the 2000 census, Mexican Americans are the fastest-growing Hispanic minority in the nation. They have passed the 20 million people mark, and led all immigrant groups coming into the country during the 1990s.

Many have settled in the southwestern states, including New Mexico, Texas, and Arizona, since the 1950s. But today, the population of Mexicans and Mexican Americans is rapidly growing in North Carolina. According to the census, nearly two of every three Hispanics in North Carolina are of Mexican ancestry.

Immigrant Contributions

Most Americans today would agree that newcomers to the states are productive residents. Some are laborers in factories and on farms. Others are professors and researchers at universities, and engineers for some of the largest companies in the world.

Immigrants have increased the ranks of professionals, including lawyers and physicians. They are in politics, helping to build an even better and stronger America. Students who study here bring their talents, new perspectives, and greater diversity to our schools.

LESSON 3 REVIEW

Fact Follow-Up
1. Why did some people oppose immigration in the early twentieth century?
2. What were immigration quotas?
3. What does it mean to be a naturalized citizen of the United States?
4. To what group of people does the term Hispanic refer?

Talk About It
1. Until the early 1900s, the United States placed no restrictions on immigration. Why were the restrictions of the early twentieth century begun?
2. Why did immigration quotas not favor immigrants from southern and eastern Europe, Asia, Africa, and Latin America?

Applying Decision-Making and
Problem-Solving Techniques to World Issues

Putting Yourself in Another's Shoes

"Just put yourself in his/her shoes and see how you'd feel."
"If you could just walk a mile in my shoes, you'd understand."

Has anyone ever said these words to you? Have you ever wondered what the words mean? Have you ever tried to put yourself in someone else's shoes? How would you begin to do that?

Look very carefully at the picture. This is an immigrant family from Italy. They are entering the United States through Ellis Island in 1901.

The girl and the older boy could be about your age. Their younger brother and a mother are with them. Why do you think the brother and not the sister is holding the baby? What do you think the mother is carrying on her head? Where—from reading Chapter 10—do you think the father is?

Concentrate on the girl and boy. How are they dressed? Do you think they are wealthy or poor? What clues does the picture give you?

Look at their eyes. Other than the camera, what do you think they see? Do you think that anything they see is familiar to them? Can you imagine any thoughts that might be running through their heads? What questions do you think they might have about America? What do you think they expect to find here? If you have answered all these questions, you have begun to put yourself into their shoes.

Next, imagine that you lived in New York City in 1901. This boy and girl are new students in your classroom. Probably they would not speak any English at all. Their clothes would probably not be like yours. They might only have one or two outfits to wear. In what other ways might they be different from you? In what ways would they be like you?

Italian immigrant family at Ellis Island

Lessons Learned

LESSON 1
Foundations of Diversity
Most early immigrants to the United States came from the British Isles and Germany. Later they were joined by Poles, Russians, Greeks, Italians, and Jews. All came for freedom and opportunity.

LESSON 2
Immigrants in American Life
Immigrants settled all over the United States. Some nationalities and ethnic groups settled together in neighborhoods. The number of Asian and African immigrants has risen. African Americans moved to northern cities to find opportunity.

LESSON 3
Immigration Patterns
At times, the United States limited immigration from certain parts of the world. New laws make it easier for naturalized citizens to bring their families to the United States. People who immigrate come to the United States in hopes of a better life. Their presence has enriched American life, too.

Talk About It

1. The first voluntary immigrants to what is now the United States came mostly from northern and western Europe. Today, more immigrants come from Asia, Mexico, and Latin America. Why has this change occurred?
2. Are the reasons why immigrants come to the United States today the same as in earlier times? Explain your answer.
3. In the early years of our nation there were no restrictions on immigration. Why have there been restrictions from time to time since then?
4. What has been the most important contribution of immigrants to American society? Explain why.
5. What is racism? How can we fight it?

Mastering Mapwork

LOCATION
Use the map on page 235 to answer these questions:

1. From what area of the world did most immigrants move to the United States between 1870 and 1920?
2. To what areas of the United States did most Europeans first move?
3. To what areas of the United States did most Asians first move?
4. From what countries in Asia did most immigrants move?
5. Was the movement of immigrants a movement of people, goods, or ideas?
6. In what direction did immigrants from Africa move as they traveled to the United States from their continent?

Becoming Better Readers

Thinking About Main Idea
When reading nonfiction information, good readers always keep in mind the main idea of what they are reading. Thinking about the main idea helps good readers organize the new information they are gathering as they read. Main ideas can be found in chapter titles and in this book, the lesson titles. What was the main idea of this chapter? Who were the many different people in this chapter?

Go to the Source

Understanding Citizenship

The passage below is from the Naturalization Oath of Allegiance to the United States. This is the oath immigrants take to become U.S. citizens. Answer the questions below using information from the oath.

I hereby declare, on oath, that I absolutely and entirely renounce [reject] and abjure [give up] all allegiance [devotion] and fidelity [loyalty] to any foreign prince, potentate [ruler], state or sovereignty, of whom or which I have heretofore [before] been a subject or citizen; that I will support and defend the Constitution and laws of the United States of America against all enemies, foreign and domestic; that I will bear true faith and allegiance to the same; that I will bear arms on behalf of the United States when required by the law; that I will perform noncombatant service in the armed forces of the United States when required by the law; that I will perform work of national importance under civilian direction when required by the law; and that I take this obligation freely without any mental reservation or purpose of evasion [avoiding]; so help me God.

Questions

1. What is the purpose of the words in the brackets?
2. When immigrants are ready to become citizens of the United States, they must take the Naturalization Oath of Allegiance of the United States of America. What is the meaning of the word oath?
3. Explain the main idea of the Naturalization Oath of Allegiance to the United States.
4. Base on the information in the oath, do you think it is fair or unfair to make all these promises? Why or why not?
5. What does the following phrase from the oath mean: "I take this obligation freely without any reservation or purpose of evasion; so help me God"?

CHAPTER 11

The United States: 1898–1945

Chapter Preview

LESSON 1
Becoming a World Power
During the twentieth century, the United States began taking a greater part in world events.

LESSON 2
American Life Between Two Wars
World War I and the Depression brought important changes to American Life.

LESSON 3
World War II
World War II made the United States into a world leader.

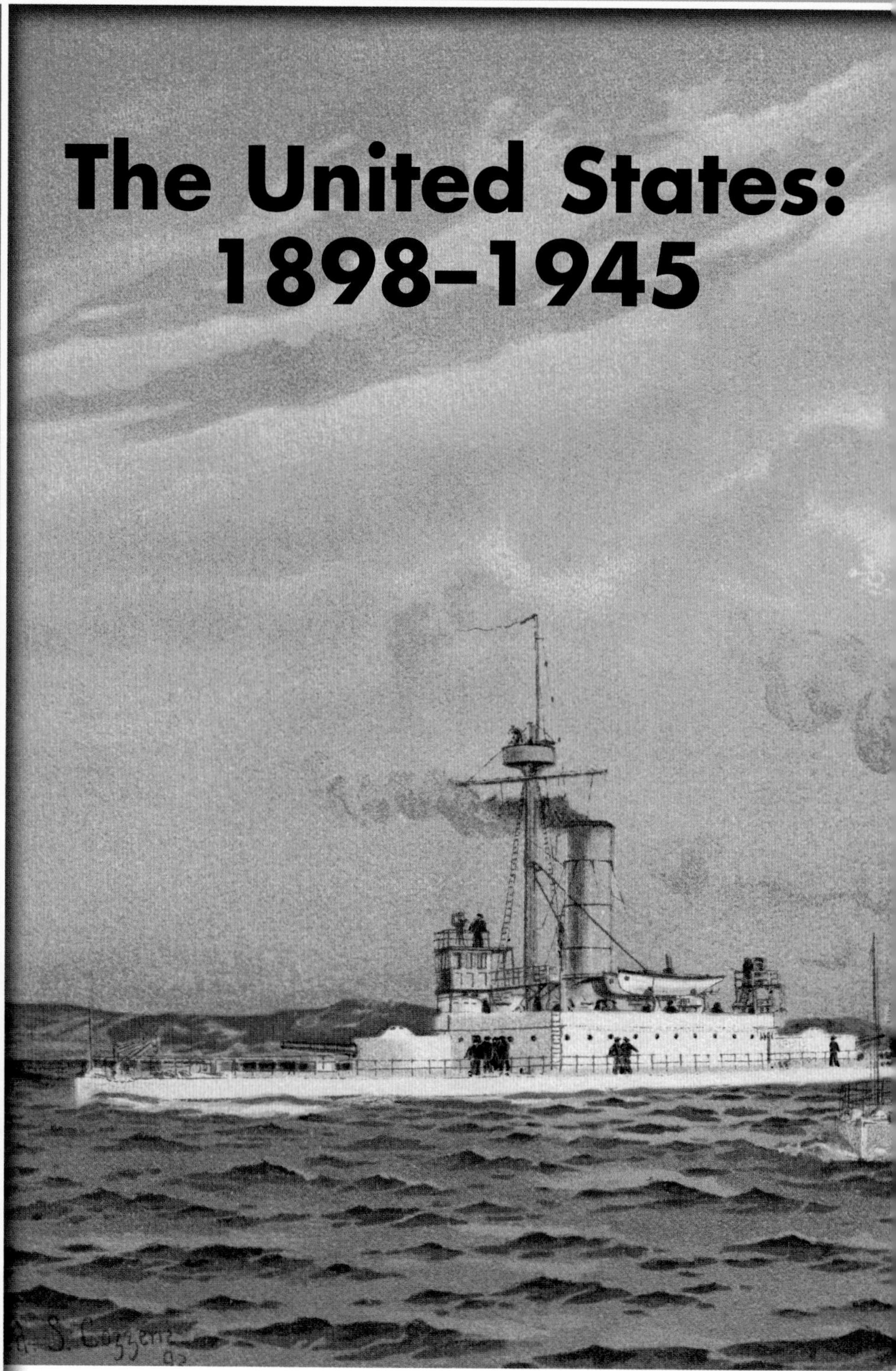

Timeline of Events

- **1898** Spanish American War
- **1900**
- **1901** Theodore Roosevelt elected president
- **1903**
  - U.S. begins Panama Canal
  - First flight at Kitty Hawk, N.C.
- **1908** Ford makes the Model T
- **1910**
- **1912** Wilson elected
- **1914**
  - Panama Canal opens
  - World War I begins
- **1915** *Lusitania* sunk
- **1917** U.S. joins Allies in World War I
- **1918** Allies win World War I
- **1919**
  - Treaty of Versailles
  - Wilson proposes "Fourteen Points"
- **1920**

In 1907, President Theodore Roosevelt ordered sixteen battleships to sail around the world. They carried some of the biggest guns in the U.S. Navy. The ships were gone for a little more than a year. They visited countries everywhere. They traveled more than 46,000 miles (74,060 km).

Roosevelt said this "Great White Fleet" was on a "good will mission." Its job was to make friends for the United States. Wherever the battleships sailed they were warmly welcomed. But the president did not talk about the other purpose for this mission. He wanted world leaders to see that the United States had a powerful navy. It could move quickly to almost anywhere in the world.

U.S. Navy vessels, 1894

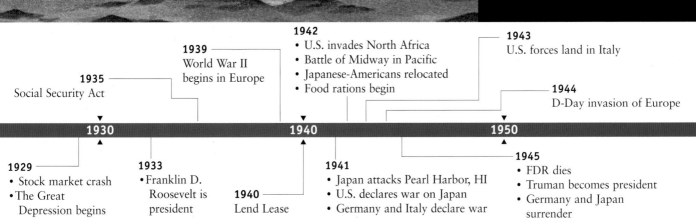

1942
• U.S. invades North Africa
• Battle of Midway in Pacific
• Japanese-Americans relocated
• Food rations begin

1943
U.S. forces land in Italy

1939
World War II begins in Europe

1935
Social Security Act

1944
D-Day invasion of Europe

1930

1940

1950

1929
• Stock market crash
• The Great Depression begins

1933
• Franklin D. Roosevelt is president
• New Deal

1940
Lend Lease

1941
• Japan attacks Pearl Harbor, HI
• U.S. declares war on Japan
• Germany and Italy declare war on the U.S.

1945
• FDR dies
• Truman becomes president
• Germany and Japan surrender
• U.S. drop atomic bombs

LESSON ① Becoming a World Power

KEY IDEAS

- President Theodore Roosevelt wanted the United States to take a strong part in world affairs.

- The United States helped European allies defeat Germany in World War I.

- President Woodrow Wilson founded the League of Nations. The United States did not become a member.

KEY TERMS

Allied Powers
Central Powers
Fourteen Points
League of Nations
Rough Riders

PEOPLE TO KNOW

Thedore Roosevelt
Woodrow Wilson

When Theodore Roosevelt was young, he was often sick. He suffered from asthma. He was short, nearsighted, and not very strong.

But Roosevelt became determined to overcome these problems. He walked hills, trained as a boxer, and roped cattle. He became a strong man. Those who knew Teddy as a boy could not have imagined that he would become a bold and outspoken leader.

The Spanish-American War

Theodore Roosevelt was a national hero before he became president. He was very interested in Cuba. This island is located less than 100 miles (161 km) south of Florida. It was a colony of Spain at the time.

Like many other Americans, Roosevelt wanted to help the people in Cuba. Spain had mistreated the Cuban people. The people rebelled.

"Remember the *Maine!*"

In January 1898, the USS *Maine*, an American battleship, was sent to Havana, Cuba. Its job was to protect Americans from the fighting. It exploded and sank. Spain was blamed.

Congress declared war on Spain. "Remember the *Maine*!" became a popular battle cry.

Roosevelt immediately formed a group of volunteers. He called them the **Rough Riders** and took them to fight in Cuba. His only battle was at San Juan Hill. There, Roosevelt led a daring attack against Spanish forces.

Teddy Roosevelt led the "Rough Riders" in the Spanish American War. **What famous toy was named after President Roosevelt?**

254   Chapter 11

The war lasted only four months. Spain's surrender brought important results for Cuba and the United States. Cuba became independent.

The United States got land for a naval base in Cuba called Guantanamo Bay. More than 3,000 American soldiers, sailors, and civilians still live and work there today.

The United States also gained new territories from Spain. These included Puerto Rico, an island in the Caribbean, and the Philippines and Guam. These are islands in the Pacific Ocean.

Roosevelt as President

President Roosevelt was a strong leader. Sending the battleship fleet around the world was only part of his plan. He acted boldly to gain the right to construct the Panama Canal (see Eyewitness to History, page 634-635). He also helped Russia and Japan end their war in Asia and sign a peace treaty. He won a Nobel Peace Prize for this work.

"Speak Softly, and Carry a Big Stick"

Roosevelt believed that the United States could use its power to make the world better. He explained that the United States should "speak softly, and carry a big stick" when dealing with other countries. This meant that the United States should step in and help or force other countries do what Americans thought was right.

Some Americans criticized Roosevelt for these beliefs. They worried that the president might take the United States into the wars of Europe or Asia.

Roosevelt, however, believed that the United States must play a larger role in world affairs. Nations were building large military forces and arguing with one another. If the United States did not help solve these disagreements, Roosevelt believed that a great war might break out. Such a war might hurt the United States.

A Great President

Theodore Roosevelt used the presidency to improve life for Americans. Even though TR (a nickname) was from a wealthy family, he did not trust wealthy businessmen. As president, he broke up a number of very large businesses.

Roosevelt called his programs the "Square Deal." The Square Deal included controlling the rates railroads charged people and passing laws to make sure foods and drugs were safe.

Theodore Roosevelt

TR's greatest legacy was the protection of the environment. He wanted Americans to use our natural resources wisely. As president, he created 150 national forests, 51 bird preserves, four game preserves, five national parks, and 18 special areas of interest, including the Grand Canyon.

Because of his successes at home and around the world, many historians rank Theodore Roosevelt as one of America's greatest presidents.

As the United States became a world power it also took on new responsibilities. It tried to to keep peace around the world. This cartoon is titled "The World's Constable." **Does the United States still function as the world's police?**

World War I

Events in Europe during the early 1900s proved Roosevelt to be right. In August 1914, the most powerful nations in Europe went to war. The **Central Powers** were Germany and Austria-Hungary. The Central Powers fought France, the United Kingdom, Italy, and Russia. They were the **Allied Powers.**

The war had three great battlefronts. Armies fought along Russia's western border. Another battleline was in Italy. The third was in eastern and northern France.

Leaders on all sides thought it would be a short war. They were wrong. The fighting went on for more than four years.

New Weapons

The war was more dangerous that any war before it. New and deadly weapons, such as the machine gun and poison gas, destroyed hundreds of thousands of lives.

The submarine was another new weapon used by the Germans. By sailing under the ocean's surface and launching torpedoes, they sank ships without warning.

As the war dragged on, it seemed to many that Europe would destroy itself.

America Stays Neutral

Woodrow Wilson was elected president in 1912. This was two years before Europe went to war. Unlike Roosevelt, Wilson was not deeply interested in foreign affairs. He wanted to solve problems at home to improve the lives of the American people.

During his first months in office, he was able to do some of these things. For example,

he started the first federal income tax. After 1914, however, his major challenges became the Great War (later called World War I) and peace negotiations.

Wilson's first response to the war in Europe was to declare that the United States would remain **neutral.** This meant that the nation would not help either side in the war.

In the early months of the war, Wilson tried to follow the American tradition of staying out of Europe's troubles. Most Americans supported this policy. Europe and its problems seemed far away.

Tanks were one of the new technologies in the war. **How was World War I different from previous wars?**

The *Lusitania*

On May 1, 1915, German submarines attacked the *Lusitania*, a British passenger ship sailing from New York City. It had 1,959 passengers on board. It was sailing to Liverpool, England.

Germany claimed that the British had put military supplies aboard the ship. After the torpedoes struck, the ship sank quickly. Rescuers saved some passengers. But 1,200 lost their lives, including 118 Americans and more than 100 children.

The American people were angry. When Germany said that it would not change the way it used its submarines to attack ships, Americans got even angrier. Finally, Germany promised that its submarines would warn ships that an attack was coming. This would give Americans a chance to climb into life boats and move away from the ship.

Going to War

Germany kept its promise to limit the use of submarines for about a year. Then, in January 1917, Germany announced that it was ordering its submarines to make surprise attacks again.

Wilson broke all ties with Germany. Then, on April 2, 1917, he asked Congress to declare war. The United States, he said, must destroy the German military to make the world safe for democracy. This, however, would be a big job.

I WANT YOU FOR U.S. ARMY
NEAREST RECRUITING STATION

German submarines like the one in this photograph became a powerful weapon during World War I. **What made President Wilson decide to enter World War I?**

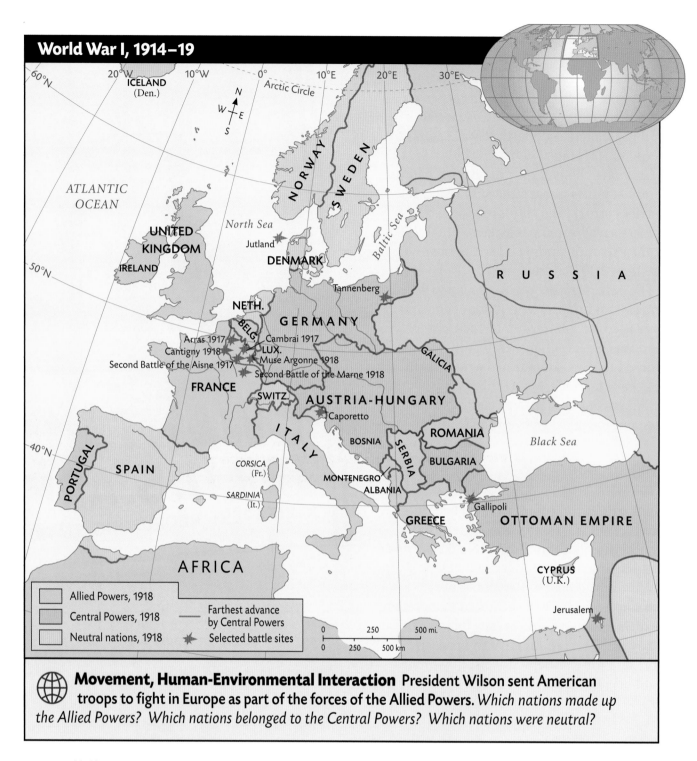

World War I, 1914–19

Movement, Human-Environmental Interaction President Wilson sent American troops to fight in Europe as part of the forces of the Allied Powers. *Which nations made up the Allied Powers? Which nations belonged to the Central Powers? Which nations were neutral?*

Building Up the Army

The United States had a large and modern navy, but its army was not ready to fight in Europe. The United States had an army of only 128,000 men. It was not big enough to win the war quickly. But many of these troops were sent into battle to help the Allied Powers.

Meanwhile, the United States began to build a larger army. Military camps opened. Men arrived for some quick basic training. They then boarded ships for Europe. There they were given more training before going into battle.

By the war's end in 1918, the United States Army had grown to about 4 million men. About half of these soldiers had been sent to Europe. American forces made a

The war ended November 11. This day is now Veteran's Day. A veteran is a person who served in the armed forces. **About how many Americans fought in Europe?**

difference. German leaders knew they could not win when fresh, well-trained Americans entered the fight.

Germany's armies were running out of men and war supplies. On November 11, 1918, the Germans agreed to stop fighting.

A Plan for Peace

The leaders of Great Britain, France, Italy, and the United States gathered in Paris in 1919. Their meeting was called the Paris Peace Conference. They were going to write the peace treaty.

Wilson had thought a lot about what caused wars. He wanted to stop wars from breaking out in the future. Wilson came up with a plan to do this. He called it his *Fourteen Points.*

He spoke about his plan for peace before the leaders started their talks. These Fourteen Points called for fair treatment of Germany. Wilson wanted democracy to grow in that country. So he did not want to make Germany pay for the war and give up too much territory. He wanted some boundaries redrawn, especially in Eastern Europe. He thought that this would help end some of the bitter rivalries that started World War I.

The Treaty of Versailles was signed in Paris in June 1919. **What did President Wilson want the treaty to accomplish?**

The United States: 1898–1945

President Woodrow Wilson (far right), and European leaders met at the Paris Peace Conference. There they planned the creation of the League of Nations. **Why didn't the United States join the League of Nations?**

The League of Nations

Above all, Wilson wanted the winners of the war to join the United States in setting up the *League of Nations.* The League would be a new kind of organization. Member nations could use it to discuss problems. They could settle disagreements without going to war.

After many long discussions in Paris, Wilson signed a peace treaty that called for a League of Nations. The president's next job was to get the United States Senate to ratify, or approve, the treaty.

According to the Constitution, the president may make treaties. But the Senate must ratify them before they become part of United States law. Wilson did not have enough votes in the Senate to ratify the treaty. Some senators did not like the idea of America joining the League of Nations.

Some advisers urged the president to compromise and accept some of the Senate's demands. Wilson refused and fought back. He rode a train across the country to speak everywhere in support of the League and his ideas. But his health failed on this trip. He was never well again. He lost his fight to win Senate approval of the peace treaty. The League of Nations was established, but the United States never joined it.

LESSON ❶ REVIEW

Fact Follow-Up
1. What territories did the United States gain after the 1898 Spanish-American War?
2. What were the opposing alliances and nations when the U.S. entered the war in 1917?
3. The United States remained neutral for the first three years of World War I. Why did President Woodrow Wilson encourage neutrality?

Talk About It
1. Should the United States have become involved in the Spanish-American War? Explain why or why not.
2. Why was World War I more dangerous than any that came before it?
3. Which president—Theodore Roosevelt or Woodrow Wilson—contributed more to the United States? Explain your choice.

Many Americans had supported joining the League of Nations when Wilson first proposed the idea. *Public opinion,* or the views of the people, changed, however, as the Senate debated the peace treaty.

Americans began to think that the League might involve the United States in another big war. That was something Americans did not want. They wanted the nation to stick with its tradition of staying out of Europe's wars.

The Roaring 1920s

As men returned from military service, Americans turned away from world problems. There was a lot to do at home.

Everyone, it seemed, had jobs. The nation had begun to enjoy a new level of *prosperity,* or economic growth, after war broke out in Europe. The nations at war had purchased a great deal of American farm products and manufactured goods.

After the war ended, sales to European customers dropped. As you will read later, this hurt American farmers. But most other American businesses continued to prosper until the late 1920s.

The Automobile Industry

The Model T Ford was not America's first automobile, but it became the most popular one in the 1920s. It was a simple machine with only 200 moving parts.

Many families could afford to buy a Model T. Henry Ford's factory built them. He perfected the assembly line process to make his cars. This meant that more cars could be made by fewer people for less money. He sold his first Model T in 1908 for $850. By the 1920s, the price had dropped to $290.

Everyone seemed to want a Model T or another automobile. In 1919, only 9 million Americans owned a car. In the next ten years, about 23 million purchased one.

These workers are building cars on the Ford assembly line in 1913. **How did the invention of the automobile change American society?**

KEY IDEAS

- With good roads and cars, Americans began to move away from cities.

- The Great Depression brought hardship to all parts of American business and society.

- President Franklin Roosevelt's New Deal helped rebuild the American economy.

KEY TERMS

Great Depression
New Deal
labor unions
prosperity
public opinion
reform
Social Security
stock
strikes
suburbs

PEOPLE TO KNOW

Henry Ford
Herbert Hoover
Franklin D. Roosevelt
Eleanor Roosevelt

Cars Fuel Growth

Booming car sales helped other businesses grow. Making cars used steel auto parts, rubber tires, glass windshields, and fabric for the seats. Other businesses that were not linked to making cars also grew.

Automobiles, for example, created a huge demand for good paved roads. For example, almost all of the roads that connected Washington, D.C., to Raleigh, North Carolina were dirt or gravel. They were rough and dusty when they were dry. If they were wet, autos could get stuck in the mud.

Changes in American Life

With good roads, automobile owners did not need to live close to their jobs. They could move to *suburbs,* communities on the edges of cities. There they could live in houses with lawns instead of in crowded apartment buildings.

In the suburbs, people needed new houses, schools, churches, libraries, and post offices. Thousands of new jobs opened for carpenters, bricklayers, and other skilled workers.

Other business grew, too. Automobile dealerships opened in cities. Service stations sold gasoline, oil, and tires. Along busy highways, food stands and motels opened.

By the late 1920s, so many cars were on the road that there were traffic jams. State and local governments had to control traffic. The first stop-and-go lights were installed in cities and at dangerous crossings. Extra police—often mounted on motorcycles—were hired to enforce traffic laws. By 1930, one out of every nine workers held a job created by the automobile industry.

Electricity in Homes

New inventions powered by electricity also helped the economy grow. Power plants built after 1900 produced cheap electricity. Electricity powered movie theaters, which opened across the country. Electricity also opened the door to radio broadcasting. About 500 stations were on the air by the end of the 1920s.

People could now afford to use electricity at home. Electric lights replaced oil lamps. Housework changed. Every modern home, it seemed, needed electric appliances—refrigerators, vacuum cleaners, washing machines, and stoves.

Electricity brought new machines like this washing machine (right) into people's homes. Some early radios were called "cathedrals" because of the design of the cabinet. Families sat together and listened to broadcasts just as they now watch TV. **Do you listen to the radio often?**

When the stock market crashed in 1929, many people had to raise money by selling possessions, such as this car, for much less than their previous value. **How long did the Great Depression last?**

The Boom Collapses

Many Americans believed that the prosperity of the 1920s would just keep going. People used the money they made at their jobs to invest in other businesses. They did this by buying *stock.* Stocks are shares of ownership in a company. When the company makes a profit, it shares the money with the stockholders.

But it is hard to keep an economy growing all the time. At the end of the decade, the economy stopped growing.

On October 24, 1929, the prices paid for stocks suddenly fell. Many people lost their savings. Even worse, many owed a lot of money.

The Great Depression

That date is often remembered as the start of the *Great Depression.* This was a period of hard times that lasted about ten years.

But some economic troubles had come much earlier than October 1929. American farmers had been suffering for several years.

When Europe's farmers went back to work after World War I, Europeans stopped buying American farm products. This meant that American farmers sold less. They did not get much for what they did sell because prices were low.

The stock market crash changed Americans' minds about the economy. They learned that prosperity could not last forever. The United States had suffered depressions before, but none had been as bad as this one.

Many, many factories closed down. They sent workers home. Millions of people were out of work for years. The Great Depression lasted through the 1930s. It did not end completely until the United States entered World War II in 1941.

Helping the Unemployed

Many people suffered in the Great Depression. With no jobs, people could not support their families. They could not buy food. They could not pay for their home.

Charities gave free meals to hungry people. Many states tried to help the unemployed. North Carolina paid men about 10 cents an hour to clear out ditches and brush along roads. But charities and state governments did not have enough money to help much. The problem was huge.

President Herbert Hoover felt bad for the American people. But he thought the Depression would not last long. He also believed help from the government would do more harm than good.

Some Americans thought that Hoover was right. Others were angry. Homeless people built themselves little huts with scraps from the city dumps. They called these huts "Hoovervilles" after the president.

Fighting the Depression

Franklin D. Roosevelt was a distant cousin of President Theodore Roosevelt. His nickname was FDR. Like his cousin, FDR was from a wealthy family. He had served as Assistant Secretary of the Navy under President Wilson. In 1920, the Democratic Party picked him as its candidate for vice president. He had a bright future in politics.

Soon after the 1920 election (he lost), FDR caught polio. Polio is an illness that can cripple people. Many thought Roosevelt's political career was over. The disease had paralyzed him from the waist down. But Roosevelt managed to keep working.

FDR was elected governor of New York. When the Great Depression hurt the people in his state, he started programs to help them.

The diagram shows how people lost their jobs. Unemployment forced people like these men to go to soup kitchens for a free meal. **Why were people out of work during the Depression?**

Depression Cycle

Factories lay off workers.

Factories do not get orders.

People lose their jobs.

Stores do not order from factories.

People cannot buy things.

Stores go out of business.

FDR in the White House

In 1932, Roosevelt was elected president of the United States. On the day he took office, he told Americans, "The only thing we have to fear is fear itself." He meant that if Americans worked together, they could solve their problems. They should not be afraid.

FDR wanted people to know that he would act quickly to solve problems. He immediately sent Congress a bill to help keep the banks in business. This was a strong message. FDR showed that he would use the powers of the government to fight the Depression.

The New Deal

Roosevelt proclaimed that he would make a "New Deal" with Americans. The *New Deal* created government programs to end the Depression. They gave help to people in need and started to fix the economy.

Roosevelt had almost the entire country behind him as he began the New Deal. Americans were terribly discouraged by three years of hardship. Many banks had closed. When they closed, people lost their savings.

About 13 million people had lost their jobs, and many had no way to make money. More than a million people roamed the country looking for work. They hitchhiked along the roads or rode in empty freight cars on the railways. But everywhere they found signs that read, "Move on. We can't take care of our own." In such bad times, people welcomed anything that FDR might try.

The First Hundred Days

During his first 100 days in office, Roosevelt sent Congress one proposal after another. These first bills were designed to help people and get the economy going again. He told Congress to borrow money. The programs that would put people back to work needed money.

Businesses could not offer people jobs. Therefore, the government would pay young

FDR walked with his wife, Eleanor, and son James on Inauguration Day, 1933. **What did President Roosevelt do to fight the Depression?**

men to do work around the nation. These people built state parks, planted trees, and built flood control projects. Construction crews used government money to build roads, athletic fields, and airports. Other funds helped farmers keep their farms going. Colleges were given money so they could give jobs to needy students. Then the students could stay in school. Still more projects put artists, actors, photographers, and singers to work.

By the end of these first 100 days, some people criticized the New Deal. Some said that the president was building a big government. It interfered too much in people's lives. Others said that the president had not done enough. But in 1936, Roosevelt won reelection to a second term in office.

Millions of Americans were still unemployed, but things seemed brighter. Banks had been saved. Industry had hired back about 6 million workers. People were no longer standing in lines for meals.

FDR and the New Deal

During the Great Depression, President Franklin Roosevelt got Congress to create many programs to get people working again. Some people made fun of the programs and their names, calling them "alphabet soup." But New Deal programs helped create jobs, improve business, and help needy Americans.

The Civilian Conservation Corps (CCC) (right) created jobs for young men between the ages of 18 and 25. It paid them about $30 per month. About 2.5 million young men took part in the program. CCC workers built trails, planted trees in our national forests, and created places to protect fish, game, and birds.

Franklin Roosevelt

The Works Progress Administration (WPA) was created in 1935. The WPA renovated and built thousands of bridges, roads, hospitals, schools, water treatment plants, theaters, and playgrounds. It also funded cultural programs for artists, musicians, actors, and writers. You may find the letters "WPA" on a wall or building in your own town.

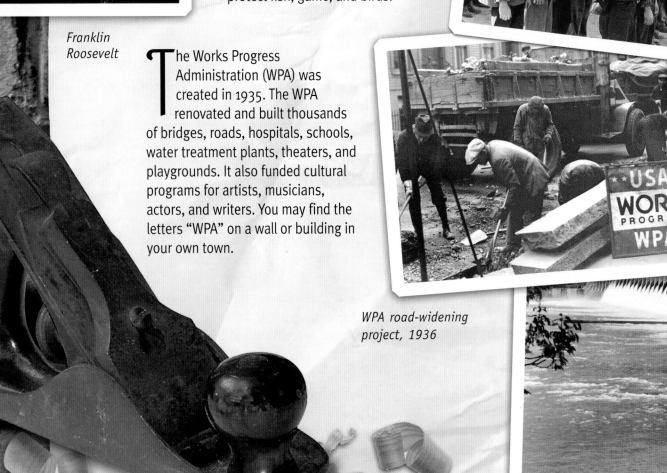

WPA road-widening project, 1936

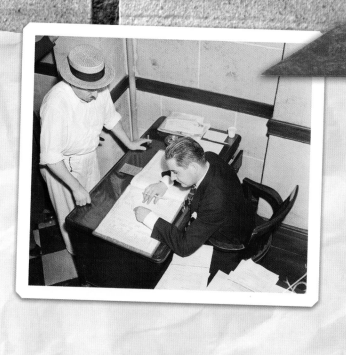

Under FDR's leadership, Congress started the Federal Deposit Insurance Corporation (FDIC). Under this program, the government protects bank deposits. Today, you can see signs on the windows of banks that say that the FDIC insures the deposits of bank customers up to $100,000.

The Social Security Administration (SSA) was another lasting New Deal program. This program made it possible for older citizens to have money after they retire.

TVA's Wilson Dam, Muscle Shoals, Alabama

Social Security card

The Tennessee Valley Authority (TVA) built dams. These stopped terrible floods. They also produced electricity. Building the dams gave construction workers jobs. Once built, the power plants created even more jobs. The TVA's low-priced electricity attracted businesses to the area. It also improved the quality of life of citizens. They could live in modern homes with electric lights, radios, and even vacuum cleaners.

The United States: 1898–1945

Hard Times for Labor

Many Americans had tough jobs with poor working conditions. They were not paid much. The workers did not have any power, so company owners ignored their complaints.

Coal mining was a dangerous job. Because of the Depression, miners' pay was very low. They worked 12 to 16 hours a day. Miners' families were desperate and starving.

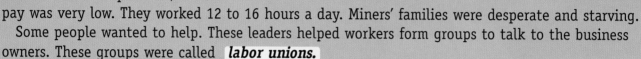

Striking miners bloacked a road in Harlan County, Kentucky. They wanted to stop people from getting in the mine.

Some people wanted to help. These leaders helped workers form groups to talk to the business owners. These groups were called **labor unions.**

The United Mine Workers of America (UMWA) was a union. It wanted to improve the lives of coal miners. After the National Industrial Recovery Act was passed, people from the UMWA crossed the country to organize all coal miners.

Unions had more power than one worker alone had. Unions could make agreements with owners for more pay, fairer treatment, and a safer place to work. The UMWA started **strikes** to try to force mining companies to make changes. Workers refused to work until they got what they wanted.

Often, the strikes worked. Sometimes companies hired people to replace the strikers. A few strikes turned violent. But overall, unions like the UMWA improved the lives of workers and their families in the first half of the twentieth century.

Another important program of Roosevelt's "New Deal" was the NRA, or National Recovery Administration.

What role did the government play in the nation's economic recovery during the 1930s?

Fixing the Economy

Now that things were getting better, Roosevelt turned to *reform.* He wanted to fix the things in the economy that did not work well.

Congress passed a law creating a *Social Security* system. This gave money each month to older citizens when they could no longer work. Laws set a minimum wage and put limits on the number of hours a day that someone could work. New rules for buying and selling stock were made. Electric power lines were built in rural areas. Western farmers were taught how to protect the soil.

These programs—and many more—did not completely end the Depression. Preparing for World War II would put everyone back to work. But the New Deal lifted America's spirits during the Depression. It changed American society. People learned that they did not stand alone. If people became victims of things that they could not control, they could ask the government for help.

Anna Eleanor Roosevelt
1884–1962

Eleanor Roosevelt was a shy and awkward child. Both of her parents died when she was young. Eleanor grew up with her strict grandmother. She had little fun or love in her childhood. When she was fifteen, she went to boarding school in France. There she made friends and became more self-confident.

When Eleanor came back to New York, she began working to help the poor. She had grown into a young woman who cared about people. Eleanor's uncle was President Theodore Roosevelt. He gave her away when she married her fifth cousin, Franklin Roosevelt. She and Franklin had six children. One son died as a baby.

When Franklin, her husband, became sick with polio and could no longer walk, she became his eyes and ears. He was elected governor of New York State with her help. Then she helped him become president, too.

America had never had a first lady like Eleanor Roosevelt. She met thousands of people and hosted parties like other first ladies. But Eleanor wanted to help people, no matter who they were. She fought discrimination against African Americans. She traveled across America to see how the government could help people. When World War II broke out, she traveled the world to visit American soldiers and sailors.

She told Franklin about what she saw. He trusted her advice. She spoke on the radio and wrote in her daily newspaper column, "My Day," about what she saw, too.

After Franklin died, she returned to her home in New York. But within a year she represented her country at the United Nations. There she helped write the Universal Declaration of Human Rights. Eleanor served her country and the world in many ways. She was called the "First Lady of the World."

Eleanor Roosevelt

LESSON 2 REVIEW

Fact Follow-Up
1. How did World War I in Europe contribute to Americas prosperity?
2. Which invention created more new businesses than any other?
3. Which Americans had experienced serious economic troubles before the Great Depression began?

Talk About It
1. When did the Great Depression begin and end?
2. Sometimes the New Deal programs were called "alphabet soup." Is this a good term to describe them? Why or why not?
3. How did Franklin Roosevelt's New Deal fight the Great Depression?

LESSON ③ World War II

KEY IDEAS

- The United States helped Britain fight Germany by lending destroyers.

- The United States entered World War II after the Japanese attack on Pearl Harbor.

- In order to bring the war to an end quickly, the United States dropped atomic bombs on two Japanese cities.

KEY TERMS

Allies
Axis Powers

PEOPLE TO KNOW

Winston Churchill
Adolf Hitler
Benito Mussolini
Emperor Hirohito
Dwight Eisenhower
Harry S. Truman

Japanese aircraft took American forces in Hawaii by surprise on Sunday, December 7, 1941. Japanese planes from aircraft carriers attacked early in the morning. They bombed America's Pacific fleet at Pearl Harbor and military planes at a nearby air field.

Fifteen warships were sunk or badly damaged. More than 150 planes were destroyed. About 2,000 sailors and soldiers were killed.

The next day a grim President Roosevelt appeared before Congress. He called December 7, 1941, "a date which will live in infamy." FDR asked Congress to declare war on Japan.

A few days after Congress declared war, Germany and Italy, allies of the Japanese, declared war on the United States. Congress immediately declared war on those two European nations. The United States was now fighting in World War II.

After the Japanese attacked Pearl Harbor in 1941 (right and far right), the United States immediately entered World War II. **What made President Roosevelt think that there would be another big war?**

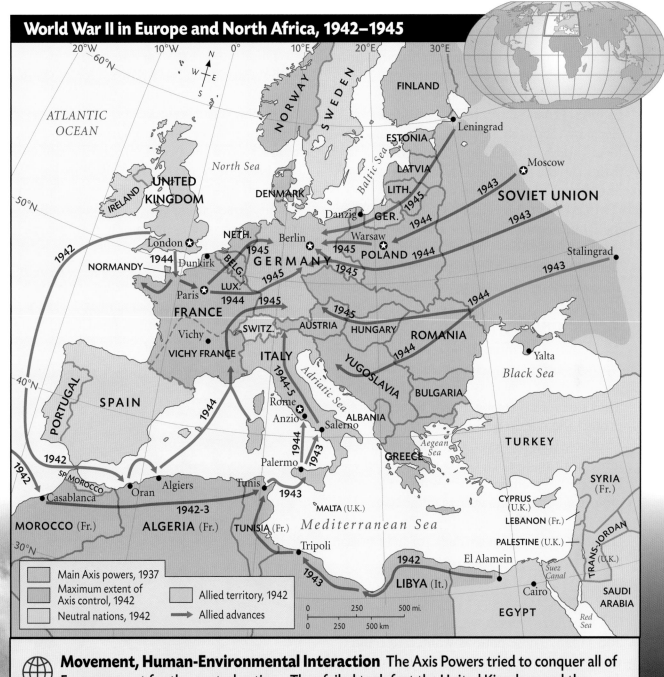

World War II in Europe and North Africa, 1942–1945

ATLANTIC OCEAN

NORWAY

SWEDEN

FINLAND

North Sea

Leningrad

Moscow

ESTONIA

LATVIA

LITH.

SOVIET UNION

IRELAND

UNITED KINGDOM

DENMARK

Baltic Sea

Danzig

GER.

London

NETH.

Berlin

Warsaw

Stalingrad

NORMANDY

Dunkirk

BELG.

GERMANY

POLAND

Paris

LUX.

FRANCE

Vichy

SWITZ.

AUSTRIA

HUNGARY

ROMANIA

Yalta

VICHY FRANCE

ITALY

Adriatic Sea

YUGOSLAVIA

Black Sea

PORTUGAL

SPAIN

Rome

Anzio

Salerno

ALBANIA

BULGARIA

TURKEY

Palermo

GREECE

Aegean Sea

SYRIA (Fr.)

SP. MOROCCO

Oran

Algiers

Tunis

MALTA (U.K.)

CYPRUS (U.K.)

LEBANON (Fr.)

Casablanca

Mediterranean Sea

PALESTINE (U.K.)

TRANS-JORDAN (U.K.)

MOROCCO (Fr.)

ALGERIA (Fr.)

TUNISIA (Fr.)

Tripoli

El Alamein

Cairo

SAUDI ARABIA

Suez Canal

LIBYA (It.)

EGYPT

Red Sea

1942, 1943, 1944, 1945 (various route labels)

Legend:
- Main Axis powers, 1937
- Maximum extent of Axis control, 1942
- Neutral nations, 1942
- Allied territory, 1942
- Allied advances

0   250   500 mi.
0   250   500 km

Movement, Human-Environmental Interaction The Axis Powers tried to conquer all of Europe except for the neutral nations. They failed to defeat the United Kingdom and the Soviet Union. *Why did FDR believe it was important to help France, the United Kingdom, and the Soviet Union?*

The Road to War

Woodrow Wilson had hoped that World War I would end all wars. By the late 1930s, however, another great war seemed to be coming. Japanese troops had invaded China. Germany and Italy had rebuilt their armed forces and had begun to expand their territories. As the 1930s ended, many Americans doubted peace in Europe would last.

Just like at the beginning of World War I, the United States again tried to stay neutral. But the Axis powers were winning. Democratic nations friendly to the United States were being attacked and conquered.

Getting Ready for War

Roosevelt wanted to be ready to fight. He worked with Congress to strengthen the army and the navy. Congress approved these steps. They knew that strong armed forces would protect the nation against an attack.

Roosevelt, however, could not do much more than that. Then Germany invaded Poland in September 1939. Within weeks almost all of Europe was again at war. Winston Churchill, the prime minister of the United Kingdom, asked FDR for help to fight the Axis.

The Axis

The *Axis Powers* were Germany, Italy, and Japan. These nations wanted to build new empires and wipe out their enemies. They were not democracies. Instead, they were led by leaders with total control.

The Germans were led by Adolf Hitler. They were called Nazis after the name of Hitler's political party in Germany. The Italians were led by Benito Mussolini. The Japanese were led by Emperor Hirohito.

Japan and Germany treated the countries that they conquered harshly. President Roosevelt feared that if the United States did not help countries like France and the United Kingdom, soon there would not be any democracies left in Europe.

Aiding the British and the French

The United States tried to help British supply ships cross the Atlantic Ocean. As in World War I, German submarines used torpedoes to sink ships.

To help defeat the submarines, Roosevelt agreed to give the British 50 old but still useful U.S. Navy destroyers, a type of ship. The British in turn gave the United States lands for military bases along the North and South American coastlines and in the Caribbean.

A few months later Roosevelt ordered the U.S. Navy into the North Atlantic. There they helped spot German submarines. This led German submarines in September 1941 to attack two American ships. The United States was coming close to war with Germany.

Adolf Hitler led Germany to defeat in World War II. More than 7 million German soldiers and civilians were killed. Among all nations involved, over 55 million people lost their lives in the war. **How did the United States first try to help the United Kingdom and France?**

These ships are being given to the British as part of the Lend-Lease program. **What did President Roosevelt mean when he compared Lend-Lease to lending a neighbor a garden hose to put out a fire?**

Lend-Lease

Most Americans supported selling military supplies to the British and the French. At first, supplies were sold on a "cash and carry" basis. This meant that those countries had to send ships to pick up the supplies. They had to pay for the supplies when they got them.

Soon, the British and French ran out of money. Roosevelt came up with the idea of "lending" those countries the supplies the needed. Congress agreed to the plan.

The president compared the Lend-Lease program to letting a neighbor borrow a garden hose if his house caught fire. You did not worry about the cost of the hose or how the neighbor would pay for it. You would simply hand the neighbor your hose and tell him to return it after the fire was out.

German submarines like this one made it hard to send Britain supplies during the early years of World War II. **How does this photo compare to the one on page 257?**

The United States: 1898–1945

WORD ORIGINS

During World War II, men who had enlisted in the United States Army became known as "G.I.'s." The initial's stand for "government issue." At first "G.I." was a way to describe the clothes and equipment used by servicemen. Later, the men used the term to refer to themselves.

Problems in Asia

Meanwhile, relations with Japan were getting worse. Japan had invaded China a few years earlier. Then Japan invaded French Indochina (now Vietnam, Cambodia, and Laos) after Germany conquered France.

To show that the United States did not like these actions, it stopped sales of scrap iron and oil to Japan. Japan responded by making an alliance with Germany and Italy. Japan made plans to attack Pearl Harbor.

Japanese leaders believed that destroying America's Pacific fleet would help them win. Japan could move into Southeast Asia and establish military bases out in the Pacific Ocean. The United States would not have ships in the Pacific to stop them.

Japan would then have a powerful empire. It would take many, many men and resources to defeat Japan. The Japanese believed that United States would be unable to force Japan to surrender.

The United States at War

All of America's energy and courage were required in the four years of war that followed Pearl Harbor. The three most powerful *Allies* were the United States, the United Kingdom, and the Soviet Union. The Allies suffered defeats in 1942. But by the next year they were beginning to turn things around. But two more years of hard fighting lay ahead in Europe and the Pacific.

The War in Europe

For the United States, World War II was fought in two separate areas of the world. In Europe and Africa, fighting centered on three fronts. German forces had driven deep into the western Soviet Union (formerly Russia). Soviet forces stopped the invaders in terrible battles. The Soviets then began to push the Germans back.

In Africa and southern Europe, American troops fought with the British against Italian and German forces. Then the Americans and British invaded Sicily. They went up through Italy. American and British naval forces brought German submarines under control.

Finally, a huge invasion force was built in the British Isles. It crossed the English Channel to France and fought its way ashore. June 6, 1944, the day of the invasion was called D-Day

American and British air forces also played important roles in preparing for the invasion of Europe. Bombs dropped on German industry and transportation weakened Germany's ability to fight the Allies.

Cologne, Germany, was badly damaged by Allied bombing. **When did United States troops land in France?**

THE HOLOCAUST

One terrible thing that happened during World War II was the Holocaust. Adolf Hitler believed that Germans were better than other kinds of people. He believed the world would be better without all different kinds of people. He especially hated Jews.

Hitler's troops rounded up all the Jewish people they could find. They sent them to concentration camps. At the camps, there was hardly anything to eat. The people were forced to do hard labor until they died. People who were too old, too young, or too weak to work were killed. About 6 million Jews died in these camps. So did 6 million other people.

When the war ended, American soldiers freed the people in the concentration camps. They were horrified at what they saw. The survivors looked like walking skeletons. Entire families had been wiped out. Some survivors spent a lifetime looking for lost relatives and friends.

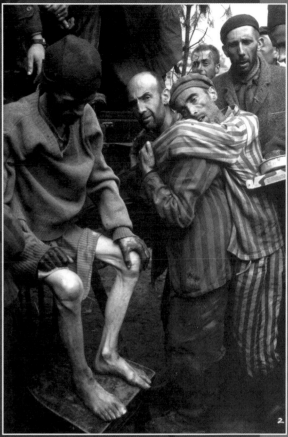

The United States: 1898–1945

275

Fort Bragg in World War II

In 1940, Fort Bragg Military Reservation was a small army base with 5,400 men. It was near Fayetteville, North Carolina. By the summer of 1941, 67,000 troops had arrived for training. In nine months, Fort Bragg had become one of the largest military bases in the United States.

Fort Bragg's population peaked at 159,000. It had hundreds of barracks to house the men, The base also had many hospitals, chapels, libraries, PXs (post exchanges: stores for servicemen), two huge laundries, a post office, and a bakery.

CAROLINA CONNECTION

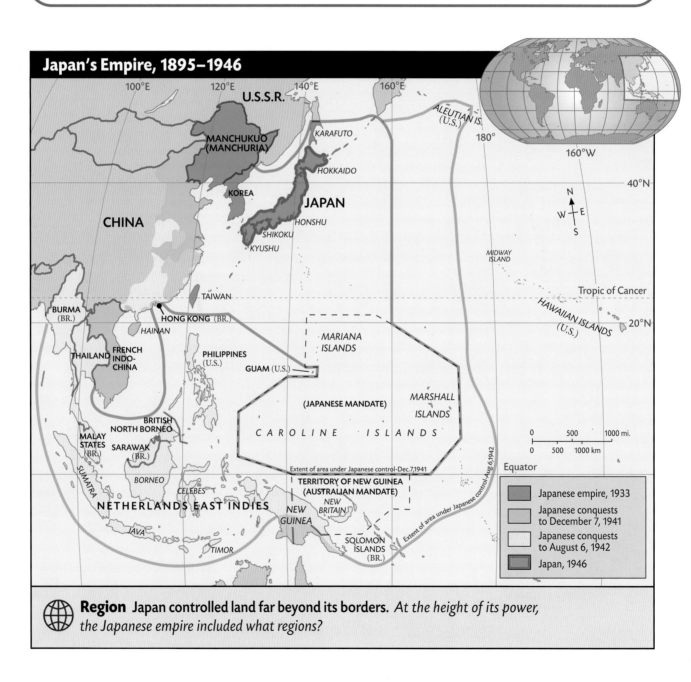

Japan's Empire, 1895–1946

U.S.S.R.

MANCHUKUO (MANCHURIA)

KARAFUTO

ALEUTIAN IS. (U.S.)

KOREA

HOKKAIDO

CHINA

JAPAN

HONSHU

SHIKOKU

KYUSHU

MIDWAY ISLAND

Tropic of Cancer

TAIWAN

HAWAIIAN ISLANDS (U.S.)

BURMA (BR.)

HONG KONG (BR.)

HAINAN

MARIANA ISLANDS

20°N

THAILAND

FRENCH INDO-CHINA

PHILIPPINES (U.S.)

GUAM (U.S.)

MARSHALL ISLANDS

(JAPANESE MANDATE)

C A R O L I N E   I S L A N D S

0   500   1000 mi.
0   500   1000 km

MALAY STATES (BR.)

BRITISH NORTH BORNEO

SARAWAK (BR.)

Extent of area under Japanese control-Dec. 7, 1941

Equator

SUMATRA

BORNEO

CELEBES

TERRITORY OF NEW GUINEA (AUSTRALIAN MANDATE)

NEW BRITAIN

Extent of area under Japanese control-Aug. 6, 1942

NETHERLANDS EAST INDIES

NEW GUINEA

JAVA

TIMOR

SOLOMON ISLANDS (BR.)

Japanese empire, 1933

Japanese conquests to December 7, 1941

Japanese conquests to August 6, 1942

Japan, 1946

Region Japan controlled land far beyond its borders. *At the height of its power, the Japanese empire included what regions?*

The War in the Pacific

Chinese armies fought thousands of Japanese troops in China. Meanwhile the British fought the Japanese in the jungles of Southeast Asia in Burma (Myanmar) and Malaysia. America's navy fought huge air and naval battles against Japanese fleets. Victories in these battles cut Japanese supply lines.

American and Australian ground forces fought together. They battled their way ashore on Japanese-held islands in the Pacific. The Allies did not try to capture all of them. After taking one island, they skipped others. This moved them closer and closer to Japan. As they neared Japan's home islands, American bombers began heavy air strikes on Japan's industrial cities.

By the late spring of 1945, World War II seemed close to an end. Germany surrendered on May 7 of that year. Japan also seemed near defeat. Only a few factories or other buildings were left in the cities. Food supplies were running low. Yet Japan refused to surrender. Would American and allied forces have to invade Japan's home islands?

The Atomic Bomb

A new president, Harry S. Truman, had to answer that question. Roosevelt died shortly after he had been inagurated for a fourth term in 1945. Truman was now president. Some of his advisers wanted to move American troops from Europe, now at peace, to Asia. Other advisers favored using a deadly new weapon, the atomic bomb.

Truman finally decided to use the bomb. He thought that an invasion would cost hundreds of thousands of lives. Truman approved dropping a first bomb on Hiroshima. The Allies demanded that Japan surrender or face "prompt and utter destruction." Japan did not comply. A second bomb would be dropped on Nagasaki. Both bombs were dropped in August 1945. Japan surrendered and World War II ended.

The War at Home

The United States built a huge military force that totaled about 16 million people. Training them was not easy. They fought in many different places—jungles, deserts, and the European countryside. Some had to learn to fly different kinds of planes. Some troops trained with special equipment.

The size of American forces meant that almost every family had a relative in uniform. The American people read news of the war. They waited for mail to be delivered. They hoped for news that loved ones were safe. Sometimes, however, the news was sad. About 290,000 Americans were killed. Another 670,000 were wounded.

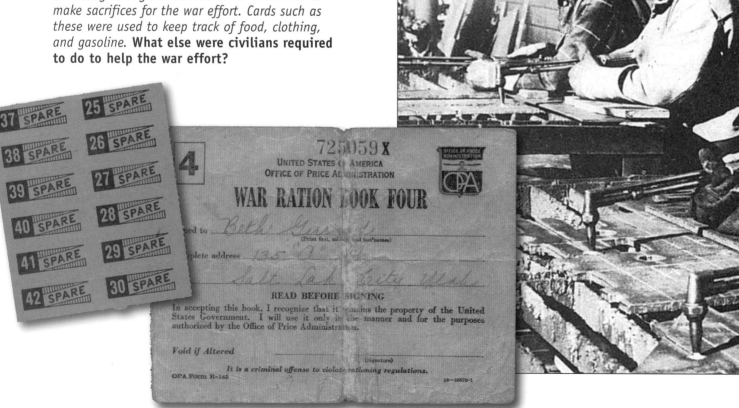

We Can Do It

Making equipment for the war quickly ended the Depression. President Roosevelt set unbelievable goals for 1942—60,000 planes, 45,000 tanks, and 20,000 antiaircraft guns. The goals were even higher in the next years. Industry and workers met them every time.

Supplying troops with uniforms and equipment created shortages at home. Food, clothing, and gasoline were rationed. Americans were encouraged to "use it up; wear it out; make it do; or go without."

Changes in American Life

World War II brought about many social changes, especially for women and African Americans. Women had worked mostly in the home before World War II. Because so many men were in the armed forces, women got the chance to work outside the home if they

Rosie the Riveter was a popular image in World War II. **What did she symbolize?**

Rationing during the war meant civilians had to make sacrifices for the war effort. Cards such as these were used to keep track of food, clothing, and gasoline. **What else were civilians required to do to help the war effort?**

wanted to do so. Many women now did jobs that men had usually done. Rosie the Riveter was a popular wartime image. She showed that a woman was strong and capable of hard work.

More than 200,000 women had nonfighting jobs with the armed forces at home and overseas. They volunteered for service in an "auxiliary force" for different branches of the military. Some served with the army or navy. Some women served as pilots on 77 different types of aircraft. They could not fly in combat. Instead they flew planes from factories to air bases. They delivered people or supplies to different places.

During the war, many women took factory jobs to replace men who were in the military. **What else did women do to serve the country during the war?**

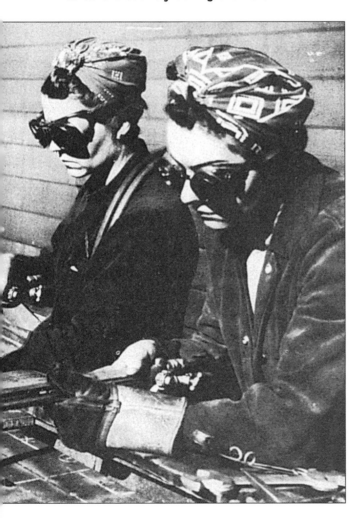

Customs

During World War II, the government rationed canned foods. Canned foods could be shipped to soldiers fighting overseas. So people at home grew vegetables in Victory Gardens. These gardens were planted in backyards and on apartment-building rooftops. Some vacant lots were used as cornfields or squash patches. At its peak, about 40 percent of all vegetables grown in the country came from Victory Gardens.

World War II Victory Gardens poster

The United States: 1898–1945

Japanese Internment

After the attack on Pearl Harbor, many Americans, especially those living on the West Coast of the United States, began to worry about Japanese Americans. Some thought Japanese Americans might be spies or supporteres of Japan.

There was no proof that the Japanese Americans were doing anything wrong. Most had been born in the United States. They thought of themselves as loyal Americans.

In February 1942, President Roosevelt ordered the removal of all Japanese from the West Coast. Japanese Americans had to leave their homes.

During the war, more than 120,000 Japanese Americans were moved to relocation centers (called internment camps). They had to sell their land and homes. Their new homes were buildings behind barbed wire.

They were only allowed to take with them whatever things they could carry—bedding, some extra clothing, and eating utensils. They had to leave their pets behind. Their radios and cameras were taken away.

Reiko Komoto was 10 years old when she and her family were forced to move. Reiko had been born in the United States. Her family was sent to a horse racing track in San Bruno, California. They slept in two cleaned-up horse stalls. The bathrooms and the dining hall were located in other buildings.

They lived there six months. Then they were sent on a crowded train to a relocation center in Topaz, Utah.

The camp in Topaz housed about 8,300 people. Each block had two rows of barracks, or group living spaces. People slept in large rooms with metal cots and army blankets. Each set of buildings had a place for meals. No one was able to leave.

Japanese men in a internment camp

As the war drew to a close, the Japanese were finally allowed to leave. The camps closed. Most people found a new place to live instead of returning to their old homes.

What would YOU do?

You are living in California during World War II. A friend who is of Japanese descent is being relocated with her family. No one in town is speaking to them, although they have been good neighbors for many years. You will not be able to write or visit your friend until the end of the war. Would you go to her home to wish her well and say goodbye?

About 1 million African American men and women served in the military during the war. Some were soldiers. Others cared for the wounded. Despite discrimination and segregation, African Americans trained as pilots at the Tuskegee Institute. This was an all-black college located in Alabama. Almost 600 pilots were trained there before the war ended. In 1948, President Truman desegregated the armed forces, opening up more opportunities for African Americans to serve their country.

The Results of World War II

World War II brought terrible destruction. More than 55 million people in all of the countries involved were killed. The war changed the world's maps. European countries had to give up their colonies in Asia and Africa after the war. The Soviet Union emerged as one of the two great world powers. The United States was the other one.

When peace came, Americans felt that their nation had been right to join the fight against the Axis Powers. Americans hoped that in the years to come the United States could use its power to make a better world. These ideals, as Americans discovered, would soon be tested.

Three "Tuskegee Airmen" go over a map before flight. **What were some of the other things African American soldiers did in World War II?**

LESSON 3 REVIEW

Fact Follow-Up
1. In what ways was the bombing of Pearl Harbor a disaster for the United States?
2. What were signs in the late 1930s that another great war was coming?
3. What steps did Roosevelt take to help the British before the United States entered the war?
4. How did World War II affect life at home in the United States?

Talk About It
1. Why can it be said that Word War II ended the Great Depression?
2. In what ways was World War II a "world" war?
3. Should the United States have forced all the Japanese Americans on the West Coast to move to internment camps? Explain.
4. Compare World War I and World War II. How were they the same? different?

The United States: 1898–1945

*Using Information for Problem-Solving,
Decision-making, and Planning*

Using Timelines

How do you find out when your favorite team is playing their next game? You look at their schedule. A schedule is a kind of timeline. Timelines organize events. They help us understand the order in which things have happened or will happen.

Every chapter in this unit has a timeline. These timelines organize events in American history. Looking at these, we can see what events occurred first, next, and last in a certain period of time.

Linear Timelines

Look at this timeline. It covers the period from 1898 to 1945. It lists events in the order they happened in time. This is called a *linear timeline*. We use a linear timeline to show one subject, like the history of the United States, in one time period, such as 1898–1945.

A linear timeline can be written horizontally (across the page) or vertically (up and down the page).

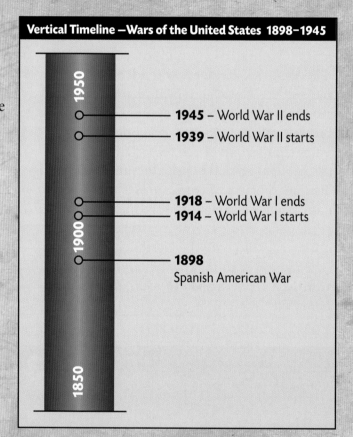

Vertical Timeline —Wars of the United States 1898–1945

1950

1945 – World War II ends
1939 – World War II starts

1918 – World War I ends
1914 – World War I starts

1898
Spanish American War

1900

1850

Answer these questions using the timeline on pages 252–253.

1. Put these events in the order in which they happened: League of Nations created, Allies win World War I, Treaty of Versailles, the United States joins World War I.
2. In which year did the building of the Panama Canal begin? When did the canal open?
3. Which happened first: World War II begins in Europe or Germany and Italy declare war on the United States?
4. Which boat was sunk later: the USS *Maine* or the USS *Lusitania?*

Comparative Time Lines

There is another kind of timeline we can use to organize events. It is called a *comparative timeline*. A comparative timeline compares two or more different topics that happened at the same time.

The TV schedule is a comparative timeline! It compares programs that will be shown on different channels at the same time.

A comparative timeline might compare historical events in two or more countries. Or it could compare two or more topics, like national events and international events. A comparative timeline could look like this:

Comparitive Timeline	
National Events 1819–1910	**International Events 1898–1903**
1901–President McKinley assassinated; Theodore Roosevelt is president	**1898**–The Spanish-American War
1903–Wright Brothers make first flight at Kitty Hawk, N.C.	**1903**–The United States begins digging the Panama Canal
1908–Henry Ford introduces the Model T	**1907**–Theodore Roosevelt sends Great White Fleet around the world

Look at these two timelines. What are they comparing? Could some events be put on both time lines? Why or why not? Is there a connection between any of the events?

Making a Timeline

Look through Chapter 11. Choose two topics to compare using a timeline. Make a list of facts and events for each topic. You may want to use other sources, too. Now you are now ready to put your facts on your timelines.

You will need to make two timelines. If you put them next to each other it will be easier to compare events. First, mark the start dates of each timeline. Next, go to the end and mark the end dates. In between these dates, list the other important dates and events in order.

Write a paragraph comparing the two timelines that answers these questions.

1. What are the topics you are comparing?
2. Can you see any relationships between events that occur at the same time?
3. Can you see any connection between an event that happens earlier on one timeline and later on another? Why or why not?

Lessons Learned

LESSON 1
Becoming a World Power
With the end of the Spanish-American War, the United States gained territories in the Caribbean and the Pacific. The United States, at first neutral in World War I, later joined the Allies. Wilson's League of Nations was formed after the war, but the United States did not join.

LESSON 2
American Life Between Two Wars
The Great Depression brought an end to the prosperity of the 1920s. President Franklin Delano Roosevelt started federal programs to help people survive and find work. Many of these New Deal programs are still part of our government.

LESSON 3
World War II
The United States entered World War II after Japanese planes bombed Pearl Harbor. The United States fought the war in Europe and Asia. At home, everyone increased production. To shorten the war and avoid a land invasion, President Truman ordered two atomic bombs be dropped on Hiroshima and Nagasaki. By the end of the war, the United States and the Soviet Union were the two world powers.

Talk About It

1. How were World War I and World War II different?
2. In what ways were Theodore and Franklin Roosevelt alike?
3. Which of the New Deal programs do you think had the most lasting impact on the American people? Explain.
4. Among the casualties of World War II were 120,000 Japanese Americans. Why can they be considered casualties?
5. How did most women and African Americans benefit from some of the changes brought about by World War II. Why?

Mastering Mapwork

MOVEMENT
Use the map on page 271 to answer these questions:

1. What city in Europe is located at the farthest eastward movement of the Axis powers?
2. What city in North Africa is located at the farthest eastward movement of the Axis powers?
3. In 1942 British forces invaded North Africa. In what directions did they move before going ashore in Oran?
4. What kinds of movement (of people, goods, or ideas) are shown on this map?

Becoming Better Readers

Recognizing Bias
Everyone has an opinion. Sometimes people reporting history mix the facts with their opinions. The mixing of facts and opinions is bias. Good readers need to recognize when what they read is fact or opinion. Facts are things that can be checked or proven. Opinions are a person's feelings about something. Chapter 11 tells the story of a time when our country was at war. Our book has taken great care to tell the facts of this time in history. Talk or write about how this chapter might have been different if it were written by someone from another country.

Go to the Source

Understanding Declarations of War

Read the passage from FDR's speech requesting Congress to Declare War on Japan. He gave this speech on December 8, 1941. Answer the questions with information from the speech.

Yesterday, December 7, 1941—a date which will live in infamy—the United States of America was suddenly and deliberately attacked by naval and air forces of the Empire of Japan.

The United States was at peace with that Nation . . . It will be recorded that the distance of Hawaii from Japan makes it obvious that the attack was deliberately planned many days or even weeks ago. . . .the Japanese Government has deliberately sought to deceive the United States by false statements and expressions of hope for continued peace.

The attack yesterday on the Hawaiian Islands has caused severe damage to American naval and military forces. I regret to tell you that very many American lives have been lost. . . .

As Commander in Chief of the Army and Navy I have directed that all measures be taken for our defense.

But always will our whole Nation remember the character of the onslaught [attack] against us.

No matter how long it may take us to overcome this premeditated [planned] invasion, the American people in their righteous might will win through to absolute victory . . . There is no blinking at the fact that our people, our territory, and our interests are in grave danger.

With confidence in our armed forces—with the unbounding determination of our people— we will gain the inevitable triumph—so help us God.

I ask that the Congress declare that since the unprovoked and dastardly attack by Japan on Sunday, December 7, 1941, a state of war has existed between the United States and the Japanese Empire.

Questions

1. One of the most famous quotes in history by FDR says: "a date which will live in infamy". What does the word infamy mean?
2. What course of action does FDR ask Congress to take?
3. According to the speech, why did the United States declare war on Japan?
4. Based on the information in the speech, who is the Commander-in-Chief of the Army and Navy of the United States?

America Since 1945

Chapter Preview

LESSON 1
The United States in World Affairs
The end of World War II brought a rivalry between the United States and the Soviet Union.

LESSON 2
Justice at Home
During the 1950s and 1960s, the laws separating blacks and whites were changed.

LESSON 3
A Changing Society
Many women now work outside the home. Immigration has made America more diverse.
The United States has changed the ways it uses technology and energy.

Timeline of Events

1946
World's first computer built

1947
Robinson is first black major league baseball player

1950–53
The Korean War

1954
Brown v. Board bans segregation in public schools

1957
Montgomery, Alabama bus boycott

1960
- Greensboro, N.C. sit-ins
- Student Nonviolent Coordinating Committee formed at Shaw University in Raleigh, N.C.

1940

1950

1960

John F. Kennedy was the first American president born in the 21st century. At his inaugural, Kennedy described the challenges facing America after World War II, and he shared his vision for the country. He said:

"Let the word go forth from this time and place, to friend and foe alike, that the torch has been passed to a new generation of Americans—born in this century, tempered by war, disciplined by a hard and bitter peace, proud of our ancient heritage—and unwilling to witness or permit the slow undoing of those human rights to which this Nation has always been committed, and to which we are committed today at home and around the world.
    Let every nation know, whether it wishes us well or ill, that we shall pay any price, bear any burden, meet any hardship, support any friend, oppose any foe, in order to assure the survival and the success of liberty."

Kennedy delivering his inaugural speech

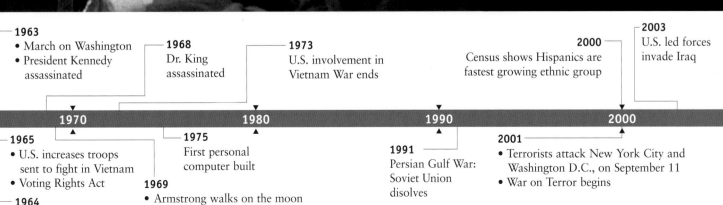

1963
• March on Washington
• President Kennedy assassinated

1968
Dr. King assassinated

1973
U.S. involvement in Vietnam War ends

2000
Census shows Hispanics are fastest growing ethnic group

2003
U.S. led forces invade Iraq

1970   **1980**   **1990**   **2000**

1965
• U.S. increases troops sent to fight in Vietnam
• Voting Rights Act

1964
Civil Rights Act

1975
First personal computer built

1969
• Armstrong walks on the moon
• Internet created

1991
Persian Gulf War: Soviet Union disolves

2001
• Terrorists attack New York City and Washington D.C., on September 11
• War on Terror begins

In 1962, President John F. Kennedy promised the world that the United States would put a man on the moon. It would be done before the end of the decade. Many people did not believe that this was possible. But President Kennedy thought this was important. He wanted his country to beat the Soviets to the moon.

The United States was in a bitter *rivalry,* or contest, with the Soviet Union. This rivalry was called the *Cold War.*

People all over the world saw President Kennedy's promise come true only seven years later. In July 1969, they watched on television as astronaut Neil Armstrong climbed down a ladder from a small spacecraft. He stepped carefully onto the moon. Then he said into his radio, "That's one small step for man, one giant leap for mankind."

The moon landing sent a powerful message around the world. Americans believed it showed that the United States was the strongest nation on the planet. They were proud of what their nation had achieved. And they had beaten the Soviets.

Buzz Aldrin also walked on the moon in July 1969 on the Apollo 11 mission. **What did Neil Armstrong mean when he said "That's one small step for man, one giant leap for mankind"?**

The Cold War

The Soviets had been the first to send a rocket carrying a small satellite into the sky. The satellite was called Sputnik. American leaders were afraid that the Soviets would control space if we did not catch up. So President Dwight D. Eisenhower ordered schools to teach more math and science. Later, President Kennedy supported the moon program. When Armstrong walked on the moon, America felt it was winning the race again.

The race into space was just one part of the Cold War. We call it the Cold War because the United States and the Soviet Union never fought each other face-to-face on a battlefield (that would be a "hot war").

Instead, the Cold War was a battle for control without an actual war between the Americans and Soviets themselves. Sometimes it was a rivalry, like the space race. A dangerous weapons race was part of that rivalry, too.

Both the Americans and the Soviets gave economic aid (money) to nations in Africa and Asia to try to win their support. Sometimes, the Americans and Soviets supported wars in other places.

The *United Nations* is the international organization that replaced the League of Nations at the end of World War II. It helped keep the Cold War from becoming a hot one. The two sides could debate their differences there. Sometimes they used the United Nations to help solve problems.

The Cold War lasted until the 1990s, a period of nearly 50 years. During that time, it affected almost the entire world.

The Rivalry

American-Soviet relations had not been good for many years. In 1917, during World War I, the *Communist Party* took control of Russia. They changed the name of Russia to the Union of Soviet Socialist Republics (USSR), or Soviet Union.

Its new leaders stated that they would help Communist parties in other nations gain power. In contrast, the United States hoped to see democracy spread throughout the world. These two systems of government were very different. This led to conflict.

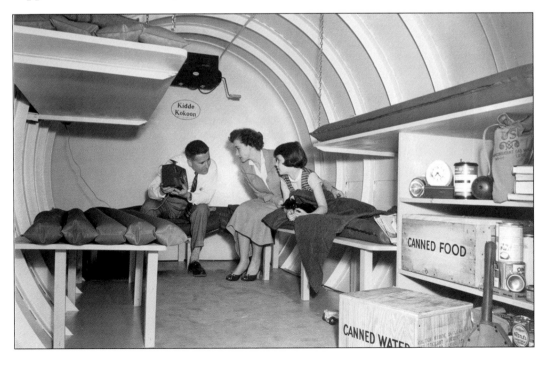

Many people built bomb shelters in reaction to the Cold War. **What were they afraid might happen?**

Allied leaders Winston Churchill (of the United Kingdom), Franklin Roosevelt, and Joseph Stalin (of the Soviet Union) met at Yalta in 1945 to discuss how World War II would end. **How did the Cold War start?**

Communism

The Soviet Union was a Communist dictatorship. Communism is both a kind of government and a kind of economic system. In a Communist system, the government owns all the goods and services. It owns all the factories and decides what to make. The government provides people with what they need, and there are not many products to choose from.

Communist governments do not allow the same freedoms as democratic ones. The Soviets did not have a Bill of Rights like America has. The government told people what jobs they must do. People were not allowed to worship according to their relegious beliefs. Leaders did not let people speak about things they did not like about the government. If someone did speak out, they could go to prison.

In World War II, the Soviets and Americans cooperated because they had the same enemy, Germany. When the war ended, the United States and the Soviet Union had become the world's strongest and most powerful nations. They were called the "superpowers." They also did not trust each other. Their governments and values were so different. This led to the rivalry.

Dividing Europe

When the war ended, the Soviet Union disagreed with the United States, the United Kingdom, and France on terms for a peace treaty. By this time, the Soviets had set up Communist governments in the countries it had freed from the Germans. The Soviets did not let these countries go back to governments they had before the war. They did not let people choose the kind of government they wanted.

This upset the Americans, British, and French. The Soviets, they said, were expanding communism. Soviet leaders replied that Western, democratic nations were trying to weaken the Soviet Union and destroy communism.

The United States, Canada, and several European nations formed the **North Atlantic Treaty Organization (NATO)** to protect each other from Communist expansion (see map, page 291). In response, the Soviet-backed nations in Europe formed the **Warsaw Pact.**

The Arms Race

Both sides built powerful weapons, or **arms.** Each nation tried to build more atomic bombs, or **nuclear weapons,** than the other. Before long, each side claimed that it could destroy the other. Nuclear weapons became symbols of a nation's power.

The use of nuclear weapons remained a threat throughout the Cold War. Conventional—non-nuclear—weapons, however, were used when fighting broke out.

Cold War Conflicts

In the Cold War, the top priority of the United States was stopping the spread of communism.

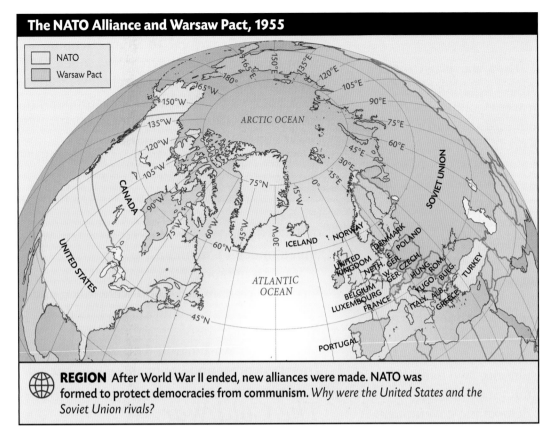

The NATO Alliance and Warsaw Pact, 1955

- ☐ NATO
- ☐ Warsaw Pact

REGION After World War II ended, new alliances were made. NATO was formed to protect democracies from communism. *Why were the United States and the Soviet Union rivals?*

In a few places round the world, some people wanted to form Communist systems. They were often poor, and thought that a Communist system would mean a better life. They believed a Communist government would take care of the people.

But other people in those places wanted to form a government more like the type the United States has. They were afraid that a Communist government would take away their freedom. These two groups of people often ended up fighting each other.

The United States did not want these places to choose communism, so it sent help to the people fighting it. The Soviets did the same for the other side. Sometimes they just sent supplies. Other times they sent troops.

What would YOU do?

Imagine that you are in charge of organizing a gathering of students your age from all around the world. The theme will be world peace through cooperation. How would you invite students to take part? What activities would you plan to promote your goal?

Number of Strategic Nuclear Weapons of the U.S. and U.S.S.R, 1945–1990

- ■ U.S.
- ■ U.S.S.R.

During the Cold War, the Americans and Soviets made thousands of nuclear weapons. **How was the arms race dangerous?**

America Since 1945

The Korean War

In the early 1950s, a war broke out in Korea. Two of Korea's neighbors, the Soviet Union and China, were Communist nations. They helped Communists in North Korea try to control all of Korea. The United Nations, led by the United States, sent troops to help stop the North Korean forces. Then China sent 200,000 men into Korea. American troops were outnumbered.

The war was difficult. More than 54,000 American troops were killed, and more than 100,000 were injured. Many people told President Truman to use a nuclear weapon against China to end the fighting. He refused. The Korean War stopped when the two sides agreed to split the country.

Korea is still split into two nations. North Korea has a Communist government. South Korea now has a democratic government. A space called the Demilitarized Zone (DMZ) separates the countries. The DMZ is 2.5 miles (4 km) wide and runs along the entire border. American troops still guard South Korea's side of the DMZ.

Vietnam

A few years after the Korean War, the United States became involved in a similar conflict in Vietnam. North Vietnamese wanted Vietnam to have a Communist government. At first, only a few Americans were sent as "advisors" to South Vietnam. Soon American troops were doing much of the fighting. They fought bravely but faced great challenges. More and more troops were sent, but the Americans and South Vietnamese could not beat the Communists.

In the United States, the war divided the American people. President Richard Nixon decided that the United States must pull out of the fighting. South Vietnam continued to fight. In 1976, its forces surrendered. Vietnam was united under a Communist government.

Over a million Americans fought in Vietnam. More than 58,000 were killed and many others were wounded. Thousands of Americans visit the Vietnam Veterans Memorial in Washington, D.C., each year. They remember and honor those who served.

The Cold War and Latin America

Cold War conflicts were not just in Europe and Asia. The rivalry also touched the countries in the Western Hemisphere.

Our Latin Neighbors

The United States has a long history of trying to keep European powers out of the Western Hemisphere. In particular, our presidents have worried about Latin America. Latin America is made up of the countries that mostly speak languages that are related to the Latin language—Spanish, French, and Portuguese. Some of these countries are Mexico, Haiti, Brazil, and Cuba.

Do you remember reading about the Monroe Doctrine in Chapter 7? That policy warned Europe to stay out of the Western Hemisphere's business. In Chapter 11, you read about Theodore Roosevelt's policy to "Speak softly, and carry a big stick." This made the United States the world's police. He used it to keep Europe out of Latin America, too. This was called the Roosevelt Corallary to the Monroe Doctrine.

American soldiers fought communists in Vietnam. **Where else in Asia did Americans fight communists?**

292

Other presidents have worked on our relationship with Latin America. Franklin Roosevelt wanted to help Latin America. He created the "Good Neighbor Policy." The relationship between the United States and Latin American nations got better.

President Kennedy wanted to help Latin America like FDR had done. He called his policy the "Alliance for Progress." But Kennedy was also worried about the Cold War. He did not want the Soviet Union helping countries in Latin America. He thought that if the United States helped Latin American countries, it would keep the Soviet Union away.

But one country had already become Communist. To make matters worse, it was working with the Soviet Union. This country was Cuba. In 1962, something happened with Cuba that led the Americans and the Soviets to the brink, or the edge, of a nuclear war.

The Cuban Missile Crisis

Cuba had had a revolution. People thought that its new leader, Fidel Castro, would have a good relationship with the United States. But he did not. Castro turned to the Soviets for help. He created a Communist system.

Cuba is very close to the United States. It is an island only 90 miles (145 km) from Florida. The Soviets were putting nuclear missiles on the island. When President Kennedy found this out, he got angry.

The Brink of War Kennedy told the Soviets that they must remove the missiles. He gave them a deadline and told them that if they did not remove them, the United States would take action to protect itself. People knew that this could mean a war with nuclear weapons. The destruction would be horrible.

The whole world waited. Four days later, the Soviets agreed to take out the missiles if the United States did two things. President Kennedy agreed not to invade Cuba and also to remove some American missiles from

Turkey, a nation near the Soviet Union. The crisis was over.

Today, the United States still does not have a good relationship with Cuba. But it does have much better relationships with many of the countries in Latin America. You will learn more about these countries in Units 6 and 7 of this book.

NAFTA

In the early 1990s, Canada, the United States and Mexico created the North American Free Trade Agreement, or *NAFTA.* The partners agreed to end tariffs, or taxes, on certain goods coming into their countries from the other partners. Our economies have become *interdependent,* meaning that each nation helps and needs help from each of the other countries.

Today, these three nations are working on the Security and Prosperity Partnership of North America. They are cooperating to solve problems related to security, transportation, the environment and public health. Their goal is to improve security, prosperity and quality of life for all citizens within North America.

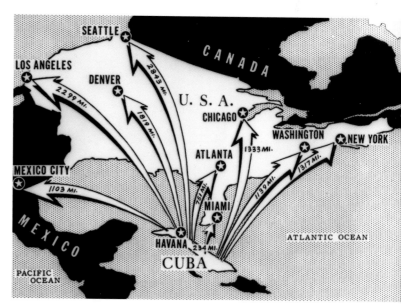

This 1962 map was printed in a newspaper. **What is it showing?**

End of the Cold War

By the 1980s, Europe and Asia had changed a great deal. Western European countries were strong democracies with good economies. But the Soviet Union had problems. Eastern European nations were becoming restless under Soviet leadership. The Soviets could no longer keep up in the arms race.

President Ronald Reagan and Soviet leader Mikhail Gorbachev signed a treaty to do away with many nuclear missiles. Two years later, Soviet troops were withdrawn from Eastern Europe. In the Soviet Union, Gorbachev began to change the economic system and allowed more freedom and democracy. His reforms started moving his country away from communism. Eastern European nations moved in the same direction.

Then the Soviet Union dissolved. Today's Russia took its place. In 1992, Russian President Boris Yeltsin and United States President George H.W. Bush declared that their countries did not consider themselves to be enemies. The Cold War was over.

In space, where the Soviets and Americans had once competed, they now cooperated. In 1998, the United States and Russia started construction of a space station.

New Challenges

The post–Cold War world has seen conflict as well as cooperation. In 1990, Iraq, a country in Southwest Asia, was led by a dictator, Saddam Hussein. Iraq invaded the small country of Kuwait. It claimed that it was taking back land that it had lost.

The United States set a deadline for Iraq to withdraw from Kuwait. When Iraq refused, the United States and many other countries sent many troops to Kuwait. Operation *Desert Storm,* a battle to free Kuwait, started. The Iraqi troops were forced back. But the United States was disappointed by Iraq's failure to change its leadership. Saddam Hussein remained as Iraq's leader.

Terrorism

There is another problem that the United States has faced since the Cold War ended. *Terrorism* is when people use violence to try to make a government change its policies.

President Ronald Reagan and Soviet leader Mikhail Gorbachev sign the historic agreement to ban intermediate-range nuclear missiles in 1987. Treaties like this one led to the end of the Cold War. **What did Gorbachev do to change his country?**

United States troops hit the ground during the Gulf War in 1991. **What event caused Operation Desert Storm?**

What is Terrorism? Terrorism can take many forms. The violence can be a bombing or a murder or kidnapping, or other things. It can be done by one person alone, a few people working together, or by a network of people working together. Terrorists are not soldiers in a nation's army. They are not usually part of a government force. Instead, they are people who fight on their own. They attack many different targets. Sometimes they attack the military or a government. Sometimes they attack civilians, people who are not in the military.

Why Do Terrorists Do This? Often terrorists are people who want to make a change. That in itself is not bad. But what America does not like is the way terrorists do this. Terrorists do not think that governments and leaders are listening to them. They believe that by blowing up a building, or hurting people, they will make people afraid. When the people are afraid, the people will tell their leaders to listen to what the terrorists say and to do what the terrorists want. But leaders of the United States disagree with terrorists. The leaders do not want any people hurt. The United States believes that there are better ways to solve problems.

It is hard to fight terrorists and stop terrorism. The United States cannot usually fight terrorists like they would another army. Fighting terrorists means that the United States and other governments have to look for

The World Trade Center towers collapsed in New York City after terrorists flew airplanes into the buildings. **What is terrorism?**

terrorists. The government wants to find them and stop them before they hurt people. Terrorism has been around for a long time. It is not new. But recently, fighting terrorism has become our nation's top priority.

September 11, 2001

On September 11, 2001, a terrorist group called al-Qaida (ahl KIE·dah) attacked the United States. Al-Qaida has been led by a man named Osama Bin Laden. Members of this group hijacked, or took over during flight, four large airplanes. They flew two of them into the World Trade Center buildings in New York. These were two of the tallest buildings in the world and many businesses had offices there. The towers burned for a short time and then collapsed.

A third plane was flown into the Pentagon in Washington, D.C. The Pentagon is the headquarters of the armed forces of the United States.

The terrorists were probably going to fly the fourth airplane into another building in Washington. Some passengers, however, struggled with the terrorists. The plane crashed in a Pennsylvania field. Everyone was killed. All together, almost 3,000 people lost their lives in these attacks. President George W. Bush promised to find the terrorists who planned these attacks and punish them.

The War on Terror

Al-Qaida's leaders were hiding in mountains in Afghanistan, far away in Asia. Afghanistan's government knew the terrorists were there but did not do anything about it. American forces invaded Afghanistan to find the terrorists. The United States removed the leaders who were letting terrorists hide there. The United States made sure people knew that it was not attacking the people of Afghanistan. Many terrorists were found, but not all of them. The search for these terrorists and the work to prevent terrorist attacks in the future are called the War on Terror.

The Invasion of Iraq Some leaders in the United States still worried about Saddam Hussein in Iraq. They thought that he was making powerful weapons, like nuclear weapons, that could hurt many people. They were afraid he might work with some of the terrorists. President George W. Bush sent American troops to invade Iraq and remove Saddam Hussein. They did remove Hussein, but they did not find any of the weapons they thought he had. Then after the invasion, the Iraqis began to fight each other. Things turned violent.

The United States and the United Kingdom have tried to help the Iraqis set up a new democratic government. It faces huge challenges. Iraqis are divided ethnically and religiously. More than 100,000 Iraqis have died in the fighting.

American troops stayed there to keep peace. But they often have been attacked by many groups there, including a branch of al-Qaida. By 2007, more than 3,000 United States soldiers have died. Many Americans want their troops to come home, but leaders of the United States have been concerned that if the American forces leave, things in Iraq would get even worse. There have been strong feelings on both sides.

Many Allies

Even though the United States is fighting a new War on Terror, it has many allies around the world. The United States is a member of the United Nations and several other international organizations that help countries try to solve problems before wars start.

As you have studied the history of the United States, you have read that the United States has had conflicts with many nations. You will read more about some of them in other chapters in this book. But although the United States has fought or disagreed with countries like Canada, Mexico, France, the United Kingdom, Japan, China, and Russia, today the United States considers them to be partners. Some, like the British and Canadians, are important allies. All these nations work for peace with the United States because they know that peace is better for their citizens.

LESSON 1 REVIEW

Fact Follow-Up
1. When and how did the Cold War begin?
2. What is the United Nations, and what was its importance in the Cold War?
3. What Soviet leader signed a treaty to do away with many nuclear missiles, and began to change the economic system in the Soviet Union?

Talk About It
1. Why did the Soviet Union and the United States engage in the Cold War?
2. How is terrorism different from the types of threats in the Cold War?
3. Which do you think was more dangerous: the Cold War or the threat of terrorism? Explain.

Chapter 12

Ernest Green was the first African American student to graduate from Central High School in Little Rock, Arkansas. After graduation, a reporter asked him about his time there.

In looking through my clippings," Ernest told him, "I think ...the most significant thing was the friendly attitude that students showed toward me on the day of the rioting. The type of thing that was going on outside, people being beaten, cursed, and the mob...we inside the school didn't realize the problems that were occurring...Continually [all the time] students were befriending us.

Desegregation

Ernest Green and nine other African American students made headlines across the United States. They were attending an all-white high school for the first time. There were angry crowds outside the school. President Dwight D. Eisenhower had to send in U.S. Army soldiers to protect them.

Green and the other students were the first to attend Arkansas' segregated schools. For more than 50 years, Southern states had required white and African American students to attend separate, or segregated, schools.

In the 1950s, however, the Supreme Court ruled that segregation violated the Constitution. That meant Green and the others could go to Central High. Having white and African American students go to the same school is called *desegregation.* But the angry people outside wanted to keep the school segregated.

KEY IDEAS

- Laws in the South separated African Americans and whites in public.

- The civil rights movement was a struggle to end unjust laws.

- Dr. Martin Luther King, Jr., led the civil rights Movement

- Civil rights are now protected for all Americans, whatever their race.

KEY TERMS

Brown v. *Board of Education*
bus boycott
civil disobedience
Civil Rights Act
de facto segregation
desegregation
NAACP
Plessy v. *Ferguson*

PEOPLE TO KNOW

Rosa Parks
Martin Luther King, Jr.
Thurgood Marshall
Jackie Robinson

Federal soldiers escort African American students to school in Little Rock, Arkansas, in 1957. **Why were soldiers needed?**

Separate but Not Equal

Do you remember reading about segregation in Chapter 8? Segregation is the separation of people of different races by law. These laws were passed after Reconstruction.

In the late 1800s, a shoemaker named Homer Plessy, an African American, got on a train. He sat in a whites-only passenger car. The railroad had him arrested.

Plessy challenged this in court. He believed that as long as he paid the price of the ticket, he had a right to sit anywhere. In 1896, the Supreme Court heard his case. It was called *Plessy v. Ferguson.*

The Court agreed with Plessy that the Constitution required citizens to be treated equally. But the Court said that if the races were separated, but treated equally, the separation of the races did not go against the Constitution. Plessy v. Ferguson became part of the law allowing segregation.

Life Under Segregation

Under segregation laws African Americans and whites could not go to the same park or playground. They could not eat in the same room at a restaurant. They were not allowed to sit in the same waiting room to see a doctor or to board a train.

These laws also made it illegal for African Americans and whites to do many things together. They could not live in the same neighborhoods, drink water from the same fountains, or even ride in the same elevator.

People could easily see that the things that African Americans had to use were not equal. Where there were two drinking fountains, the one for whites was better. Whites sat in front of the screen in movie theaters. African Americans watched films from the balcony.

Southern states set up two school systems. One was for whites. The other was for African Americans. This kept the races apart, but the schools were almost never equal.

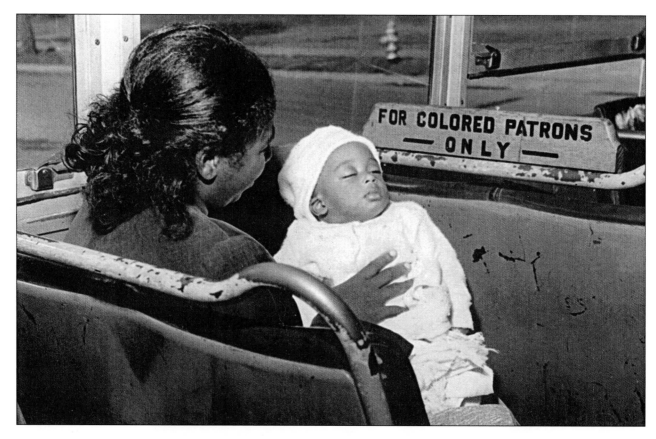

Prior to the civil rights movement, African Americans were made to feel inferior to whites because of things like restricted seating on buses and in theaters. **What is segregation?**

The school buildings for white students were better than those for African Americans. African American schools received less money for supplies. When white schools bought new textbooks, the old ones were sent to African American schools.

NAACP

A group of African American and white leaders decided that segregation must end. They set up the National Association for the Advancement of Colored People (**NAACP**). The NAACP attacked segregation. It showed that separate but equal did not work.

The NAACP showed the Supreme Court that things like colleges, court trials, and other programs were not always equal for both whites and African Americans. Everything that was supposed to be equal had to be examined to see if it was really equal to what whites' had. They examined colleges, court trials, law schools, and voting rights to see if they were really equal or fair.

The court began to agree with the NAACP. So the NAACP decided to show the court that the schools were not equal.

Changing the Law

Oliver Brown and his family lived in Topeka, Kansas. His daughter Linda, a third grader, went to a segregated school. To get to school, she had to walk a long distance and cross railroad tracks. Linda lived near an all-white school. Her father wanted her to go there.

Brown went to the NAACP. The lawsuit against the school system was called *Brown v. Board of Education.*

An Important Decision

Thurgood Marshall argued the family's case to the Supreme Court. Marshall was a smart lawyer. He would later become the first African American to serve on the United States Supreme Court.

Thurgood Marshall argued that segregation caused unequal treatment of African Americans. **What case did he win that declared school segregation illegal?**

In *Brown* v. *Board of Education*, the Supreme Court decided that having separate schools for different races was wrong. The court said that even if the buildings and supplies were made the same, white children would feel that they were better than African Americans because they were separated. The court also said that some African American children would feel that something was wrong with them.

The court decided that segregation laws went against the Constitution. The court ordered states to end segregation in education. But ending segregation was a very slow process. It took many people more than a decade to make changes.

Breaking Other Barriers

The *Brown* case showed that challenging segregation in court was a good way to end other segregation laws. For example, laws in the South made buses have different seats for whites and African Americans. These unfair laws were challenged by Rosa Parks.

Montgomery Bus Boycott

African Americans had to sit in the back of city buses. If the white section filled up, African Americans had to give their seats to whites. Then they had to stand.

Rosa Parks lived in Montgomery, Alabama. She worked in a tailor shop. One night in 1955, Parks was riding a bus home from work. She sat in the African American section. When the white section filled up, the driver ordered her to give up her seat. She was tired from a hard day at work. When she refused to move, the police arrested her.

A young man, Dr. Martin Luther King, Jr., was a minister at a church in Montgomery. He helped the African American citizens decide what to do. They started a *bus boycott.* They refused to ride the buses until the seating policy changed.

This was a great sacrifice. Instead of taking the bus, people walked or drove. But many poor African Americans did not have cars. So they carpooled, or got rides with,

WORD ORIGINS

In a **boycott**, people stop doing business with a person or group. They want a change to be made. The word comes from the name of Captain C. C. Boycott. He was a landowner in Ireland during the nineteenth century. The people who rented and worked on his land wanted a fair rent. So they stopped working for him. They would not serve him in stores. Today, boycotts are a form of nonviolent protest.

others who had cars. Some whites also helped by giving African Americans rides.

The boycott made the white leaders of the city and the bus company angry. The leaders did not like that the African Americans were fighting the law. The bus company was upset because they were losing a lot of money. But they learned that African Americans, working together, had power. The African Americans learned this about themselves, too.

The boycott lasted for a year. African American leaders took the city to court. The Supreme Court agreed that the law separating the races on buses was unconstitutional.

After this decision, the city agreed to hire African American bus drivers. It also let whites and African Americans sit wherever they liked on buses.

Dr. Martin Luther King, Jr.

In Montgomery, Dr. King introduced his ideas of *civil disobedience.* Civil disobedience is a nonviolent protest against unjust laws. It was not a new idea. But Dr. King wanted to try using it to get justice and equal treatment for African Americans. It became a powerful tool.

Dr. King suggested that his followers join together in large groups. Then the group would break a law that they believed to be wrong. Instead of resisting the police when

Rosa Parks (right) rode a bus in Montgomery, Alabama, in 1955, and started the civil rights movement. **Does it make a difference when one person stands up for what he or she thinks is right?**

they were arrested, they would go to jail peacefully. Dr. King knew that when hundreds of African Americans showed they would rather go to jail than live under laws that were wrong, the American public would become angry. Americans would demand that the laws be changed. This, Dr. King thought, would be the best way to end segregation.

After the bus boycott, he helped organize other protests. Almost 10 years later, he won the Nobel Prize for his leadership.

An important group that followed Dr. King's teachings was formed at Shaw University in Raleigh, North Carolina. The Student Nonviolent Coordinating Committee (or SNCC, pronounced "snick") was formed in 1960. Some of its student members had led sit-ins at segregated lunch counters in the South (see the Carolina Connection, below). SNCC's goal was to help people attack segregation and other forms of racism. SNCC helped desegregate buses and register African Americans to vote all over the South.

The Greensboro Sit-in

Four students from North Carolina Agricultural and Technical College made a big impact on the civil rights movement. On February 1, 1960, Ezell Blair, Jr., David Richmond, Joseph McNeil, and Franklin McCain entered the F.W. Woolworth store. They sat on stools in the all-white section of the lunch counter and asked to be served.

The men thought they would be arrested, but they were not. They were not served either.

The next day, they went back. Others joined them. The students sat from 11 A.M. until 3 P.M. Again, they were not served. They went back the next day. So many students went with them that they filled all the seats in the store. But they were still not served.

By the end of the first week, more than 1,000 students were protesting segregation in Greensboro. By the end of February, the sit-in movement had spread to 15 cities in five states. By the end of March, the sit-in movement had spread to 54 cities in 12 states.

AMERICAN PORTRAIT

Martin Luther King, Jr.
1929–1968

Dr. Martin Luther King, Jr., was the most famous leader of the civil rights movement. He was also a Baptist minister. He and his wife Coretta Scott King had four children.

Dr. King helped start the Southern Christian Leadership Conference (SCLC). This group helped African American churches in the South lead nonviolent protests. These protests were part of the civil rights movement.

Dr. King followed the example of nonviolent civil disobedience used by Mahatma Gandhi in India. Gandhi had used nonviolent protest to force the British to withdraw from India. King used these teachings in the SCLC's protests.

All over the South, and in several northern cities, Dr. King led marches for the right to vote, desegregation, and other civil rights. Dr. King gave his famous "I Have a Dream" speech on the steps of the Lincoln Memorial, in Washington, D.C., in 1963. He was awarded the 1964 Nobel Peace Prize for his work.

Dr. King was assassinated in 1968. Three-hundred-thousand people attended his funeral. Each January, we honor Dr. King and all he achieved on Martin Luther King, Jr. Day.

A National Movement

In the North, segregation existed, but it was not usually because a law required separation. Instead, segregation was based upon people's prejudices. For example, if an African American family moved into a neighborhood, the whites would all move away. Or a company would just not hire an African American person to do certain jobs, even though the person was able to do the job well. This kind of segregation is called *de facto segregation.*

Major league baseball was segregated this way. In 1947, Jackie Robinson became the first African American to play baseball on a major league team. He desegregated baseball. This led to the desegregation of other sports and activities.

In 1963, more than 200,000 African Americans and whites gathered in Washington, D.C., to demand racial equality. It was here that Dr. King delivered his ringing "I Have a Dream" speech of hope. His dream, Dr. King said, was that the day would come when a person would be judged by how he behaves and not by the color of his skin.

In 1964, Congress passed the *Civil Rights Act.* This law ended segregation. In 1965, Congress passed the Voting Rights Act. This made it against the law to to not let someone vote because of race.

Jackie Robinson played for the Brooklyn Dodgers and today is in the Baseball Hall of Fame. **How did Jackie Robinson help end segregation?**

LESSON 2 REVIEW

Fact Follow-Up
1. What was the importance of the case of *Plessy* v. *Ferguson* in 1896?
2. How did the NAACP attack segregation?
3. What was the Montgomery bus boycott?
4. In what city did the sit-ins against racial discrimination begin?
5. What is civil disobendience?

Talk About It
1. What was the difference between the racial segregation permitted because of the *Plessy* v. *Ferguson* decision and *de facto* segregation?
2. How could the Soviet Union have used racial segregation as propaganda in the competition with the United States during the Cold War?

Recently, Julie, Biff, and their two-year-old son moved from Chapel Hill, North Carolina, to Salt Lake City, Utah. They will live there for three years while Julie finishes her studies.

Julie will be a pediatrician. Pediatricians are doctors who care for young people. In Utah, she is working at a children's hospital. There she will learn to care for young people who are seriously ill.

Julie is an example of just one of the changes that has taken place in America since the end of World War II. As you have read, the Cold War and the civil rights movement were important. But other key things have shaped our life in the twenty-first century.

Rights for Women

Julie is one of the millions of women who work full-time. Today, a woman may be a teacher, firefighter, governor, reporter, president of a big company, nurse, chief of police, sailor, truck driver, electrical engineer, or general in the army.

This is a recent change in the lives of Americans. Before World War II, women who worked outside the home could only choose from a few types of jobs. They usually became store clerks, factory workers, nurses, secretaries, or teachers. Most other jobs were thought of as "men's work."

Television in the 1950s often portrayed family life in traditional ways with two parents, a stay-at-home-mom, and obedient children. **Does television portray family life in similar ways today?**

America Since 1945

THE WOMEN'S MOVEMENT

During the nineteenth century, women in the United States did not have many rights. They could not vote. Only a few colleges would accept them. Women could not work in certain jobs. Therefore women began to work together to fight for equal rights.

Elizabeth Cady Stanton joined Lucia Mott and many others to work for women's equality. They met in Seneca Falls, New York, in 1848. The women wrote their beliefs in words that reminded readers of the Declaration of Independence. "We hold these truths to be self-evident: that all men and women are created equal."

Elizabeth Cady Stanton

For more than 70 years after that meeting, women struggled to gain the right to vote. Finally, in 1920, the Fifteenth Amendment to the Constitution was ratified. This gave women the right to vote. Now female political candidates are common. Women are mayors, governors, and senators. Nancy Pelosi became the first female Speaker of the House of Representatives in 2007.

Women demonstrating for the right to vote, 1911

W omen have made great strides in education and work. In times of war, women did the jobs that were held by men. During World War II "Rosie the Riveter" was the symbol of women working in factories that made things for the war.

The more WOMEN at work the sooner we WIN!

WOMEN ARE NEEDED ALSO AS:

FARM WORKERS   WAITRESSES   TIMEKEEPERS   LAUNDRESSES
TYPISTS   BUS DRIVERS   ELEVATOR OPERATORS TEACHERS
SALESPEOPLE   TAXI DRIVERS MESSENGERS   CONDUCTORS
                             — and in hundreds of other war jobs!

SEE YOUR LOCAL U.S. EMPLOYMENT SERVICE

Equal Rights Amendment support rally

D uring the 1960s and 1970s, many women supported an Equal Rights Amendment (ERA). The ERA would grant equality under the Constitution. The ERA was not ratified, but women continued to make progress. More and more women go to college. Many women choose to work outside the home.

Equal Rights Amendment button

S ince the 1960s, new laws protect and help women. Under **affirmative action** laws, employers who receive money from the federal government must hire a certain number of women and minorities. The Family Leave Act of 1993 made it possible for women to care for a new baby or for sick family members without losing their jobs.

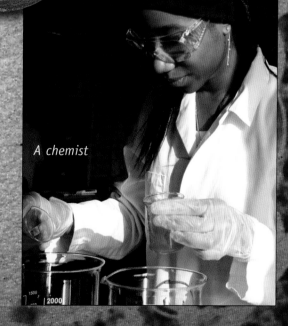

A chemist

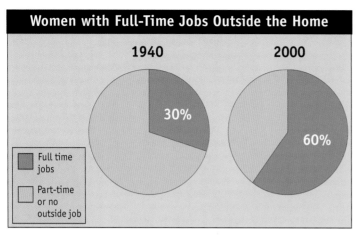

Women with Full-Time Jobs Outside the Home

1940   2000

30%   60%

Full time jobs

Part-time or no outside job

These pie charts show the number of women who had full-time jobs in 1940 and 2000. **What led to this change?**

Working Outside the Home

Look at the pie charts. Since the start of World War II, the number of women who work outside their homes grew by 60 percent. Part of this growth was mothers with children younger than eighteen years old. Some of these children are cared for by fathers who stay at home. Some are cared for by grandparents. Some go to day care.

It took many years for these changes to take place. Your parents and grandparents probably know an old saying: "A woman's place is in the home." This saying reflects an older tradition. Earlier, most Americans lived

Today, women do the same jobs as men. **How has this changed society?**

on farms or in small towns. We call these places *rural.* Rural means in the country, away from cities.

"Keeping House"

Homes did not have machines like vacuum cleaners, clothes washers and dryers, gas or electric stoves, or microwave ovens. Caring for a home and family was a lot of work.

In addition to running a farm, a husband might split wood or carry coal for the stoves. Older children had assigned chores. They might empty ashes from the stoves or feed the chickens.

Without cars or grocery stores, families had to grow and make most of their food. Women tended vegetable gardens. They canned vegetables and fruits so the family would have more food in the winter. Although things like flour and sugar may have been bought at a store, bread was baked at home. Making meals took a lot of time each day.

Women in Careers

As you have read, these rural ways of life began to disappear. Girls and boys went to school instead of working to help the family. More people moved to cities. Cities are *urban* areas.

During World War I and World War II, many women took jobs to help the war efforts. Industries needed them to replace men that had been drafted. Many women realized that they liked working. Women found that they could do the same work as men.

More women went on to college, too. Now they had the education needed for jobs like doctors, lawyers, and engineers.

By the 1970s and 1980s, many young women began to think of building careers. They no longer thought of working as something to do until they married. Women are much more independent today. If they marry, many combine marriage and children with their jobs.

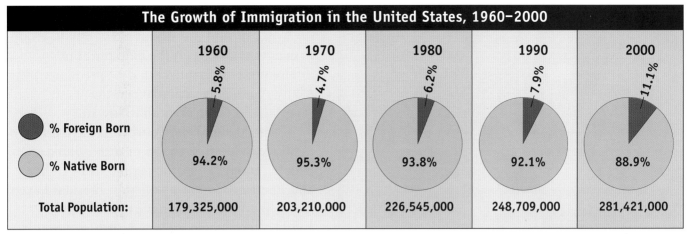

The Growth of Immigration in the United States, 1960–2000

	1960	1970	1980	1990	2000
% Foreign Born / % Native Born	5.8% / 94.2%	4.7% / 95.3%	6.2% / 93.8%	7.9% / 92.1%	11.1% / 88.9%
Total Population:	179,325,000	203,210,000	226,545,000	248,709,000	281,421,000

These pie charts show how the percentage of immigrants in the United States has increased. **Why are people coming to the United States today?**

Changing Families

Many women decided that they liked working. They did not feel that they had to get married to have a full life.

Many of today's families are different from the families people watched on TV in the 1950s, with a mom who stayed home, a dad who worked, and children. Now, it is common for children to have two parents who work. Some families are headed by only a working mother. Some are headed by only a working father. Some children live with their grandparents. But what is the same is that families love and support their children in the best way they can.

Some Americans—both men and women—did not agree that women should work when their children are young. But, as you have read, the women's movement has changed American life. It has already changed the nation's family patterns. It has also added a great deal of talent to the nation's workforce.

Changing Population

In October 2006, the U.S. Census Bureau estimated the number of Americans to be 300,000,000 (see Eyewitness to History, page 330). The number of Americans has grown by about 50 million people since 1990. The United States is one of only three countries in the world with more than 300 million people. The population will likely hit 400 million in 2043.

Our population is growing because people are being born in the United States at a faster rate than people are dying. It is estimated that a child is born every seven seconds, but someone dies only every 13 seconds.

Immigration also plays a role. The Census Bureau estimates that a new immigrant comes here every 31 seconds.

Top 10 Foreign-Born Populations in the United States, 2010*	
Mexico	23.7%
China	4.7%
Philippines	4.2%
India	4.0%
Vietnam	3.0%
El Salvador	2.7%
Cuba	2.7%
Dominican Republic	2.3%
Canada	2.3%
Korea	2.2%
*U.S. Census Bureau projection based upon 2000 U.S. Census and 2004 Yearbook of Immigrant Statistics	

These are the top ten nations from where many of today's immigrants come. **Why do you think so many people come from Mexico?**

America Since 1945

Hispanic business executives chat at a meeting. **Why do people from other countries see the United States as the "land of opportunity"?**

New Immigrants

Over time, America's *ethnic* make-up, or the nationalities, races and religions of people, has changed. Americans are also living longer. These things have changed our culture.

Do you remember reading about immigration in Chapter 10? About 100 years ago, the immigration laws were changed. Immigration from Asia and Eastern Europe was limited.

These laws were changed again after World War II. The doors opened once again to all Europeans, Asians, Africans, and Hispanic people from Latin America.

About 1 million immigrants arrive every year. Look at the table and chart on page 307. It shows the percentage of people living in the United States who are immigrants (were born in foreign countries). It lists the top ten countries they left. Some new immigrants are *refugees.* They come because things were not safe in their homelands. Many have been persecuted for their political beliefs.

Hispanics More than half of all immigrants today are Hispanic. In 2005, the Hispanic population became the nation's largest ethnic group. Hispanics made up about 14 percent of the total population.

Making Homes

You can find just about every ethnic group in every major city in the country. But different ethnic groups are not spread evenly. Many Asian Americans live in the West, especially in California and Hawaii.

California and the Southwest have for many years been home to most Hispanic people. Today, Hispanic people from Cuba and Puerto Rico have settled in Florida. Large numbers of Mexicans have moved into southeastern states such as North and South Carolina. The Midwest has attracted the fewest new immigrants.

The new immigrants are like those who came earlier. They come for a better life. They come for good jobs or better educations. They help our society grow.

An Aging America

There is another important thing to know about America's population. It is getting older. In 2003, about 36 million Americans were over the age of 65. Experts estimate that number will double in the next 30 years.

Why is this happening? We live safer, healthier lives in many ways than people did before World War II. We have better medicines and eat healthier foods. Today, people live about 30 years longer than they did a century ago.

New Technology

When Julie and Biff moved to Utah, Biff did not need to look for a new job. Computer technology has allowed him to work in Utah for his company in North Carolina. Computers are another big change in American life.

Early computers made just after World War II were the size of a large room. They used as much power as a few thousand of today's laptop computers. Now, computers are small enough to fit into a watch or cellular phone. Today's personal computers, or PCs, were invented in the early 1970s. PCs have gotten much more powerful and faster since then.

Bill Gates and Paul Allen wrote the first software for the modern PC. They founded the company Microsoft. Companies like IBM, Dell, and Hewlett-Packard have grown very large making computer hardware.

TVs and PCs Today

New technologies, like PCs, cell phones, and televisions have changed American life since the end of World War II. They all help us communicate with one another.

Television was first developed in the 1930s, but it did not become popular until after World War II. Now, almost all American homes have a TV set. First, TV was only black and white, then came color. Today, a new type of television has come into our homes. Called HDTV, it has a bigger and better picture than TVs of the past.

Television changed the way we learn about the world around us. People were able to watch civil rights marches and images from the Vietnam War right in their living rooms. People could decide for themselves what they thought about these events. Today, a similar change is taking place because of the Internet.

The Internet

Imagine you just scored a goal in your soccer match. Your friend takes a picture of you with his cell phone, and e-mails it to another friend. This is all made possible by computers and the *Internet.* The Internet is a network of connected computers from all over the world. We can use a PC or a cell phone to connect to it. We can instantly share information, pictures, music, video, and data across thousands of miles.

The Internet is a powerful resource. People use it to shop, take classes, chat with friends, and listen to music or watch movies. The people who wrote this textbook used the

"Telecommuting" has made it possible for many people to work from home. **How is technology changing the way people work?**

Internet to research information around the world.

Now telecommuters like Biff have more choices because of technology. Some people telecommute so they can live where they want or need to, like Biff. Others telecommute to be able to be at home with children during the day. Americans use technology to better balance work and family life.

Together, computers and the Internet have already changed the ways Americans work and play. Many more changes will come in the future.

Customs

Since the 1970s, American families have been using personal computers in their homes. These PCs are as powerful as the machines that used to take up a whole room.

People use these PCs to connect to the Internet. Americans write to their families and friends by e-mail, do homework, and shop online.

Energy for America

Americans drove big cars in the 1950s. Big cars used a lot of gasoline, a product made from oil and also a source of energy. Oil is one of our natural resources. Because the United States had enough, or a good *supply* of oil, it did not cost much to buy. As long as gasoline did not cost a lot of money, Americans could afford to drive big cars.

Americans knew their country was rich in natural resources. Many could not imagine a day when it would be hard to get gas for their car. They believed that our country had more than enough oil, or a *surplus,* to last a very long time. But natural resources are not endless. They are limited. More and more

A Journey to WATERGATE

Keeping Government Honest

Some people make poor choices, like lying or cheating. If a leader like the president lies or cheats, then people feel they cannot trust their government. This is what happened in the Watergate scandal.

President Richard Nixon was a Republican. He worried that he would not win re-election. People working for his campaign hired five men to break into the Democratic Party's office. They were looking for information that might help President Nixon win. This was against the law.

The men, called burglars, were discovered and arrested. The office the burglars broke into was in the Watergate Building, so the scandal was called "Watergate."

Two reporters working for the *Washington Post* started looking into the burglars' backgrounds. They

President Richard M. Nixon

found a connection between the burglars and people working at the White House. The reporters wrote about this in the paper.

The Senate thought that this was a serious problem. They set up hearings to look into the events. Senator Sam Ervin from North Carolina led the hearings. Americans watched on TV as people who worked for President Nixon told what they knew.

It became clear that many important people who worked with the president, and probably the president, too, had broken the law and then lied about it. Americans were upset that their leaders had done this.

In 1974, President Nixon resigned, or left, the presidency before he could be charged with a crime. He is the only president to resign. Several people who worked for him went to jail.

Americans do not trust their government as they once did. But some good things did come from Watergate. Today, laws make it easier to get information about our government. Reporters watch our leaders closely to make sure they are honest in their work. Watergate shows how it is important for citizens to pay attention to government and not to be afraid to ask questions.

Americans used gasoline in their cars and oil to heat their homes and businesses. Trucks and trains used fuels that also came from oil. This increased *demand,* or the amount people needed and wanted to use. The amount of oil resources decreased. America began to buy more and more oil from other countries.

The Energy Crisis

In the early 1970s, some of these nations began to cut back on the amount of oil it sold to the United States. They also raised their prices. This caused big problems. Oil and the fuels made from it were now scarce. Many people needed these fuels. This demand made the price go way up. *Scarcity* is when there is not enough supply to meet demand.

First, there were huge shortages of oil and all products, such as gasoline, that were made from oil. Gasoline had to be rationed. Drivers of cars that had license tags ending with an odd number could buy gas only on odd-numbered days of the month. Drivers of cars with even-numbered tags were allowed to purchase fuel only on even-numbered days.

Power companies that used oil to make electricity had to charge more for the electricity. In turn, things that used electricity, like factories, had to charge more for the goods they made. Trucks and trains needed fuel to transport goods. The higher cost of fuel was added to the cost of the goods.

Conservation

The government also wanted people to start to save, or *conserve,* energy. People turned off lights they were not using. To use less fuel, a speed limit was put on all highways. Driving slower used less gas. New cars were smaller and used less gas, too.

America began to look for new types of energy. Hydropower (power from water), nuclear power, solar (sun power), and wind power are energy sources that have begun to be used more and more. Today, the United States is still looking for new sources of energy and better ways to use solar and wind power.

People waited in long lines to get gas during the energy crisis in the 1970s. **What does scarcity mean?**

LESSON 3 REVIEW

Fact Follow-Up
1. How have job opportunities for women changed over the last 60 or 70 years?
2. In 2000, what percentage of women were working in full-time jobs?
3. Why have Americans been looking for new types of energy?

Talk About It
1. Why do you think women's opportunities for work have increased? Explain.
2. How is the new immigration similar to and different from the older immigration?
3. How did having less oil and gasoline make everything more expensive in the 1970s?

skill

Accessing a Variety of Sources; Gathering, Synthesizing, and Reporting Information

Organizing Information

In the last century, the United States made several alliances. Some of them were made to fight wars. Others were made to keep peace. Still others were made to help the economies of the partners.

Remember the Monroe Doctrine? It warned European powers to stay out of the countries in the Western Hemisphere. Since then, the United States has been involved in many world affairs.

A simple graphic organizer, like the one on the bottom of page 313, will help you keep track of these alliances. A timeline (below) is another way to track alliances. So is the flow chart (right).

To fill in the graphic organizer, you will need to use information from several chapters in this book. You might even use other sources such as an encyclopedia or the Internet.

Once you have filled in your table, you will be ready to discuss America's alliances. You will answer such questions as these:

- Have we participated more in military or peaceful alliances?
- With which countries have we mostly been allied?
- What countries have we been allied against?
- Have we ever been allied with former enemies? If so, which enemies have become allies?
- Which alliances seem to have been most effective?
- Which alliances seem to have been least successful?

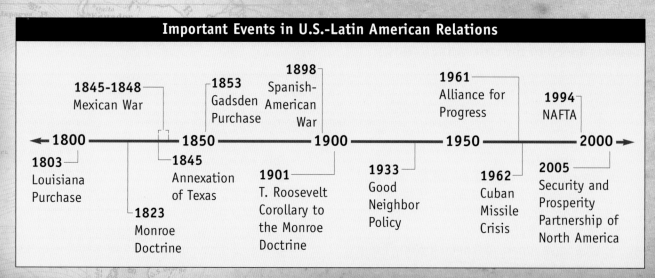

Important Events in U.S.-Latin American Relations

- **1803** Louisiana Purchase
- **1845-1848** Mexican War
- **1845** Annexation of Texas
- **1823** Monroe Doctrine
- **1853** Gadsden Purchase
- **1898** Spanish-American War
- **1901** T. Roosevelt Corollary to the Monroe Doctrine
- **1933** Good Neighbor Policy
- **1961** Alliance for Progress
- **1962** Cuban Missile Crisis
- **1994** NAFTA
- **2005** Security and Prosperity Partnership of North America

← 1800 — 1850 — 1900 — 1950 — 2000 →

U.S.-Latin American Relations Flow Chart

Adding Territories

Louisiana Purchase
Gadsden Purchase
Annexation of Texas

Conflicts

Mexican War
Spanish-American War
Cuban Missile Crisis

Policies

Monroe Doctrine
Roosevelt Corollary
Good Neighbor
Alliance for Progress

U.S. — Latin America Relations

Partnerships

NAFTA
Security and Prosperity
 Partnership

Issues

Immigration
Terrorism / Security

United States Alliances

Alliance	When Started	When Ended	Nations Involved	Purposes

Lessons Learned

LESSON 1
The United States in World Affairs
After World War II, the United States fought the Cold War with the Soviet Union. The United States has a long history of relationships with Latin America. Since the end of the Cold War, the United States has been concerned more and more with terrorism.

LESSON 2
Justice at Home
In the nineteenth century, segregation laws kept blacks and whites apart. During the 1950s and 1960s, African American leader Dr. Martin Luther King, Jr., led a movement to end segregation. The Civil Rights Act now protects all citizens.

LESSON 3
A Changing Society
Women have entered the workforce in large numbers. Many new immigrants are coming to the United States. Computers have made great changes in the way we live. The energy crisis made Americans conserve energy.

Talk About It

1. Why was the Cold War so very dangerous?
2. Which action do you think was more important in ending segregation and racial discrimination—the legal approach of the NAACP or civil disobedience? Explain your answer.
3. Three heroes of the civil rights movement—Rosa Parks, Thurgood Marshall, and Dr. Martin Luther King, Jr.—are mentioned in this chapter. Which do you think was the greatest leader? Explain why.
4. Do you think the saying "A man works from sun to sun, but a woman's work is never done" is still true today? Explain your answer.
5. How have new inventions changed the ways people work in the United States?

Mastering Mapwork

LOCATION
Use the map on page 291 to answer these questions:
1. Which two NATO nations are in North America?
2. Looking at this map, why do you think this alliance is called the North Atlantic Treaty Organization?
3. Which NATO nations are partly or totally located south of 45°N?
4. Which Warsaw Pact nation is completely located west of 15°E?
5. Which four NATO nations have land above 60°N?

Becoming Better Readers

More on Bias
Every person has a different viewpoint on important issues. A viewpoint is the way someone thinks about something. Someone's viewpoint is affected by where they live, how they were raised, by their education, and many other factors. This chapter is about many differing viewpoints. Choose one issue mentioned in this chapter and write your viewpoint on the issue.

Go to the Source

Analyzing a Speech

The Reverend Dr. Martin Luther King, Jr., gave his "I Have a Dream" speech on August 28, 1963, at the Lincoln Memorial in Washington D.C. He spoke to 250,000 who had gathered in support of the civil rights movement. Read the passage below and answer the questions with information from the document.

Five score (100) years ago, a great American, in whose symbolic shadow we stand today, signed the Emancipation Proclamation. This momentous decree came as a great beacon light of hope to millions of Negro slaves . . . It came as a joyous daybreak to end the long night of their captivity.

But one hundred years later, the Negro still is not free. . . .

And so even though we face the difficulties of today and tomorrow, I still have a dream. It is a dream deeply rooted in the American dream.

I have a dream that one day this nation will rise up and live out the true meaning of its creed: "We hold these truths to be self-evident, that all men are created equal."

I have a dream that one day on the red hills of Georgia, the sons of former slaves and the sons of former slave owners will be able to sit down together at the table of brotherhood.

I have a dream that one day even the state of Mississippi, a state sweltering with the heat of injustice, sweltering with the heat of oppression, will be transformed into an oasis of freedom and justice.

I have a dream that my four little children will one day live in a nation where they will not be judged by the color of their skin but by the content of their character.

I have a dream today!

I have a dream that one day, down in Alabama. . . .little black boys and black girls will be able to join hands with little white boys and white girls as sisters and brothers.

I have a dream today!

_____

Questions
1. What is the effect of Dr. Martin Luther King, Jr.'s repetition of the phrase, "I Have a Dream"?
2. Based on the text of the speech do you think Dr. King's dream has come true? Why or Why not?
3. What is the tone/mood of the speech?
4. Based on the speech, what characteristic would best describe Dr. King?

Unit 4

One flag, one land,
one heart, one hand,
One nation, evermore!

Oliver Wendell Holmes wrote this to describe the unity of our nation. These fifth graders are raising the flag on a beautiful spring morning. They are saying the Pledge of Allegiance. When they do actions like these, they are joining Oliver Wendell Holmes. They are showing their loyalty to our country.

Fifth graders raise the flag at a Raleigh public school.

Our Nation Today

A Rich Land

President Eisenhower initiates the national highway system.

Dwight D. Eisenhower was commander of Allied forces in World War II. He later became president of the United States. Eisenhower learned from the war the importance of a good transportation system. He asked Congress to build the Interstate Highway System. This cost billions of dollars. Today, the highways have paid for themselves. They have helped our economy grow.

These highways connect the resources and businesses of the United States. On the highway you can see trucks carrying goods—like the one belonging to Jim in Chapter 1. You can see the varied landforms and vegetation of our nation. You can also see the ways in which Americans have changed the land.

Chapter Preview

LESSON 1
A Vast and Varied Land
All of the types of climates can be found in the United States. The land is rich in vegetation and resources.

LESSON 2
Modern Economy and Agriculture
The United States economy is based on free enterprise. American industries trade with partners throughout the world.

LESSON 3
Promises and Problems
Americans have good health care, education, and quality of life. But Americans face many challenges, too.

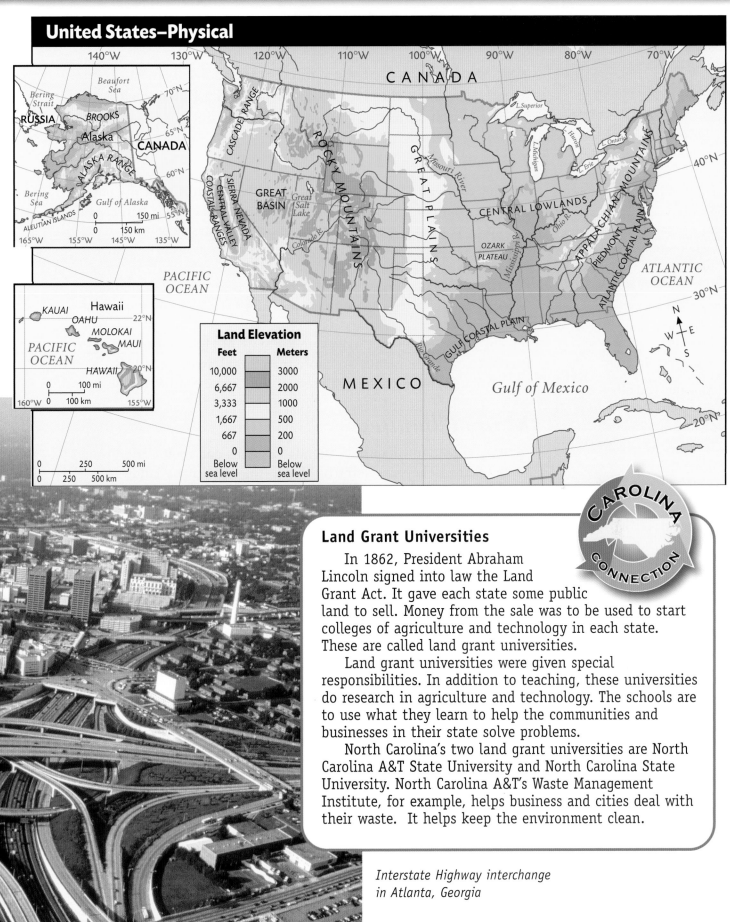

United States–Physical

Land Elevation

Feet	Meters
10,000	3000
6,667	2000
3,333	1000
1,667	500
667	200
0	0
Below sea level	Below sea level

Land Grant Universities

In 1862, President Abraham Lincoln signed into law the Land Grant Act. It gave each state some public land to sell. Money from the sale was to be used to start colleges of agriculture and technology in each state. These are called land grant universities.

Land grant universities were given special responsibilities. In addition to teaching, these universities do research in agriculture and technology. The schools are to use what they learn to help the communities and businesses in their state solve problems.

North Carolina's two land grant universities are North Carolina A&T State University and North Carolina State University. North Carolina A&T's Waste Management Institute, for example, helps business and cities deal with their waste. It helps keep the environment clean.

Interstate Highway interchange in Atlanta, Georgia

You know that the United States has 50 states. Forty-eight of these states are contiguous. That means that each state touches at least one other state.

Locating the United States

The *contiguous* states are located on the North American continent. They are south of Canada and north of Mexico. They are bordered by the Atlantic Ocean to the east and the Pacific Ocean to the west.

Two states, Alaska and Hawaii, are not contiguous. The state of Alaska is north of the contiguous states. It borders Canada on the east and the Pacific Ocean on the south. To the west is the Bering Sea, and the Arctic Ocean is to the north. Alaskans call the contiguous states "the lower forty-eight."

The island group that makes up the state of Hawaii is found in the Pacific Ocean. The islands are more than 2,000 miles (3,220 km) west of California. Hawaiians often call rest of the United States "the mainland."

Many Climates

As you read in Chapter 1, Brendan and his dad took a trip around the United States. They saw some of North America's many landforms. There are many climates, too.

Climate, you remember, means all the weather conditions in an area over a long period of time. The average temperatures for various seasons are part of a place's climate. So is average rainfall, snowfall, and humidity.

All the world's climate types are found in the United States. No other nation has so many.

Summers in Florida are hot and humid (right). This snowboarder shows off his skill (far right). **What kind of climate does Florida have? What kind of climate allows snowboarding?**

What Affects Climate?

Look at the map on page 45. It shows the different climates of the United States. As you learned in Chapter 3, there are three major things that influence a place's climate. One is its nearness to the Equator. Another is landforms, like mountains. The third is its nearness to large bodies of water, like oceans.

In general, the part of a country that is farthest from the oceans has colder winters and hotter summers. Large bodies of water, such as oceans, can make climates milder.

San Francisco, California, and Kansas City, Missouri, are about the same distance from the Equator. But San Francisco is much warmer in winter and cooler in summer. That is because San Francisco is on the shore of the Pacific Ocean.

The climate becomes warmer as you move closer to the Equator. So Arkansas is usually warmer than Montana. Elevation is height above the earth's surface. It affects climate, too. It is colder and snowier at higher elevations, like mountain tops, than at lower ones.

Where is Which Climate?

Florida has the hot, humid summers and rainy winters of the humid subtropical climate. So does most of the south. In the North, from the Rockies to the Atlantic, people live in a continental climate. Winters are cold and snowy there. Summers are warm.

In the West, the climate is drier. Many areas receive only a little rainfall in the steppe climate. This dry desert climate is found in the southwestern United States.

Along the southern California coast the climate is Mediterranean. Winters are mild and rainy, and summers are hot and dry. The northern Pacific Coast enjoys a Marine West Coast climate. It is mild and rainy all year.

Most of Alaska has a subarctic climate. Summers are short and winters are long, cold, and snowy. Northern Alaska has a cold tundra climate. There it is cold and dry all year with short, cool summers.

At the tip of Florida and in much of Hawaii, it is hot all year with wet and dry seasons. Here you will find tropical rain forest and tropical savanna climates.

A Rich Land

Vegetation

Climate and soil affect the kinds of trees and plants that can grow in an area. The soils and climates of the United States help create the richest land in the world. Many different types of vegetation grow here.

Trees

Two types of trees grow in the forests of the eastern United States. Deciduous trees, such as maples and oaks, lose their leaves every year. They are amazing in the autumn. Their leaves change from green to gold, red, and orange before falling.

Evergreens stay green all year. The Douglas fir and the spruce thrive in eastern mountains. Other kinds of evergreen trees, especially pine trees, grow well in the Coastal Plain.

Grasses

The natural plant of the Central Plains is grass. If humans did not farm, grasses would cover the area from Iowa all the way westward to Wyoming. They would also cover from Montana and North Dakota southward all the way to Texas.

Prairie grass was a challenge for the first farmers on the plains. But the grass protected the rich soil from erosion. *Erosion* is when the top soil blows away or runs off with the rain. This rich soil provided the rich farmland of the plains states.

Sage and short grass are found in the western desert regions. Cactus plants love the

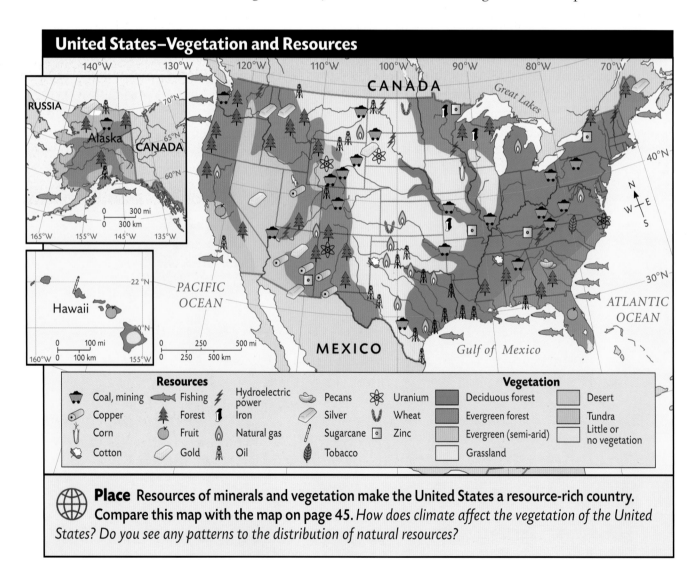

United States—Vegetation and Resources

Resources

- Coal, mining
- Copper
- Corn
- Cotton
- Fishing
- Forest
- Fruit
- Gold
- Hydroelectric power
- Iron
- Natural gas
- Oil
- Pecans
- Silver
- Sugarcane
- Tobacco
- Uranium
- Wheat
- Zinc

Vegetation

- Deciduous forest
- Evergreen forest
- Evergreen (semi-arid)
- Grassland
- Desert
- Tundra
- Little or no vegetation

Place Resources of minerals and vegetation make the United States a resource-rich country. Compare this map with the map on page 45. *How does climate affect the vegetation of the United States? Do you see any patterns to the distribution of natural resources?*

Chapter 13

George Washington Carver
1864–1943

Science Helps Farmers

During the 1900s, scientists and inventors solved problems and invented new products that made life easier. One of these scientists was from Missouri.

George Washington Carver was born at the end of the Civil War. His parents had been slaves. He never knew his father. When Carver was a baby, Confederates kidnapped him and his mother. Moses Carver, his owner, went searching for them. He found only little George.

The Carver family raised George. As he grew, he was often sick. He did not have the strength to work in the fields. Instead, he helped Mrs. Carver in the house and in the garden. He spent his free time outdoors.

Going to School

Mrs. Carver taught George to read and write because there was no school in Diamond for black children. When he got a little older, George left the Carvers and walked to Neosho to go to school. George was very smart and did well in schools.

George spent his teenage years traveling all over the Midwest. He worked and went to school when he could. It was a hard life. Finally, George ended up in Iowa. He became the first African American to graduate from Iowa State University. He was the first African American to teach there, too. Later, he taught at Tuskegee Institute in Alabama. It was a famous school for former slaves and their children.

A Famous Professor

Carver taught at Tuskegee for almost 50 years. He became one of the most famous scientists in the world. He found better ways to grow plants such as peanuts. He found hundreds of uses for peanuts, pecans, soybeans, and sweet potatoes.

Carver also helped people be better farmers. For decades, southern farmers had grown only cotton. This was bad for the soil. It left the soil with few minerals. Carver said farmers should plant cotton one year and peanuts, peas, or soybeans the next year. These crops put minerals back into the soil. His advice saved many farms.

After he became famous, Carver spoke all across the nation. He told young people that all races could get along.

dry conditions of the desert. Arizona chose the bloom of the Saguaro Cactus as its state flower.

Much of Alaska is tundra, a treeless plain. Only a few low-growing plants, such as grasses, lichens, and mosses, are able to survive.

Flowers, vines, and other plants grow in Hawaii. Many are found nowhere else. Some plants once thought to be native to Hawaii, such as coconuts and pineapples, were imported.

Natural Resources

The United States has become an industrial giant. This is partly because its land contains so many different raw materials.

Look at the map. Very few other countries have so many different kinds of resources or as large amounts of them.

A Rich Land

How Do We Get Petroleum?

Petroleum is another word for crude oil. People build large machines to pump oil out of the grown. After drilling to get to the oil, the machines pump the oil to the surface.

1. Workers remove the derrick and set up a pump like this one. Can you see why this is called a "grasshopper pump?"

2. A motor makes the gear box move a lever. This gives the pump power to draw up the oil.

3. The oil is pumped into a pipe at the surface. The pipe moves the oil to tanker trunks. Trucks and barges carry oil to the refinery.

Fossil Fuels

For example, there are three types of *fossil fuels* in the United States. *Petroleum* (the oil you read about in Chapter 12), natural gas, and coal are found in many states. They come from decayed plants and animals from thousands of years ago.

Petroleum is found mainly in Alaska, Texas, Oklahoma, and Louisiana. The country's need for oil is greater than the amount those wells can produce. So America must import oil from other countries.

Minerals

When our nation was young, many raw materials were found in the East. This gave new industries the resources to grow.

As the nation expanded westward, cities were built near places where raw materials could be found. For example, boomtowns sprung up where copper or silver mines were built in places like Arizona. When the metal was gone, people sometimes left. Other towns found new industries upon which to build.

The largest deposits of iron are in Minnesota. Most copper is mined in western states. Both of these minerals can also be found in other parts of the country.

An offshore oil rig pumps crude oil from beneath the Gulf of Mexico. **What is an alternative to fossil fuel for generating power?**

Energy

During the 1900s, electricity became more and more important as an energy source. Much electric power has been generated with fossil fuels.

As the demand for electricity has grown, the nation has turned to its many waterways to make electric power. The water is used to turn electric generators.

If you have visited Fontana Dam in western North Carolina, you have seen how water from a river can generate an endless supply of electricity. Hundreds of dams like Fontana are found throughout the United States.

LESSON 1 REVIEW

Fact Follow-Up

1. Define climate and give examples of differences between climate and weather.
2. What influences determine the climate of an area?
3. Name two types of deciduous trees that grow in the eastern United States.
4. Where are grasslands areas in the United States?
5. Name four minerals or three fossil fuels that have been important to the nation.

Talk About It

1. What can a farmer in Hawaii raise that a farmer in Minnesota cannot?
2. What sports do Minnesota children play that Florida children don't? Why?
3. Why are minerals and fuels important to a nation?
4. How would our resources be different if the nation still had only 13 colonies?
5. What did George Washington Carver do?

A Rich Land

KEY IDEAS

- The United States' economy is a system of free enterprise.

- The economy of the United States includes manufacturing, high-technology, agricultural, and service industries.

- Many industries can produce more goods and services with fewer people.

- American businesses trade with countries all over the world.

KEY TERMS

capital resources
competition
consumers
entreprenuer
export
foreign trade
free enterprise
gross domestic product
human resources
import
mechanized farming
monopoly
scientific farming
service industry
software
telecommuter

Do you remember reading about Julie the doctor in Chapter 12? She, her husband Biff, and their son moved to Utah so Julie could work in a hospital there. Their family has made choices about where to live and how to work. These are economic choices.

America's Economy

Economics is the study of how people get the goods and services they need and want. There are different kinds of economic systems. A traditional economy is one where people grow or make what they need. There is very little trading. Many of the Native American societies you read about in Chapter 4 had traditional economies.

Do you remember reading about the Soviet Union in Chapter 12? It was Communist. In that system, the government decided what people needed and what factories should make. That is a command economy.

The United States has a capitalist economy. Capitalism is a *free enterprise* system. Private citizens, not the government, make the decisions. They can make or buy what they want. People are free to choose how to spend their money and what type of work to do.

Our system also has **competition.** This means that more than one company may make the same item or provide the same service. *Consumers,* people who buy the item or service, have a choice. They can buy the product or service they like best. Companies compete to make the best products. They improve the products they sell to make them better. This helps our economy grow.

Our free enterprise system does have some limits. As you read in Chapter 9, the government passed laws to protect people and the environment. For example, the government limits things like the number of hours a person can work in a day. It also makes sure that places to work are safe, and that the food and drugs we have are safe, too.

The government also wants to make sure that the competition is fair. If one company gets too big and does not allow competition, this is called a **monopoly.** The government makes rules to prevent monopolies.

WORD ORIGINS

Scottish economist Adam Smith wrote in 1776 about a new system of economics. In "An Inquiry into the Nature and Causes of the Wealth of Nations," Smith wrote that wealth is created through **free enterprise**. This would be fair competition among people in the marketplace. He argued for an economy free from government controls.

Using Our Resources

An economy's resources can be placed into three groups: natural, human, and capital. As you read in Lesson 1, the United States is rich in natural resources.

Human Resources

Human resources are the people who do the work, or our workforce. Human resources include truck drivers, teachers, doctors, farmers, and sales clerks.

An educated workforce is an important resource. Today, businesses need educated people to work with computers or complicated machines. To do some jobs, like doctors, nurses, lawyers, or engineers, people need to go to college.

Many people try to learn new skills. That way, they can find a new job if they have to.

Capital Resources

Capital resources are the things people use to make, grow, or deliver goods or services. These include tools, equipment, and buildings. Capital resources may be used over and over during a long period of time without being used up. Trucks, ovens, computers, and desks are capital resources.

Things that are used up in making a product to sell are not capital resources. The nails used to build a bookcase would not be a capital resource. But the hammer used to hit the nails would be a capital resource.

Henry Heinz
1844–1919

Do you like ketchup on your hamburgers? Henry Heinz started in the food business when he was eight years old. He sold extra vegetables from his mother's garden near Pittsburgh, Pennsylvania.

Heinz grew up and formed the H. J. Heinz Company. Starting it made him an *entreprenuer.* Heinz made ketchup, pickles, sauerkraut, and vinegar. Business soared. By the time he started advertising "57 Varieties," the company already sold more than 60 products.

To make sure its foods were top quality, the company owned its own farms. It also owned the factories for processing and packing foods. Heinz packed whatever he could in clear glass bottles, not cans. He wanted people to see the quality of his products.

To make more money, other food manufacturers added fillers. They added chalk to milk and sawdust to bread and hot dogs. Heinz believed this was unsafe and dishonest. He urged Congress to pass the Pure Food and Drug Act, which made this kind of dishonesty against the law.

Heinz also ran his factories differently. He treated workers fairly and paid them well. They got free medical care. They got manicures to keep hands clean for handling food. The factories had special lunchrooms with music and art. Washrooms had hot and cold showers, which most homes did not have at the time.

Henry Heinz started his family's tradition of giving back to the community. He founded the Sarah Heinz House in Pittsburgh. It was a place for immigrant children to go after school to learn English and have fun. It was named for Henry's wife.

Teaching is part of the service industry. **What percentage of workers in the United States are in service jobs?**

The New Economy

Biff's and Julie's jobs are part of big changes taking place in the economy of the United States. Julie's work as a doctor reflects another new trend. She works with patients, helping them get well. In doing this, she is not producing a product. Products come from farms, factories, or mines. Instead, she is providing a service to other people.

Service Industries

The many different kind of jobs that help people are part of the *service industry.* These jobs now make up the largest part of the nation's economy. Schools, law firms, insurance companies, restaurants, real estate firms, and repair shops are a few examples of service industries.

Manufacturing

One of the first industries created during the Industrial Revolution was manufacturing. It is still an important part of our economy. United States factories make products others want to buy, especially automobiles, food products, and chemicals. Sometimes the parts of products are made in other countries, but the final product is assembled in America. This section of our economy is shrinking as more and more things are made overseas.

The construction industry builds all our new buildings: houses, factories, offices, and schools.

High-Technology Industries

The United States is now a world leader in high-technology (high-tech) industries. High-tech industries are businesses that require special systems, such as computers, to make something.

For example, Boeing Aircraft continues to be one of the world's largest makers of large airplanes. IBM, Microsoft, and other companies lead in making computer hardware and software. Companies that research and produce medicines are also part of the high-tech industry.

Agricultural Industries

As you read in Chapter 9, new machines were invented to help farmers grow more crops. Farms grew in size. Machines were needed to run them. *Mechanized farming* is farming that needs machines to do the work.

Scientific farming uses science to improve farming. This has brought great changes. Scientists help farmers get more from their crops. When our nation was young, a farm family could feed itself and three other people. Most people farmed for a living. Today, the number of farms and farmers continues to decrease. But the size of farms is getting larger.

Most jobs require basic computer skills. **Why is education important to finding a job?**

Chapter 13

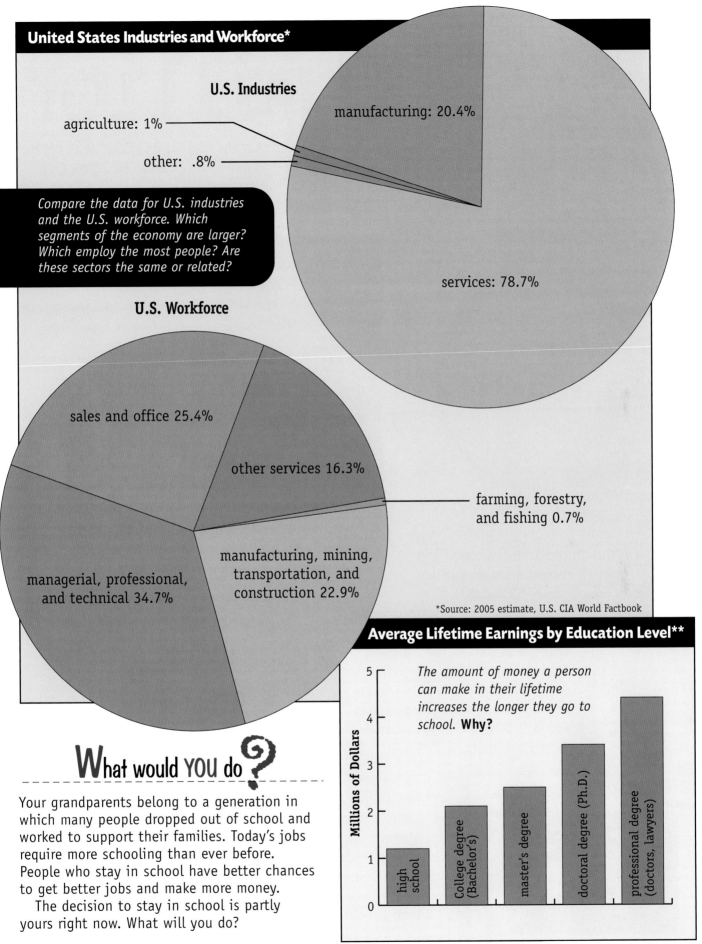

United States Industries and Workforce*

U.S. Industries

agriculture: 1%

other: .8%

manufacturing: 20.4%

services: 78.7%

Compare the data for U.S. industries and the U.S. workforce. Which segments of the economy are larger? Which employ the most people? Are these sectors the same or related?

U.S. Workforce

sales and office 25.4%

other services 16.3%

farming, forestry, and fishing 0.7%

managerial, professional, and technical 34.7%

manufacturing, mining, transportation, and construction 22.9%

*Source: 2005 estimate, U.S. CIA World Factbook

Average Lifetime Earnings by Education Level**

*The amount of money a person can make in their lifetime increases the longer they go to school. **Why?***

Millions of Dollars

- high school
- College degree (Bachelor's)
- master's degree
- doctoral degree (Ph.D.)
- professional degree (doctors, lawyers)

**2002 U.S. Dept. of Commerce

What would YOU do?

Your grandparents belong to a generation in which many people dropped out of school and worked to support their families. Today's jobs require more schooling than ever before. People who stay in school have better chances to get better jobs and make more money.

The decision to stay in school is partly yours right now. What will you do?

A Rich Land

Passing 300 million

EYEWITNESS TO HISTORY

The U.S. Census Bureau estimated that the population of the United States reached the historic milestone of 300 million on October 17, 2006. This happened almost 39 years after the 200 million mark was reached on November 20, 1967.

Immigrants arrive at Ellis Island, New York, 1907

The United States averages one birth every 7 seconds and one death every 13 seconds.

Immigrants arriving and Americans leaving to live overseas were also included as part of the estimate. This movement adds one person every 31 seconds. Together, these numbers mean that one person is added to America's population every 11 seconds.

In 1915, America's population reached 100 million. In 1967 it reached 200 million. Let's compare some figures from these years to 2006.

There are only two other countries with populations larger than the United States. India and China (left) both have more than 1 billion people.

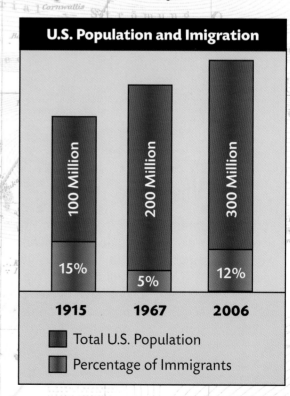

U.S. Population and Imigration

100 Million	200 Million	300 Million
15%	5%	12%
1915	**1967**	**2006**

■ Total U.S. Population
■ Percentage of Immigrants

In 2006 there were 34.3 million immigrants living in the United States. They made up 12 percent of the total population. Most of the immigrants came from Mexico. In 1967 there were 9.7 million immigrants living here. They made up 5 percent of the total population. The most immigrants had come from Italy. In 1915, there were 13.5 million immigrants living here. They made up 15 percent of the total population. The most immigrants had come from Germany.

In 1915, only 13.5 percent of Americans had graduated from high school. By 1967, that number had grown to 51. 1 percent. In 2006, more than 85 percent of Americans graduated from high school.

In 1915, the average life span of an American was 54.5 years. In 1967, it grew to 70.5. In 2006, it was 77.8. Americans are living much longer than they were almost 100 years ago. This affects the number of people who live past 65. In 2006, 36.8 million people were age sixty-five and older. In 1967, 19.1 million people were age sixty-five and older. In 1915, there were only 4.5 million people age sixty-five and older.

Moving Goods, People, and Ideas

Do you remember reading about the importance of ports early in our history? Or how canals and trains moved goods to market? Today, moving people, goods, and ideas is still important to our economy.

America's transportation network is huge. Airplanes, trains, trucks, and ships move people and goods across the country. They also connect us with other countries.

Another way we move things today is with computers. We do not send a package over a computer network or the Internet. But we do send information and ideas.

Some companies use and sell information. Newspapers, magazines, radio, and TV are all businesses that provide information.

Scientists share ideas over the Internet. Sometimes this leads to new products or faster ways of doing things. Sharing infomation has made our economy grow.

People also move. Just like Julie and Biff, people move to where there are jobs. They also move to go to special schools. As people move, they bring new ideas with them.

Our Future

Throughout its history, America's economy has had times of growth and depression. Over the long run, however, the economy has grown.

By 2004, the United States' GDP, or **gross domestic product,** had reached about $10,756 trillion. The GDP is the value of all the goods and services in a nation. America's GDP was the largest in the world. It means that the United States is still a giant in agriculture, manufacturing, the production of natural resources, and newer industries such as services and high-tech.

What will our economy look like in the future? Economists, people who study the economy, tell us that the service industry will be very strong. High-tech businesses will be important.

The United States economy has changed with the times. Once, farms and factories made the economy grow. Today, the service and high-tech industries help make the economy strong. The United States' economy is the world's strongest.

The Interstate System

President Eisenhower is credited with creating the interstate highway system. This idea was talked about for a long time. Eisenhower had traveled across the country as a young Army officer. He went from Washington, D.C., to San Francisco on a series of dirt roads. It took him two months to make the trip.

The United States needed a national interstate system in case the mainland was ever attacked. An uninterrupted system of roads would allow the military to move troops and equipment quickly.

After Eisenhower became president, he convinced Congress to fund the project. The government paid for most of the work. Interstates had to be at least two lanes in each direction. The roads had to handle speeds of 50 to 70 miles (80 to 112 km) per hour. The national system of roads that Eisenhower and others imagined is called the Dwight D. Eisenhower National System of Interstate and Defense Highways.

Million, Billion, Trillion

What does a trillion look like? The United States' economy is measured in trillions of dollars.

A trillion looks like this:
1,000,000,000,000

The U.S. Gross Domstic Product in 2004 was $10,756,000,000,000!!

A container ship unloads in Los Angeles harbor. **What are some of our imports?**

Trading with the World

Foreign trade is the buying and selling of items between the United States and other countries. Look around your house. You will probably find many things made overseas.

What you may not see so easily are the products Americans sell, or *export*. For example, North Carolina exports medicines.

Our nation's biggest exports are transportation equipment, computers, chemicals, plastics, metals, and paper. We also export many agricultural products.

We also *import*, or buy from other countries. America imports many everyday items such as clothing, shoes, and toys. We buy TVs, DVD players, and many of our cars from other nations. We also import oil, iron, steel, other metals, and chemical products. In the winter, much of our fruit and vegetables come from countries with warmer climates.

World Trade

Many large United States buinesses have locations in other countries. General Electric and IBM have offices and factories worldwide. In turn, foreign-owned companies have opened offices and factories here.

As you read in Chapter 12, the United States is linked with the economies of other nations. Trade policies such as NAFTA link us to our neighbors Canada and Mexico. More and more, the United States' economy is tied to the economies of the nations in North America and the world.

LESSON 2 REVIEW

Fact Follow-Up

1. What are high-technology industries?
2. What is the difference between a command economy and a free-enterprise system?
3. What are service industries?
4. What are our nation's most important exports?

Talk About It

1. Why is education more important today than ever before in our history?
2. Why do you think United States corporations open offices in other countries?
3. Should the United States import as much as it does? Explain your answer.

A Rich Land

- Changes in the uses of land changed air and water too, especially as cities and industries grew.

- Since the late nineteenth century, Americans have shown concern for protecting resources of air, land, and water.

- Cleaning up pollution and living with the changes to the environment are important issues.

KEY TERMS

Earth Day
ecology
Environmental Protection
  Agency (EPA)
global warming
National Park System
smog
spawn
recycling

Early Europeans discovered in North America a land of Native American villages. The Native Americans and Europeans had different ideas about land.

Native Americans lived by using resources on the land around them. They killed game and caught fish. They cleared land for farming. Native Americans lived lightly on the land. Most believed that they must not take too much from nature.

European settlers brought with them different ideas. They had crossed the ocean searching for new opportunities. They wanted to own the land. They wanted to build communities by using the many resources they found.

American Achievements

As you have read, the United States is a resource-rich nation. These resources have been used to support a growing population. They also have been used to improve our quality of life.

Most families in the United States make more money than families in other nations of North America. This is because of America's strong economy. Most Americans can afford healthy food and a place to live.

Healthcare

America's resources also have created a good health care system. In many Middle American countries, 22 to 72 babies out of every 1,000 die soon after birth. The infant death rate in the United States is 12 out of every 1,000. Our young people also may expect to live for a long

Appalachian State University is one of the many universities in North Carolina. **Why is college education important?**

time. People born in these times generally live until they are almost eighty years old. Among our neighbors, only Canadians live as long.

Educating Everyone

When America was founded, only the very wealthy sent their children to school. Often they had private tutors. Usually only boys were educated.

Public Schools The first American public school was created in 1643 by the town of Dedham in the Massachusetts Bay Colony. Later, Virginia's constitution required the legislature to "provide for a system of free public elementary and secondary schools for all children of school age."

Americans believed that being able to read, write, and do math was important. Freed slaves and immigrants valued their education. Many times education included learning a trade.

By the twentieth century most children went to elementary school. But by the time World War II ended, most children completed high school. As you read in Chapter 12, desegregation brought better education to African Americans.

Colleges and Universties The colonies also saw a need for higher education. Colleges trained ministers and lawyers. Harvard College (now Harvard Univeristy) was founded in 1636.

The University of North Carolina was the first public, state-run university. It was created by the state assembly in 1789. Building it in Chapel Hill began in 1793.

In the 1800s, colleges in the West gave more opportunities to women and African Americans. Many Eastern schools would not allow them to attend.

Congress passed the G.I. Bill of Rights in 1944. This let World War II veterans go to college and graduate school. Most of these people could not have afforded college before the war. This opened the door for many to better jobs in business, law, and medicine. Desegregation of colleges and universities in the 1960s again opened doors to African Americans.

Yellowstone National Park is home to different types of wildlife. **Why does the government create national parks?**

Chapter 13

Future Challenges

Our nation used its vast resources to achieve health, educate its people, and grow the economy. To support the growing population, sometimes people or businesses damaged the land. Sometimes they wasted resources. Now we try to take better care of nature's gifts while improving the quality of life for all.

Preserving Wilderness

John Muir loved America's wilderness. In 1892, he founded the Sierra Club to "do something for wildness." During a camping trip he asked President Theodore Roosevelt to protect forests from being destroyed.

Roosevelt loved the outdoors. But he also knew that the United States needed to use its resources wisely. He preserved a number of forests. Yet he also believed lumber companies and farmers should be able to use the forests to cut timber or grow crops.

National Parks

Other government lands began to be set aside for protection. These were soon called national parks.

Yellowstone became the world's first national park in 1872. Congress set aside more than 2 million acres in Idaho, Wyoming, and Montana to protect the geysers, waterfalls, canyons, and wildlife of the region.

Congress created the **National Park System** in 1916. There are now 390 places protected by the National Park Service. Eighty million acres of wilderness and historic sites are protected.

Other Protected Land

Millions of acres, mainly in the West, are controlled by other parts of the national government. The Fish and Wildlife Service's 96 million acres protect animals' habitats and migration routes. The Bureau of Land Management oversees 261 million acres. The Forest Service runs 155 national forests. These agencies allow some logging and mining companies, ranchers, and others to use the land.

Customs

Earth Day is celebrated annually in April. It is one way Americans show their concern about the environment. Schools and local governments plan events to show the importance of caring for the environment. We are learning to reduce the amount of waste thrown away. Schools teach us to reuse things instead of throwing them away, and to recycle plastic, glass, paper, and metal.

John Muir (right) convinced President Theodore Roosevelt (left) to preserve "wildness" by protecting forest land. **How does the government preserve wilderness today?**

Pollution

The United States had begun to be polluted long before the government began to protect our land, water, and air. Cities were choked with the smoke of factories. Streets were filled with horse and cow manure. People heated their homes and cooked their food with wood and coal stoves.

As industry grew, pollution grew. One famous river, the Cuyahoga in Cleveland, Ohio, was so full of oil and chemicals that it often caught fire. The shores of the Great Lakes were full of dead fish. They were killed by pollution dumped into the lakes. The air in many cities was so dirty that laundry hung outside in the morning was dark with gritty dirt by evening. Farmers used chemicals to kill diseases and insects that hurt their crops.

Finally, Americans began to see what was happening. The author Rachel Carson sounded an alarm with her book *Silent Spring* in 1962. *Silent Spring* showed that some chemicals used to kill bugs and insects on crops were doing more harm than good. The chemicals got into the water and killed fish, birds, and other wildlife. Because of Carson's book and other studies, the government banned the use of the dangerous chemical DDT.

Over the next two decades, Americans learned with horror that poisons in the air and in the water were causing serious illnesses. The poisons came from the trash from factories or from the chemicals sprayed on crops.

Rachel Carson's Silent Spring *helped awaken citizens to the effects of chemicals on the environment.* **What are ways that you daily protect the environment?**

What would YOU do?

In parts of the Northwest, dams have been built to harness electricity and provide water for irrigation and drinking. Some dams prevent salmon from swimming upstream to **spawn,** or lay their eggs. Experts have found that the numbers of salmon have dropped since the dams were built. Imagine you are in charge of figuring out a way to modify the dams to get the salmon past them to their spawning grounds. What would you do?

Americans also began to worry about the waste from nuclear power plants. Such waste, if not handled correctly, can cause terrible problems for many, many years.

Ecology

All over the country, Americans began to think about the environment. People began to learn about **ecology.** That is the study of the way plants and animals relate to one another and to the environment.

In 1970, the government created the ***Environmental Protection Agency (EPA).*** Its job is to protect the environment and help clean up pollution.

People began to look for ways to fix some of the damage from pollution. Although we have made great progress in cleaning up, there is still plenty of work to do.

Smog

One of the most difficult pollution problems is **smog.** The word smog is a combination of two words: smoke and fog. Smog is like smoky fog.

Smog is made when warm, dry air high above the ground traps cooler air underneath it. The cooler air collects polluted air, like factory smoke or the exhaust, or air, from a car's engine. Until automobile exhaust is clean, pollution will remain a problem.

Pollution choked the air of Pittsburgh and other cities during the nineteenth and early twentieth centuries. Pollution is still a problem, as shown above (inset) by the Exxon Valdez oil spill in Alaska. **What forms of pollution are found today?**

A Rich Land

Schoolchildren observe Earth Day at Blue Jay Point in Wake County, North Carolina. They examine water for insect life to test its quality. **What do you do on Earth Day?**

make the earth warmer by trapping the sun's warmth and energy.

Global Warming is the average increase in the earth's temperature. The warmer temperature causes changes in climate. A warmer earth may lead to other changes, too. Things like more rain in certain places, a rise in sea level, and other changes to plants, wildlife, and humans might happen. When scientists talk about the issue of climate change, their concern is about global warming caused by human activities.

Global Warming

The earth has warmed by about 1°F over the past century. Many of the world's scientists think that things people do are making the earth warmer.

Greenhouse Effect Scientists know that the greenhouse effect is happening. Gases in the air, like carbon dioxide, are increasing. Burning fossil fuels, for example, puts carbon dioxide into the air. Carbon dioxide is one kind of greenhouse gas. Greenhouse gases

Reduce, Reuse, Recycle

Young people all across the United States share the chore of taking out the trash. Many experts worry that soon we will run out of places to put it all. The average American throws away about 1,000 pounds of trash each year. That is close to 4 pounds (1.8 kilograms) of trash every day.

Recycling is one way to reduce this huge trash pile. Glass, steel, iron, tin, aluminum, paper, and plastic can be reused.

Many Americans are working hard to find ways to make a cleaner environment. Many of our rivers are cleaner. The air over many of our cities is clearer. No one, however, thinks the job is done.

LESSON 3 REVIEW

Fact Follow-Up
1. What is ecology?
2. What age do Americans generally live to be?
3. What is global warming?

Talk About It
1. Why do we need the National Park System? Explain.
2. Describe the effects of Rachel Carson's book *Silent Spring*.
3. Why is recycling important?

Where Should We Build the Factory?

American businesses build factories and offices in other countries. Other countries, in turn, build factories in the United States. Is there a foreign-owned business in your community? If there is, do you know why it is located in your area?

Businesses choose where to locate factories or offices based on several things, called criteria:

The labor supply: Is the workforce trained to make the business successful?

Transportation: Will it be easy to bring in raw materials and send out finished products?

Available land: Is there land available at a reasonable cost?

Markets: Are there good markets for the products nearby?

Raw materials: Are there nearby sources of important raw materials?

Think about a foreign-owned business in your own community. Which of these criteria does your community meet?

You now have a challenge: Imagine that you represent a foreign-owned business. You work as a member of a team to choose a place in the United States where a factory will be built. This factory will make three kinds of balls for playing sports: basketballs, footballs, and soccer balls.

You will choose the location of the factory from among these states: California, Texas, Iowa, and Florida.

You may use information from this chapter and from Chapters 14, 15, and 16. You may also use any other information your teacher may suggest.

Good luck in meeting your challenge!

What criteria will you use to make your decision? Is one item more important than others? Be sure that you can justify your decision.

*A Toyota assembly
line in California*

Lessons Learned

LESSON 1
A Vast and Varied Land

Most of the states of the United States are contiguous. Alaska and Hawaii are not. All of the world's climate types can be found in the United States. The varied climates in the United States allow all kinds of vegetation to grow here. Minerals and other resources make the United States a rich land.

LESSON 2
Modern Economy and Agriculture

The United States' economy is a system of free enterprise. It includes the manufacturing, high-technology, agricultural, and service industries. Today, many industries can produce more goods and services with fewer people. American businesses trade with countries all over the world.

LESSON 3
Promises and Problems

The United States has good health care and educational systems. Protecting wilderness is a challenge. Americans now work harder to protect the environment.

Talk About It

1. How do you think the United States might be different without the interstate highway system?
2. How is the story of the United States a story of environmental change?
3. How is it possible to produce more goods with fewer workers? What does this mean for the workers of the future?
4. Native Americans lived lightly on the land. European settlers wanted to build communities by using the plentiful resources they found. How did they change our environment?

Mastering Mapwork

LOCATIONS
Use the map on page 319 and the map on page 682 in the atlas to answer the following questions.

1. Describe the relative location of the Great Plains.
2. Which three physical features noted on this map lie in North Carolina?
3. Describe the relative location of the Great Basin.
4. Which three physical features noted on this map lie in California?
5. What plateau is located between the Central Lowlands and the Gulf Coastal Plain?
6. Describe the relative location of the Brooks Range in Alaska.
7. Which two mountain ranges lie roughly south of the Cascade Range?
8. Which landform identified on the map lies along the Gulf of Mexico?

Becoming Better Readers

More on Main Idea

Good readers are continually looking for ways to remember what they read. One way to do this is by mapping out the information. You make a graphic organizer by writing the main idea in the center and then writing the details around the main idea. In Lesson 1, the main idea is "A Vast and Varied Land." What are the three main features that make the United States vast and varied?

Go to the Source

Understanding Culture Through Art

Study and compare the two paintings below. Answer the questions based on what you see in the artwork.

Christina's World *by*
Andrew Wyeth

100 Cans *by Andy*
Warhol

Questions

1. What is happening in Andrew Wyeth's painting?
2. What effect is created by Warhol's painting?
3. Andy Warhol's painting *100 Cans* turns advertising into art. Where else can we see art in everyday things?
4. Both of these paintings were done in the twentieth century. What do they say about modern American life?
5. List the differences you notice about the two styles of the paintings.

Eastern Regions of the United States

Enjoying ice cream in Pennsylvania

What do you call the small candies sprinkled on ice cream cones? In different places of the United States, they are called jimmies, ants, sprinkles, dots, or nonpareils. What do you call a carbonated drink? Soda? Pop? Soft drink? Tonic?

Different regions of the United States use different words to describe everyday things. Regions are places on the earth that share common features. Language and words like soda or tonic are one of those features.

In the next three chapters, you will discover other features each of our nation's regions have in common.

Chapter Preview

LESSON 1
The Northeast Region: New England
The states of Maine, New Hampshire, Vermont, Massachusetts, Rhode Island, and Connecticut make up New England.

LESSON 2
The Northeast Region: The Mid-Atlantic
The region is made up of New York, New Jersey, Pennsylvania, Delaware, Maryland, and the District of Columbia.

LESSON 3
The Southeast Region
Virginia, West Virginia, Kentucky, Tennessee, North Carolina, South Carolina, Georgia, Florida, Alabama, Mississippi, Louisiana, and Arkansas are the states of the Southeast.

The Appalachian Trail

United States—Major Regions

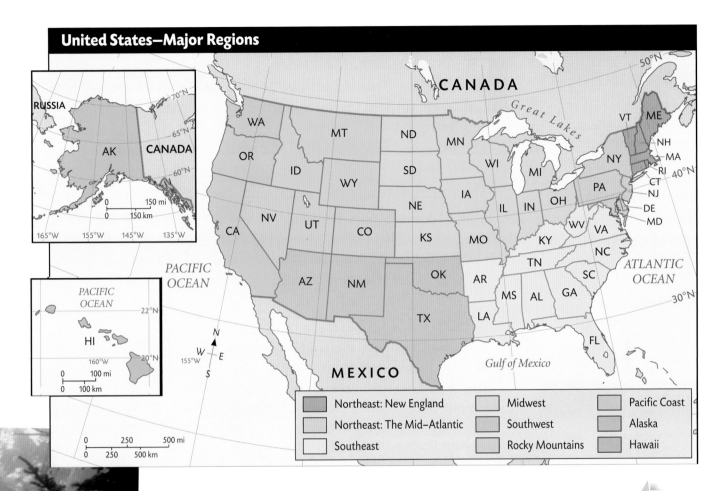

Legend:
- Northeast: New England
- Northeast: The Mid–Atlantic
- Southeast
- Midwest
- Southwest
- Rocky Mountains
- Pacific Coast
- Alaska
- Hawaii

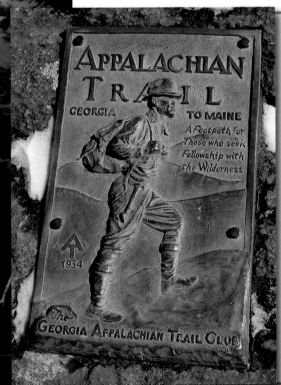

The Appalachian Trail

What is a valley road, a mountain footpath, a field, and a city street all at the same time? The Appalachian Trail!

The trail runs more than 2,000 miles (3,220 km) through the eastern United States. It starts at Spring Mountain in Georgia. It runs through the North Carolina mountains to the peak of Mount Katahdin in Maine.

Parts of the trail are hiked by nearly 40,000 people a year. A few hikers start out from Georgia in early March, intending to hike all the way to Maine before winter. Most of them reach the North Carolina mountains in time to see the mountain laurels bloom in April.

CAROLINA CONNECTION

Every morning, the first rays of morning sun in America shine on West Quoddy Head. That is an island off the coast of Maine. This is the easternmost point in the United States.

Then the sun hits the mainland at the top of Mount Katahdin (ka·TAH·din), one peak of the Appalachian Mountains.

The northeastern states of Maine, New Hampshire, Vermont, Massachusetts, Rhode Island, and Connecticut make up the region called **New England.** When people picture New England, they may think of rocky beaches or colorful fall foliage. Some may think of farmland bordered by stone walls and maple trees.

Soil and Climate

As beautiful as New England is, the land poses some challenges. The soil is rocky. Stone walls dot the fields and woods of New England. They were built by farmers who took the rocks from the fields. They placed them along the borders with other farms.

The mountains and rocks make much of New England a poor place to grow crops such as wheat. The land is better for other types of agriculture, such as dairy farming—raising cows for milk.

This is a view of the White Mountains in New Hampshire. **What are some of New England's challenges?**

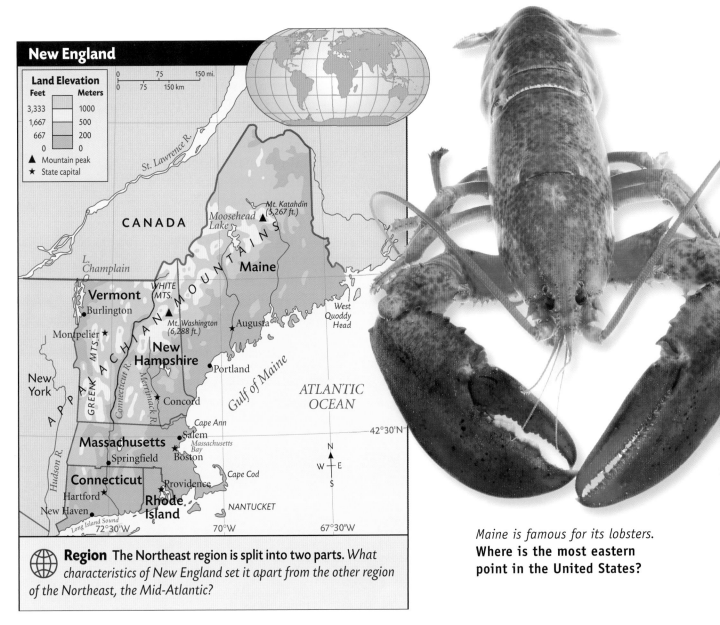

New England

Land Elevation

Feet	Meters
3,333	1000
1,667	500
667	200
0	0

▲ Mountain peak
★ State capital

0 — 75 — 150 mi.
0 — 75 — 150 km

St. Lawrence R.

CANADA

Moosehead Lake

Mt. Katahdin (5,267 ft.) ▲

L. Champlain

Maine

Vermont
• Burlington

WHITE MTS.

Montpelier ★

Mt. Washington (6,288 ft.) ▲

★ Augusta

West Quoddy Head

New Hampshire

• Portland

Gulf of Maine

New York

• Concord

ATLANTIC OCEAN

APPALACHIAN MOUNTAINS

GREEN MTS.

Connecticut R.

Merrimack R.

Cape Ann

42°30'N

Massachusetts

Salem
Massachusetts Bay

• Springfield   Boston ★

Hudson R.

Connecticut

Cape Cod

N
W — E
S

Hartford ★

Providence ★

New Haven •

Rhode Island

NANTUCKET

Long Island Sound

72°30'W   70°W   67°30'W

Region The Northeast region is split into two parts. *What characteristics of New England set it apart from the other region of the Northeast, the Mid-Atlantic?*

Maine is famous for its lobsters.
Where is the most eastern point in the United States?

Climate

New England has a humid continental climate. The winters are cold and snowy. Summers can be warm and humid. The cities and towns in northern Vermont, New Hampshire, and Maine, and those along the coast enjoy milder summers. The mountains also have cooler summers because of their elevation. New Englanders enjoy the variety of weather that the four seasons bring.

New England's long coastline, huge forests, and strong rivers helped industries grow.

Economy

From colonial times through the 1800s, many New Englanders made a living from the sea. Shipbuilding, trade, and fishing were the center of the economy.

WORD ORIGINS

The word **Appalachian** came from the name of a Native American group called the *Apalateans.* They lived in part of these mountains. The Appalachians run from Maine south to Georgia.

Shipbuilding

There are many tall trees in New England's forests. These gave shipbuilders wood for masts and decks. The pitch and tar from pine trees made the ships watertight. They used turpentine made from the pines as a cleaner and paint thinner.

Fewer ships are needed today. Large ships are no longer made from wood. But ships are still built in Bath, Maine, and New London and Groton, Connecticut. New London is also the home of the United States Coast Guard Academy.

Trade and Whaling

Boston and Salem, Massachusetts, were the home ports of sea captains who sailed worldwide. New England's coastline has many good harbors. Several towns on the water grew into important trading centers.

New England's merchants became wealthy. They exported New England's timber and ship stores (materials for ship construction). Then they imported English products. They sailed to China. Then the traders sold China's tea and porcelain in world markets.

Some coastal New England towns were centers of the whaling industry. Whales were used to provide many household goods in the 1700s and 1800s.

Scrimshaw on this whale's tooth shows scenes from the whaling industry. **Why was the sea important?**

Whaling was an important industry in New England. **What made New England a center for international trade?**

Henry David Thoreau
1809–1865

A Young Boy in Concord

Henry David Thoreau was born in Boston, Massachusetts. When he was a young boy, his family moved to Concord. Thoreau loved Concord. He explored the woods and took long walks. As he walked, he looked and listened. He liked to think while he was in the woods.

Thoreau went to Harvard and was the only one of the four children in his family to go to college. He became a teacher but soon quit. Thoreau did not want to whip his students when they did not behave. Later, he tried teaching again with his brother John. They started a school together, but John died. Theoreau was too sad to go on with the school alone.

In Good Company

Thoreau had a group of friends who liked to think and write. One of his friends was named Ralph Waldo Emerson. Emerson taught Thoreau many things, including how to keep a journal. Thoreau wrote his thoughts in his journal for the rest of his life. He wrote about nature and people.

"In warm evenings I . . . sat in the boat playing the flute, and saw the perch [fish], which I seemed to have charmed, hovering around me, and the moon traveling over the ribbed bottom, which was strewed with the wrecks of the forest."

"I Went to the Woods . . ."

To live out his ideas, Thoreau built a small cabin next to Walden Pond. He lived there for two years. He worked in his garden and read books. He fished and wrote in his journal. Every day he spent time enjoying nature. He studied plants, animals, and the weather.

Although he liked to be alone, every few days he went to the village. He visited friends and heard the latest news. Sometimes he had friends over.

Some of Thoreau's best writings came from the time he spent at Walden Pond. His most famous book is called *Walden*. Thoreau had a good sense of humor. He wrote about changing the week to six days of rest and one day of work. It wasn't all a joke—he wanted people to see that they did not need to rush around busy all the time. They could make or grow what they needed to live. They could do things for themselves.

One Can Make a Difference

After living at the pond, Thoreau kept writing and doing important things. He hated slavery, so he and his family helped runaway slaves escape to freedom. He wrote about a time when he spent a night in jail for standing up to a law he thought was wrong. He tried to show that one person can make a difference.

Thoreau died in Concord when he was only 44 years old. He was buried near many of his friends on Author's Ridge in Sleepy Hollow Cemetery.

Fishing always has strengthened New England's ties to the sea.
What other industries closely connect the region to the ocean?

Fishing

Fishing also brought wealth to the region. Many kinds of fish filled the ocean near New England. Ships from around the world caught cod and lobster.

Fishing has declined in recent years. Too many fish have been caught. Strict rules now limit fishing so the population can grow again. But there are very few fishermen left. Many can no longer make a living like their fathers and grandfathers did.

Rivers and Mills

New England's rivers are shallow. Loggers used the rivers to float logs to the coast. There they were used to make ships or were exported.

Rivers were an important source of power for factories. Textile mills were built on rivers like the Merrimack. The region became an important center of the Industrial Revolution.

Today's Economy

After World War II, New England, like many other parts of the United States, became a center for service industries. Service industries help other people and businesses.

High Tech and Higher Education

New England has become an electronics and engineering center. These companies work with experts from the almost 270 colleges and universities in the region. Harvard and Yale are two of the nation's oldest and most respected universities. The Massachusetts Institute of Technology (M.I.T.) is known worldwide for research in science and technology. These schools provide many jobs.

Resources

A profitable product in New England is maple syrup. In March, pipes are tapped into trees to create a spout. The pipe catches the running sap, which is caught in a pail. The sap is collected from the pails. It is cooked in boilers until the sap turns into maple syrup. Vermonters made 460 thousand gallons of syrup in 2000.

The largest granite quarry in the world is located in Vermont near its capital, Montpelier. Granite from this quarry is used for buildings all over the country.

Tourism is an important industry in New England.
What other industries are important there?

Tourism

New England's beautiful scenery has helped build a strong tourism industry. They come to see its historic sites, to ski, and to play on the beaches. Autumn is the peak tourist season. During the crisp fall days, the deciduous trees, especially the maples, turn to brilliant yellows, reds, and oranges.

Culture

The area is also famous for its many libraries and museums. Theaters and orchestras enrich the region's culture. Many famous writers come from New England, too. Louisa May Alcott, Nathaniel Hawthorne, Robert Frost, and Emily Dickenson are just a few of the region's authors. Norman Rockwell, a famous painter, was also inspired by New England.

LESSON 1 REVIEW

Fact Follow-Up
1. What states are included in New England?
2. What are some physical features of New England?
3. What were important parts of the New England economy in its early history?
4. How did shipbuilding develop as an industry?

Talk About It
1. How might New England be different if the soil were fertile?
2. How has New England's economy changed over time?
3. How is a service industry different from a manufacturing industry?

There is a chain of cities along the coast of the Northeastern United States. This area runs from Washington, D.C., north to Boston, Massachusetts. This chain of cities is called a *megalopolis,* which means a huge urban area where cities sprawl into one another. The area's population was about 53 million in 2004.

About one sixth of the nation's population is squeezed into the small but diverse **Mid-Atlantic** part of the Northeast. It is very diverse. Both the Asian and Hispanic populations here grew by more than 50 percent in the last decade.

Location and Landforms

The Mid-Atlantic region lies southwest of New England. It is bounded on the east by the Atlantic Ocean and on the west by the Appalachians.

The Mid-Atlantic contains more varied landforms than New England. The Coastal Plain widens in the Mid-Atlantic states of New York, New Jersey, Pennsylvania, Delaware, and Maryland.

In southern New Jersey and Delaware the shoreline is sandy and marshy. Farther north, in Pennsylvania, there are wooded hills and lakes as well as miles of rolling farmland.

The Appalachian Mountains run through the northwest corner of New Jersey and through much of Pennsylvania.

Pittsburgh, Pennsylvania, grew where the Monongahela and the Allegheny Rivers meet. **What river is formed as those two rivers flow together?**

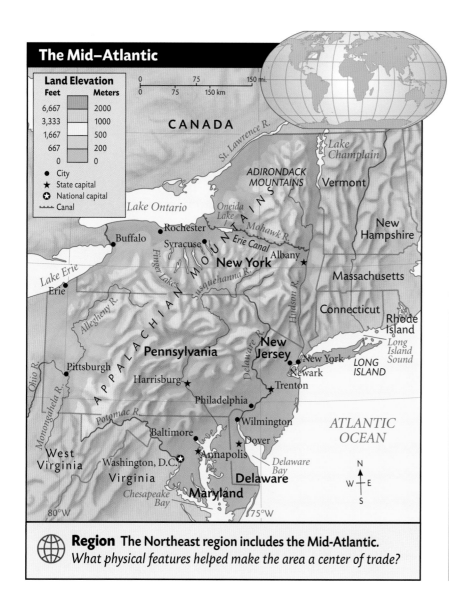

The Mid–Atlantic

Land Elevation

Feet	Meters
6,667	2000
3,333	1000
1,667	500
667	200
0	0

• City
★ State capital
⊛ National capital
┈┈ Canal

CANADA

St. Lawrence R.

Lake Champlain

ADIRONDACK MOUNTAINS

Vermont

Lake Ontario

Oneida Lake

Rochester

Buffalo

Syracuse

Mohawk R.

Erie Canal

New York

Albany

New Hampshire

Finger Lakes

Lake Erie

Erie

Susquehanna R.

APPALACHIAN MOUNTAINS

Allegheny R.

Massachusetts

Connecticut

Rhode Island

Hudson R.

Pennsylvania

New Jersey

Long Island Sound

Pittsburgh

Ohio R.

Monongahela R.

Harrisburg

Delaware R.

New York

Newark

LONG ISLAND

Trenton

Philadelphia

Potomac R.

Baltimore

Wilmington

ATLANTIC OCEAN

West Virginia

Washington, D.C.

Annapolis

Dover

Delaware Bay

Virginia

Delaware

N
W + E
S

Chesapeake Bay

Maryland

80°W

75°W

Region The Northeast region includes the Mid-Atlantic. *What physical features helped make the area a center of trade?*

The Empire State Building in New York City is a symbol of New York state. **What is New York City's relative location?**

Bodies of Water

Many important rivers flow through the Mid-Atlantic. Several carried early settlers away from the coast. They still carry goods today. In the east there are the St. Lawrence, the Hudson, and the Delaware Rivers.

The Ohio River is in the west. It begins where the Allegheny River and the Monongahela River flow together. Pittsburgh, Pennsylvania, is located at that point.

The eastern Great Lakes, Ontario and Erie, have connected the Mid-Atlantic states with the Midwest since the early 1800s. The Erie Canal and Hudson River linked the Great Lakes with New York City.

The **St. Lawrence Seaway** is a series of canals and locks built by Canada and the United States in the 1950s. It lets ocean-going ships sail directly from the Atlantic to the ports of the Great Lakes.

To the south, the Chesapeake Bay almost divides Maryland into two parts. The **Tidewater** is the area of rivers and inlets affected by the changing tides. It is a sporting paradise. Boaters can sail and explore, catch crabs, fish, or watch ducks and shore birds. In a good year, about 60 million pounds of blue crabs are harvested from the Tidewater.

Eastern Regions of the United States

In the Catskills *(1836) by Thomas Doughty captures the beauty of the rural Mid-Atlantic state of New York.*
Despite its high population, why does the Mid-Atlantic still have many rural areas?

The Economy

The Mid-Atlantic region has many industries. It is a center of world trade.

Ports

Many ports connect the Mid-Atlantic states to the world. Bays, coves, and islands create many harbors along the Atlantic coast. Deepwater ports have been major points of entry to the United States since colonial times.

The nation's busiest port is New York City. Other important ports are Philadelphia and Baltimore. Philadelphia is the nation's largest freshwater port. It is located on the Delaware River, about 90 miles (145 km) from the Atlantic. Baltimore has direct access to the Atlantic Ocean through the Chesapeake Bay.

Agriculture

The fertile soil of the Mid-Atlantic has always helped farmers. Today, about one third of New Jersey is farmed. Its nickname is the Garden State. New Jersey's farms are called *truck farms.* Farmers once brought their produce into Philadelphia and New York City in their trucks. They sold it from the backs of their trucks. Some still do.

New York State has about 38,000 working farms. They produce several kinds of fruit. Grapes for its famous wines are grown in vineyards around Lake Ontario, Lake Erie, and in the Finger Lakes regions.

Pennsylvania and Delaware produce corn, hay, and poultry. Pennsylvania also is known for its beautiful dairy farms.

The Mid-Atlantic, like New England, has varied landform, from the Atlantic Coast to the Appalachian Mountains. **What are some important bodies of water in this region?**

New Jersey

Fenwick Island Lighthouse in Delaware

Antietam Bridge in Maryland

Eastern Regions of the United States

Before steel is produced, the iron ore is smelted. **What industries are important in the Mid-Atlantic states?**

Industry

The key to the Mid-Atlantic economy today is business, finance, and communications. New York City's Wall Street is the headquarters of finance. The New York and American stock exchanges are located there. New York is also the home of the fashion industry, TV networks, and other communication businesses.

Coal from the mountains of Pennsylvania was, and still is, an important power source. The nation's petroleum industry also began here. Iron ore is the basic raw material for the steel industry. It was taken by ships on the Great Lakes from Minnesota to Pittsburgh and other steel manufacturing cities.

The area around Philadelphia and northeastern New Jersey became an industrial powerhouse. In Delaware, a gun powder plant was started in the early 1800s by the Dupont family. It has become the world's largest chemical producer.

Changing Times

Industry is still important here. But most of the steel plants are gone now. They were either forced to close by competition from other countries or they moved to other parts of the United States.

New Jersey is still one of the most heavily industrialized states. Buffalo, New York, is on the Great Lakes. It still has a few small steel mills and some auto assembly plants, chemical plants, and flour mills. Nearby, Rochester, New York, is known for plants that make optical (lenses), photographic, and office equipment.

Tourism is an important industry in the Mid-Atlantic. Tourists flock to New York City to see plays on Broadway. They visit the Liberty Bell at Independence Hall in Philadelphia, the Naval Academy at Annapolis, Maryland, and Niagara Falls in upstate New York.

LESSON 2 REVIEW

Fact Follow-Up
1. What states are in the Mid-Atlantic region?
2. What are some physical features of the Mid-Atlantic region?
3. What are the important parts of the Mid-Atlantic economy?

Talk About It
1. How did the physical characteristics of place encourage trade in the Mid-Atlantic region?
2. Why has the economy of the Mid-Atlantic region changed in this century?

The rapidly changing Southeast was once mostly a rural region. It is now the home of a growing population. Many people live in such cities as Charlotte, North Carolina; Miami, Florida; and Atlanta, Georgia. The Southeast is growing more urban.

Location and Landforms

The *Southeast* extends from the Ohio River to the Gulf of Mexico. In the east it stretches from the southern Chesapeake Bay to the southernmost tip of Florida. In the west the region reaches from Kentucky south to Arkansas and Louisiana.

The Southeast covers about 460,000 square miles (1,196,000 sq km). It includes 12 states: Virginia, North Carolina, South Carolina, Georgia, Florida, Alabama, Mississippi, Louisiana, Arkansas, Tennessee, Kentucky, and West Virginia.

This southern Arkansas farm field is part of the wide Coastal Plain of the Gulf Coast.
Why do you think the Gulf Coastal Plain is wider than the Atlantic Coastal Plain?

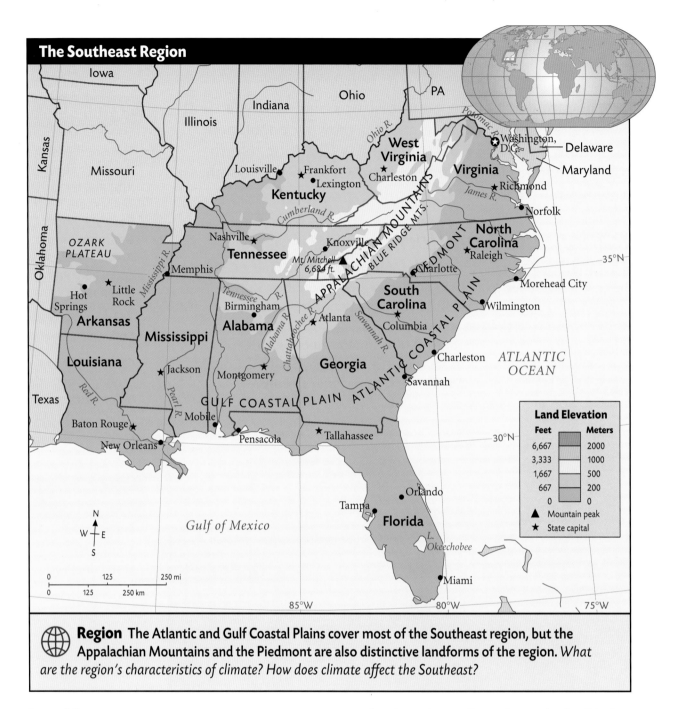

The Southeast Region

Land Elevation

Feet	Meters
6,667	2000
3,333	1000
1,667	500
667	200
0	0

▲ Mountain peak
★ State capital

Region The Atlantic and Gulf Coastal Plains cover most of the Southeast region, but the Appalachian Mountains and the Piedmont are also distinctive landforms of the region. *What are the region's characteristics of climate? How does climate affect the Southeast?*

Landforms

The Coastal Plain widens from about 100 miles (161 km) along the Atlantic Coast to 200 miles (322 km) along the Gulf Coast. The Mississippi River flows through the Gulf Coastal Plain on its way to the Gulf of Mexico.

Inland from the Coastal Plain, the Piedmont begins to rise. The plain meets the Piedmont at the *fall line.* The Potomac and other rivers flow through the Piedmont. They often flow over waterfalls at the fall line. Most of the Southeast's industry is located along the fall line.

West of the Piedmont are the Appalachians. Fertile lowland is good for raising corn, soybeans, peanuts, and tobacco. It is found west of the Appalachians in Kentucky, Tennessee, and Alabama. Dairy cattle and the famous race horses of Kentucky thrive there.

Strip mining, such as shown above in Kentucky, is an efficient method of extracting coal.
Why are some opposed to this way of mining?

Climate

The climate of most of the Southeast is warmer than the Northeast. Crops have a longer growing season. In the southernmost states and along the coast, temperatures are mild. Parts of the Southeast enjoy a humid subtropical climate.

Hurricanes often threaten the Southeast coast. They can cause millions of dollars of damage. In 2004, four hurricanes hit Florida. They caused great damage. In 2005, however, Hurricane Katrina hit Louisiana and Mississippi. It was the costliest natural disaster in American history (see Eyewitness to History, page 360).

Resources

The Southeast benefits from many natural resources. Coal deposits are found in West Virginia, Kentucky, Virginia, Alabama, and Tennessee. Alabama contains large deposits of iron ore. Tennessee produces zinc and pyrites. Pyrites are used to refine copper and make chemicals. Florida and North Carolina produce phosphate rock that is used for fertilizer.

Louisiana, Mississippi, and Kentucky have petroleum deposits. There are great oil deposits in the waters of the Gulf of Mexico.

Forestry is an important industry in the Southeast. Trees grow quickly in the warm, moist climate. North Carolina is famous for its fine wood furniture.

Fishing is important to the Southeast. Shellfish from the Chesapeake Tidewater and the Gulf Coast are shipped throughout the country. Mississippi catfish farmers produce most of the catfish eaten in the United States.

What would YOU do?

One kind of coal mine found in the Southeast is called a **strip mine.** In strip mining, huge earth movers, bulldozers, and shovels strip soil to find the coal. Strip mining is used to mine a great deal of coal cheaply.

People who are against strip mining say it hurts the environment. They believe it causes erosion. Yet coal fuels many industries. It provides heat and electricity for many homes. How would you try to mine the coal without damaging the environment? Explain why.

Eastern Regions of the United States

Hurricane Katrina

On August 29, 2005, Hurricane Katrina made landfall in southeast Louisiana and along the Louisiana-Mississippi state line. It left a trail of unbelievable destruction behind it.

Katrina was so large, it destroyed much of the Gulf Coast for 100 miles (161 km) from the storm's center. It was the sixth-strongest Atlantic hurricane ever recorded. It was also the third-strongest hurricane to hit the United States on record.

The storm surge wiped out much of the Gulf Coast. The cities of Mobile, Alabama, Waveland, Biloxi, and Gulfport in Mississippi, and New Orleans and other towns in Louisiana were crippled.

In New Orleans, there were levees, or barriers, that separated Lake Pontchartrain from New Orleans. These were damaged by the massive amounts of water coming in from the storm. Then they broke. Water rushed in. Eighty percent of the city was flooded (below). Many neighborhoods were flooded for months after the storm.

Hurricane Katrina makes landfall

Although leaders of Louisiana and New Orleans told people to leave the city, some did not. People had to be rescued from their rooftops by helicopters or boats (below). The city was in chaos.

Thousands of houses were destroyed like the one above. People had to relocate to other cities such as Houston and Dallas, Texas; Atlanta, Georgia; and Baton Rouge, Louisiana. Some went as far away as Maine and Utah.

Sadly, the governments at the federal, state, and local levels were not prepared for a storm that size and its great damage. It took several days to get all the people out of New Orleans. At least 1,836 people lost their lives in Hurricane Katrina and the floods. The storm is estimated to have caused $81.2 billion in damage. It will take years to rebuild the region.

*Atlanta, Georgia, is one of the key cities of the Southeast region. It is a financial and transportation center. **What are other important cities in the region?***

Economy

For much of its early history, the Southeast was an agricultural region. As you read in Chapter 8, cotton was the most important crop before the Civil War. After the war, planters still produced cotton. Then the cotton-eating insect called the boll weevil forced farmers to grow a wider variety of crops.

Alabama produces cattle, peanuts, and poultry. Large poultry farms also can be found in Arkansas and North Carolina. North Carolina is now a leading hog producer. It still grows more sweet potatoes and tobacco than any other state.

Florida, has a long growing season. It produces more than half of the nation's oranges and grapefruit. Even cotton has returned to the region. Memphis, Tennessee, is home to the nation's largest cotton market.

In recent years, the economy of the Southeast has changed in many exciting ways. New industries have started or moved into the region because of lower wages and less costly land. The fastest growing state economies are those of Arkansas, Georgia, North Carolina, and Florida.

Tourism

Many people visit the sunny south. Atlanta, Georgia, drew huge crowds for the 1996 Summer Olympics. Golfers enjoy playing in Florida and the Carolinas. The Kentucky Derby horse race is watched around the world on television each May.

Florida's warmth attracts people year-round. People enjoy boating in the Florida Keys. The Keys are a string of small islands off the tip of Florida. Families relax on sunny beaches and visit Disney World.

LESSON 3 REVIEW

Fact Follow-Up
1. Describe the landforms of the Southeast.
2. What are the resources of the Southeast?
3. What was Hurricane Katrina? What did it do?

Talk About It
1. How has the economy of the Southeast region changed over time?
2. What are some of the challenges facing the Southeast after Hurricane Katrina.

Using Geography's Themes: Region

This skill lesson focuses on the fifth theme of the Five Themes of Geography: Region. You practiced using the first four themes in earlier chapters. Now you are studying the regions of the United States.

A region is an area on the surface of the earth that contains many similar features. One feature might be political. A city, county, state, or nation may be a political region.

Another feature might be physical. What landforms or climates are shared? For example, why is the Coastal Plain thought of as a physical region?

You have been reading about the three eastern regions of the United States. In the next two chapters you will learn about six other regions of our nation.

Below is a graphic organizer that will help you organize information about the eastern regions. Review Chapter 14 to complete the chart.

Why is the Northeast divided into New England and the Mid-Atlantic regions? What similar features make the Southeast all one region?

After you have completed this chart, look again at the chart you made earlier of the three cities. Can you tell which political regions each city occupies? What economic regions do they occupy? How are they alike or different?

Comparing Regions		
	Northeast Region	Southeast Region
1. Political Units (states)		
2. Landforms		
3. Climate		
4. Natural Resources		
5. Size		
6. Economic Activities		

Lessons Learned

LESSON 1
The Northeast Region: New England
New Englanders made their living from shipbuilding, trade, and fishing. Today, New England is an important region for education and service industries.

LESSON 2
The Northeast Region: The Mid-Atlantic
The land and resources made the Mid-Atlantic states an early center for industry and trade in the United States. Manufacturing, finance, communications, and tourism are important parts of the economy.

LESSON 3
The Southeast Region
The Southeast has changed from a rural and agricultural region to one that is more industrialized and urban. Agriculture is still important. Its resources and mild climate attract new residents.

Talk About It

1. What are some reasons for the recent rapid growth of industry in the Southeast region?
2. Describe the boundaries of the Southeast region.
3. Explain the importance of tourism in New England and the Mid-Atlantic region?
4. Imagine that you and your family could live for a year in any state in New England, the Mid-Atlantic, or the Southeast. In which state would you choose to live? Give reasons for your answer.
5. Why is education said to be a New England product? Is education more a product of New England than of the Mid-Atlantic or the Southeast? Explain your answer.
6. What are some reasons why businesses are moving to the Southeast? Which do you think is the most important reason?
7. The Mid-Atlantic in the early years of our nation's history was called the "breadbasket" of the United States. Why do you think it was given this name?

Mastering Mapwork

REGIONS
Use the maps on page 347, 353, and 358 to answer these questions:

1. Use the map on page 347 to describe the relative location of the tallest peak in New England.
2. Through what states of the Mid-Atlantic region (see map, page 353) does the Susquehanna River flow?
3. Use the map on page 358 to describe the location of the tallest peak in the Appalachian chain, found in the Southeast region.
4. New England is a region as are the Mid-Atlantic states and the Southeast. Are the Appalachian Mountains also a region?

Becoming Better Readers

Finding Details
Good readers know how to read to find detail. Details provide more information and support for the main ideas. If books only had main ideas, readers would be left with lots of questions. When reading a textbook or a nonfiction book, heads and subheads give clues to where to find the details. Go back to page 351 and reread the section titled, *Today's Economy*. Find three details that support how technology, resources, and tourism affect today's economy in the New England states.

Go to the Source

Reading a Recipe

This recipe features two important products of the Northeastern United States. People use maple sugar or syrup to sweeten and flavor food. They get maple from trees that grow well in the region. Dairy farming is a key part of the region's agriculture. Read the recipe below and answer the questions using information from the recipe.

Maple Walnut Ice Cream

1 cup maple syrup
2 cups heavy cream
1 cup whole milk
1/4 teaspoon salt
2 large eggs
1/3 cup walnuts,
    toasted and chopped

DIRECTIONS:

Boil syrup in a 2-quart pot over medium high heat until it has reduced to 3/4 cup (about 5 to 10 minutes). Stir in cream, milk, and salt. Bring to a boil.

Whisk eggs in a large bowl. Add the hot cream mixture in a slow stream, whisking all the time.

Transfer this mixture, now a custard, to the pot. Cook over medium low heat, stirring constantly, until slightly thickened and a thermometer registers 170 degrees, about 1 to 2 minutes. Do not let it boil!

Pour and strain custard into a clean metal bowl. Cover and chill until cold, at least 3 hours. Freeze custard in an ice-cream maker until soft-frozen. Then with the motor running, add the nuts. Continue churning until frozen. Transfer to an airtight container and put in freezer to harden.

1. What are the two important products of the Northeastern United States featured in the recipe?

   a. Eggs and maple syrup   **c.** Walnuts and maple syrup
   b. Dairy and maple syrup   **d.** Eggs and dairy

2. What is the first step in making maple walnut ice cream?

   a. Wisk eggs in a bowl   **c.** Boil syrup in a 2 quart heavy saucepan
   b. Mix cream, milk & salt   **d.** Add hot cream into a bowl

3. What do you do to the ice cream after it is frozen?

   a. Put it in the freezer to harden   **c.** Cover and chill for three hours
   b. Keep churning until frozen   **d.** Add nuts

4. What does the mixture become when you whisk the eggs and add hot cream in a slow stream?

   a. Pudding   **b.** Ice cream   **c.** Yogurt   **d.** Custard

Western Regions of the United States

cowboy boots

Where is the West?
Who shall fix its limits?
He who attempts will soon learn that
it is not a fixed but a floating line.
— Eleuthoros Cook, 1858

In colonial days, "the West" meant the land along the Appalachian Mountains. In the early days of the new nation, the West was the Ohio territory. Later the West was California and Oregon, then New Mexico and Arizona. Today, the West includes the Midwest, the Southwest, the Rocky Mountains, and the Pacific Coast. Today's West is still a vast, varied, rich, and promising region.

Chapter Preview

LESSON 1
The Midwest Region
The Midwest includes Ohio, Illinois, Indiana, Michigan, Wisconsin, Missouri, Iowa, Kansas, Minnesota, Nebraska, North Dakota, and South Dakota.

LESSON 2
The Southwest Region
Arizona, New Mexico, Oklahoma, and Texas make up the Southwest.

LESSON 3
The Rocky Mountain Region
Colorado, Wyoming, Montana, Idaho, Utah, and Nevada are states of the Rocky Mountain region.

Spring Turning (1936) by Grant Wood

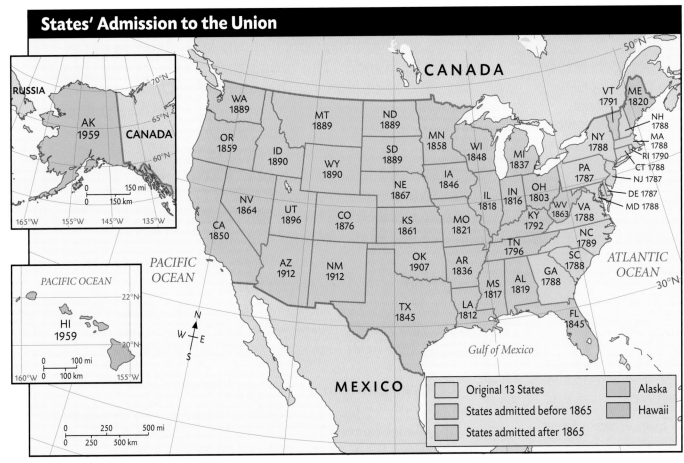

States' Admission to the Union

RUSSIA

AK 1959 — CANADA

150 mi
150 km

165°W 155°W 145°W 135°W

70°N
65°N
60°N

PACIFIC OCEAN

22°N

HI 1959

20°N

0 100 mi
0 100 km

160°W 155°W

CANADA

50°N

WA 1889
OR 1859
ID 1890
MT 1889
ND 1889
SD 1889
MN 1858
WI 1848
MI 1837
NY 1788
VT 1791
ME 1820
NH 1788
MA 1788
RI 1790
CT 1788
NJ 1787
DE 1787
MD 1788

NV 1864
UT 1896
WY 1890
CO 1876
NE 1867
IA 1846
IL 1818
IN 1816
OH 1803
WV 1863
KY 1792
VA 1788
PA 1787

CA 1850
AZ 1912
NM 1912
KS 1861
MO 1821
TN 1796
NC 1789
SC 1788

OK 1907
AR 1836
MS 1817
AL 1819
GA 1788

TX 1845
LA 1812
FL 1845

PACIFIC OCEAN

ATLANTIC OCEAN

30°N

Gulf of Mexico

MEXICO

Original 13 States		Alaska	
States admitted before 1865		Hawaii	
States admitted after 1865			

N
W E
S

0 250 500 mi
0 250 500 km

As people settled in western territories, additional states were added to the Union.

Donner Pass

The Donner family of Rowan County, North Carolina, decided to move west. They met many hardships on their journey.

George Donner first settled west of the Appalachians in Kentucky in 1818. A decade later he moved to Indiana, then Illinois. George married his third wife, Tamsen Eustis Donner. She was a teacher from Elizabeth City, North Carolina. They sold their farm and joined a wagon train headed to California in 1846.

The Donner party was trapped by early snows in a high pass of the Sierra Nevada mountains. George and Tamsen did not survive. Their children were rescued. The Donner's descendants live today in California. The site of the Donners' deaths is now named Donner Pass (above).

CAROLINA CONNECTION

KEY IDEAS

- The Midwest is the nation's heartland because of its location. It is also the center of rich farmland.

- The fertile soil of the Midwest has made it the nation's breadbasket. Dairy, corn, and hogs are also important farm products.

- Its great rivers and lakes are key transportation links.

- Resources include iron ore, lead, limestone, and soft coal.

- Making automobiles is still an important industry here.

KEY TERMS

loess
prairie
tributaries

Wallace Stegner called the West "Hope's native home." This means that people look to the west with hope for the future. The Donners of North Carolina headed west with hopes for a better life. Millions of other settlers moved west, too. They shared the same dreams.

The 12 states of the Midwest make up a huge territory. Ohio, Illinois, Indiana, Michigan, Wisconsin, Missouri, Iowa, Kansas, Minnesota, Nebraska, North Dakota, and South Dakota are often called the nation's heartland. That means they are the center of the nation.

Location and Landforms

The Midwest is best known for miles of rolling plains. The plains are also called the *prairie.* There we can find "amber waves of grain." We sing about these fields in the song "America the Beautiful."

The Central Lowlands

Much of the Midwest is part of the Central Lowlands (see map, 369). It includes central Ohio, Indiana, Illinois, northern Missouri, eastern Kansas, Iowa, most of Minnesota, southern Wisconsin, and the eastern edges of Nebraska and the Dakotas. This is some of the most fertile farmland in the world.

The Mississippi River and its tributaries flow through this region. *Tributaries* are rivers that flow into a larger river. The Ohio and Missouri Rivers are two tributaries of the Mississippi.

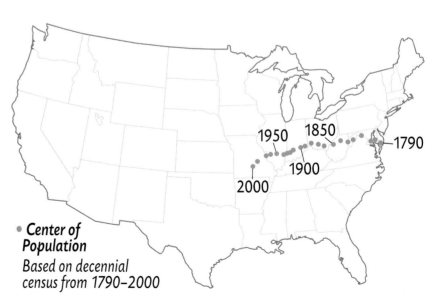

As people moved westward, the population center moved westward. Today it is in southwest Missouri. **Why do you think the center moved toward the Southwest from 1950 to 2000?**

● **Center of Population**
Based on decennial census from 1790–2000

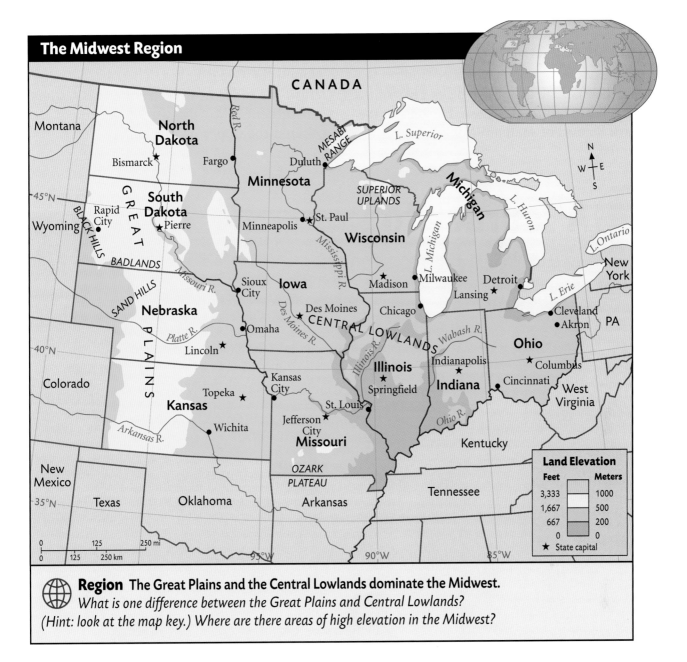

Region The Great Plains and the Central Lowlands dominate the Midwest. *What is one difference between the Great Plains and Central Lowlands? (Hint: look at the map key.) Where are there areas of high elevation in the Midwest?*

The Great Plains

West of the Central Lowlands are the Great Plains. These plains are dry. There are few trees. As you have read, the first European explorers called the plains the "Great American Desert."

Farming the Plains The pioneers moving west did not think anything useful would grow on land that did not have trees. All they could see were the thick prairie grasses. Sometimes the grass grew as tall as a person on horseback.

New inventions and new farming methods helped them grow wheat and other crops on the dry land. John Deere invented a steel plow that could tear through the toughest prairie grass. Farmers also learned ways to save water as they worked the land.

But the plowed soil of the Midwest rewarded the farmers' hard work. The thick, rich soil was formed by glaciers millions of years ago. In some areas, the soil is powdery, with no rocks at all. This deep soil is called *loess* (LOH·ehs). In some parts of Iowa the soil reaches down 600 feet (180 m) into the earth.

Hills of the Midwest

The Midwest does have other landforms. Some parts are not flat. The Black Hills of the Dakotas are hilly and rugged. The hills of the Ozark Plateau of southern Missouri are forested.

There are forests in the hilly areas around the Great Lakes. They are what is left of the miles of "big woods," as settlers called them. The "big woods" once covered the upper Midwest.

 A Journey to THE MIDWEST

Living on the Plains in a Sod House

Pioneers settled the vast plains of the American Midwest. They found fertile soil, broad, grassy pastures there. But there was little wood.

Building a home without wood was a challenge. A lot of settlers had to use sod. Sod is the thick, grassy, top layer of prairie soil. They used it to build the floors, ceilings, and walls of their new homes.

Glen Rounds wrote in his book *The Treeless Plains* about the settlers and their sod houses:

But for folk who for months had been living in a dugout canoe, a sod house was a luxury simply to be able to look out of the doorway or through the tiny window hole and see the horizon instead of the face of another cutbank [riverbank]. Even when divided into rooms by hanging canvas or blankets, the tiny building seemed almost spacious [roomy]....

But in spite of the improved view, the increased living space, and the added ventilation [air flow]—due to having a window as well as a door—the sod houses did have certain drawbacks [problems]. The interiors were dark even on the sunniest days. And after the grass underfoot had worn away, the floors, even when carefully smoothed and packed, were dusty in dry weather and muddy in wet.... Bits of earth

fell from the rough surfaces of the walls at the slightest touch, making housekeeping difficult. Mice, gophers, and a dozen kinds of beetles quickly took advantage of the ease with which burrows and nests could be made.... Somehow the discovery of a mouse swimming in the water bucket, or a huge beetle dropping into the flapjack batter did little to improve [one's] temper.

Home with a sod roof

Chapter 15

The Gateway Arch, symbolic of the city's position as the Gateway to the West, rises above downtown St. Louis, Missouri. **What major rivers join each other at St. Louis?**

Climate

The Midwest usually enjoys hot summers and long, cold winters. These are features of a continental climate. In the eastern part of the region, the average precipitation (rain and snow) is about 36 inches (91 centimeters) per year. The climate is excellent for farming. There is a long growing season and, usually, plenty of rain.

In the western part, there is much less rainfall. Some parts of western Nebraska, for example, receive only about 16 inches (41 cm) of precipitation in an average year.

Natural Resources

The Midwest has more to offer than just rich farmland. Waterways also are an important resource.

Transportation

As you have read, the Great Lakes and the Midwest's long rivers have played a key role in the region's growth. Four of the five Great Lakes form the Midwest's northern boundary. The Mississippi River runs through its center. Other rivers include the Missouri, the Ohio, the Platte, and the Arkansas.

Easy and cheap water transportation helped Midwestern cities grow. For example, St. Louis, Missouri, is located where the Missouri River flows into the Mississippi. It is known as the Gateway to the West. Many pioneers left St. Louis on wagon trains to follow the western trails to Oregon, California, and Utah.

Chicago and other Midwest cities developed as trading posts for travelers. Chicago became a railroad hub, as you read in Chapter 9. Today, its airports are also transportation hubs, too.

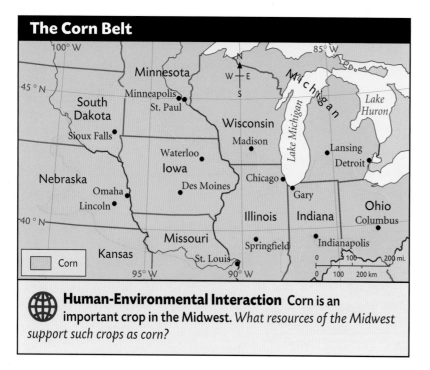

The Corn Belt

Human-Environmental Interaction Corn is an important crop in the Midwest. *What resources of the Midwest support such crops as corn?*

Raw Materials

The region's location and natural resources helped industries grow. The area around the Great Lakes is rich in iron ore, copper, and limestone. In the Mesabi Range of Minnesota, there are rich deposits of iron ore. This provided much of the nation's iron. Some of the richest deposits have been used up.

There are other important minerals in the Midwest. There is lead in Missouri, limestone in Indiana, and soft coal in Illinois. South Dakota has gold. Kansas produces salt and petroleum.

Customs

Corn Toys Many settlers farming the Midwest found some things in short supply. Materials used to make toys—like cloth or wood—were usually scarce. But the settlers knew how to make do.

Settlers on the plains used corn husks and cobs to make toys for their children. They carved whistles and miniature pipes out of cobs. They used the husks to make dolls. Today, many of these old corn toys are valuable. People like to collect them.

Farming

The farmers of the Midwest grow much of America's food. So the region is often called the nation's "breadbasket." The Midwest also exports food to other countries. The dairy farms of Wisconsin have a total of about 1.25 million cows. They produce more dairy products, such as milk, butter, cheese, and ice cream, than any other state.

Eighty-nine percent of Iowa is farmed. Iowa leads the nation in the production of pork, corn, soybeans, and eggs. Iowa also is putting in place programs that protect the soil and water. The land and water are important resources.

The Midwest once was home to many small family farms. Today, most farms in the region are large. Fewer people are needed to grow the enormous amounts of food produced each year. As you read in Chapter 13, improved farm machinery and science have increased the amount of food a farmer can raise.

Industry

Most Midwesterners today do not live on the farm. They live in the region's many cities. The urban areas around Minneapolis and St. Paul, Minnesota; Chicago, Illinois; St. Louis, Missouri; Detroit, Michigan; Milwaukee, Wisconsin; and Columbus, Ohio, have more than a million people each.

Food Processing

Since the Midwest produces so much food, food processing became a key industry. Food processing plants turn the raw foods into products we buy in grocery stores. For example, pork from hogs is made into sausage. Milk is bottled or made into cheese.

The region's transportation system carries farm products to cities where they are processed. Then they are shipped to markets around the country and around the world.

Factories

Good transportation is important for other Midwestern industries. Gary, Indiana, became a major steel manufacturing center. Iron ore could be shipped cheaply from Minnesota on the Great Lakes.

Being close to the production of steel helped make Detroit, Michigan, the home of the automobile industry. Auto production, in turn, helped grow related industries in neighboring cities.

As you read in Chapter 13, these manufacturing industries have undergone significant changes. Some steel plants closed in the 1970s and 1980s. Since then, auto factories have modernized and today produce more cars with fewer workers.

Culture

Even though many people now live in cites, the rural heritage of the Midwest influences its culture. Midwesterners are viewed as open, friendly, and plain-speaking people.

Food processing plants are built close to regions of food production. This meatpacking plant in Chicago is near the hog-producing state of Iowa. **What kinds of food processing are done near your home?**

As you read in Chapter 10, Many African Americans moved north to work in Midwestern factories. In Detroit, African Americans created the "Motown Sound" of rock and roll.

The area has many professional sports teams. College football is important in Nebraska, Indiana, and Michigan. Many teams have won national championships. Auto racing is popular. The Indianapolis 500 is run each spring in Indiana. Music fans visit the Rock and Roll Hall of Fame in Cleveland, Ohio.

LESSON 1 REVIEW

Fact Follow-Up
1. What are the Midwestern states?
2. What landforms are in the Midwest?
3. Describe the climate and natural resources of the Midwest.

Talk About It
1. Why did the farming and food processing industries develop in the Midwest?
2. Explain why good transportation has been so important to the Midwest's economy.

As far as we know, the oldest continuously settled community in the United States is located in the Southwest. Native Americans have lived at the Acoma Pueblo in New Mexico for more than 1,000 years. The Southwest is the home of many Native Americans.

The Spanish heritage is also still strong in the Southwest. Families descended from Spanish explorers have lived in the region for hundreds of years. Newcomers from Mexico are attracted by its familiar culture and wider economic opportunities.

The Southwest attracts people from other places, too. It is one of the fastest-growing regions of the country.

Location and Landforms

The Southwest is a place where people want to live because of its beauty. Some of the most thrilling natural wonders in the United States are in Arizona, New Mexico, Oklahoma, and Texas.

Visitors to the Grand Canyon are awed by its size and beauty. It has inspired artists and storytellers. **What kind of story would you write using the Grand Canyon as your setting?**

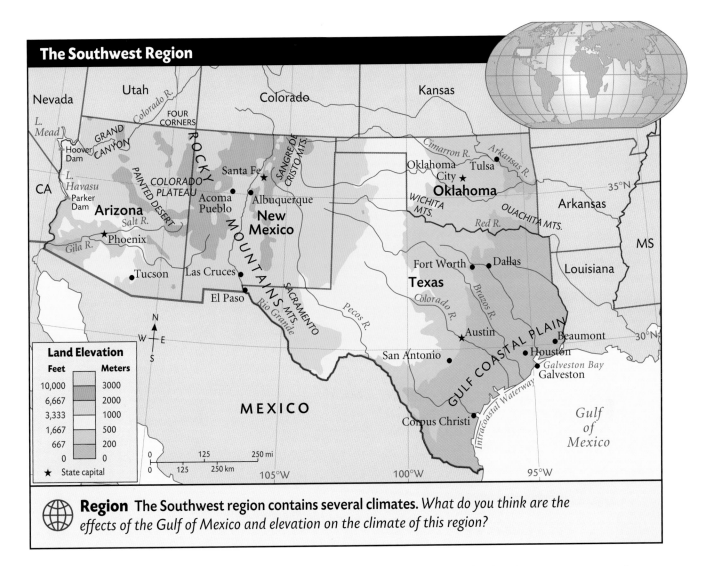

Region The Southwest region contains several climates. *What do you think are the effects of the Gulf of Mexico and elevation on the climate of this region?*

Texas

Many think of flat desert when they think of the Southwest. Yet the eastern part of the region has rolling woodlands. Fields of wildflowers bloom in the Hill Country of Texas, between Austin and San Antonio.

Along Texas' Gulf Coast, the Coastal Plain is sandy. There are many swamps and offshore islands. The Gulf Coastal Plain also has wide stretches of fertile farmland. Here farmers grow cotton, rice, fruit, and vegetables.

The Ozark Plateau borders the region to the east. The Great Plains extend into eastern Texas and Oklahoma. Cattle country, home to hardy beef cattle and the tough cowboys who herd them, is in northwest Texas and in eastern New Mexico. This is high plains country—dry, and mostly treeless.

Plateau

Southwest Texas, western New Mexico, and Arizona lie in the *plateau* (plah·TOE) country. Plateaus are flat highlands. Rivers have flowed across the plateaus for millions of years. They have cut deep canyons into the land. The most spectacular is the Grand Canyon of Arizona. It was carved 6 to 10 million years ago by the Colorado River.

The borders of Arizona, New Mexico, Colorado, and Utah meet at a point called the *Four Corners.* Novelist Willa Cather described its beauty: "Elsewhere the sky is the roof of the world; but here the earth was the floor of the sky."

Western Regions of the United States

The Settlement of Oklahoma

By the end of the 1880s, almost all of the western frontier had been settled. The only unsettled area left was the Oklahoma Territory. This had been controlled by Native Americans. But on March 23, 1889, President Benjamin Harrison declared that the Oklahoma Territory would be opened to settlement. Land would be given away in "runs" and lotteries.

Before each run, thousands of people gathered at the line, ready to stake their claims to farmland. "At last the revolvers barked, and along the line pandemonium broke loose. Men whipped up their horses, wagons careened wildly forward—all was hurrah and excitement. Noise and confusion reigned."

Many of them met people who had already staked claims in the Oklahoma Territory several hours or days before. These people were called "sooners." They arrived in the territory sooner than they were allowed to.

Racing to stake a claim in Oklahoma during the Cherokee Outlet run, 1893

Tent city in a cornfield in the Oklahoma Territory

L and offices helped settle claim disputes between settlers. For some African Americans, a homestead in Oklahoma was their first chance to own land. By 1910 there were 138,000 African American Oklahomans.

African American homesteaders in Oklahoma

The Central Arizona Project is a water-control system that supplies Arizona's cities with water. **How do limited water resources impact the growth of cities in the Southwest?**

Deserts and Mountains

This part of the Southwest is very dry. Deserts reach toward the Rocky Mountains. The Rio Grande (rio means river in Spanish) begins in the Rockies and flows southeast. It forms the border between the United States and Mexico.

The Southwest is called the "land of open sky." It has thousands of acres of unspoiled land, national parks, and forests. As one resident says, "The land is so full of silence that there is no room for sound."

Climate

The Southwest makes up a large part of the nation's Sun Belt. The Southeastern region and southern California are also part of the Sun Belt.

The region's climates change with elevation and nearness to water. The Texas Gulf Coast is humid subtropical. People in the higher mountain areas have the highlands climate.

The mostly dry parts of the Southwest are in the steppe and desert climates. This dry part of the Southwest receives fewer than ten inches (25 cm) of precipitation a year. Because of the scarcity of rain, farms depend on irrigation. Irrigation brings water to the plants, like using a sprinkler on your lawn.

Natural Resources

Great reserves of oil and natural gas lie below the surface of Texas and Oklahoma. The oil industry began in both states in 1901. They soon replaced western Pennsylvania as the center of the nation's oil industry.

Oil

The discovery of oil was like a gold strike. Oil wells were called gushers. Wells gushed, or exploded, in great fountains of "black gold."

People from everywhere rushed to the oil fields of Texas and Oklahoma. They hoped to strike it rich. Boom towns, such as Beaumont and Houston, Texas, and Tulsa, Oklahoma, grew with the oil industry.

Other Resources

The Southwest contains many other minerals. More than half of the nation's copper supply is found in Arizona. The region also is mined for gold, silver, lead, uranium, and zinc.

Other natural resources are found here, too. The almost constant sunshine is ideal for solar power. Flat land and clear air make the Arizona deserts perfect for United States air bases and military sites.

Water

One resource has created major problems and challenges in the dry Southwest. Its future depends on water.

Hundreds of years ago, Native Americans living in this region watered their crops using irrigation ditches. Today, farmers also irrigate the land to grow crops.

The Southwest's growing population has greatly increased demand for water. The Central Arizona Project is a system of 336 miles (541 km) of pipes and canals. It brings water to Phoenix and Tucson from Lake Havasu on the Colorado River.

The Colorado River provides much of the water in the Southwest. Much of the river is used for irrigation, hydroelectric power, and

Chapter 15

drinking water. These uses have reduced the river to a trickle before it empties into the Gulf of California.

As the Southwest continues to grow, making sure people, animals, and crops have enough water will be a serious problem.

Industry

Petroleum and its related industries are the biggest industries in the Southwest. Oil is used to make gasoline and many other products, such as nylon and plastic. Houston is the capital of the oil industry. Houston is connected to Galveston Bay and the Intercoastal Waterway by the Houston Ship Canal.

Major crops are grown in the Southwest. They include cotton, wheat, fruit, and vegetables.

The Southwest is famous as cowboy country. Texas leads the nation in cattle production. The cattle now are processed for market right in Texas.

Mining was the center of the Southwest's economy for many years. Copper mining is still important in Arizona. Uranium, is used to make nuclear power. It is mined in New Mexico. Electronics has grown into a major industry in Texas.

Houston is a "space" city. The space shuttle and other spacecraft are guided on their journeys from "Mission Control." Mission Control is located at the Lyndon B. Johnson Space Center in Houston.

Agriculture in the Southwest depends on irrigation. Mobile irrigation pipes used on this New Mexico farm keep the soil fertile. **How would population patterns change if water supplies ran out in the Southwest?**

Culture

The Southwest has a diverse culture. Native Americans, Spanish, European, and African American settlers have all influenced each other.

Many tourists visit the area to see the amazing landscapes. They buy lovely crafts like silver jewelry from Native American artists. They enjoy delicious foods.

Texans are famous for beef barbeque. Corn and peppers are used in many Southwestern dishes. These flavors show the region's Spanish and Mexican heritage.

LESSON 2 REVIEW

Fact Follow-Up
1. Describe the landforms, soil, and vegetation of the Southwest.
2. Describe the changing economy of the Southwest.
3. Why is irrigation important here?

Talk About It
1. Which natural resource is most important to the Southwest?
2. How did settlement change the Southwest's landscape?
3. Which groups influence culture here?

LESSON **3** The Rocky Mountain Region

KEY IDEAS

- The Rocky Mountain states are Montana, Idaho, Wyoming, Colorado, Utah, and Nevada.

- The Rocky Mountains are the central landform of the region.

- Like the Southwest, the lack of water is a problem.

- Farming is important in Idaho, but elsewhere the economy is based on mineral production.

KEY TERMS

cardinal directions
Continental Divide
intermediate directions
map key
north arrow
scale
symbols

Do you remember reading about the Mormon Trail in Chapter 7? Brigham Young led members of the Mormon church to the site of present-day Salt Lake City, Utah. He was looking for "a place on this earth nobody else wants."

Today, Salt Lake City is a modern city. It hosted the 2002 Winter Olympic Games. The city is located in one of the most rapidly changing regions of the country—the Rocky Mountain region.

Location and Landforms

Colorado, Idaho, Montana, Nevada, Utah, and Wyoming are not densely populated. Less than 4 percent of the nation's population live here. Stretches of these states are undeveloped. The open landscape is dotted with tourist resorts or small mining towns. Most people live in the region's cities.

Rocky Mountain states are in a region named for its major landform. **What climate is common in mountain regions?**

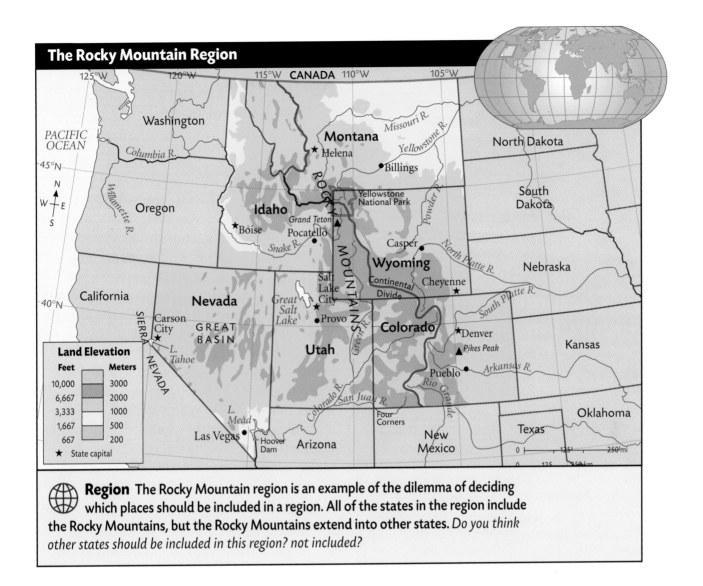

The Rocky Mountain Region

CANADA

Region The Rocky Mountain region is an example of the dilemma of deciding which places should be included in a region. All of the states in the region include the Rocky Mountains, but the Rocky Mountains extend into other states. *Do you think other states should be included in this region? not included?*

The Rockies

The Rocky Mountain region, of course, takes its name from the mountains. They reach from Canada all the way south to Mexico.

The highest peaks are located in the southern part of the Rocky Mountains. The Rockies stretch from Canada down through Wyoming, Montana, Idaho, and Colorado.

The *Continental Divide* twists through the mountains. Water on the eastern side of the divide flows toward the Mississippi River. It makes its way into the Gulf of Mexico. Water on the western side of the divide flows toward the Pacific Ocean.

Other Features

Many other different features mark the Rocky Mountain region. One of the most beautiful is the Great Salt Lake. There

Brigham Young brought the Mormons to settle in peace.

The Great Salt Lake covers almost 1,500 square miles (3,900 square kilometers). It is located in the Great Basin, a huge area of desert. It has such a high salt content that swimmers cannot sink.

Climate

In most of the region, the highlands climate changes with elevation. In higher elevations, winters are colder and summers are shorter. Lower elevations have the cold winters of the continental climate. The amount of precipitation varies greatly within the Rocky Mountain region. The entire region is dry. Nevada is the driest state in America. It averages about 9 inches (23 cm) of rainfall a year.

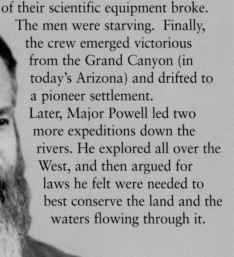

John Wesley Powell
1834–1902

In 1869, Major John Wesley Powell was thirty-five years old. He had lost an arm fighting in the Civil War. Despite this, he rode a train to Wyoming, bringing four wooden boats with him. He and nine men set out to explore the Green and Colorado Rivers, which until that time were largely unknown.

Powell and his crew bravely followed the Green River into a steep canyon, rowing through foaming rapids. To get samples of rocks and plants above the river, the men struggled to scale the red rock cliffs in sweltering heat. One boat crashed; supplies were lost. Food was running out. Only some rotting ham and damp sacks of rice, beans, and dried apples were left.

The Green River flowed into the Colorado. Day after day, the men floated through canyons so rough that the last of their scientific equipment broke. The men were starving. Finally, the crew emerged victorious from the Grand Canyon (in today's Arizona) and drifted to a pioneer settlement.

Later, Major Powell led two more expeditions down the rivers. He explored all over the West, and then argued for laws he felt were needed to best conserve the land and the waters flowing through it.

Natural Resources

Like the rest of the West, the Rocky Mountain states are also rich in resources.

Water

As in the Southwest, the supply of water is a problem in the Rockies. The Colorado River brings water from the Rockies to the growing populations of California and Arizona.

Drier Utah and Colorado must provide for their growing cities. The Central Utah Water Project should provide enough water for Salt Lake City until 2020. The Colorado Water Conservation Board has more than nine agreements with other states that regulate water usage.

Idaho, on the other hand, has a smaller population. It also has many rivers. So Idaho does not have major water problems.

Minerals

Miners have raced to the mountain states since the 1800s. They found gold, copper, uranium, and silver. Nevada leads the nation in the mining of gold and silver. Large reserves of oil are also located in the mountain states.

The region has some unusual minerals. Vermiculite is used in insulation. It and talc are found in Montana. Wyoming has the largest supply of trona in the world. Trona is a mineral used to make glass, detergent, and baking soda.

The soil and climate of the Snake Valley in Idaho are perfect for growing the famous Idaho potatoes. More potatoes are harvested in Idaho than any other state. Many of the "spuds" are turned into french fries and potato chips before they ever cross the state's borders.

Chapter 15

Las Vegas, Nevada, is one of the fastest-growing cities in the United States, partly because of the tourists attracted to such places as the MGM Grand Hotel. **Where would you want to live in the Rocky Mountain region?**

The Economy

"It's spring in the Rockies!" declare business owners and employees in the mountain states. The economies of Colorado, Idaho, Montana, Nevada, Utah, and Wyoming are growing faster than the economy of the nation as a whole. Las Vegas is the fastest-growing city in the region.

Las Vegas, Nevada

In 1931, the state of Nevada made gambling legal. This brings many people to Nevada on vacation. About 27 percent of Nevada's population now work in tourism.

Each month, 2.5 million visitors and 6,000 new residents go to Las Vegas. Las Vegas has ranked first in the nation for employment growth since 1995. The current population is estimated at 1.6 million.

Other Changes

In other areas of the region, new technologies like computers help people live and work in more rural areas. Many people have wanted to live in the mountains. But it has been hard to earn a living there unless you were a miner or a rancher.

Today, small businesses or individuals can work where they like. A telecommuter is the name for a person who works at home and communicates with coworkers and customers by telephone and computer.

Of all the mountain states, Colorado has the most varied economy, with government facilities, mines, resorts, farms, ranches, and industry.

What would YOU do?

Imagine you are in charge of managing the water supply for a town in the dry western part of the United States. You know that your town needs more water for its people and businesses.

But more water used today will mean less water in the future. That will stop economic growth in your town. Some businesses might close. Jobs will be lost. How would you try to solve the problem?

Skiing, bicycling, hiking, rock climbing, and rafting are popular recreations in the Rocky Mountain region. **If many people visit wilderness areas, how will that affect the environment?**

Land Use

The future of large sections of this region depends on the decisions of its owner—the United States government. The government owns about 50 percent of the land in Wyoming and about 80 percent of the land in Nevada.

Some people in these states would like to control how this land is used. They might mine the rich minerals, pump the large oil reserves, or ranch. Others want the federal government to keep control of the land.

Culture

The population of Utah is about 62 percent Mormon. Some of them are descended from the followers of Brigham Young. When Young chose a site on the Great Salt Lake for settlement, his followers irrigated the desert and built an attractive city.

Despite the area's growth, there are still plenty of wide open spaces in the Rockies. Much of Idaho and northwestern Montana are wilderness, welcoming hikers, campers, and rafters. Wyoming, with the smallest population of any state, attracts skiers and tourists.

Yellowstone National Park is the largest and most famous national park. It was founded in 1872. Today, Yellowstone attracts more than 4 million visitors annually.

Many Native Americans also call the Rocky Mountain region their home. The Rockies provide a good quality of life for people who love the outdoors.

LESSON ③ REVIEW

Fact Follow-Up
1. How is the Rocky Mountain region changing?
2. Describe the climate and landforms of the Rocky Mountain region.
3. What are some of the activities taking place in the Rocky Mountains?

Talk About It
1. Why is the Rocky Mountain region growing in population? What problems does growth bring?
2. How did gambling change Nevada?
3. How does this region use its resources?

*Analyzing, Interpreting, Creating,
and Using Resources and Materials*

Using Maps

This lesson will help you read maps better. Maps provide a lot of information.

Finding Your Direction

On most maps you will find a *north arrow.* This is a small arrow that shows the direction to the North Pole.

Find the north arrow on the maps in this chapter. These maps have been drawn so the top of the map points north. East points toward the right. West points left. South points to the bottom.

Always find the north arrow on a map, and you can figure out how to look at it.

Cardinal Directions

North, south, east, and west are called *cardinal directions.* They are the major directions. Halfway between each of the cardinal directions are the *intermediate directions.* These are northeast, southeast, southwest, and northwest.

a north arrow

Using Scale

Every map in this book is much, much smaller than the area shown by the map. The *scale* shows what the distances are on the map. On some maps, 1 inch may equal 50 miles. On other maps, 1 inch might represent 500 or 1,000 miles.

Look at the maps on pages 369, 372, 375, and 381. Note that each has two scales. The top line tells you how many miles are represented by one inch. The bottom scale line tells you how many kilometers (km) are represented by two centimeters (cm).

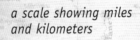

*a scale showing miles
and kilometers*

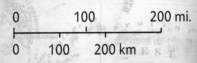

Symbols

Mapmakers use different kinds of *symbols* to give us information. These keep the map from getting crowded with too many words. The *map key* tells us the meanings of the symbols.

Now look at the map on page 322. Look at the key called Resources. The symbols represent different natural resources. You can see where our nation's resources are by matching these symbols with those on the map.

What other symbols are used on maps you have used already this year?

Lessons Learned

LESSON 1

The Midwest Region

The Midwest region is the nation's heartland because of its location, farming, and industrial activities.

LESSON 2

The Southwest Region

The Southwest region has a variety of landforms. The region is rich in mineral resources, but it lacks water.

LESSON 3

The Rocky Mountain Region

The Rocky Mountain region is dominated by the Rocky Mountains. The region attracts newcomers who are telecommuters.

Talk About It

1. In each region discussed in this chapter, what problems are faced in protecting the environment? Are problems much the same in all four regions, or are they different? Explain.
2. Which of the regions described in the chapter do you think is the most important to the national economy? Give reasons for your answer.
3. Which of the regions described in the chapter is most like the Southeast region? least like the Southeast region? Give reasons for your answer.
4. What is the impact of climate on the economy of the Midwest region? Explain.
5. Which of the regions in this chapter are most like the Northeast region? Explain.

Mastering Mapwork

LOCATION

Use the maps on pages 369, 372, 375, and 381 to answer these questions:

1. How many states make up the Midwest region?
2. Describe the elevation of the Midwest region.
3. Compare the elevation of the Midwest and the Southwest.
4. Which regions have the highest and lowest overall elevations?
5. All of the states in the Rocky Mountain region include the Rockies. Into which other regions do the Rockies extend?

Becoming Better Readers

Understanding the Text

To help understand the text, good readers have to think outside of what is written on the page. A good reader will organize the information into a sequence, look for cause and effect relationships, and make inferences. Chapter 15 is part of a unit called, *Our Nation Today.* Read the Unit Preview on page 317. How has the author organized this unit? How does Chapter 15 fit in with rest of the unit?

Go to the Source

Understanding Advertisements

You have read about resources of the West. You have also read in Chapter 9 about railroads advertising for people to move to the West. This poster is one of those advertisments. Study it and answer the questions using information from the advertisement.

Questions

1. Who is the poster trying to attract?
2. What clues show you who the poster is trying to attract?
3. What resources does the poster claim are available in southwestern Kansas?
4. What crops can be grown in Southwestern Kansas according to the poster?
5. If you wanted to move West in the 1870's, what in this poster would attract you, why or why not?
6. Using clues from the pictures on the poster, why is the prairie a better place to start a farm rather than the woodlands?

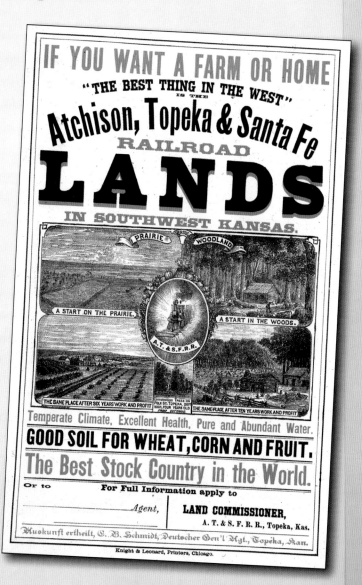

pineapple

The Pacific Region of the United States

The Pacific Region is the largest and most diverse of all regions in the United States. Imagine you are drawing a giant triangle. You start from the beaches of Honolulu. Then go north to the summit of Alaska's Mount McKinley. After that, go south, down the coast of the Pacific Ocean, to southern California. The triangle is completed when you go back to Hawaii. In that triangle, you would find several active volcanoes, old growth forests, large cities, huge stretches of wilderness, rich farmland, and miles and miles of ocean.

Chapter Preview

LESSON 1
The Pacific Coast Region
The Pacific Coast states are California, Oregon, and Washington.

LESSON 2
Alaska
The Land of the Midnight Sun is our nation's largest state.

LESSON 3
Hawaii
The fiftieth state is a chain of tropical islands formed by volcanoes.

Glacier Bay, Alaska

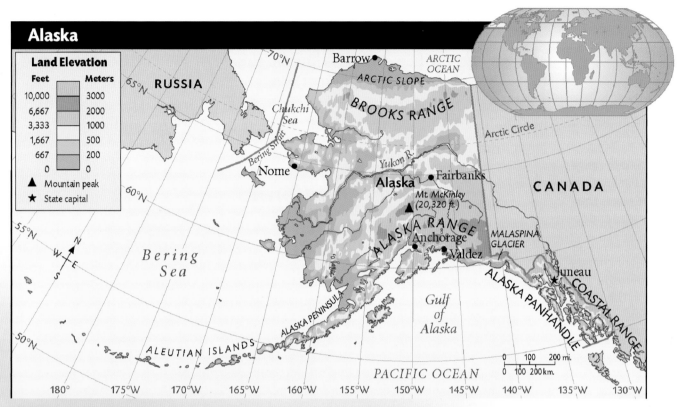

Alaska

Land Elevation

Feet		Meters
10,000		3000
6,667		2000
3,333		1000
1,667		500
667		200
0		0

▲ Mountain peak
★ State capital

RUSSIA

70°N
65°N
60°N
55°N
50°N

Barrow

ARCTIC OCEAN
ARCTIC SLOPE
BROOKS RANGE

Arctic Circle

Chukchi Sea

Bering Strait

Nome

Yukon R.

Alaska

Fairbanks

Mt. McKinley (20,320 ft.) ▲

CANADA

ALASKA RANGE

Anchorage

Valdez

MALASPINA GLACIER

Juneau ★

COASTAL RANGE

Bering Sea

N
W E
S

Gulf of Alaska

ALASKA PENINSULA

ALASKA PANHANDLE

ALEUTIAN ISLANDS

PACIFIC OCEAN

0   100   200 mi.
0   100 200 km.

180° 175°W 170°W 165°W 160°W 155°W 150°W 145°W 140°W 135°W 130°W

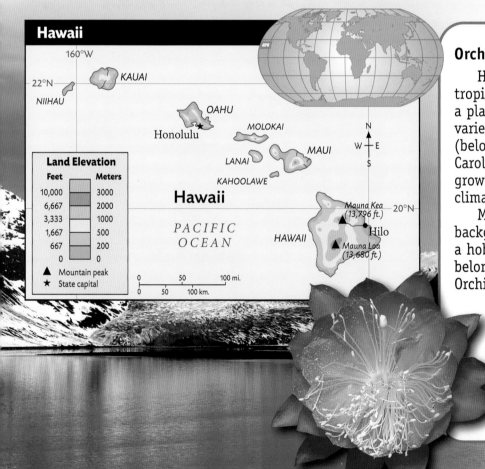

Hawaii

160°W

22°N

NIIHAU

KAUAI

OAHU

Honolulu ★

MOLOKAI

MAUI

LANAI

KAHOOLAWE

N
W E
S

Land Elevation

Feet		Meters
10,000		3000
6,667		2000
3,333		1000
1,667		500
667		200
0		0

▲ Mountain peak
★ State capital

Hawaii

PACIFIC OCEAN

HAWAII

Mauna Kea (13,796 ft.) ▲

20°N

Hilo

Mauna Loa (13,680 ft.) ▲

0   50   100 mi.
0   50 100 km.

Orchid Societies

Hawaii has a tropical climate. it is a place where many varieties of orchids (below) grow naturally. In North Carolina, however, orchids must be grown in greenhouses or indoors. Our climate is cooler.

Many people from different backgrounds enjoy growing orchids as a hobby. Some orchid hobbyists belong to groups such as the Triangle Orchid Society. Society members share information and tips about growing lovely orchids. They have meetings and also chat over the Internet. Members compete to see who can grow the most beautiful orchids.

CAROLINA CONNECTION

389

- The Pacific Coast States are California, Oregon, and Washington.

- Three mountain ranges rise in the Pacific Coast: the Coast Range, the Sierra Nevada, and the Cascades.

- Many types of climate and natural resources are found in the Pacific Coast states.

- The Pacific Coast states are leaders in mineral production, timber, farming, fishing, and high technology.

KEY TERMS

Silicon Valley

When you walk on the shores of the Pacific Ocean in the contiguous United States, you might be in Washington, Oregon, or California. These states of the Pacific Coast region have a great diversity of landforms, climate, and resources.

Location and Landforms

These three states are found on the western edge of the United States. The Pacific Ocean breaks upon all of their coastlines. In the north, Washington state borders Canada. In the South, California borders Mexico.

Mono Pass, Sierra Nevada Mountains California *by William Keith, shows the stunning beauty of the Pacific Coast region.* **Where in California is this range?**

Mountains

Three mountain ranges give the Pacific Coast states some of their incredible scenery. The ranges also affect climate.

You might think of these mountains as making the shape of the capital letter H. The Coast Range forms one long side of the H. It extends north to south along the Pacific Ocean. Farther east, higher mountains make the second long side. In the north, these are the Cascades. In the south, they are the higher Sierra Nevada. The Klamath Mountains form the cross line of the H.

Valleys and Deserts

Fertile river valleys stretch between the long lines of the H. North of the Klamath Mountains are rich lands along Puget Sound in Washington and the Willamette River in Oregon. South of the mountains lies California's great Central Valley.

Across southeastern California stretches a low-lying desert. It is part of the Great Basin. Death Valley is located here. It is the lowest point in the nation at 280 feet (84 m) below sea level.

The Pacific Coast Region

Puget Sound
Grand Coulee Dam
Seattle
Spokane
Olympia
Washington
Mt. Rainier (14,411 ft.)
CASCADES
Mt. Saint Helens (9,677 ft.)
Columbia R.
Mt. Hood
Portland
Salem
45°N
COASTAL RANGE
Willamette R.
Oregon
Idaho
Snake R.
PACIFIC OCEAN
Crater Lake
KLAMATH MOUNTAINS
Lassen Peak
Great Salt Lake
Nevada
40°N
Sacramento R.
SIERRA NEVADA
L. Tahoe
Utah
CENTRAL VALLEY
Sacramento
San Joaquin R.
San Francisco
Mt. Whitney (14,495 ft.)
L. Mead
DEATH VALLEY
California
35°N
Hoover Dam
L. Havasu
Parker Dam
Los Angeles
IMPERIAL VALLEY
San Diego
125°W   120°W   115°W

N W E S

0   125   250 mi
0   125   200 km

Land Elevation

Feet		Meters
10,000		3000
6,667		2000
3,333		1000
1,667		500
667		200
0		0
Below sea level		Below sea level

▲ Mountain peak
★ State capital

Region The Pacific Coast region of the United States has grown quickly in population as barriers to movement were overcome. *What were some of the barriers, and how were they overcome?*

Fault Lines and Volcanos

The Coastal Range mountains are young. They rise along the line where two huge plates of the earth's crust bump into each other. These two plates are the oceanic plate and the continental plate.

You can see the crack in the earth's surface where the plates meet. It is called the San Andreas Fault. Occasionally, the two plates shift. Great vibrations shake the land in the form of earthquakes.

Volcanic activity formed the Cascade mountains. Several volcanoes remain active there.

About 7,000 years ago, a volcano created Crater Lake. It is the deepest lake in the nation. Crater Lake attracts tourists to the eastern Cascade Mountains in Oregon. Volcanic ash also helped form the rich, loamy soils of the valleys of Washington, Oregon, and northern California.

Crater Lake in Oregon is now a national park.
How was the lake created?

Mount St. Helens Washington's Mount St. Helens erupted in 1980. It caused great damage and the loss of 57 lives. In 2004 it became active again. The volcano emits occasional steam and ash. Small earthquakes occur from time to time. Scientists say that an eruption similar to the one in 1980 is still possible, but the chances are very low. People can still camp and hike on the mountain.

Climate

The western parts of Washington, Oregon, and northern California have a cool and wet climate. This is a feature of the Marine West Coast climate. This is the result of warm, wet winds blowing off the Pacific Ocean.

Western Oregon can receive 130 inches (330 cm) of precipitation a year. Western Washington has about 140 inches (355 cm). East of the Coastal Range of the Cascades, the climate of both states is much drier. People there live in a continental climate.

Most of California has a rainy season and a dry season. In northern California, the rainy season lasts from October to April. Southern California's rainy season lasts from November to March or April. The southern part of the state's climate is warm and dry. They have a Mediterranean climate.

Natural Resources

Like the rest of the country, the Pacific Region has a varity of natural resources.

Forests

In California's great forests, you can find many amazing trees. The world's oldest living tree is the bristlecone pine. The world's tallest is the Douglas fir. The world's largest is the giant sequoia.

Oregon's forests cover about 28 million acres of land. Washington is close behind with about 21 million acres of forests. Together, these produce about 30 percent of the nation's timber.

Today, people debate about how best to use the forests of the Pacific states. Some "old growth" forests have never been cut. The trees have been growing for hundreds of years. Some think these trees should never be cut.

But lumber companies prize the tall old-growth trees because they have a fine grain and few knots. Others are concerned that endangered species may be wiped out if forests are cut.

Fish

Fish are another resource here. California harvests anchovies, tuna, and mackerel. Salmon is important in Oregon and Washington.

Salmon was very important to Native Americans of the Northwest. A Kwakiutl (kwa·CUE·til) chant describes the respect and joy of a person eating a freshly caught fish:

When a man eats salmon by the river, he sings the salmon song. It is in the river in the roasting in the spearing in the sharing in the shoring in the shaking shining salmon. It is in the song too.

Logging is a source of income for many in the Pacific Coast region. Conservationists are concerned about the effects logging has on the land. **How would you balance logging and the environment?**

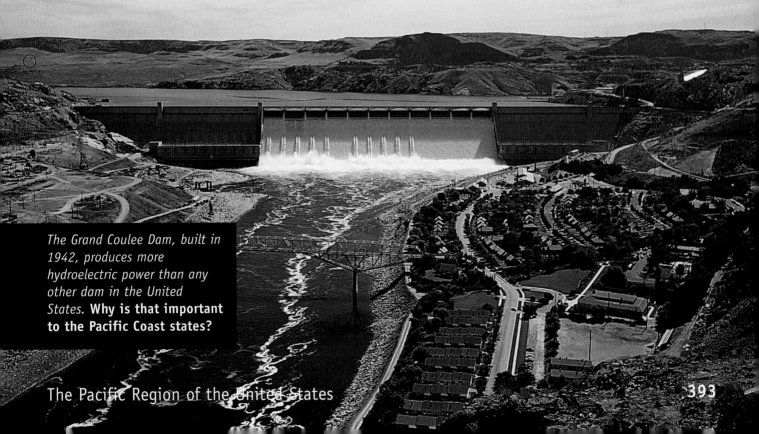

The Grand Coulee Dam, built in 1942, produces more hydroelectric power than any other dam in the United States. **Why is that important to the Pacific Coast states?**

The Pacific Region of the United States

Minerals

These states are rich in minerals and oil. California is the fourth-largest state in oil production. Nickel comes from Oregon. It is the only state that produces the mineral. All three states contain gold, silver, copper, zinc, lead, sand, gravel, and coal.

Water

These states have rich soils and favorable climates. Water is either supplied by nature or by irrigation. These factors make the valleys of the Pacific Coast states productive farmland.

The dams spanning the great rivers of Washington State produce hydroelectric power. The Grand Coulee Dam on the Columbia River is the largest concrete dam in America.

Economy

The Pacific Coast states contribute a great deal to the nation's economy. California alone produces many different goods and services. If it were a separate country, it would be in the top ten richest countries in the world.

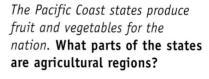

Farming

The Pacific Coast states rely on agriculture as part of their economies. Washington and Oregon grow fruit, especially apples, pears, and cherries. California produces most of the nation's canned and frozen fruit and vegetables. Crops can grow 300 days a year in the Imperial Valley in southern California.

In Oregon and Washington, logs and timber are the most important products. Oregon has led the nation in lumber production for 40 years.

Ships and Ports

Many activities involve the Pacific Ocean. Fishing, as you have read, is a key activity. In the ports of Washington, many people work in shipbuilding.

United States' trade with Asia depends on the ports of the Pacific Coast, especially San Francisco, California, and Portland, Oregon. Most of the cars imported to the United States from Japan arrive in Portland.

Manufacturing

The Pacific Coast states make different products. California's **Silicon Valley** is the headquarters for many companies that manufacture computer hardware and software. The region's nickname comes from silicon, the key component in computer chips.

Microsoft is a giant software developer. Its headquarters are in Seattle, Washington. It employs thousands of people.

The Boeing Company began building

The Pacific Coast states produce fruit and vegetables for the nation. **What parts of the states are agricultural regions?**

airplanes in Washington in 1916. The industry really took off during World War II. Today, aviation and aerospace companies employ engineers and scientists in Seattle, Washington, and San Diego, California.

Urban Populations

Although agriculture and lumber are important, most people of the region live in cities. About 94 percent of all Californians are city dwellers. Los Angeles is second only to New York City in population.

Washington's largest city is Seattle. More than half of the state's residents live within 50 miles of Seattle. Oregon's largest city is Portland.

Culture

Tourism makes up a major part of California's income. People visit Hollywood and tour movie studios. They also want to see the California coast, the famous redwood trees, San Francisco's Golden Gate Bridge, the San Diego Zoo, and, of course, Disneyland.

California has a large Hispanic population. Many have lived in California since the first missions were founded by the Spanish hundreds of years ago. This heritage can be seen in the many Spanish names of cities and towns scross the state.

AMERICAN PORTRAIT

William E. Boeing
1881–1956

Bill Boeing was a young man when he took his first plane ride. It was 1909, just a few years after airplanes were invented, and people didn't know much about them yet. Boeing decided he could build a better one.

He and a friend began to work. They hired men to help make a plane and a pilot to fly it. The first one flew pretty well, but they knew they could do better. They kept on planning and testing new ideas.

The U.S. Navy bought the first 50 airplanes. Boeing, however, could see that planes had uses in peacetime as well as in war. Boeing made planes to carry the mail, then he made planes to carry people. Within 50 years, it was the biggest company in Washington state. Today, Boeing's planes are used all over the world.

LESSON ❶ REVIEW

Fact Follow-Up
1. What landforms dominate this region?
2. What is Silicon Valley, and how did it get its name?
3. What are the most important economic activities in this region?

Talk About It
1. Which state in this region would you prefer to visit if you could? Explain why.
2. Why are there so many climates in the region?
3. Why do you think most people live in cities?
4. Describe California's Spanish heritage.

- Alaska is the largest of the 50 states.

- It is a region of mainly tundra and subarctic climates.

- Its landforms make getting resources, such as oil and timber, expensive.

permafrost

I n summer, the largest state, Alaska, is the land of the midnight sun. Wintertime means the dark of night almost all day for Alaskans living north of the Arctic Circle.

Alaska's 591,004 square miles (1,536,610 sq km) contain our 15 highest mountains, our largest glacier, and our longest chain of volcanoes. Alaska has more than 3 million lakes. It also has about 100,000 glaciers and about 1,800 islands.

Alaska's wildlife includes brown bears, caribou, bald eagles, puffins, seals, and whales. No wonder the Native American Aleuts of Alaska call their state "Great Land."

Location and Landforms

Alaska juts out from the landmass of Canada to form a huge peninsula. Bodies of water surround Alaska on three sides. The Arctic Ocean is on Alaska's north. The Chukchi Sea and the Bering Sea are to its west. The Gulf of Alaska and the Pacific Ocean lie to the south.

Look at the map on page 389. Do you see the "panhandle" of Alaska? The Alaska Panhandle points southeast. It is a narrow strip of land along the Gulf of Alaska. Juneau, the capital of Alaska, is located here. It sits at the edge of mountains that rise straight out of the water.

The Alaska Peninsula and the Aleutian Islands are also narrow. They extend from the southern coast toward the southwest. Volcanoes and glaciers dot the Alaska Peninsula and the Aleutian Islands.

Mount McKinley, the tallest mountain in North America at 20,320 feet (6,096 m), towers above mile-high mountains in front of it. Native Americans call the mountain Denali. **Would you want to climb this mountain? Why or why not?**

Mountains

Mountains ring Alaska. The Coastal Range runs from the United States through Canada and into southern Alaska (see map, page 389).

Mountains surround the interior. Land there has hills and wide valleys. The Brooks Range, part of the Rocky Mountains, forms the interior's northern boundary.

The Alaska Range marks the southern edge of the interior. Mount McKinley, the highest mountain in North America, dominates the Alaska Range.

Water and Glaciers

The Yukon River is the fourth-largest river in the United States. It flows from Canada through the interior of Alaska. It empties into the Bering Sea.

Most of Alaska's glaciers, including its largest and longest, are located in the south and southeastern part of the state. Malaspina Glacier covers 850 square miles (2,210 sq km). The Bering Glacier extends 100 miles (161 km).

The northernmost point in the United States is in Alaska at Point Barrow on the Arctic Ocean.

Summer cruise ships visit Juneau, the state capital. **Can you tell from this picture or the map on page 389 why visitors to Juneau can get there only by boat or plane?**

Climate and Vegetation

The climate of Alaska's southern coast gives it cold winters and warm summers. Heavy rain falls along the southeast coast and in the Aleutian Islands. The Alaska Panhandle also receives a great deal of precipitation. Most Alaskans live here along the southern coast.

Few people settle in the state's interior. Its subarctic climate features severely cold winters and short, cool summers. It has moderate rainfall.

The Arctic

The most northern region of Alaska is called the Arctic Slope. It stretches to the Arctic Ocean. This area has the Arctic tundra climate. Temperatures range from very cold to cool in the middle of the summer. Summer here lasts only about two months.

This cold region is north of the timberline. No trees grow here. The ground is **permafrost,** permanently frozen subsoil. It thaws only a bit at the surface during the arctic summer.

Glaciers flow throughout Alaska, even in southern Alaska. **What kind of climate keeps glaciers from melting and Alaskans cold most of the year?**

The Pacific Region of the United States

Natural Resources

Russia first claimed the land that is now Alaska. In 1867, the United States purchased Alaska from the Russians. The price was $7.2 million—or 2 cents per acre. Back then, some people thought that price was too high. Today, very few people would even try to put a price tag on Alaska's riches.

Fish are an important resource in Alaska. Valuable varieties include salmon, halibut, and herring. Alaskan king crab is important, too. Overfishing is a problem. To protect this resource, the Alaskan fishing industry operates under strict regulations. About 6 billion pounds of fish and seafood still are caught each year.

Logging is important in the Panhandle. Transportation costs are too high to make cutting lumber profitable in other parts of the state.

The climate of Alaska does not allow much farming. Garden vegetables grow in the Panhandle, in the Matanuska Valley around Anchorage, and in the Tanana Valley near Fairbanks. Alaskans must import almost 90 percent of their food.

Oil

In 1957, oil began being pumped in Alaska. In 1968, huge oil reserves were discovered at Prudhoe Bay on the Arctic Slope. However, tankers had to ship the oil all the way around the huge state.

A Journey to ALASKA

Building the Trans-Alaska Pipeline

The Trans-Alaska Pipeline cuts through the Alaskan wilderness. it stretches 800 miles (1,288 km) from Prudhoe Bay on the Arctic Slope to Valdez on the Gulf of Alaska.

Construction began on the pipeline in 1973. The cold climate affected pipeline construction in many ways. Engineers had to design the Trans-Alaska Pipeline carefully.

The biggest difficulty was permafrost, the permanently frozen ground. Engineers worried that the weight of the pipeline would melt the ice in the ground and cause the pipeline to sink. So engineers filled the pipeline's supports with liquid ammonia. The ammonia cools the ground beneath the pipeline. The permafrost stays frozen. The pipeline stays stable.

Another problem was keeping the oil in the pipeline warm enough to be pumped. So workers wrapped the pipeline in insulation. There is enough insulation to keep more than 21,000 homes warm.

Still another problem was how to inspect the inside of the pipeline after construction. Designers built a small, tube-shaped car called a "snoopy." Rolling down the pipeline inside the snoopy, workers checked welds. They made sure the pipeline was strong. It had to hold up to the pressure of thousands of gallons of oil being pumped through it every day.

In 2006, part of the pipeline was closed for repair. When the shutdown was announced, the price of oil went up briefly. The pipeline is very important to America's economy.

An 800-mile (1,288-km)-long pipeline was built to solve the problem. It carries oil from Prudhoe Bay to the port of Valdez. The pipeline is above the ground so it will not melt the permafrost.

Oil Spills When the pipeline was planned, people worried about the terrible damage that could be caused by even small leaks in the pipeline or a spill from an oil tanker.

A major oil spill did occur in Prince William Sound in 1989. The tanker Exxon Valdez spilled 11 million gallons of oil into the sound after hitting a reef. The loss of wildlife was huge. Birds, fish, otters, and seals died in large numbers.

The Athabascan people placed this fish wheel in the Tanana River. The water current turns the wheel that scoops up fish in a wire trap and deposits them in a holding pen. **Why is fishing an important industry in Alaska?**

Trans-Alaska Pipeline

ARCTIC OCEAN
ARCTIC SLOPE
Prudhoe Bay
Alaska
Valdez
Gulf of Alaska

Other Minerals

Alaska holds even more oil and many minerals that are not being pumped or mined. Some of these are gold, silver, nickel, tin, lead, zinc, and copper. It will be hard to mine these materials without harming the delicate environment. Transportation will also be costly.

Alaska's People

Alaska has the second-smallest population of all the states. Even in Alaska, most people make their homes in cities. About 70 percent of the population live in urban areas. More than 42 percent live in Anchorage, the state's largest city.

Native Americans make up about 19 percent of the population. This is the largest percentage of any state. The three groups of native peoples are Inuit, Aleuts, and other Native Americans.

The number of people who leave the state to find work elsewhere is on the rise. People move to the contiguous states for education and jobs.

Fishing is an important industry in Alaska. **How many pounds of fish and seafood are caught each year?**

The Economy

The high cost of transportation limits the economic activities of Alaskans. There are very few roads. This is due in part to natural barriers such as mountains and glaciers.

During World War II, the Al-Can Highway was built. This links Alaska with the states to the south. You can drive for hours on this 1,500-mile (2,415-km) highway without seeing another vehicle.

Economic activity also is limited because the federal government owns 47 percent of the land. About 48 million acres of Alaskan's land are in national parks. The U.S. Fish and Wildlife Service protects another 71 million acres. Alaskans disagree about how much land needs protection.

The government employs more people than any company in Alaska. More than 27 percent of Alaskan workers work for the federal, state, or local governments. This includes those who work on military bases.

Culture

Many tourists visit Alaska. Some watch the annual Iditarod sled race in March. Drivers mush dogs from Anchorage to Nome to win prizes. The tough trip takes from 10 to 15 days. Other tourists cruise on ships along the coast, seeing glaciers, whales, and other wildlife.

The Matanuska Valley near Anchorage is one of the few agricultural regions of Alaska. The short growing season is intense because of the long hours of sunlight. **What other areas of Alaska can grow garden vegetables?**

Alaska's native peoples are divided into eleven cultures. They speak twenty different languages. Many Alaska natives have kept their customs. Some natives still hunt and fish as they have done since "the creation times."

LESSON 2 REVIEW

Fact Follow-Up

1. Describe the landforms and climate of Alaska.
2. What were some challenges faced by the people who built the Trans-Alaskan Pipeline?

Talk About It

1. What are some examples of human-environmental interaction in Alaska?
2. Who lives in Alaska? Where do they live? How do climate and landforms influence life?
3. What is Alaska's most valuable resource? Why?

LESSON ③ Hawaii

KEY IDEAS

- Hawaii is made up of volcanic islands in the Pacific Ocean.

- Hawaii is in the Tropics. It receives a lot of rainfall and is usually hot.

- Tourism, the military, and government employment are the important parts of the economy.

KEY TERMS

leeward
Pacific Rim
taro
tsunamis
windward

Which state is not located in North America? Which state has both a former royal palace and a coffee plantation? Which state contains a volcano that erupts regularly? Which state is an island once ruled by kings and queens?

Hawaii (hah·WIGH·ee) is the answer to all of these questions. Hawaii became the fiftieth state in 1959. It is our most southern and most western state.

Hawaii is unique in many other ways. Its great beauty, resources, and location have made it an important part of the nation.

The Island State

The state of Hawaii is a chain of eight big islands and 124 smaller ones. A strong ruler, King Kamehameha, brought the islands together in 1810.

When the land of all the islands is measured and totalled up, we can see that Hawaii is the fourth smallest state. But the chain of islands stretches very far. The chain is about 1,500 miles (2,415 km) long!

The eight large islands are Niihau, Kauai, Oahu, Molokai, Lanai, Maui, Kahoolawe, and Hawaii. Because it is the largest, the island of Hawaii is often called the Big Island.

This volcanic beach gives a clue to how islands of Hawaii were formed. **What do the palm trees tell you about Hawaii?**

WORD ORIGINS

The name for our fiftieth state comes from **"Hawaiki."** That is the Hawaiian word for homeland. British explorer James Cook wrote the word as "Owhyhee" on sea charts during his visit in 1778.

Cook named the islands the Sandwich Islands after Lord Sandwich, British First Lord of the Admiralty. But the native name for the islands, spelled Hawai'i, is the name we use today.

Location and Landforms

If you have a globe, you can see just how far Hawaii is from North America. The state is located in the North Pacific Ocean. It is 2,397 miles (3,859 km) southwest of San Francisco.

Volcanoes

The Hawaiian islands were formed when volcanoes pushed up from the floor of the Pacific Ocean. Two volcanoes on the Big Island are still active. The volcano Kilauea (kee·lou·WAY·ah) erupts regularly. Fortunately, the lava from this volcano flows slowly. Usually no one is hurt.

The islands in the north of the chain are the oldest. Scientists expect that another island will rise up from the ocean in the next 2,000 to 20,000 years.

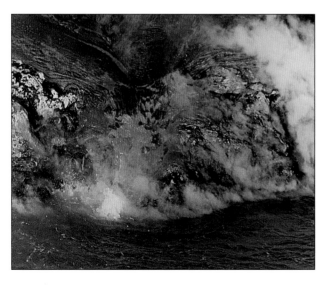

PRONOUNCING HAWAIIAN WORDS

Almost all Hawaiians speak English. But most place names and some other words are in the native Hawaiian language.

Hawaiian is different from English. The Hawaiian alphabet has only 12 letters: A E H I K L M N O P U W. Every Hawaiian word and syllable ends with a vowel. Two consonants never occur without a vowel between them.

Here are the vowel sounds: a—ah, e—ay, i—ee, o—o (as in cone), u—oo (as in moon). The letters "au" together sound like the "ou" in "house". Spoken words have an almost musical sound when pronounced correctly. It takes practice to learn how to say Hawaiian words.

Let's Practice!

Honolulu
(HOH·noh·LOO·loo)

Haleakala
(hah·lay·ah·kah·LAH)

Waikiki
(WIGH·kee·KEE)

Kamehameha
(kah·MAY·hah·MAY·hah)

Kalakaua
(kah·LAH·kah·ou·wah)

Nuuanu Pali
(noo·oo·ah·noo PAH·lee)

A volcano can be dangerous when lava flows or hot ash erupts. **How did volcanoes form the islands of Hawaii?**

Other Landforms

The major islands are cone-shaped. There are mountains near their centers. The eroding slopes of volcanoes gave Hawaii its soil.

Hawaiians have a unique way of giving directions. It comes from the slope of the land. Instead of north, south, east, and west, Hawaiians use two main directions. *Mauka* (MOW·kah) means toward the mountains *Makai* (mah·KIGH) means toward the sea.

There are few lakes and only two rivers in Hawaii. They are the Hanapepe (hah·nah·PAY·pay) and the Wailua (wigh·LOO·ah). Both are located on Kauai.

The People of Hawaii

The first Hawaiians came from Polynesia in the South Pacific. British Captain James Cook was the first European to visit Hawaii. He came in 1778. By then, native people had been in the islands for centuries.

This dancer performs the hula. Hula is a form of prayer and storytelling.
How are Hawaiians both American and Polynesian?

Customs

The Lei

The custom of the lei (lay) was brought to Hawaii by Polynesian travelers. They journeyed from Tahiti to Hawaii in canoes. They used the stars as a guide.

A lei is a garland of flowers, leaves, shells, seeds, nuts, or feathers worn around the neck. Leis are symbols of friendship and welcome. You should never refuse a lei. Hawaiians believe that it is rude to take off a lei in the presence of the person who gave it to you.

Many other sailors, missionaries, and business people followed Cook. As in the Americas, Europeans carried new diseases to the islands. Many thousands of Hawaiians died.

Between 1852 and 1905, about 184,000 immigrants came to Hawaii. They came from Japan, China, the Philippines, Korea, Southeast Asia, Puerto Rico, Spain, and Portugal. These immigrants made Hawaii one of the most diverse states in our country.

Culture

Hawaii is a cultural crossroads. Hawaiians value their heritage. Children learn to speak Hawaiian in school. They learn about their Polynesian ancestors. People feel a connection to the ocean and the land.

But Hawaiians are citizens of the United States, too. Hawaii has modern cities with tall buildings. It even has federal interstate highways! And, like the culture of the mainland states, Hawaii has adopted traditions from the immigrants who have made the islands their home.

Have you ever been to a luau or done a hula dance? These are Hawaiian traditions. Hawaii's culture has influenced American culture, too.

The population of the state of Hawaii is about 1.3 million people. About 75 percent live on the island of Oahu (oh·AH·hoo). Most of them live in the capital city of Honolulu (HOH·noh·LOO·loo).

The Eight Big Islands

Oahu is the third largest of the islands (see map, page 389) but has 70 percent of the state's population. Oahu's nickname is "the Gathering Place." Legends say that Hawai'iloa, the Polynesian navigator who discovered the islands, named Oahu after a son.

Lush and beautiful **Kauai** (kah·WAH) contains many rare plants and animals.

Fertile fields form the center of **Molokai** (MOH·loh·KAH·ee). Mountains and canyons are on the eastern part of the island. Sandy beaches stretch along the western part.

Lanai (LAH·nigh) used to be the pineapple island. The Dole Corporation grew pineapples on a huge plantation that covered most of the island. Pineapple is no longer grown commercially on Lanai.

Maui (MOU·ee) has stunning landforms. Its mountains spread across the interior. Rugged sections cover western and eastern parts of the island also. Most people live along the shore. Maui's beaches are very popular.

The United States armed forces use **Kahoolawe** (koh·ho·o·LAH·vay), an uninhabited island, for military practice.

Niihau (nee·ee·HOU) is privately owned. Few people are allowed to visit. Naturally, it is called the Forbidden Island.

Farmers grow many products on the Big Island of **Hawaii.** They produce sugarcane, fruit, coffee, and macadamia nuts. Cattle are raised on one of the largest ranches in the United States.

Climate and Vegetation

The climate of Hawaii is tropical. It has almost no change in seasons. The

Mount Waialeale on Kauai is said to be the wettest spot in the world, receiving more than an inch of rain a day. **How does that amount of rainfall compare to North Carolina's?**

temperature generally stays between 70° and 85°F (21° and 29°C).

However, the temperature drops with elevation. The tops of Hawaii's highest mountains, Mauna Loa (MOU·nah LOH·ah) and Mauna Kea (MOU·nah KAY·ah), are sometimes covered with snow.

Rainfall

Most islands have a wet, windy *windward* side and a drier, calmer *leeward* side (away from the wind). The dry side receives as little as 8 inches (20 cm) of rain per year.

The wet sides can be very wet. Mount Waialeale (WIGH·ah·lay·AH·lay) on Kauai is the wettest place on earth. It receives an average of 460 inches (11.6 m) of rain per year.

Sometime hurricanes and tsunamis hit Hawaii. *Tsunamis* (soo·NAH·meez) are destructive ocean waves caused by earthquakes. When a hurricane in the Pacific Ocean crosses the International Date Line, it is called a typhoon.

The wind and birds brought the first seeds and insects to the islands. Today lush rain forests cover the land. Two mammals, the monk seal and the hoary bat, came to Hawaii on their own. Other animals were brought or came along with people.

PRINCESS KAIULANI

The last royal family to rule in what is now the United States was not King George III and Queen Charlotte of Great Britain. Hawaii was ruled by royalty until it became a territory of the United States in 1898.

Queen Liliuokalani

In 1877, powerful American owners of sugarcane plantations banded together. They forced King Kalakana to accept a constitution. This limited his authority. It also allowed non-natives to vote.

Queen Liliuokalani succeeded King Kalakana. About that time, businessmen from America worked to get the United States to annex Hawaii. Princess Kaiulani, the heir to the throne, was in school in the United Kingdom. While she was there, U.S. Marines marched into Honolulu and forced Queen Liliuokalani to give up her throne.

Princess Kaiulani was only 17 years old. Yet she sailed to the United States to ask President Grover Cleveland to stop annexation.

Princess Kaiulani

Cleveland told the princess he would investigate what happened. He promised her the Hawaiian people would be treated fairly. But the Americans in Hawaii would not give up power. President Cleveland would not use force to make them give up power. All he could do was block annexation.

Annexation ceremonies,
Iolani Palace

A group of young Hawaiians tried to restore the throne, but Queen Liliuokalani was forced to give it up. Princess Kaiulani decided to sail home.

In 1898, After President Cleveland left office, Congress voted to annex Hawaii. Hawaiians did not celebrate. Princess Kaiulani stayed home alone, sitting under a banyan tree. Six months later, the last princess of Hawaii died at age twenty-three. Some said she died of respiratory [lung] illness. Others said she died of sadness about her land.

Sugar plantation mill

The Pacific Region of the United States

Economy

Hawaii's climate is important to the islands' economy. It is a key influence on many of the island's industries.

Natural Resources

The climate and rich volcanic soil help orchids, ferns, and many rare plants grow. For example, the silversword plant grows only on Maui and Hawaii. After sprouting a stalk of purple flowers, the plant dies.

There are many edible plants and fruits that grow here. These include 50 different kinds of bananas, guavas, and, of course, pineapples. Taro also grows easily here.

Taro is a plant that produces a tuber, a swollen underground stem much like a potato. Hawaiians cook the tuber and pound it into poi (POH·ee). Poi is a sort of pasty pudding that many Hawaiians love.

Industry

Hawaii's environment contributes to the state's most important industry, tourism. In 2005, more than 7.5 million tourists visited Hawaii. That was the highest number ever. Tourists spend more than $11 billion a year.

Government and defense are important parts of the economy. More than 10 percent of Hawaii's population is made up of military personnel and their families.

The high cost of shipping materials makes Hawaiian-made goods very expensive in other places. Manufacturers try to make small items that are not costly to ship but have high market value.

Today, agriculture makes up only about 1 percent of Hawaii's total income. Flowers and nursery plants, sugarcane, coffee, macadamea nuts, and pineapple are the leading crops. Sugarcane processing was an important industry but is now declining.

Cost of Living

Hawaii's cost of living is high. Life here costs 35 cents more for every dollar spent on the mainland. Much of this comes from the expense of shipping goods long distance. Even transportation among the islands is costly.

The Pacific Rim

Hawaii occupies what has been called "one of the world's most fortunate locations." Honolulu used to be known as the Crossroads of the Pacific. Today, people call the countries that lie within or border the Pacific Ocean the *Pacific Rim.*

These nations include Japan, Korea, Taiwan, and China. The Pacific Rim now produces more than half of the world's manufactured goods. Pacific Rim nations are already important markets. They will continue to be good customers for America.

With Hawaii's diverse population and close connections with Asia, its leaders believe their islands will serve as a link with the Pacific Rim for the United States.

Tourism is an important industry in Hawaii.
What "resource" attracts tourists?

The Shrinking Pineapple Industry

Once sugarcane and pineapple fields covered most of Hawaii's islands. Now you'll find houses, hotels, and fields with such other crops as coffee, macadamia nuts, and flowers.

The Pineapple Industry

In 1901, Harvard graduate James Dole moved to Hawaii. He created a company to grow and can pineapples. By 1922, Dole had bought the entire island of Lanai. It had been a cactus-covered island with 150 people. Lanai became the largest pineapple plantation in the world. It had 20,000 acres of pineapples. More than 1,000 pineapple workers and their families lived there.

Pineapple harvest in Hawaii

By the middle of the last century, Hawaii was the pineapple capital of the world. It grew more than 80 percent of the world's pineapple. There were eight pineapple companies there. More than 3,000 people worked in the pineapple industry. Pineapple production was Hawaii's second largest industry (sugarcane was first).

Changing Times

Now it costs more to hire workers and raise pineapples in the United States. So companies have moved their plantations to countries where it is less costly. Fresh Del Monte, Produce Inc., announced in 2006 that they would stop growing pineapples in Hawaii in 2008.

Today, Hawaii is no longer among the top ten of the world's pineapple producers. Now Thailand, the Philippines, and Brazil together grow about a third of the world's pineapple. Hawaii produces only about 2 percent of the world's pineapple today.

LESSON 3 REVIEW

Fact Follow-Up

1. Describe the climate and vegetation of Hawaii.
2. How have Hawaii's location, resources, and climate influenced the state's economy?

Talk About It

1. Describe the different Hawaiian islands.
2. Why is climate Hawaii's most valuable resource?
3. What happened to the pineapple industry?

Alaska

Hawaii

Analyzing, Interpreting, Creating,
and Using Resources and Materials

Asking Questions

Imagine that your parents or grandparents have decided to move to Alaska or Hawaii. They have asked you to find information that will help them make their decision.

You need to take two steps. First, you must identify your family's needs. Second, you need to research the information they will use to make the decision. To do this, you'll need to ask more questions. You need to take two steps. First, identify your family's concerns. Second, ask questions that will give you information about how to meet your family's needs.

What Are Our Needs?

Think about your family's wants and needs. These questions will help you.

- Do people in your family need jobs? What jobs do they do now?
- Would your family like a climate warmer or cooler than North Carolina's?
- Does someone have a health problem and need a doctor or hospital nearby?
- Does the family need to be near schools?
- Would children in your family have friends their age?

What other questions are on your list?

Research Questions

Look at the first question we asked. It's about jobs. Here are some questions you could ask about jobs:

- What kinds of jobs are in the state?
- Do they match the kinds of jobs your family members have now?
- Are employers hiring?
- What are the wages?

Finding Answers

Reading is one way of finding answers to questions. This chapter may have some answers. Your media center will have more answers. You can also do research on the Internet.

You may also interview someone who knows a lot about Alaska or Hawaii. An adult you know may have served on a military base in one of the states. You could interview other people through letters or e-mail. Could you send questions to other fifth-graders in Alaska or Hawaii using the Internet?

A Menu for Research

Let's make a graphic organizer. A menu will help us choose the types of research questions we need to ask.

Fold a piece of paper in half. On the front, come up with a name for your restaurant that relates to your state, for example, "Hawaii Haven" or "Alaska Trails." Be creative. You can decorate the menu with pictures and symbols of your state, too.

Make a list of your research subjects. We have discussed one subject you can use, Jobs. What other subjects do you need to research?

Open your menu. Divide the paper into the same number of boxes as the number of subjects you have. Make them big enough to fit your questions.

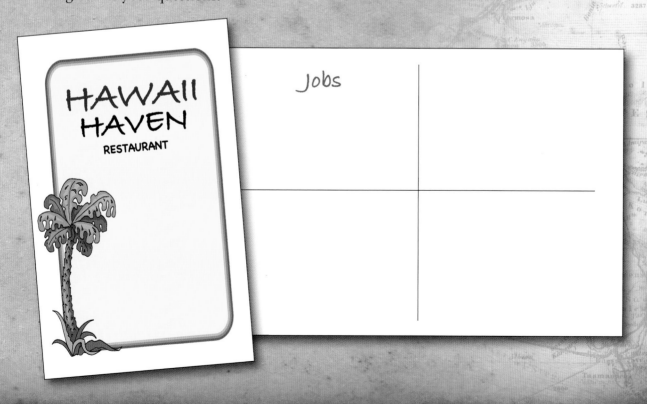

Lessons Learned

LESSON 1
The Pacific Coast Region
The Pacific Coast region enjoys a varied climate. California, Washington, and Oregon have more resources for agriculture and industry than some countries.

LESSON 2
Alaska
Alaska is a mountainous state with a cold climate and few people, but it is rich in mineral, forest, and ocean resources. Most Alaskans live in cities. Forty percent live in its largest city, Anchorage.

LESSON 3
Hawaii
Hawaii is a state of many volcanic islands set in the Pacific Ocean. The eight large islands of Hawaii contain beautiful landforms. Tourism is Hawaii's main industry. Sugarcane and pineapple are Hawaii's main crops.

Talk About It

1. Which of these—volcanic activity or earthquakes—has been more important in the Pacific Coast states? Explain why.
2. Why do you think most people in the Pacific Coast states live in cities?
3. How does relative location affect the economy of the Pacific Coast region?
4. The Aleut people of Alaska call it Great Land. Could the same term describe Hawaii? Explain your answer.
5. Which state—Alaska or Hawaii—has the more endangered environment? Explain your answer.
6. Compare the means by which Alaska and Hawaii were acquired by the United States.

Mastering Mapwork

HUMAN-ENVIRONMENTAL INTERACTION
Use the maps on page 389 to answer the following questions.

1. Locate Honolulu on the island of Oahu in Hawaii. What patterns of human-environmental interaction would you expect to see?
2. Locate the intersection of 70°N and 150°W and Anchorage, Alaska, which lies farther south on 150°W. What differences in human-environmental interaction would you expect to see in these two places?
3. Locate Hilo at 155°W on the island of Hawaii. From what you have read in this chapter, what human-environmental interaction would you expect to see in this place?

Becoming Better Readers

More Strategies for Understanding the Text
Another strategy that good readers use to understand the text is to make comparisons. To understand the Pacific Coast Region, a good reader would think about how the land compares to the other regions in the United States. How does climate of the Pacific Coast Region (see page 392) compare to the climate of the Midwest Region (see page 371)?

Go to the Source

Photo by Mike Green

Analyzing Song Lyrics

Builders of the Grand Coulee Dam wanted to tell people how important making hydroelectric power was. They hired a famous folk singer for one month. His job was to write songs for a film about the dam.

Woody Guthrie wrote "Roll On, Columbia." In 1987, it became Washington's state folk song. Answer the questions using information from the lyrics and text below.

At the Grand Coulee Dam, a metal sculpture shows Woody Guthrie singing one of his Columbia River ballads.

Roll On, Columbia

Roll on, Columbia
Roll on, Columbia, roll on,
Roll on, Columbia, roll on.
Your power is turning the darkness to dawn,
Roll on, Columbia, roll on.
And far up the river is Grand Coulee Dam,
The mightiest thing ever built by man,
To run the great factories and water the land,
It's roll on, Columbia, roll on.

Questions

1. What is the Columbia?
2. Why is the Grand Coulee Dam important?
3. What is the effect of using the phrase: "Roll on, Roll on Columbia" over and over in the song?
4. Based on the context of the song, what does "Your power is turning the darkness to dawn" mean?
5. Who wrote "Roll on Columbia" and why?

VOTE

Government of the People

History is a story. The history of voting in the United States is a story of struggle. It takes us from the Founding Fathers writing the Constitution to the amendment allowing eighteen-year-olds to vote.

At first, America only allowed white male property owners over twenty-one to vote. Then after the Civil War, the Thirteenth Amendment gave African American males the right to vote. But many states prevented them from voting.

In 1920, the Nineteenth Amendment gave all women the right to vote. The Civil Rights Act of 1964 and the Voting Rights Act of 1965 made it possible for African American men and women to vote in all states. Finally, in 1971, the Twenty-sixth Amendment gave eighteen-year-olds the right to vote.

Voters across the country, like these voters in Detroit, cast their ballots for the 2000 United States presidential election.

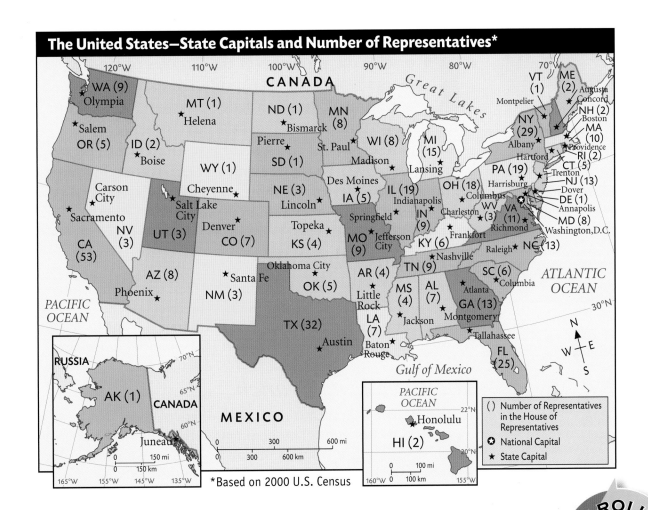

The United States—State Capitals and Number of Representatives*

CANADA

Great Lakes

WA (9) ★ Olympia

★ Salem
OR (5)

MT (1) ★ Helena

ND (1)
★ Bismarck

MN (8)
St. Paul ★

WI (8)

MI (15)
★ Lansing

VT (1)
Montpelier

ME (2) ★ Augusta
Concord

NH (2)
Boston
MA (10)

ID (2)
★ Boise

Pierre ★
SD (1)

Madison ★

Des Moines ★

NY (29)
Albany ★

Providence
RI (2)
Hartford
CT (5)

Carson City

WY (1)
★ Cheyenne

NE (3)
Lincoln ★

IA (5)

IL (19)
Springfield ★

OH (18)
★ Columbus

PA (19)
★ Harrisburg

Trenton
NJ (13)
Dover
DE (1)

★ Sacramento

NV (3)

UT (3)

Denver ★
CO (7)

Topeka ★
KS (4)

MO (9)
Jefferson City ★

Indianapolis ★
IN (9)

Charleston ★
WV (3)

VA (11)
Richmond ★

Annapolis
MD (8)
Washington, D.C.

CA (53)

AZ (8)
Phoenix ★

Santa Fe ★
NM (3)

Oklahoma City ★
OK (5)

AR (4)
Little Rock ★

TN (9)
★ Nashville

KY (6)
Frankfort ★

Raleigh ★ NC (13)

SC (6)
★ Columbia

ATLANTIC OCEAN

PACIFIC OCEAN

TX (32)
★ Austin

LA (7)
Baton Rouge ★

MS (4)
Jackson ★

AL (7)
Montgomery ★

Atlanta ★
GA (13)

Tallahassee ★

30°N

N
W E
S

Gulf of Mexico

FL (25)

RUSSIA

AK (1)

CANADA

70°N
65°N
60°N

Juneau

0   150 mi
0   150 km

165°W   155°W   145°W   135°W

MEXICO

0   300   600 mi
0   300   600 km

*Based on 2000 U.S. Census

PACIFIC OCEAN

22°N

Honolulu

HI (2)

20°N

0   100 mi
0   100 km

160°W   155°W

( ) Number of Representatives in the House of Representatives
✪ National Capital
★ State Capital

120°W   110°W   100°W   90°W   80°W   70°W

James Iredell

James Iredell was a colonial leader of North Carolina. He had a great influence on both our state and national governments. Iredell was born in England in 1751 and moved to Edenton when he was seventeen. Iredell became a lawyer and was well respected. From the start of the Revolutionary War, he supported the Patriot cause. During the Revolution he served as attorney general of North Carolina.

Iredell was a delegate to the Constitutional Convention of 1788. As the leader of the Federalists of North Carolina, he argued in favor of the adoption of the new Constitution. President Washington appointed him to be a justice of the new United States Supreme Court. He gave speeches to juries that explained the meaning of the Constitution. They were published all over the country.

Iredell County is named after him.

CAROLINA CONNECTION

James Iredell

415

KEY IDEAS

- The federal government is divided into three parts: legislative, executive, and judicial.

- The executive branch is led by the president. It enforces laws.

KEY TERMS

Democratic Party
diplomats
electoral college
Executive
party
President
Republican Party
vice president

To solve the problems of the Articles of Confederation, the writers of the Constitution created a new government. It was a federal system. We call our national government the "federal" government.

The main offices of the federal government are located in Washington, D.C. The abbreviation D.C. stands for District of Columbia. The city of Washington, D.C., was built to be the headquarters of the national government.

Three Branches

The federal government has three branches. First is the legislative branch, called Congress. Second is the executive branch. The president is the head of the executive branch. The third branch is the judicial branch. The Supreme Court is the highest court in the judicial branch.

The Executive Branch

The *executive* branch is the branch of government that carries out the laws passed by Congress. The *president* is the head of the executive branch. The president enforces the laws passed by Congress. When we read about the history of the United States in this book, we are learning about many of the decisions our past presidents have made.

The eagle on the presidential seal represents the country. **What do you think the arrows and the olive branch represent? Why might the eagle be facing the olive branch?**

Vice President

The *vice president* is second-in-command to the president. The vice president replaces the president if the president dies while in office or if the president cannot do his or her duties. Often, the president asks the vice president to represent the United States at special events or meetings in other countries.

The vice president also serves as the president of the Senate in Congress. He or she can only vote to break a tie in the Senate.

The President's Responsibilities

The jobs of the president have grown over time. Today, the president has seven major responsibilities. Some of these jobs are listed in the Constitution. Some have been added in times of crisis, like wartime. These make up the president's five official responsibilities.

Head of State The first role of the president is *head of state*. In some nations, the head of state is a king or a queen. The president is the American head of state. He or she is a living symbol of the nation.

As head of state, the president stands for the highest values and ideals of our country. The president acts as head of state when he awards medals to war veterans.

Chief Executive The president is also the *chief executive*. As head of the executive branch, the president is the "boss." The president decides how the laws of the United States are to be enforced.

He or she oversees all government workers in the executive branch. The branch is divided into departments. Each department deals with a different government job.

The federal government is our nation's largest employer! There are many, many government workers—almost 2 million. The soldiers and sailors in the military are also government workers. There are another 1.4

million active duty people in the military.

As chief executive, the president hires people to help run the executive branch. The heads of the departments make up the cabinet. The president meets with the cabinet to talk about what the government is doing. You read about the cabinet in chapter 7.

Federal Workers

- Military Workers 1.4 million
- Civilian Workers 2 million

Chief Diplomat *Chief diplomat* is the third role of the president. The president makes the foreign policy of the United States. The advisors help him or her. The president decides what our *diplomats* should say to foreign governments. Diplomats are people who represent our country to other nations.

When the president travels to meet with the heads of other governments, such as the president of Mexico, he is acting as the chief diplomat.

The U.S. Fish and Wildlife Service is one of the many executive departments. **How many people work for the federal government?**

Ronald Reagan
1911–2004

Ronald W. Reagan was born in Illinois. He worked his way through Eureka College. In addition to his studies, he played on the football team and acted in school plays. After graduation he became a radio sports announcer and then an actor in Hollywood, California.

Reagan had a long career in movies and on television before he became a politician. His wife, Nancy, was also an actress. He was elected the thirty-third governor of California and served two terms.

Reagan became the fortieth president of the United States. At age 69, he was the oldest person ever elected president. He was also the only president to be shot by an assassin (on March 30, 1981) while in office and live.

Reagan was nicknamed the "Great Communicator." He had excellent public speaking skills and a great sense of humor. He was one of our most popular presidents. In the last several years of his life, Reagan suffered from Alzheimer's disease. It is a disease that slowly destroys a person's memory and ability to talk or do daily tasks. When he died he was buried at the Ronald Reagan Presidential Library in Simi Valley, California.

President George H. W. Bush visited American troops in Saudi Arabia in 1990. **What powers are granted the commander-in-chief?**

Commander-in-Chief In wartime, the president's job as *commander-in-chief* is easy to see. The president is in charge of the nation's armed forces: the army, navy, air force, marines, and Coast Guard. All military generals and admirals take their orders from the president. The president decides where troops, ships, and equipment should be sent and how weapons shall be used.

Chief Legislator Only Congress has the power to pass laws. But the Constitution does give the president power to advise Congress about what laws are needed. As *chief legislator* the president may propose legislation to members of Congress. He or she can ask Congress to pass new laws. The president can also veto bills that he or she does not like.

Unofficial Responsibilities

Head of Party One job of the president that is not an official one is *head of party*. As the leader of his or her political party, the president helps members of that party get elected. The president campaigns for party members who have supported his or her policies.

Chief Guardian of the Economy The last role is also an unofficial role. The president does not control the economy. But citizens and businesses expect that the president will keep it running smoothly.

As *chief guardian of the economy*, the president thinks about such things as unemployment, high prices, taxes, business profits. He or she looks at the general well being of Americans.

The president meets with economists, people who study the economy, and business leaders. They discuss the country's needs and problems. The president makes decisions with their help.

The President's Cabinet

The Constitution says that the president "may require the opinion, in writing, of the principal officer in each of the executive departments, upon any subject relating to the duties of their . . . offices . . . " But the Constitution does not tell us how many executive departments should be created. It does not tell us which departments should be made.

This is an example of the flexibility of the Constitution. As the nation has grown, more departments have been added. We have not had to amend, or change, the Constitution to do this. Over time, some departments have been combined, broken apart, or renamed.

Cabinet Secretaries

The executive departments are led by people we call secretaries. The secretaries make up the president's cabinet. They are appointed by the president. But before they can start to work, they must be approved by a majority vote of the Senate. That is 51 votes.

The president is the "boss" of the department secretaries. Only the president can fire them. They are expected to resign, or quit, when a new president takes office.

President Bill Clinton spoke at the 2000 Democratic National Convention. **What is one of the unofficial duties of the president?**

There is no official schedule for cabinet meetings. Most presidents try to meet with their cabinets about once a week. Besides the president and department secretaries, cabinet meetings are usually attended by the vice president, the United States ambassador to the United Nations, and a few other top-level officials.

Executive Branch Departments in the Cabinet
Secretary of Agriculture
Secretary of Commerce
Secretary of Defense
Secretary of Education
Secretary of Energy
Secretary of Health and Human Services
Secretary of Homeland Security
Secretary of Housing and Urban Development
Secretary of Interior
Attorney General
Secretary of Labor
Secretary of State
Secretary of Transportation
Secretary of Treasure
Secretary of Veteran Affairs

Cabinet members oversee specific areas of government and report to the president. **What does the Constitution say about the role of the cabinet?**

Government of the People

The Electoral College and the Elections of 1876 and 2000

The presidential election of 1876 has some similarities to the election of 2000. In 1876, Republican Rutherford B. Hayes ran against Democrat Samuel J. Tilden. In 2000, Republican George W. Bush ran against Democrat Albert Gore.

In both 1876 and 2000, politicians had to solve disagreements in the electoral college. In both elections, the electoral vote and the popular vote were won by different candidates. In each case, the Democrat won the popular vote and the Republican won the electoral college.

The 1876 election was undecided. There were problems with the voting in Florida. Congress appointed a special Electoral Commission to work things out. The commission made a backroom deal known as the Corrupt Bargain. It voted to make Hayes president. In return, Hayes promised to end Reconstruction and remove federal troops from Southern states. The election controversy's shadow never left Hayes. He was nicknamed "Rutherfraud."

Senate President Ferry announces the results of the close 1876 election.

Rutherford B. Hayes (left) and Samuel J. Tilden (right)

People rally for their candidate at the Supreme Court in December 2000.

The 2000 election had similar problems. The winner of Florida would get 21 electoral votes. On election day, news organizations first announced that they thought Gore would win Florida. Then early on election night, they called Bush the winner. They said that with Florida's 21 electoral votes, he had a total of 271 electoral votes. That was one more than Bush needed to win the presidency.

But Florida's votes were very close. Later in the night, the news organizations changed what they said again. They said the election was too close to call.

It looked like Gore had lost Florida by about 2,000 votes. Democrats argued that Gore had lost because of fraud, or cheating, and counting mistakes.

Democrats went to court. They asked judges to force Florida to recount thousands of votes. The Florida Supreme Court told the state to recount only ballots that had not been counted correctly the first time.

The election of 2000 was decided in the courts. The United States Supreme Court settled the dispute. It overturned the decision of the Florida Supreme Court. It told Florida that there would not be any more recounts. Florida then made Bush the official winner by 537 votes.

George W. Bush was then certified, or made official, as the winner of Florida's electors. Therefore he won a majority in the electoral college. He became our forty-third president.

George W. Bush (left) greets Albert Gore (right)

Presidential Elections

We elect a president and vice president every four years. Presidential elections are exciting and expensive events. They officially begin when political groups select candidates to run for president and vice president. An organized political group is a political party.

Political Parties

The United States has two major political parties, the *Democratic Party* and the *Republican Party.* . Most Americans consider themselves to be either a Democrat or Republican. Some people do not want to belong to a political party. They call themselves "independents."

There are other political parties (not the Democratic Party or the Republican Party) that sometimes offer candidates. They are called third-party candidates.

Primaries Parties choose the candidates for president. The political parties in each state have either an election, called a primary, or a special meeting, called a caucus. This is how the party decides who it will nominate to run for president. The person who wins the most primaries becomes the nominee.

The Democratic Party nominee and the Republican Party nominee, along with any third-party nominees, are the candidates for president.

The Election

The candidates campaign across the country. In a campaign, the candidates go out to meet people and ask for votes. They usually debate on television. Candidates spend millions of dollars campaigning. They buy many advertisements on television.

Finally, the citizens decide by voting on election day. Election day is always the Tuesday after the first Monday in November. This is when the Constitution says the vote should take place.

Electoral College The vote of the citizens is called the popular vote. But it is not the end of the election. In the popular vote, citizens are actually voting for members of the *electoral college.* The electors officially elect the president and vice president.

Each state has as many electors in the

> **Democracy:** rule by the majority (more than half the voters)
>
> **Republic:** the people elect representatives to make the laws

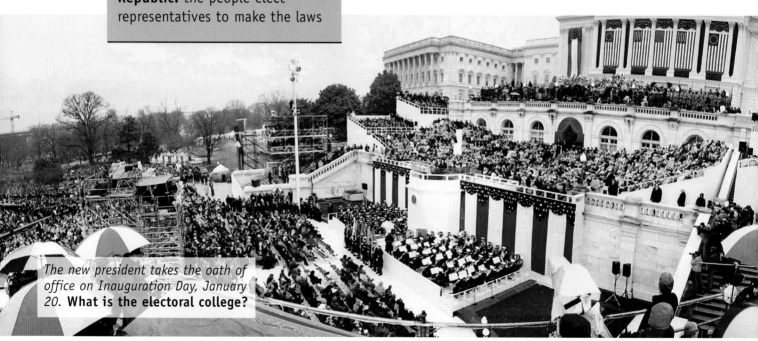

The new president takes the oath of office on Inauguration Day, January 20. **What is the electoral college?**

electoral college as it has senators and representatives in Congress. The District of Columbia has three electors. So with 100 senators, 435 representatives, and three electors from Washington, D.C., there are 538 electors.

The electors usually vote according to the popular vote in their state. For example, in most states, if a candidate wins 51 percent of the popular vote in a state, all of that state's electors will vote for that candidate.

To win the office of president, a candidate must win 270 electoral votes. If no candidate has a majority of electoral votes, the House of Representatives chooses the president. That has happened twice, in 1800 and 1824.

The person the electoral college chooses becomes the president-elect. Inauguration Day, when the new president and vice president take office, is January 20th.

What would YOU do?

Elections are exciting. They can stir up deep feelings. You want to have a discussion about an upcoming election in your class. You also want to avoid anger and hurt feelings among your classmates. What rules would you make to guide the discussion?

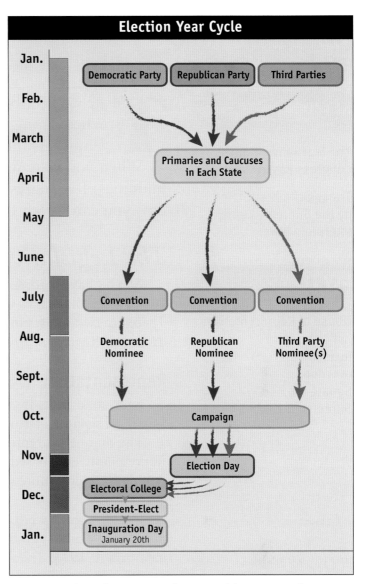

It takes about a year for a president to run for office and be inaugurated. **What are primaries?**

LESSON 1 REVIEW

Fact Follow-Up
1. What are the official responsibilities of the president of the United States?
2. What are the unofficial responsibilities of the president?
3. What is the president's cabinet?
4. What is the electoral college?

Talk About It
1. The cabinet of the president is an example of the flexibility of the Constitution. Why?
2. What happens if no presidential candidate wins a majority of the electoral votes?
3. Why was the Election of 1876 called a "corrupt bargain"?

Government of the People

KEY IDEAS

- The legislative branch of Congress passes laws.

- The judicial branch, led by the Supreme Court, interprets laws.

KEY TERMS

House of Representatives
judicial
legislative
override
Senate
Supreme Court

The Capitol is where Congress meets. **Which branch of government is Congress? What are its two houses?**

The Capitol Building is located in Washington, D.C. It is where Congress meets. Across the street from the Capitol is the Supreme Court Building.

When you visit Washington D.C., you can tour both buildings. If Congress or the Supreme Court are meeting that day, you can watch from the galleries.

The Legislative Branch

As you have read, Congress writes the laws for the nation. This lawmaking role makes Congress the *legislative* branch of government. There are two houses in Congress. They are the *Senate* and the *House of Representatives.*

Representation

Each state elects two senators. There are a total of 100 senators in the Senate. A senator's term is six years.

The number of representatives a state has in the House of Representatives is based on the state's population. States with larger populations elect more representatives. Representatives are elected to two-year terms.

In 1789, there were 65 members of the House. That number grew as more people and states were added to the country. It reached 435 members in 1913. Then Congress voted to make that number the limit.

States may gain or lose representatives as they gain or lose population. North Carolina has 13 representatives in Congress.

Making Laws

The main job of Congress is to make, change, or end the laws of the federal government. Congress decides what taxes American citizens must pay.

Before a law becomes a law, it is a bill. Members of Congress submit bills. Even if the president suggests an idea for a law, the bill for that law must be submitted by either a senator or a representative. All bills that propose to raise taxes must be submitted in the House.

Next, a bill is studied by a committee in the chamber of Congress where it was submitted. If the committee thinks the bill should be voted on, it gets sent out for a vote. The Senators or the House members vote on the bill. It must get a majority of votes to pass.

Say a bill passes in the Senate. Next, it gets sent to the House. A bill must pass both houses of Congress. After it has passed out of Congress, it is sent along to the president. If the president signs the bill, it becomes law.

Vetos

The president might not want the new law. If he rejects the bill, this is called a veto. The bill returns to Congress. It is voted on again. Both houses of Congress must pass the bill again with a two-thirds majority. Then the bill becomes law without the president's signature. This is called an *override.*

AMERICAN PORTRAIT

Sandra Day O'Connor
1930–

Sandra Day O'Connor grew up on the Lazy B Ranch in Greenlee County, Arizona. As a young girl, she was the first female to go on a cattle roundup on her father's ranch. O'Connor later became the first female to do some important things in the government.

She was the first female in the nation to serve as Senate majority leader. Later, President Ronald Reagan made her the first female to serve on the U.S. Supreme Court. She helped make important decisions for our country. She retired from the court in 2006 after serving 25 years.

Few cases are heard before the Supreme Court, but those that do often change the interpretation of the Constitution. **Why is it important to have a Supreme Court in our government?**

The Judicial Branch

The *judicial* branch is the third branch of the federal government. The United States **Supreme Court** and federal courts make up the judicial branch.

The Supreme Court decides what the laws passed by Congress mean. It also makes sure that laws do not go against the Constitution. There are many Supreme Court decsions discussed in this book.

The president appoints the justices of the Supreme Court. The Senate must approve those choices. Justices may hold office for life or until they choose to retire.

Customs

Americans enjoy displaying the national flag, "the Stars and Stripes," on Independence Day, Memorial Day, and other holidays. A special day to honor the flag is Flag Day (June 14). It started as a class project in 1885. Teacher B. J. Cigrand and his class wanted to celebrate the anniversary of when America chose the stars and stripes as its flag. Now Flag Day is celebrated throughout the country.

Other federal courts include 13 federal courts of appeal and 95 federal district courts. The judges of these courts are also appointed by the president, with the approval of the Senate. They hold office for life.

A case may be heard in a federal court when it involves the Constitution, the laws of the federal government, or a conflict between states.

Checks and Balances

The writers of the Constitution created three branches of the federal government. Each branch "checks," or limits, the power of the others. One branch has the power to check the power of the other two branches.

An example of this is when the president appoints a new justice to the Supreme Court. The Court does not have the power to choose its own members. And the Senate has to approve of the person the president wants. So the president (executive branch) and the Senate (legislative branch are checking the power of the Supreme Court (judicial branch).

This system of checks and balances prevents any one branch of government from becoming too strong. The skill lesson at the end of this chapter will help you learn how this system works.

LESSON ② REVIEW

Fact Follow-Up
1. What two bodies make up the legislative branch of government?
2. What is the job of the legislative branch of government?
3. What is the job of the judicial branch of government?
4. What are checks and balances?

Talk About It
1. Why does our national government have a system of checks and balances?
2. Why do you think the number of members of the House of Representatives was set at 435?
3. When may a case be heard in a federal court?
4. Describe a veto.

LESSON (3) State and Local Government

The last amendment in the Bill of Rights is important. It says that any powers in the Constitution that were not given to the national government belong to the states and to the people. This is called a federal system of government.

All states have their own constitutions. Each of these makes the rules for its state government. These state constitutions give certain rights to the state governments. They give other rights to local governments and to the citizens of the state.

The Federal System

In our federal system of government, the national government shares power with the states. Both can tax the people, make laws, enforce laws, and decide what laws mean. A state government makes state laws.

Sometimes state and national governments deal with different sides of the same problem. A state government, for example, may pass laws for companies that make medicine and sell the medicines in the state. The national government can make rules for the same companies, but only if they sell their medicines in more than one state.

KEY IDEAS

- In our federal system of government, the national government shares power with the states.

- State governments are similar to the federal government.

- State governments deal with matters within state borders.

- County and local governments provide services.

KEY TERMS

appeal
General Assembly
governor
juries
municipal

Our Federal System		
Level	**Place**	**Examples of Power**
Local	Cities and counties	• city police and firefighters • county roads and bridges • water and sewer
State	North Carolina	• state lands and resources • state roads • drivers' licenses
National	United States	• national defense • printing money • relations with other countries

Government of the People

WORD ORIGINS

National Government Powers

The Constitution gives the power to print money and declare war only to the national government. There would be problems if all the states printed their own money, or if one state wanted to go to war but the rest did not. For the same reason, only the national government can make relationships with the governments of other countries.

State Government Powers

Under the Constitution, powers that are not given to the national government are given to the states. State laws, however, cannot go against the laws passed by Congress.

State governments act on many things close to our everyday lives. For example, each state creates its own education system. The state government makes laws about how schools shall be run.

State Government

State governments must cooperate with the federal government. They are set up much like the national government. But each state government is slightly different from the other states.

Like the federal government, state governments have three branches. They have a legislature, an executive, and a judicial branch. These branches also have checks and balances, just like the national government.

In North Carolina, the three branches of state government have their headquarters in Raleigh. Raleigh is the capital of our state.

The General Assembly

The legislative branch in North Carolina is called the *General Assembly.* It has two branches, just like Congress. North Carolina's senate has 50 members. North Carolina's house of representatives has 120 members.

The job of the General Assembly is to make laws for the state. Adults vote to elect state senators and representatives every two years.

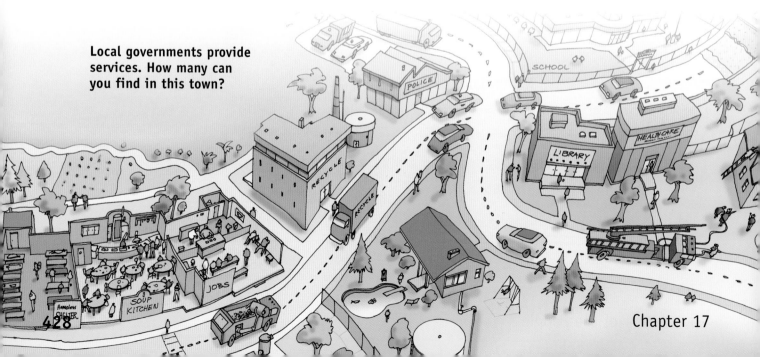

Local governments provide services. How many can you find in this town?

Sales Tax

When you buy a toy at the store, you pay a sales tax. The sales tax in North Carolina is 4.5 percent. That means that for every dollar you spend, you must pay about four cents. The money from the taxes goes to state government.

Local governments also add on a sales tax of at least 2.5 percent.

Income Tax

People and businesses pay taxes on the money they make. This is called an income tax. Your parents have to pay income tax every year.

They pay federal income tax to the United States government. They also pay state income tax to North Carolina.

Property Tax

If you own land, a home, or a building, you have to pay property tax.

If you rent your home, the landlord uses part of your rent to pay property taxes.

The property taxes go to local governments.

The Governor

The job of the executive branch of government is to carry out the laws passed by the General Assembly. The executive branch is led by the *governor.* In North Carolina, the governor is elected every four years. He or she can serve two consecutive, or back-to-back, terms.

The executive branch prepares the state budget. It must then be passed by the General Assembly. Like the president at the national level, the governor is the "boss" of state workers. The governor appoints the heads of state agencies.

State Agencies State agencies are the departments of state government. In North Carolina, these include the Division of Crime Control and Public Safety, the Department of Agriculture, the Department of Labor, the Department of Cultural Resources, and the Department of Public Instruction.

State agencies have offices across the state to help people. When you are helped by a State Highway Patrol Trooper, or visit a state historic site, or even open your textbook, you are using services provided by state agencies.

One role of county government is police protection. **What other services do citizens receive from county governments?**

The Court System

The judicial branch of the state government of North Carolina has several levels. These levels make up the court system.

The Supreme Court The highest state court is the state supreme court. It is made up of seven justices. The head justice is called the Chief Justice. North Carolinians vote to elect the justices. They serve eight-year terms.

Other Courts Cases are first heard in superior and district courts. Superior courts hear serious criminal and civil cases. District courts hear less serious criminal and civil cases. The decisions in these courts are made by juries.

Juries are groups of ordinary people picked to make the decision. The Bill of Rights says that all Americans have the right to be tried by a jury. Serving on a jury is a responsibility of being a citizen.

Sometimes people believe that these courts did not follow the law in deciding their case. A person can ask, or *appeal,* to a higher court to review their case.

Appeals The main job of both the state supreme court and the court of appeals, like the U.S. Supreme Court, is to review cases. The court of appeals is the second-highest court in our state. Many people appeal, but not every case gets to be heard again. The judges and justices of these higher courts choose which cases should be heard again.

Local Government

Within each state there are also county and *municipal* (city or town) governments. These also are close to our daily lives. They provide law enforcement, help the state build roads, and assist with the support of schools.

Adults vote for the leaders of county and municipal governments, too. Voting is another responsibility of being a citizen.

The capitol building in Raleigh, North Carolina, is the seat of government for the state. **Where else can you find state government in action?**

LESSON ③ REVIEW

Fact Follow-Up
1. What things does the Constitution allow only the national government to do?
2. What are three levels of government in our state?
3. Describe the legislative branch of government in North Carolina.
4. What are the jobs of county and municipal governments in North Carolina?

Talk About It
1. Why is printing money one of the powers given only to the national government?
2. Why do we have both national and state court systems?
3. Even though powers not given to the national governments are given to the states, states cannot pass laws that go against laws passed by Congress. Why?

Analyzing, Interpreting, Creating,
and Using Resources and Materials

Reading a Chart

The United States government has a system of checks and balances. Each of the three branches of government has certain powers. These powers "check," or limit, the powers of the other two. In this way, the authors of the Constitution hoped that one branch of government would not have more power than the other branches.

Look at the chart below. With your finger, trace the path of each arrow between each of the branches. What are the three branches of government? What powers do they have? What powers do they not have?

Now, answer the following questions.

1. Which branch of government passes laws?
2. Which branch can veto legislation, or laws?
3. Which branch can declare legislation unconstitutional, or against the Constitution?
4. Which branch can propose or suggest legislation?
5. Which branch can override a presidential veto?
6. Which branch can impeach, or remove, judges?
7. Which branch can appoint federal judges?

Checks and Balances

EXECUTIVE BRANCH

- Vetoes bills
- Makes annual speeches to Congress
- Calls special sessions of Congress
- Recommends legislation

- Grants pardons and reprieves to federal offenders
- Appoints federal judges

- Can impeach and remove the president
- Can overrule the president's veto
- Can refuse to ratify treaties or confirm appointments

- Declares executive acts unconstitutional
- Serves for life so is free from control by the president

- Declares laws unconstitutional

LEGISLATIVE BRANCH

- Can impeach and remove judges
- Denies judicial appointments
- Creates lower federal courts

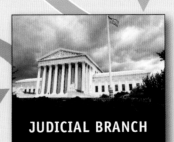

JUDICIAL BRANCH

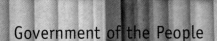

Lessons Learned

LESSON 1
The Executive Branch
The federal government has three branches: legislative, executive, and judicial. The executive branch, led by the president, enforces laws. The vice president becomes president if the president dies while in office. The president is advised by the cabinet, which is made up of the heads of government departments. The electoral college votes for the president.

LESSON 2
The Legislative and Judicial Branches
The legislative branch of Congress passes laws. The judicial branch, led by the Supreme Court, interprets laws.

LESSON 3
State and Local Government
The United States has a federal system of government. The national government shares power with the states. States have three branches of government. Local governments provide many services.

Talk About It

1. Which job of the president do you think is most important? Explain why.
2. Many people believe that the electoral college is no longer needed and that the president should be chosen by the direct vote of the people. Why might they feel this way?
3. Should federal judges be elected instead of appointed? Explain your answer.
4. Why do you think local governments have the responsibilities they have?
5. If you could hold any job in the United States or North Carolina government, which job would you choose? Explain why you would choose this job.

Mastering Mapwork

LOCATION
Use the map on page 415 to answer these questions:

1. How many representatives does North Carolina have in the House of Representatives? How many senators? How many electors in the Electoral College?
2. Which state has the largest number of electoral votes, and in which region is it located?
3. Which political region has the second-largest number of electoral votes?
4. A person needs 270 electoral votes to be elected president of the United States. Is it possible for New England to elect the president?

Becoming Better Readers

Using Graphic Organizers
　　Graphic Organizers are good tools to build understanding. Good readers use graphic organizers to think about important ideas. Make a Graphic Organizer to show your understanding of the Checks and Balance system.

Go to the Source

Understanding an Inaugural Speech

This is an excerpt from President Ronald Reagan's Inaugural Address on January 20, 1980.
It is the first speech he made as president. The inauguration is the ceremony that makes the president-elect become the actual president. After presidents are sworn into the office, they make a speech to thank Americans and to tell them what they will do as their leader. Read the speech below and answer the following questions using information from the speech.

To a few of us here today, this is a solemn [serious] and most momentous [grand] occasion; and yet, in the history of our Nation, it is a commonplace occurrence. The orderly transfer of authority as called for in the Constitution routinely takes place....In the eyes of many in the world, this every-four-year ceremony we accept as normal is nothing less than a miracle.

Mr. President [Carter], I want our fellow citizens to know how much you did to carry on this tradition. By your gracious cooperation...you have shown a watching world that we are a united people pledged to maintaining a political system which guarantees individual liberty to a greater degree than any other, and I thank you...for all your help...

Those who say that we are in a time when there are no heroes just don't know where to look. You can see heroes every day going in and out of factory gates. Others...produce enough food to feed all of us and then the world beyond. You meet heroes across a counter—and they are on both sides of that counter...They are individuals and families whose taxes support the Government and whose voluntary gifts support church, charity, culture, art, and education. Their patriotism is quiet but deep. Their values sustain [support] our national life.

I have used the words "they" and "their" in speaking of these heroes. I could say "you" and "your" because I am addressing the heroes of whom I speak—you, the citizens of this blessed land. Your dreams, your hopes, your goals are going to be the dreams, the hopes, and the goals of this administration, so help me God.

Questions
1. Who was leaving the office of President during this ceremony?
2. Based on the information in this speech, why do many in the world consider this ceremony nothing less than a miracle?
3. Why did Reagan take the time to describe the everyday heroes in his speech?

Unit 5

During the early 1900s, Canadian artists called the Group of Seven wanted to capture the spirit of Canada in their images of Canadian landscapes. Paintings like The Solemn Land *(right)*, *by J. E. H. MacDonald, expressed the importance of Canada's wilderness to Canadians. MacDonald and the rest of the group showed the majesty, splendor, and power of Canada in their paintings of mountains, streams, and prairies. The Group of Seven helped Canadians appreciate their country. As you read about Canada's land and people, you also may come to appreciate our northern neighbors.*

The Solemn Land *by J. E. H. MacDonald*

434

Canada

Unit Preview

CHAPTER 18

The Land and People

The night sky in Canada is often filled with colorful light. It is not starlight. It is the Northern Lights, also known as the Aurora Borealis. Green, pink, yellow, and blue lights arc and dance across the sky.

These are not special effects. The lights are actually collisions between electrically charged particles from the sun that enter the earth's atmosphere. The lights are seen above the poles of the Northern and Southern Hemispheres. They are known as Aurora Borealis in the north, meaning "dawn of the north."

The Northern Lights can be seen from anywhere in Canada, but the best places are the far northern territories of Yukon, Nunavut, and the Northwest Territories. The best time of year to see them is winter, when nights are long and often clear.

The Northern Lights are just one of the amazing sights to see in Canada. It is a land of wide-open spaces, high mountains, and modern cities. Canada's people have come from all over the world. They have created a country that honors their many backgrounds.

Chapter Preview

LESSON 1
Location and Size
Canada is the world's second-largest country. It is north of the United States, in North America. Canada has many of the same landforms as the United States.

LESSON 2
Climate and Vegetation
Canada's northern location and its cold climate affect the land, vegetation, animal life, and people.

LESSON 3
Canada's Changing Environment
Canada faces environmental challenges in overfishing, logging, and energy development.

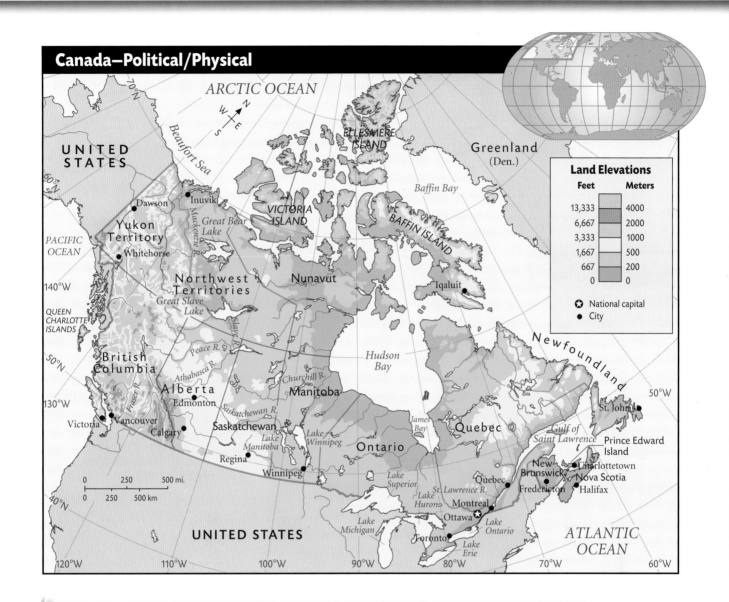

Canada—Political/Physical

Land Elevations

Feet	Meters
13,333	4000
6,667	2000
3,333	1000
1,667	500
667	200
0	0

⊛ National capital
● City

ARCTIC OCEAN

UNITED STATES

ELLESMERE ISLAND

Greenland (Den.)

Baffin Bay

Beaufort Sea

Dawson • Inuvik •

VICTORIA ISLAND

BAFFIN ISLAND

Yukon Territory

Great Bear Lake

Mackenzie R.

Whitehorse •

PACIFIC OCEAN

Northwest Territories

Nunavut

Iqaluit •

140°W

Great Slave Lake

Slave R.

Hudson Bay

Newfoundland

QUEEN CHARLOTTE ISLANDS

50°N

British Columbia

Peace R.

Athabasca R.

Fraser R.

Churchill R.

130°W

Alberta

Edmonton •

Manitoba

50°W

St. John's •

Victoria • Vancouver •

Saskatchewan R.

Calgary •

Saskatchewan

Lake Manitoba

Lake Winnipeg

Ontario

James Bay

Quebec

Gulf of Saint Lawrence

Prince Edward Island

Regina •

Winnipeg •

Lake Superior

Lake Huron

St. Lawrence R.

New Brunswick

Charlottetown
Nova Scotia

Fredericton •

Halifax •

UNITED STATES

Lake Michigan

Montreal •

Ottawa ⊛

Lake Ontario

Lake Erie

Toronto •

Quebec •

ATLANTIC OCEAN

0 250 500 mi.
0 250 500 km

120°W 110°W 100°W 90°W 80°W 70°W 60°W

Canadian Snowbirds

If you and your family like to go to the beach during the fall or spring, you might see cars with Canadian license plates. Many Canadians take their vacations in the late fall or early spring. Favorite destinations are the North Carolina beaches.

There Canadians can fish, walk, and wade through surf instead of winter sports like skiing, snowshoeing, or ice skating. Year-round beach residents call the visitors "snowbirds." Canadians also have come to Carolina beaches in the fall to windsurf on the Outer Banks. The water off Avon is sometimes called the "Canadian hole" because so many Canadians visit there.

The Land and People

Canada is a huge country. It runs almost 2,900 miles (4,669 km) from north to south. It is more than 3,200 miles (5,152 km) from east to west. Russia is the only country in the world with more territory than Canada.

Provinces and Territories

Canada's lands are divided into ten southern provinces and three northern territories. *Provinces* are political divisions similar to states in our country. *Territories* are also divisions. But they have less power than provinces. The national government has more control in territories.

The sizes of the provinces and territories go from very small to very large. The Canadian province of Manitoba is almost five times the size of North Carolina. But Canada's small eastern provinces of Prince Edward Island, Nova Scotia, and New Brunswick would fit inside North Carolina.

Canada's territories are huge. The Yukon, the Northwest Territories, and Nunavut together are three times larger than Alaska. Canadians call the territories "the North."

Location and Landforms

Canada covers most of the northern half of North America. Its coastlines touch the Atlantic, Pacific, and Arctic Oceans (see map, page 437). Alaska is on Canada's northwest border.

Canada shares many North American landforms, such as the Appalachian Mountains, the plains, and the Rocky Mountains. But much of Canada has a far northern coastline. Therefore, some Canadian landforms are different from any in the United States.

Canada's Size

Location Canada's larger area is contained within ten provinces and three territories. Some provinces are similar to the size of our states. *Where are those provinces?*

Bodies of Water

Water is very important to Canada.

Canada has more lakes than any other nation. The Great Lakes of Ontario, Superior, Erie, and Huron make up part of Canada's southern border with the United States. The Great Lakes contain about 18 percent of the world's fresh water supply.

The Hudson Bay covers about a third of mainland Canada. The bay is usually frozen. During the short summer months, Hudson Bay is a waterway to the inside of Canada.

Rivers

Because of its location, the St. Lawrence River is key to Canada's economy. It links the Great Lakes with the Atlantic Ocean through the St. Lawrence Seaway. This seaway was built by the United States and Canada. It is Canada's most important waterway.

Canada's other great rivers are the Columbia, the Fraser, and the Yukon. These empty into the Pacific Ocean. The MacKenzie River is the second longest in North America. It moves away from cities, north into the Arctic Ocean. Its outlet is usually locked in ice.

Montreal in Quebec was built along the St. Lawrence River. **What does the St. Laurence connect?**

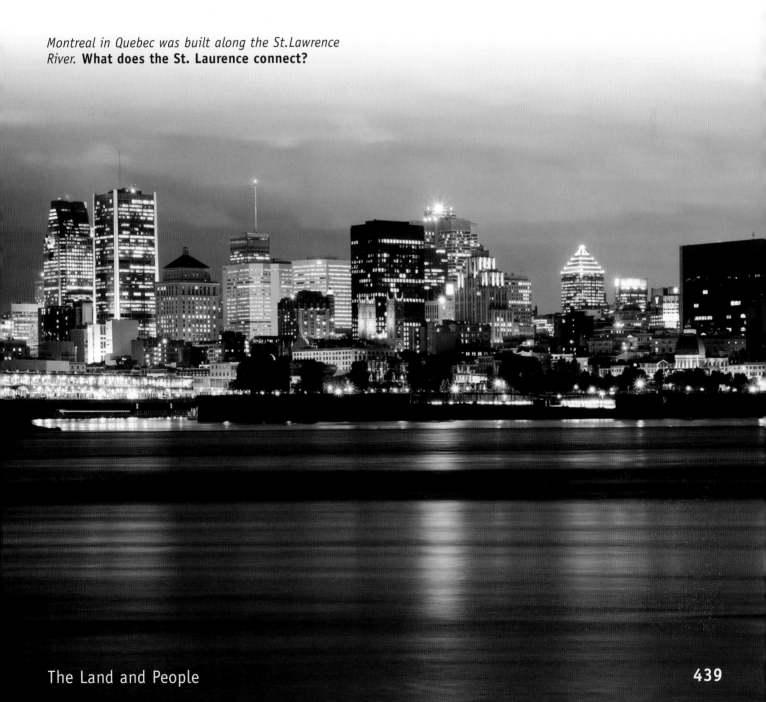

The Land and People

Canada's Regions

Geographers divide Canada into six regions. They are the Arctic Plains, the Appalachian Highlands, the Great Lakes-St. Lawrence Lowlands, the Canadian Shield, the Interior Plains, and the Western Mountains.

The Arctic Plains

Most arctic land is flat tundra plain. Tundra is so cold and dry that no trees can grow. But wildlife does live there. Canada's tundra is home to more polar bears, foxes, seals, and caribou than to people.

The Arctic Plains contains many minerals and energy resources. The costs of mining or drilling have limited their use. So have the fears of hurting the environment.

The Appalachian Highlands

The Appalachian Highlands run north from the United States into eastern Canada. These rolling hills are often covered with forests. Glaciers and ocean tides have carved the region's coast into bays and inlets. These are great natural harbors.

The four Atlantic provinces of Newfoundland, Prince Edward Island, Nova Scotia, and New Brunswick make up this region. Because these provinces are on the coast, they are also often called "the Maritimes."

The Appalachian Highlands includes such coastal areas as the Bay of Fundy in Newfoundland (below), where swift tides carve rocks. These tiny flowers (right) bloom on the tundra. **Why do only small plants grow on the Arctic Plains tundra?**

The Great Lakes–St. Lawrence Lowlands

The Great Lakes–St. Lawrence Lowlands region is Canada's smallest. But more than half of all Canadians live here. It is Canada's most southern region.

Americans often think that all of Canada lies north of the United States. But this is not the case. Look at the map. The land in this region extends south into the Great Lakes. Parts of the region are south of at least 13 states of the United States, including all of New England.

The region's good farmland, central location, and transportation links have made it Canada's industrial center. The region is located in the provinces of Quebec and Ontario.

The Canadian Shield

The Canadian Shield covers more than half of the nation. It touches parts of the Northwest Territories, Saskatchewan, Manitoba, Ontario, Nunavut, and Quebec.

More than 18,000 years ago, a huge glacier covered Canada. It moved south like a giant bulldozer. The ice sheet scraped away most of the soil. This left hard rock and thousands of holes. Over time, these holes filled with water and became rivers, bays, and lakes.

Parts of the shield that are not water or hard rock are flat and swampy lowland areas. These are called *muskeg.*

Under the ground in this region are many minerals. Iron, gold, lead, zinc, copper, and nickel can be found here. Do you remember what Brendan and his father picked up in Canada on their trip, way back in Chapter 1? Paper! Forests cover the surface of the Canadian Shield. Lumber, paper, and pulp from trees are important industries in Canada.

Kingston, Ontario, is a port city on Lake Ontario where the St. Lawrence River begins in the Great Lakes–St. Lawrence Lowlands. Glaciers scraped rock into layers in the Canadian Shield (above). **In which region do more people live? Why?**

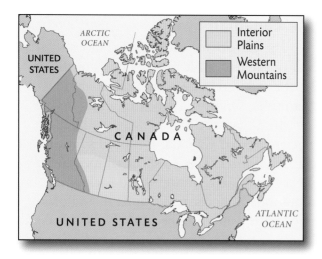

The Interior Plains

The southern parts of Alberta, Saskatchewan, and Manitoba make up the Interior Plains. The plains are west of the Canadian Shield.

The flat grasslands and low hills of the Interior Plains contain deep, fertile soil. The southern Interior Plains connects to the Great Plains of the United States. Evergreen forests cover the northern plains.

The Western Mountains

Huge mountains near the Pacific Coast run through North America. Look at the map of Canada on page 437. You can see the mountains between the Pacific Ocean and the plains. On the western side near the ocean are the Coast Ranges. On the eastern side, near the plains, are the Rocky Mountains.

The region covers almost all of British Columbia and the Yukon territories, and a small part of Alberta and the Northwest Territories.

Lake Louise in Alberta reflects the beauty of the Western Mountains region. **What might be some challenges that face people who live in this region?**

"Fifty-four Forty or Fight!"

The western border between Canada and the United States was undecided for many years. The United Kingdom controlled Canada. It and the United States both claimed the Oregon Territory.

This area covered from the Pacific Ocean eastward to the Rocky Mountains, and between 42°N and 54°40'N (see the map, page 437). The parallel of latitude at 54°40'N marked Alaska's southern boundary (Russia claimed Alaska then).

The Americans wanted to divide Oregon along the 49th parallel. That was the border between the United States and Canada east of the Rocky Mountains to New England. The British wanted a border further south along the Columbia River. They could not agree, so the two countries decided in 1818 that they would share the region. This worked for several years.

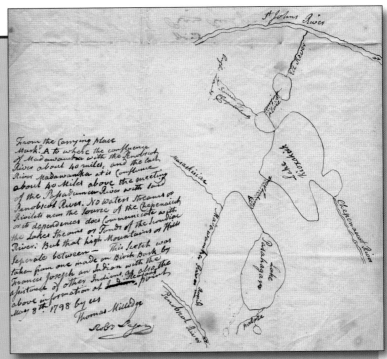

This sketch was made to determine the boundary between the United States and Canada.

By the 1840s, American settlers were moving to the region along the Oregon Trail. The land could no longer be shared. In 1844, James K. Polk a North Carolina native was elected president. Democrats told Polk that the United States position should be: "Fifty-four Forty or Fight!" This meant that they wanted to take control of all Oregon territory. They were willing to go to war for the land.

Polk compromised and the two countries came to an agreement. The Treaty of Oregon set the border at 49°N. Vancouver Island in Puget Sound went to Canada (see page 481 for more information about this part of the border). This border still exists today between the United States and Canada.

LESSON 1 REVIEW

Fact Follow-Up

1. How large is Canada? How large is it in comparison to other world areas?
2. How many physical regions does Canada have? What are their names?
3. What is the most northerly physical region of Canada? The most southerly? The farthest west? The farthest east?

Talk About It

1. In what ways is the Mackenzie River different from the Mississippi River? How important are the differences?
2. Why do you think President Polk wanted all of the Oregon Territory for the United States?

LESSON 2 Climate and Vegetation

KEY IDEAS

- Canada's northern location and cold climate affect the land, vegetation, animal life, and people.

- Canada has three types of vegetation: tundra, forests, and grasslands.

KEY TERMS

lichens

Winter in Quebec City means snow and low temperatures. It also means cross-country skiing and ice skating. **How does the climate affect life there?**

One of Canada's best-known writers is Stephen Leacock. He once joked that life in Canada could be divided into three seasons. He called them, "preparing for winter, enduring [getting through] winter, and recovering from winter."

Many Canadians might agree with Leacock. In most of Canada, the winters are long and cold. The summers are warm but short.

The warmer parts of Canada have climates similar to the cooler parts of the United States.

Climate

In northern Canada, winter brings cold temperatures, fierce winds, and big snowstorms. Just how cold? North of the Arctic Circle temperatures can stay below –20°F (–29°C) for more than four months.

Winter turns the town of Churchill, located on the Hudson Bay, into an icebox. People bundle up. It can get so cold that parts of the body not covered by clothes, hats, gloves, or scarves can freeze quickly.

In the large southern cities it is not quite so cold. But it is much colder than North Carolina. The thermometer may not rise above 0°F (–17.8°C) for more than half the year.

Tundra and Subarctic

Look at the climate map of North America on page 45 in Chapter 2. Northern Canada, including all of the Arctic Plains and much of the Canadian Shield, has short, cool summers. These regions have tundra and subarctic climates.

Steppe and Humid Continental

In southern Canada, summers are warm enough for raising crops. In the prairie provinces, farmers harvest large fields of grain, such as rye. They also grow a special type of wheat that does well in shorter growing seasons. Here, the southern Interior Plains region has steppe and humid continental climates.

The Appalachian Highlands, the southern part of the Canadian Shield, and the Great Lakes-St. Lawrence Lowlands regions also have a humid continental climate. All of these regions have cool, instead of warm, summers.

A Journey to THE CANADIAN PRAIRIE

Life on a Large Farm

Life in the prairie provinces of Manitoba, Saskatchewan, and Alberta often means life on a large farm.

Read the following from William Kurelek's *A Prairie Boy's Summer*. How is your life is similar to or different from the life of William, the boy in the story?

Haying was an important early summer job on dairy farms. When his father went into dairying William had to learn many of the steps necessary to make a haystack out of a field of grass. His father planted grass, but his neighbors rented sections of the bog to the east and cut natural grass. William envied the neighbors' boys, for they sometimes stayed out on the bog for two whole weeks cooking out in the open and sleeping under the wagon just like gypsies.

The first machine that was used in haying was the mower, and it had to be oiled often. William liked the scent of fresh-mown hay.

William had to learn how to build the stack properly and at the same time catch bundles of hay thrown up by his father. Once, after they had begun building a stack of clover, an approaching thunderstorm during the night forced the family to get up at 2:00 A.M. to put a peak on the stack to shed the rain. They finished just before the downpour and returned to the house at dawn.

Marine West Coast and Highlands

Some Canadians took part in a survey. They were asked in which province they would most like to live. British Columbia ranked first.

Unlike the rest of Canada, the coast of British Columbia has mild winters and cool summers. Mild, warm winds blow into British Columbia from the Pacific Ocean. So it has the Marine West Coast climate.

This area also has the wettest climate in the country. Parts of British Columbia get more than 100 inches (254 cm) of precipitation a year. Very little of that is snow.

Mild winters and heavy rainfall have been good for the trees. This part of Canada has the tallest trees in the country. There are thick forests of fir and cedar. Stephen Leacock called the province "an ideal home for the human race, not too cold, not too hot, not too wet, not too dry."

The mountains of the Western Mountains region have the highlands climate. As you have learned, climate gets cooler the higher you go above sea level.

Plant Life and Animals

Three types of vegetation cover most of Canada. In each region, temperature and rainfall affect plant life.

In the Arctic Plains, most of the land is tundra. South of there, forests cover about half of Canada. Long and short grasses once covered the Interior Plains. Today, the Plains has Canada's most fertile farmlands.

Tundra

Winter temperatures can fall as low as −60°F (−51°C) in the Arctic Plains. It is too cold and dry for roots to take hold. Roots that reach down into the tundra soil freeze and die.

Most of the tundra is permafrost. That means the top layer of soil is frozen all the time, all year long. During the few weeks of arctic summer, the very top of the permafrost thaws to a soggy mud mixture.

Butchart Gardens, on Vancouver Island in British Columbia, displays the lovely results of a mild climate. **Why is the climate here less harsh than in other parts of Canada?**

Chapter 18

Mosses, *lichens* (LIE·kens), and other small plants grow on the tundra. Lichen is a fungus. It grows together with algae and forms a kind of crust on rocks or tree trunks.

Arctic Animals Birds return for the short summer. Thousands of caribou cross the tundra. They grow fat by grazing on lichens and grasses.

By September, birds have flown south. Caribou have headed for the forests. By October, musk oxen, arctic foxes, and polar bears are the only large animals left on land. Walruses, seals, and whales can survive the cold, cold Arctic waters.

Caribou (below) live on the tundra, a frozen plain where only mosses, grasses, and flowers grow during a short summer. **Why do this Inuit mother and child wear such heavy clothing in the summer?**

The Land and People

Terrence "Terry" Fox
1958–1981

Terry Fox was born in Manitoba and raised in British Columbia. He played many sports as a teen. When he was eighteen, doctors told him he had bone cancer. Terry had to have his right leg amputated (removed) 6 inches (15 cm) above his knee.

While in the hospital, Terry met other cancer patients. Many were young children. He decided that he would run across Canada to raise money for cancer research. He trained for 18 months to get ready. He called his run the "Marathon of Hope."

Terry began by dipping his artificial leg in the Atlantic Ocean in Newfoundland on April 12, 1980. His goal was to dip his leg in the Pacific Ocean at the end. He wanted to run about 26.2 miles (42 km) a day. No one had ever done anything like this before.

During his run Terry kept a journal. Early in the trip he wrote, "Today we got up at 4:00 A.M. As usual, it was tough. If I died, I would die happy because I was doing what I wanted to do. How many people could say that? . . . I want to set an example that will never be forgotten."

As he ran, people heard Terry's story. They gave him money and support. He made it through Newfoundland, Nova Scotia, Prince Edward Island, New Brunswick, Quebec, and Ontario.

But after 143 days and 3,339 miles (5,373 km), Terry had to stop running. He had cancer in his lungs. Everyone was shocked and sad. Terry died the following year.

Terry is an inspiration to many people. He did not let physical challenges get in his way. He did something with only one leg that many able-bodied people would not even try.

Terry is still one of Canada's greatest heroes.

Customs

Curling is a popular winter sport in Canada. It is played on ice, but is not like hockey. In curling two teams of four players each slide 42-pound granite rocks toward the center of a 12-foot diameter target.

Each player throws two rocks toward the target, alternating with the opponent. The team with the rock closest to the center scores points. A unique part of curling is the sweeping. Players brush the ice in front of the rock to keep it moving. The friction of the brooms melts a thin layer of ice in front of the rock allowing it to travel farther and straighter.

Canada's Women's Olympic Curling Team won the bronze medal in 2006.

Most of Canada's regions, such as the Appalachian Highlands, are heavily forested. **Which regions lack forests?**

Forests

South of the tundra, the subarctic climate is still too cold for farming. The soil is poor, too. But trees grow well here.

Forests cover almost half of Canada's land area. Mountain wilderness spreads over the Yukon and part of the Northwest Territories. Forests also stretch across southern Canada. They run from Queen Charlotte Island on the Pacific Coast to Newfoundland, a large island in the Atlantic.

The West Coast has heavy rainfall. It also has Canada's longest growing season. There you can find giant evergreen trees. Douglas fir, cedar, and hemlock grow well.

The St. Lawrence Lowlands and other parts of southern Canada have huge maple forests. Maple syrup is an important product. The maple leaf is the country's symbol. Canada's flag has one large maple leaf in the center.

Grasslands

Like the plains in the United States, the grasslands in Canada are good for farming. The prairie provinces of the Interior Plains are Canada's breadbasket. Farmers there grow wheat and barley for their nation and the world. Farmers also raise hay, corn, and grain for cattle ranches and dairy farms.

LESSON 2 REVIEW

Fact Follow-Up
1. Describe Canadian winters in detail.
2. What are the three types of vegetation of Canada? How do they differ?
3. Why are the prairie provinces called Canada's "breadbasket"?

Talk About It
1. Why is the West Coast climate unlike that of the rest of Canada? How is it different?
2. Do differences in the region's climates affect the lives of people? Do they affect the economy?

The Land and People

LESSON (3) Canada's Changing Environment

KEY IDEAS

- Canada faces environmental challenges in overfishing, logging, and the development of hydroelectric and petroleum energy sources.

- Opposition to development has caused Canadians to rethink their use of the environment.

KEY TERMS

acid rain
James Bay Project
overfishing

Canada is one of the richest and most advanced countries in the world. Canadians want to be sure that they also protect their environment. Their land is important to them.

A Haida Native American artist worried about the effects of Canada's growth on the land. The artist wrote,

This is a great place, but we take it for granted. When I go back to my home, I see the scars of logging everywhere. The abalone is fished out.... It's really scary for me. We don't seem to notice the good things until they are gone.

Often choices are difficult. Cleaner air and water may mean fewer factories and fewer jobs. Canadians look to the North to find more resources. There are challenges there, too.

Canada's Resources

Canadians are slowly beginning to tap the resources of the Arctic Plains. Some of its many resources are found here. It costs a lot of money to mine metals and minerals in weather with temperatures below zero.

Transportation also is a major problem. The Arctic has only a few good roads. Most of the year, northern rivers are frozen solid or clogged with chunks of ice.

At a zinc and lead mine in the Arctic, the only way for workers to get to and from the mine is by airplane. The nearest port is free of ice for only a month and a half in the summer. Then a ship rushes in with enough food supplies for the entire year. The ship carries out all of the zinc and lead mined there.

Even with high pay, a heated underground swimming pool, and a gym, not many skilled workers want to work away from their homes for a long time.

The Confederation Bridge was completed in 1997, replacing a ferry service. The bridge connects Prince Edward Island to mainland Canada. **How could the bridge improve the island's economy?**

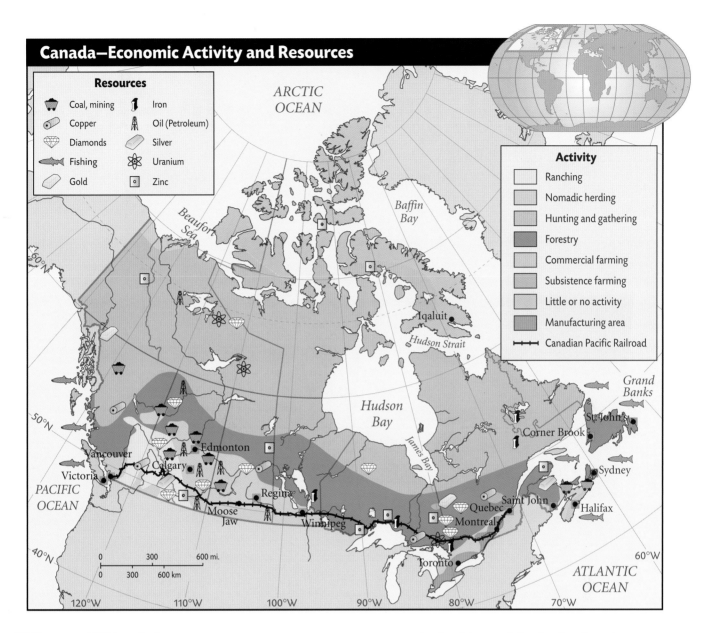

Canada—Economic Activity and Resources

Resources
- Coal, mining
- Copper
- Diamonds
- Fishing
- Gold
- Iron
- Oil (Petroleum)
- Silver
- Uranium
- Zinc

Activity
- Ranching
- Nomadic herding
- Hunting and gathering
- Forestry
- Commercial farming
- Subsistence farming
- Little or no activity
- Manufacturing area
- Canadian Pacific Railroad

ARCTIC OCEAN

Beaufort Sea

Baffin Bay

Hudson Strait

Iqaluit

Hudson Bay

James Bay

Grand Banks

St. John's

Corner Brook

Vancouver

Edmonton

Calgary

Victoria

PACIFIC OCEAN

Regina

Moose Jaw

Winnipeg

Sydney

Quebec

Saint John

Montreal

Halifax

Toronto

ATLANTIC OCEAN

300   600 mi.

300   600 km

120°W   110°W   100°W   90°W   80°W   70°W

60°W

60°N   50°N   40°N

Water Wealth

In the last 50 years, Canadians have been tapping another resource. Water resources, like rivers and waterfalls, can be put to use. Much of the energy used in Canada's factories and homes comes from hydroelectric power. It is cleaner for the environment than burning fossil fuels like coal or oil.

But water power is not without problems. Some Canadians are worried that hydroelectric plants will hurt the environment and the people of Canada.

During the building of the hydroelectric **James Bay Project,** large areas of land in Quebec were flooded. Many Native Americans were forced to find new homes.

The government, the Inuit, and the Cree of northern Quebec came to an agreement. The native peoples received 5,400 square miles (14,040 sq km) of land and more than $225 million (Canadian dollars) for their losses.

Several phases of the project have been completed. But other plans were cancelled and others were put on hold. Today, Quebec is planning to build a new dam in a new phase of the project.

The Land and People

451

Harnessing Hydroelectric Power

One resource Canada will not run out of is water. Canada has found ways to use the water to produce energy for its people and to sell to the United States.

Some large power plants are driven by water. They are called hydroelectric plants. Hydro means "water." The plants convert the water power into electricity.

To harness the power of the water, most hydroelectric plants are built near dams. Hydroelectric plants work when some of the water behind the dam rushes through pipes into the plant.

In the plant, water turns a wheel connected to a shaft, or large pole. The shaft runs a turbine where it spins powerful magnets. The magnets spin inside the turbine close to copper wire. This creates a strong electric current.

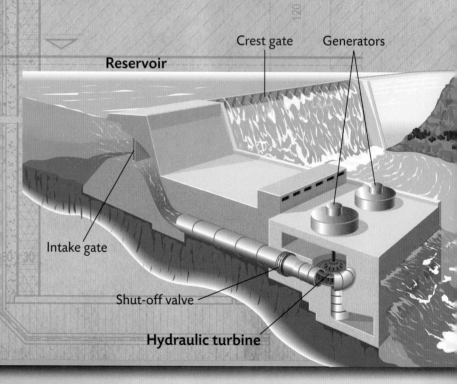

Crest gate Generators

Reservoir

Intake gate

Shut-off valve

Hydraulic turbine

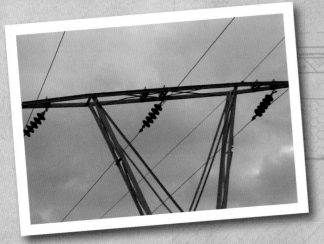

The electricity flows out of the plant on power lines. The electricity is then sent to thousands of homes, factories, and businesses. The power of water meets almost 75 percent of Canada's electricity needs.

The James Bay Project has built several hydroelectric power stations. They are on the La Grande River in northwestern Quebec at James Bay. The courses of La Grande and a few other rivers were moved. Then dams were built to create reservoirs. Water from the reservoirs powers the turbines.

The project covers an area of the size of the state of New York. It is one of the largest hydroelectric systems in the world. It makes enough power to meet the needs of half of Quebec. Planning began in 2004 to build a new dam on the Rupert River.

The Land and People

The Fishing Crisis

For many centuries, the Grand Banks off the Atlantic coast of Canada (see map, page 451) had many, many fish. It was the center of a huge fishing industry. Fishing boats netted all the fish they could. Few people thought the fish supply would be in danger.

But in the late 1980s, things began to change. Catches got smaller. The region was overfished. *Overfishing* means more fish are caught than hatched each year. Overfishing means that the fish population has dropped.

In the Grand Banks, the fish numbers are dangerously low. Commercial fishermen from around the world have hurt the fish populations. Technology has helped them find and catch the fish.

In 1994, the Canadian government stopped all cod fishing to give the cod population a chance to come back. Although some flounder species have come back, the cod has not. For now, the ban will continue.

In Canada's Atlantic Provinces, the fishing industry employed most people. The ban has caused many to lose their jobs and has hurt the economy.

Acid Rain

Some years back, park officials on Mount Mitchell, North Carolina's highest mountain, noticed trees on the mountain top were dying. Forests on surrounding mountains were already dead.

Scientists said that *acid rain* was the cause. This form of air and water pollution is caused by gasses from cars, factories, and power stations. The gasses mix with drops of water. Lakes, fish, and wildlife can be hurt by acid rain.

Many fishing boats on the Atlantic coast remain idle in harbors of the Appalachian Highlands because the Canadian government restricts cod fishing. **Why is fishing restricted?**

Acid rain is a serious problem for southern Ontario. Pollution comes from the smokestacks of factories and power plants. It is carried by winds to the lakes and forests of Canada. In Ontario alone, the fish in more than 1,000 lakes have been killed off by acid rain. Air pollution also threatens Canada's maple trees, the nation's symbol.

In the 1980s, Canada and the United States blamed each other for this problem, but in the 1990s they began working together to solve it. In 2004, the Canadian government said that in order to protect the environment, more needed to be done. Acid rain is still a problem.

These same sources of pollution also cause global warming. Canada requires power plants to keep harmful gases from leaving factory and power plant smokestacks. The United States is working with Canada to reduce the pollution.

Hard Choices

The James Bay Project has sharpened the debate over the use of Canada's resources. Should projects that bring such huge changes to the environment be repeated? Supporters say that the project brings jobs. It also brings money. Critics argue forests were destroyed and can never be replaced. The project was just too costly. The issues are still not settled.

What would YOU do?

If you lived in Canada, you would have to weigh the importance between people having jobs and the possible destruction of the environment. **What would you do? Would you argue for development? for preserving the environment? or something else?**

During a visit from the Queen of the United Kingdom and Canada to British Columbia, citizens protest against logging in the province. **How have Canadians encouraged protection of the environment?**

LESSON ③ REVIEW

Fact Follow-Up
1. How has Canada's physical environmental changed?
2. What are some of the difficulties of tapping the resources of the Arctic?
3. How do hydroelectric plants affect Canadians?

Talk About It
1. Why is it said there are too many fishermen and not enough fish in Canada?
2. What are some of the hard choices Canada faces? Which choice do you think will be most difficult? Explain why.

Applying Decision-Making and
Problem-Solving Techniques to World Issues

Acid Rain in Canada

Imagine that you live in a suburb of Toronto. One day you see a notice on a bulletin board in the shopping mall. It says:

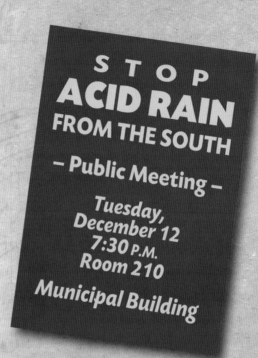

STOP
ACID RAIN
FROM THE SOUTH
– Public Meeting –
Tuesday,
December 12
7:30 P.M.
Room 210
Municipal Building

You must make a choice. As a citizen, should you attend the meeting? How do you decide whether to go? First, you might consider what you already know about the topic (in this case, acid rain.) What do you need to know in order to make good choices? Will this meeting (left) help you learn more?

A second way of deciding is to look at your reasons. List all the reasons to go to the meeting and all the reasons not to go on a piece of paper. Look it over. You can make your choices based on your reasons.

A *third* way of deciding is to find out which group is holding the meeting. Are you likely to learn new information? Will you only hear one side of the issue?

If you are likely to hear only one side of the issue, you might want to learn about the other side. You can read about other points of view or attend other meetings.

If you decide to attend the meeting, you will need to learn about the issue. How will you do this?

First, if there have been any articles about the subject in the newspaper, read them. Write down any questions you have after reading.

Second, watch TV news shows to learn more about the issue. Remember, though, that sometimes people say things on TV that may not be totally true. To get more information, use your school's media center and the Internet. They are good places to start your research.

Here are some facts you may learn about acid rain in Canada:

1. More than $1 billion worth of damage is caused by acid rain each year.

2. Eighty percent of Canadians live in areas of high acid rain levels.

3. More than 80 percent of the most productive agricultural land in eastern Canada receives more than acceptable levels of acid rain.

What do you decide to do to reduce levels of acid rain?

A copper-nickel mine and acid rain killed foliage on a hillside in Ontario.

Lessons Learned

LESSON 1
Location and Size

Canada is the second-largest country in the world. It includes six physical regions: the Arctic Plains, Appalachian Highlands, Great Lakes-St. Lawrence Lowlands, Canadian Shield, Interior Plains, and Western Mountains.

LESSON 2
Climate and Vegetation

The Canadian climate is cold, except in British Columbia on the West Coast, where the climate is mild. The climate allows the growth of three major types of vegetation: tundra, forests, and grasslands.

LESSON 3
Canada's Changing Environment

Canada faces the environmental challenges of overfishing, logging, acid rain, and discovering safe energy sources.

Talk About It

1. Imagine that you and your family are moving to Canada. In which region would you choose to live? Explain your answer in as much detail as you can.
2. Imagine that a visitor from Canada is coming to your school. What questions can you ask the visitor to find out the most about the climate, resources, and people of Canada? Why would you ask these questions? Explain your answer.

Mastering Mapwork

HUMAN-ENVIRONMENTAL INTERACTION

Use the map on page 451 to answer these questions:

1. Locate Vancouver in British Columbia and Dawson in Yukon Territory. How might human-environmental interaction in these two places differ even though both are located in the Western Mountains of Canada?
2. From this map and your reading in Chapter 18 would you say that people in the Arctic Plains region affect the environment more or that the physical environment affects people more? Explain.
3. Eight out of ten Canadians live within 200 miles of the United States border. Does this fact show more environmental influence on people or more human influence on the environment? Explain.
4. Would you expect to see similar patterns of human-environmental interaction in Regina, Saskatchewan, and Winnipeg, Manitoba? Are those patterns similar to or different from those in the United States?

Becoming Better Readers

More Graphic Organizers

Graphic organizers come in a variety of shapes and sizes. Graphic organizers are tools to help organize information. Make a graphic organizer to help organize all the information you learned about Canada in this chapter.

Go to the Source

Understanding Rankings

Read the document below from the Environment Canada division of the Canadian Government. Answer the questions using information from the data.

Canadian Cities are Weather Winners!

From St. John's to Victoria, Canadians love to brag about the weather that they endure (or enjoy!). Surely their community must get the most in the entire country! But which Canadian city really is the rainiest, the snowiest or the windiest? And where is the sunshine capital?

To find the answers, David Phillips, Environment Canada's Senior Climatologist, and the nation's favorite weather guru, has analyzed 30 years of recent weather data for Canada's 100 largest cities.

Weather Category*	First place	Second place	Third place
Coldest year-round	Yellowknife NT	Thompson MB	Whitehorse YT
Warmest year-round	Chilliwack BC	Vancouver BC	Abbottsford BC
Wettest (rain and snow)	Prince Rupert BC	Port Alberni BC	Chilliwack BC
Snowiest	Gander NL	Corner Brook NL	Sept-Îles QC
Most foggy days	St. John's NL	Halifax NS	Saint John NB
Sunniest year-round	Medicine Hat AB	Estevan SK	Swift Current SK
Windiest city year-round	St. John's NL	Gander NL	Summerside PEI

*Selected categories

Questions

1. Which city gets the most snow?
2. Which city is the third-wettest in Canada? the second-wettest?
3. Explain the difference between the meaning of the "Wettest" city and the "Snowiest" city?
4. Which city is the windiest and has the most foggy days?
5. Which city is the warmest and one of the wettest?

The Land and People

Settling a Nation

Chapter Preview

LESSON 1
People of Canada
Canada's citizens are diverse. Native American and Inuit peoples, descendants of the French and British settlers, and new immigrants from Asia, Africa, Latin America, and Europe, make up Canada's population.

LESSON 2
First Settlers
Native Americans and Inuit first settled in Canada. Europeans began to arrive about 450 years ago.

LESSON 3
Moving West
Gold and railroads brought settlers to the prairie provinces and the North.

Timeline of Events

1497
Cabot explores coasts of Newfoundland and Cape Breton

1583
Gilbert claims Newfoundland for Britain

1610
Hudson discovers Hudson Bay

1627
New France founded

1400   1500   1600

1534
Cartier claims Gulf of St. Lawrence for France

1608
Champlain founds Quebec City

1642
Montreal founded

1670
Hudson's Bay Company created

A photographer walked through a wilderness park in western Canada. He said,

Most places in North America, no matter how far you go into the wilderness, you find signs of people—a fire ring on the shore, the sound of a logging operation, a footpath. But here I've never even seen a jet trail. The birds own the sky and the only footprints come in sets of four.... If you're a person, you're a foreigner."

In some places in Canada, people are the "foreigners." The land is untouched. In other places, Canadians have reshaped the environment. In this chapter you will see ways Canadians have changed the land.

French Voyageurs were accustomed to demanding and difficult work as they transported goods and people from place to place.

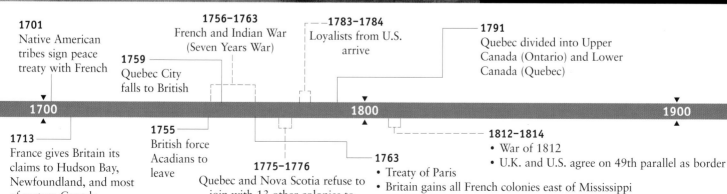

1701
Native American tribes sign peace treaty with French

1759
Quebec City falls to British

1756–1763
French and Indian War (Seven Years War)

1783–1784
Loyalists from U.S. arrive

1791
Quebec divided into Upper Canada (Ontario) and Lower Canada (Quebec)

1700

1800

1900

1713
France gives Britain its claims to Hudson Bay, Newfoundland, and most of eastern Canada

1755
British force Acadians to leave

1775–1776
Quebec and Nova Scotia refuse to join with 13 other colonies to rebel against Great Britain

1763
• Treaty of Paris
• Britain gains all French colonies east of Mississippi
• New France becomes British colony of Quebec

1812–1814
• War of 1812
• U.K. and U.S. agree on 49th parallel as border

LESSON ① People of Canada

KEY IDEAS

- The first settlers of Canada probably came thousands of years ago from Asia across the land bridge.

- Other Canadians are descendants of French and British settlers and new immigrants from Asia, the Middle East, and Europe.

- Most Canadians live along the United States border.

KEY TERMS

mosaic
New France

Canadian artist Robert Davidson was asked to describe what he liked about his country. "I like to be alone a lot. Canada is a good place to feel alone."

Why would he say this? Canada is a country of wide open spaces. But it does not have many people.

Think about the United States. Canada is bigger than our country. We have about 300 million people. Canada has about 33 million.

Canada's population is not spread out evenly across its land. Eighty percent of Canadians live within 200 miles (322 km) of the United States. The northern two thirds of Canada's land have few people.

Settlement Patterns

Several of the largest cities in Canada are found in the Great Lakes–St. Lawrence Lowlands region. These include Toronto, Montreal, and Ottawa. Ottawa is Canada's capital.

These cities are located close to other large cities in the United States. They are also located on important waterways. This has made them important for transportation and manufacturing.

On the Pacific Coast, Vancouver is in the southern part of British Columbia. It is a busy port city.

The huge spaces of northern Canada have less than 1 percent of Canada's people. Fewer people live in the Northwest, Yukon, and Nunavut Territories combined than in the city of Durham, North Carolina.

Because most of Canada is so thinly populated, even Canada's major cities are not far from the wilderness. In almost all parts of Canada, unsettled lands are no more than a few hours' drive away.

A Mosaic of Peoples

People from all over the world live in Canada today. The 2001 Census found that more than 18 percent of Canada's people were born in other countries.

Canadians compare their country to a mosaic. A *mosaic* is a type of artwork. It is made of many different small pieces. They are put together to create one large image. Canadians come from many different countries with different customs and beliefs. Together, these groups form the Canadian nation.

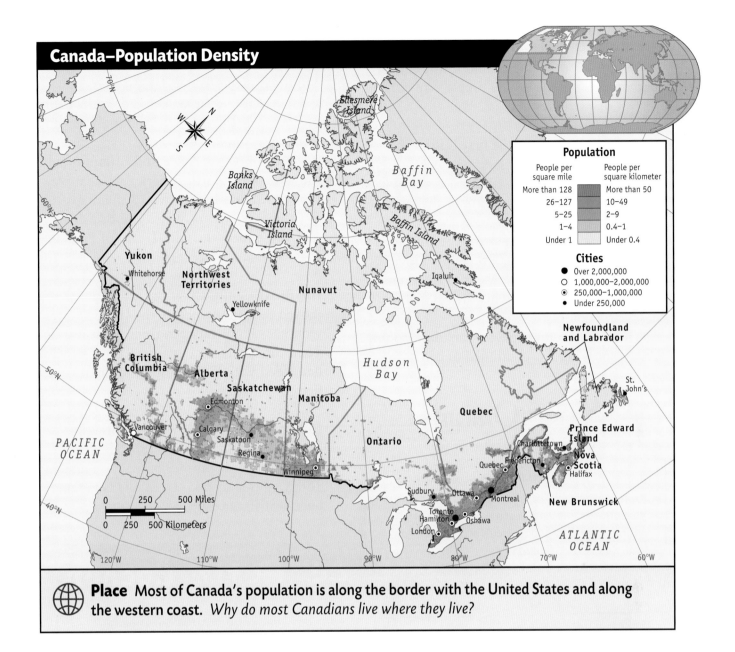

Canada–Population Density

Population

People per square mile	People per square kilometer
More than 128	More than 50
26–127	10–49
5–25	2–9
1–4	0.4–1
Under 1	Under 0.4

Cities
- ● Over 2,000,000
- ○ 1,000,000–2,000,000
- ◉ 250,000–1,000,000
- • Under 250,000

Place Most of Canada's population is along the border with the United States and along the western coast. *Why do most Canadians live where they live?*

The First Peoples

As you read in Chapter 4, the first settlers of Canada were Native Americans. The first people most likely walked over the land bridge from Asia. This bridge connected Asia and North America during the Ice Age. Canadians call these peoples the First Nations.

Other people, now known as the Inuit, also came from Asia. But they came near the end of the Ice Age. By then the land bridge was disappearing. Many Inuit probably came in boats.

Today, Inuit mostly live in the northern parts of the Northwest Territories, Nunavut, and Quebec. They make up less than 1 percent of Canada's people. Other Native American groups live in Canada. Many make their homes in the forest lands of the north.

At one time the Inuit and other Native Americans (First Nations) lived mainly by hunting, gathering, and fishing. After the arrival of Europeans, they rapidly lost their land to the new settlers. About 70 percent live on reservations that the government created for them. They work hard to preserve their cultures.

The French and British

Except for the Native Americans, almost everyone in Canada at one time spoke either English or French.

The French France was the first European country to explore and claim parts of Canada. French trappers and traders traveled by canoe and sled, learning about the land from Native Americans.

France started a permanent colony called *New France.* About 10,000 people moved there to build the colony. Most of the French people now living in Canada are related to these early colonists.

The number of people in Canada who are French-speaking has continued to grow.

Word Origins

In 1535, Jacques Cartier first sailed the St. Lawrence River. He asked Huron villagers what their land was called. Thinking he meant their town, they replied, "kanata." *Kanata* is a Huron-Iroquois word meaning "a settlement." Cartier returned to France and claimed discovery of a new land. He called it **"Canada."**

Today, people from many French-speaking countries move to Quebec. The city of Montreal is the second-largest French-speaking city in the world. (Paris, the capital of France, is the largest). About 23 percent of Canada's population is French-speaking.

In the 1700s, France and Britain fought for control of North America in what we call the French and Indian War (Canadians call this the Seven Years War). The British won. The war ended with the Treaty of Paris in 1763.

The British Only a few British colonists moved to Canada before the United States won its war for independence from Britain. Then thousands of Loyalists, colonists who had sided with Great Britain in the revolution, fled to Canada.

Loyalists were soon followed by people from other parts of Britain—especially Scotland and Ireland. By 1867, English-speaking people outnumbered the French. Today, about 25 percent of all Canadians have British ancestry.

This is a cafe in Quebec. **What in this picture shows French culture?**

Other Europeans

In the late 1800s, Canadians opened up their west to settlers. They built a railroad and offered free land. People from Iceland came to settle. Mennonites from Russia escaping religious persecution also came. People from Norway, Sweden, and Ukraine arrived. They all knew how to survive in a challenging climate.

After World War II ended, people from Italy, Greece, and Portugal settled in Canada. They were joined in the 1950s and 1960s by people from Hungary and Czechoslovakia. These refugees sought freedom in Canada after their countries were taken over by the Soviet Union.

Related to Raleigh
Several members of Sir Walter Raleigh's family explored the New World. Raleigh founded Roanoke. Sir Humphrey Gilbert, his half-brother, founded Newfoundland. Raleigh's son, Walter, was killed exploring South America; his half-nephew founded Fort St. George.

These Russian immigrants came to Canada in the early 1900s. **When did people from Italy, in southern Europe, move to Canada?**

The Canadian Colonies

You will learn more about how Canada formed a government in Chapter 20. But did you ever wonder about Canada's colonies? Were they like the 13 colonies that became the United States?

After the American Revolution, the colonies to the north of the United States were part of British North America. All of today's Canada was ruled by Great Britain.

Eastern Canada New France was founded by the French. After the French and Indian War (Seven Years War), it became a British colony. The British divided it into two parts, Ontario and Quebec. Later, these two colonies became the Province of Canada.

New Brunswick, Newfoundland and Labrador, Nova Scotia, and Prince Edward Island were all separate British colonies before joining Canada. Like the 13 American colonies, they each had their own governments.

Western Canada British Columbia was part of the Oregon Territory given to the United Kingdom and the United States by Spain. It became a British colony.

Manitoba and Northwest Territories were created in 1870 from lands bought from the Hudson's Bay Company. The Northwest Territories at one time covered most of northern and western Canada. Yukon, Alberta, Saskatchewan, and Nunavut were all once part of the Northwest Territories.

Canadians from Asia and Africa

In the 1880s, more than 15,000 Chinese workers helped build Canada's first railroad in the west. They became the first Asian settlers of Canada. From these roots, the Chinese community in Canada has grown.

In recent years, the cities of Toronto, Vancouver, Calgary, and Edmonton have attracted Asian immigrants.

People of African descent make up less than 1 percent of Canada's population. Many have come to Canada from island countries in the Caribbean. Other have come from South Africa, Somalia, and other areas of Africa.

Immigrants from the United States

Before the Civil War, many enslaved African Americans escaped to Canada. Slavery had been outlawed in Canada. Most Canadians were against slavery. Some of them wrote a song about the goals of the runaway slaves:

I'm on my way to Canada
That cold and distant land
The dire effects of slavery
I can no longer stand—
Farewell old master,
Don't come after me.
I'm on my way to Canada
Where men are free.

The Vietnam War in the 1960s again brought United States citizens to Canada. More than 32,000 young men moved across the border rather than serve as soldiers in that war. Many stayed and settled. Some did come back to the United States when they were allowed to return several years after the war ended.

Asian immigrants first moved to Canada to help build a railroad across the country. Many wealthy Asians now invest in the country. **To what part of Canada do most Asians move? Why?**

LESSON 1 REVIEW

Fact Follow-Up
1. Who were the first Canadians? Where did they settle?
2. From what areas of Europe have people moved to Canada? When did each group move?

Talk About It
1. What are some challenges facing a country with two or more languages spoken by entire provinces?
2. Why have European and other groups moved to Canada? Has life in Canada lived up to their expectations?

Analyzing, Interpreting, Creating,
and Using Resources and Materials

Population Distribution in Canada

The same information can be shown in different ways. So it is good to learn how to read different kinds of graphs, tables, maps, and charts.

Reading a Table or Graph

Look at these two different charts. They both show the population distribution in Canada. One shows this data in a table. The other shows this data in a bar graph.

The table shows information with words and numbers. It is a list. Look at the table. You can see the percentage of Canada's total population for each province and territory.

You can take data from the table. Use it to make a bar graph.

Reading a Map

The population density map on page 463 gives different information. Colors show you how the population is spread out in different areas. From the map you can learn how many people live in one area.

Using the Information

Being able to see information in different ways can be helpful. For example, suppose that you are opening a business to sell HDTVs in Canada. Your company needs to have one warehouse for each 1 million people. You know that Canada has about 33 million people.

How could you use these tables to figure out how many warehouses you need? Will these tables also help you decide on how many warehouses will be needed in each province? Can you use the map to help locate the warehouses? How?

Canadian Population Distribution, 2001	
Province/Territory	**Percentage of Total Population**
Alberta	9.9%
British Columbia	13.0%
Manitoba	3.7%
New Brunswick	2.4%
Newfoundland	1.7%
Nova Scotia	3.0%
Ontario	38.0%
Prince Edward Island	0.45%
Quebec	24.1%
Saskatchewan	3.26%
Northwest Territories	.124%
Yukon Territory	.095%
Nunavut	.089%

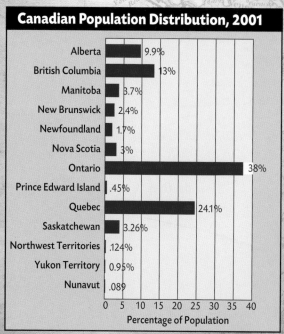

Canadian Population Distribution, 2001

Alberta 9.9%
British Columbia 13%
Manitoba 3.7%
New Brunswick 2.4%
Newfoundland 1.7%
Nova Scotia 3%
Ontario 38%
Prince Edward Island .45%
Quebec 24.1%
Saskatchewan 3.26%
Northwest Territories .124%
Yukon Territory 0.95%
Nunavut .089

Percentage of Population

*2001 Census of Canada

LESSON ② First Settlers

KEY IDEAS

- Native Americans adapted to Canada's climate.
- European explorers used the land's resources.
- Fish and furs were important for trade.

KEY TERMS

beavers
coureurs de bois
deportation
Grand Banks
umiaks
wigwams

The wind blows cold. The temperature drops below zero. Six sleds pulled by dogs cross the ice. Everyone is warm inside sealskin coats. The Inuit villagers cross the tundra. Tatatuapik (ta·ta·TOO·ah·pik) signals everyone to stop. He has found a lake under the snow and ice. He takes out his ice-cutting knife. He scrapes away the snow from the ice below him to make a fishing hole. Now there will be fish for dinner.

It is time to stop for the night. Everyone will need a place to sleep. There are few building materials on the treeless tundra. So Tatatuapik and the others use their long bone knives to carve blocks out of the packed snow. They stack the blocks to build a snowhouse.

The Inuit

It takes special skills to live in the Arctic. Knowing which way to go on flat, snow-covered ground takes great skill. An Inuit person will carefully look for the patterns the wind makes on snowdrifts. This helps him or her find their direction.

For thousands of years the Inuit have survived in the harsh environment of the Arctic. They use the resources of the sea and land. They have fished and hunted to get food and clothing.

They have used the skins of seals, caribou, and other animals. They make soft fur-lined jackets and sealskin boots to keep out the cold. They stretch animal skins over a whalebone frame. This makes lightweight summer tents. They use kayaks and *umiaks,* sealskin boats, to cross rivers and oceans. Whale oil gives heat and light. Meat, fat, and bone have their uses, too.

The Inuit have lived in the Arctic for thousands of years. **How do they survive in this environment?**

Natives in the Northern Forests

Like the Inuit, Native American settlers of Canada's forests also lived off the land. The Slave (slah·VAY), Cree, and Ojibwe (oh·JIB·way) hunted, gathered, and fished. The forests gave wood to build homes. But the cold climate and the rocky ground of the Canadian Shield made them work hard to live.

In the northern forests, Native Americans built homes called *wigwams.* These were made from trees and animal skins. Native Americans made clothing from the soft skin of deer, caribou, and elk.

They also made canoes out of bark. Canoes were good boats for small streams and rivers. Paddlers could easily carry the light boats from one body of water to another.

Along the Yukon River, the Athabascan (ah·THAH·bas·kahn) people hunted rabbits. They ate the meat and used the fur for warmth. In summer the Athabascans fished for salmon. They hunted moose in the fall. In the winter, caribou were hunted for food and fur. The wood of the forests fueled cooking fires and provided logs for cabins.

Both Inuit and other Native Americans respected their environment. They lived close to the land. They taught their children to treat it wisely. These peoples valued its resources. They took only what they needed.

This is a replica of a western red cedar totem pole. It was carved by Native Americans of the northern forests. **How else did the native peoples use trees?**

Customs

Bone Game: The Inuit play variations on a bone game. It uses a small caribou leather bag with about 40 seal and bird bones. There are a few different ways to play. In one game, players compete to rebuild the skeleton of a seal's flipper or bird's foot. In another, players try to take bones from the bag using a noose on the end of a leather thong to hook the bones.

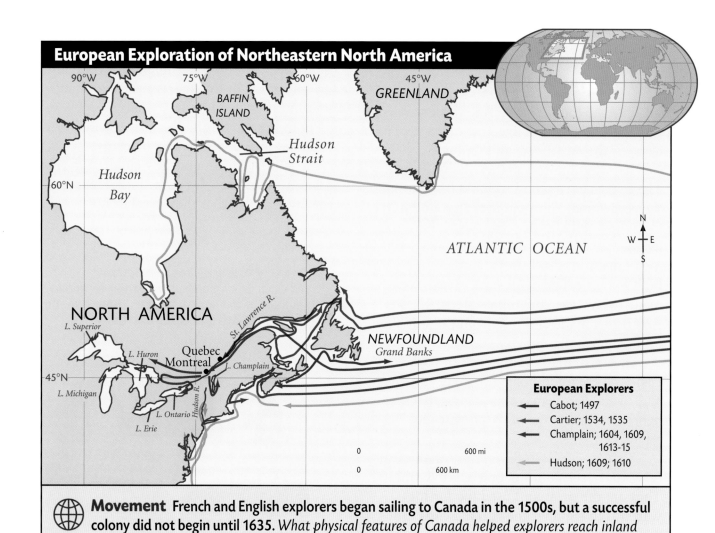

European Exploration of Northeastern North America

90°W 75°W 60°W 45°W GREENLAND

BAFFIN ISLAND

Hudson Strait

Hudson Bay

60°N

ATLANTIC OCEAN

N
W   E
S

NORTH AMERICA

L. Superior

St. Lawrence R.

NEWFOUNDLAND
Grand Banks

L. Huron Quebec
Montreal L. Champlain

45°N

L. Michigan

Hudson R.

L. Ontario

L. Erie

0   600 mi
0   600 km

European Explorers
← Cabot; 1497
← Cartier; 1534, 1535
← Champlain; 1604, 1609,
      1613-15
← Hudson; 1609; 1610

Movement French and English explorers began sailing to Canada in the 1500s, but a successful colony did not begin until 1635. *What physical features of Canada helped explorers reach inland areas? From the map key can you tell why the French were the first Europeans to begin settling Canada?*

John Cabot, in his search for the Northwest Passage, explored the waterways of what is now eastern Canada. **What was the Northwest Passage?**

470

European Explorers

Dreams of gold and spices brought the early European explorers to Canada. But fish and furs made them stay.

When the Europeans came, they saw the land differently than the Native Americans did. The Europeans changed Canada's environment. They changed how natural resources were used.

Cabot

One of the first explorers was John Cabot. He sailed in 1497 and claimed the island of Newfoundland for England. He also found the **Grand Banks.** This is a rich fishing area off the Atlantic coast. His men could easily catch many codfish. They just attached baskets to ropes and trailed them over the side of the ship.

Reports of this great fishing spot attracted people from England, Portugal, and France. The coves and bays of the Atlantic coast made good harbors. Fishing boats used them when sailing to or from the Grand Banks.

Almost 40 years after Cabot left, French King Francis I sent Jacques Cartier to Canada. The king wanted him to claim land for a colony called New France.

Cartier

Cartier wanted to find a water route to Asia. Europeans called this legendary route the Northwest Passage. They believed this route would be found in the far north of North America. The nation that could find it first would be very lucky. It would control the trade in silk, jewels, and spices from Asia.

Cartier made three trips to Canada. On the second he went up the St. Lawrence. He sailed more than 900 miles (1,449 km) up the St. Lawrence from where it flows into the Atlantic. His travels were stopped by giant rapids near the hill he called Mont Réal (later called Montreal).

Champlain

In 1608, another French explorer sailed for Canada. Samuel de Champlain followed Cartier's old route up the St. Lawrence. He stopped at the hill the natives called Quebeck, meaning where the river narrows in Algonquian. There he started a colony.

Natives brought the colony food to eat and furs to trade. The fur trade helped the colony do well. This became Quebec City, the capital of New France.

Samuel de Champlain built an outpost for France at Quebec. **How was this French settlement like the English settlement in Massachusetts?**

WORD ORIGINS

The city of **Montreal** is named for a hill. The hill was near the rapids that kept explorer Jacques Cartier from going farther up the St. Lawrence River. Cartier named the hill Mont Réal. It means "Royal Mountain" in French.

Coureurs de Bois

The *coureurs de bois* (coo·RUHR duh bwah) were French scouts. They traded with Native American tribes in Canada. They learned how to live in the Canadian wilderness from the tribes they traded with. *Coureurs de bois* means runners of the woods in English.

*T*he object of the *coureurs de bois'* trade was fur. They traded with native leaders for pelts [furskins] of beaver, mink, otter, and bear. Native Americans got knives, pots, guns, blankets, and new metal fishing hooks.

Beaver pelts

Trading with Native Americans

*C*oureurs de bois had to know several Native American languages in order to do the trading.

Indians Portaging Furs *by Cornelius Krieghoff*

The *coureurs de bois* became skilled woodsmen. Native Americans taught them how to build sturdy shelters. These would protect them from heavy winter snows. They also learned how to make birch bark canoes. The canoes were small, light, and steady. They made traveling Canadian rivers easier. The *coureurs de bois* who paddled the canoes came to be called *voyageurs*.

Even with their skill and new knowledge, *coureurs de bois* were often cold and lonely. One wrote in his diary: "I long to see the smoke from the chimneys of Jonquiere [a colonial settlement] curling up to meet the sky. I am tired and wet... In a month I will rent a room ... and bask before the fire, warming my poor feet and drinking spiced tea."

Hudson's Bay Company *voyageurs*

The Fur Trade

European explorers never found gold. They did not find the Northwest Passage to Asia. But, they did find *beavers.* Europeans wanted to buy beaver pelts (skins) because of their special fur.

French traders called *coureurs de bois* loaded their canoes with trade goods. They left New France and searched the forests for furs.

Montreal became the center of the French fur trade. Montreal was located on the St. Lawrence River, the highway of the colony. It was a natural place to store fur pelts, buy supplies, and rest.

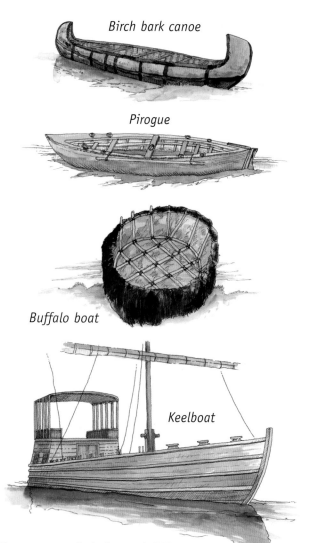

Birch bark canoe

Pirogue

Buffalo boat

Keelboat

The coureurs de bois *used different types of boats to travel North America's rivers.* **Why would they need more than one kind of boat?**

Fur was used in Europe to make clothing, and beaver hats, like this man's cloak and hat. **What city was the center of the French fur trade?**

Hudson's Bay Company

The English saw the success of the French. They also wanted a share of the fur trade. They, too, had colonies in North America. They also had a claim to Canada.

Two centuries earlier, English explorer Henry Hudson had claimed what he thought was a giant sea for England. That sea is called Hudson Bay. Hudson's travels ended badly—his unhappy crew left him to starve to death.

Hudson's explorations did lead to a rich reward for the English. This reward was a share in the fur trade. In the late 1600s, England founded the Hudson's Bay Company. The company became a rival to New France's traders.

Besides beavers, Canada's forests held minks, wolves, and otters. The search for these furs drew both English and French traders farther and farther west.

Tragedy for the Acadians

"Acadian" was the name for the French people who lived in the French colony of Acadia, centered in today's Nova Scotia. They first settled there in 1604 and lived mostly along the coast. Their villages were located on the border of two great colonial empires. They were often caught in the middle of conflicts between the French and British. Acadians tried to stay neutral.

In 1713, the French gave Acadia to the British. The British disliked Acadians for many reasons. One reason was because the French and British had been enemies for hundreds of years. Religion was another reason. The French were Catholics. Most of the British were Protestants.

In 1756, the first year of the French and Indian War (Seven Years War), the British wanted the Acadians to help fight the French. The Acadians refused. So the British decided to make them leave. They burned the Acadians' homes and took their land. About 12,000 men, women, and children were forced onto ships. Most were taken to the southern colonies. Forcing people to leave their homes is called **deportation.**

Later, some of the Acadians made their way back to Nova Scotia. Others headed southwest to Louisiana. There they became known as the *Cajuns*. The word cajun comes from the word Acadian. Many descendants of the Cajuns still live in Louisiana today.

In 2003, Queen Elizabeth II issued a proclamation. It recognized the wrongs the Acadians suffered during the removal. Starting in 2005, Canada's government made July 28 a day to remember the Acadian deportation.

The Acadians were forced to leave their homes right away. They had little time to pack anything, and many had to leave all of their belongings. **How would you feel if you were forced to leave your home and all your possessions?**

The Story of Evangeline

Historians write about important events in the past. But sometimes we can also learn from stories of people who lived through those events.

Some poets, novelists, and playwrights write about the past, too. Their stories are fiction. But the setting of the story may be based in history. The setting is where and when the story takes place. Characters in the story show us what life may have been like for people who lived in other times.

Almost 100 years after the Arcadians were forced to leave, Henry Wadsworth Longfellow wrote a poem. He imagined what it must have been like for these people. His poem is called "Evangeline." It tells the story of a young Acadian girl named Evangeline Bellefontaine and her love for Gabriel Lajeunesse.

In the story, Evangeline and Gabriel have just become engaged. They look forward to a happy life together. But before they are married, the British navy arrives. The captain tells the villagers that they must move.

Namely, that all your lands, and dwellings, and cattle of all kinds

Forfeited be [given over] to the crown; and that you yourselves from this province
Be transported [moved] to other lands. God grant you may dwell there
Ever as faithful subjects, a happy and peaceable people!
Prisoners now I declare you; for such is his Majesty's pleasure [wish]!"

The British soldiers force everyone in the village from their homes. The Acadians board ships to be taken away.

...forth came the guard, and marching in gloomy procession [lines]
Followed the long-imprisoned, but patient, Acadian farmers.

Evangeline stands on the shore and watches as Gabriel and his father sail away. Before she can board a ship, Evangeline's father dies.

Evangeline spends the rest of her life searching for Gabriel. She sails down the Mississippi River. She does not know that Gabriel has passed by her on a raft going the other way. When Evangeline arrives in Louisiana, she finds Gabriel's father. He tells her his son has gone north to look for her.

Others tell Evangeline that they are sure Gabriel lives in Michigan. So Evangeline travels there. But when she arrives, Gabriel cannot be found.

After wandering for many more years, Evangeline arrives in Philadelphia. There, she decides to become a nun. She spends the rest of her life caring for the poor and the sick.

When many people come down with an illness, Evangeline finds Gabriel among the sick. He is now an old man. Gabriel dies in her arms. Evangeline dies a short time later. She is buried next to Gabriel in a graveyard in Philadelphia.

All was ended now, the hope, and the fear, and the sorrow,
All the aching of heart, the restless, unsatisfied longing,
All the dull, deep pain, and constant anguish of patience!

At the end of the poem, Longfellow reminds the reader that now another people "with other customs and language" lives in Acadia.

Today, this poem helps us think about history. We know that Evangeline was not a real person. We also know that some things in the poem did not really happen.

Yet we can still think about why the British made the Acadian leave. We can also think about other people in history who have been forced to leave their homes. We have read about some of those groups in our study of North America.

The Loyalists

Supporters of the British in the 13 colonies that became the United States were called Loyalists. They believed the Americans were wrong to separate from Britain.

Many feared for their lives. Some lost their homes. Others were persecuted for their beliefs.

Many fought back. British Captain Banastre Tarleton was the commander of the "loyal legion" of Loyalists. Tarleton was called "Bloody Tarleton" because of his attacks on the Patriots. One historian wrote that Tarleton "wrote his name in the letters of blood all across the history of the war in the South."

After the American Revolution ended, about 40,000 Loyalists moved from the United States to Canada.

The Move North

The Loyalists packed all they could into trunks. Some were wealthy merchants and landowners. Others were carpenters and craftspeople.

They closed their houses, stores, and workshops. When they left, many did not think they would ever see their homes again.

Once they reached the safety of their new homes, many Loyalists had more hardships ahead of them.

In 1783, a young barrelmaker wrote that Loyalists from Virginia and the Carolinas were living in a ship "crowded like a sheep-pen." Other Loyalists were lucky to be on shore. They made do with houses "built from sods, where men, women, children, pigs, bugs, mosquitoes and other insects all mingl'd [mingled, or lived together] in society."

Loyalists helped develop the areas where they settled in Canada. They were loyal to the British government.

Loyalists fled the new United States to Canada. **Why did they have to leave their homes?**

LESSON 2 REVIEW

Fact Follow-Up
1. How did the earliest Canadians interact with their physical environment?
2. Who were the first Europeans to visit Canada? Why did they visit?
3. How did Europeans interact with the physical environment of Canada?

Talk About It
1. The French claimed a large empire in North America and settled it mainly with a few thousand fur traders. Compare this to how the English settled their colonies.
2. Compare and contrast the Loyalists and Acadians.

Settling a Nation

LESSON ③ Moving West

KEY IDEAS

- Railroads opened Canada's west to settlement.
- The Prairie Provinces and the Western Mountains changed as settlers found new resources.
- The Lowlands changed as Canada became urban and industrial.

KEY TERMS

Canadian Pacific Railway
"last best west"

The first European settlers of Canada found riches in its oceans and forests. Later, settlers found other treasures. They were oil, gold, and wheat.

These resources were hard to reach. Canada is wide. The climate is cold. The landscape can be rough. Yet Canadians met nature's challenges. They changed the environment. They claimed the land's resources.

Opening the West

Canada's prairie provinces are some of the world's top wheat farmlands. But about 100 years ago, this land was almost all grassland. Few people lived here.

This photograph shows an 1876 steam locomotive of the Canada Pacific Railway.
How did the railroad open the west?

Then the *Canadian Pacific Railway* was built. It opened the land to settlers from Europe and the United States. They settled on the plains. Trains were as important to prairie settlers as canoes had been to the fur traders.

Building the Railroad

Canada's landscape made building the railroad hard work. In the east, builders had to carve the rock in the Canadian Shield to make a place to lay the track. In other places, rock was not a problem. But the muskeg was so soggy the roadbeds sank.

Workers had a different challenge in the West. A way had to be found through the Western mountains. About 15,000 Chinese workers had a dangerous job. They used dynamite to blast tunnels through the mountains. Explosions and falling rocks killed or injured many people.

The map on page 451 shows how the railroad opened the west. Find Toronto and Moose Jaw on the map. It took trappers and traders in canoes three months to make the trip from Toronto to Moose Jaw. The railroad shortened the trip to three days.

The railroad would also help bring new industries to the plains. It linked farms to ports on the Great Lakes and the St. Lawrence River.

New Immigrants

The railroad was finished in 1885. It stretched from the Atlantic to the Pacific Coast. Railroads took out newspaper ads in Europe and the United States. They wanted people to come to the *"last best west."* Many did. They came for free land and the hope of a better life.

Most people came from eastern Canada, the United States, Germany, Italy, Ukraine, and northern European countries. By 1905, enough people had come to create two new provinces, Alberta and Saskatchewan.

CANADIAN PORTRAIT

Mary Ann Shadd Cary
1823–1893

Mary Ann Shadd Cary was a writer, teacher, lawyer, abolitionist and the first African American newspaperwoman in North America. She spoke out against slavery and fought for equal rights for all people.

Cary was born in Wilmington, Delaware. She was the oldest of 13 children. Her family helped runaway slaves when she was young. They moved to Pennsylvania so the children could go to school. Cary became a teacher. She taught African American children in Delaware, New York, and Pennsylvania.

When the Fugitive Slave Law was passed in the United States, Cary moved to Canada with her brother. She wrote a pamphlet, "Notes on Canada West." This was read by many African Americans in the United States. It told about the opportunities for them in Canada. She then founded Canada's first anti-slavery newspaper, the *Provincial Freeman*. She was nicknamed the "rebel" by her friends. During the Civil War, Mary Shadd Cary was made a "Recruiting Officer" for the Union Army. She moved back to the United States. After the war, Cary became active in the women's rights movement. She studied law at Howard University. When she graduated, she became one of the first female African American lawyers in the country.

Industries on the Plains

Agriculture was the first industry on the plains. Oil became another important industry several years later.

Farming

Settlers had to work hard to turn the prairie into farmland. Whole families plowed and planted wheat. They worked from sunup to sunset in the few months of the growing season. Days are long in the summer because of the rotation of the earth. There are more hours of sunlight in Canada in the summer than in lands closer to the Equator (see Chapter 3).

Summer temperatures could reach more than 95°F (35°C). Fires sometimes swept across the fields. They destroyed homes and crops. A season's work could be gone in minutes.

Settlers overcame these problems. They changed grasslands into productive wheat farms. They also raised cattle on ranches.

Ships on the St. Lawrence carried farm products across the Great Lakes to Chicago. They also took Canada's products out and across the Atlantic Ocean to London.

Oil

In 1947, oil was discovered in Alberta. The wheat fields gave way to oil fields.

Soon Alberta had more than 1,200 oil wells. The oil business boomed. Edmonton, Alberta, turned from a small farm town to a large center. There oil was made into gasoline and other products.

Other cities in Canada also were affected by the oil industry. For example, back east in Hamilton, Ontario, there were steel mills. They rolled out the steel for Alberta's pipelines.

The discovery of oil in Alberta drew people to the Plains Provinces and to the west. **How did oil wells in Alberta change the eastern provinces?**

Farming on the Canadian frontier in the 1800s was challenging. **What did settlers grow?**

Chapter 19

Gold Mines

In 1856, Vancouver, British Columbia, and New Caledonia were British colonies on the Pacific coast. They were mainly made up of trading posts for the Hudson's Bay Company. The population was very small. The 700 people in Vancouver, for example, were mostly traders and trappers.

Only a few people had reasons to make the long journey west. But in 1858, that changed. A prospector found gold nuggets the size of marbles in the Fraser River.

Miners search for gold in the Gold Rush. **What is a gold rush?**

The Gold Rush

News of the gold discovery spread. More than 20,000 gold seekers came into the area. They were part of the gold rush.

After the gold rush ended, many stayed anyway. They liked the mild climate of the west coast. Leaders in Canada agreed to extend the railroad to the Pacific coast.

These three colonies joined to form today's province of British Columbia. Mining, forestry, fishing, and farming were the main industries of the region.

The Klondike Gold Rush

Another gold rush happened in 1898. The Klondike Gold Rush brought miners even farther north to the Northwest Territory. Dawson was the closest town to the gold fields. It grew from a few hundred people to 50,000. Most of these people went home when the gold rush ended.

The Canadian government decided to make a second territory, the Yukon, out of the Northwest Territories.

The Pig War of 1859

Which war killed only a pig? The Pig War of 1859, of course!

The 1846 Oregon Treaty set the border between Canada and United States at the 49th parallel of latitude. The border stretched from the Great Lakes to the Pacific coast. Both sides agreed that all of Vancouver Island would stay British. But the treaty was not clear about the other islands in Puget Sound.

The treaty said the border was "in the middle of the channel." But there were two channels of water around the islands. Both nations claimed the Gulf Islands and San Juan Island. There were about 18 Americans on San Juan Island. The British thought they should not be there. They believed the land was owned by the Hudson's Bay Company.

An American settler there named Lyman Cutlar shot and killed a pig that was rooting in his garden. The pig belonged to the Hudson's Bay Company. The British wanted to arrest Cutlar. The Americans asked the United States government to protect them. Soldiers were sent. This made the British angry. They brought in forces, too.

When the British and American leaders far away heard of this, they were shocked. They did not want to fight each other because of a pig. They asked the leader of Germany, Kaiser Wilhelm I, to settle the dispute. The border was finally set in 1872. Today, the San Juan Islands belong to Washington state. The Gulf Islands belong to British Columbia.

Settling a Nation

Industry Grows

Once fur trappers had paddled canoes on their way west. Today, giant ships filled with grains, steel, and ore dock in the cities.

The railroad was finished in 1885. It gave Canadians a way to move wheat, lumber, iron ore, and many other natural resources. These could be brought from farms, forests, and mines in the west to cities in the east.

The railroads helped industry grow. They opened up new markets for goods. Industries bought western resources. They needed iron, steel, and fuel to run factories.

Factories

New factories were built in the St. Lawrence Lowlands. Lumber from the forests of British Columbia, farm products from the prairie provinces, and oil from Alberta were loaded onto trains. They went by rail to factories in Quebec and Ontario. There these raw materials became cereal, paper, or gasoline for Canada, the United States, and Europe.

The Great Lakes–St. Lawrence Lowlands became Canada's manufacturing center. This region was close to where most of the

Toronto grew as industries grew. **Why did people move to the cities?**

country's people lived. It was connected by the Great Lakes and rivers to the Great Plains of Canada and the United States.

Cities Grow

As industry grew, more people came to Canada's cities. The largest, Toronto and Montreal, built highways and subways so that people could live in suburbs and work downtown.

Canada remained a largely rural nation until after World War II. In the 1940s, Canada's manufacturing centers became urban centers. Now about 80 percent of all Canadians live in cities.

Changes for Native Americans

These changes to Canada's open lands also changed life for the native peoples. Not all of these changes were good.

Inuit

Before the 1960s, the Inuit lived in temporary snowhouses or tents. They tracked caribou or seal. They hunted beluga whales. Many Inuit still hunt and trap, but they do it part-time. Now most use snowmobiles instead of dog sleds to cross over the Arctic tundra.

Most of the year the Inuit live in modern houses. Under their fur-lined parkas they wear jeans and T-shirts. Satellites link the Arctic with the rest of Canada. Almost every home has a television. Igloos and tents are used only on hunting trips now.

Many Inuit still hunt and eat caribou, fish from the Arctic, and other traditional foods. They also eat snack foods and hot dogs and drink soda flown to the Arctic. They share the culture of modern Canada. They also work to keep their own culture alive.

Other Native Americans

There are about half a million other Native Americans (First Nations) in Canada. Almost half live on the country's 2,200 reservations. These are owned by the Native Americans but managed by the government. The Canadian government is responsible for the Native Americans' schools, housing, and health care.

Native Americans in Canada and the United States have had a similar history. European settlers moved westward. The claims of Native Americans were often ignored. By the late 1880s, almost all Native Americans had lost their land.

Since the 1970s, many Native Americans have united. They have won more rights and better treatment from the government. The government has had to pay some Native American peoples for the loss of hunting and fishing grounds.

LESSON 3 REVIEW

Fact Follow-Up
1. How did building the Canadian Pacific Railroad change Canada?
2. Describe the life of a farm family in the Prairie Provinces.
3. What things happened to turn grasslands into wheat fields and oil fields?

Talk About It
1. How did changes like the building of railroads or the discovery of gold and oil change life for Native Americans?
2. How did these discoveries change life for the Western settlers? for people who lived in eastern Canada? Were all the changes good?

Lessons Learned

LESSON 1
People of Canada
Canada's first settlers were the early Native Americans and Inuit. Settlers from France and Great Britain came in the 1600s. In the past 200 years, immigrants have come from Asia, the Americas, and Europe. Today's population mainly lives along the United States border, especially in the Great Lakes–St. Lawrence Lowlands region.

LESSON 2
First Settlers
The French were the first to use the resources of Canada as trappers. English settlements followed. The British forced the Acadians to leave. Loyalists from the new United States settled in Canada.

LESSON 3
Moving West
The Canadian Pacific Railroad opened the Canadian west to settlement. New settlers changed the environment of the prairies, the west and the north. The area along the Great Lakes and St. Lawrence River became Canada's industrial and population center.

Talk About It

1. Someone has said that "Canadian history is the history of human environmental interaction." Do you agree or disagree with this statement? Explain why.
2. Which event in Canada's history was more important the discovery of gold in the Fraser River and the Yukon or the completion of the Canadian Pacific Railroad? Explain your answer.
3. Which early Canadian settlers—the French or the Native Americans—lived more within the physical environment? Explain your answer.
4. Given the environmental problems facing Canada today, does the description, "last best west" still apply? Explain.

Mastering Mapwork

Movement
Use the maps on pages 451 and 463 to answer these questions:
1. British Columbia was made a province and the Yukon a territory because of the gold rushes of 1858 and 1898. Which kind of movement—of people, goods, or ideas—caused these changes?
2. Many Inuit still hunt and trap, but they do it part-time, racing snowmobiles instead of dogsleds over the Arctic tundra. What kind of movement is this–of people, goods, or ideas?
3. Was the movement of the *coureurs de bois* into the wilderness the movement of goods or of ideas?
4. The Canadian Pacific Railroad united Canada east to west. Along this route much movement occurred. Was this the movement of people, goods, or ideas?
5. According to the map on page 451, how might coal move across Canada? What type of movement does the map show most clearly? Why do you think this is the case?

Becoming Better Readers

Asking Questions
Good readers continually ask questions as they read. Being able to ask questions shows understanding of what is important in the text. Write two good questions about how the western part of Canada was opened. Refer to pages 478 and 479.

Go to the Source

Judging the Accuracy of Historical Fiction

Compare the two quotations below from people involved with the deporation of the Acadians. Think about how these relate to what you read in Lesson 2. Answer the questions with information from the documents.

The inhabitants, sadly and with great sorrow, abandoned their homes. The women, in great distress, carried their newborn or their youngest children in their arms. Others pulled carts with their household effects and crippled parents. It was a scene of confusion, despair and desolation.

—Colonel John Winslow, British officer in charge of Acadian deportment

Since these people arrived consumed in wretchedness and in the greatest possible need, through the orders of the French General and mine they were helped immediately with fresh bread and biscuits which had been prepared for the first needy ones who might arrive. I ordered that an ox and a calf, which I had sent for upriver for my own consumption [use], and that of those who are with me, be given to them. This was done on the same night that they had encountered the launch [boat] which was transporting them, and the pilot assured me that immediately upon receiving these animals they slaughtered them and ate the meat raw.

—Antonio de Ulloa, colonial governor of Louisiana

Questions
1. What is the overall mood or tone of the quotes?
2. How are the sources different from one another?
3. What characteristic would best describe Antonio de Ulloa?
4. Compare these to what you read about the poem "Evangeline." How accurately do you think the poem describes what happened?

Economy and Government

Canadians believe in a strong partnership between government and business. The building of the railroad across Canada is a good example of this.

There were no private companies that could do the job alone. So the government created the Canadian Pacific Railway. It gave the new company money and land.

This partnership paid off. The railroad united the country. It helped Canada's economy grow into one of the strongest in the world.

Construction of the Canadian Pacific Railroad

The last spike of Canada's first transcontinental railroad is driven into the ground on November 7, 1885.

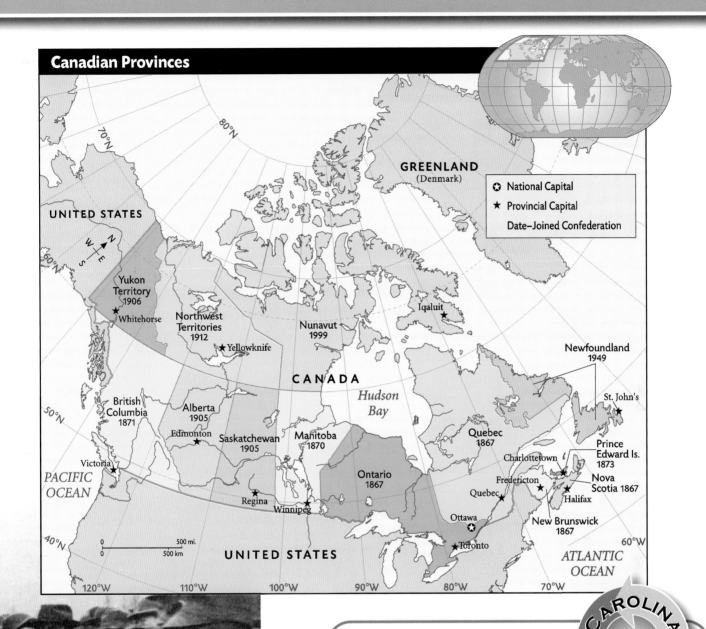

Canadian Provinces

GREENLAND
(Denmark)

UNITED STATES

☮ National Capital
★ Provincial Capital
Date–Joined Confederation

Yukon
Territory
1906
★ Whitehorse

Northwest
Territories
1912
★ Yellowknife

Nunavut
1999

Iqaluit

CANADA

Hudson
Bay

Newfoundland
1949

St. John's

British
Columbia
1871

Alberta
1905
★ Edmonton

Saskatchewan
1905

Manitoba
1870

Quebec
1867

Charlottetown

Prince
Edward Is.
1873

Victoria

Ontario
1867

Fredericton

Nova
Scotia 1867

PACIFIC
OCEAN

Regina
★ Winnipeg

Quebec

Halifax

Ottawa ☮

New Brunswick
1867

UNITED STATES

★ Toronto

ATLANTIC
OCEAN

Nortel Networks

North Carolina has a key link with one of Canada's biggest private businesses. Nortel Networks is Canada's largest maker of telephone equipment. It is also one of the largest in the world.

In 1980, Northern Telecom (now called Nortel Networks) chose Research Triangle Park to be one of its research and manufacturing centers.

Research Triangle Park is often called RTP. It is located in between Raleigh, Durham, and Chapel Hill.

CAROLINA
CONNECTION

KEY IDEAS

- Crown corporations play a large role in Canada's strong economy.

- Most Canadians work for private businesses.

- Canada has both primary and secondary industries.

KEY TERMS

crown corporations
primary industries
secondary industries

Getting to some of Canada's resources can sometimes be hard. Also, it can cost a lot of money. So the government works closely with private companies. Together, they work to develop the nation's resources.

The government wants private companies to drill for oil and mine for minerals. So it lowers taxes for businesses that do those things. This helps these businesses save some money. They can then use that money to pay for the extra costs of drilling or mining.

The government has done even more to help businesses that will go into the far north. It has built roads, airstrips, and telephone lines. These help companies save money in a place where costs are high.

The government has also invested in Canada's people.

Education

Canada has one of the best education systems in the world. With a good education, people can do many different kinds of jobs. Canada's well-educated people are an important resource.

Many Languages

Each province runs its own educational system. In Quebec, most children go to a school where everything is taught in French. Other provinces have mostly English-speaking schools. In some provinces,

The National Film Board of Canada runs the nation's movie industry. Here a crew makes a film about Canada for an international trade show. **What other Canadian businesses are run by the government?**

parents can choose to send their children to a French- or English-speaking school. Most children in Canada learn both French and English.

In Nunavut, children are taught only in Inuktitut (in·OOK·tih·toot) until they finish fifth grade. Inuktitut is the language of the Inuit. Students are taught in English from then on.

Many Canadians go on to college. Several Canadian universities, such as McGill in Montreal, are world famous. People come from all over the world to study in Canada.

People who graduate from college use what they have learned at work. This helps Canada's economy grow.

Government and Business

Canada's economy is similar to the economy of the United States. It is a free market economy. As in the United States, Canada's government also makes rules for businesses to follow. But it also is slightly more involved in the economy than is the government in our country.

Crown Corporations

Government ownership of businesses has been much more common in Canada than in the United States. Companies owned or controlled by the national and provincial governments are called *crown corporations*.

Canada chooses to own businesses that are important for the country. It used to own more. But the government decided that many businesses could do well on their own. So it sold them. Some of the Canadian businesses that started as crown corporations include Air Canada, an airline; the Canadian National Railway; Petro-Canada, a gasoline company; Nova Scotia Power, and several provincial telephone systems.

Today, crown corporations deliver the mail (Canada Post), oversee the nuclear energy programs, and do other important jobs for the nation.

TV, Radio, and Film

Canada still owns the National Film Board of Canada. It makes movies. The government also makes radio and television shows. The Canadian Broadcasting Corporation broadcasts news and entertainment programs in English and French.

Why does the government own these companies? Canada wants to make sure that its national culture is presented in film and on television. This might not happen if all Canada's television shows and movies were made in other places, like in Hollywood, London, or Paris.

Other Government Aid

The national and provincial governments own about 90 percent of all Canada's forests. Private lumber companies pay the government for the right to harvest trees on publicly owned land.

Look at the Canadian Energy map below. The oil shipped from Norman Wells in the Northwest Territories has a long trip to the cities where it will be used. Pipelines built with government money help carry oil to the United States and Canada.

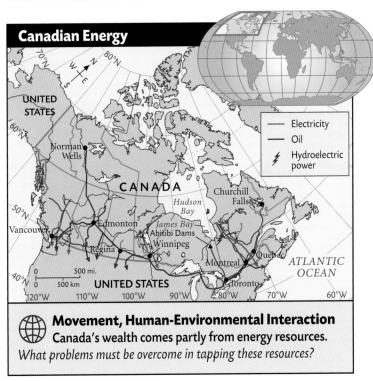

Movement, Human-Environmental Interaction
Canada's wealth comes partly from energy resources.
What problems must be overcome in tapping these resources?

Industry

Canada is a large country with many different natural resources. These resources can be found in different parts of the country. Forests can be found in British Columbia, so timber and paper are important industries there. The oil industry is key in Alberta. Mining is important in Ontario. And fishing is still important along the Atlantic Coast.

Primary Industries

Natural resources are raw materials. They are also called primary products. Businesses that gather them are called *primary industries.*

Some of Canada's primary products include oil and natural gas, timber, and minerals. Farm crops, such as wheat and barley, and fish, such as salmon and cod, are also primary products. Selling these products is important to Canada's economy.

About 100 years ago, 70 percent of Canadian families worked in farming. Look at the pie chart on the next page. Now only about 3 percent do.

Secondary Industries

Industries that make goods from primary products are called *secondary industries.* Look at the pie chart again. About 15 percent of Canada's workforce has jobs in these manufacturing industries.

Canada's top secondary industry is the making of transportation equipment. Canadian iron ore is made into steel and then sold to car and truck manufacturers in Windsor, Ontario, Detroit, Michigan, or elsewhere.

Other important secondary industries are food processing and paper products.

High-Tech

Canadians also have a strong high-tech industry. They have invented diving suits for exploring underwater. They have also written computer programs that control satellites.

Engineers in Ontario built a camera that takes a perfectly clear photo of a car license plate. But it takes the picture from an airplane flying half a mile up in the sky! Police and military officers use this camera for detective work around the world.

Primary and Secondary Industries

Primary industries are those that gather or sell products such as oil and natural gas, timber, minerals, wheat, barley, salmon, and cod. This is a pump drawing oil from a well in Saskatchewan.

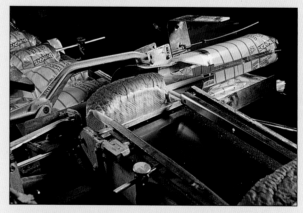

Secondary industries are those that make goods from raw materials. Examples of products produced by secondary industries include transportation equipment, processed foods, and paper. This is a food processing plant in Ontario.

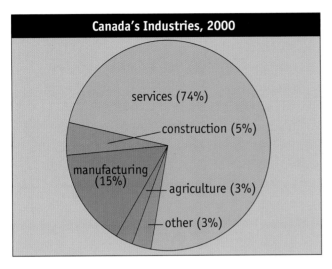

Canada's Industries, 2000

services (74%)

construction (5%)

manufacturing (15%)

agriculture (3%)

other (3%)

Compare this chart to the one on page 329. **How are the economies of Canada and the United States alike?**

Services

Look at the pie chart again. About three fourths of all Canadians work in service jobs. Many of these workers are teachers, doctors and nurses, or lawyers. Others work in banks, hotels, restaurants, or stores.

There is another type of service that is growing in both Canada and the United States. These are businesses that protect the environment. They clean up pollution.

Taxes Pay for Services

We just read that Canada's different regions have different resources and industries. Some of these industries make more money than others.

Canada's government taxes provinces such as Ontario, Alberta, and British Columbia. These provinces have strong economies. The taxes are used to pay for services in the provinces and territories that do not have as much. Some of the services that the government provides with this money are healthcare and education.

Some people want this policy to change. They want each province to pay its own way. Canadians are discussing this issue right now.

CANADIAN PORTRAIT

Frederick Banting
1891–1941

Frederick Banting was a doctor who won a Nobel Prize. He discovered how to make insulin. Insulin is a product your body makes to turn sugar into energy. People with diabetes (di·ah·BEE·tees) have too much sugar in their bodies. Their bodies cannot make (or do not make enough) insulin. Banting's work brought hope to these people.

Banting was the youngest of five children. He grew up in Alliston, Ontario. While at the University of Toronto, he decided to study medicine. During World War I, he joined the Canadian Army Medical Corps. He was wounded in France, and he won a medal for bravery.

After the war, Banting finished his studies and became a doctor. At the time, diabetics, people with diabetes, faced shorter lives. They often went blind or had to have a foot or leg amputated. They faced many challenges.

Banting read an article about diabetes research. It gave him an idea. He decided to try to find a way to give insulin to people with diabetes.

Banting formed a team of researchers. They found that they could use dogs to make insulin for people. The people they tested the insulin on got much better quickly. With the insulin, diabetics could bring their blood sugar level under control. The discovery did not cure diabetes. But it made life much better for diabetics all over the world.

Economy and Government

491

The Newest Province

Newfoundland and Labrador is Canada's newest province. It joined the Confederation in 1949. Newfoundland is a large island. Labrador is part of mainland Canada.

About 90 percent of the province's people live in Newfoundland. People get to and from the island and Labrador mostly by airplane or boat.

Labrador is nicknamed "the Big Land." It has a big, open sky and many hours of summer sunlight.

People who live in Newfoundland and Labrador enjoy lots of activities. In the summer, you can watch a boat race called the Royal St. John's Regatta. It is North America's oldest sporting event. You may also kayak, fish, hike, or go iceberg or whale watching. Music lovers enjoy the province's orchestra. There are festivals and cultural events year-round.

Winters here are long. They last from about November to April. It can be a challenge. But winters are a great time for adventure, too! There is a winter snowmobile trail network that runs throughout Labrador. It is almost 932 miles (1,500 km) long.

This province also has important natural resources. Almost 80 percent of eastern Canada's offshore oil resources are located in the ocean off Newfoundland and Labrador.

LESSON 1 REVIEW

Fact Follow-Up

1. What are the differences between crown corporations and privately owned businesses?
2. What are the differences between primary and secondary industries?
3. How many Canadians work in agriculture? in service industries? Explain why.

Talk About It

1. Compare Canadian and American attitudes toward government's involvement in business.
2. In Canada, wealthier provinces pay more in taxes than they receive in government benefits. Why?
3. Why are there fewer crown corporations today?

LESSON ② World Partners

The Ambassador Bridge stretches between Windsor, Ontario, and Detroit, Michigan. More than 10,000 trucks cross the bridge each weekday. One quarter of all the goods and services traded between Canada and the United States each year crosses this bridge.

North American Neighbors

The border between the United States and Canada is 5,500 miles (8,855 km) long. It is the longest undefended border in the world. Every day, Canadians and Americans go back and forth across this border. They travel for work and for play.

Good Friends

There are many reasons for this friendly relationship. The United States and Canada share the English language and a similar heritage. They also have similar economic systems and similar ways of doing business. They are important trading partners. *Trading partners* are countries that trade closely together.

Sports bring them together too. Teams from Canada and the United States compete against one another in baseball, basketball, and hockey.

The two countries, as you read in Chapter 18, also work to clean up the environment together. Canada and the United States share waters in the Great Lakes and the oceans. They also share air pollution. So they work together to clean the air and to protect the waters and fish.

KEY IDEAS

- The St. Lawrence Seaway was built by the United States and Canada.

- The economies of Canada and the United States depend on each other.

- NAFTA strengthened those economic ties.

- Canada's trade with Pacific countries is growing.

KEY TERMS

NORAD
St. Lawrence Seaway
trading partners

International Peace Park

Waterton-Glacier International Peace Park was the world's first international peace park. It is a symbol of the cooperation and good will between the United States and Canada. It celebrates the longest peaceful border between two nations in the world.

The park runs along the frontiers of both nations. Glacier National Park is on the American side. It is in northwestern Montana. Waterton National Park is on the Canadian side. It is in Alberta. The parks were joined as an International Peace Park in 1932.

Wolves, bears, big horn sheep, and mountain lions live in the park. There are high mountains and cold lakes. The park reminds us that our natural resources belong to everyone.

Bison in Waterton Park

Differences

Canada is a sovereign nation and makes its own decisions. At times, Canadians disagree with the policies and decisions of the United States. Canada did not participate in the the 2003 invasion of Iraq. But it later gave support to rebuild Iraq.

Defense and Terrorism

The United States and Canada want to keep their nations safe. The governments are worried about terrorist attacks. The open border can be a challenge. The freedom of the border is good for citizens and businesses. But the two countries also want to make sure that terrorists or other people doing illegal things do not take advantage of the open border.

The American and Canadian military forces have cooperated for more than 50 years. The North American Aerospace Defense Command *(NORAD)* center was set up during the Cold War. It was designed to protect the United States and Canada from a nuclear weapons attack. In 2006, a new agreement was signed. It will help the two countries fight terrorism, too.

The St. Lawrence Seaway

Canada and the United States have strong economic ties. Ships sail back and forth on the Great Lakes and the St. Lawrence River. They carry wheat from Saskatchewan and ore from northern Quebec. They also carry corn from Illinois, iron pellets from Minnesota, and coal from New York.

Large freighters sail from United States or Canadian ports on the Great Lakes to the Atlantic Ocean. They use the *St. Lawrence Seaway.* Long ago, canals opened a passage from Lake Erie to the Atlantic Ocean for small boats. But large ships needed something deeper.

The seaway has locks and many canals and channels. These help large ships go from

Trade between the United States and Canada all along the St. Lawrence Seaway (above and right) represents a key partnership. **Why have the Canadian and United States governments agreed to trade freely?**

the Great Lakes through the St. Lawrence River and Gulf of St. Lawrence to the Atlantic Ocean.

The United States and Canadian governments planned and built the seaway in the 1950s. Each year, more than 43 million tons of cargo pass through the system, strengthening the economic connection between the United States and Canada. The seaway is the best example of their close cooperation.

Look at the Eyewitness to History on page 496. Find the map of the seaway. It shows how the seaway connects large parts of both countries.

Trade

Relative to size, Canada's population is small. Therefore, it has always needed to find markets outside Canada for its products. Trading primary products with other nations has been important. Canada's exports include wheat, zinc, and newsprint.

The United States and Canada are each other's most important trading partners.

Imports and Exports

About 84 percent of all Canadian exports go to the United States. About 56 percent of Canada's imports are from the United States.

Canadians buy many of their winter vegetables and fruit from the United States and Mexico. American automakers have factories in Canada. They make cars, trucks, subway cars, and airplanes for buyers at home and abroad.

The two countries also trade electricity. Hydro-Quebec sells power to New England states. So do electric companies in Canada's Atlantic provinces.

Economy and Government

THE BUILDING OF THE

The Canadian city of Toronto is a long way from the Atlantic Ocean. Yet, thanks to the St. Lawrence Seaway, freighters from Japan, the United Kingdom, and France sail to Toronto and other inland cities. At the same time, other freighters leave Toronto. They sail to places around the world with loads of iron ore, grain, and wood.

Building the St. Lawrence Seaway began in August 1954. Millions of cubic feet of dirt were moved. Workers built 15 locks. These raise and lower ships between the Great Lakes and the Atlantic Ocean.

The seaway was finished in 1959. It is 2,342 miles (3,771 km) in length. It allows ships to travel more than 9,500 miles (15,295 km). They can now reach the North American heartland.

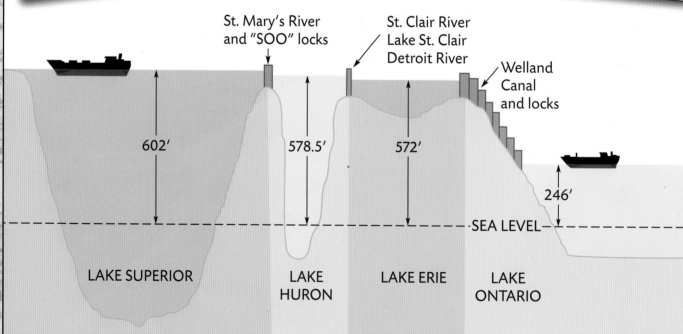

St. Mary's River and "SOO" locks

St. Clair River
Lake St. Clair
Detroit River

Welland Canal and locks

602'

578.5'

572'

246'

SEA LEVEL

LAKE SUPERIOR

LAKE HURON

LAKE ERIE

LAKE ONTARIO

ST. LAWRENCE SEAWAY

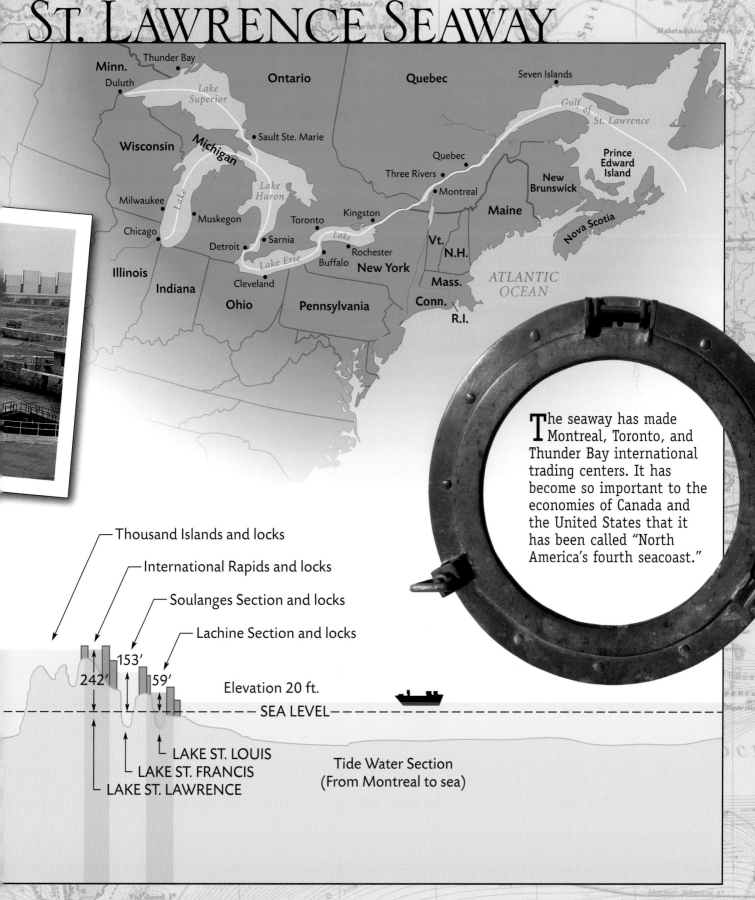

Minn.
Thunder Bay
Duluth
Lake Superior
Ontario
Quebec
Seven Islands
Gulf of St. Lawrence
Wisconsin
Michigan
Sault Ste. Marie
Quebec
Three Rivers
Prince Edward Island
New Brunswick
Milwaukee
Lake Huron
Montreal
Maine
Muskegon
Lake
Toronto
Kingston
Nova Scotia
Chicago
Sarnia
Lake
Detroit
Rochester
Vt.
Illinois
Lake Erie
Buffalo
N.H.
ATLANTIC OCEAN
Indiana
Cleveland
New York
Mass.
Ohio
Pennsylvania
Conn.
R.I.

The seaway has made Montreal, Toronto, and Thunder Bay international trading centers. It has become so important to the economies of Canada and the United States that it has been called "North America's fourth seacoast."

Thousand Islands and locks

International Rapids and locks

Soulanges Section and locks

Lachine Section and locks

153'

242'   59'   Elevation 20 ft.

SEA LEVEL

LAKE ST. LOUIS
LAKE ST. FRANCIS
LAKE ST. LAWRENCE

Tide Water Section
(From Montreal to sea)

NAFTA

In 1993, Canada signed a three-way trade agreement with the United States and Mexico. This was the North American Free Trade Agreement, or NAFTA (nahf·tah). Under this agreement, the three countries cut tariffs, taxes on goods coming into their countries.

Not all Canadians supported NAFTA. Some factory workers feared it would result in fewer jobs for Canadian workers. Factories might move south to the United States or Mexico. Canadian merchants worried their Canadian customers might buy cheaper goods from the United States or Mexico.

But other Canadians support Canada's part in NAFTA. They believe the country must find markets for its products. As one Canadian businessman said, "We are realizing that we are North Americans, not just Canadians. And this is a North American market, not just a Canadian and a United States market."

NAFTA has had some clear effects on Canada's economy. Canadian exports to both Mexico and the United States almost doubled between 1994 and 2000. NAFTA has made Canada more attractive to foreign and domestic investors.

FTAA

Canada is talking with the United States, Mexico, and 32 other democratic

A large archway makes this street look like an entry into a Chinese city, but this is in Victoria, British Columbia. **Why is the archway there?**

governments in the Western Hemisphere. They are working to create a new free trade zone. This would be called the Free Trade Area of the Americas (FTAA).

The Pacific Rim

Canada is strengthening its ties with countries outside North America, too. Like the United States, it is a Pacific Rim nation. Five provinces have important trade relations with the Pacific region. They are British Columbia, Alberta, Saskatchewan, Ontario, and Quebec. Vancouver, British Columbia, is Canada's busiest port for trade with such countries as China and Japan. Canada is working on ways to grow trade with this region.

Canada also has good relations with Australia and New Zealand in the Pacific. They share a similar heritage. They are both important customers for Canadian goods. You will read more about their special relationship in the next chapter.

LESSON ② REVIEW

Fact Follow-Up

1. Describe North Carolina's connections with Canada.

2. How are the United States and Canada interdependent?

3. Why is NAFTA important to Canada?

Talk About It

1. How do Canada and the United States cooperate for defense?

2. What are some signs of Canada's interdependence with Asia? Does this interdependence affect all Canadians? Why or why not?

Diane France is a Canadian writer. Someone asked her what she liked about Canada. She had no trouble deciding.

Canada is wonderful because it has . . . safe streets. Democracy. Good schools. Phones that work. . . . Roads and bridges that are plentiful and safe. Power at the flick of a switch. Good medical care. Little poverty. Water you can drink.

Many Canadians would agree with this point of view. Canada has one of the world's highest standards of living. Its citizens tend to live longer than citizens of other countries. Fewer Canadian babies die in infancy.

Canada's strong government has helped the country achieve this success.

Role of Government

Americans and Canadians have similar ideas about the rights of citizens. Both believe people's rights should be protected. Both believe that all people have the right to equal treatment under the law.

Different Views

Yet the two nations have different views about the role of government in their lives. Researchers asked people from both countries if government should "help citizens get a job and a good standard of living" or "let each person get ahead on his own." Many more Canadians thought the government should help its citizens. More than half of the United States citizens said government should stay out of people's lives.

These different views can be seen in the different healthcare systems. The Canadian government provides all citizens with healthcare. In the United States, most people pay for healthcare by buying insurance from private companies. Only people older than sixty-five get help with heath care costs from the government in the United States.

KEY IDEAS

- Canada is a parliamentary democracy.
- Provincial governments share power with the national government.
- The Canadian constitution maintains strong ties with the United Kingdom.

KEY TERMS

Canada Day
confederation
Constitution Act of 1982
Dominion Day
governor general
prime minister
Separatists

A Parliamentary Democracy

The Canadian and American forms of government are alike in key ways. Both are democracies. The people elect representatives. They are different in other ways.

Parliament

Canada's legislature is the Parliament. It makes laws for the national government. It has two houses. The smaller house is the Senate. The larger house is called the House of Commons.

In the United States, the lawmaking and executive branches are separate. The members of Congress make the laws, and the president and executive branch carry them out. In Canada, the Parliament combines the lawmaking and executive branches of government.

The Prime Minister

Parliament chooses the leader of Canada's government. The leader is called the *prime minister.* He or she is a member of Parliament. The majority party in Parliament gets to pick the prime minister. The parties that do not have a majority are called "the opposition."

In the United States, the president serves a four-year term. He or she must step down if not reelected. A parliamentary system is different.

The prime minister stays in office as long as the House of Commons supports the programs he or she recommends. A prime minister must resign when his or her party no longer has a majority of representatives in the House.

Elections

But sometimes members of the prime minister's party do not support a program important to him or her. A special vote is taken. This is called a "vote of no confidence." If the prime minister loses this vote, a new election must be held. Then the party that wins the most seats will form a new government. That means the majority party will choose a new prime minister.

With support or not, the prime minister must call an election at least once every five years.

The Governor General

Canada still has ties with the United Kingdom. The king or queen of the United Kingdom is also Canada's head of state. The king or queen appoints a *governor general* to represent him or her in Canada.

The governor general, like the king or queen, does not take part in politics. One important job the governor general does is represent the king or queen to officially open Parliament's session. Today, the governor general mostly takes part in ceremonies.

The size and beauty of Canada's Parliament building (left) reflects its importance. **Inside (right), why does it look much like the British Parliament?**

CANADIAN PORTRAIT

John A. Macdonald
1815–1891

Sir John A. Macdonald is called the founding father of Canada. He united the French and English-speaking people. He also helped start the Canadian Pacific Railway.

Sir John was born in Scotland. When he was five years old, his father's business was not doing well. The family wanted a new start. They moved to Upper Canada (today's Ontario).

Sir John was well respected and successful in business. When he was 28, he married his cousin Isabella Clark. Soon after the wedding, she became ill. No one knew the cause of her sickness. They had two sons. One died when he was thirteen months old. Isabella died in 1857.

He was elected as a Conservative representative in the Province of Canada's assembly. Later Sir John was chosen to be attorney general. He served as co-premier from 1856 to 1862.

In 1867, Sir John married again to Susan Agnes Bernard. They had one daughter.

About this time, Sir John decided it was important for the colonies in British North America to join together. The colonies in the east did not all agree. But after the American Civil War and other events, they decided it would be best to form a confederation.

Sir John wrote the British North America Act that created Canada. He was chosen to be the first prime minister of this new country. He worked to bring more provinces into Canada.

He served Canada until his death.

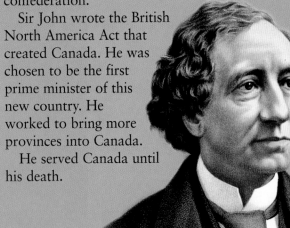

Confederation

Do you remember reading in Chapter 19 about the French and Indian War? The Canadians call that the Seven Years War. Great Britain won that war. The French colonies were taken over by the British. Most of North America north of New Spain became a British colony.

Then the 13 southern British colonies rebelled. They became a new nation, the United States of America. The remaining colonies were called British North America. These colonies became today's Canada.

A New Nation

The colonies in British North America were much like the other 13 colonies before the American Revolution. They were not united together. They were each their own colony.

On July 1, 1867, British North America joined together to form a new country. There was no revolution. Instead, Canada became a "dominion." A dominion was a country that governed itself but stayed part of the British Empire.

The provinces joining together to make the country of Canada is called *confederation.* But the new country had only four provinces. They were New Brunswick, Nova Scotia, Ontario, and Quebec.

Customs

Canadian Thanksgiving Canadian Thanksgiving is celebrated on the second Monday of October. Around 1578, the English navigator Martin Frobisher held a ceremony in today's Newfoundland. He gave thanks for surviving his journey.

Around 1750 this celebration of harvest came to Nova Scotia. Settlers from the southern New England colonies brought it with them. At the same time, French settlers were also holding feasts of "thanksgiving."

Early celebrations of Dominion Day (left) included parades. Today, Canada Day is an event that attracts families to big-city parks. **What does Canada Day celebrate?**

Canada's 1887 constitution created a national government. This gave the United Kingdom of Great Britain and Ireland power over Canada's laws. The *Constitution Act of 1982* put Canadians in charge of their own government.

July 1st is a national holiday. It was called *Dominion Day.* Now it is called *Canada Day.* Which date in American history does this remind you of?

The Mounties

The Royal Canadian Mounted Police (RCMP) are nicknamed the Mounties. They are the national police force of Canada. The Mounties are famous for their red uniforms and flat-brimmed hats. They are a symbol of Canada. The RCMP are called mounted police because they used to ride horses. Today, Mounties are a regular police force. Horses are ridden for special ceremonies.

The RCMP began as the North-West Mounted Police. Sir John A. Macdonald, the first prime minister of Canada, created this force. He wanted to bring law and order to the North-Western Territories.

Today, the RCMP enforces federal laws. It also is the provincial or territorial police for Canada's three territories and eight of its provinces. This would be similar to the State Highway Patrol in North Carolina. Ontario, Quebec, and parts of Newfoundland and Labrador have their own provincial police forces. Many towns and cities in Canada also use the RCMP as their local police force.

The RCMP is the largest police force in Canada. The Mounties do many jobs. They patrol towns and cities. They protect the prime minister and other leaders. They enforce federal laws. They fight terrorism. The RCMP often cooperates with police in the United States to solve crimes and protect citizens of both countries.

Economy and Government

Provinces and Territories

Today, Canada has ten provinces and three territories. It took 132 years for all the provinces and territories to join Canada. The provinces work both independently and together. Confederation allows each province to keep its special culture. For example, the many French-speaking people in eastern Canada wanted to keep their language. They did not want to lose their French traditions.

A Federal System

Like the United States, the national and provincial governments of Canada have different powers. The national government directs transportation and trade, banking, defense, and relations with other countries. Canada's leaders wanted the new national government to unite the country and strengthen its economy.

Provinces are set up like the national government. But the leaders of provinces are called premiers. Territories have less power than provinces. They are supervised by the national government.

Provincial governments are responsible for education, health, town and city government, and natural resources. Canada's provinces have strong governments. Ontario and Quebec, not the national government, decide how to spend money earned from their sale of hydroelectricity. Alberta decides how it will export oil.

WORD ORIGINS

In April 1999, Canadians redrew the map of their country. The Inuit people were given their own territory. It was carved out of the eastern half of the Northwest Territories. The Inuit chose the name **Nunavut** for the territory. This means "our land."

The Inuit are the people once called Eskimos. The word Eskimo means "eaters of raw meat." Inuit, the name they prefer, means "the people" in their own language.

Quebec

Quebec has a strong French heritage. A large portion of its citizens want Quebec to separate from Canada. They think that Canada's government cannot protect their French culture. These people are called *Separatists.*

In the past 30 years, there have been two votes in Quebec. Citizens were asked if they wanted to stay a part of Canada or separate from it. The Separatists lost both votes, but only by a little. Therefore, Quebec has stayed a part of Canada.

Canada's national government has passed laws to help protect French culture and heritage in Quebec. Many Canadians, particularly in the western provinces, do not like Quebec's requests for special treatment. This sometimes causes conflict among the provinces.

LESSON 3 REVIEW

Fact Follow-Up

1. What is a prime minister, and who elects him or her?
2. How is the Canadian government dealing with native peoples?
3. Explain why Canadians speak of the French and British as "two founding peoples."

Talk About It

1. What are some differences between a parliamentary system of government and the form of government in the United States? some similarities?
2. How are Canadian provinces similar to states in the United States? How are they different?

Charting the Organization of Canada's Government

There are many kinds of charts. Charts can tell us different things. The chart below is called an organizational chart. This kind of chart tells us how a group is set up. Usually, the person in the top block is the leader. He or she is responsible for the organization.

Everyone else is listed in the boxes under the leader. They report to him or her. The lines show who supervises, or is the boss of, whom. Different people have different jobs.

Governments also have organizational charts. This chart shows how Canada's government is set up. At the top, the monarch is the king or queen. Next, the governor general is shown. In Parliament, the House of Commons is shown equal to the Senate. The dotted lines show that the prime minister and the cabinet are members of Parliament, too.

Reading the Charts

Compare this chart with the United States Government chart on on page 431. Answer these questions.

1. Compare the position of the president of the United States to the positions of prime minister and governor general in Canada.

2. What are the differences and similarities between the two governments?

3. In Canada, what is "the opposition," and how do Canadians determine what the opposition is?

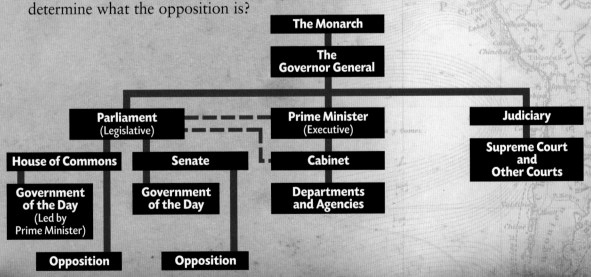

Lessons Learned

LESSON 1
The Economy
Canada has one of the world's strongest economies. It has important primary and secondary industries, plus a growing high-tech industry. Most Canadians work in service industries.

LESSON 2
World Partners
Canada and the United States are good neighbors. They cooperate in things like the St. Lawrence Seaway, defense, and trade.

LESSON 3
How Canada's Government Works
Canada is a parliamentary democracy. It is modeled on the system of the United Kingdom. Provinces share power with the national government.

Talk About It

1. Imagine that a Canadian teacher is coming to visit your class. What are the three best questions to ask your guest in order to learn more about Canadian government? Explain why your questions are the best.
2. Canada and the United States have different beliefs about government involvement in business. Most Canadians believe that government should be involved. Many Americans disagree. Why?
3. Which system of government has more advantages: the confederation of Canada or the federalism of the United States? Explain your answer.

Mastering Mapwork

LOCATION
Use the map on page 487 to answer the following questions.

1. Which two provincial capitals are located nearest 50°N?
2. Latitude 60°N forms the boundary of four provinces and one territory in Canada. Why do you think this is the case?
3. Which two provinces share 110°W as a boundary?
4. Describe the location of Toronto relative to Ottawa, the national capital.
5. Describe the relative location of the province of Manitoba.

Becoming Better Readers

Strategies While Reading
Good readers continually ask themselves if they understand what they read. They make predictions about what they will read. What strategies did you use to understand what you read in this chapter?

Go to the Source

Understanding a National Symbol

Canada's national anthem "O Canada" and coat of arms are symbols that unite Canadians. Canada's motto is on the coat of arms. In Latin it means, "A Mari Usque Ad Mare." In English it means, From Sea to Sea. Read the lyrics below and study the coat of arms. Then answer the questions below using information from the sources.

O Canada!
Our home and native land!
True patriot love in all thy sons command.
With glowing hearts we see thee rise,
The True North strong and free!
From far and wide,
O Canada, we stand on guard for thee.
God keep our land glorious and free!
O Canada, we stand on guard for thee.
O Canada, we stand on guard for thee.

Go to the Source

Questions
1. When viewing the Canadian coat of arms, what evidence shows that Canada and the United Kingdom were associated with one another?
2. How is patriotism represented in Canada's national anthem?
3. What do you think is the purpose for putting the motto *From Sea to Sea* on the Canadian coat of arms?

Society and Culture

The Caribana Festival brings together thousands of people in Toronto each summer. They dress in glittering costumes and dance through the streets. They beat steel drums and sing songs. This parade celebrates the culture of people from the Caribbean islands who now live in Canada.

This parade also shows us the cultural mosaic of Canada. Other festivals honor this, too. People at the Winnipeg Folkarama celebrate the many different cultures in Canada. The Calgary Stampede celebrates western ranch life. The Inuit, Native American, British, and French cultures continue to have a strong presence in everyday life.

Caribana Festival parade in Toronto

Chapter Preview

LESSON 1
A Changing Society
Canada has changed as its major cities have grown.

LESSON 2
Tradition Lives
The British and French heritages still affect the lives of Canadians.

LESSON 3
A Cultural Mosaic
The cultures of Canada are like the different pieces of a mosaic that are part of a whole.

The Winnipeg Folkarama attracts Canadians of many cultures.

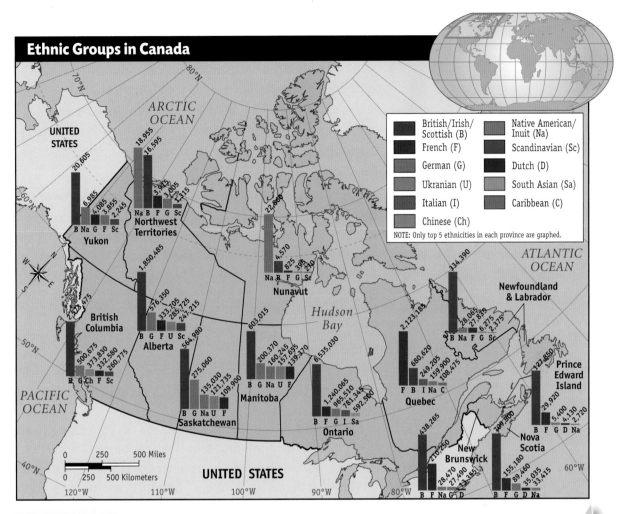

Ethnic Groups in Canada

British/Irish/Scottish (B)
French (F)
German (G)
Ukranian (U)
Italian (I)
Chinese (Ch)

Native American/Inuit (Na)
Scandinavian (Sc)
Dutch (D)
South Asian (Sa)
Caribbean (C)

NOTE: Only top 5 ethnicities in each province are graphed.

Yukon
20,605
6,985
4,085 3,855 2,245
B Na G F Sc

Northwest Territories
18,955
16,595
3,912 3,005 1,315
Na B F G Sc

Nunavut
22,800
4,570
825 395 250
Na B F G Sc

British Columbia
2,112,475
B G Ch F Sc
500,675 373,830 332,580 260,775

Alberta
1,850,485
576,350
333,705 285,725 247,215
B G F U Sc

Saskatchewan
564,980
275,060
135,030 121,735 109,900
B G Na U F

Manitoba
603,015
200,370 160,245 157,695 139,370
B G Na U F

Ontario
6,535,030
1,240,065 965,510 781,345 592,500
B F G I Sa

Quebec
2,123,183
680,620
249,205 159,900 108,475
F B I Na C

Newfoundland & Labrador
334,390
28,065 27,895 6,275 2,375
B Na F G S

Prince Edward Island
127,850
29,920 5,400 4,130 2,720
B F G D Na

Nova Scotia
409,800
155,190 89,460 35,035 33,415
B F G D Na

New Brunswick
438,265
210,250
28,470 27,490 13,355
B F Na G D

F. Blount Drane

In 1915, a young North Carolinian reached the village of Fort Yukon. His name was Frederick Blount Drane. His mission was to minister to Native Americans. They lived along the Yukon River north of the Arctic Circle.

It was a cold place for a man from North Carolina. Drane learned from the villagers. He wore a caribou-skin parka, sealskin boots, and snowshoes. He ate the same foods they ate.

After a decade in the Arctic, Reverend Drane returned to North Carolina. During the rest of his life, he looked back fondly on his days of living in the north.

CAROLINA CONNECTION

LESSON **1** A Changing Society

KEY IDEAS

- Most Canadians live in cities, and each city gives its residents a unique way of life.

- Life has changed in the Arctic for native people because of television, satellites, and airplanes.

Today, 80 percent of all Canadians live in cities. They move there for jobs. City life is also exciting. Canada's cities are some of the safest, cleanest, and best-run in the world.

Most immigrants to Canada move to cities, too. Newcomers look for jobs. But they also want to live near people from their homeland. They share customs and language.

Let's take a walk through five of Canada's cities. Each shows the different ways of life in Canada.

Montreal

Montreal is Canada's third-oldest and second-largest city. It was founded around 400 years ago on the St. Lawrence River.

An Inland Seaport

This location helped Montreal grow. It was once a small settlement in New France. Today it is one of the world's great ports. Montreal is now a major transportation and financial center.

The city is on an island in the middle of the St. Lawrence River. The island is 30 miles (48 km) long and less than 10 miles (16 km) wide. The city was built at a point where the river narrowed. Here rapids stopped boats from sailing farther up the river. Therefore, many early travelers had to leave the river and carry their canoes overland.

Several streets in Montreal look like Paris. **What are some less obvious signs of French culture in Montreal?**

This view of Montreal's skyline makes the city look different from Toronto (see below). **Why do you think they do not look alike?**

Until the St. Lawrence Seaway opened, Montreal was the farthest point inland that large oceangoing ships could reach. It is about 1,000 miles (1,610 km) from the Atlantic Ocean. But even so, it is one of the world's largest inland seaports.

People

Montreal has more French-speaking people than any city except Paris, France.

Many people of British, Irish, Russian, Chinese, and West Indian heritage also make their home there. But the city still has a strong French flavor.

Montreal is a showcase for French culture in North America. It has many theaters, movies, and art exhibits by French and French-Canadian artists. One proud resident stated that it was "possible to see the latest French movies as soon as they see them in Paris. We hear French orchestras and see French theater and ballet."

Toronto

Toronto is Canada's largest city. It is also Canada's banking and business center. The city is located on Lake Ontario and the St. Lawrence Seaway. It has many businesses that make and ship products from the mines and forests of the Canadian Shield.

Like many cities, Toronto has an underground shopping center. But Toronto's is the largest in the world. There are 16 miles (26 km) of walkways. You can shop in any of 1,200 stores.

From a distance, Toronto looks like many big cities in the United States. **What has Toronto built underground?**

People

In Toronto we can see the mosaic of Canada's culture. There are many ethnic groups that call the city home. Greeks, Italians, South Asians, Chinese, and many other ethnic groups have their neighborhoods. You will see restaurants, grocery stores, and gathering places.

Tomson Highway is a Native American who writes plays. He once wrote,

In Toronto, I can see the skin colorings of every race on the planet . . . . And I can hear the sound of languages from the four corners of the world . . . . This diversity, this richness of cultures, this electric mixture of so many strands of humanity . . . makes this country so unique, so lovable.

Sports

Sports fans enjoy the Rogers Centre. Its roof can open and close depending on the weather. Fans can watch games year-round. In the summer they go see the Blue Jays play baseball.

Hockey is Canada's national sport. Fans of the Toronto Maple Leafs can watch them shoot pucks into the net at the Air Canada Centre.

Vancouver

Vancouver is on the West Coast. It is the largest city in British Columbia. It is the third-largest urban area in Canada.

The city is located on a peninsula that points into the Pacific Ocean. Vancouver has a mild climate. Its harbor stays ice-free all year. Because of this and its location on the West Coast, Vancouver is a key port. It is Canada's main gateway for trade with Pacific Rim countries and the northwestern United States. It is Canada's busiest port.

Like Toronto, Vancouver is an English-speaking city. Its citizens come from many cultures. People of many faiths live and worship there. Some go to Buddhist temples. Others go to synagogues or churches.

Asian Cultures

Many people of Asian descent live in Vancouver. Its first Asian settlers were from China. They came to mine the gold fields on the Fraser River. Later, more Chinese were brought over to build railroads.

Recently, many Chinese have come from Hong Kong. They left there before the British turned the city over to China in 1997. Chinese residents make up about 17 percent of the city's population. Vancouver also has strong Vietnamese, Japanese, and South Asian communities.

Many tourists from the United States like to visit Vancouver as well as Seattle when they visit the Pacific Coast. **Would you like to travel there? Why?**

Winnipeg

Rivers and railroads helped Winnipeg grow. The Hudson Bay Company owned the land in what is now Manitoba. Fur traders and trappers built a trading post at the place where the Red and Assiniboine (as·SIN·ih·BOIN) Rivers meet. This became the town of Winnipeg.

The tracks of the Canadian Pacific Railway were laid through Winnipeg. The new railroad helped the prairie town grow. Farmers brought their grain to the railroad to ship it east.

Winnipeg built farm supply centers and grain elevators. These stored the wheat until the trains came to take it to market. Today, Winnipeg is a large city. Canadians call it the "Gateway to the West."

Winnipeg started as a small prairie town. It is now a big city. **Are there any signs it is a place linked to nearby grain and cattle industries?**

Iqaluit

Canada's newest and most northerly capital city is Iqaluit. Only about 7,250 people live there. It has a unique history.

The Inuit people did not build permanent cities. They followed and hunted game in the summer. In the winter they lived along the coast and hunted seals.

In the 1800s, Europeans came to the area to hunt whales. They built a village that became Iqaluit. Inuit later settled there, too. Some took jobs working for the Europeans.

In the 1970s, the Inuit told the government of Canada that they wanted their own territory. This dream came true. In 1999, Nunavut was created out of land that was part of the Northwest Territories.

Iqaluit is the capital of Nunavut. **Why was it important for the Inuit to have their own territory?**

The City Today

Iqaluit is the capital of Nunavut. It is Canada's fastest-growing community. It only officially became a city in 2001. Iqaluit's economy is based on being the capital. It now has many government offices. People usually travel to Iqaluit by airplane.

Iqaluit is located on the Arctic tundra on Baffin Island. In the summer, it has 21 hours of sunshine a day. But in the winter, it is extremely cold. During December, days are short. The sun rises and sets within four hours.

Blizzards and high winds can stop travel in the Arctic. So winter visitors sometimes have to spend an extra night or two in the North. This is called being "weathered-in."

Wildlife in Churchill

The Canadian town of Churchill in Manitoba is alive with wildlife.

Each fall, Churchill becomes the polar bear capital of the world. About 1,200 bears gather on the icy tundra. They are waiting for the the Hudson Bay to freeze. Then they will wander out on the ice to find seals.

Special tour buses called tundra buggies take visitors to see the polar bears. The buggies have huge tires. The tires do not hurt the tundra as much as regular bus or car tires can. Bears come right up to the buggies. Bears are beautiful, but dangerous.

In summertime, Beluga whales swim in the Hudson Bay and Churchill River. These are small whales that look much like porpoises. They are born gray, but turn snow-white when adults. Belugas are friendly and curious. They let people swim with them. People enjoy whale watching trips to see the Belugas.

Other species that can be seen in the area are caribou, harp seals, arctic foxes, and ptarmigans (snow chickens).

LESSON 1 REVIEW

Fact Follow-Up
1. What are some similarities among the five cities described in the text?
2. Why is Vancouver a center for Asian culture?
3. How have the changes in arctic life affected the Inuit?
4. What is Churchill, Manitoba, famous for?

Talk About It
1. How do differences among Canada's cities reflect the variety of the nation's people?
2. Why do you think it was important for the Inuit to have their own territory? Explain.
3. How is life in Canada's cities similar to and different from life in cities in the United States?

LESSON **2** Tradition Lives

The United States fought a revolution to free itself from Great Britain. The Canadians did not. They loosened their ties slowly and peacefully.

Canadians still have strong British connections. Parts of Canada also have deep roots in French culture. Both traditions are alive today. This unites some people. It also brings challenges.

British Ties

Canada is still part of the **British Commonwealth of Nations.** This group is made up of the United Kingdom and some of its former colonies. Some of the other countries that belong are Australia, India, Kenya, Jamaica, and other nations. They are connected by their history as British colonies.

The British legacy is everywhere in Canada. It can be seen in the English language, the form of government, and the court system. British style has influenced the design of buildings and cities. Ottawa, the nation's capital, and Toronto, Canada's largest city, have many British-style buildings.

During World Wars I and II, the British and Canadians fought side by side. During World War II, Canadian warships escorted supply ships across the Atlantic. They brought badly needed aid to the British.

KEY IDEAS

- Canada has strong ties with the United Kingdom.

- Signs of Canadian culture are the national flag and song.

- Descendants of French settlers preserve their French culture and customs.

KEY TERMS

British Commonwealth of Nations
"God Save the Queen"
"O Canada"

Is this the United Kingdom? No, it is Canada. The ceremony and uniforms look British. **If you were Canadian, what might you be proud of in Canada's British heritage?**

Society and Culture

515

Quebec City:
Capital of New France

July 3, 2008, was the 400th anniversary of Quebec City. Only a few cities in North America have reached this milestone. Today it is the capital of the province of Quebec.

Early French map of the St. Lawrence River

Fur traders and Roman Catholic missionaries were the first people who came to the colony. It grew and became the center of New France. The colonists built walls to protect the city. Quebec City is the only North American city north of Mexico that still has its walls today.

The French explorer Samuel de Champlain founded Quebec City. He named his settlement "Kebec" (kay • BEHK). This is from the Algonquian Native American language. It means "place where the river becomes narrow." He built his trading post on the tip of Cape Diamond. The city overlooks the St. Lawrence River.

Quebec City

Quebec City has a long and rich history. In 1759, the British and French fought a famous battle on the Plains of Abraham. The British won and took control of the city. This led to France's surrender of North America in the Seven Years War (French and Indian War).

Illustration of Quebec City in the 1700s

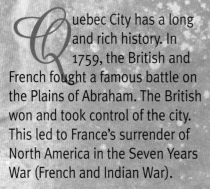

After Great Britain controlled the colony, parliment passed the Quebec Act. It gave religious freedom to the people of Quebec. This was one reason why the French there chose not to join in the American Revolution. So the 13 colonies invaded Quebec instead. In the winter of 1775–1776, American troops tried to capture Quebec City. But they failed. The walls protected the city until more British troops arrived in the spring.

In World War II, two conferences were held in Quebec City with the leaders of the United States, the United Kingdom, and Canada. There they made plans for the invasion of Europe in 1944.

United States President Franklin Roosevelt and the Prime Minister of the United Kingdom Winston Churchill (standing, right) met with other officials at the Quebec Conference in 1943.

Society and Culture

CANADIAN PORTRAIT

Lucy Maud Montgomery
1874–1942

Lucy Maud Montgomery was born on Prince Edward Island. Her mother died before she turned two. After his wife's death, her father went to live in the western territories of Canada. Montgomery went to live with her grandparents. When she turned sixteen, she was to Saskatchewan to live with her father and stepmother. She only stayed one year. Then she returned to Prince Edward Island.

Montgomery went to Prince of Wales College in Charlottetown on the Island. She graduated with a teaching certificate and taught at several schools on the Island. She also briefly worked for two newspapers for a short time. Then Montgomery moved back home to care for her grandmother.

During this time she began to write stories and poems. In 1908, she published her first book, *Anne of Green Gables*. She wrote more than 500 short stories and poems and 20 novels. Nineteen of the novels were set on Prince Edward Island.

After her grandmother's death, Montgomery married Ewan Macdonald, a minister, and they moved to Ontario. They had three sons. One died at birth. She lived in Ontario for the last years of her life.

Montgomery's stories are still read by people around the world. After World War II, *Anne of Green Gables* was translated into Japanese. Today, people join Lucy Maud Montgomery book clubs in Japan. They meet to read and talk about her books. Thousands of people from Japan and other nations visit her home on Prince Edward Island each year.

This is the Maple Leaf flag. It replaced the Union Jack as Canada's national symbol. **Why did Canada want a new flag?**

New Symbols

Canada's first flag was called the Union Jack. It also showed Canada's close ties with the United Kingdom. The United Kingdom's flag is also called the Union Jack.

For many years, Canadian bands played *"God Save the Queen"* at official ceremonies. Children sang it in school. This song is the United Kingdom's national anthem.

Canadians thought it was important to create their own national symbols. In 1965, Canada chose the Maple Leaf flag to be its new symbol. *"O Canada"* became Canada's national anthem in 1980.

French Identity

French language and French customs also have a long tradition in Canada. It was a French colony for more than 150 years. It only became a British colony in 1763.

Quebec Province was the home of French settlers. It is still home to the majority of French-speaking Canadians today (see map, page 509).

WORD ORIGINS

The Montreal **Canadiens** are an NHL hockey team. But why do they call themselves the Canadiens and not the Canadians?

People who live in Canada call themselves by two different names. English speakers call themselves "Canadians." People who speak French use the word "Canadien." It is the French spelling.

To French speakers, the name and the team are symbols of their ties with France.

I Remember

Many French Canadians take great pride in their French ancestry, culture, and language. The provincial flag has four white *fleur de lis*, the symbol of France. Quebec's motto is *Je me souviens*. This means "I remember" in English. It means that the people of Quebec remember their French heritage.

A French-Canadian businessman spoke proudly of Quebec's ties with France:

Our French-Canadian writers are published in France, our best students go to France . . . . Even for the average person, Paris is just around the corner. In the last 30 years we have grown back together with France.

He and others want to make sure that Quebec stays French in culture. More than 80 percent of the people in Quebec speak French as their first language. Only about 10 percent of people who live in Quebec consider English their first language. Most live around Montreal. Many of them speak French as well.

Until 1974, both English and French were official languages of Quebec. That year, Quebec voters decided to make French the only official language. All children must attend French-speaking schools.

Some large businesses did not like this. So they moved their headquarters from

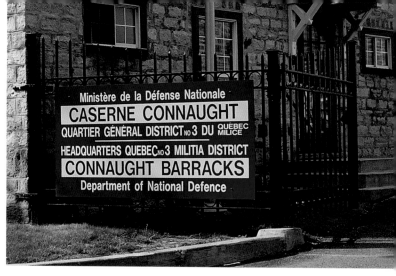

Signs in Quebec are written in French and usually do not include an English translation, such as the one at left. **Why do you think that sign is written in both English and French?**

Montreal to Toronto. Many English-speaking families left as well.

About 40 percent of Canada's population is Roman Catholic. Membership in that church is a reminder of the strong French culture in Canada.

What would YOU do?

If you walk down a street anywhere in Quebec, you might have trouble finding your way unless you speak French. Due to a law passed in the 1980s, all signs must be written in French.

Supporters of the law say it is fair. Most of the province's residents speak French. Some of Quebec's English speakers disagree. They feel discriminated against. They have asked for the law to be repealed. What would you do? Why?

LESSON 2 REVIEW

Fact Follow-Up
1. How do both British and French traditions persist in Canada today?
2. What are Canadian connections to Britain? to France?
3. What are some signs of British culture in Canada? of French culture?

Talk About It
1. Why do you think some French-speaking Canadians might want Quebec to separate from Canada?
2. Why might the British and French cultures not always fit together? How can the government help people get along?

Society and Culture

KEY IDEAS

- Canadian culture is called a mosaic.
- Each ethnic group maintains its important traditions.
- Canadians share a love for the outdoor life and hockey
- Inuit and Native American art is highly valued today.

KEY TERMS

Calgary Stampede
ice hockey
Stanley Cup

Many people who have studied Canada and its people say that Canadian culture is hard to define. It includes the favorite sports, art, music, festivals, and other ways Canadians enjoy themselves. Canada's culture is a mosaic made of many people and traditions.

A Year of Festivals

Throughout the year, many Canadian cities hold festivals. These highlight the customs of different groups and regions in Canada.

Icelandic The largest settlement of Icelanders outside Iceland is in Gimli, Manitoba. They hold a three-day festival to celebrate that town's Icelandic heritage.

Scottish Nova Scotia means "New Scotland." The community of Antigonish there holds the Highland Games. They are the world's longest running highland games outside of Scotland.

Chinese Vancouver hosts North America's largest Chinese fair each January. The festival is the biggest of its kind anywhere in the world outside of China.

There are other festivals that celebrate things unique to Canada.

These are scenes from Scottish (left) and Icelandic (below) festivals. The festivals celebrate those cultures in Canada. **Why is it important to celebrate different cultures?**

Maple Sugar

The maple leaf is Canada's national symbol. Maple festivals in Quebec, Ontario, and the Maritimes are popular. Many communities host these festivals each spring. The sap runs in maple trees in March. It is tapped and boiled down to make maple syrup.

Eastern Canada produces 85 percent of the world's maple syrup. The rest is made in the northeastern United States.

Calgary Stampede

In early July, Calgary, Alberta hosts the *Calgary Stampede*. It is Canada's largest annual event. It is also the world's largest outdoor rodeo. It celebrates Canada's western heritage.

The stampede has many events in addition to the rodeo. There are concerts, agricultural competitions, chuckwagon races, Native American exhibits, and other things to do. You can eat at one of the many pancake breakfasts held around the city, too.

Canadians show their pride in their heritage and their country in all of these special celebrations.

The Calgary Stampede features chuckwagon races and other events to celebrate the western heritage of Canada. **If your town had a festival, what would it be like?**

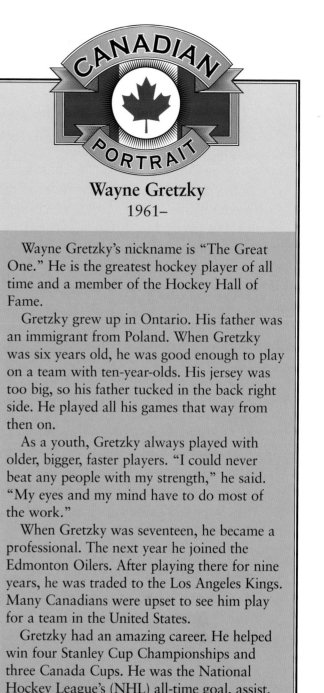

CANADIAN PORTRAIT

Wayne Gretzky
1961–

Wayne Gretzky's nickname is "The Great One." He is the greatest hockey player of all time and a member of the Hockey Hall of Fame.

Gretzky grew up in Ontario. His father was an immigrant from Poland. When Gretzky was six years old, he was good enough to play on a team with ten-year-olds. His jersey was too big, so his father tucked in the back right side. He played all his games that way from then on.

As a youth, Gretzky always played with older, bigger, faster players. "I could never beat any people with my strength," he said. "My eyes and my mind have to do most of the work."

When Gretzky was seventeen, he became a professional. The next year he joined the Edmonton Oilers. After playing there for nine years, he was traded to the Los Angeles Kings. Many Canadians were upset to see him play for a team in the United States.

Gretzky had an amazing career. He helped win four Stanley Cup Championships and three Canada Cups. He was the National Hockey League's (NHL) all-time goal, assist, and points leader. He retired in 1999.

He is the only player who will ever wear the number 99. The NHL retired that number for all its teams.

Gretzky is still active in hockey. He managed the Canadian men's hockey team for the 2002 Winter Olympics. He became a coach for the Phoenix, Arizona, Coyotes NHL team in 2005.

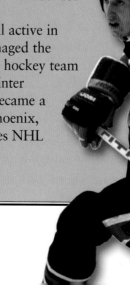

Being Canadian

Canada is a proud nation. Its citizens enjoy their lifestyle. They also appreciate the quality of life that their nation provides.

But Canadians also face challenges. Some come from having such strong provincial governments. Other challenges come from having strong but different cultural backgrounds.

First Nations

Canadians call the Native Americans who live in their country the First Nations. Canada has tried to be more respectful of First Nations cultures than it has in the past. Inuit peoples are not part of the First Nations.

Canadians appreciate and showcase Native American arts and crafts. In British Columbia at a Kwakiutl (kwa·ki·YOO·tul) village, carvers make woodcarvings known as totem poles. These carvings honor their ancestors.

Regional Loyalties

Within regions like the prairie provinces or the Atlantic provinces, people have much in common. Some Canadians may feel greater loyalty to their province than to the country as a whole.

It is as though, said one Canadian, "there is an Ontario patriotism, a Quebec patriotism, or a western patriotism, but there is no Canadian patriotism." These loyalties have made it harder for Canadians to come together as a nation.

But Canadians are united by a love of hockey and the outdoors.

Ice hockey is the perfect game for Canada. Its frozen lakes are great places to learn to ice skate in the winter. Ex-Montreal Canadien goalie Ken Dryden described hockey. He said it was a game that grew from "long northern winters uncluttered by things to do." With a net, a stick, and a small disk called a puck, it can be played on frozen ponds and in snow-covered streets.

The Outdoors

There is a saying, "Scratch a Canadian and you'll find a backwoodsman." This describes how Canadians enjoy the outdoors. Even though it is cold, winter is not a stay-inside season. People wear warm hats and coats and put on boots. They put snow tires on cars. Canadians make sure snow plows are ready to roll.

Canadians ski in the mountains, ice skate on frozen lakes, or play ice hockey on neighborhood rinks. The Rideau Canal in Ottawa freezes solid each winter. It then becomes the world's longest skating rink.

Many Canadian families spend their summer vacations at the beach or in the woods. One Canadian woman remembered how she felt when her family first arrived at their summer cabin. She wrote about their vacation on a lake in the Manitoba woods:

Cool fresh air of the woods hit me: a strong smell of spruce and balsam, pine needles, . . . wildflowers, rotting logs, wet moss, and beneath it all, the cold, slightly fishy smell of the lake.

Customs

Ice Hockey

Canada gave the United States and the world ice hockey. It has dominated the sport. The National Hockey League awards the **Stanley Cup** trophy to the champion each year. Since 1927, Canadian teams have won it 41 times.

Canada's teams are the Toronto Maple Leafs, Edmonton Oilers, Calgary Flames, Ottawa Senators, Vancouver Canucks, and Montreal Canadiens.

Inuit Art: From Drawings to Stone to Cloth

Canadian artist and art collector James Houston helped start interest in Inuit art. He began the West Baffin Inuit Co-operative. There Inuit sculptors and artists make carvings and prints.

Cape Dorset artist Pitaloosie Saila (pih·tah·LOOS·ee SAY·lah) (shown here) drew a scene called "Stopping to Rest." It showed two women. They each had a young child.

Eegyvudluk Pootoogook (EE·gie·vud·luk poo·TOO·gook) then traced the drawing onto a smooth stone. He inked the stone and carved the design. Then he covered the stone with paper. He rubbed the paper with his fingers. This put the design on the paper.

On Holman Island, Stanley Eloknak Klengenberg's (el·o·NAHK KLEN·gen·BERG) made a stencil called "Cold and Hungry." It shows the hardships his ancestors faced to survive life in the Arctic. He named another of his stencils "Ancestors' Song for Survival." It shows how Inuit want to preserve their traditions.

Klengenberg's drawings were printed on paper by Louis Nigiyok (NIG·ee·yok). Some artists, however, do both parts of the printmaking process.

In other communities in the Arctic, the Inuit transformed drawings into beautiful tapestries. Other Inuit carve traditional scenes in stone or walrus ivory. They also use bones from whale and caribou.

All of their creations help us learn about the Inuit way of life.

LESSON ③ REVIEW

Fact Follow-Up

1. What are some bonds that bind Canadian provinces together? that bind all of Canada together?
2. Why is the maple important to Canada?
3. What are some developments in Inuit art?

Talk About It

1. Why might it be said of Canadians, "Scratch a Canadian and you'll find a backwoodsman"?
2. Why might it be said that Canadians celebrate differences?

Learning about Canada and Its Provinces Using Flags

Study the flags on this page. What can we learn from them about the people of North Carolina, the United States, and Canada?

First, look closely at the colors in the flags. Did you know that blue is the most popular flag color in the world? Blue can stand for loyalty or patriotism. Red can stand for courage. What else could blue and red represent? What might white represent?

By the colors they use in their flags, nations, states, or provinces tell us what they think is important about themselves.

Patterns on flags, like the colors, can also tell us about the places they represent. The flag of the United States has stars and stripes. The Canadian flag has a maple leaf. What do these symbols mean?

Flags are Symbols

Look now at the North Carolina flag. What colors are used? There are two dates written on the flag. What do they represent?

The Canadian flag has changed from the Union Jack to the Maple Leaf. Why? How has the flag of the United States changed? Has the flag of North Carolina changed?

Look now at the figures on the province flags. Many province flags contain symbols of the United Kingdom, such as a lion or parts of the British flag. The rampant, or rearing, lion on Nova Scotia's flag is a symbol of Scotland. Scotland is part of the United Kingdom.

What do the *fleurs-de-lis* symbolize on Quebec's flag? How does Alberta's flag represent its landforms? What do the symbols on Ontario's flag mean?

You will study more about Canada's flags in Go to the Source in the Chapter Review.

North Carolina

Alberta

Quebec

Ontario

Nova Scotia

Lessons Learned

LESSON 1
A Changing Society
Most Canadians live in cities. Vancouver, Montreal, Toronto, Winnipeg, and Iqaluit show different parts of Canada's culture.

LESSON 2
Tradition Lives
Canada's culture is influenced by the British and French.

LESSON 3
A Cultural Mosaic
Each province celebrates unique ways of living. Canadian ethnic groups celebrate their own customs. Together, Canadians share an appreciation for the outdoors and ice hockey. Canada calls its Native Americans First Nations.

Talk About It

1. In 1980 and 1995, the people of Quebec voted not to separate from Canada. The issue will come up again. Imagine that you are a French-speaking resident of Quebec. Will you favor separation or not? Explain your choice.
2. It has been said that each Canadian province has its own culture but that Canada as a nation does not have a "Canadian culture." Do you agree or disagree with this statement? Give reasons for your answer.
3. Imagine that you are a Russian who plans to move to Canada. Where will you choose to live? Explain the reasons for your choice.
4. "Canadians identify with their regions and United States citizens identify with their country." Do you agree or disagree with this statement? Why or why not?
5. Is Canada more like the United States than it is different, or is it more different than it is similar? Explain your answer.

Mastering Mapwork

PLACE
Use the map on page 509 to answer these questions:
1. Examine the ethnic groups in Quebec. Given what you know about Canada and Quebec, what cultural characteristics of place would you expect to observe in Quebec?
2. Which province other than Quebec would be most likely to have the French language as a major cultural characteristic of place?
3. In which province is the British ethnic group most important as a cultural characteristic of place?
4. In which province or territory is there the most important Native American or Inuit presence?
5. Which province has the most people of Chinese heritage?

Becoming Better Readers

Taking Notes
We become better readers so that we can become better learners. Good readers know how to read a text and pull out the important information. What was the most important information about Canada's culture? What were the important details you wanted to remember?

Go to the Source

Flags of Canada

Study the provincial flags of Quebec, Nunavut, and British Columbia, and answer the questions below.

Quebec

Blue and the *fleur-de-lis* were chosen by King Louis VII of France in the twelfth century and were on the French flag at that time. The cross represents the cross that was on the banner flying from Jacques Cartier's ship in 1534.

Nunavut

The colors, blue and gold, symbolize the riches of the land, sea, and sky. Red is a reference to Canada. The inuksuk (in·NUK·shuk) symbolizes stone monuments which guide people on the land and mark special places. The star is the North Star. It is the traditional guide for navigation. It is symbolic of the leadership of elders in the community.

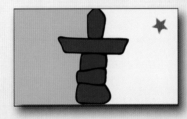

British Columbia

The Union Jack, or British flag, on the shield symbolizes its colonial origins. Its geographic location between the Pacific Ocean and the Rocky Mountains is represented by the wavy blue and silver bars and the setting sun.

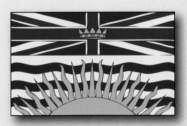

1. How are the three flags above different?
2. On British Columbia's flag, what do the wavy blue and silver bars and the setting sun symbolize?
3. What is the significance of the North Star on the Nunavut flag?
4. What symbol on the Quebec flag was also on the banner that was flying on Jacques Cartier's ship in 1534?

Unit 6

Waves from the Gulf of Mexico and the Pacific Ocean both crash upon Mexico's shores. Tall mountains divide the nation from north to south. The land has plains and deserts. It also has rain forests.

Mexico's history goes back to the Maya and Aztecs. The Maya people lived at the same time as ancient Egyptians. Hundreds of years later the Spanish brought their customs to the Americas. Today Mexico looks forward to a bright future with the other nations of North America.

Mexican folk dancers

Mexico

Unit Preview

The Land and People

Hernán Cortés

There is a story that the king of Spain once asked the explorer Hernán Cortés to describe the land of Mexico. Cortés simply took out a sheet of paper. He crumpled it and laid it out before the king. The bumps and ridges on the wrinkled paper showed the king the great variety of landforms in Central Mexico.

The people of Mexico are just as different as its landforms. They are united by a Spanish colonial heritage dating back more than 500 years. This European influence can be found in religion and government. It is also in the language and customs.

This influence has blended with Native American traditions to form modern Mexico.

Chapter Preview

LESSON 1
Location and Size
Located south of the United States, Mexico has many landforms.

LESSON 2
Climate and Plant Life
Mexico has warm deserts and cool mountains. It also has rain forests and evergreen forests.

LESSON 3
People of Mexico
Mexico's people descend mainly from Native Americans and Spanish settlers.

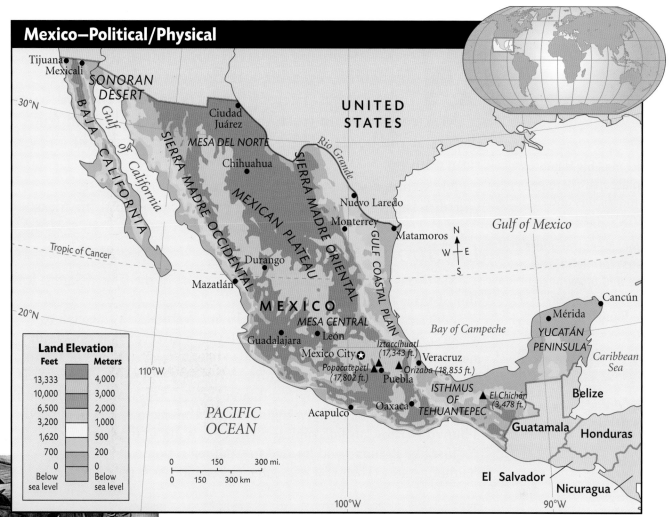

Mexico—Political/Physical

Tijuana
Mexicali
SONORAN DESERT
BAJA CALIFORNIA
30°N
Gulf of California
Ciudad Juárez
MESA DEL NORTE
Chihuahua
SIERRA MADRE OCCIDENTAL
MEXICAN PLATEAU
SIERRA MADRE ORIENTAL
Rio Grande
UNITED STATES
Nuevo Laredo
Monterrey
GULF COASTAL PLAIN
Matamoros
Gulf of Mexico
Tropic of Cancer
Durango
Mazatlán
MEXICO
20°N
MESA CENTRAL
Guadalajara
León
Bay of Campeche
Cancún
Mérida
YUCATÁN PENINSULA
Caribbean Sea
Iztaccíhuatl (17,343 ft.)
Mexico City ☆
Popocatepetl (17,802 ft.)
Veracruz
Orizaba (18,855 ft.)
Puebla
El Chichón (3,478 ft.)
Belize
Oaxaca
ISTHMUS OF TEHUANTEPEC
Acapulco
110°W
PACIFIC OCEAN
Guatamala
Honduras
El Salvador
Nicuragua
100°W
90°W

N
W + E
S

Land Elevation

Feet	Meters
13,333	4,000
10,000	3,000
6,500	2,000
3,200	1,000
1,620	500
700	200
0	0
Below sea level	Below sea level

0   150   300 mi.
0   150   300 km

James K. Polk

James K. Polk was born in North Carolina in 1795. He was elected the eleventh president of the United States in 1844. One of his goals was to expand the size of the United States. Texas had gained its independence from Mexico in 1837. In 1846, President Polk sent United States troops to help the Republic of Texas settle a border dispute. This turned into the Mexican War.

Texas became a state. The United States won the war. The territories that would become New Mexico, Colorado, Arizona, Utah, and California became part of the United States. This war caused bad feelings between the two countries for many years.

CAROLINA CONNECTION

531

LESSON ⑴ Location and Size

North Carolinians get many good things from Mexico. In the winter, vegetables are brought by truck to the United States. Factory products are also shipped from Mexico. American truck drivers often meet Mexican truck drivers at the border. There they exchange their freight and return home.

Mexicans come to North Carolina to work. North Carolinians travel to Mexico on both vacation and business.

Location

Mexico is located south of the western part of the United States. It is almost three times larger than Texas.

Let's imagine that your family is driving from North Carolina to Mexico. To drive through Mexico, you will need a car that can climb up and down high mountains. It must also handle long stretches of flat and dry plains. You will pass through steep canyons and open country. You will see areas with few people and large modern cities as well. High in the mountains it will be chilly at night. On the coast you will be reminded of a humid North Carolina summer. The heat is dry in the plains.

Just like Brendan and his dad in Chapter 1, you will cross many southern states. Then you will enter Texas and reach the Mexican border.

Mexico City is the largest city in Mexico. **What landforms might you see in Mexico?**

Driving Through Mexico

The border between the United States and Mexico is 2,000 miles (3,220 m) long. This is one of the busiest borders in the world.

On your trip you cross the border near Brownsville, Texas. The first Mexican city you reach is Matamoros (ma·tah·MOR·as). The highway becomes a black ribbon running through miles of sand. You have reached the Mesa del Norte.

You continue to take the highway south. Once you reach the capitol of Mexico City, you begin to travel southeast.

South of Mexico City, the highway enters the Isthmus of Tehuantepec (teh·WAHN·ta·PEK). An isthmus is a narrow land bridge. The isthmus lies between the Gulf of Mexico and the Pacific Ocean. If you continue on this road you will reach the countries of Central America. The nations of Guatemala and Belize border Mexico to the south.

WORD ORIGINS

The word "Mexico" comes from a Native American language. The word *"mexico"* was the name of a group that lived in Mesa Central before the Spanish arrrived.

The Copper Canyon—Barranca del Cobre—is part of the Sierra Madre mountains.
What two bodies of water border Mexico?

Mexico's Regions

Like the United States and Canada, Mexico can be divided into regions. These are the Mesa del Norte, the Mesa Central, and Southern Mexico.

Mesa del Norte

Mountains rise along the eastern and western sides of the *Mesa del Norte.* To the southeast there are low and rolling mountains like those of the eastern United States. These are the Sierra Madre Oriental. Little rain falls here and in the southeastern area of the plateau. Mexico's western mountains are tall with deep canyons. Mountain streams created the canyons over many years. These mountains are called the Sierra Madre Occidental.

Throughout much of the Mesa del Norte, the climate is dry. Cactus and wild scrub are the only plants that can survive in areas that receive only 2 inches of rain a year. Some dry areas have been changed into farmland through modern watering systems.

Farmers grow things like beans, corn, and chili peppers. They also grow cotton and wheat. Ranchers raise cattle in some parts of the Mesa del Norte. Beef has become an important industry. Large numbers of sheep and hogs are raised as well. Livestock has been raised in Mexico for almost 500 years.

The Land and People

Mexico's Spanish settlers forced Native Americans to dig for silver. Today, the nation's silver mines continue to produce this precious metal. Much is used for jewelry. In this region the Mexican states of Zacatecas (zah·kah·TAY·kas) and San Luis Potosi are silver mining centers. Northern states such as Sonora and Chihuahua have large mining operations.

Mesa Central

The *Mesa Central* is the middle region of the Mexican Plateau. It is an area of high plateaus near tall mountains. This region is cool and dry. Mexico City and Puebla are the two large cities located in this region.

Near Mexico City is an active volcano, Popocatepetl (po·pah·KAH·teh·peht·l). It stands almost 18,000 feet (5,400 m) tall. Popocatepetl is an important symbol of Mexico.

Years ago in this region, melting snow formed large lakes. Many of these lakes have been drained to create more land for living.

Some of Mexico's best cropland is found in the Mesa Central. Most Mexicans eat a lot of corn and beans. These crops grow well here. Squash and chili peppers grow well on the plateau, too. A large portion of Mexico's people have lived on the rich farmland of the Mesa Central since before the Spanish came.

When you leave the Mesa Central you begin a steady descent from the plateau to the Isthmus of Tehuantepec and the Yucatán Plain. The highway then takes you directly to southern Mexico through the city of Oaxaca (wah·HAH·kah).

Southern Mexico

The Yucatán Plain is part of Southern Mexico. Look at the map on page 531. The Yucatán Plain begins at the edge of the Mexican Plateau south of the Bay of Campeche (kam·PEE·chee). It stretches through the Yucatán Peninsula and into the countries of Guatemala and Belize.

Here the elevation is lower and the land flatter. Oak and pine trees grow alongside cactus. Rain forests thrive in the hot and humid climate of the southern Yucatán Plain.

A farmer in Oaxaca walks among dry corn stalks. **What are some differences between the Mesa del Norte and the Mesa Central?**

Chapter 22

The ground beneath the Yucatán Plain is made of limestone. Rainwater seeps through limestone quickly. No rivers run through the Yucatán Plain. Instead there are holes in the limestone called *cenotes* (say·NO·tays). These holes collect and provide water for the people. The ancient lowland Maya people built cities here using the *cenotes* for water.

During the dry season farmers grow wheat and alfalfa. They harvest their crops during the wet season. Farmers also grow cotton and sisal, a fiber used to make rope and textiles. These are plants that do not require a lot of water. Farmers grow sugar and coffee further south.

At Mexico's most southern tip is the state of Chiapas (CHEE·ah·pahs). There you will find another range of tall mountains and some volcanoes. This is also the home of the modern highland Maya. The Highland Maya split away from the lowland Maya centuries ago.

Coffee and corn are important crops here. Logging and beef production are major industries.

In the south, the state of Guerrero (GWAH·reh·ro) has silver, copper, and iron. Oil is found in the humid lowlands along the Gulf of Mexico. Mexico exports some of these raw materials. Most are used in Mexico's own factories.

These men are drying sisal fibers on racks in Yucatán, Mexico. Sisal is an important crop. **What are the other important crops in Mexico?**

LESSON ① REVIEW

Fact Follow-Up
1. What is an isthmus?
2. What are the three regions of Mexico?
3. In which region is Mexico City located?
4. Which region has the best cropland?
5. What are the features of Southern Mexico? of the Mesa del Norte? of the Mesa Central?

Talk About It
1. If you could visit one of the three regions of Mexico, which would you choose? Why?
2. Why do no rivers run through the Yucatán Plain?
3. How does relative location contribute to trade between the United States and Mexico? What factor might discourage trade?

The Land and People

KEY IDEAS

- Mexico is warmer than most of the United States. In Mexico's mountains and plateaus, the climate is much cooler.

- Mexico contains forests, grasslands, and deserts.

- Rain forests grow on Mexico's low plains. Evergreen forests are found at higher elevations.

Mexico is warmer than most parts of the United States. As in the United States, elevation and nearness to water affect the climate. The highest mountain peaks may have snow. Other places in Mexico have more tropical climates with miles and miles of thick plants.

There are also places with dry, sandy deserts that get little rain. Here, cactus and scrub grasses grow. There are even places in Mexico with many pine trees. There the countryside looks similar to the Appalachian Mountains of western North Carolina.

Climate

As you climb higher into the mountains, you'll feel it get cooler. You will also notice differences in rainfall and humidity. These differences are linked to elevation, as you read in Chapter 3.

In the western parts of the Mesa del Norte the land is flat and the climate is hot and dry. The mountains have cooler weather. Along the eastern coast of the Mesa del Norte, near the Texas border and Gulf of Mexico, the damp winds blow off the water. These winds and low elevation create warm temperatures and humid conditions.

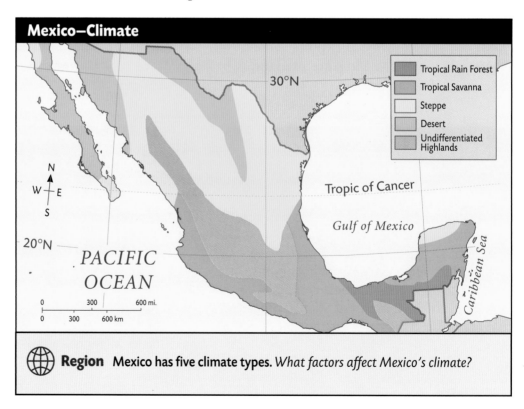

Mexico—Climate

Legend:
- Tropical Rain Forest
- Tropical Savanna
- Steppe
- Desert
- Undifferentiated Highlands

30°N

Tropic of Cancer

Gulf of Mexico

Caribbean Sea

20°N

PACIFIC OCEAN

0   300   600 mi.
0 300 600 km

Region Mexico has five climate types. *What factors affect Mexico's climate?*

The Mesa Central is dry and cool. Most people live at an elevation of more than 8,000 feet (2,400 m). People in the Mesa Central live near the Equator. But they enjoy a pleasant climate due to the higher elevation.

People living on the Yucatán Plain have homes very close to sea level and not far north of the Equator. Their climate is hot. Since they also are near the ocean, the air is moist. Rain falls often.

Farther south in the highlands of Chiapas, the climate is once again cool. That is due to their higher elevation.

Plant Life

Mexico also has many kinds of plant life. It has forests and grasslands. There are also plants in the desert. These are three of the four main types of plant life you learned about in Chapter 3. Climate and elevation affect what types of plants grow in each region.

Grasslands in Mexico are much less common than forests and desert plants. Do you remember reading about deserts? Deserts receive less than 10 inches of rain per year. Yet you will find a great variety of plant life in these areas. Some of the driest areas have

cactus, scrub brush, and even small trees. These plants are able to bud and bloom when it rains.

The Mesa del Norte sits at a high elevation, around 6,000 feet (1,800 m) and is quite level. The plateau is mainly covered with evergreen and leafy forests. The highest mountain ranges are cool and dry. Only small hardy trees and some grasses grow in this region. People have a hard time growing crops here.

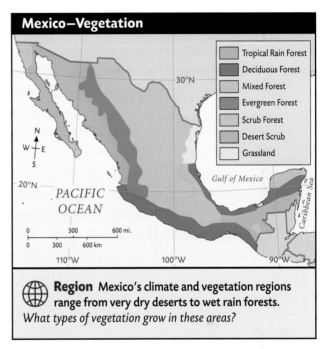

Mexico—Vegetation

- Tropical Rain Forest
- Deciduous Forest
- Mixed Forest
- Evergreen Forest
- Scrub Forest
- Desert Scrub
- Grassland

Region Mexico's climate and vegetation regions range from very dry deserts to wet rain forests. *What types of vegetation grow in these areas?*

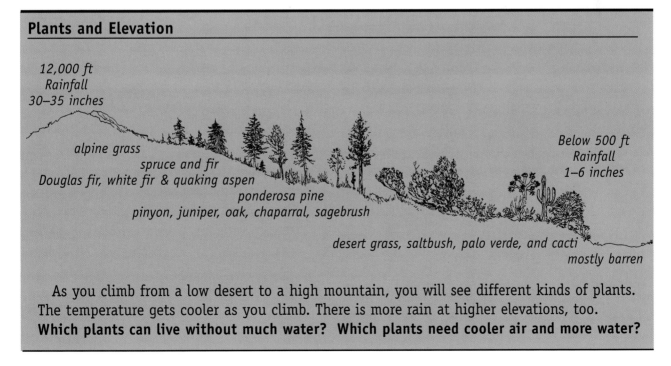

Plants and Elevation

12,000 ft
Rainfall
30–35 inches

alpine grass
spruce and fir
Douglas fir, white fir & quaking aspen
ponderosa pine
pinyon, juniper, oak, chaparral, sagebrush

Below 500 ft
Rainfall
1–6 inches

desert grass, saltbush, palo verde, and cacti
mostly barren

As you climb from a low desert to a high mountain, you will see different kinds of plants. The temperature gets cooler as you climb. There is more rain at higher elevations, too.
Which plants can live without much water? Which plants need cooler air and more water?

The Land and People

In Mexico's Mesa Central, climate and plant life are much like those of the Mesa del Norte. On land cleared of the forests people grow corn and wheat.

Southern Mexico is not far north of the Equator, but climates and plant life change with height above sea level. Tropical rain forests and moist plains grow on the low, hot lands of the Yucatán Plain. Rain forests are also found at higher elevations.

At the southern tip of Mexico the state of Chiapas has several different elevations so different types of plants grow there. Tropical rain forests grow in some areas. Forests also grow there. Some even have oak trees.

Changing the Land

At the higher elevations of Mexico, a few people terrace the land. Terracing is when a mountainside is shaped into a series of flat steps. Terraces let farmers grow crops on slopes that otherwise would be too steep.

What would YOU do?

You have an opportunity to live with your family for a year in a small town in Mexico. You will learn Spanish and go to the local school. What should you do to prepare? How would you make sure you are ready for life in a new place?

A saguaro cactus grows in a wheat field in the Baja area of Mexico. **How does this photograph show human-environmental interaction?**

LESSON 2 REVIEW

Fact Follow-Up
1. How does elevation affect climate in Mexico?
2. Of the four main types of plant life, which three does Mexico have?
3. Where in Mexico are there tropical rain forests?
4. Why have mountainsides been terraced?

Talk About It
1. Southern Mexico lies in the Tropics. How is it possible that there are snowcapped mountains in Mexico?
2. Where in Mexico would you go to visit an area least like the southeastern United States? What type of plants would you find there?

A Journey to CHIAPAS

San Cristobal de las Casas

The state of Chiapas is in the southern part of Mexico. There the city of San Cristobal de las Casas lies in a valley more than 7,000 feet (2,133 m) high. The mountains rise to more than 9,000 feet (2,743 m). A Spanish settler founded the city in 1528.

At first the town was called San Cristobal. "Las Casas" was added to the city's name later. It honors Father Bartolome de las Casas. Many years earlier he fought for the rights of the Native Americans in the Spanish colonies.

Today, San Cristobal de las Casas is a center of highland Maya culture. It is also a vacation spot for tourists from all over the world. Around the city lay many Maya villages. San Cristobal is the area's market town.

In the hills and valleys around San Cristobal, the Maya grow their crops on terraces. Most dress in traditional clothes. Most Maya speak their own languages and Spanish.

Visiting San Cristobal can be a journey into the past. Many of the streets in the town are made of cobblestones. This makes for a rough ride in a car or truck.

Yet modern technology is also present here. Computers and satellite dishes bring news of the world. Airplanes from Mexico City land at the local airport every day.

The Land and People

KEY IDEAS

- Most Mexicans live in the cities of the Mesa Central.

- Mexico's culture combines Native American customs with Spanish traditions.

- Trade is bringing Mexico and the United States closer together.

KEY TERMS

mestizo
mezcla
tiendas

People from Europe and North America came together to build Mexico. The Mexican people descend mainly from Native Americans and the Spanish. A small population with African ancestors lives along the Gulf of Mexico.

Mexican writers and artists began calling themselves *La Raza Cosmica* (the Cosmic Race) after the revolution. They believe each ethnic group helps make their nation strong.

Where People Live

The most densely settled area of Mexico is the Mesa Central. Its four largest cities are all located here.

This region is also the home of Mexico's ancient cities. People have lived and worked there for thousands of years. Mexico has a thinly populated northern desert region. But the northern region's border towns have growing populations. Their closeness to the United States draws people and businesses to the border.

Much of Mexico is a patchwork of open spaces mixed with urban areas. In the southern highlands there are fewer people than in the Mesa Central. The rain forests of the Yucatán Peninsula are also thinly populated.

As you drive along you might find yourself alone on long stretches of isolated highway. But you might also find yourself in crowded places along the coast. Many people live there, too.

Mexico City's Paseo de la Reforma shows how Mexico honors its past while being a busy, modern city. **What does *mezcla* mean? How does it describe Mexico?**

Guadalajara's cathedral is one sign of European influence in Mexico. **What is another sign of Spanish influence?**

A Mezcla of Peoples

The Spanish word *mezcla* means mixture. It describes the population of Mexico. Before the Spanish came, Mexico was home to the Maya and Aztec empires. Everyone spoke their own Native American language and worshiped their own gods.

Language

The Spanish brought their language and the Roman Catholic Church. So modern Mexico is mostly a combination of Native Americans and Europeans. There is also a small number of Africans.

The majority of Mexicans speak Spanish. Ninety-one percent use Spanish as their principal language. There are several Native American languages spoken there as well. More than 6 percent of Mexicans speak one of these Native American languages.

Native American languages have given us both Spanish and English words. The words chocolate and tomato come from Nahuatl words. Throughout Mexico, Spanish is mixed with Native American words for places and animals. The same is true for many plants.

About half of the Mexican people are *mestizo,* or persons of mixed Native American and European ancestry. Around one third of the population is Native American. About 15 percent are European. About 1 percent of the population falls into other categories.

Customs

Mexicans celebrate the coming of Christmas with a *posada*. Posada is a Spanish word that means "shelter." Sometimes they have a little pageant where children portraying Mary and Joseph knock at three doors and ask to come in. They are turned away at the first and second doors. They are welcomed in and offered special foods and drinks at the third door. The children break open a *piñata*. Out pours all kinds of candy. There might also be some fruit and coins in the *piñata* as well.

WORD ORIGINS

The word "mestizo" refers to Americans of both Native American and European backgrounds. The phrase comes from the spanish word *"metizar"* and means "to mix" or "cross". Mestizo people have ansestors who are both European and Native American.

The Meeting of Cortés and Moctezuma

Hernán Cortés was the leader of the Spanish forces that conquered the Aztec Empire. Moctezuma II was the Aztec emperor at that time. The meeting of these two leaders was one of the most dramatic moments in the history of Mexico.

In 1519, the Spanish governor of the island colony of Cuba sent Hernán Cortés (left) to the mainland. Cortés' goal was to make contact with the people there. His orders were to explore, not to conquer. Cortés did not follow his instructions. He conquered the Aztecs.

Moctezuma II (left) was the Aztec ruler . In 1517, when Moctezuma first heard of the Spanish landing on the coast, he posted people to watch the foriegners and to let him know when more arrived. When Cortés arrived in 1519, Moctezuma's people told him about the newcomer. Moctezuma sent gifts and people to meet Cortés.

Aztec Empire

Teotihuacán

Tenochtitlán

Cortés and the Spanish brought many things that the Aztecs had never seen. They had guns, huge fighting dogs, horses, and steel armor.

Cortés fought his way from the coast to the Mesa Central. The Spanish made an alliance with enemies of the Aztecs. Then Cortés traveled to the Aztec capital. The two men met.

Cortés meets Moctezuma

Moctezuma II was dressed in a great cape of colorful feathers. Cortés wore shiny armor. Cortés gave Moctezuma II a necklace of pearls and diamonds. Moctezuma II gave Cortés a chain hung with large gold figures. Moctezuma invited the Spanish to stay with him in his palace.

Eventually Cortés kidnapped Moctezuma II. With the help of the Aztecs' enemies, the Spanish soldiers, and European diseases, the Aztec empire fell. Moctezuma was killed in a battle with the Spanish, but it is unclear whether he was killed by the Spanish or his own people.

Cortés conquers the Aztecs

The Land and People

The Roman Catholic Church has been an important influence in Mexico for more than 400 years.
What culture did the European explorers encounter when they first arrived?

Native Americans

Chapter 4 explained how the first settlers of the Americas moved from Asia. Many of these people traveled as far south as modern Mexico. They built great cities in the Mesa Central and Yucatán Peninsula.

Others remained nomads for a time or moved about the land according to the season. There were also highly advanced cultures that developed in other parts of Mexico.

Europeans and Africans

The Spanish came to Mexico in 1519. They conquered the Aztecs. Over time many more Spanish people came to Mexico. They started the colony of New Spain. Its capital was Mexico City. Then the Spanish spread out across the land. They built cities in many places. Most of these cities exist today.

Few people from places other than Spain came to Mexico. Over the years some Asians and other Europeans made the journey. Africans arrived in Mexico as free men and women. Sometimes they came as the result of shipwrecks in the Gulf of Mexico.

Others escaped slavery on Caribbean islands and then came to Mexico. A small number were brought to Mexico as slaves. More recently, some Africans have moved to Mexico.

Mexico Today

Beginning in the 1980s, many Central Americans began to flee to Mexico. They left political conflicts in their own countries. Many of these people spend time in Mexico on their way to the United States. They travel north seeking work and freedom.

There are also some communities in Mexico with a large number of United States citizens. Many of these are retired people. There are 9,000 foreigners in the state of Guanajuato (gwan·ah·WA·to) alone. About 350,000 United States citizens live in Mexico today.

Mexico is a country of young people. More than half of its people are under 20 years of age. The nation's total population is almost 110 million.

In the second half of the 1900s, many Mexicans moved from the country to the cities. Today Mexico is an urban nation. Around 71 percent of the population lives in cities or towns. Mexico City is the second-largest urban area in the world.

This modern building is the stock exchange in Mexico City. **Do more Mexicans live in urban or rural areas?**

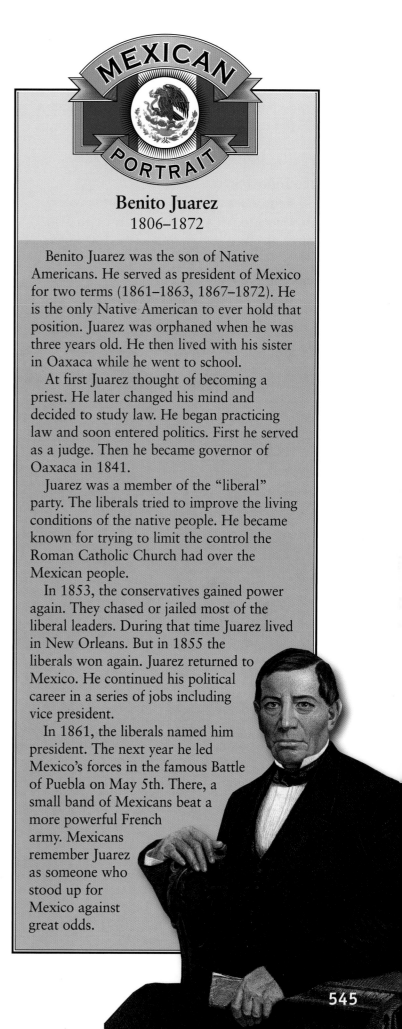

MEXICAN PORTRAIT

Benito Juarez
1806–1872

Benito Juarez was the son of Native Americans. He served as president of Mexico for two terms (1861–1863, 1867–1872). He is the only Native American to ever hold that position. Juarez was orphaned when he was three years old. He then lived with his sister in Oaxaca while he went to school.

At first Juarez thought of becoming a priest. He later changed his mind and decided to study law. He began practicing law and soon entered politics. First he served as a judge. Then he became governor of Oaxaca in 1841.

Juarez was a member of the "liberal" party. The liberals tried to improve the living conditions of the native people. He became known for trying to limit the control the Roman Catholic Church had over the Mexican people.

In 1853, the conservatives gained power again. They chased or jailed most of the liberal leaders. During that time Juarez lived in New Orleans. But in 1855 the liberals won again. Juarez returned to Mexico. He continued his political career in a series of jobs including vice president.

In 1861, the liberals named him president. The next year he led Mexico's forces in the famous Battle of Puebla on May 5th. There, a small band of Mexicans beat a more powerful French army. Mexicans remember Juarez as someone who stood up for Mexico against great odds.

The Land and People

Relations with North Carolina

Mexico is one of North Carolina's biggest trade partners. Several of North Carolina's textile companies have started partnerships with Mexican firms. Some have built new factories there and closed other factories in the United States.

Industries here export a number of products to Mexico. North Carolina also buys produce and manufactured products from Mexico. Truckers travel long distances hauling these goods.

Coming Closer

The people of Mexico and North Carolina come into contact with one another all the time. Mexicans are learning to speak English and North Carolinians are studying Spanish.

In the cities and small towns of North Carolina you see *tiendas,* or shops selling food and magazines from Mexico. The country that seemed so far away only 20 years ago has come to the very doorstep of North Carolina.

These women are sewing clothes at a Mexican factory. **What do Americans buy from Mexico?**

LESSON ③ REVIEW

Fact Follow-Up
1. What is the most densely settled area of Mexico?
2. How does the Spanish word *mezcla* describe the population of Mexico?
3. Describe the diversity of the population of Mexico.
4. What is a *tienda?*

Talk About It
1. Which country is more a country of youth: Mexico or the United States? Explain why.
2. More and more United States citizens are moving to Mexico to live and work. Why?
3. What might be some effects of a North Carolina company building a new factory in Mexico?

Comparing the Regions of North America

Just as you have learned about regions of the United States and Canada, you have now begun to learn about the regions of Mexico. In your studies of regions in the United States and Canada, you learned about both physical and political regions. You may even remember learning about cultural and language regions.

Do you recall any differences between French-speaking and English-speaking regions in Canada?

Let's compare the regions of Canada, the United States, and Mexico. This will help you learn about the things these three countries share and about their differences. To begin these comparisons, you will need to make two important decisions.

First, you will need to choose which regions you will study. Choose one region from each country. They are listed below.

The Mesa del Norte in Mexico

A. The United States regions: New England, the Mid-Atlantic, the Southeast, the Midwest, the Southwest, the West, and the Pacific.
B. The Canadian regions: the Arctic Plains, the Appalachian Highlands, the Great Lakes-St. Lawrence Lowlands, the Interior Plains, the Canadian Shield, and the Western Mountains.
C. The Mexican regions: the Mesa del Norte, the Mesa Central, and Southern Mexico.

You might use the maps in Chapters 14, 15, 16, 18, and 22 to refresh your memory of these regions. You will need to decide the best way to compare these regions. You might choose landforms, climate, minerals, and other economic resources. What other things might you use? population? economic activities? You could even use recreation as one of the things you compare.

Your teacher will guide you as you make these decisions and compare the regions of the United States, Canada, and Mexico.

Lessons Learned

LESSON 1
Location and Size
Mexico lies south of the western United States. It includes many highlands. The best land for farming is in the Mesa Central, where the Aztecs and other ancient peoples settled.

LESSON 2
Climate and Plant life
Although Mexico's climate is warmer than most of the United States, the air is cooler in the mountains and plateaus. Rain forests grow on the low plains, and evergreen forests grow in the highlands.

LESSON 3
People of Mexico
The cities of the Mesa Central are highly populated. Mexico's culture is a mixture of Native American and Spanish traditions. In recent years, trade has brought the United States and Mexico closer together.

Talk About It

1. Which region, the Mesa Central or Southern Mexico, do you think has more valuable resources for Mexico's future? Explain why.
2. How did Africans arrive in Mexico?
3. Is the word *mezcla* a more accurate description of the population of Mexico or the United States? Explain.
4. Why have contacts between North Carolina and Mexico increased in recent years?
5. Suppose Hernán Cortés had not disobeyed orders and kidnapped Moctezuma II. How do you think life in Mexico might have been different? Explain why.

Mastering Mapwork

Movement
Use the maps on page 531, 536, and 537 to answer these questions:
1. Locate Veracruz. What physical characteristics of place would you expect to find in Veracruz?
2. Locate Ciudad Juarez. What physical and cultural features of place would you expect to find in this place?
3. Using only the information from this map, what cultural features of place would you expect to find in Mexico City?
4. Locate Merida on the Yucatán Peninsula. What physical features of place would you expect to find in this location?
5. Locate the Gulf Coastal Plain. What physical features of place would you expect to find in this place?
6. Which of these cities is likely to be cooler: Chihuahua or Mexico City? Explain why.
7. Which city is likely to be warmer: Monterrey or Mazatlan? Explain why.

Becoming better readers

More on Taking Notes
In order to remember what they read, good readers will sometimes take notes. To take notes, good readers write the main idea and one or two details that tell more about the main idea. Reread the portrait of Benito Juarez on page 545. Write down the key points of his life and one or two details that support those points.

Go to the Source

Gathering Information from Letters

Letters to friends and family can be primary source documents. They describe people, places, and events at a particular point in time. People often also write of their thoughts and feeling about things that are happening. Historians often use letters to learn more about a culture or other things that may have been happening during a a particular period of time.

Read the letter from the pen pal to her friend below. Answer the questions using information from the letter.

Translation:

> Hi, how are you Christian? Good, I hope. I am from Mexico and I live in the state of Querétaro in the town of Jalpan, and my name is Ana Guadalupe. I am going to explain a little about Mexico. Mexico is a place where there are many ecosystems: aquatic, aerial, terrestrial. In the aquatic live fish, serpents, and more other things. In the air live birds, butterflies, and other things. On land there live horses, mountain lions, turkey, snakes, spiders and other things. Now I have explained Mexico to you. I would like you to tell me about California and about your customs and I hope that we will be good friends.
>
> Sincerely,
> Your new friend:
> Ana Guadalupe

Questions

1. Where does Ana live?
2. What are the three ecosystems in Mexico that Ana describes?
3. Why would Ana want Christian to tell her about customs in California?
4. What is Ana's purpose in writing this letter?
5. What is Ana's tone in this letter?

People and Their Environment

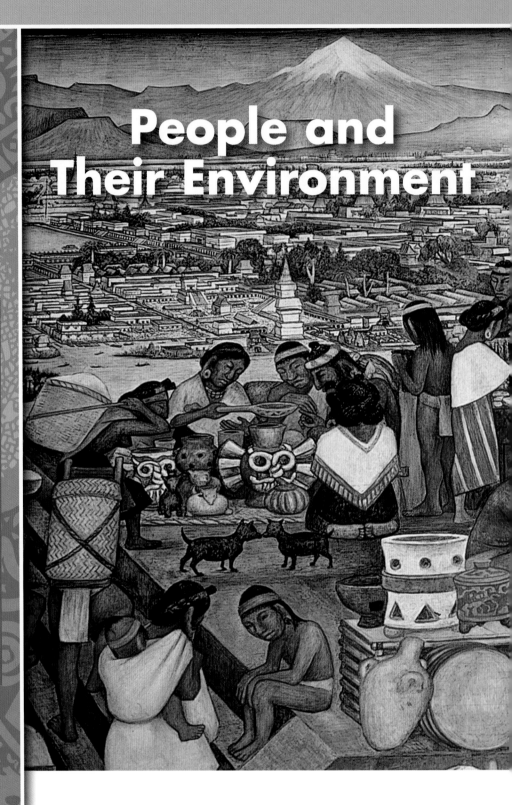

Timeline of Events

2600 B.C.

100 B.C.

100 B.C.
Teotihuacán founded

2600 B.C.
Maya civilization
begins

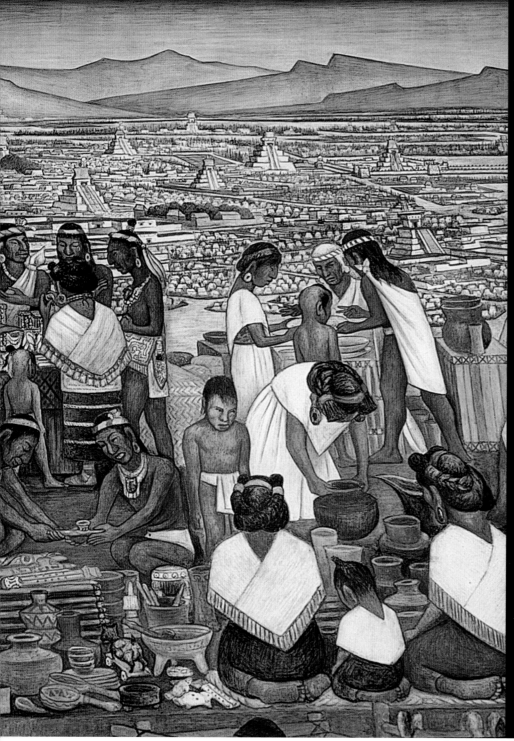

In the center of the Mexican flag is a picture of an eagle. It is sitting on a cactus with a snake in its mouth. This was a sacred symbol to the Aztecs. They had once wandered the earth searching for a place to build their homes.

They believed that the gods would give them a signal when they reached the right place. When they saw the eagle with the snake in its beak, they would know that they had reached the right place.

Diego Rivera's The Gran Tenochtitlán

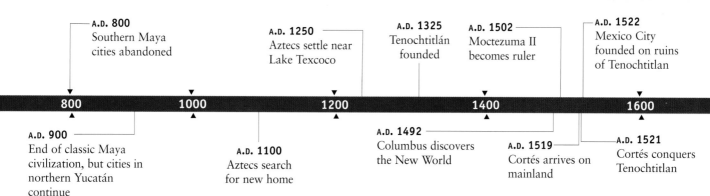

A.D. 800
Southern Maya cities abandoned

A.D. 1250
Aztecs settle near Lake Texcoco

A.D. 1325
Tenochtitlán founded

A.D. 1502
Moctezuma II becomes ruler

A.D. 1522
Mexico City founded on ruins of Tenochtitlan

800 | 1000 | 1200 | 1400 | 1600

A.D. 900
End of classic Maya civilization, but cities in northern Yucatán continue

A.D. 1100
Aztecs search for new home

A.D. 1492
Columbus discovers the New World

A.D. 1519
Cortés arrives on mainland

A.D. 1521
Cortés conquers Tenochtitlan

KEY IDEAS

- Mexico was the center of the Maya and Aztec cultures.

- The Maya developed a written language. They were also skilled in farming and math.

- The Aztecs built great cities that were centers of religion and culture.

KEY TERMS

drought
obsidian
rituals
slash-and-burn farming
specialization

Long before the Spanish came there were already several great cultures in today's Mexico. Two of the most important were the Aztec and the Maya. These ancient peoples built great cities. Both had a complex system of laws. Like other great civilizations, both knew how to farm native plants and best use their natural resources.

The Aztecs had created a huge empire by the time the Spanish arrived. Sometimes the empires fought wars just as European kingdoms did. Kings ruled these empires. The kings claimed the gods chose them to rule.

Native American Culture

The Spanish conquered the Native Americans. But they did not destroy all of their culture. Native American traditions still have a great influence in Mexican society.

The Three Sisters

Corn and beans were very important to the early people of Mexico. They also grew different kinds of squash. These plants grow well together. The wide leaves of the corn plant shade the beans and squash from the harsh sunlight.

The bean and squash vines can climb the corn stalks. The squash plant's leaves and vines in turn cover the ground. This protects the soil and keeps it moist. It also prevents weeds from growing. The beans put nutrients in the soil that helps the corn and squash grow. This combination of plants even attracts certain insects that feed on other more harmful insects.

Successful farming means people have plenty of food. A community that has extra food allows people to share the work. This is called *specialization.* This means that people can divide the work, or specialize, based on their skills and talents. When the Native Americans became successful farmers, more people in their empires could do other jobs. Some people were able to do special jobs in the cities. They could be priests, or make pots, or build pyramids.

The people planted corn or maize, squash and pumpkins, and beans together. **Why are these crops called the "three sisters?"**

The Lowland Maya

The Lowland Maya people lived in the Yucatán Peninsula. They had to prepare the land there to plant crops. They used a *slash-and-burn* method to clear the land. They cut down and burned what they had cut. The burning helped return nutrients to the soil.

The lowland Maya built a system of canals to bring water from rivers to their fields. After a while, Mayan farmers began to produce more food than they needed to feed everyone.

A market system tied Mayan towns together. Priests were important because people believed that the priests brought messages from the gods. The messages told them when to plant crops and predicted the weather. Priests also led the people in *rituals* (special ceremonies) and prayers for successful farming.

In the cities of the Yucatán Plain, the Maya built pyramids of stone for religious rituals. The rituals sometimes included a human or animal sacrifice.

The Maya also created a written language. They wrote in picture-symbols called hieroglyphs.

The Maya used astronomy to create an accurate calendar. This means that they studied the position of the sun, moon, and stars. This helped them keep track of the seasons. They even invented an advanced system of mathematics.

The Decline of the Maya

The Mayan way of life thrived for nearly 1,000 years. The Maya left their cities around A.D. 900. That was about 600 years before the Spanish arrived. Historians still do not know why they did this. But they have some theories about what happened.

Some think that the Mayan population grew too fast. Not enough people were farming and too many poeple were doing other jobs. The Maya system of farming may have used up too much land. Maya farmers might not have been able to grow enough food to feed everyone in the cities. The problem with this theory is that we know that Maya farmers often grew more food than they needed.

Another theory is that a severe *drought,* or lack of rain, may have hurt food production and caused starvation. People may have moved away to find food.

Others think that a war within the Maya society caused many to flee into the jungle. Some moved to the highlands of modern Guatemala and the Mexican state of Chiapas. There they had to adapt to life in the mountains.

Today, more than 3 million people continue the Maya way of life. They are still adapting to the modern world while trying to keep many of their ancient ways. These are the Highland Maya. We will learn about their culture in Chapter 26.

This statue was used as a marker in a Maya ball game.
Why do you think the figure is wearing knee pads?

The Temple of the Moon at Teotihuacán took more than 7,000 laborers about 15 years to build. **Why do you think the temple was important to Native Americans?**

The Aztecs

The Aztec way of life developed on the Mexican plateau around the year A.D. 1300. There the Aztecs began to farm and work as soldiers in the other nearby cities. They lived around a series of large connected lakes. In the middle of one lake was a large island. There they built the splendid city of Tenochtitlán (tay·noke·tee·LAHN).

The Native Americans began free schools where children could learn different professions. Some learned astronomy. Others learned to be doctors or priests. Schools also taught young girls the necessary skills for running a household or serving the religious community.

Farming

The Aztecs created a special way of farming the wet land. They dammed the lakes in certain spots and drained them in other places. Then they cut thick mats of floating water plants into long strips. They piled these on top of one another. As they added more strips, the water plants sank to the bottom.

The farmers kept piling on strips until the last was above the water. Then they scooped the rich mud from the lake bottom and covered the mat of water plants. Here they planted crops. These gardens were called *chinampas.* The Aztecs also created ways to bring water from the lake to their crops.

Aztec Cities

The Aztecs were good at taking the ideas of other peoples and improving them. They borrowed ideas about building and farming from their neighbors.

A nomadic people, the Aztecs invaded the Valley of Mexico looking for a new home. they often were brutal and violent rulers. They built great cities, but also made many enemies. More than 300,000 people lived in Tenochtitlán by the mid-1400s. It was one of the largest cities in the world. The ruins of Tenochtitlán lie beneath present-day Mexico City.

Ruins of the Past

Today the ruins tell us how Native Americans lived before the Europeans came. The ruins were once painted bright colors. Tall pyramids have Native American carvings that tell us about the animals they saw. You can see the domed buildings the Maya used to observe the stars. There are even huge open courts where the people played ball games.

The lakes where the Aztec cities began are now gone. The canals used by the Maya to water their fields are covered by centuries of plant growth. But you can still imagine cities with thousands of people. The squares were busy markets filled with buyers and sellers trading goods from across the region.

This stone marked a boundary of a Maya court game.
What do you think happened to the Maya?

The City of the Gods

Teotihuacán (tay·oh·tee·wah·KAHN) was, at the time, the largest city in the Americas. It had a population of more than 100,000 at its peak.

Historians are not quite certain which Native American group founded the city. It may have been the Toltecs or the Tolonacs. But many different Native American peoples lived in the city over several centuries.

Teotihuacán was carefully laid out in blocks like our modern cities. It had many temples. Its pyramids influenced the Maya and Aztec cultures. There was even a drainage system under the streets to carry away the rainwater from sudden storms.

The city became a trading center. Merchants traded things like obsidian knives and tools used to cut beautiful feathers and precious stones. **Obsidian** is a mineral created by volcanoes. It looks like black glass. Obsidian was the hardest substance known to the Native Americans. When chipped, it made a sharp edge that was excellent for cutting.

The Calendars of Mexico

Astronomy and religion were closely linked for both the Aztecs and the Maya. They believed that the movement of the sun, moon, and stars told them the will of the gods. Both cultures developed an advanced system of mathematics to help them in track this movement. They used it to make accurate calendars. The calendars allowed them to predict things such as eclipses and comets.

The priests and royalty were astronomers. This means that they studied the stars. They used their learning in colorful rituals. They wore special costumes made of beautiful feathers and golden cloth.

These ceremonies were held in huge temples or on the great pyramids. We know that structures of that size could not have been planned and built without a strong knowledge of math and geometry.

The calendar was important to life in ancient Mexico. People believed that time moved in a great circle. Their calendars were even round. Knowing when to expect the dry or rainy season or when to look for storms helped them survive. Knowing the best times to plant or harvest were also important for farming.

Their knowledge of astronomy and math made the priests powerful. They held high positions in society. Understanding the ancient calendar is important to many of the descendants of the Aztecs and Maya today.

LESSON 1 REVIEW

Fact Follow-Up

1. Describe the relative location of the Lowland Maya and Aztec cultures.
2. What crops did both the Maya and Aztecs grow?
3. How did they make use of their water resources?
4. What were the major cities of the Aztec people?

Talk About It

1. How did the farming practices of the Maya and Aztecs help them develop cities?
2. What were some of the similarities between the Maya and Aztecs?
3. What is specialization? Why is it important for creating civilizations?
4. What happened to the Maya culture?

LESSON 2   Lands and Resources

In the 1490s the Spanish and other Europeans were searching for a water route to Asia. They wanted to trade with China and the islands in Southeast Asia. Europeans believed that the earth was round. They thought if they sailed west they would eventually reach Asia. Europeans did not know that America lay in between Asia and Europe.

Finding the Americas was a surprise to the Europeans. They were also surprised to find that there were people and many valuable natural resources in this New World. The Spanish started colonies in the Americas in order to take the resources back to Spain.

The Spanish Arrive

The Spanish first colonized the islands of the Caribbean. Next they sent missions to the west to explore. They did not know whether they would find more islands or a new continent. They hoped they would find a route to Asia and its spices and other riches. Instead, the mainland of North America blocked their way.

The Spanish forces led by Cortés and his Native American allies conquered the Aztec empire. Then Spanish colonists started to move onto the mainland. The sights they saw dazzled them.

The Spanish learned a great deal from the Native Americans. The Spanish enjoyed eating the chili peppers and corn grown by Native American farmers.

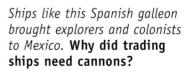

Ships like this Spanish galleon brought explorers and colonists to Mexico. **Why did trading ships need cannons?**

KEY IDEAS

- Mexico was part of the Spanish colony of New Spain.

- Spain started the colony to benefit Spain rather than the Native Americans.

- The Spanish built large silver mines and large farms to supply the mine workers.

- Catholic priests from Spain worked to convert Native Americans to Christianity.

KEY TERMS

haciendas
plaza

People and Their Environment   **557**

This drawing shows the design of a village planned by Spanish colonists. The church faces the plaza. You can also see the grid pattern of the streets. **Why were the villages so carefully planned?**

New Towns and Settlements

The Spanish believed in an orderly world. This affected the way they built towns. Buildings were placed around a central square called a *plaza.* This is where the people gathered in the evenings. There were strict rules about how a town should be built. Streets were laid out in a grid pattern. The Catholic Church and town hall were built around the plaza.

These two large buildings reminded everyone that the Catholic Church and the Spanish Crown were the two most powerful things in the colony.

The marketplace was the heart of the town's life. People went there to buy food and other necessities. There they could have their wagons repaired. Goods were brought in from the countryside to be sold in the market.

Colonial Economy

The Spanish called Mexico "New Spain." Mexico was a colony of Spain. It helped Spain grow rich and powerful.

Trade

Spain made Mexico and other Spanish colonies in the Americas ship all goods such as sugar and gold back home. Fleets of Spanish ships armed with cannon brought this wealth across the Atlantic Ocean. The cannon protected the ships from pirates. Twice each year Spanish ships arrived in New Spain and other colonies full of cargo from Spain. They then returned to Spain filled with gold, silver, and sugar.

Spain insisted that its colonies buy all their goods from Spain. The Spanish government also limited what the people in its colonies could produce. The colonists were only allowed to raise food and make some types of rough clothing. Everything else had to come from Spain. This helped Spain make money from their exports to the colonies in addition to the things the colonies shipped back to them.

Buying goods from Spain cost a lot of money. For example, the colonists needed wine for rituals in their Catholic churches. Many places in Mexico were suitable for growing wine grapes. But this was forbidden. They had to be grown in Spain and only by wine growers approved by the Spanish government. Gunpowder and tobacco were controlled in much the same way. These controls prevented the colonies from taking business away from Spain.

Spain wanted its colonies to increase production. The colonies expanded sugar plantations on Spain's islands in the Caribbean and in the humid land along Mexico's coast.

Mining

Spain also wanted all the gold and silver in Mexico. Soon thousands of Native Americans were digging for precious metals from mines in the ground.

Mining had a great effect on the wealth of the growing colony. The mines required many workers. Therefore, they also needed plenty of such supplies as food and building materials.

The areas around the mines supported the miners. Food was grown to feed the miners. The mine shafts were braced with lumber and stone. The miners used leather to make containers to carry water and earth out of the mine shafts. They also needed candles. These materials had to be brought to the mines.

Haciendas

The farms where these mining supplies were produced were called **haciendas.** The Spanish owners of *haciendas* usually had a house on the farm as well as one in town. Owning a *hacienda* made a colonist wealthy and powerful.

A *hacienda* was a large piece of land, like a ranch or farm. The main role of the *hacienda* was to feed the people in the cities and keep the mines supplied. There

were always plenty of horses and cows on a *hacienda*. They needed a lot of land for grazing. Native Americans had never seen so many large animals. The largest ranches were in the northern Mexico.

At first, Native Americans were given to the landowners as virtual slaves. Later, Spain's government allowed colonists to make Native Americans work on the *haciendas* without paying them. But the colonists were responsible to educate and convert Native Americans to Christianity. It was not much of an improvement for the Native Americans.

The owners also had to provide food and shelter for the workers. The owners of the *haciendas* did not always keep their word. Sometimes they treated the Native Americans on their land well. But sometimes they mistreated them. Owners forced the Native Americans to work long hours at very hard jobs. Many died of disease and overwork.

The *hacienda* system had another long-lasting effect. Native Americans had lived on the land that became *haciendas* long before the Spanish arrived. The newcomers took that land. As a result, much of the land in Latin America is still owned by a limited number of people today.

Haciendas like this were once centers of wealth. **How did mining affect the local economy?**

People and Their Environment

SILVER MINING in Mexico

The Spanish seized the gold and silver of the Aztecs and the other peoples of Mexico. Then they looked for more. The deposits of gold in Mexico were soon gone. But silver existed in great amounts. In northern Mexico, large deposits of silver ore were found.

The Spanish made the Native Americans work in the mines. Most of the time their labor was forced. Often they were made to stay deep within the mine for a week at a time. They were forced to journey long distances from their homes to work in the mines.

The conditions in the mines were poor. The mines were damp. The air was bad. The hours were long. The mines sometimes caved-in on the workers.

Native American miners

In the sixteenth century, Judge Alonso de Zorita described these conditions of the Native American workers to the Spanish king. "They died in the mines or along the road, of hunger and cold or extreme heat, and from carrying enormous loads of implements for the mines or other extremely heavy things; for the Spaniards, not satisfied with taking them so far away to work, must load them down on the way."

Spanish coins made from Mexican silver

Etching depicting harsh conditions in the mine

Silver belt buckle

Today mining is still hard work. But Native Americans are no longer enslaved and forced to work in the mines. Modern techniques and machinery are used throughout northern Mexico. They produce not only silver but also copper, iron, zinc, lead, and gold.

Modern silver mine in Mexico

People and Their Environment

WORD ORIGINS

Mesa is a Spanish word that means "table." Spanish people called high plateaus in Spain and in parts of the Americas mesas because they are high and flat, like a table.

Mexican families gather on December 31 to celebrate the coming of the new year. They have a special tradition. When the clock starts to strike twelve, everyone eats twelve grapes. Each person must finish the grapes before the clock stops striking. The grapes represent the twelve months of the coming year. Finishing all the grapes as the clock strikes is said to give one good luck all through the new year.

MEXICAN PORTRAIT

Dona Marina: "La Malinche"
1496—c.1529 or 1551

In 1519, Cortés and his men were making their way across Mexico. In one place he received a gift of 20 slave women from a Maya king. Cortes had the women baptized as Christians.

One woman was given the Spanish name Dona Marina. Her family was Aztec, but they had sold her to the Maya as a slave when she was young. She was the only one who spoke the language of the Maya and the language of the Aztecs. In Cortés' party there was a Spanish priest who also spoke Maya. This meant that when Cortés reached the Aztec capitol he could communicate with King Moctezuma II through the priest and Dona Marina.

She helped Cortés understand Aztec culture. She also convinced him not to kill so many Aztecs. Because she helped Cortés, some people called her a traitor. Others think she is a heroine because she saved many lives.

Dona Marina translates for Cortés

LESSON 2 REVIEW

Fact Follow-Up
1. What goods did the Spanish government require to be shipped from New Spain to Spain?
2. What products were the people of New Spain required to buy from Spain?
3. What were *haciendas*?

Talk About It
1. Describe the cultural features of place in the towns of New Spain.
2. Why was the *hacienda* system developed?
3. Which people did the *hacienda* system serve better: the Spanish or the Native Americans? Explain why.

LESSON ③ Mexico's Environment

hen Cortés and his army of Spanish *conquistadors* arrived in Mexico, they brought with them many things that the people there had never seen. One of the most amazing things they brought was the horse. The Native Americans had never seen an animal so large. The horses were covered in shining armor. They were also fast.

At first the Native Americans even believed that the rider and horse were one animal and that they could not be killed. The Native Americans were frightened. Horses gave the Spanish a great advantage over the Aztecs and other Native Americans.

Changes to the Environment

Both before and after colonization, human beings altered and changed the land of Mexico. The Spanish used more wood in building houses than had the Native Americans. They had mostly used stone and adobe. Using timber meant trees were cut. Slowly but steadily, forests began to disappear in the Spanish colonies. This problem expanded over time.

The Spanish also brought livestock such as cattle and horses to New Spain. These animals required great amounts of grazing land. Overgrazing soon ruined the vast grasslands of Mexico. The Spanish brought with them new crops like wheat and barley. These crops soon replaced fields that were once corn.

Changes in Diet

In general, the *haciendas* worked well to support the operation of mines and plantations. They also supplied food that the Spanish liked to eat. But *haciendas* cut into the production of traditional Native American foods.

Many Native Americans had to work in mines and on *haciendas*. They worked on sugar plantations, too. They no longer had as many chances to grow food for themselves. They were working full-time for the Spanish. Many Native Americans had lost their land. Others lost the water that they needed for their crops when the Spanish set up their own watering systems. So fewer traditional foods were raised.

Sometimes Native Americans living on *haciendas* were allowed to grow crops for their families. Yet they rarely could raise what they needed. The plots of land were usually very small and of poor quality. These changes led to a decrease in the production of food by the Native American people. The richness of the Native American diet was gone within decades of the Spanish conquest.

KEY IDEAS

- The colonization of Mexico changed the environment.

- Many Native Americans lost their lands to the Spanish *haciendas.*

- The Spanish brought to the New World animals and technology that Native Americans had never seen.

- Many Native Americans died of diseases brought by the Europeans.

KEY TERMS

Columbian Exchange

This figure of a conquistador *on a horse, was made around 1650.* **What do you think life was like in America before there were horses?**

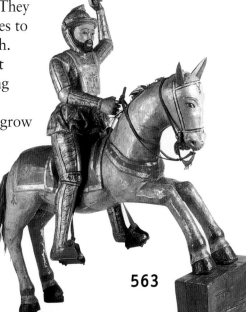

The Columbian Exchange

The Spanish and the Native Americans exchanged, or shared, many things. This process was called the **Columbian Exchange.** It was named after Christopher Columbus. The Columbian Exchange involved plants and animals. It also involved ideas and even diseases.

Plants and Farming

Europeans brought many different grains, vegetables, and fruits from Europe. The Americas gave Europe foods like corn and potatoes. Fruit such as tomatoes and avocados also were first found in the Americas.

Three other important American plants became popular throughout the rest of the world. Cacao (cah·COW), from which chocolate is made, and vanilla beans are still important crops today. People in Europe also became fond of another plant, tobacco.

New ways of growing plants were shared between the people of Europe and the Americas. Africans made contributions as well. Europeans and Africans showed the Native Americans how to plow the ground, toss seeds, and then cover them with dirt. Native Americans taught the Europeans and Africans how to carefully select seeds and plant them in combinations that complemented one another.

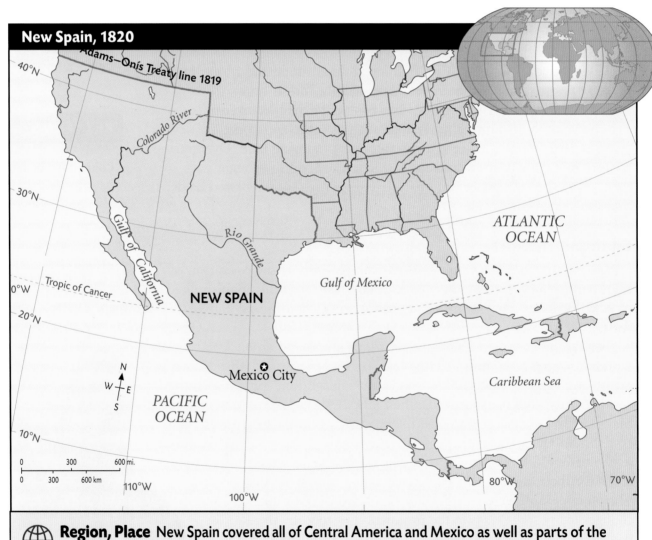

New Spain, 1820

Region, Place New Spain covered all of Central America and Mexico as well as parts of the United States and the Caribbean. *What did Spain want from these colonies?*

Chapter 23

Animals from Europe

The Americas had few large animals. Only the llama in South America and the buffalo in northern North America were large. The buffalo were too difficult to tame. The llama, because of its spindly legs, could not carry as much weight as a man. Neither animal lived in Mexico or Central America.

Even the dogs in the Americas were small. Almost all farm animals such as chickens and cows came from Europe. Only the turkey and a few other species of birds were raised by the Native Americans before the arrival of the Spanish.

Exchange of Ideas

Spanish *conquistadors* brought new ideas to the Americas. One of the most powerful was Christianity. Priests of the Roman Catholic Church began to convert Native Americans wherever the Spanish founded colonies.

The Spanish idea of government also had a great effect on the Americas. For the first time, from the southwestern United States through Mexico to South America, all the people (except in Brazil) were brought under the same type of government. This was New Spain.

The Spanish language unified the region. For the first time the majority of the people spoke the same language. Today almost all of Latin America shares a common heritage of church and state from their rulers.

Technology from Europe

Technology was also shared. The Spanish brought gunpowder and explosives and great wagons pulled by large work animals. This gave Native Americans a better understanding of the wheel. They also brought the knowledge of how to create stronger metals such as iron and steel.

The Native Americans taught the Europeans new ways to water and farm the land. Native Americans also helped Europeans better understand the movement of the stars and planets.

Disease from Europe

Unfortunately for the Native Americans, Europeans also brought diseases. Deadly diseases such as smallpox, malaria, yellow fever, measles, cholera, typhoid, and the bubonic plague were new to the Americas. The Native Americans had no natural immunities to these diseases. This means that their bodies could not fight these illnesses.

Historians still debate how many native people lived in the Americas before the Europeans arrived. They are also unsure exactly how many died due to these diseases. But they do know that diseases did kill many, many native people. This may have made it easier for Europeans all over the Americas to conquer and settle the region.

Signs of Mexican Culture in North Carolina

You probably can see signs of Mexican life in North Carolina in your local supermarket. Many grocery stores stock Mexican products and fruit. People from Mexico and other parts of Latin America enjoy tropical fruit and vegetables that are not grown here. "Many of our best customers are people from Mexico and Latin America," said one grocery store manager. "They miss the foods that they grew up with and have become used to. We try to fill that gap."

Now most products made in the United States have both English and Spanish directions on them. This helps Spanish-speaking customers buy and use them.

CAROLINA CONNECTION

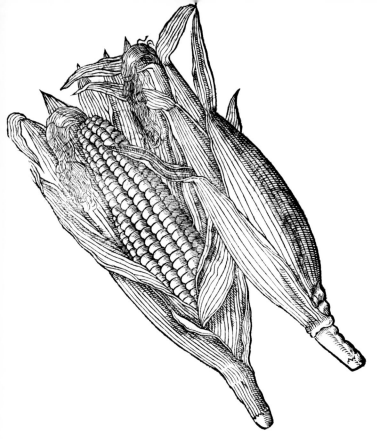

This drawing of maize, or corn, appeared in a European book in 1633. **Along with corn, what were the other important plants that originated in America?**

The Colonial Legacy

Imagine Mexico before the arrival of the Spanish. There was no wheat with which to make bread, only corn for tortillas. No peaches or pears or sugar to sweeten the daily diet. There were no large animals to carry heavy burdens.

Now think about Europe and the rest of the world without chocolate, vanilla, corn, potatoes, and tomatoes. Exchanges of ideas and technology have changed people's lives in positive ways on both sides of the Atlantic.

There is also a negative side to this exchange. Disease killed millions of Native Americans in the years after contact with the Europeans. Many Native Americans lost their land and were made to work as slaves.

These legacies still sometimes cause prejudice. They led to great inequalities of wealth in the region that exist today. The story of people, the environment, and Mexico is a complex one. It is filled with positives and negatives. People often disagree about how to measure the value of colonization.

What would YOU do?

Throughout Middle America, a major issue is deciding how to best use limited farmland. Imagine you are in charge of deciding how land is to be used. If you allow the land to be always growing crops, the soil will lose all its nutrients. It will be useless for farming. But if you let the land rest, farmers and their families will suffer. What would you do?

LESSON 3 REVIEW

Fact Follow-Up
1. What large animals did the Spanish bring to New Spain?
2. What new crops did the Spanish bring to New Spain?
3. How did Spanish building practices and large animals change the physical environment of New Spain?
4. What was the Columbian Exchange?

Talk About It
1. Describe human-environmental interaction in New Spain after the Spanish conquerors arrived.
2. How did the Columbian Exchange give almost all the people of Latin America a common heritage?
3. What are the costs and benefits to the region of the Columbian Exchange?

Analyzing, Interpreting, Creating,
and Using Resources and Materials

Was the Columbian Exchange an Exchange?

You read in Chapter 22 about the encounter between Hernán Cortés and Moctezuma II, and you have been reading in this chapter about the Columbian Exchange. After reading Chapters 22 and 23, you might be left with this question: Was the Columbian Exchange really an exchange, or was it something else?

What is an exchange? Have you ever traded lunch treats or stuffed animals or sports cards with a friend? If you have, you have engaged in an exchange.

When you trade with your friends, both sides must be willing to trade. If you have something your friend wants but you want to keep, you will not be willing to trade it away. If you have something someone wants and that person simply takes it from you, giving you nothing in return, there has been no trade. There has been a theft.

Finally, you would never consider trading something you already have for another object that you don't even want, would you? Of course not! You would never make a trade like that, would you?

A true exchange then has three parts:

1. A willingness to exchange: Both sides have to be willing to trade or exchange.
2. Reciprocity: Each side exchanges something and gets something else.
3. Satisfaction: Unless both sides are pleased with the exchange, it doesn't go through.

Using these three parts, can you decide whether the Columbian Exchange was an exchange or something else? This is a question you must consider carefully before making a decision. There are a number of questions to be answered beginning with these:

1. What was exchanged, and for what was it exchanged?
2. Was the Columbian Exchange planned (intentional), or did it just happen?
3. If the exchange was not intentional, was it really an exchange?

Lessons Learned

LESSON 1
Native American People of Mexico

Mexico was the center of two great Native American cultures: the Maya and the Aztec. The Maya developed farming, mathematics, and a written language. No one knows why the Maya left their cities. The Aztec built great cities that were centers of religion and culture. They irrigated their crops.

LESSON 2
Lands and Resources

Mexico was part of the Spanish colony of New Spain. Spain set up the colony to benefit its own economy. The Spanish built large silver mines and *haciendas*. Silver and farm products were sent to Spain. Goods the colony needed had to be gotten from Spain. Catholic priests from Spain worked to convert Native Americans to Christianity.

LESSON 3
Mexico's Environment

Spain's colonization of Mexico changed the environment. The Spanish brought animals and technology to the New World. Native Americans taught the Spanish new farming techniques. Many Native Americans died of diseases brought by the Europeans.

Talk About It

1. Which of the civilizations—the Mayan or the Aztec—do you believe was more creative? Explain your choice.
2. What do you think was the greatest achievement of the Maya and Aztec civilizations? Explain why.
3. Both the Aztecs and the conquering Spanish planned complex cities. In what ways were their cities similar and different?
4. Which do you think had the greatest consequence for Mexican society today: the *hacienda* system, sugar plantations, or the silver mines? Explain why.
5. Was the Columbian Exchange a benefit or a burden for America? Explain your answer.

Mastering Mapwork

LOCATION
Use the map on page 564 to answer these questions:
1. Describe the absolute location of the northwestern border of New Spain.
2. What is where the Rio Grand runs today?
3. Esitmate how far it is from the Adams-Onis Treaty Line to Mexico City using the scale.

Becoming Better Readers

More Strategies While Reading

Good readers do not try to memorize all the details of what they read. Instead they look for key ideas and some important details that support the key ideas. Reread the "Eyewitness to History" on pages 560–561. Write two or three main ideas of this article. Then write one or two details that support the main idea.

Go to the Source

Understanding Legends

Corn was the most important food crop in Mexico for hundreds of years. Maya, Aztecs, and other Native Americans worshiped corn gods and developed myths and legends about growing and harvesting corn. Read the legend below. Answer the questions using information from the legend.

Many years ago, a man and his son went from Aramberri to Tamulipas to look for work. They came back with 20 burros (donkeys) loaded with corn. On the way, night fell. They unloaded the burros, and tied the 20 bushels of corn, all together, to a big tree trunk. Later, they started a fire to make dinner and, after that, they went to bed behind where they had left the 20 bushels of corn.

The next morning, they got up before dawn, had breakfast and went to get their burros to feed them. Then they looked for the corn to load it onto the burros, but they couldn't find it. All they found was a very big trail. The man and his son gathered the burros and followed the trail the bushels left. After several hours on the road, they found a very large snake carrying all of the corn. Then they realized that they had tied the corn not to a tree trunk, but to the snake.

At night, when the beast was hungry, it went looking for food and dragged the 20 bushels of corn after it. Legend has it that the trail left by the snake and the bushels of corn is now the road going from Aramberri to La Boquilla.

_____

Questions
1. What is the significance of the snake dragging 20 bushels of corn?
2. Based on the selection, what will most likely happen?
3. What part of the selection is exaggerated?

Go to the Source

Economy and Government

Chapter Preview

LESSON 1
From Colony to Nation
Strong leaders took charge after Mexico won independence in 1820. One party ruled the country during most of the twentieth century.

LESSON 2
The Economy
Mexico's government controlled the chief industries after the revolution. Now NAFTA has increased free enterprise in Mexico.

LESSON 3
Challenges
NAFTA offers hope for Mexico's economic future. Health and environmental problems must be solved before all Mexicans can benefit.

Timeline of Events

1810-1821
Mexican War of Independence

1836
• Santa Anna attacks the Alamo
• Battle of San Jacinto
• Texas declares independence

1861
Juarez president

1800

1850

1846
U.S. declares war on Mexico

1848
U.S. gains almost half of Mexico's land

1862
Mexico wins Battle of Puebla

One of the most famous of New Spain's leaders was Bernardo de Galvez. Galvez was the Spanish governor of the territory of Louisiana. Galvez helped the 13 colonies become independent from Great Britain. He led Spanish troops against British forts from Florida to Louisiana.

Galvez became viceroy of New Spain in 1784. He died of yellow fever only two years later. He had lots of ideas about how New Spain could be governed better. Many were put into practice.

The United States honored Galvez' descendants. It named them members of the Sons and Daughters of the American Revolution.

In Baja California, Mexico, stand sculptures of some of Mexico's important political leaders: Venustiano Carranza, Benito Pablo Juares, and Miguel Hildalgo y Costilla.

1867
- Maximilian executed
- Republic is restored
- Juarez regains presidency

1929
The Institutional Revolutionary Party (PRI) wins presidential election

1994
Zapatistas in Chiapas rebel

1992
NAFTA

1900

1950

2000

1876
Diaz leads revolt

1910
Mexican Revolution

1917
New constitution approved

2000
Fox elected president

KEY IDEAS

- Mexicans won independence from Spain in 1821. They fought against taxes.

- Mexico's constitution provided for free public education and land reform. It also provided for fair wages and a system of health and welfare.

- The Mexican–American War and civil war weakened Mexico's economy. President Porfirio Díaz brought economic development to Mexico.

- One party ruled Mexico for most of the twentieth century.

KEY TERMS

Creoles
caudillo
Institutional Revolutionary Party (PRI)

PEOPLE TO KNOW

Bernardo de Galvez
Father Miguel Hidalgo
Porfirio Díaz
Francisco Madero
Venustiano Carranza
Vicente Fox Quesada
Emiliano Zapata
Antonio Lopez de Santa Anna

By 1800, the Spanish colonists had become tired of the lack of freedom. Much like the American colonists, they were unhappy with heavy taxes. The examples of the American and French Revolutions helped them decide to form their own nation.

Mexico Wins Independence

Father Miguel Hidalgo was a priest. He was called the "Father of Mexican Independence." In 1810 he and other rebels began to resist Spanish rule. Thousands of poor farmers followed Father Hidalgo. These followers were not an organized army. They were just people who believed that Spain had not treated them fairly. They believed a county run by Mexicans would be better.

Hidalgo's followers armed themselves. They attacked the Spanish leaders. At first, the rebels had support from many people. But later they could not unite all the Mexican people. The Creoles (KREE·ohls), did not want Father Hidalgo's followers to gain power. *Creoles* were wealthy Spanish people born in New Spain.

Creoles owned Mexico's *haciendas*. Their families had become important leaders in Mexican affairs. The Creoles wanted Spain to give Mexican leaders more freedom to run the colony. They did not support Father Hidalgo's call for independence at first.

Spanish troops crushed the unrest. They killed its leaders, including Father Hidalgo. The Creoles made no protests. But the Spanish king made the mistake of thinking that all Mexicans were traitors.

He ordered the Creoles to pay more taxes. He also ordered a large army to stop any trouble. These actions made the Creoles decide that they could no longer trust Spain.

In 1820, there was political unrest back in Spain. The king faced a revolt. Juan Odonojú (oth·on·oh·HOO) was the commander of Spain's army in Mexico. He was convinced that the colony should be free. He made no effort to keep Mexicans from declaring their independence. By the end of the next year, the last Spanish officials went home. Mexico had gained the freedom to govern itself.

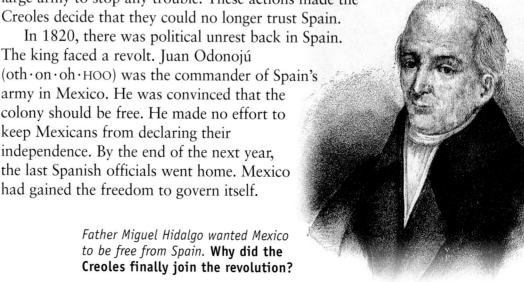

Father Miguel Hidalgo wanted Mexico to be free from Spain. **Why did the Creoles finally join the revolution?**

Portrait of a Gentleman, artist unknown, shows a Creole gentleman of Mexico in the 1700s. **How was Mexico's fight for independence similar to that of the United States?**

Independent Mexico

Becoming independent from Spain was easier for Mexico's new leaders than creating a new government.

The Early Years

The leaders could not agree on the type of government they wanted. Some wanted a strong central government. They also wanted the Roman Catholic Church as Mexico's official religion. Others wanted Mexico's states to have more power than the central government. This group also wanted religious freedom.

Mexico's leaders adopted a constitution. It called for a president and a congress heading the national government. Each of Mexico's states was to have a governor and legislature.

Mexico's leaders had never made laws or governed themselves. Military men often revolted against the young country. One of them was General Antonio Lopez de Santa Anna. He was a **caudillo** (kaw·DEE·yo). Caudillo means strong man. Santa Anna was the president 11 times between 1833 and 1855. He also commanded the Mexican army during the Mexican–American War.

The United States won this war. The treaty of Guadalupe Hidalgo brought peace, but Mexico had to turn over almost half of its territory to the United States.

The Mexican–American War left Mexico broke. Its people were bitterly divided. Then civil war broke out. French troops took control for a short time. Several groups revolted against the government.

The Porfiriato

Porfirio Díaz seized power in 1876. He was a hero in the fight against the French. Díaz formed good relations with some of Mexico's important leaders. He used his army to control those who opposed him. He began a dictatorship that ruled Mexico until 1911.

Díaz's long rule is called the Porfiriato (por·fee·ree·AH·toh). The Porfiriato brought economic development to Mexico. Díaz built railroads and improved the mining industry. He also invited people from other countries to invest in Mexico.

Most people stayed loyal to Díaz for a long time. Many believed that the economic development helped the whole country. But later they learned that the only people who made money were a few wealthy Mexicans and people from other countries. Díaz's opponents saw that the people who spoke out against Díaz were usually violently attacked. Mexicans got tired of the government's failure to bring democracy.

The CAUDILLO
in Mexican History

In the nineteenth century, men with military backgrounds led many Latin American governments. Most had shown bravery in battle. These leaders usually had powerful personalities. Their word was law. Each leader believed that only he knew what was best for his nation. These types of leaders were called *caudillos* (koh·DEE·yohs).

General Antonio Lopez de Santa Anna was one of the first Mexican *caudillos*. From 1824 to 1853, Santa Anna was the center of Mexican government. He was brave in battle. He lost half of his left leg to a cannon ball. Santa Anna commanded the army that lost the Mexican–American War.

General Antonio Lopez de Santa Anna

The mural People in Arms *by David Siqueiros*

*General
Porfirio Díaz*

General Porfirio Díaz was another great caudillo. He was a hero when Mexico defeated the French invasion. He ruled Mexico from 1876 to 1911. Mexico made economic progress during his rule. But his government was not democratic. It neglected the poor.

Because of this, the Mexican people rose up against Díaz. This rebellion is known as the Mexican Revolution. During the revolution, Emiliano Zapata became an important figure. He was also a *caudillo*. Zapata led Native American farmers to defend their land.

Zapata died in 1919, but he is still a hero to many Mexicans. His rallying cry was "Land and Liberty." It insipres the modern-day Native American rebels in Chiapas. The *caudillo* tradition is still important in Latin America.

Emiliano Zapata

Emiliano Zapata and Pancho Villa ride into Mexico City in 1910 during the Mexican Revolution. **What did Zapata do in the Mexican Revolution?**

The Mexican Revolution

In 1908, Díaz told the country that he would allow elections. Francisco Madero was a wealthy Mexican businessman. He challenged Díaz. Madero wanted to fix the government and create a democracy.

The Mexican assembly said that Díaz won the election. Madero decided that violence was the only way to remove the dictator. He called for a national revolt against Díaz.

The Mexican Revolution began in November 1910. The Mexican people united against Díaz. They quickly won their freedom. Several months later, Díaz quit and fled to Europe. Then the fighting started again. The revolution became a war between Mexicans with different ideas about their country's future.

By 1916, most Mexicans saw Venustiano Carranza (veh·noos·tee·AH·noh kah·RAHN·zah) as their leader. Carranza called a meeting to write a new constitution. The Constitution of 1917 used Carranza's ideas and those of his rivals.

The constitution said that there must be free public education. It also contained a system of public health and welfare. Limits were also placed on the ownership of land and businesses by people who did not live in Mexico. The constitution called for the president to serve only a single term. The government took over all of Mexico's oil resources. The Roman Catholic Church also had new government controls.

Customs

On May 10, Mexican school children honor their mothers with a celebration. The students invite their mothers to school, which has been decorated for the occasion. In a special ceremony students recite poetry. They also sing and dance to show their love for their mothers. At the end of the program the students give their mothers something they have made.

The PRI

From 1921 until 2000 a single political party ruled Mexico. It is called the *Institutional Revolutionary Party,* or *PRI.* For many years the PRI worked for the ideas of the revolution. The government took over the privately owned *haciendas*. It split them up among millions of landless farmers.

The development of new industry was also supported by the PRI. Labor unions were allowed to set up. A national school system was created. Many hospitals and housing projects were built. The Roman Catholic Church agreed to stay out of politics. The government supervised Catholic churches and schools.

The presidents of Mexico between 1921 and 2000 were all members of the PRI. Candidates for other offices who did not belong to the PRI had little chance of being elected.

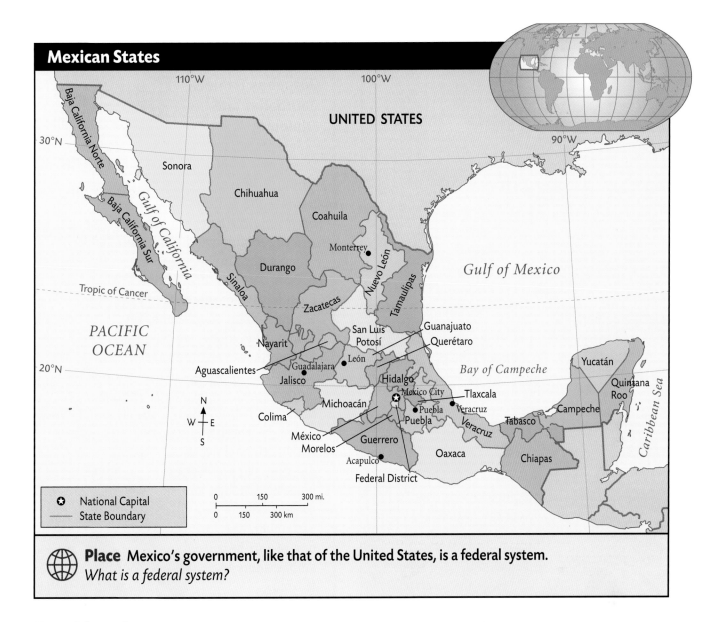

Mexican States

UNITED STATES

Baja California Norte
Baja California Sur
Gulf of California
Sonora
Chihuahua
Coahuila
Monterrey
Nuevo León
Tamaulipas
Durango
Zacatecas
Sinaloa
Nayarit
San Luis Potosí
Guanajuato
Querétaro
Aguascalientes
Guadalajara
León
Jalisco
Hidalgo
Mexico City
Tlaxcala
Michoacán
Puebla
Veracruz
Colima
Puebla
Veracruz
Tabasco
Campeche
México
Morelos
Guerrero
Oaxaca
Chiapas
Acapulco
Federal District

PACIFIC OCEAN

Gulf of Mexico

Bay of Campeche

Yucatán

Quintana Roo

Caribbean Sea

Tropic of Cancer

30°N
20°N
110°W
100°W
90°W

N
W E
S

⊛ National Capital
— State Boundary

0   150   300 mi.
0 150 300 km

🌐 **Place** Mexico's government, like that of the United States, is a federal system. What is a federal system?

New Direction

People wanted more political parties from which to choose leaders starting in the 1980s. In 1988, the PRI's critics claimed the PRI stole the presidential election. Opponents also blamed the PRI for serious economic problems. Some Maya in southern Mexico revolted.

New election laws gave other parties a chance to compete with the PRI. The PRI lost seats in one of the houses of Congress. In 2000, Vicente Fox Quesada of the National Action Party became Mexico's new president.

This is a PRI rally in Mexico City in 1982. **Why did the PRI lose support?**

Emiliano Zapata
1879–1919

Emiliano Zapata was born during the dictatorship of Porfirio Diaz. At this time Mexico's economy centered on the *hacienda*. Almost all of Mexico's wealth was controlled by a few landowners. Zapata spoke Spanish but he also spoke the Native American language. He became a leader in his town. Everyone understood him when he spoke up for the peasants. When he saw the *hacienda* owners burn the village of the peasants he got angry.

Then the revolution began. Zapata became a popular hero. He helped take control of the *haciendas*. The new leaders divided the land equally among the people.

Zapata was killed in an ambush in 1919, by people who wanted to go back to the old way of life before the revolution.

Today there are groups who call themselves Zapatistas. That name means that they follow his idea that everyone should have a small piece of land, rather than a few people having most of it.

Josephus Daniels, Journalist and Diplomat

Josephus Daniels was born in 1862 in Washington, North Carolina. When he was thirty-three he became the editor of *The Raleigh Observer* (*The News and Observer* today). His paper supported public-funded schools and universities.

From 1913 to 1921, Daniels served as President Woodrow Wilson's secretary of the navy. Daniels became the ambassador to Mexico when Franklin Roosevelt was elected president in 1932.

The United States' relationship with Latin America was called "The Good Neighbor Policy" under FDR. This policy called for the United States to cooperate with Latin American nations. Daniels helped make this policy a success. He is remembered as one of our best ambassadors to Mexico.

LESSON 1 REVIEW

Fact Follow-Up
1. In Mexico, who were the Creoles?
2. Why was Father Miguel Hidalgo known as the "Father of Mexican Independence"?
3. What is the PRI?

Talk About It
1. Why did the Creoles, who had not supported Father Hidalgo, finally turn against Spain?
2. Which *caudillo*—Santa Anna or Díaz—was more important to Mexico? Explain why.
3. Why do you think the *caudillo* tradition developed in Mexico?

LESSON 2 The Economy

merican movies and television often show Mexico as a land of farmers in sombreros. But Mexico has changed greatly in recent years. It has become a nation of huge cities with high-tech factories. There are also modern farms. Tourist resorts attract people from around the world. Mexico changed a great deal economically as well as politically in the twentieth century.

But Mexico's economy also faces many challenges. There is a large gap between the rich and poor. Many people are unemployed or do not have jobs that pay enough to support their families. Mexican states in the south with large Native American populations are usually poorer than states in northern Mexico.

Many poor people move to cities for jobs. The Petroleum Mexico (PEMEX) refinery near Mexico City is one business that attracts them. **What type of economy does Mexico have?**

The Mexican Economy

Before the revolution of 1910, most Mexicans lived in the countryside. Today most Mexicans live in cities and work in manufacturing or service industries. The political system has moved from one run by *caudillos* to a democratic republic. The Mexican economy has also changed. A state-controlled economy has become a free-market system. Trade agreements with more than 40 nations now guide Mexico's economy.

Mexico has a tradition of state-owned industry. After the revolution, the government owned most utilities and factories. Many of these industries needed a lot of money to help them run. The Mexican government became the only source of funding. This was because the constitution stopped businesses from other countries from owning businesses in Mexico.

Growth of Private Industry

During the 1990s, the Mexican government began to sell the state-owned businesses to private citizens and corporations. Some of these were foreign. This was part of the PRI's plan to open trade. They wanted to bring the Mexican economy more into line with that of the United States.

The government made it legal for foreigners to own land and resources in 1993. NAFTA went into effect in 1994. This further reduced the Mexican government's participation in the economy.

This new emphasis on free enterprise has also affected the way privately owned industries operate. Until recently, the government closely watched privately owned businesses. Mexico's government once decided which resources a business might have and what types of products it might make. These rules have now been loosened.

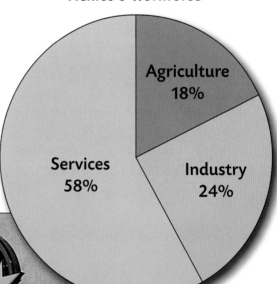

Mexico's Workforce

- Agriculture 18%
- Industry 24%
- Services 58%

Compare this chart to the charts on pages 329 and 491. **How is Mexico's workforce different from that of the United Sates and Canada?**

The Mexican government has sold many industries to private citizens and companies. United States' businesses have invested in Mexico. **What is Mexico's most important natural resource?**

Chapter 24

Industry

Early in the last century, Mexico's economy began to develop. An iron and steel plant in Monterrey was built. During the 1950s other factories were built, especially around Mexico City. Products such as textiles and glass were made. Goods made using Mexico's own oil have been important. Look at the pie chart on page 580. Today, about 24 percent of the workforce works in industry.

Mining is still important (see map, page 583). Iron, copper, and some less well-known minerals are mined as well. Mexico produces about 15 percent of the world's silver.

Oil is now the most important natural resource. Large deposits of natural gas and petroleum mean that Mexico has enough energy for now. Most of the oil and natural gas deposits are located along the coast of the Gulf of Mexico. Mexico's minerals are largely found in the northern parts of the country.

New Factories

The *maquiladora* (mah·kee·lah·DOH·rah) factories are one of Mexico's most important industrial activities. *Maquiladoras* assemble parts or raw materials that come from the United States. Products that are built here range from electronic equipment to clothing and furniture.

There are thousands of such plants on the Mexican side of the border. Before NAFTA, companies paid small fees to ship the finished goods back into the United States. NAFTA ended these fees. Goods and people steadily flow back and forth between border cities and the two nations.

There are more than 1 million people, mostly women, working in the *maquiladoras*. This is about one third of Mexico's industrial labor force.

These changes are part of globalization. This means that the economies of many countries are connected and depend on one another. But globalization brings challenges.

Just as jobs from the United States and North Carolina moved to Mexico, now jobs are leaving Mexico for other places, such as China.

Maquiladoras are slowly expanding southward into the heart of Mexico. Mexico's government and people hope that the foreign companies will build more than assembly plants. They would like to have factories that manufacture and assemble parts. This type of expansion has already taken place in the auto industry. Big car companies have built large manufacturing plants in Mexico.

Another key part of Mexico's economy is electronics. **What effect have the *maquiladoras* had on the border?**

Economy and Government

Cancún's beaches are crowded year-round. **What are some of the other tourist attractions in Mexico?**

Tourism

Tourism is Mexico's third-largest industry. Mexico's beautiful beaches and climate are major attractions. Wintertime travelers from the United States and Canada visit resorts like Acapulco and the Yucatán Peninsula. The beaches of Cancún and Cozumel attract travelers from around the globe.

The wonders of ancient Native American cultures also attract tourists. The ruins of the ancient Aztec and Maya cultures in such places as Teotihuacán and Chichén Itzá also bring thousands of visitors to Mexico every year. People come to see the other unique cultures found in the country.

Farming

Mexican farming has a colonial heritage. About 18 percent of the population works in a job related to agriculture. Many of these people are small farmers. In the south corn is Mexico's leading crop (see map, page 583). Most of it is used to make tortillas. They are a part of most Mexican meals.

The cattle industry has also been important since the Spanish arrived. Most ranches are found in the north. Sheep and goats are raised in some of the higher elevations.

Large-scale commercial farming is also important in Mexico. Some of the crops feed the Mexican people. Most of it goes north. Most all of the fresh vegetables and fruit on the shelves of supermarkets in the United States and Canada during the winter come from Mexico.

Much of this food enters the United States in air-cooled trucks through Nogales, Arizona. All of it is usually sold to supermarkets before it even arrives. When you have a tomato on your sandwich or salad this winter, it may have passed along this same route.

Chapter 24

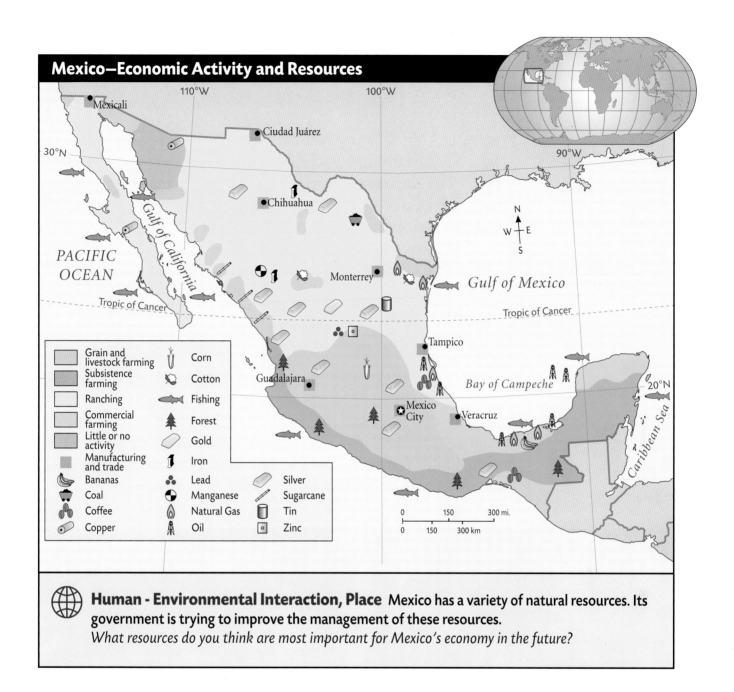

Mexico—Economic Activity and Resources

110°W · 100°W · 90°W

Mexicali

Ciudad Juárez

30°N

Chihuahua

PACIFIC OCEAN

Gulf of California

Monterrey

Gulf of Mexico

Tropic of Cancer · Tropic of Cancer

Tampico

Guadalajara

Bay of Campeche

20°N

Mexico City

Veracruz

Caribbean Sea

Legend:

Grain and livestock farming	Corn
Subsistence farming	Cotton
Ranching	Fishing
Commercial farming	Forest
Little or no activity	Gold
Manufacturing and trade	Iron
Bananas	Lead	Silver
Coal	Manganese	Sugarcane
Coffee	Natural Gas	Tin
Copper	Oil	Zinc

Scale:
0 — 150 — 300 mi.
0 — 150 — 300 km

Human - Environmental Interaction, Place Mexico has a variety of natural resources. Its government is trying to improve the management of these resources.
What resources do you think are most important for Mexico's economy in the future?

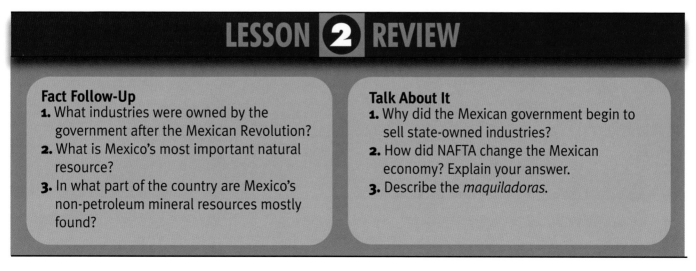

LESSON 2 REVIEW

Fact Follow-Up
1. What industries were owned by the government after the Mexican Revolution?
2. What is Mexico's most important natural resource?
3. In what part of the country are Mexico's non-petroleum mineral resources mostly found?

Talk About It
1. Why did the Mexican government begin to sell state-owned industries?
2. How did NAFTA change the Mexican economy? Explain your answer.
3. Describe the *maquiladoras*.

LESSON ③ Challenges

KEY IDEAS

- Increased trade among the nations of North America helped improve Mexico's economy.

- The Mexican economy continues to reform.

- Many Mexicans are moving to the cities and to the United States to improve their lives.

- Mexico faces serious problems.

KEY TERMS

guerilla war

The United States, Canada, and Mexico signed an important agreement in 1993. It was called NAFTA. The Mexican government wanted to link its economy to those of the United States and Canada. Taxes on goods moving across the two borders are to be taken away by 2009.

The government's leaders believed that NAFTA would get companies from the United States and Canada to build plants in Mexico. They were right. The agreement also made it easier to export Mexico's products to its northern neighbors.

In these ways, NAFTA has helped the economy grow and provide jobs for a growing population.

This was not the first time that the Mexican government encouraged growth. The *caudillo* Díaz had brought new industries into Mexico. But only a few Mexican people and foreigners profited. The government expected more people to benefit under NAFTA. Many people have, but the gap between them and those on the outside looking in is growing.

North American leaders (standing) Carlos Salinas, George H.W. Bush, and Brian Mulroney sign the North American Free Trade Agreement in 1992. **What did they hope NAFTA would accomplish?**

Ciudad is one of Mexico's growing cities. **How has Mexico's economy changed since NAFTA?**

Movement

Great numbers of people are moving away from the Mexican countryside. People leave rural areas because pay is low and work is scarce. Healthcare and education can also be hard to find in the country.

In some places political unrest makes life difficult. They hope to find in a city all of the things that are missing in rural communities.

Migration to the Cities

Mexico's cities do not have enough resources to provide for everyone. Mexico City has become the world's second-largest city. It does not have enough places for newcomers to live.

Water and electric services cannot be built fast enough to keep up with its growing population. Smoke and exhaust fumes have polluted the air. Many of the city's neighborhoods have become dangerous and unhealthy places to live.

At least 71 percent of Mexico's people live in cities today. Guadalajara and Puebla are growing rapidly. Border cities of Ciudad Juárez and Monterrey each have more than 1 million residents. All of these cities are overcrowded.

WORD ORIGINS

Every day of the year more than two thousand Mexican people pack up their belongings. They move to Mexico City in search of a better life. Mexico City dwellers call them *paracaidistas* (pah·rah·cay·DEES·tahs), or "parachutists." There are so many people arriving in Mexico City every day that they just seem to fall out of the sky.

Migrant farmworkers load watermelons in Mississippi. **Who would harvest crops in the United States if the migrant farmers stayed in Mexico?**

Moving to the United States

People move to the United States for the same reasons that some others move to Mexico's cities. Some Mexicans come to the United States to make it their permanent home. Others come only at certain times of the year to work during harvests.

Still others commute every day between the towns on the border. Mexicans enter the United States because they can't make enough money in Mexico to support a family.

Mexicans who come to work in the United States usually send money home each month to Mexico. The sacrifices made by the workers help improve the lives of their families back home.

Push and Pull Factors of Immigration

UNITED STATES

PULL
- Jobs
- Higher pay
- Access to healthcare
- Quality of life
- Opportunity
- Political freedom

PUSH
- Poverty
- Unemployment
- Lack of opportunity
- Insecurity
- political oppresssion

MEXICO

Push factors are things that might influence a person to emigrate, or leave, their country. Pull factors are things that attract a person to move to a particular country. Immigrants weigh the costs and benefits of all these factors when they make a decision to move. **What pull factors attract Mexican immigrants to North Carolina?**

Chapter 24

Going to School in Mexico

In Mexico, all children between the ages of five to fifteen must attend school. They go to school from first grade to ninth grade. Just like students in most American schools, Mexican children must pass tests.

At the age of eleven, students must pass the *Certificado de Educación Primaria* (Primary Certificate) exam. It is a national test. Then the student goes on to one of two different schools for three more years. One school prepares students to go on to college. The other prepares students to work in a trade. They study to be nurses, mechanics, secretaries, or other jobs.

In rural areas students attend these schools by watching lessons on TV. It is called *Telesecondaria*.

At sixteen, students who want to go to college or have a special trade go to school for another three years.

Mexican classroom

Mexico's school systems face many challenges. About 15 percent of children do not go to school. The federal government funds the schools. But schools in rural areas do not have as many resources as schools in the cities. Many people move to cities so their children can go to better schools.

Private schools are better than public schools. Families that can afford it send their children to private schools. They get a better education and can get better jobs.

Mexico continues to improve it schools. More people in Mexico can read than ever before. This attracts more high-tech and other businesses to Mexico.

The Environment

Mexico's environment is being affected by the nation's rapid growth.

Water Pollution

Mexico has a problem with water pollution. This is true not only in the cities. It is also true in the country. The government of Mexico calls this problem one of "national security."

More than 12 million Mexicans have problems getting safe drinking water. Almost 75 percent of Mexico's water is unsafe to drink. Farms and cattle ranches receive their water free of charge. So do the mines.

Deforestation

Mexico's shrinking forests are also part of the "national security" problem. Trees help hold the soil in place during rainstorms. When many trees are cut, soil washes away. Farmland is ruined. This abuse of the land means even more people are being forced to move to the cities and the United States. When people cannot farm their land they must move to find work.

Some people in Mexico cut trees illegally. The Mexican government says that people cutting the trees threaten violence or actually fight if someone tries to stop them. That makes other people afraid to try.

This group of Zapatista supporters in Chiapas are protesting Mexico's federal government. **Why are the Zapatistas against NAFTA?**

The Zapatista National Liberation Army

On January 1, 1994, NAFTA went into effect. On that same day, a radical group of Maya farmers began a *guerrilla war* against the Mexican government. They named their group after Emiliano Zapata, the hero of the Mexican Revolution and of Native Americans in Mexico.

They wore masks to hide their faces and protect their families. The Zapatistas protested the parts of NAFTA that they believed threatened the land reform promised by the Constitution of 1917 and the Mexican Revolution. They were also worried about self-government and the survival of their Native American culture.

The Mexican army reacted swiftly to the uprising. The rebels were driven back into the forests.

The Zapatistas, who are mainly from Chiapas, are concerned that the poorest parts of the country are being left out by NAFTA's free trade reforms. The rebels fear losing control of their traditional, community-owned lands through privatization. Their spokesman, Subcomandante Marcos, has delivered many speeches and messages to Mexico and the world pleading for greater respect for the civil and human rights of Native American people.

What would YOU do?

In January of 1994 hundreds of armed guerrillas took over a small town in southeastern Mexico. They claimed that the Mexican government had ignored the region's extreme poverty. Imagine you are either the leader of the guerrillas or in the Mexican government. How would you have handled the conflict? Why?

Dealing with Population and Pollution

Mexico City is one of the fastest-growing cities in the world. The city's population is growing so fast that utility companies have to ration water and electricity.

Water and power to one area of the city are sometimes shut off. This allows water and power service to flow to another area. Most people save jugs of water to use when water service is cut off to their area. Even when the water does come out of the tap, it often comes out at a trickle instead of a stream. Filling the jugs takes a long time.

The Mexican author Carlos Fuentes wrote a book about Mexico City. Fuentes describes polluted air that can stay trapped over the city for days. It is not uncommon for pollution to be so bad that people can see only halfway across the city.

The snowcapped volcano Popocatepetl (po·po·CAH·teh·pet·l) is often hidden by smog. On really bad days the air begins to leave a taste in your mouth like metal. Breathing it for extended periods of time can cause headaches and chest pains for some people.

LESSON ❸ REVIEW

Fact Follow-Up
1. What three nations signed the NAFTA treaty?
2. Why did Mexico want NAFTA?
3. Why are Mexican people moving from the countryside to cities?

Talk About It
1. Why does the Mexican government describe problems of water pollution and cutting too many trees as a threat to "national security"?
2. What did the Zapatistas want? Why were they worried about NAFTA?

Economy and Government

Analyzing, Interpreting, Creating, and Using Resources and Materials

Studying Mexico's Economic and Political Development

Mexico has been an independent country for nearly 200 years. In that time there have been many changes in government. Let's look at the relationship between the kind of government Mexico has had and how well its economy works?

Government and the Economy in Mexico		
Government	Dates	Economic Development

To help you answer this question, you will need to compare different periods in Mexican history. A chart like the one shown above will help you do this. You will need to make some notes on two kinds of information before you make the chart.

1. What are the different governments that have been in power since the country became independent?
2. What economic changes have taken place in Mexico since independence?

Remember to note specific dates whenever you can. Dates are convenient "hooks" for hanging ideas on. You will notice that the middle column of the chart on this page has spaces for dates and time periods.

Your notes will give you the information you need to complete the chart. You can think about questions such as these:

- When has Mexico's government been most democratic?
- When has Mexico's economy been strongest? When has it been the weakest?
- Which groups in Mexico have generally held political power?
- Have the people in power in government generally been wealthier than other Mexicans?
- At what times have poorer people benefited most? Finally, is there a relationship between Mexico's government and how well its economy works?

Palacio de Bellas Artes, Mexico City

Lessons Learned

LESSON 1
From Colony to Nation
Mexicans won their independence from Spain in 1821. Their constitution provided free public education and land reform. It also provided for fair wages and health care. Strong leaders ruled Mexico after the revolution. A single party has remained in power during most of the time since the revolution.

LESSON 2
The Economy
The Mexican government controlled chief industries after the revolution. Now Mexico's businesses belong to individuals or companies. *Maquiladoras* form the most important part of Mexico's industry today. Farming and tourism also continue to be important parts of Mexico's economy.

LESSON 3
Challenges
NAFTA has generally improved the Mexican economy by making trade easier and less expensive. Mexico must now improve its environment. The problems of overcrowding and pollution are important challenges for Mexico today.

Talk About It

1. In earlier chapters you read that the United States after its revolution against Great Britain successfully developed democratic institutions that worked fairly well. Why do you think Mexico's revolution against Spain did not have the same results?
2. Why do you think the *caudillo* system lasted so long in Mexico?
3. Maquiladoras provide employment for many Mexican workers. Why do many Mexicans want to produce goods from start to finish rather than assemble products in the maquiladoras?
4. Which do you think changed more during the twentieth century: the Mexican economy or the Mexican government? Explain your answer.
5. If you could solve one of the problems facing Mexico today, which would you choose? Explain why.

Mastering Mapwork

LOCATION
Use the map on page 583 to answer these questions:
1. Which economic activity is more widely practiced: ranching or family farming?
2. What economic activities and resources are located nearest Guadalajara?
3. What economic activities and resources are located nearest Mexico City?

Becoming Better Readers

Using Literature Techniques
Good readers recognize genre and theme when they are reading. Social studies books usually are one genre: nonfiction. A technique you can use to help you understand what you are reading is to read as though your book were a story that is unfolding. It is! Write a story about Father Miguel Hidalgo. Use factual information to tell your story.

Go to the Source

Comparing Maps Over Time

These maps show Mexico's territory before and after The Mexican-American War, and before the Treaty of Guadalupe (the peace treaty that ended the war). Study both maps and answer the questions below.

Questions

1. Based on the maps, how did the Treaty of Guadelupe affect Mexico?
2. According to the maps, which country acquired land from Mexico?
3. Estimate how much land Mexico lost.

"Little burro" piñata

Culture and Society

Festivals are a big part of Mexican culture. Each town has a holiday each year to honor its patron saint. Mexicans celebrate Easter and Christmas as people do in the United States.

There are some other holidays that Mexicans celebrate. The Day of the Dead and the Day of the Virgin of Guadalupe (gwah·deh·LOO·pay) are special. There is also Cinco de Mayo and Independence Day. Holidays are both serious and joyful. They can include fireworks and live music.

People like to dance and eat on Mexican holidays. There are often religious ceremonies, too. People in the country celebrate in more traditional ways. Native American customs are often part of the festivities. Celebrations in the cities are more modern.

Worshippers carry a picture of Our Lady of Guadalupe in Chiapas.

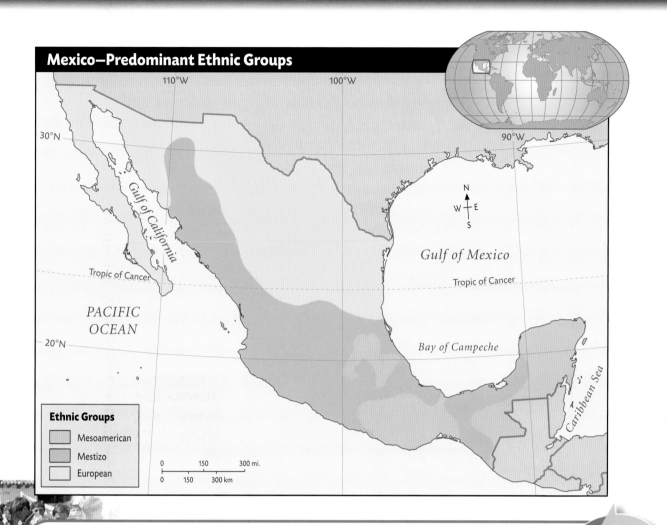

Mexico—Predominant Ethnic Groups

110°W
100°W
90°W
30°N
Gulf of California
PACIFIC OCEAN
Tropic of Cancer
20°N
Gulf of Mexico
Tropic of Cancer
Bay of Campeche
Caribbean Sea

Ethnic Groups
- Mesoamerican
- Mestizo
- European

0   150   300 mi.
0   150   300 km

Native American Artifacts

The largest museums in North Carolina have art and artifacts from the Maya and Aztec cultures. These works show the importance of nature to the Native Americans of the time.

Works of art tell the tales of the people who made them. They are important primary resources.

Art made today about people and places long ago are also important. They tell stories, too. But the artists were not there when what they painted or sculpted happened. So these are secondary sources.

Exhibits of modern works of art by Latin American painters and sculptors can also help us understand Latin America.

CAROLINA CONNECTION

KEY IDEAS

- Mexico City is the capital of the country. It mixes ancient and colonial cultures with modern ways.

- Acapulco was once an important port. Now tourists enjoy the city.

- Monterrey is the third-largest city in Mexico. It is an important manufacturing center.

KEY TERMS

El D.F.

Mexico City is home to over 25 million people. **What are some of the museums you can visit in Mexico City?**

Mexico is a country with many cultures and customs. It has huge areas of open space as well as growing cities. Mexico City is rich in ancient history. But it also has a modern subway system.

Acapulco (ah·kah·POOL·koh) is a popular tourist spot. It has beautiful beaches and exciting entertainment. The daring Cliff Divers of La Quebrada (lah keh·BRAH·dah) are famous.

The very modern Lighthouse of Commerce is in Monterrey. It shines its gleaming green laser beam out across the city.

Regional differences are often distinct in Mexico. Mexico City is in the center. Acapulco is in the west. Monterrey is in the east. Each offers its own individual flavors and lifestyles.

Mexico City

Most Mexicans do not call their capital Mexico City. They call it *"El D.F."* (ehl day effe). That is short for Federal District. This is similar to Americans calling our capital "D.C." for District of Columbia. Mexicans sometimes call the capital simply Mexico. Mexicans refer to their country as "the Republic."

Old and New

Mexico City was built on the ruins of the Aztec city Tenochtitlán. When the Spanish conquerors arrived there, they smashed almost every piece of Aztec culture. They even drained the lakes and filled them in. But visitors can still see signs of Aztec culture in the city today.

The Plaza of Three Cultures shows this history. Here are the ruins of the Aztec village of Tlatelolco. There are also Spanish colonial churches

Plaza in Spanish means simply "place." But in Mexico the plaza is the center of activity. People gather in the plaza daily to sell goods and just be together in a shared space.

and a modern high-rise apartment building. Ancient and colonial houses are still used in modern Mexico.

People visit the Floating Gardens of Xochimilco (so·chee·MIL·koh) to experience Old Mexico. It is the last of the Aztec lagoons. These were the lakes around which the Aztecs built their culture.

At Xochimilco you can hire a boat and a pilot to guide you around the chinampa (chee·NAHM·pah) flower gardens. There are

boats selling tacos and drinks. Strolling musicians offer to play favorite songs for visitors.

To experience twenty-first century Mexico, visitors go to Reforma Avenue in the Zona Rosa. It is the heart of modern Mexico. There they shop and stay in lovely hotels.

Mexico has one of the world's finest subway systems. The Metro can quickly take you to one of Mexico City's many museums. The most famous are the museums of Anthropology and Modern Art. There is another museum dedicated to the Revolution.

The National Palace is like the White House in the United States. Leaders of Mexico from New Spain to today's president have made this their home. Diego Rivera painted beautiful murals here.

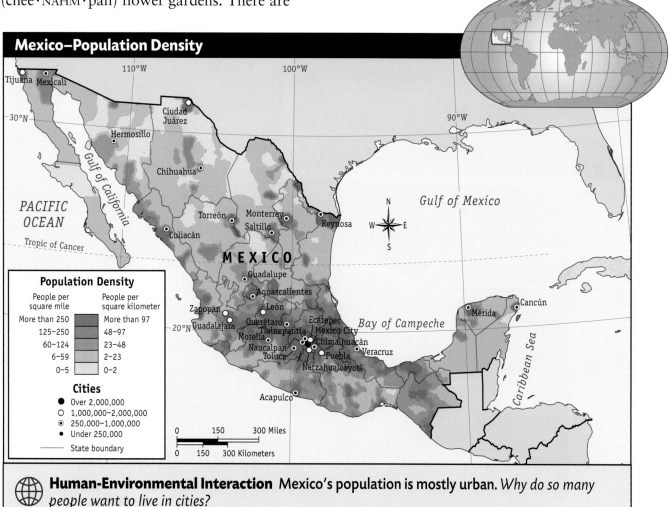

Mexico–Population Density

Population Density

People per square mile	People per square kilometer
More than 250	More than 97
125–250	48–97
60–124	23–48
6–59	2–23
0–5	0–2

Cities
- ● Over 2,000,000
- ○ 1,000,000–2,000,000
- ◉ 250,000–1,000,000
- • Under 250,000
- ----- State boundary

Human-Environmental Interaction Mexico's population is mostly urban. *Why do so many people want to live in cities?*

Guanajuato

Rich silver and gold deposits surround Guanajuato (gwah·nah·HWAH·toh). It was the wealthiest city in Mexico for centuries. The city is located on the Mesa Central, north of Mexico City. Guanajuato was built on the hillsides of a valley. The town's roads are steep and rolling (below). Some are actually alleyways with stairs.

In 1988, the United Nations named Guanajuato a World Heritage Zone. Because of this, the town bans traffic lights and neon signs. Buildings that do not fit with its colonial design are not allowed. The landscape of the valley means that there is little room for new buildings anyway.

Guanajuato was the site of one of the first battles of the Mexican War for Independence. On September 29, 1810, Father Hidalgo's followers attacked the place where people loyal to Spain had taken refuge. The building was burned to the ground. Many were killed. Later, Hidalgo was captured and executed. His head was displayed here to remind people not to go against Spain.

The name Guanajuato comes from the Nahuatl language. the word Quanax-huato (qua·nas·HWAH·toh) means "Hill of Frogs." Because of the Native American name, the image of the frog is can be seen throughout the town. This is similar to they ways that a Ram, a Wolf, or a Blue Devil might be seen in Chapel Hill, Raleigh, or Durham.

The Basillica Nuestra Señora

Acapulco

Acapulco is a port city on the Pacific Ocean. It is a popular tourist spot. In the 1500s it was one of the most important harbors in the Spanish empire. It was a major port for ships from Asia. These brought silks and spices to Mexico. From Acapulco these treasures were taken overland to Veracruz. Then they were shipped to Spain.

The riches attracted pirates. Acapulco's port was raided many times. The Spanish built the Fortress of San Diego at the harbor entrance. Today you can visit this star-shaped fort.

Tourism

Acapulco became a quiet fishing village after Mexico's independence. In the late 1920s, the Mexican government built a road and airport. It wanted to promote the city to tourists because of its beauty.

The government also brought in electricity and a drainage system. Then nice hotels were built. Hollywood stars in the 1930s and 1940s began to visit Acapulco. The city has grown from a population of barely 20,000 in 1950 to more than 2 million people today. More than 1.5 million tourists visit every year.

People visit Acapulco for its beaches and nightlife. Visitors enjoy many forms of entertainment. There are also parks where people can go boating and roller-blading. They watch trained dolphins and go on water rides.

Cliff Diving

Acapulco is famous for the Cliff Divers of La Quebrada. La Quebrada is a steep mountain ledge overlooking the bay.

Daring young men put on diving shows several times a day. They dive gracefully into the water from a height of 140 feet (42 m). They must time their dives with the tide and waves. If they were to hit the water at low tide they would get hurt. The final diver of the day dives holding a pair of flaming torches.

Monterrey

Monterrey is the third-largest city in Mexico. It is a center of international trade and manufacturing. The city is located near the border with the United States. It is surrounded by mountains. A famous one is Cerro de la Silla (seh·roh·deh·lah·see·yah), or Saddle Mountain.

Monterrey is a modern city. But the heart of the old city is the colonial Plaza Zaragoza (zah·rah·goh·zah). It is also known as the Macroplaza. It has beautiful fountains and statues.

Monterrey has a twenty-first-century side as well. The Lighthouse of Commerce is a stunning, bright red tower. It stands over the

Acapulco has long been an important vacation spot in Mexico. **Why do tourists vacation in Acapulco?**

entire town. The Lighthouse flashes a laser beam across the city at night. To some it resembles a red hot iron bar.

The Alfa Cultural Center is an example of modern architecture. Some people think it looks like a telescope pointing to the sky. It symbolizes the importance of science to the city. Inside is the Science and Technology Museum. It has an interactive center where students can study astronomy and physics. There is also a planetarium there.

The mountains are only 30 miles (48 km) from Monterrey. Twelve miles (19 km) to the south is the Mesa de Chipinique (CHEE·pee·NEE·keh). You can drive through a cool forest of oak and pine to reach that plateau. There visitors enjoy a beautiful view of the city.

Just a bit farther south is the Cola de Caballo (kah·BIGH·yoh) waterfall. The Boca Dam forms an artificial lake near the waterfall. There people sail and water ski.

Driving west from Monterrey you will pass through dry plains and great mountains. You will arrive at some caves called Garcia Grottos (gar·SEE·ah·GROHT·tohs). In the caves are a series of interesting rock formations. Their names come from their shapes, such as "Indian Head" or "Hand of the Dead."

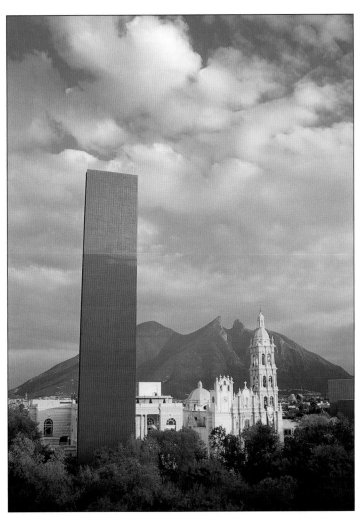

The modern Faro del Comercio, translated as the Lighthouse of Commerce, is a monument to business. It mixes the old and the new in Monterrey. **What is another example of modern architecture there?**

LESSON 1 REVIEW

Fact Follow-Up
1. What holidays do Mexicans celebrate?
2. Most Mexicans do not call their capital Mexico City. What do they call it?
3. In the past Acapulco was a seaport. What is it known for today?
4. Which city is known as a center of trade and manufacturing?

Talk About It
1. If you could visit one of these four cities, which would you choose? Why?
2. Which of the four cities described in this lesson do you think is most modern? Explain why.
3. How do these cities blend Native American and European cultures?

Culture and Society

LESSON (2) Tradition and Religion in Mexico

KEY IDEAS

- Mexican tradition includes many reminders of Native American religions.

- Some Native Americans helped Catholic priests convert people.

- The Virgin of Guadalupe is an important religious symbol for Mexicans.

- Masks play a dramatic part in Mexican cultural traditions.

KEY TERMS

Day of the Dead
missions
patron saint
Virgin of Guadalupe

The Spanish monarchy and the Roman Catholic Church were closely linked. Missionaries from Spain were among the first to settle in Latin America. They came because Spain wanted to convert Native Americans to Christianity. The priests arrived with the explorers. The native people managed to blend parts of their own religions with those from Europe. This can be seen throughout Mexico and Central America today.

Native American Beliefs

In Mexico there are many reminders of Native American religions. Some people still worship the old gods. Some have merged them with Catholic Christian beliefs. The missionaries looked for common themes in the Catholic and native religions. They used these similarities to teach the native peoples.

The story of the Aztecs wandering in search of a homeland is one example of this. Priests may have compared it to the Bible story of the Jews searching for the Promised Land. Priests also built churches in places that were already sacred to the Native Americans. Sometimes they even destroyed old temples and used the same materials to build new churches.

The old religions were difficult to erase from the hearts and minds of the Native Americans. There are still reminders of these older religions. A trip to Mexico would not be complete without visiting the Aztec and Mayan pyramids.

You can also see the observatories where these people studied the stars. You have read how the stars and planets were part of their religion. People in rural areas still watch the movements in the sky. These help the farmers know when to plant and harvest crops. Although their numbers are small, a few people still worship the old gods and follow the old religion.

Catholicism in Mexico

In the early years of the conquest two or three priests would travel to a Native American village. They explained the Christian religion to Native Americans. They baptized them. Then they built a church. These priests were the first to learn the Native American languages. They taught the Native Americans how to speak Spanish.

The priests also built *missions.* The missions were centers of worship and learning. They were built to convert and educate Native Americans. Spanish settlers built towns around the missions.

Most Native Americans did not like the idea of giving up their religious beliefs for Christian ones. Many fled into the surrounding countryside. Others stayed in the villages but did not follow the priests' teachings.

Other Native Americans wanted to convert to Christianity. Many helped the missionaries convert others. They traveled with the priests to other villages. There they translated and taught Spanish. They also protected the priests from harm.

Over time, the Catholic religion in Mexico and Central America came to combine Catholic beliefs with Native American religious views. Catholic saints replaced Aztec and Maya gods. Often the two came to be associated with one another. Some Catholic holy days were arranged to fall on Aztec and Maya feast days.

This drawing shows a Catholic missionary preaching to Native Americans. **What role did Spanish missions play in colonial Mexico?**

Small churches are at the center of village life. This one was built in the early 1800s in San Luis Potosí, Mexico. **How is this church different from other churches you have seen?**

Culture and Society

Many Catholics in Mexico say the Catholic Church must help the people wherever it can. Others say the Church should support the government more. They fear the Church will become too powerful if it does too much on its own.

Imagine you are a government official serving a poor community. Would you let the Church try to help them? Why or why not?

The Virgin of Guadalupe appears to Juan Diego. **In what ways has Mexico blended Catholic and Aztec traditions?**

The Virgin of Guadalupe's image appears on candles and other religious artifacts. **Why is her image seen in many places?**

The Virgin of Guadalupe

The Virgin Mary is a sacred figure in the Roman Catholic religion. She is the mother of Jesus Christ.

Every Mexican child learns the legend of the Virgin of Guadalupe. It is one of the most popular stories in Mexico. It takes place in the early years of New Spain.

Juan Diego was a Native American who had converted to Christianity. In December of 1531, he was walking to the new Catholic church in Tlatelolco. He climbed a hill that had been a sacred spot to an Aztec goddess. He heard someone singing.

Then he saw a brilliant vision of the Virgin Mary. Mary told Juan Diego to go to the Spanish bishop and tell him to build a church on the hill. She spoke to him in his native language. Bishop Zumarraga did not believe Juan Diego. A few days later the Virgin Mary reappeared. She told Juan Diego to gather roses from the top of the hill and take them to the bishop. This seemed impossible because roses did not bloom at that time of the year. But Juan Diego found bright red roses growing on the hill. He gathered them in his cloak and took them to the bishop.

He opened his cloak to remove the roses and they tumbled out. But the image of the Virgin Mary was imprinted on the cloth of his cloak. This Virgin Mary was dark-skinned and Native American. The cloak today hangs above the altar in a giant church built to honor the Virgin.

No one is sure why the name Guadalupe was given to the Virgin Mary vision Juan Diego saw. But that vision has become a symbol of Mexico.

The *Virgin of Guadalupe* is the *patron saint* of Mexico. Patron saints are special guardians of a person, place, or activity. You will see the Virgin of Guadalupe's image among the Mexicans living in North Carolina.

A family decorates a tomb on the Day of the Dead.
On what day is the Day of the Dead?

The Day of the Dead

The day after North Carolinians celebrate Halloween, Mexicans celebrate a holiday called the *Day of the Dead.* Some people go to the cemetery and honor their dead ancestors at midnight.

Everything that day has the theme of death. People wear masks resembling skulls. They eat candy and special bread shaped like bones. People also cover graves with yellow marigolds. They leave small amounts of the dead person's favorite foods. The towns of Pátzcuaro (PAHTZ·kway·roh) and the state of Michoacán (mee·chah·wah·KAHN) are famous for their festivals.

Mexican Family Life

Families are the center of Mexican life. In many homes, grandparents, parents, and children may live together. Families in rural areas might be large.

Most Mexican families are traditional. The father is the head of the family. Mothers are greatly respected, but the father usually makes most decisions. In the cities, many women have jobs. Women who live in rural areas work on the farms.

Mexican girls do not have as much freedom as do girls in the United States and Canada. Boys in rural areas work in the fields. Young people in the cities sometimes have part-time or full-time jobs.

Mexicans believe that they should help family members. They might help a family member find a job or go to school.

Masks

In Mexico, masks are worn not only for the Day of the Dead but for other holidays, too. Some Mexicans wear happy masks at Christmas. Some wear sad masks at Easter.

The Native Americans wear masks while dancing. These special dances tell tales of the conquest and their fight against the Spanish. Other dances tell fables and legends.

Masked dancers at a carnival in Huejotzingo, Mexico. **Do you think the dance about the fight with the Spanish would be happy or sad?**

LESSON 2 REVIEW

Fact Follow-Up
1. Why did Roman Catholic priests and missionaries arrive in Mexico so early?
2. What elements of Native American religions can still be observed in Mexico?
3. What are patron saints, and who is the patron saint of Mexico?

Talk About It
1. Why does Catholicism in Mexico blend ancient traditions with Christian teachings? Is it the same in other countries?
2. Which of all the religious holiday celebrations would you most like to experience? Explain why.

LESSON ③ Culture in Mexico

Mexico is large. It has many states and regions. Each area of the country has a special culture, much like the United States and Canada.

The areas of Mexico closest to the northern border are a lot like the southwestern United States. Southern Texas or Arizona might seem much like the northern Mexican states of Coahuila (koh·HWEE·ah) or Sonora (soh·NOHR·rah).

The culture is more international in the Mesa Central. In the more isolated southern states Native American customs are common.

Sports and the arts are important in Mexico. The brightly colored costumes of the mariachi and the rhythms of Latin dance music often fill the air. There are also soccer and wrestling fans.

Music

Ranchero (rahn·CHAH·roh) music is very popular. It might remind a person from North Carolina of country music. It has a similar rhythm and tells sad stories. Another popular form of music is *mariachi.* You may have seen a mariachi band on television or even playing in North Carolina. The musicians dress in silver-studded pants and jackets. They wear wide-brimmed sombreros. They look like Mexican cowboys of old.

Another Mexican musical tradition is the *conjunto* (coh·HOON·toe). Small groups of musicians play conjunto. They play accordions and a special kind of guitar called a bajo (BAH·hoe) sextos. This folk music is popular in northern Mexico.

City streets are often filled with the sounds of music coming from stores and shops. Bands play in the town plaza on Sunday evenings and for special occasions. Children learn to dance at an early age. Boys and girls are generally not shy at all about dancing. Young people and adults often attend the same dances. Most popular music in Mexico is created with dancing in mind.

KEY IDEAS

- Mexican music has many forms, from traditional to rock 'n' roll.

- Literature, art, and film are important in Mexican culture.

- Soccer and baseball are the most popular sports. Wrestling is very popular, too.

KEY TERMS

fútbol
mariachi

Senorino Alvarez, age ninety, plays in a mariachi band in Mexico City's Garibaldi Square. **Have you heard mariachi music?**

MEXICAN PORTRAIT

Diego Rivera
1886–1957

Diego Rivera was born in the town of Guanajuato. He began drawing at an early age. Soon he began to paint. He married Frida Kahlo. She was an equally important Mexican artist. She was the subject of many of his paintings and murals.

Diego Rivera was a master of painting. He could imagine how his paintings would look before he had finished them. His subjects rarely had to even be in the same room with him once he began to paint.

To Diego Rivera, art was public. He wanted it to be displayed where everyone could see it. He also wanted his work to be enjoyed by Mexicans from all walks of life. Painting murals was the way he brought his art to all people.

A mural is a large picture painted directly on the walls or ceilings of buildings. Rivera liked using murals because many people could see the painting at one time.

Diego Rivera's murals are colorful. They most often show Mexico's people past and present. Aztec warriors and Spanish conquistadors are featured in some murals. Others portray people working in fields or factories.

There are several of Rivera's murals in this book. Look at them and think about which ones you like best and why.

Diego Rivera,
Self-Portrait, 1941

The Fine Arts

In Mexico you will also find a rich tradition of painting and sculpture. After the Mexican Revolution, the government hired artists to paint great murals in many places. Diego Rivera and José Clemente Orozco (oh·ROH·skoh) were famous muralists. They painted scenes of Mexican history and daily life on the walls of public buildings.

Frida Kahlo was another famous Mexican artist. She painted a fantasy world full of strange images. These were paintings of Mexican life as she saw it. These artists were all inspired by the ancient paintings and buildings around their nation.

There is also a great craft tradition in Mexico. Pottery is painted with beautiful designs copied from the walls of ancient pyramids and temples. The Mexican government helps make sure these traditional crafts continue.

Taxco is located in the state of Guerrero (geh·REH·roh). It is famous for beautiful silver jewelry. Around the lakeside city of Pátzcuaro, coppersmithing has been a trade since before the Spanish conquest.

Architecture

Architecture is also an important art in Mexico. Mexicans take great pride in the way their buildings look. In cities like Monterrey you will see buildings decorated with glass and colored tiles. Some are built in new and interesting shapes. In other places like Guanajuato, the architecture will be in the beautiful Spanish colonial style.

This silver bracelet is an example of one of Mexico's many fine arts. **What other crafts does Mexico produce?**

Movies and TV

Mexico has an important film and television industry. Mexican films are shown all over Latin America and Europe. There have been many films made about the Mexican Revolution. Just as many have been made about singing cowboys (rancheros). These have introduced Mexican music to the rest of the world.

Cantinflas (kahn·TEEN·flahs) was a Mexican comedian who made more than 80 films. They were shown all over the world. When he died in 1986, thousands of people and presidents from other countries in Latin America attended his funeral.

This is a self portrait of Frida Kahlo, a famous Mexican artist. **When did the Mexican government begin promoting the arts?**

MEXICAN PORTRAIT

Frida Kahlo
1907–1954

Frida Kahlo was the most famous female Mexican painter of the twentieth century.

Kahlo's mother was Mexican and her father was German. Her early life was difficult because she suffered from polio when she was six.

When she was eighteen, she was in a very serious bus accident. This caused health problems for the rest of her life. She started to paint because she was bored from staying in bed after the accident.

Kahlo decided to change her studies from medicine to painting after the bus accident. She often chose Maya and Aztec themes for her paintings. She liked the bold colors and costumes of the native people.

The Mexican Revolution began when Kahlo was three years old. She was interested in politics her whole life. She supported the working class. She did not want only a few people to have all the power.

Kahlo also painted many self-portraits. She frequently showed herself in some sort of physical or emotional pain. In 1933 she married Diego Rivera. He was a famous muralist. Their marriage was difficult. They later divorced and then remarried a few years later.

Rivera said of his wife, "Frida Kahlo is the greatest Mexican painter. Her work is destined to be multiplied by reproductions and will speak, thanks to books, to the whole world."

Mexican poet Octavio Paz won the Nobel Prize in Literature in 1994. **Why do people say that Latin American literature has a social conscience?**

Literature

Mexico has produced great writers. Both Octavio Paz (ahk·TAH·vee·oh PAHZ) and Carlos Fuentes (foh·EHN·tehz) are world famous for their books and essays. Paz won the Nobel Prize in Literature in 1990. In their books they explored the theme of what it means to be a Mexican.

Paz and Fuentes, like many Latin American authors, write about the history of their nation. They want readers to think about solutions to Mexico's problems. Because of this, people say that Latin American literature has a social conscience.

Customs

Mexican Names First names are used only for family and close acquaintances. Mexican children are generally given two last names. The first is their father's family name (the last name he gained from his father). The second is their mother's family name (the last name she gained from her father). Many Mexicans refer to themselves using the last name gained from their father.

Sports

Soccer is the most popular sport in the world. It is number one in Mexico as well. Soccer is called *fútbol* throughout Latin America. There are many professional leagues across Mexico. Teams from the big cities play annually for a national championship. One of the biggest games is Mexico City versus Guadalajara (GWAH·dah·lah·HAH·rah).

The national team has participated in the World Cup Tournament many times. The World Cup tournament was held in Mexico in 1970 and 1986.

Baseball is also played in Mexico. Teams from Mexico's major cities play in the Mexican League. More than 80 players born in Mexico have played in the major leagues in the United States. In the 1980s, Fernando Valenzuela was a star pitcher for the Los Angeles Dodgers. Roberto Avila led the American League in batting in 1954.

Wrestling

One of the most popular forms of entertainment in Mexico is professional wrestling. They call it lucha libre (LOO·chah LEE·brah). Almost every night of the week in major cities there are matches. Thousands of fans go to watch. Mexican wrestlers are divided into two groups. The *rudos* (ROO·dohs) are the bad guys. The *técnicos* (TEHK·nee·kohs) are the good guys. Most Mexican wrestlers wear masks.

One Mexican wrestler was more famous than all the others. His name was El Santo (ehl SAHN·toh), "The Saint." El Santo was a *técnico* and wore a silver mask. He made more than 20 movies. A series of comic books were written about him.

Mexican wrestlers have begun to come out of the ring and act almost like real super-heroes. One wrestler named Superbarrio (SOO·pehr BAH·ree·roh) (Super neighborhood) began trying to help people who rented apartments in Mexico City. They fought for fair rent and decent housing in the months after the 1985 earthquake. Today he speaks out about other political issues.

Superecologista Verde (SOO·pehr eh·koh·loh·HEE·stah) (Super Ecologist Green) protests damage to the environment. Another masked wrestler named Superanimal (SOO·pehr·ah·nee·MAHL) (Super Animal) speaks out against cruelty to animals.

A wrestler in costume meets with children at a match in Mexico City. **What have some Mexican wrestlers begun to do?**

LESSON 3 REVIEW

Fact Follow-Up
1. Describe music in Mexico.
2. After the Mexican Revolution the government promoted the painting of great murals in many places. Who were famous muralists?
3. In what places are the people known for their beautiful silver jewelry and copper work?
4. What is the most popular sport in Mexico, and what is it called?

Talk About It
1. Which sport in Mexico is of most interest to you? Explain why.
2. Why do people say that Latin American literature has a social conscience?
3. Why is visual art important in Mexican culture?
4. To what extent are Mexico and the United States dependent on one another?

Accessing a Variety of Sources; Gathering,
Synthesizing, and Reporting Information

What is Mexican Culture?

Earlier this school year we studied the geographic theme of place. You have used this theme to look at what makes different places in North America similar to and different from others.

Remember that all places have both physical and cultural (or human) features. In this chapter you have learned about three cities in Mexico: Mexico City, Acapulco, and Monterrey. How are these places alike and different?

Charting Cultural Differences

Web charts can be useful to study the cultural features of these places. An example of a web chart is shown at right. You will need to sketch and complete three charts. That is one for each city you read about in this chapter.

How will you do this? Begin by rereading the information on each city and making notes. You can then group information from your notes into categories. Use these categories in your charts.

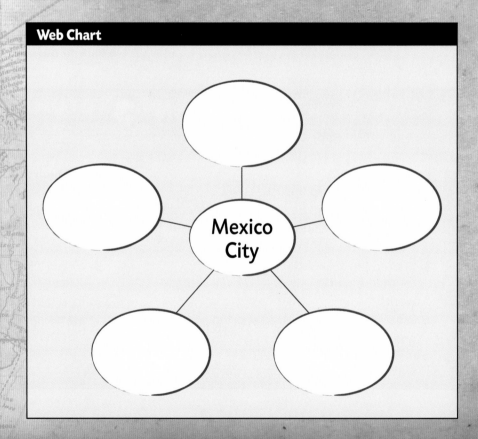

Web Chart

Mexico City

For example, there is information about important buildings in every city; so one of your categories might be Buildings. What other categories can you use? Should you use the same categories for each city?

Once you have completed the web charts, try to answer the question: What is "Mexican culture"?

Review Lessons 2 and 3 closely. These might help you answer the question more completely. Can you construct a web chart using information from all the lessons in this chapter? Can you write a paragraph describing Mexican culture? Are there other ways you can describe Mexican culture? What might some of these ways be?

Finally, is Mexican culture so diverse that you cannot explain it in just one paragraph? Is there other information that you need?

Playing soccer in Mexico

Lessons Learned

LESSON 1
A Tale of Three Cities
Mexico's cities offer variety in atmosphere and culture. Mexico City is the capital of the country. Acapulco attracts many tourists. Monterrey is a manufacturing and trade center.

LESSON 2
Tradition and Religion in Mexico
Most Mexicans are Catholic. Many Native American religious traditions survive today. Some religious traditions mix Roman Catholic and Native American cultures. The Virgin of Guadalupe inspires devotion and pride.

LESSON 3
Culture in Mexico
Mexicans art is known around the world. The most popular sports are soccer and baseball. Wrestling is popular, too.

Talk About It

1. Which of the cities described in this chapter do you think best reflects the nation of Mexico? Explain why.
2. The Roman Catholic missions established in Mexico had two purposes: to convert and educate Native Americans. Did they accomplish these purposes? Explain.
3. Do you think art is more a part of everyday life in Mexico than it is in the United States? Explain your answer.
4. If a visitor from Mexico City were to come to your classroom, what three questions would you ask him or her in order to learn the most about the city? Explain why you would choose these three questions.
5. Mexican writers are said to have a social conscience. Do you think that other artists have a social conscience as well? Consider Diego Rivera. Explain your answer.

Mastering Mapwork

LOCATION
Use the map on page 595 to answer these questions:
1. Which ethnic group is concentrated in northern Mexico?
2. Which ethnic group is concentrated in southern and southeastern Mexico?
3. Which ethnic group is concentrated in western and central Mexico?
4. Which ethnic group is most numerous in the area surrounding Monterrey?
5. Which ethnic group is most numerous in the area surrounding Merida?
6. Which ethnic group is most numerous in the area around Acapulco?
7. Which ethnic group is most numerous in Tijuana and Ciudad Juárez?

Becoming better Readers

Using Resource Materials
Good readers use many sources to gather information. Sometimes they read a book. Sometimes they use the internet. What are some of the ways you find information about topics that interest you?

Go to the Source

Newspaper Articles

Read the newspaper article below. Answer the questions using the information from the article.

Cinco de Mayo
U.S. celebrates holiday more than some parts of Mexico

by Paul Huggins

Jesus Chavez grew up in Mexico but never witnessed a Cinco de Mayo celebration until he came to the United States.

Alberto Carbajal grew up in Mexico and practiced months to march in Cinco de Mayo parades.

The contrasting experiences of the two restaurant managers can be as confusing as the origins of the holiday itself, which many Americans mistakenly believe is Mexican Independence Day. It actually commemorates Mexico's 1862 victory over the French at the Battle of Puebla.

But don't let any misunderstanding stop you from enjoying dinner and drink specials local Mexican restaurants will offer Thursday. Truth is, American's enjoyment of those discounts is part of the tradition.

"It's just a bigger holiday here than in Mexico," he added with a clueless shrug. "When I got to the United States is when I started celebrating Cinco de Mayo."

Some Spanish students in Elizabeth Cheatham's class at Calhoun Community College came to the same conclusion.

Because she knew many of the students mistakenly believed Cinco de Mayo was like the Fourth of July in the United States, Cheatham assigned them to research the origins of the holiday.

"One student said 'When I was doing my research on Cinco de Mayo, I learned it is really an American tradition,' " Cheatham said.

World Book Encyclopedia agreed. It has no mention of Cinco de Mayo in its vast Mexico section, but does list it under Mexican-American cultures.

Questions

1. What holiday do Americans mistakenly believe Cinco de Mayo represents?
2. Why is Cinco de Mayo a bigger holiday in the United States than in Mexico?
3. When did Jesus Chavez start celebrating Cinco de Mayo?
4. What are the professions of Jesus Chavez and Alberto Carbajal?
5. Explain what one student meant when she said, "When I was doing my research on Cinco de Mayo, I learned it is really an American tradition"?

Central America and the Caribbean

Central America and the Caribbean are regions of contrasts. Volcanoes, rugged mountain ranges, steaming rain forests, deserts, and hurricanes can make life difficult. But there are also areas with fertile soil, great natural beauty, and year-round, springlike weather.

Central America and the Caribbean are in the Tropics. Central America is made up of temperate mountains, volcanoes, and hot, coastal lowlands. Islands formed from volcanoes and coral deposits make up the Caribbean.

The diverse geography in this region is matched by the variety in the histories of the nations and territories found there.

Carnival, Martinique

617

Central America

A male quetzal

The most magnificent bird in Central America is the quetzal (KET·sahl). This bird was sacred to the Maya. The Aztecs prized its bright red and green feathers. The quetzal cannot live in captivity. For this reason it is a symbol of freedom in Central America. It is the national bird of Guatemala.

Its tail feathers can be up to 5 feet (1.5 m) long. Because poachers have killed and captured so many of these birds, it is difficult to spot one today. But there are some protected zones where, with luck, one might see a quetzal perched among the high branches of the forest.

Chapter Preview

Mayan temple in Tikal, Guatemala

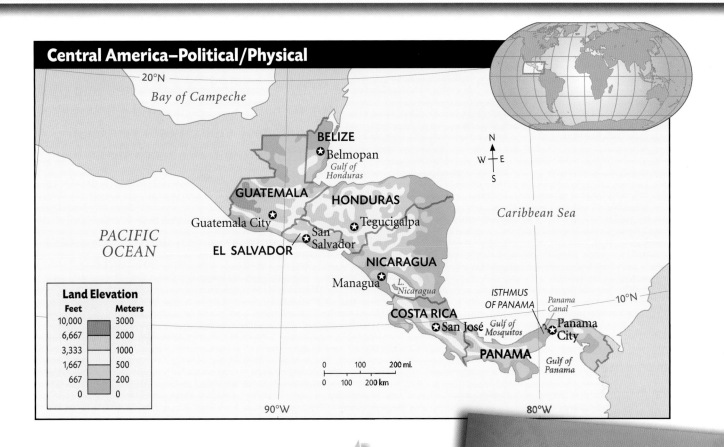

Central America–Political/Physical

20°N

Bay of Campeche

BELIZE
⊗ Belmopan
Gulf of Honduras

GUATEMALA

HONDURAS

Guatemala City ⊗

⊗ Tegucigalpa

Caribbean Sea

PACIFIC OCEAN

San ⊗ Salvador

EL SALVADOR

NICARAGUA

Managua ⊗

L. Nicaragua

ISTHMUS OF PANAMA

Panama Canal

10°N

Land Elevation

Feet	Meters
10,000	3000
6,667	2000
3,333	1000
1,667	500
667	200
0	0

COSTA RICA

⊗ San José

Gulf of Mosquitos

⊗ Panama City

PANAMA

Gulf of Panama

0   100   200 mi.
0   100   200 km

90°W

80°W

O. Henry and Honduras

William Sydney Porter was born in Greensboro in 1862. He is one of North Carolina's most famous authors. He used the pen name O. Henry. His stories usually had surprise endings. You may have read his Christmas story "The Gift of the Magi."

While O. Henry lived in Texas he was accused of stealing. Instead of going to jail, he fled to Honduras. He learned that his wife was sick. So he returned to the United States. He was arrested. In prison he wrote a book of short stories set in Honduras. The book, *The Cabbages and Kings*, was published in 1904.

COUNTRIES
of Central America

- Belize
- Costa Rica
- El Salvador
- Guatemala
- Honduras
- Nicaragua
- Panama

619

LESSON 1 Land and People

KEY IDEAS

- The nations of Central America lie in southern North America. They are close to South America.

- Many of the mountains of Central America are volcanoes.

- Central America is hot and humid in areas close to the coast and in valleys. In the mountains, the climate is cool or very cold.

- Central America is rich in plant and animal life.

KEY TERMS

ecotourism
Ring of Fire
Tierra Caliente
Tierra Fria
Tierra Helada
Tierra Templada

Some people have called Central America "the Land of the Shaking Earth." It has many volcanoes and earthquakes. People get used to living near volcanoes. Even small children know what to do if the ground begins to shake beneath their feet.

In Central America you will see corn planted almost everywhere, even on the side of a volcano. Warm weather vegetables and cool weather vegetables both grow year-round. Central Americans are trying to make a living through preserving their forests and wildlife.

This market in Antigua, Guatemala falls in the shadows of the Pacaya Volcano. **Why is Central America nicknamed the "Land of the Shaking Earth."**

Location and Landforms

The nations of Central America are on a narrow strip of land called an isthmus. The isthmus separates the Caribbean Sea and the Pacific Ocean. It also connects North and South America. High mountains and volcanoes run along this land like a pointy spine.

Central America is part of a huge ring of volcanoes. This is called the Pacific *Ring of Fire.* The ring circles the Pacific Ocean. It reaches from Asia to Alaska to the tip of South America. In this circle volcanic eruptions and earthquakes are common.

Volcanoes have helped and harmed Central America. The ash from volcanoes has enriched the soil. This helps plants grow. But earthquakes have also destroyed cities and taken lives.

Elevation and Climate

Central America lies in the Tropics. This means that temperatures remain fairly stable throughout the year.

In between its two coasts, the land rises to mountains over 12,000 feet (3600 m) above sea level. The mountains are a barrier to transportation, communication, and agriculture. But their elevation provides a climate with spring-like weather all year.

The map on page 623 shows the three main land types. They are tropical rain forest, tropical savanna, and highlands.

The rainy season lasts from May until November. Every year it brings storms and flooding to many areas. Hurricanes from the Caribbean Sea often destroy crops, bridges, and buildings and sometimes kill many people.

In 1998, Honduras was devastated by Hurricane Mitch. For more than two days the winds howled at speeds of more than 150 miles (241.5 km) per hour. Four feet (1.2 m) of rain fell. Floods and mudslides killed thousands. The homes of more than 1 million people were destroyed.

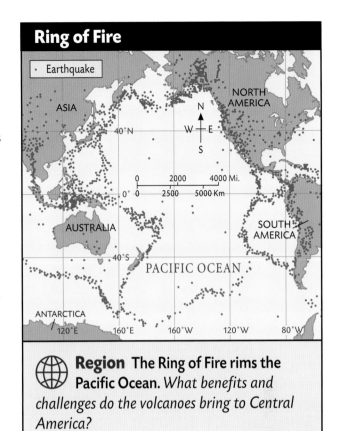

Ring of Fire

Earthquake

ASIA

NORTH AMERICA

AUSTRALIA

SOUTH AMERICA

PACIFIC OCEAN

ANTARCTICA

Region The Ring of Fire rims the Pacific Ocean. *What benefits and challenges do the volcanoes bring to Central America?*

A family inspects a parched cornfield in Los Rojos, Nicaragua. **What do you see in the background of this photo?**

The *Tierras*

Central America also has several elevation zones (see map, page 619).

Along the coasts, from sea level up to about 2,500 feet (750 m), is the zone called *Tierra Caliente,* or Hot Land. Here temperatures are hot, like summer in the Coastal Plain of North Carolina. The main crops are bananas, sugarcane, and rice.

The next elevation zone, the *Tierra Templada,* or Temperate Land, is found at elevations between 2,500 feet (750 m) and 6,000 feet (1,800 m). Major crops here include coffee, corn, wheat, and vegetables. The temperatures are mild, like spring in North Carolina.

Most people live in this zone. Several capital cities are above 3,000 feet (900 m) in elevation. North Carolina's capital, Raleigh, is 434 feet (130 m) above sea level. Asheville, North Carolina, is 2,140 feet (642m) in elevation.

At 6,000 feet (1,800 m) above sea level is the *Tierra Fria,* or Cold Land. Fewer people live here. They grow potatoes and grains. They raise livestock such as sheep for wool.

The last zone is the *Tierra Helada,* or Icy Land. It is above 12,000 feet (3,600 km). In Central America there is very little land at this elevation.

Plant Life

People around the world believe certain trees are sacred. For the Vikings it was the ash tree. For the Native Americans in North Carolina it was the elm.

One of the special trees of Central America is the *ceiba* (SAY·bah). It grows wide, above-ground roots. Above its huge trunk, its branches stretch up 130 feet (39 m) high. To the ancient Maya people, the *ceiba's* roots represented the underworld. Its branches represented the heavens. Its trunk represented human life on earth.

The *sapodilla* (sah·poe·DEEL·yah) tree is famous for its juice, called *chicle* (CHEE·clay). The Maya boil and harden *chicle*. You may know it as chewing gum.

A third important tree of Central America is the *caoba* (cah·OH·bah), or mahogany tree. Its hard and beautiful wood is prized for making furniture. Sadly, most of the caoba trees in Central America have been cut down to make furniture.

Deforestation

Like nations around the world, Central American nations have cut down much of their forests for logging, fuel, and farmland. Now they are facing the problems of deforestation.

The country of Costa Rica leads the way in preserving its forests. It has established a national network of parks and wildlife refuges. Tourists from all over the world come to visit these parks.

The entry fees to these national parks help pay for programs to protect plants and animals. This new kind of tourist industry is called ecological, or *ecotourism.*

This ceiba *tree grows in a tropical rain forest in Guatemala.* **What is made from a sapodilla tree?**

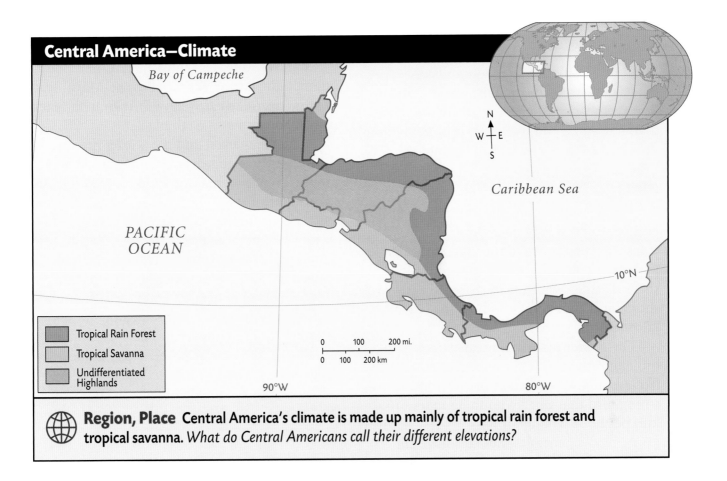

Central America—Climate

Bay of Campeche

Caribbean Sea

PACIFIC OCEAN

10°N

Tropical Rain Forest

Tropical Savanna

Undifferentiated Highlands

0   100   200 mi.

0   100   200 km

90°W   80°W

Region, Place Central America's climate is made up mainly of tropical rain forest and tropical savanna. *What do Central Americans call their different elevations?*

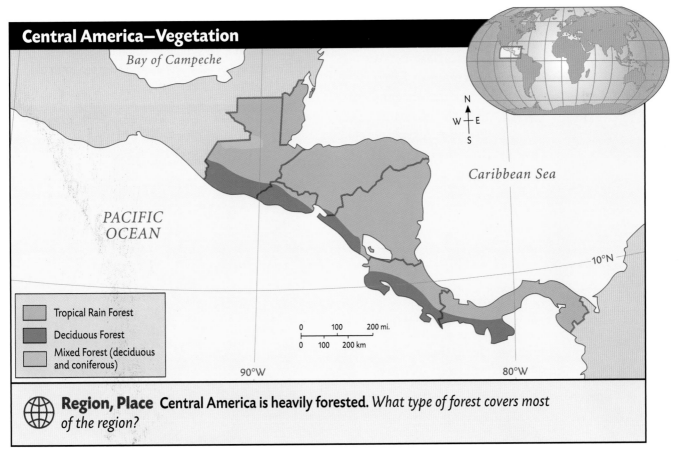

Central America—Vegetation

Bay of Campeche

Caribbean Sea

PACIFIC OCEAN

10°N

Tropical Rain Forest

Deciduous Forest

Mixed Forest (deciduous and coniferous)

0   100   200 mi.

0   100   200 km

90°W   80°W

Region, Place Central America is heavily forested. *What type of forest covers most of the region?*

Central America

Wildlife

Central America has thousands of remarkable birds, mammals, reptiles, and insects. In Costa Rica alone, there are more than 850 kinds of birds. This is more than in the United States and Canada combined.

Birds

The quetzal is only one of many beautiful birds in Central America. On the Pacific Coast, parakeets live in the wild. Toucans with multicolored, banana-shaped beaks share the skies with the long-legged egret, a shore bird. Can you guess how the laughing falcon got its name?

The scarlet macaw, a noisy parrot with brilliant red, yellow, and blue feathers, looks like a rainbow perched in the treetops. It is a strong bird that can fly up to 35 miles (56.4 km) per hour. Though it has very few natural enemies, humans have cut down the trees where it builds its nests. Today only 300 scarlet macaws remain in Central America. Because of this, the governments of Belize and Guatemala have started programs to protect them.

The jaguar (right) is sacred to the Maya. The scarlet macaw (left) is a type of parrot. **What is the problem facing these animals?**

Mammals

Central America's most magnificent animal, the jaguar, is sacred to the Maya. It is a large tiger-like cat, yellow-brown with black spots. Sometimes it is all black.

Like the quetzal and the scarlet macaw, however, the jaguar has become rare. It is in danger of extinction due to hunting and loss of habitat.

The pizote (pee·zoe·tay) has a striped tail. It might remind you of a raccoon. But its long snout and way of running make it seem like a cousin of both the anteater and house cat.

There are also several types of monkey in Central America. Species include the spider monkey and the howler monkey. Despite its small size, the howler monkey can make a huge racket. Once you have heard it screaming in the jungle night, it is impossible to forget.

Word Origins

The name "**quetzal**" comes from the Aztec word *quetzalli*. It means "brightly colored tail feathers." The feathers of the quetzal are vivid green, with red and blue flashes underneath.

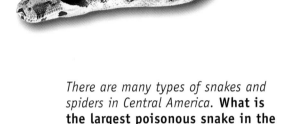

Insects, Spiders, and Reptiles

There are many insects, spiders, and reptiles in Central America. Army ants and tarantula spiders live in the thick forests. There are thousands of types of butterflies.

Central America is home to many frogs. Some of them are poisonous to the touch. Alligators and their cousins, caimans, are found along some Central American waterways. Many large snakes live here. Species include the fer-de-lance and the bushmaster. The bushmaster is the largest poisonous snake in the Americas. The boa constrictor is another native snake.

There are many types of snakes and spiders in Central America. **What is the largest poisonous snake in the Americas?**

Ecotourism gives Central American nations a way to preserve their wildlife while they earn money. Imagine that you are placed in charge of a national preserve. What rules would you lay down for visitors to the preserve? How would you explain the importance of these rules to your visitors? What consequence would there be for breaking the rules?

LESSON 1 REVIEW

Fact Follow-Up
1. Describe the climate of Central America.
2. What are Central America's elevation zones? What crops are grown in each zone?
3. What are some important trees in this region?
4. What are some important birds, mammals, and insects and reptiles of Central America?

Talk About It
1. How can the location of Central America be a hazard to its people?
2. How might deforestation threaten animal life in Central America?
3. What do the quetzal, the scarlet macaw, and the jaguar have in common?

LESSON 2 People and Environment

KEY IDEAS

- The Maya have lived in Central America for more than 2,500 years.

- *Mestizos* have a mixture of Native American and Spanish heritage.

- Many descendants of Africans live along Central America's Caribbean Coast.

KEY TERMS

garifuna
indigo

Central America is not rich in gold or silver. Because of this, Spanish colonists there had to look for other products to send back to Spain. Native Americans taught the Spanish many things about the environment.

The People

People have lived in Central America for thousands of years. Native Americans were the first people here.

In the 1500s the Spanish came as conquerors. They stayed as settlers. They forced people from Africa to come to Central America as slaves. All of these people, Native Americans, Spanish, and Africans, have influenced Central America's culture.

Tourists can visit the Temple of the Giant Jaguar in Tikal, Guatemala. **What do you think happened to the people of Tikal?**

These Miskito children are first graders at a school near the Hondoran-Nicaraguan border. **Which group makes up the majority of people living in Central America?**

Native Americans

The Maya lived in much of the northern part of Central America. The ruins of Tikal (tee·KAHL) have been found in the jungles of Guatemala. Tikal was the center of a civilization of great builders and astronomers. It flourished between 1,000 and 2,500 years ago.

No one knows for certain why this great city was abandoned. Perhaps the people used too many of the area's natural resources. Perhaps their civilization collapsed after wars with rival Maya cities.

Today, the ruins have become a national park. People from around the world visit it. They can climb the Pyramid of the Masks and see the magnificent Pyramid of the Jaguar.

The Highland Maya still live in the mountains of western Guatemala. They created their own complex civilization. Though the Spanish conquered them in the early 1500s, their culture was not destroyed.

The Highland Maya continue to live in the *Tierra Templada* and the lower elevations of the *Tierra Fria*. They maintain many of their traditions. They do not mix much with other people.

Other Native Americans live in Central America, too. The Chibcha live in southern Costa Rica and Panama. Today, these groups are struggling to maintain their culture. The ancestors of the Miskito people of Honduras and Nicaragua married Africans but kept their way of life.

Mestizos

In every Central American nation except Belize, *mestizos* make up the majority of the population. *Mestizos* is the name for people who have both Native American and Spanish ancestors. Their communities mix their ancestors' different cultures.

Garifuna

Garifuna are people of mixed African and Native American descent. They live in communities along the Caribbean coast from Belize to Nicaragua. They have their own language. They keep a strong connection with African traditions.

In Belize, the *garifuna* culture is changing. *Mestizos* and Maya have arrived from neighboring countries. These newcomers are adding their ways of life to those of the *garifuna*.

Ethnic Heritage in Society

People in Central America today do not always treat one another as equals. This inequality is partly based on a person's ancestry, or ethnic heritage. As you have read, Central America's people are descended from different ethnic groups and nationalities. Many groups have their own language and ways of life. They also differ in wealth and social standing.

As in all the Americas, the most powerful people have mainly been of families whose only ancestors were Spanish or other Europeans. They are generally the ones with the most wealth. They also have better educations.

Few Native Americans, *mestizos,* or *garifuna* have become rulers of Central American nations. Some, though, have gained wealth and high social standing.

Many Central Americans experience discrimination because of their ethnic group. Some of this discrimination came from the way the original European settlers treated them. Gaining a better life has been harder for people who face these prejudices.

The Belize woman makes a simple meal in her home.
How does ancestry affect social standing?

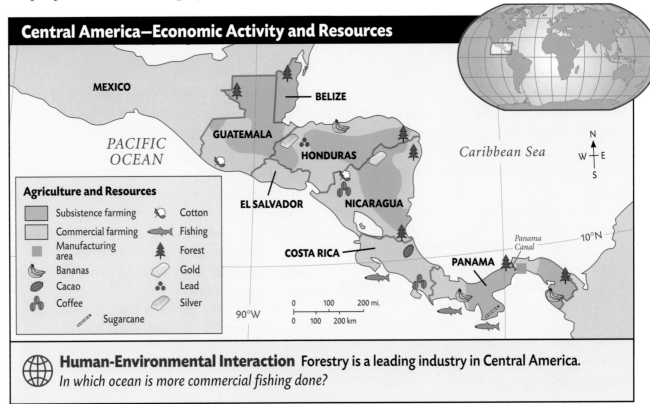

Central America—Economic Activity and Resources

MEXICO

BELIZE

PACIFIC OCEAN

GUATEMALA

HONDURAS

Caribbean Sea

N
W—E
S

Agriculture and Resources

- Subsistence farming
- Commercial farming
- Manufacturing area
- Bananas
- Cacao
- Coffee
- Sugarcane
- Cotton
- Fishing
- Forest
- Gold
- Lead
- Silver

EL SALVADOR

NICARAGUA

COSTA RICA

PANAMA

Panama Canal

10°N

0   100   200 mi.
0   100   200 km

90°W

Human-Environmental Interaction Forestry is a leading industry in Central America. *In which ocean is more commercial fishing done?*

Chapter 26

Land and Resources

Since the Spanish did not find much gold and silver in Central America, they concentrated on agriculture. As in Mexico, the Spanish carved large *haciendas* out of land occupied by Native American people. Native Americans and enslaved Africans were put to work on plantations.

Unlike in Mexico, these *haciendas* were not used to feed people working in mines. Instead, their products were shipped to Spain. As you will see, these *haciendas* became Central America's biggest and most important businesses.

Chocolate

Colonists found three Central American products to export. The first of these was chocolate.

Chocolate is made from cacao (cah·COW) beans. Europeans knew nothing about cacao or how the beans could be used. Then they saw Native Americans growing cacao trees and making a drink from their seeds.

Europeans quickly found that they liked chocolate, too. They began drinking huge quantities of chocolate after mixing it with sugar, cinnamon, vanilla, and milk.

Other Exports

By the 1800s, cacao was being grown in other parts of the world. Central America lost many of its cacao markets.

To replace them, the Spanish turned to the fruit of the *xiquilite* (see·key·lee·tay) plant. From this fruit they made a deep-blue dye called **indigo.** A red dye called cochineal (coh·KEE·neel) was made from the dried skeletons of a native bug. It became the third major export.

These cacao beans and pods are important products of Central America. **According to the map on page 628, where does cacao come from?**

LESSON 2 REVIEW

Fact Follow-Up
1. What group of people makes up the majority of the population in most Central American nations?
2. Who are the *garifuna*, and where do they live?
3. What products replaced cacao as important exports?

Talk About It
1. What three groups of people have influenced Central America's culture?
2. Why do the *garifuna* mostly live along the Caribbean coast of Central America?
3. How did the *hacienda* systems in Central America and Mexico differ?

Cochineal

Cochineal is an insect that lives on the Prickly Pear Cactus. The cochineal's body is bright red. Native Americans used the dye to color robes, weapons, and even their bodies.

European red dyes were not as bright as that of cochineal. Cortés saw the Aztec nobles dressed in this color. He knew that Europeans would want it. He immediately shipped bags of the dried skeletons of the cochineal to Spain. By 1600, cochineal was the second most valuable export.

In Europe, cochineal dye was used to color the robes of Roman Catholic Cardinals and royalty. Even the jackets of the "Redcoats" in the British army were dyed with cochineal.

The Spanish tried to keep the source of cochineal a secret. For years they made people believe that it came from a seed. They even called it the "cochineal grain." A Dutch scientist finally viewed one of these "seeds" under a microscope. He saw that it was an insect.

In the late 1800s, a substitute for the dye was discovered. For a time less cochineal was produced. Recently, cochineal production has grown. It is a natural and safe coloring for foods and lipstick.

Cochineal dye

Cochineal on a Prikly Pear-Cactus

LESSON ③ Economy and Government

Spain ruled Central America as a colony for more nearly 300 years. During that time, Spain controlled the economy. Everything was done to benefit the Spanish empire and its rulers.

Much of the food and other agricultural products were sent overseas. Spanish merchants shipped cacao, indigo, and cochineal to new European markets.

The countries of the region are now independent. Central Americans are no longer forced to send everything to Spain. They can sell it for their own profit.

Yet Central America's economy still is the same in some ways. Much of their income comes from agricultural products. There are few factories. Many goods must be imported.

Along with cacao, bananas are a major export of Central America.
What are some other exports?

Central America

The United States imports bananas from Central America. **Who owned the banana plantations in the 1800s and 1900s.**

The Export Economy

Plantation agriculture grew after the Spanish gave up their colonial empire in 1821. By the late 1800s, plantation owners in Guatemala, Honduras, and Costa Rica were making a profit by exporting coffee beans.

Plantation owners grew rich. They could afford to buy imported goods from other countries. The rest of the people were not so lucky. Many worked for very low wages on the coffee plantations.

At this same time, governments wanted foreigners to invest in banana plantations. The governments offered these people money or land. Some offered the foreigners low taxes. Others promised that people would work for low wages.

British and United States companies rushed into Central America to make money growing bananas. Foreign companies set up plantations in Guatemala, Panama, Honduras, and Costa Rica. The foreign owners took most of their earnings out of these countries.

Today's Economy

Today, in addition to coffee and bananas, Central America exports sugar, cacao, and beef.

The problems of plantation agriculture still have not been solved. Profits from the plantations have enriched wealthy local or foreign owners.

Wages for plantation workers are still low. Those who have managed to buy their own small farms are also poor.

Some industries and businesses have opened in cities. They do not have enough jobs, however, for all those who want to work. This means that the majority of Central America's people continue to live in poverty.

Government

Spain granted independence to these nations in 1821. Afterward, Central American leaders tried to unite the region into one country. When the effort failed, the region

Anastasio Somoza was a Nicaraguan caudillo. *This photo was taken prior to becoming president in 1937.* **How did the caudillos bring wealth to local landowners?**

split into nations named Guatemala, El Salvador, Honduras, Nicaragua, and Costa Rica. Panama joined the group later when it broke away from Colombia.

Only recently has Central America become home to democratically elected governments.

Caudillos and Military Dictators

The new nations of Central America tried to set up democracies but they had no experience. Spain was not a democracy. It did not run its colonies democratically. As a result, control was taken by strongmen *caudillos. Caudillos* often made alliances with other powerful landowners to protect their own interests.

In the twentieth century, *caudillos* were often military dictators who controlled the country with military force. They made sure that their private partners could get cheap land and cheap labor. With this support, plantation owners did not think they needed to pay workers more or to improve working conditions.

Many times these leaders were backed by the United States especially during the Cold War. The United States supported dictators who promised not to make the country Communist.

The powerful military dictators and their partners grew rich. They were often not willing to use their profits to help most of the people. For example, a dictator might promise to build a railroad to help small townspeople and farmers. In reality, the railroad usually helped only the plantation owners by carrying coffee or banana to ports where it was loaded on ships for export.

Most people continued to live in poverty on small farms and in isolated towns. Governments did little to provide public education or health care. Many people suffered from disease and poor nutrition. Most Central Americans could not read or write.

Guerrilla Wars

At times the people banded together to fight the government. These conflicts are called guerrilla wars. Guerrilla comes from the Spanish word for war, *guerra*. It means "little war."

Sometimes people have fought because they wanted democratic government. Other times they wanted a different system of government, such as communism or socialism. Often they just want a chance to feed and educate their families.

The men are part of the Sandinista army in Nicaragua. **What are some reasons for guerilla wars in the region?**

Building the Panama Canal

The Panama Canal crosses the Middle American mainland at its narrowest point. It was one of the largest building projects in the world. It is the most direct route between the Atlantic and Pacific Oceans. Thousands of ships pass through its locks every year.

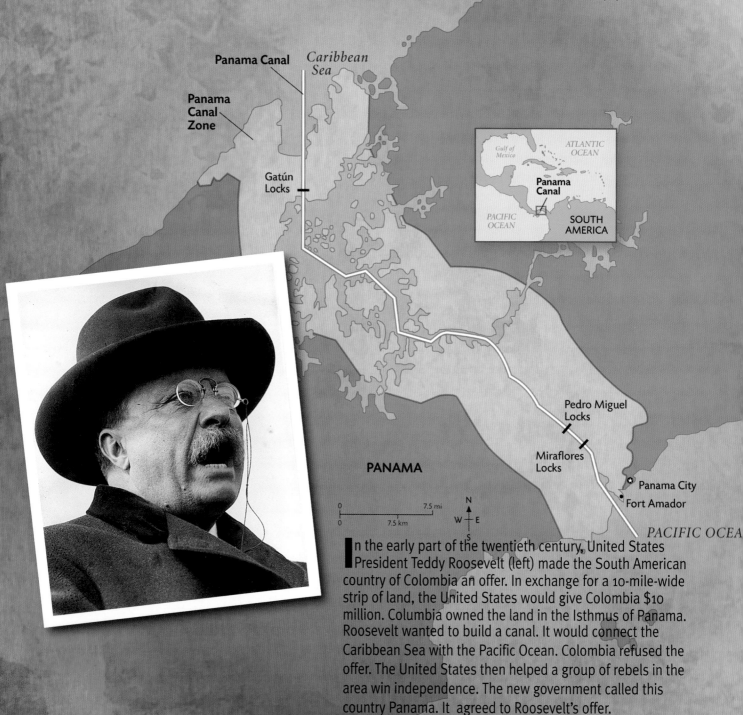

In the early part of the twentieth century, United States President Teddy Roosevelt (left) made the South American country of Colombia an offer. In exchange for a 10-mile-wide strip of land, the United States would give Colombia $10 million. Columbia owned the land in the Isthmus of Panama. Roosevelt wanted to build a canal. It would connect the Caribbean Sea with the Pacific Ocean. Colombia refused the offer. The United States then helped a group of rebels in the area win independence. The new government called this country Panama. It agreed to Roosevelt's offer.

Steam shovels cleared earth from the "big ditch." That was a popular nickname for the Canal. Workers even used a new invention. Dynamite helped workers blast through mountains.

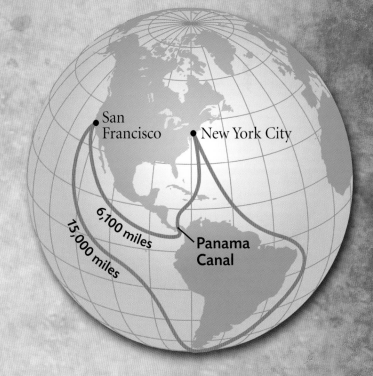

The Panama Canal took more than 43,000 workers eight years to dig. It took two more years to install machines to control the flowing water. Many of the workers came from the Caribbean. Workers earned only 10 cents an hour. They worked nine to ten hours a day.

The Canal cut the distance between San Francisco and New York City by almost 9,000 miles (14,490 km). In 1978, a treaty was signed between Panama and the United States. It passed control of the Canal Zone from the United States to Panama in 1979. This same treaty transferred the ownership of the Canal from the United States to Panama in 2000.

San Francisco

New York City

6,100 miles

15,000 miles

Panama Canal

Central America

Growing Democracy

Nicaragua, Guatemala, El Salvador, Panama, and Honduras were ruled by dictators until recently. In Nicaragua, Guatemala, and El Salvador, long guerrilla wars were fought to end the rule of dictators.

In 1987, Oscar Arias Sanchez, the president of Costa Rica, invited the leaders of Nicaragua, Guatemala, Honduras, and El Salvador to a meeting in San Jose. He wanted to talk about democracy.

In the meeting Arias said Central American governments were wasting their resources on the military. He urged them instead to improve their countries. He said governments ought to be peaceful. He said Central Americans should have the right to vote in free elections.

Today, democratically elected officials lead all the countries of Central America.

However, this has not solved the old problems. A few people still own most of the land. Powerful people control resources. This limits the growth of equality and democracy.

Oscar Sanchez

CENTRAL AMERICAN PORTRAIT

Oscar Arias Sanchez
1940–

In 1941 Oscar Arias Sanchez was born into one of Costa Rica's richest coffee-growing families. As a young man, he studied briefly in the United States and then in Britain, where he earned a law degree. After returning to Costa Rica, he held several government positions. In 1986, voters elected Arias president of Costa Rica. As president, he began his work as a peacemaker in the region. He worked tirelessly to end armed conflict and bring stability to the war-torn region. He convinced the leaders of Guatemala, El Salvador, Honduras, and Nicaragua to talk to him and to each other. In 1987 he proposed a regional peace plan. It called for free elections in Central American countries and other things to bring peace. For his efforts, Arias won the 1987 Nobel Peace Prize. In his acceptance speech Arias said, "I accept for Costa Rica, for peace and for Central America, where 25 million human beings deserve to look to the future with optimism and some hope of progress."

LESSON 3 REVIEW

Fact Follow-Up
1. What products have Central American nations exported to the rest of the world?
2. What, in general, have Central American nations imported?
3. What are caudillos, and how did they become successful?

Talk About It
1. Although many Central American countries are now democratic, their democracy is fragile. Why?
2. What are guerrilla wars?
3. Did *caudillos*, military dictators, and landowners cause guerilla wars? Explain.

Along Central America's Caribbean and Pacific Coasts are cultures much like those of the Caribbean islands. The Maya culture survives in the volcanic mountains. In the *Tierra Templada* cities are centers of *mestizo* culture.

Plantation-style farming has left its mark in coffee and banana plantations throughout Central America. Central Americans look more and more to manufacturing and assembly industries to make a living, but farming is still important.

A Tale of Three Nations

Central America is a region of diverse climates and natural resources. Yet the nations of Central America also share a common Spanish heritage and economic base. Let's look at the similarities and differences in three Central American countries.

San José, Costa Rica, is a modern city. **In what ways is Costa Rica different from other Central American countries?**

Tourists ride through the middle layer of a rain forest canopy in Costa Rica. **What is the idea of ecotourism?**

A cornfield ruined by drought in La Jagua, 200 miles north of Managua, Nicaragua. **Who were the Sandinistas?**

Costa Rica

Costa Rica differs in several ways from the rest of Central America. The biggest difference is the nation's long history of free elections. Only twice since 1889 has Costa Rica strayed from democracy.

Costa Rica abolished its army in 1948. Costa Rica also has the most developed public education system in Central America.

Most of the people in Costa Rica live in the *Tierra Templada*. That is where the capital of San Jose is located. There are hot lowlands near the Atlantic coast. There farm families live on whatever they can grow. In the west, along the Pacific, bananas were the major crop between 1930 and 1960.

Recent efforts have been made to help farmers. Farmers are getting help to try planting new crops. One of Costa Rica's most important economic projects is developing the ecotourism industry.

The country has stopped destroying its beautiful rain forests. Costa Rica now encourages tourists to visit its forests and relax on its beaches. Costa Ricans used to make money by selling the lumber from trees. Now, instead of cutting trees down, they take tourists on nature walks and charge money. The plan is working. People from all over the world are visiting Costa Rica. Ecotourism provides money to preserve the environment and create jobs for Costa Ricans.

Nicaragua

Nicaragua is Central America's poorest country. It was ruled by dictators for much of the last century. One family, the Somozas, ruled Nicaragua with the military and a small group of landowners. Foreign companies owned huge coffee and banana plantations.

Most Nicaraguans had few opportunities to improve their lives. This caused an uprising beginning in the 1960s. The fighting lasted for almost 30 years. Many people were killed. Others were forced to flee the fighting. The fighting also destroyed bridges, roads, and crops. It drained the nation's wealth and energy.

In 1979, a group known as the Sandinistas overthrew the Somoza dictatorship. They wanted to re-distribute land more evenly to citizens. Not all Nicaraguans supported the Sandinistas. People argued over land redistribution. The United States supported Nicaraguans fighting against the Sandinista government. In 1990, the war ended. Nicuragua became democratic. An anti-Sandinista government was elected. Several years later, in 2006, the leader of the Sandinistas, Daniel Ortega, was elected president. He has vowed to work within the democratic system.

Nicaragua is a beautiful country and her people are hard workers. Still, Nicaragua has many obstacles in the path to prosperity. Solutions to basic problems, such as feeding the population, are most important.

Guatemala

Guatemala has Central America's biggest population and also the largest Native American population.

Throughout the 1800s, *caudillos* ruled Guatemala. A revolution created a democratic government in 1944. It was overthrown in 1954. From that point until 1986, Guatemala was again ruled by a military dictatorship. Since 1986, Guatemala has been a democracy.

Elections alone have not brought political stability. Guatemala suffered from guerrilla warfare between 1961 and 1996. Maya make up half of the nation's population. They are discriminated against by *mestizos* and people of European ancestry. Poor farmers resent the wealth of rich plantation owners.

Guatemala has great potential. Volcanic ash makes the soil in the *Tierra Templada* fertile. Mineral wealth, such as oil, lies beneath the ground. There are beautiful volcanoes and waterfalls, beaches and lakes. The ruins of the ancient Maya cities and the culture of the modern Maya could also attract tourists.

Customs

During the week before Easter, in Antigua, Guatemala, people create carpets of colored sawdust and flower petals. These carpets are prepared for a procession of people who will carry statues representing the saints. After the procession is over, the sawdust and petal carpets are destroyed.

Many Maya traditionally carry bundles in tzutaes, *or carrying cloths, on their heads.* **How are the Maya important to Guatemala?**

This Catholic priest is celebrating Semana Santa (Holy Week) in Guatemala.
What challenges face both the Catholic Church and governments in Central America?

Religion in Society

The Roman Catholic Church is the largest Christian denomination in Central America. Roman Catholics and Protestants still work to convert the Native Americans. They send missionaries to work with and teach the poor.

Some religious missionaries teach new farming methods. Others work against drug abuse. Still others take care of the large numbers of homeless children found in many Central American cities.

Private church schools are an important alternative to public schools in Central America. Overcrowding is a problem in public schools in the larger cities. Schools in rural areas sometimes close due to lack of money. Church schools provide a good education to many children at a low cost.

Central American governments look to the Catholic Church to help them give aid to poor citizens. This can lead to problems between the government and the Church.

Priests in poor areas have encouraged citizens to request services that the government cannot provide. Government authorities fear that these requests will cause poor people to rise up against them. Uprisings like these have already happened in some poor areas of Guatemala.

Culture

Central American festivals overflow with games and music. There is also lots of food and dancing. Religious services are important to many festivals.

Patron Saints

Many towns in Central America are named for saints. The patron saint of a town is honored every year with a celebration called a *fiesta patronal.* The feast of San Jose is celebrated on March 19 in Costa Rica.

A *fiesta patronal* usually starts with a service in the town church. The townspeople parade through the streets carrying a statue of the patron saint. The mayor of the town and other important citizens such as priests participate. In some regions a local *mariachi* or *marimba* band will march in the parade.

The *marimba* is a kind of xylophone played by several people at once.

People gather in the plaza to celebrate after the parade. This means there is lots of singing and dancing. Firecrackers and rockets are also set off.

Eating is a big part of the *fiesta patronal.* The foods reflect many centuries of combined Spanish and Native American cooking. Corn is an important part of the diet of Central Americans.

Corn tortillas and tamales are filled with meat, cheese, and beans. They are prepared and eaten by the basketful. If you visit someone's home on fiesta day, you can expect to be served a local specialty.

Bands continue to play past sundown. People dance far into the night. There is often a carnival in the plaza with a Ferris wheel and rides. *Futbol* (soccer) and other games are played. Fireworks light up the night sky.

These dancers take part in a festival in Masaya, Nicaragua. **What celebration in the United States does the description of the *fiesta patronal* bring to mind?**

Central America's Future

Most of Central America is poor. But there is hope for Central America's future. Governments and private organizations are cooperating to give people a better chance. Democratic elections are giving more people a say in their government. Governments have begun to pass laws against discrimination based on ethnic heritage or skin color.

But much hard work lies ahead. One of the toughest problems is land distribution. Some governments have tried to redistribute the land among the poor. Many landowners oppose this type of solution. Sometimes, governments have to seize private property to redistribute the land. This could easily lead to war. It did in Nicaragua.

Central America is important to the United States. There is growing trade with the United States because of more investment in the region by American companies. The Panama Canal has also increased our nation's economic and political interest in this region.

Another important link between Central America and the United States is people. Many people leave their Central American nations to seek a better life in the United States. Others fled to the United States to escape the military dictatorships and wars. As you have read, the three big nations of

North America signed a free-trade agreement called NAFTA in 1994. A similar agreement went into effect in Central America in 2006. Some people believe that this will open up new markets for Central America and improve their economies. Others see it only as a way to increase profits for large American companies while straining Central American's already weak economies.

Central America is an important trading partner for the NAFTA nations. **What might happen to further these relationships?**

LESSON 4 REVIEW

Fact Follow-Up
1. In what ways does Costa Rica differ from other Central American countries?
2. What events in the twentieth century have contributed to Nicaragua being Central America's poorest country?
3. What is the largest religious denomination in Central America?

Talk About It
1. Why are religious rituals a part of many celebrations in Central America?
2. Of all the promising signs, which one offers the greatest hope for the future of Central America? Explain your choice.
3. Why is Guatemala said to have great potential?

Analyzing, Interpreting, Creating,
and Using Resources and Materials

Thinking About Population

By now you have had lots of experience in reading maps and graphs. This table provides you with some information about population in four countries of North America that you have studied this year. They are Canada, Mexico, Costa Rica, and Nicaragua.

What do the population figures in the graph below mean? What does it mean that life expectancy in Costa Rica is nearly the same as the life expectancy in Canada? Does it mean that Costa Rica is a wealthier country and better able to care for its elderly citizens?

What does it mean that nearly half (44 percent) of Nicaragua's population is under the age of fourteen while just over one fifth (21 percent) of Canada's population falls in that category? Does it mean that Nicaragua values children more than Canada does?

How can these population figures be used? How can decision makers in government use this information? What might nations like Costa Rica be doing to provide for their elderly population? What might nations like Nicaragua be doing to provide for their youthful population?

Young school children in Managua, Nicaragua

Comparing Population Statistics				
Countries	Age 1–14 years	Age 15–64 years	Age 65 years and older	Life expectancy at birth
Canada	16%	70%	14%	81.4 years
Mexico	28%	66%	6%	77.3 years
Costa Rica	26%	68%	6%	79.4 years
Nicaragua	36%	60%	4%	77.3 years

*2010 estimate, United Nations Population Division

Lessons Learned

LESSON 1
Land and People
Central America contains coastal plains and valleys. It also has mountains and volcanoes. The climate is hot and humid in low-lying areas. It is cooler in the mountains. The region's animal and plant life is rich and diverse.

LESSON 2
People and Environment
The Maya have lived in Central America for thousands of years. During colonial times, Europeans and Africans came to the region. *Mestizos* are descendants of Native Americans and Europeans.

LESSON 3
Economy and Government
Central American resources were used for European gain during colonial times. After independence, plantations grew crops for other countries. Now Central American nations are building their own stable economies.

LESSON 4
Society and Culture
Some Central American nations have a long history of democracy. Others have struggled under dictators. The region is now becoming more democratic. All Central American governments are democracies today. But conditions relating to plantation-style farming and poor land distribution still exist.

Talk About It

1. Native Americans, Spanish, and Africans have all influenced the culture of Central America. Which do you think has influenced the culture most? Explain your answer.
2. Mexico and Central America had different hacienda systems. Which do you think had the greater lasting influence? Explain.
3. Of the three nations—Costa Rica, Guatemala, and Nicaragua—which would you prefer to visit? Explain your choice.
4. How does a celebration such as a fiesta patronal show both Spanish and Native American influences on Central American society?
5. The role of the Catholic Church in Central America has changed over the years. Which change do you think will be most beneficial to the future of Central America? Explain why.

Mastering Mapwork

Movement
Use the map on page 619 to answer these questions:

1. Which Central American capital city is located nearest 80°W?
2. Which Central American capital city is located nearest 10°N?
3. 90°W passes near which three Central American capital cities?
4. Describe the relative location of Belmopan.
5. Describe the relative location of the Panama Canal.

Becoming Better Readers

Taking a Test
When taking a test, good readers read slowly to be sure they understand the questions. Good readers look for key words that provide clues to the answers. Words like *best*, *except, least likely*, and *more likely* all provide clues to the test taker. Write a test question using one of these words. Do you see how the word changes the question?

Go to the Source

Panama Canal Statistics

An average of 40 vessels pass through the locks of the Panama Canal each day. Compare the information in the bar graph and the data about what type of ships carry cargo to the canal. Answer the questions below using specific information from the documents.

Vehicle Trips Through the Panama Canal*

1999	14,336
2000	13,653
2001	13,492
2002	13,183
2003	13,154

Most Important Cargo by Percentage—2003

Type of Cargo	Percentage
Containerized cargo (goods shipped in large containers)	24.9%
Grain	18.9%
Petroleum and petroleum products	8.6%

Questions

1. Which year had the most number of trips through the Panama Canal?
2. Which year had the least number of trips though the canal?
3. Is the number of trips through the canal each year increasing or decreasing?
4. What item is shipped the most in Panama Canal?
5. In 2003, which item made up 18.9 percent of all materials shipped in the canal?

*Source: 2001 and 2003 Annual Reports, Panama Canal Authority

Go to the Source

Sugar cane

The Caribbean Islands

In the sixteenth and seventeenth centuries, pirates used the islands of the Caribbean for their winter headquarters. Blackbeard often sailed between the coast of North Carolina and Port Royal, Jamaica.

The islands and the waters of the Caribbean have been the site of hundreds of encounters between pirates, European navies, merchants, and Native Americans. Naval battles, accidents, and storms caused many ships to sink. Millions of dollars of gold and silver from the mainland lie buried in shipwrecks beneath the Caribbean's waves.

But for the world's tables, the real treasure of the Caribbean has been sugarcane. Europeans brought it to the region from Asia. The Caribbean islands were an ideal place to grow sugarcane.

Chapter Preview

Carnival girl in Trinidad

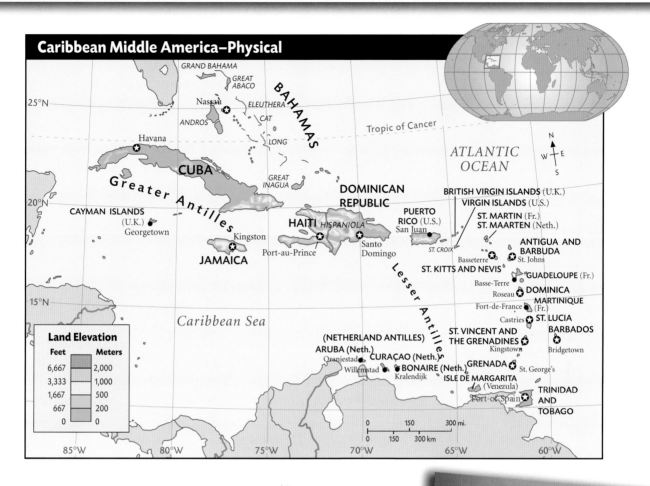

Caribbean Middle America–Physical

GRAND BAHAMA
GREAT ABACO
BAHAMAS
Nassau
ELEUTHERA
ANDROS
CAT
25°N
Tropic of Cancer
Havana
LONG
CUBA
ATLANTIC OCEAN
Greater Antilles
GREAT INAGUA
DOMINICAN REPUBLIC
BRITISH VIRGIN ISLANDS (U.K.)
VIRGIN ISLANDS (U.S.)
20°N
CAYMAN ISLANDS (U.K.)
Georgetown
PUERTO RICO (U.S.)
San Juan
ST. MARTIN (Fr.)
ST. MAARTEN (Neth.)
HAITI HISPANIOLA
Kingston
Port-au-Prince
Santo Domingo
ST. CROIX
ANTIGUA AND BARBUDA
St. Johns
JAMAICA
Basseterre
ST. KITTS AND NEVIS
GUADELOUPE (Fr.)
Basse-Terre
DOMINICA
Roseau
MARTINIQUE
Fort-de-France
(Fr.)
15°N
Caribbean Sea
Lesser Antilles
Castries
ST. LUCIA
BARBADOS

Land Elevation

Feet	Meters
6,667	2,000
3,333	1,000
1,667	500
667	200
0	0

ST. VINCENT AND THE GRENADINES
Kingstown
Bridgetown
(NETHERLAND ANTILLES)
ARUBA (Neth.)
Oranjestad
CURAÇAO (Neth.)
Willemstad
BONAIRE (Neth.)
Kralendijk
GRENADA
St. George's
ISLE DE MARGARITA (Venezula)
TRINIDAD AND TOBAGO
Port-of-Spain

0   150   300 mi.
0   150   300 km

85°W   80°W   75°W   70°W   65°W   60°W

Hurricanes

Occasionally a major hurricane hits the North Carolina coast. Many hurricanes gain strength in the warm Caribbean Sea after forming off the coast of Africa. Some come ashore on the islands in the Caribbean.

In 1996, Hurricane Fran first skirted north of Cuba and brushed the Bahamas. In 1999, Hurricane Floyd blew through the Bahamas but managed to miss most of the other Caribbean islands. In 2003, Hurricane Isabel passed Caribbean islands but created a new inlet near Cape Hatteras.

COUNTRIES
of the Caribbean

- Antigua and Barbuda
- Bahamas
- Barbados
- Cuba
- Dominica
- Dominican Republic
- Grenada
- Haiti
- Jamaica
- St. Kitts and Nevis
- St Lucia
- St. Vincent and the Grenadines
- Trinidad and Tobago

647

LESSON ① Land and People

KEY IDEAS

- The Caribbean contains three island groups: the Bahamas, the Greater Antilles, and the Lesser Antilles.

- The Caribbean climate is warm all year, with dry and rainy seasons.

- Hurricanes can bring destruction to the region.

- Tourism is an important industry in the Caribbean.

KEY TERMS

asphalt
bauxite
leeward
trade winds
windward

The Caribbean Islands lie between the Atlantic Ocean and the Caribbean Sea (see map, page 647). The islands spread out in a curve. The northern end of the curve is near the coast of southern Florida. The curve stretches southeast to the islands of Trinidad and Tobago. These two islands are very close to the northern coast of South America.

Location and Landforms

The island at the western tip of this curve is Cuba. It points into the Gulf of Mexico at 85°W. Barbados is the most eastern island at 59°W. The most northern island in the region is in the Bahamas at 28°N. The most southern island nation is Trinidad and Tobago at 10°N.

Some of the islands are much larger than the others. The largest is Cuba. The next largest is Hispaniola. Puerto Rico is followed by Jamaica.

But even the largest island is much smaller than North Carolina. Cuba would fit within North Carolina with about 8,000 square miles (20,800 sq km) left over.

Other islands, such as Dominica and St. Kitts and Nevis, are tiny specks of land. Some measure only a few square miles. All the rest of the Caribbean islands together would fit inside of Cuba with room left over!

The Bahamas are in the northern area of the Caribbean Sea. **What is the largest Caribbean island?**

Many islands in the Caribbean have volcanoes. These on St. Lucia are dormant. **What two nations share one island?**

Three Island Groups

The Caribbean Sea contains three sets of islands. To the north lie the Bahamas. Farthest to the west lie the Greater Antilles. To the southeast lie the Lesser Antilles.

The Bahamas to the north are made up of about 700 islands. Only two islands have large populations. They are called Grand Bahama and New Providence. The Bahamas are warmed by the Gulf Stream. They share the tropical climate of the islands to the south.

South of the Bahamas is the group of islands called the Greater Antilles. These are the largest islands in the Caribbean. They include Jamaica, Cuba, Puerto Rico, and Hispaniola. The two countries of Haiti and the Dominican Republic share the island of Hispaniola. The French colonized Haiti. The Dominican Republic was a colony of Spain.

The third group is the Lesser Antilles. These islands extend east from Puerto Rico. Then they curve southeast to the coast of Venezuela in South America. They include the U.S. Virgin Islands, the British Virgin Islands; St. Martin/St. Maarten, St. Christopher (St. Kitts) and Nevis, Antigua and Barbados, St. Vincent and the Grenadines, and Grenada.

Trinidad and Tobago are two islands. Together they form one country. That is also true of St. Kitts and Nevis, as well as Antigua and Barbuda.

Curving around westward are the Netherlands Antilles. They are made up of the three islands of Aruba, Bonaire, and Curaçao. These islands are sometimes called the "ABC" islands. These three islands still maintain a close relationship with the Netherlands. The Netherlands cares for their defense and foreign relations.

The Caribbean Islands

Palm trees of many varieties grow on Caribbean Islands. Some palms have thin, needle-like leaves. Other palms have broad, fan-shaped leaves. **On what side of an island do you think the broad-leafed palms grow? the needlelike palms?**

Climate and Plant Life

Most of the Caribbean Islands are south of the Tropic of Cancer. The weather stays warm all year. Instead of being either cold or warm, the seasons are either rainy or dry. Most places in the islands never have chilly temperatures. Rainfall is heavy, especially from April to December.

Because the islands are warm year-round, farmers are able to harvest several crops a year. Sugarcane, bananas, coffee, and spices are grown on large plantations. Other farmers raise corn, beans, squash, and peppers on smaller plots of land.

Many plants and trees that grow on the Caribbean Islands have wide and heavy leaves. This helps them absorb large amounts of rain and sunshine. Tall palm trees line the streets of many Caribbean towns and villages.

Parrots are endangered species in the Caribbean. **How do you think they should be protected?**

Brightly colored birds fly from tree to tree.

Many of islands in the Caribbean are volcanic. Many have mountains. On some, there is little flat land to farm.

As you learned in Chapter 3, elevation affects the climate. The tops of these mountains are cool. Farmers make good use of the cooler climate and fertile soil of the hillsides.

Trade Winds

Winds blowing toward the Caribbean Islands from the northeast are called *trade winds.* European sailors gave them that name many years ago. These winds filled the sails of ships traveling from Europe.

Columbus reached the Caribbean by first sailing south to the Canary Islands. They are a small group of islands owned by Spain off the coast of Africa. From there he turned west and picked up the trade winds. They carried him across the Atlantic Ocean.

Ships driven by engines do not need those winds today. Yet trade winds remain important. They keep steady breezes blowing over many of the Caribbean islands. This cools the tropical heat and makes the islands pleasant to live on or to visit.

Trade winds also pick up moisture as they blow over ocean water. Islands located in the path of the trade winds are called the Windward Islands. They receive rainfall during most of the year. Vegetation on these islands is thick and green all the time.

High mountains divide some of these Windward Islands. Do you remember reading about the rain shadow effect in Chapter 3?

The mountains cause the rain shadow effect on the islands. They act as a block to the winds. Most of the rain falls on the *windward* side. That is the side that the winds first hit.

The opposite side is called the *leeward* side. On the leeward side little or no rain falls. Desert scrub plants and palm trees with needlelike leaves grow there. Some islands receive so little rainfall that food must be imported.

Hurricanes

The sea brings food and money. The sea also creates the conditions that form powerful hurricanes. The word hurricane is the name Native Americans gave to these storms.

Tropical storms develop in the Atlantic Ocean off the coast of Africa during the summer. They often move west across the Atlantic and into the Caribbean Sea. The warm water of the Caribbean feeds the dangerous storms.

The storms build strong winds. The high speed of the wind destroys life and property. An average hurricane measures about 250 miles (403 km) across. Its winds blow from 75 to 150 miles (121 to 242 km) an hour.

Hurricanes drive the level of the ocean up as they approach the coastline. This is called the storm surge. Waves get higher and higher as the storm gets closer. The storm surge floods coasts and small, low islands. This causes even more damage than high winds.

Many of these storms stay in the Caribbean. They pound islands and the mainland of Middle America and the United States. Sometimes they turn northward and move out of the Caribbean. They move along the Atlantic coast of North America. Sometimes they strike North Carolina.

Weather forecasters today can often predict the paths of these storms. This cuts the loss of life. People can take shelter or move out of a storm's path.

Customs

From December through January 6, Puerto Ricans celebrate what is called *Parrandas Navideñas,* a kind of surprise Christmas caroling. A family goes to the house of another family. They play music or sing Christmas carols. Soon the other family invites the group in. After they visit for about an hour, the two families go to another house of a relative or friend.

Hurricane Michelle hit the Bahamas in November 2001. **What causes the most damage during a hurricane?**

Many cruise ships stop in the harbor of Charlotte Amalie, St. Thomas, U.S. Virgin Islands. **How many tourists visit the Caribbean each year?**

Tourism

The waters surrounding the islands of the Caribbean are an important resource for the people.

The sea has always been a source of food. The sea now brings tourists to the Caribbean. Tourists love to swim in the sparkling saltwater and walk along the clean, sandy beaches.

There are beautiful coral reefs in the Caribbean. Tourists who enjoy adventure scuba dive and snorkel there.

More than 25 million people vacation in the Caribbean every year. Many arrive aboard cruise ships that sail among the islands. Visitors from around the world spend money. This helps support the Caribbean nations' economies.

After 1950, tourism became the way most people earned money in the Caribbean. It is particularly important on islands where farming is difficult or impossible. Many Caribbean islanders work in hotels, restaurants, and shops that serve tourists.

Coral Reefs

Coral reefs are spectacular, living marine ecosystems. Reefs are built up over many years from the skeletons of dead coral. Coral reefs are a habitat for many kinds of sea life. They also help the Caribbean economy. The animals that live on the reef are a source of food. Reef tourism provides jobs. The reefs also help protect the coastline from storms.

Scientists studying coral reefs have found that reefs all over the world have been rapidly declining. Many of the problems coral reefs face are caused by humans. These problems combine with natural events such as hurricanes, high water temperature, and disease to stress corals and hurt or destroy reef habitats.

Puerto Rico is surrounded by over 3,107 miles (5,000 km) of coral reef ecosystems (below). However, the island's high population density, pollution, overfishing, and other factors have hurt the reefs. The United States government and the other organizations are working to save and protect the coral reefs of Puerto Rico.

A bauxite mine in Jamaica provides the mineral to make aluminum. There are a few other minerals in the Caribbean. **What important mineral is refined in the Caribbean but is found in nearby South America?**

Other Resources

Few minerals have been found in the Caribbean Islands. Trinidad mines and exports asphalt. *Asphalt* is a black, sticky material that is used to pave roads. Pitch Lake is one of that island's most famous sights. It is a reservoir of black tar. During colonial times, this natural material was used to coat the hulls of ships.

In Jamaica a large deposit of bauxite was found. *Bauxite* is the mineral from which aluminum is made. Huge shovels scoop the ore from open pit mines. It is loaded into train cars and taken to port. From there the ore is shipped to the United States and Canada.

Bauxite is Jamaica's most important export. The United States and Canada buy most of their bauxite supplies from Jamaica.

Oil is refined on several islands. Antigua and Barbuda, Aruba and Curaçao, and Trinidad and Tobago ship petroleum products to world markets. Some oil is found in these islands. Most of the petroleum refined there comes from nearby South American oil fields.

Most metals and other industrial raw materials are brought to the Caribbean from other places. Mexico provides much of the raw materials for the small amount of Caribbean manufacturing.

LESSON 1 REVIEW

Fact Follow-Up
1. Describe the relative location of the Caribbean Islands.
2. What are the largest of islands?
3. What is the importance of the trade winds for the Caribbean Islands?
4. What is the importance of tourism?

Talk About It
1. Why did pirates make use of the Caribbean Islands in the sixteenth and seventeenth centuries?
2. Describe how the climate can be both a benefit and a hazard for the Caribbean Islands.

The Caribbean Islands

The Caribbean Islands are a meeting ground. People from many backgrounds have settled there. Descendants of Native Americans, such as the Caribs and the Tainos, have mixed with people from Africa, Spain, Portugal, France, the United Kingdom, the Netherlands, Asia, and India. They have formed unique combinations of culture, language, cooking, and music.

Many Peoples

People from across the world have influenced the farming, building, government, and religion of the Caribbean. When thinking about these islands, we must remember that each one is unique.

Native Americans

Tainos and the Caribs were two of the most numerous Native American groups in the Caribbean when Europeans arrived. Under the Spanish, many Native Americans died from disease, overwork, and starvation. Some survivors from both groups mixed with Europeans and Africans.

Tainos were the first Native Americans to be incorrectly called "Indians" by Columbus. As you read in Chapter 5, he believed that he had reached Asia's East Indies. The Tainos welcomed the Europeans and helped them survive. The Tainos introduced the hammock and tobacco to the Europeans. The word barbecue also comes from the Taino language.

Today, the Taino's descendants are found in many places in the Caribbean. They live in Cuba, Puerto Rico, the Dominican Republic, and the Virgin Islands.

The Caribs were another Native American group in the region. They came to the islands from South America. They traveled on canoes with sails. The Caribs arrived around the same time as the Spanish.

The Spanish and the English accused the Caribs of being cannibals. Cannibals are people who eat human flesh. There is little evidence that this was true. But this claim was used as an excuse to attack and enslave the Caribs.

Today, about 3,000 Caribs live on the island of Dominica. Their ancestry is mixed with that of Europeans and Africans.

This eighteenth century engraving of a Carib Indian of the Antilles shows what Caribbean Native Americans looked like when the Europeans arrived.
Where can you find descendants of the Caribs?

These two Carib girls are wearing their school uniforms. They live on Dominica. **Why are most people in the Caribbean today of African descent?**

African Heritage

Most people in the Caribbean have African ancestors. Spain brought Africans to the Caribbean as slaves as early as 1502. Africans were brought to replace Native Americans who had died or escaped into the mountains of the islands. The Africans served as builders and craftsmen. They also fished and farmed.

Just three years after Africans arrived on the island of Hispaniola, there was a huge slave rebellion. Native Americans and Africans joined forces against their Spanish masters.

Many escaped to live in the mountains, forests, and swamps. Some went to Cuba or Puerto Rico. Others made it to Jamaica and the smaller islands. In these safe havens, African culture survived. It blended with Native American ways of life.

Today, Afro-Caribbean culture is rich all over the Caribbean. In every Caribbean nation the food, music, and traditions are very much based on African culture.

Spanish Heritage

The first Spanish ships brought soldiers, priests, and craftspeople to the colony. Later they brought tools, seeds, livestock, and other items to run a colony.

The Spanish laid the first claims to most of the Caribbean islands. The first to gain independence from Spain was the Dominican Republic. As you read in Chapter 11, Cuba and Puerto Rico remained colonies until the Spanish–American War.

Cuba gained independence from Spain in that war. But it came under United States supervision. The United States took possession of Puerto Rico. It is still a territory of the United States. Spanish influence remains strong in language, law, architecture, and religion.

Spain wanted colonies that supplied gold and silver. Very little of these metals were found in the Caribbean. Mexico, however, filled ship after ship with treasures bound for Spain. To reach Spain the ships had to sail through the Caribbean.

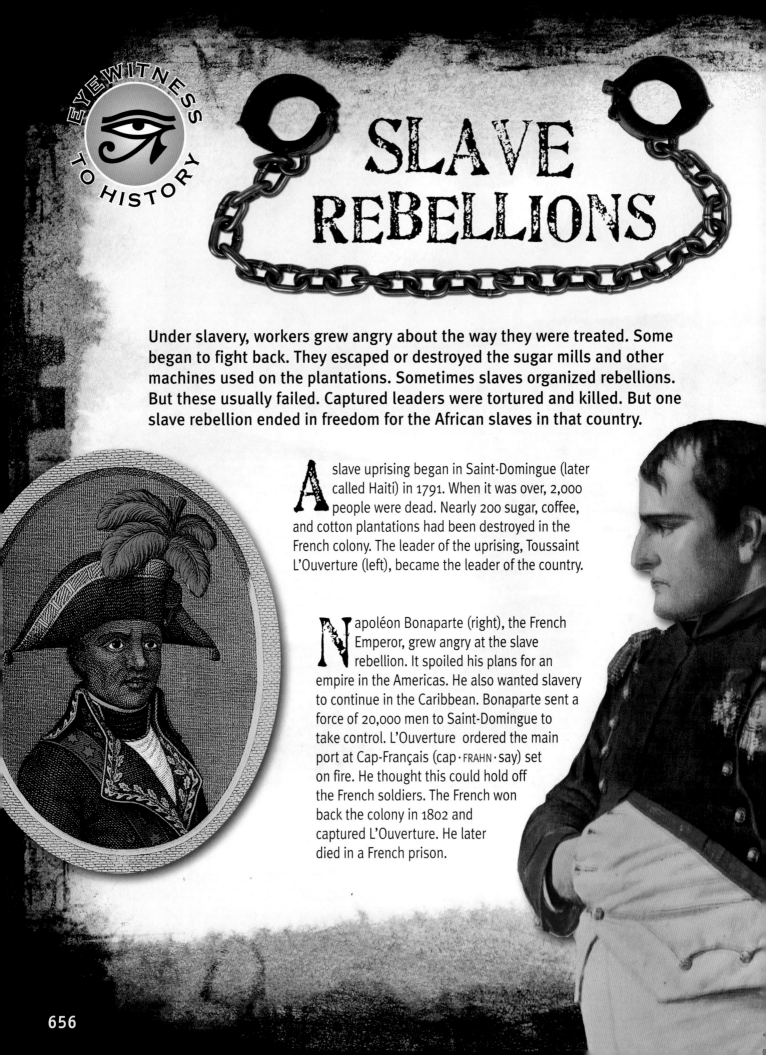

SLAVE REBELLIONS

Under slavery, workers grew angry about the way they were treated. Some began to fight back. They escaped or destroyed the sugar mills and other machines used on the plantations. Sometimes slaves organized rebellions. But these usually failed. Captured leaders were tortured and killed. But one slave rebellion ended in freedom for the African slaves in that country.

A slave uprising began in Saint-Domingue (later called Haiti) in 1791. When it was over, 2,000 people were dead. Nearly 200 sugar, coffee, and cotton plantations had been destroyed in the French colony. The leader of the uprising, Toussaint L'Ouverture (left), became the leader of the country.

Napoléon Bonaparte (right), the French Emperor, grew angry at the slave rebellion. It spoiled his plans for an empire in the Americas. He also wanted slavery to continue in the Caribbean. Bonaparte sent a force of 20,000 men to Saint-Domingue to take control. L'Ouverture ordered the main port at Cap-Français (cap·FRAHN·say) set on fire. He thought this could hold off the French soldiers. The French won back the colony in 1802 and captured L'Ouverture. He later died in a French prison.

The French tried to reestablish slavery but failed. Slaves continued their struggle. At this point, British and Spanish troops invaded the island. These European powers also were against slaves taking over a country.

An army of freed slaves and native-born mulattoes (people of mixed European and African heritage) formed. Jean-Jacques Dessalines led the group. They finally won independence in 1804 after years of fighting. The leaders did not want the name Saint-Domingue. They renamed their new country a native word, Haiti. It means "land of the mountains."

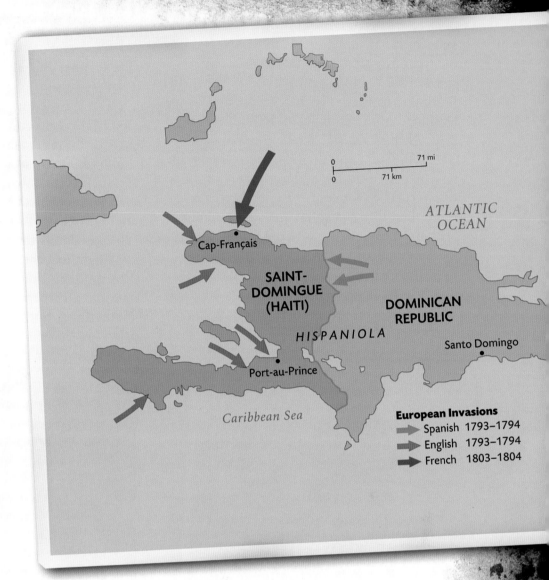

ATLANTIC OCEAN

Cap-Français

SAINT-DOMINGUE (HAITI)

DOMINICAN REPUBLIC

HISPANIOLA

Santo Domingo

Port-au-Prince

Caribbean Sea

71 mi
71 km

European Invasions
➤ Spanish 1793–1794
➤ English 1793–1794
➤ French 1803–1804

Soon after the victory, abolitionists began a movement to free slave workers in Middle America. Abolitionists called slavery brutal and barbaric. They tried hard for many years to end it. They first succeeded in 1833. The United Kingdom ended slavery in its Caribbean colonies. Soon after, the French and the Dutch colonies abolished slavery. Spain ended slavery in its colonies last. By 1886 freedom had come to all slaves on the Caribbean Islands.

Spain's Legacy

To guard these treasure ships, the Spanish built fortresses. They built them in the best and safest harbors in the Caribbean. There the treasure ships could be repaired and stocked for the long journey to Europe. San Juan, Puerto Rico; Havana, Cuba; and Santo Domingo in the Dominican Republic were three of the most important colonial ports.

Both Cuba and the Dominican Republic have experienced the Spanish legacy of the *caudillo*. The Dominican Republic was ruled more than thirty years by the strongman Rafael Trujillo. Cuba suffered under the dictatorships of Gerardo Machado and Fulgencio Batista. Cuba today is ruled by another strongman, Fidel Castro.

This turret is part of El Morro Fort, built by the Spanish in Puerto Rico. **When did Puerto Rico gain independence from Spain?**

Other European Influences

France, the Netherlands, and England colonized some Caribbean islands. In the late 1500s, Spain's power in Europe weakened. These other European nations began to slowly take possession of Spanish territories.

During its war for independence from Spain, the Netherlands seized the islands of Aruba, Bonaire, and Curaçao. It also took some of Spain's other islands. Denmark controlled the other Virgin Islands for a time, before the United States came to govern them in 1917. Great Britain gained some of the Virigin Islands from the Dutch.

Spain lost the islands of Guadeloupe and Martinique to the French in 1635. Haiti became a French colony in 1677. The Netherlands and France share ownership of the island of St. Martin (which the Netherlands call St. Maarten) in the Lesser Antilles.

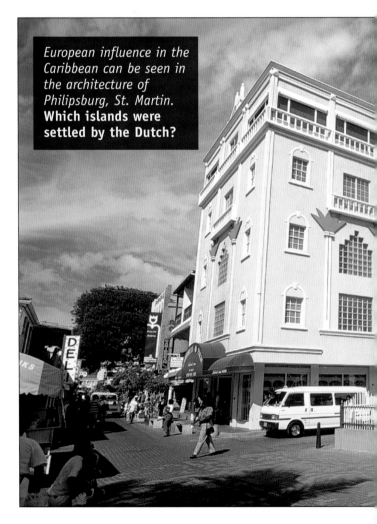

European influence in the Caribbean can be seen in the architecture of Philipsburg, St. Martin. **Which islands were settled by the Dutch?**

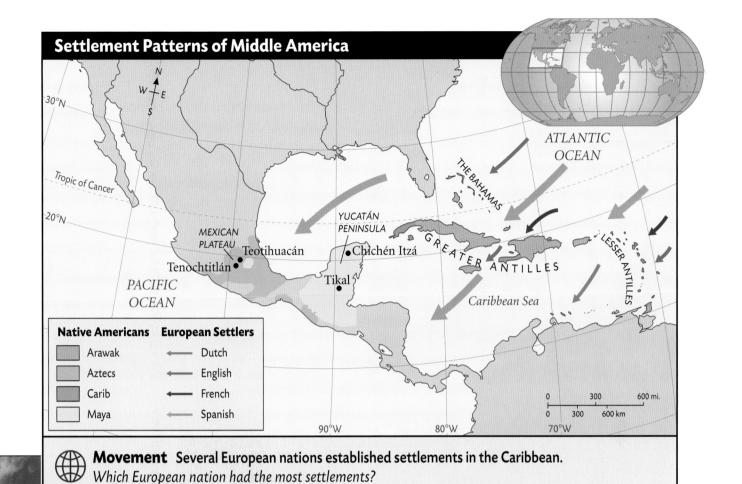

Settlement Patterns of Middle America

Native Americans
- Arawak
- Aztecs
- Carib
- Maya

European Settlers
- Dutch
- English
- French
- Spanish

30°N
Tropic of Cancer
20°N

ATLANTIC OCEAN

THE BAHAMAS
GREATER ANTILLES
LESSER ANTILLES

MEXICAN PLATEAU
YUCATÁN PENINSULA
• Teotihuacán
• Tenochtitlán
• Chichén Itzá
• Tikal
PACIFIC OCEAN
Caribbean Sea

0   300   600 mi.
0   300   600 km

90°W   80°W   70°W

Movement Several European nations established settlements in the Caribbean. *Which European nation had the most settlements?*

The English settled the uninhabited islands of Barbados and St. Kitts-Nevis in the early 1600s. Between 1647 and 1802, they took control of the Bahamas, Jamaica, St. Vincent, and Trinidad and Tobago.

The Environment

Each group of Europeans brought its own way of life to the Caribbean. Yet, like the Spanish, they found that the tropical environment changed their food and housing.

Plantations

Throughout the Caribbean, Europeans started plantations to grow sugar, cotton, and coffee. At first the Spanish used Native Americans to search for gold. After gold supplies ran out and Native Americans died, they turned quickly to plantations and sugar production.

The Caribbean Islands

The Spanish already knew that operating plantations with slave labor would make money. They had operated plantations on islands near the African coast. The other Europeans hoped to repeat Spain's success.

Plantations were Europe's most important way of changing the Caribbean environment. Many plantations are there still. Sugar grows in lowland areas. Coffee is raised at higher elevations. Cuba and Puerto Rico grow sugar. Hispaniola and Jamaica's high hills produce coffee.

These farmers are loading harvested sugarcane onto trucks on a plantation in San Germán, Puerto Rico. **What has been the cost of development in the Caribbean?**

Challenges

The system of plantation agriculture has sometimes damaged the Caribbean's land. Soil erodes quickly when it is over planted. It is also lost when trees are cut down and not replaced.

In Haiti, people suffer great poverty. They have had long years of undemocratic government. To survive, people cut down trees for fuel and building homes. There is now a huge problem with deforestation. Thousands of acres of land have become useless.

Humans changed the environment in other parts of the Caribbean. Wherever mining and industry developed, the land, water, and air became polluted. The bauxite mines of Jamaica and the oil refineries of Trinidad bring jobs to those places. But those areas have a hard time keeping the air, water, and land clean.

What would YOU do?

Imagine that your father is a Spanish plantation owner in the Caribbean during colonial times. He thinks he treats the workers well, but you see that the plantation system is unjust. Would you leave your comfortable home and try to change the system?

LESSON 2 REVIEW

Fact Follow-Up
1. What were the most numerous Native American groups when the Spanish arrived in the Caribbean?
2. What is the most numerous population group in the Caribbean today?
3. What were the three most important fortified ports during colonial times?

Talk About It
1. Why did the Spanish import African slaves to the Caribbean islands?
2. Why were plantations important? How did they change the landscape?
3. How did the Caribbean Islands become important ports? How did the Spanish use the ports?

LESSON ③ Economy and Government

Many people from North Carolina and around the world vacation in the Caribbean. You may know people who went there on their honeymoon. Before tourism, farming was the most important industry. Farmers grew mainly sugar, coffee, and tobacco. Today, both farming and tourism are important to the livelihoods of the people of many of the islands.

KEY IDEAS

- Plantation agriculture brought hardships to the Caribbean.

- Cuba's Castro led a revolution but has not allowed free elections.

- Deforestation and erosion are problems in Haiti. Trinidad and Tobago has a successful economy.

The Sugar Economy

Christopher Columbus brought sugar to Hispaniola in 1493. The crop grew well there. But it was over a hundred years before there was a strong demand for sugar in Europe. That happened when Europeans began to enjoy drinking coffee and chocolate.

By the 1600s, sugarcane plantations began to spring up across the Caribbean. Growing sugar required a huge investment. Large plots of land had to be cleared and planted. Mills had to be built to process the sugar. Storehouses and transportation were needed.

Sugar also needed many hands to harvest it. Turning the sugarcane into a finished product was hard work. The Native American population was too small. Therefore, Africans were brought to the Caribbean. They were enslaved to do the work.

The cane was cut during the dry season, between January and May. It was crushed in a mill. The juice left from the crushing was boiled in a huge vat. After the liquid sugar cooled, it became either molasses or sugar crystals. Rum was made from molasses. The sugar crystals were packed in great barrels and shipped to Europe.

These people are harvesting sugarcane on Guadaloupe in 1905. **Why did it take 100 years for the sugar industry to develop?**

Governments and *Caudillos*

Plantation farming has sometimes led to undemocratic rule by governments in the Caribbean. Plantation owners supported governments headed by dictators. In return, the dictator helped owners pay little for land and labor. Workers stayed poor. The owner did not have to increase wages or improve the workers' living conditions.

As in Central America, dictators and plantation owners in Caribbean nations formed alliances. These often resulted in brutal dictators coming to power. *Caudillos* and military dictators have ruled a number of Caribbean islands. They were helped by a few rich countrymen and foreign companies.

The Caribbean Islands

661

A Tale of Three Countries

Some islands have continued close relationships with their former colonial masters. In other places, moves have been made to bring democracy. In Cuba, however, the government went yet another way.

Cuba

Cuba is the largest island in the Caribbean. It has a blend of Spanish and African heritage. More than half of the Cuban population is descended from both African and European ancestors.

Cuba remained a Spanish colony until 1898. The United States stepped into the Cuban war for independence (the Spanish-American War). After Spain lost, the United States ran the Cuban government for several decades. American forces were stationed there, too.

Sugar has always been the most important crop in Cuba. For years dictators and plantation owners worked together and shared the profits. These dictators ruled with the help of the Cuban army. Foreign companies were happy with the situation and supported the dictators.

Castro In 1959, a group of Communist guerrillas won a victory over the dictator, Fulgencio Batista. These guerrillas were led by Fidel Castro. Castro promised to distribute the wealth of Cuba more fairly. Many Cubans were tired of being ruled by dictators. They supported Castro and his ideas.

Castro's new government redistributed the land and wealth. Some Cubans did not agree with this. They fled the island. Many came to the United States.

Years passed. Castro continued to rule. He became an ally of the Soviet Union. This upset the Americans. Congress banned all trade with Cuba. But still Castro continued to rule.

A tour bus near a sugarcane field symbolizes Cuba's changing economy. **What has prevented tourism from growing in Cuba?**

Chapter 27

Colorful masks are a popular art form throughout the Caribbean. These are from Cuba. **In what way is Cuban culture similar to that of Central America?**

CARIBBEAN PORTRAIT

Fidel Castro
1926–

Fidel Castro became the absolute leader of Cuba after the revolution there in 1959. Long before the revolution, Castro was politically active while he was studied at the University of Havana in the 1940s. After his marriage, he began practicing law.

During the 1950s, he became more interested in communism. He became a champion of the poor and disadvantaged. At this same time, he began to publicly question the role of United States businesses in Latin America and Cuba. He gained popular support by calling attention to corruption and injustice in Fulgencio Batista's government. Castro led the rebels that forced Batista out in 1959.

Castro is a hero to some and a cruel dictator to others. He has dealt with all United States presidents since Eisenhower in the 1950s.

The most important event in American-Cuban relations was the Cuban Missile Crisis in 1962. You may remember reading about this in Chapter 12. President Kennedy threatened to use military force if Cuba and the Soviet Union did not remove nuclear weapons from Cuba. The missiles were removed. But Castro continued to oppose the United States.

With the fall of the Soviet Union in 1991, Cuba lost its greatest sponsor. Because of America's restrictions on trade with Cuba, the island nation is cut off from a great deal of trade. So Cuba's economy does not grow as quickly as other North American nations. Despite these hard economic times for Cuba, Castro's family today enjoys great wealth and privilege. These are some of the same things Castro fought against in the revolution.

The Caribbean Islands

Workers sift stones from a rice crop in Haiti. Rice is one of its staple foods. Deforestation has decreased the rice crop. It has hurt the soil and irrigation systems. **Who ruled Haiti from 1957 until 1986?**

Haiti

Haiti occupies the western portion of the island of Hispaniola. The Dominican Republic covers the eastern two thirds of the island. Haiti is one of the poorest countries in the world.

Haiti became a French colony in 1677. Haitians speak a form of French called creole. Haiti was the second European colony in the Western Hemisphere, after the United States, to win independence.

About 95 percent of the population is of purely African descent. The rest are of mixed African and European descent. But this small minority holds most of the important jobs in government and business.

About 70 percent of the people work in farming. There is a severe shortage of fertile land. Deforestation and erosion are major problems.

In the cities almost half the people have no work. For those with jobs, the pay often is not enough to survive.

Dictators In the years since independence, Haiti has seen a long line of dictators and unstable governments. During the nineteenth century there was much

unrest. United States Marines occupied the country from 1915 to 1934.

Between 1957 and 1971, François Duvalier ruled Haiti with the help of the military. His son, Jean-Claude Duvalier, ran the country from 1971 until he was overthrown in 1986. The Haitian military ruled the nation until elections were held in 1990.

The 1990 elections were won by a Roman Catholic priest, Jean-Bertrand Aristide. He promised to halt corruption. He wanted to end poverty and bring democracy to the people.

Wealthy business and land owners did not support Aristide. His government was overthrown in 1991. Once again the military ruled Haiti. The United States helped him regain the presidency. In 2000 Aristide was reelected president. But then four years later there was another uprising. Elections were supposed to be held in 2006, but were delayed. Only time will tell whether democracy will succeed in Haiti.

The Haitian economy is almost completely based on farming. Yet in recent years the sugar harvest has gone way down. Deforestation has spoiled the land. Because of the nation's instability, tourism is almost zero.

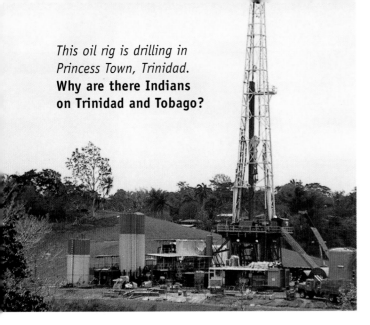

This oil rig is drilling in Princess Town, Trinidad.
Why are there Indians on Trinidad and Tobago?

Trinidad and Tobago

Trinidad and Tobago is one nation made up of two islands. The islands are located close to the coast of Venezuela. They lie in the southernmost part of the Caribbean. The capital is Port of Spain. It is on Trinidad.

Trinidad is larger and has a more ethnically diverse population. Most of the nation's industry is in Trinidad. Tobago has a much more easygoing pace. It attracts tourists because of its beautiful natural environment.

Columbus claimed Trinidad for Spain in 1498. Europeans did not settle there until 1592. Late in the 1700s, the Spanish king wanted more people to colonize Trinidad. He offered free land to any Roman Catholics who would settle there. Some French planters moved in and built sugar and cacao plantations.

In 1797, the British seized Trinidad. They seized Tobago in 1814. African slaves were brought in to work the plantations. Then in 1838, the United Kingdom outlawed slavery in its territories. So large numbers of laborers were brought to Trinidad from India. These Indians signed contracts to work for five years. After that time they could choose either 5 acres of free land or free passage home. Many stayed.

Multiculturalism Today, about 40 percent of the population of Trinidad and Tobago is Indian. People of African heritage make up another 40 percent. The remaining people are Europeans, Chinese, Southwest Asians, and South Americans. This makes the nation one of the most multicultural in the Caribbean.

Trinidad and Tobago has one of the most successful economies in the region. This is partly due to its supply of oil and natural gas.

The islands gained their independence from the United Kingdom in 1962. It became a member of the British Commonwealth in 1976. Healthcare and education are generally available to most of the population. There were some problems with the military in the early 1990s. Overall, the democratic government is stable.

LESSON 3 REVIEW

Fact Follow-Up
1. What was the basis of the Caribbean economy before tourism became important?
2. What guerrilla leader came to power in Cuba in 1959? What strongman did he replace?
3. What measures does the United States government take against Cuba? What are the effects of these measures?

Talk About It
1. Which of these nations, Cuba or Haiti, do you think has greater chance of economic success? Explain why.
2. How did Trinidad and Tobago become one of the most multicultural nations in the Caribbean?

The Caribbean Islands

KEY IDEAS

- The culture of the Caribbean is very diverse.

- Caribbean food is a mixture of African, European, and local ingredients.

- Afro-Carribbean music includes reggae, steelpan, and calypso.

- The people of the Caribbean enjoy water sports, baseball, and cricket.

KEY TERMS

calypso
Carnival
Lent
Mardi Gras
reggae
steelpan

People from many places in the world have come to live in the Caribbean. The culture there is diverse. There is great variety in religious customs, food, music, and recreation. Many languages are spoken. The Caribbean is a crossroads of world culture.

The people of the Caribbean have taken contributions of Africa and Europe, Asia and the Americas. They have created distinct societies and cultures on their islands. The roots of Caribbean culture lie in North and South America, Spain, Portugal, England, France, the Netherlands, Africa, and Asia. There is no one true Caribbean culture. But all of the islands show a common African thread in their societies.

Food

Food in the Caribbean will often be a combination of European and African recipes and local ingredients. Seafood is always available, since they are surrounded by the ocean. Lobster and crab are the base of many dishes. So are octopus and clams. Native fruits are important to the Caribbean diet. Have you ever eaten a guava, mango, or plantain?

Religion

Religion plays a big role in people's lives in the Caribbean. Roman Catholicism is a powerful force. This faith came mostly with settlers from France and Spain.

Unlike Central America and Mexico, Catholicism is not the only major religion. There are many followers of Protestant Christian religions. Many are in the former British colonies. On some islands there are also followers of African religions.

A Catholic priest leads an outdoor mass in the Dominican Republic. **In what way is the religious tradition in the Caribbean unlike Central America?**

Chapter 27

Carnival in the Caribbean

Not everyone is Roman Catholic. But Roman Catholicism has contributed the tradition of carnival to the entire region. Carnival (CAR·nih·vahl) is a winter festival. In some places it begins on January 6 and ends about two months later.

The final celebration is on **Mardi Gras,** the day before Lent begins. **Lent** is a time of solemn prayer as Catholics prepare for Easter. The Carnival season is a time of many parties and parades before the quiet season of Lent.

Mardi Gras is the climax of carnival season. People dress in fancy costumes called *mas* (from the word masquerade). These costumes can take months to make and sew. People dressed as butterflies, dragons, and birds fill the streets. Bands play on floats pulled through the streets. Bystanders dance to the beats of Caribbean music.

French Catholic settlers brought the tradition of Carnival to the island of Trinidad. There, clubs called "mas camps"

These children are celebrating carnival in the streets of Jacmel, Haiti. **When is Carnival celebrated?**

work together. They create costumes with the same theme. The mas camps perform their street dances as if they were on stage.

In the days leading up to the parades, bands compete in contests to find the best group. They compete in different categories. During the celebrations there are parties lasting late into the night.

WORD ORIGINS

Mardi Gras means "Fat Tuesday." The French words describe the day before the beginning of Lent. This day is the last time many Catholics enjoy meat and other rich foods before the 40 days of Lent.

Bob Marley of Jamaica made reggae music world famous. He spread Caribbean culture wherever he performed. **What other kinds of culture come from the Caribbean?**

Afro-Caribbean Music

Long ago, Caribbean plantation owners tried to destroy the traditions of the African slaves. The owners wanted to control the slaves. They wanted to keep them from revolting. So plantation owners made the slave workers wear European clothing. They made them learn the language of the masters.

One way that the African people saved their culture was through their music. The music was based on complex drumming and other percussion instruments. The Africans made their own instruments. They continued to play music that came from their African heritage. They kept alive their sacred African rhythms.

Reggae and Steelpan

Today, Jamaica is known as a center of *reggae* music. The strong, steady African beats and chanted words of reggae are popular in the Caribbean. In other parts of the Caribbean, *steelpan* music is a favorite. Steelpan musicians make their music on oil drums that have been hammered into shiny, rounded bowls.

Calypso

Calypso is also another type of music that was invented in the Caribbean. Calypso is distinctive because of the lyrics rather than the instruments played. In one type of calypso, called picong, the words are made up on stage. They usually tease a well-known person or even someone in the audience. Calypso songs even mock local politicians.

In some ways, calypso may be considered an ancestor to rap music.

The Caribbean has also given the world some of the most popular types of dance music and dance. *Mambo*, *merengue*, and the *limbo* were created in the Caribbean. People all over the world learn these dances.

Sports in the Caribbean

Beaches and clear blue water offer the people of the Caribbean opportunities for fun. Fishing, swimming, and sailing are popular pastimes. Caribbean people also enjoy sports brought to the island from other parts of the world.

Baseball

Baseball came from the United States. But it is even more popular in the Caribbean than in our country. If you are a baseball fan, you already know that many of the great players in our major leagues come from the Dominican Republic, Puerto Rico, and Cuba.

Sammy Sosa, the only baseball player to hit more than 60 home runs in back-to-back seasons, is from the Dominican Republic. Roberto Clemente, an outstanding Puerto Rican outfielder for the Pittsburgh Pirates, was elected to baseball's Hall of Fame in 1972.

Chapter 27

In all, there are regularly close to 100 players from the Caribbean playing major league baseball in a given season. Even the tiny islands of Curaçao and Aruba have sent players to the major leagues.

Today, major league teams from the United States run clinics and camps in places like the Dominican Republic. Baseball scouts go there to search for the next Sammy Sosa or Roberto Clemente. Often young boys see baseball as a way out of poverty.

Cricket

Cricket is a sport similar to baseball. It uses a ball and a bat. Cricket is mainly popular in former British colonies like Jamaica, Barbados, and Antigua. There cricket is followed with a passion, like college basketball is in North Carolina. Calling themselves the West Indies, the best players from the Caribbean team up. They challenge larger members of the British Commonwealth, including Australia, New Zealand, India, and Pakistan.

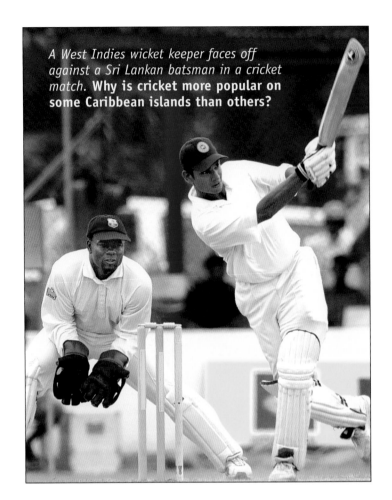

A West Indies wicket keeper faces off against a Sri Lankan batsman in a cricket match. **Why is cricket more popular on some Caribbean islands than others?**

CARIBBEAN PORTRAIT

Derek Walcott
1930–

Derek Walcott is the most important living Caribbean author. He won the Nobel Prize for Literature in 1992.

Walcott was born on the island of St. Lucia. His father was a painter who died when Derek was still quite young. He first attended St. Mary's College in St. Lucia. His mother was a teacher there. He got a love of poetry from his mother. He was soon very familiar with the great works of English literature. Walcott got a scholarship to study at the University College of the West Indies in Jamaica. He studied Latin, French, and Spanish.

He also started writing plays about European influence in Caribbean culture. Walcott moved to New York for a time, and then settled in Trinidad to teach and write. He later became a professor of poetry at Boston University.

Walcott is the author of more than twenty plays. He has been a central figure in Caribbean theater throughout his life. His plays often use the island music and storytelling traditions that form the core of Caribbean culture.

The Caribbean Islands

An Island of Historic Beauty

Imagine you are sailing into Saint Anna Bay harbor in Curaçao's capital city of Willemstad. The first thing you notice are the bright yellow, pink, and green Dutch row houses along the waterfront.

The city was recently added to the United Nations' World Heritage List for its history and beauty. It is home to Mikve Israel Synagogue. This is the oldest continuously used Jewish temple in the Western Hemisphere.

Curaçao is the largest island in the Netherlands Antilles. The island is dry. The land is covered with cactus and short divi-divi trees. These are twisted and bent by the constant ocean winds.

You can explore caves with ancient paintings. The crystal clear water is ideal for diving. Christoffel Park is perfect for a day of watching tropical birds.

The explorer Amerigo Vespucci landed on the island in 1499. He claimed it for Spain. The Spanish built very little on the island. In 1634, the Dutch seized Curaçao. The Dutch West India Company turned Curaçao into one of the main slave ports in the Caribbean.

People of Spanish, Portuguese, Dutch, and African origin came to Curaçao. While Dutch is the official language of the island, everyone speaks Papiamento. Papiamento is a new language. It is a blend of the various languages brought to the island by each wave of immigrants.

In 1918, Curaçao opened its first oil refinery. This industry brought prosperity to the island. Today the inhabitants have many more comforts than do most of their neighbors in the Caribbean.

LESSON 4 REVIEW

Fact Follow-Up
1. What is one common thread in the cultural makeup of Caribbean societies?
2. What is Carnival, and how does it end?
3. What are reggae, steelpan, and calypso?
4. Who are two great major-league baseball players native to the Caribbean?

Talk About It
1. Why can the Caribbean be said to be a crossroads of world cultures?
2. Why was music an important way enslaved Africans Africans preserved their culture?
3. What is your favorite part of Caribbean culture? Why?

Analyzing, Interpreting, Creating, and Using Resources and Materials

How Diverse is North America?

You have learned this year about many societies in North America, Central America, and the Caribbean. You have read about the word "diverse" just as many times. Do you remember studying diverse landforms and climates, diverse plant and animal life, diverse governments and national histories, and diverse peoples and traditions?

The United States has the most diversity in climate and landforms because of its large size. The states of Alaska and Hawaii also add to our country's diversity.

But of all the societies you have studied this year, which has the most diversity in its people and their lives? Here is information about five countries. This will help you begin to answer this question. What conclusions can you draw from this information?

*2006 CIA World Factbook
** U.S. Census Bureau, 2005 American Community Survey.

COUNTRIES	ETHNIC GROUPS	RELIGION	LANGUAGES
United States 300,500,000	White 74.7%, Hispanic** 12.1%, African American 12.1%, Asian 4.3%, Native Americans and Alaska Natives .8%, Native Hawaiian or Other Pacific Islander .1%, two or more races 1.9%	Protestant 52%, Roman Catholic 24%, Mormon 2%, Jewish 1%, Muslim 1%, other 10%, none 10%	English 82.1%, Spanish 10.7%, other Indo-European 3.8%, Asian and Pacific island 2.7%, other 0.7%
Canada* 33,098,932	British Isles origin 28%, French origin 23%, other European 15%, Amerindian 2%, other 6%, mixed 26%	Roman Catholic 42.6%, Protestant 23.3%, other Christian 4.4%, Muslim 1.9%, other 11.8%, none 16%	English (official) 59.3%, French (official) 23.2%, other 17.5%
Mexico* 107,449,525	*mestizo* (Amerindian-Spanish) 60%, Amerindian 30%, white 9%, other 1%	Roman Catholic 89%, Protestant 6%, other 5%	Spanish, various Maya, Nahuatl, and other regional indigeous languages
Costa Rica* 4,075,261	white (including mestizo) 94%, black 3%, Amerindian 1%, Chinese 1%, other 1%	Roman Catholic 76.3%, Evangelical 13.7%, Jehovah's Witnesses 1.3%, other Protestant 0.7%, other 4.8%, none 3.2%	Spanish (official), English
Haiti* 8,308,504	black 95%, mulatto and white 5%	Roman Catholic 80%, Protestant 16% (Note: roughly half the population practices Voodoo)	French (official), Creole (official)

Lessons Learned

LESSON 1
Land and People
The Caribbean Islands lie between southern Florida and the northern coast of South America. The three island groups are the Bahamas, the Greater Antilles, and the Lesser Antilles. The climate is warm all year, with dry and rainy seasons.

LESSON 2
People and Environment
Each island in the Caribbean is different, but all are diverse. Native Americans, Africans, and Europeans have all played a part in the history of the region. Their descendents live in the islands today.

LESSON 3
Economy and Government
Plantation agriculture brought slavery to the Caribbean. Sugar has been an important crop. Today's Caribbean economy depends on both agriculture and tourism. Since independence, many Caribbean nations have continued to struggle with poverty and injustice.

LESSON 4
Society and Culture
The Caribbean is a crossroads of world culture. Festivals, food, music, and sports combine many cultural influences in unique ways.

Talk About It

1. Has the sugar economy been a benefit or a burden for the people of the Caribbean? Explain.
2. If you could visit one place in the Caribbean, where would you choose to visit? Explain why.
3. Compare Fidel Castro with other such Caribbean strongmen as Trujillo, Duvalier, and Batista.
4. What resource of the Caribbean Islands do you think will be most important in the future? Explain why.
5. Europeans, especially the Spanish, brought many things with them when they conquered the Caribbean Islands. Which of these things do you think has had the most impact on the people living on the islands today? Explain why.

Mastering Mapwork

LOCATION
Use the map on page 647 to answer these questions:

1. The national capital of a Caribbean nation is located at 70°W. What is the capital, and what is the nation?
2. What national capital is located nearest the Tropic of Cancer?
3. The national capitals of two countries are located very near the northern coast of South America. What are the capitals, and what are the nations?
4. What national capital is located at 25°N?

Becoming Better Readers

What Good Readers Do
Congratulations! You have become a better reader this year. You have learned how to preview a chapter, how to look for main ideas, and how to find important details to support your main idea. What reading strategy do you use the most when reading a nonfiction text?

Go to the Source

Writing to Government Leaders

Fidel Castro wrote this letter to President Franklin Roosevelt on November 6, 1940. FDR had just been elected to a third term as President. Read Castro's letter below. Answer the questions using information from the letter.

My good friend Roosevelt I don't know very English but I know as much as to write to you. I like to hear the radio and I am very happy because I heard in it that you will be president for a new (periodo). I am twelve years old. I am a boy but I think very much but do not think that that I am writing the President of the United States.

If you like, give me a ten dollar bill green american, in the letter, because never I have not seen a ten dollar bill green american and I would like to have one of them.

My address is: Sr. Fidel Castro Colegio de Bolover Santiago de Cuba Oriente, Cuba

I don't know very English but I know very much Spanish and I suppose you don't know very Spanish but you know very English because you are American but I am not American.

Thank you very much, Good by. Your friend, Fidel Castro

If you want iron to make your ships I will show you the bigest [sic] mines of iron of the land. They are in Mayori, Oriente Cuba.

Questions

1. How old was Fidel Castro when he wrote this letter?
2. Was Fidel Castro supportive of Roosevelt?
3. What was the goal of Fidel Castro for writing this letter to President Roosevelt?
4. Based on the information in the letter, do you think Castro will keep a positive attitude toward the United States. Why?

Appendix

ATLAS

Atlas Key

United States Postal Abbreviations

State	Abbreviation	State	Abbreviation	State	Abbreviation	State	Abbreviation
Alabama	AL	Illinois	IL	Montana	MT	Rhode Island	RI
Alaska	AK	Indiana	IN	Nebraska	NE	South Carolina	SC
Arizona	AZ	Iowa	IA	Nevada	NV	South Dakota	SD
Arkansas	AR	Kansas	KS	New Hampshire	NH	Tennessee	TN
California	CA	Kentucky	KY	New Jersey	NJ	Texas	TX
Colorado	CO	Louisiana	LA	New Mexico	NM	Utah	UT
Connecticut	CT	Maine	ME	New York	NY	Vermont	VT
Delaware	DE	Maryland	MD	North Carolina	NC	Virginia	VA
Florida	FL	Massachusetts	MA	North Dakota	ND	Washington	WA
Georgia	GA	Michigan	MI	Ohio	OH	West Virginia	WV
Hawaii	HI	Minnesota	MN	Oklahoma	OK	Wisconsin	WI
Idaho	ID	Mississippi	MS	Oregon	OR	Wyoming	WY
		Missouri	MO	Pennsylvania	PA		

World–Political

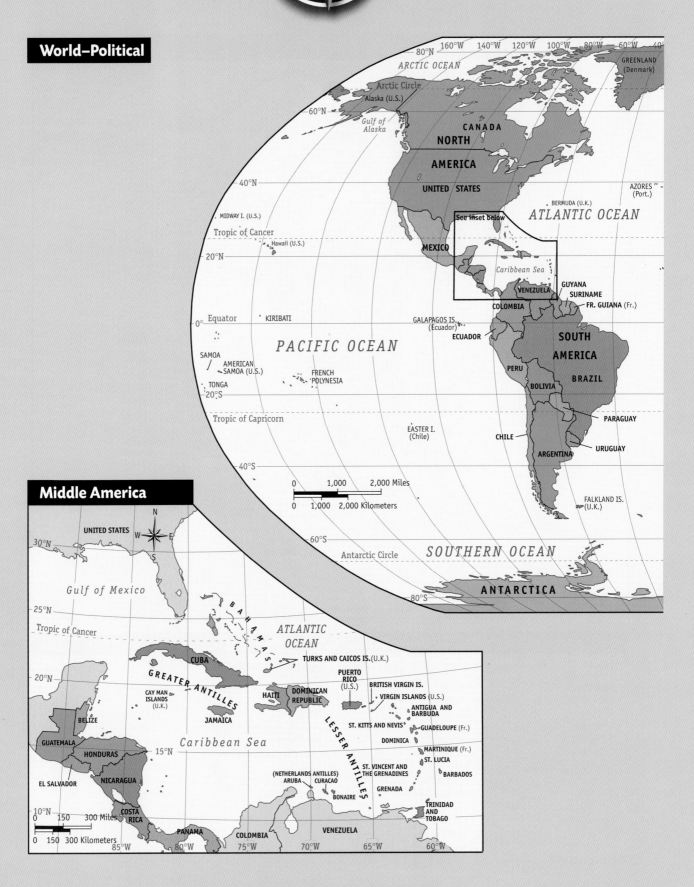

ARCTIC OCEAN

GREENLAND
(Denmark)

80°N

160°W 140°W 120°W 100°W 80°W 60°W 40°

Arctic Circle

Alaska (U.S.)

60°N

Gulf of
Alaska

CANADA

NORTH

AMERICA

40°N

UNITED STATES

AZORES
(Port.)

BERMUDA (U.K.)

ATLANTIC OCEAN

MIDWAY I. (U.S.)

See inset below

Tropic of Cancer

Hawaii (U.S.)

20°N

MEXICO

Caribbean Sea

VENEZUELA   GUYANA
             SURINAME
COLOMBIA   FR. GUIANA (Fr.)

Equator   KIRIBATI

0°

GALAPAGOS IS.
(Ecuador)

ECUADOR

SOUTH

AMERICA

PACIFIC OCEAN

SAMOA

AMERICAN
SAMOA (U.S.)

FRENCH
POLYNESIA

PERU

BRAZIL

BOLIVIA

TONGA

20°S

Tropic of Capricorn

EASTER I.
(Chile)

PARAGUAY

CHILE

URUGUAY

ARGENTINA

0   1,000   2,000 Miles

0   1,000   2,000 Kilometers

40°S

FALKLAND IS.
(U.K.)

60°S

SOUTHERN OCEAN

Antarctic Circle

80°S

ANTARCTICA

Middle America

N
W   E
S

UNITED STATES

30°N

Gulf of Mexico

25°N

Tropic of Cancer

BAHAMAS

ATLANTIC
OCEAN

CUBA

TURKS AND CAICOS IS. (U.K.)

20°N

GREATER ANTILLES

CAYMAN
ISLANDS
(U.K.)

HAITI

DOMINICAN
REPUBLIC

PUERTO
RICO
(U.S.)

BRITISH VIRGIN IS.

VIRGIN ISLANDS (U.S.)

ANTIGUA AND
BARBUDA

JAMAICA

BELIZE

ST. KITTS AND NEVIS

GUADELOUPE (Fr.)

GUATEMALA

Caribbean Sea

LESSER ANTILLES

DOMINICA

MARTINIQUE (Fr.)

HONDURAS

15°N

ST. LUCIA

EL SALVADOR

NICARAGUA

(NETHERLANDS ANTILLES)
ARUBA   CURACAO

ST. VINCENT AND
THE GRENADINES

BARBADOS

BONAIRE

GRENADA

COSTA
RICA

0   150   300 Miles

TRINIDAD
AND
TOBAGO

0   150   300 Kilometers

PANAMA

COLOMBIA

VENEZUELA

85°W   80°W   75°W   70°W   65°W   60°W

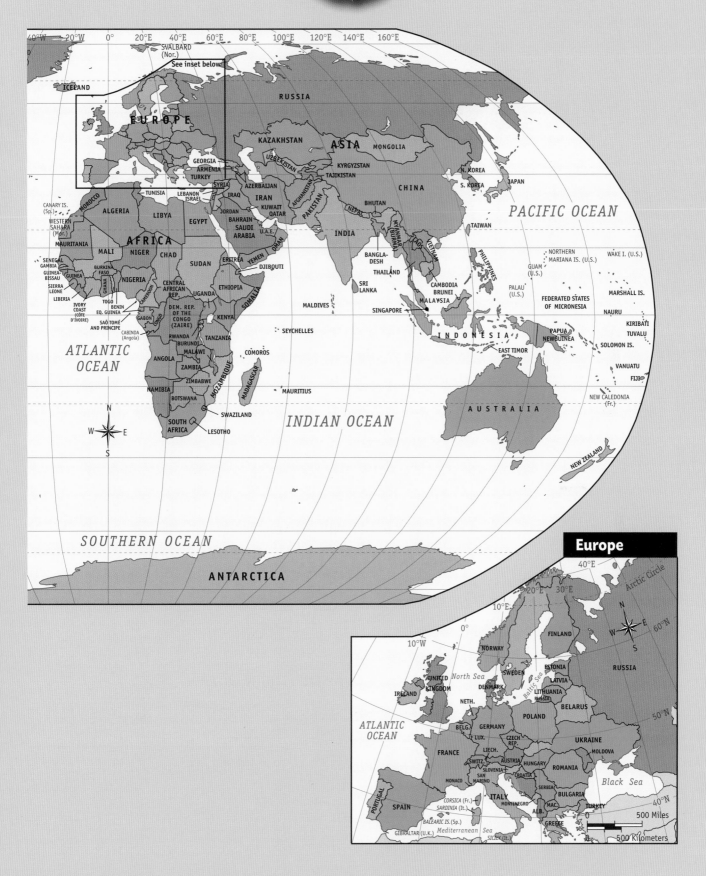

40°W 20°W 0° 20°E 40°E 60°E 80°E 100°E 120°E 140°E 160°E

SVALBARD
(Nor.)

See inset below

ICELAND

RUSSIA

EUROPE

ASIA

KAZAKHSTAN

MONGOLIA

GEORGIA
ARMENIA
TURKEY

UZBEKISTAN

KYRGYZSTAN

N. KOREA

TAJIKISTAN

S. KOREA JAPAN

CANARY IS.
(Sp.)

TUNISIA

SYRIA

LEBANON
ISRAEL

AZERBAIJAN

IRAQ

AFGHANISTAN

CHINA

MOROCCO

ALGERIA

LIBYA

IRAN

KUWAIT
QATAR

PAKISTAN

NEPAL

BHUTAN

TAIWAN

PACIFIC OCEAN

WESTERN
SAHARA
(Mor.)

EGYPT

BAHRAIN
SAUDI
ARABIA

U.A.E.

INDIA

MYANMAR
(BURMA)

MAURITANIA

AFRICA

MALI

NIGER

CHAD

SUDAN

OMAN

YEMEN

BANGLA-
DESH

LAOS

VIETNAM

NORTHERN
MARIANA IS. (U.S.)

WAKE I. (U.S.)

SENEGAL
GAMBIA
GUINEA-
BISSAU GUINEA

BURKINA
FASO

NIGERIA

ERITREA

DJIBOUTI

THAILAND

GUAM
(U.S.)

SIERRA
LEONE

GHANA

CENTRAL
AFRICAN
REP.

ETHIOPIA

UGANDA

SRI
LANKA

CAMBODIA
BRUNEI
MALAYSIA

PHILIPPINES

PALAU
(U.S.)

FEDERATED STATES
OF MICRONESIA

MARSHALL IS.

NAURU

LIBERIA

IVORY
COAST
(CÔTE
D'IVOIRE)

TOGO
BENIN
EQ. GUINEA

CAMEROON

GABON CONGO

DEM. REP.
OF THE
CONGO
(ZAIRE)

KENYA

SOMALIA

MALDIVES

SINGAPORE

INDONESIA

KIRIBATI

TUVALU

PAPUA
NEW GUINEA

SOLOMON IS.

SÃO TOMÉ
AND PRINCIPE

CABINDA
(Angola)

RWANDA
BURUNDI

TANZANIA

SEYCHELLES

ATLANTIC
OCEAN

ANGOLA

MALAWI

ZAMBIA

COMOROS

EAST TIMOR

VANUATU

FIJI

NEW CALEDONIA
(Fr.)

ZIMBABWE

MADAGASCAR

MAURITIUS

NAMIBIA

BOTSWANA

MOZAMBIQUE

INDIAN OCEAN

AUSTRALIA

N
W   E
S

SWAZILAND

SOUTH
AFRICA

LESOTHO

NEW ZEALAND

SOUTHERN OCEAN

ANTARCTICA

Europe

40°E

Arctic Circle

20°E 30°E

10°E

FINLAND

N
W   E
S

60°N

NORWAY

10°W

ESTONIA

SWEDEN

RUSSIA

North Sea

Baltic Sea

UNITED
KINGDOM

LATVIA

0°

DENMARK

LITHUANIA

50°N

IRELAND

RUSSIA

NETH.

BELARUS

ATLANTIC
OCEAN

BELG.

GERMANY

POLAND

LUX.

LIECH.

CZECH
REP.

UKRAINE

FRANCE

SWITZ.

AUSTRIA

HUNGARY

MOLDOVA

SLOVENIA

ROMANIA

MONACO

SAN
MARINO

CROATIA

SERBIA

Black Sea

PORTUGAL

CORSICA (Fr.)

SARDINIA (It.)

ITALY

MONTENEGRO

MAC.

BULGARIA

TURKEY

40°N

SPAIN

BALEARIC IS.(Sp.)

ALB.

GREECE

0

500 Miles

GIBRALTAR (U.K.)

Mediterranean
Sea

SICILY (It.)

500 Kilometers

World–Physical

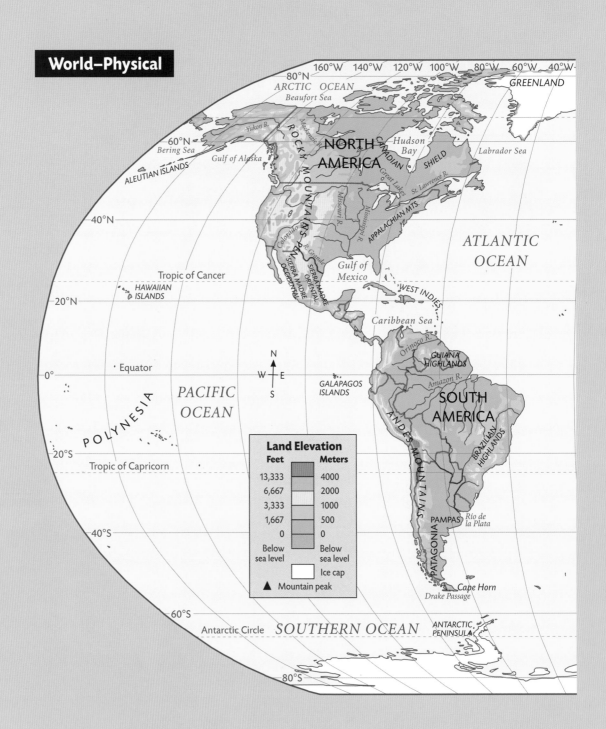

160°W 140°W 120°W 100°W 80°W 60°W 40°W

80°N
ARCTIC OCEAN
Beaufort Sea
GREENLAND

60°N
Bering Sea
Yukon R.
Gulf of Alaska
ALEUTIAN ISLANDS
ROCKY MOUNTAINS
Mackenzie R.
CANADIAN
NORTH AMERICA
Hudson Bay
SHIELD
Great Lakes
Labrador Sea

40°N
Colorado R.
Rio Grande
SIERRA MADRE OCCIDENTAL
SIERRA MADRE ORIENTAL
Missouri R.
Mississippi R.
St. Lawrence R.
APPALACHIAN MTS.
ATLANTIC OCEAN

Tropic of Cancer
HAWAIIAN ISLANDS
Gulf of Mexico
WEST INDIES

20°N

Caribbean Sea

PACIFIC OCEAN
GALAPAGOS ISLANDS
Orinoco R.
GUIANA HIGHLANDS

0° Equator
Amazon R.
SOUTH AMERICA

POLYNESIA
ANDES MOUNTAINS
BRAZILIAN HIGHLANDS

20°S
Tropic of Capricorn

Land Elevation

Feet		Meters
13,333		4000
6,667		2000
3,333		1000
1,667		500
0		0
Below sea level		Below sea level
		Ice cap
▲ Mountain peak		

PAMPAS
Río de la Plata

40°S
PATAGONIA

Cape Horn
Drake Passage

60°S
Antarctic Circle SOUTHERN OCEAN
ANTARCTIC PENINSULA

80°S

N
W E
S

ATLAS

20°W 0° 20°E 40°E 60°E 80°E 100°E 120°E 140°E 160°E

ARCTIC OCEAN

Arctic Circle

SCANDINAVIAN PEN.

Yenisey R.

Ob R.

SIBERIA

Lena R.

KOLYMA RANGE

BRITISH ISLES
North Sea
Volga R.
URAL MTS.
WEST SIBERIAN PLAIN

L. Baikal

KAMCHATKA PENINSULA

NORTHERN EUROPEAN PLAIN

EUROPE

Amur R.

ALPS

Aral Sea

ASIA

ALTAI MTS.

IBERIAN PEN.

BALKAN PEN.
Black Sea
CAUCASUS MTS.
Caspian Sea

TIEN SHAN

GOBI DESERT

NORTH CHINA PLAIN

ATLAS MTS.

Mediterranean Sea

ZAGROS MTS.

PLATEAU OF IRAN

KUNLUN SHAN
TIBETAN PLATEAU

Huang

Nile R.

S A H A R A
D E S E R T

ARABIAN PEN.

Indus R.

HIMALAYAS
Ganges R.

Mt. Everest
29,035 ft
8,850 m

Yangzi R.

Tropic of Cancer

Niger R.

SAHEL

Persian Gulf

DECCAN PLATEAU

AFRICA

ETHIOPIAN HIGHLANDS

Arabian Sea

Bay of Bengal

South China Sea

PHILIPPINE ISLANDS

PACIFIC OCEAN

MICRONESIA

Horn of Africa

Congo R.

L. Victoria

INDIAN OCEAN

SUMATRA

BORNEO

CELEBES

EAST INDIES

NEW GUINEA

MELANESIA

ATLANTIC OCEAN

Zambezi R.

MADAGASCAR

KALAHARI DESERT

AUSTRALIA

GREAT DIVIDING RANGE

Darling R.

Cape of Good Hope

0   1000   2000 Miles
0   1000   2000 Kilometers

SOUTHERN OCEAN

ANTARCTICA

ATLAS

Western Hemisphere–Political

ARCTIC OCEAN

GREENLAND
(Denmark)

Beaufort Sea

ALASKA
(U.S.)
Fairbanks
Anchorage

Baffin Bay

Arctic Circle

Nuuk

Yukon R.

Yellowknife

Iqaluit

Davis Strait

Juneau

Mackenzie R.

CANADA

Hudson Bay

Labrador Sea

St. John's
Gulf of St. Lawrence

Edmonton

NORTH AMERICA

Vancouver
Winnipeg

Quebec

Seattle
Portland

Montreal
Ottawa
Toronto

Halifax

Salt Lake City

Missouri R.

Minneapolis

Boston

San Francisco

UNITED
Chicago
Denver

Detroit

New York
Washington, D.C.

ATLANTIC OCEAN

St. Louis

STATES

Colorado R.

Los Angeles
Phoenix

Atlanta

Raleigh

BERMUDA
(U.K.)

Tropic of Cancer

Houston

Mississippi R.

Monterey
New Orleans

MEXICO
Gulf of Mexico

Miami

See inset

Guadalajara
Mexico City

MIDDLE AMERICA

Belmopan
BELIZE
HONDURAS

Caribbean Sea
(Netherlands Antilles)

GUYANA

GUATEMALA
Guatemala City
San Salvador
EL SALVADOR

Tegucigalpa
NICARAGUA
Managua

Maracaibo

Georgetown
Cayenne

PACIFIC OCEAN

San José
COSTA RICA

Panama City

Caracas
VENEZUELA

Paramaribo
FRENCH GUIANA (Fr.)

PANAMA

Bogotá

SURINAME

ECUADOR

COLOMBIA

Equator

GALAPAGOS ISLANDS
(Ecuador)

Quito

Belém

Guayaquil

Amazon R.

Manaus

Recife

PERU

BRAZIL
SOUTH AMERICA

Bahia

West Indies

ATLANTIC OCEAN

Nassau

Tropic of Cancer

Callao
Lima

Santa Cruz

Brasília

Havana
BAHAMAS

La Paz
BOLIVIA

20°S

CUBA

DOMINICAN REPUBLIC

PUERTO RICO
(U.S.)

VIRGIN ISLANDS
(U.S./U.K.)

Sucre

São Paulo

Rio de Janeiro

CAYMAN ISLANDS
(U.K.)

JAMAICA

HAITI
Port-au-Prince

San Juan

Santo Domingo

ANTIGUA AND BARBUDA

Antofagasta

Tucumán

PARAGUAY

Pôrto Alegre

Asunción

Kingston

Basseterre
ST. KITTS AND NEVIS
GUADELOUPE (Fr.)
ST. VINCENT AND THE GRENADINES

St. John's
DOMINICA
MARTINIQUE (Fr.)
ST. LUCIA

CHILE

ARGENTINA

URUGUAY

Caribbean Sea

Roseau
Castries

Santiago

Rosario
Montevideo

(NETHERLAND ANTILLES)
ARUBA   CURAÇAO
BONAIRE

Kingstown
St. George's
GRENADA
Port-of-Spain

BARBADOS
Bridgetown

TRINIDAD AND TOBAGO

Buenos Aires
Concepción
La Plata
Mar del Plata

Comodoro Rivadavia

FALKLAND ISLANDS
(U.K.)

Punta Arenas

Strait of Magellan

SOUTH GEORGIA
(U.K.)

⊛ National capital
• Major city

680

North Carolina Journeys

ATLAS

Western Hemisphere–Physical

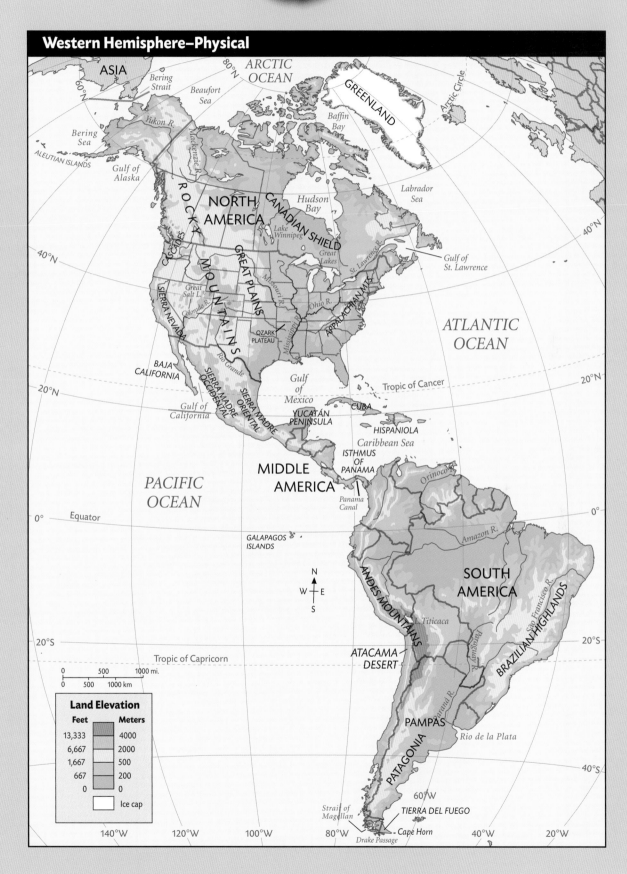

ASIA

ARCTIC OCEAN

80°N

60°N

Bering Strait

Beaufort Sea

GREENLAND

Arctic Circle

Bering Sea

Yukon R.

Baffin Bay

ALEUTIAN ISLANDS

Gulf of Alaska

Mackenzie R.

NORTH AMERICA

Hudson Bay

Labrador Sea

ROCKY

CANADIAN SHIELD

40°N

Lake Winnipeg

Gulf of St. Lawrence

40°N

CASCADES

GREAT PLAINS

Great Lakes

St. Lawrence

MOUNTAINS

Missouri R.

Great Salt L.

Ohio R.

APPALACHIAN MTS.

ATLANTIC OCEAN

SIERRA NEVADA

Colorado R.

Mississippi R.

OZARK PLATEAU

BAJA CALIFORNIA

Rio Grande

Gulf of Mexico

Tropic of Cancer

20°N

20°N

SIERRA MADRE OCCIDENTAL

SIERRA MADRE ORIENTAL

CUBA

Gulf of California

YUCATÁN PENINSULA

HISPANIOLA

Caribbean Sea

PACIFIC OCEAN

MIDDLE AMERICA

ISTHMUS OF PANAMA

Orinoco R.

Panama Canal

Equator

0°

0°

GALAPAGOS ISLANDS

Amazon R.

SOUTH AMERICA

ANDES MOUNTAINS

N

W   E

S

L. Titicaca

São Francisco R.

BRAZILIAN HIGHLANDS

Paraguay R.

20°S

20°S

Tropic of Capricorn

ATACAMA DESERT

0   500   1000 mi.

0   500

1000 km

Paraná R.

Land Elevation

Feet	Meters
13,333	4000
6,667	2000
1,667	500
667	200
0	0
	Ice cap

PAMPAS

Rio de la Plata

PATAGONIA

40°S

60°W

Strait of Magellan

TIERRA DEL FUEGO

Cape Horn

Drake Passage

140°W   120°W   100°W   80°W   40°W   20°W

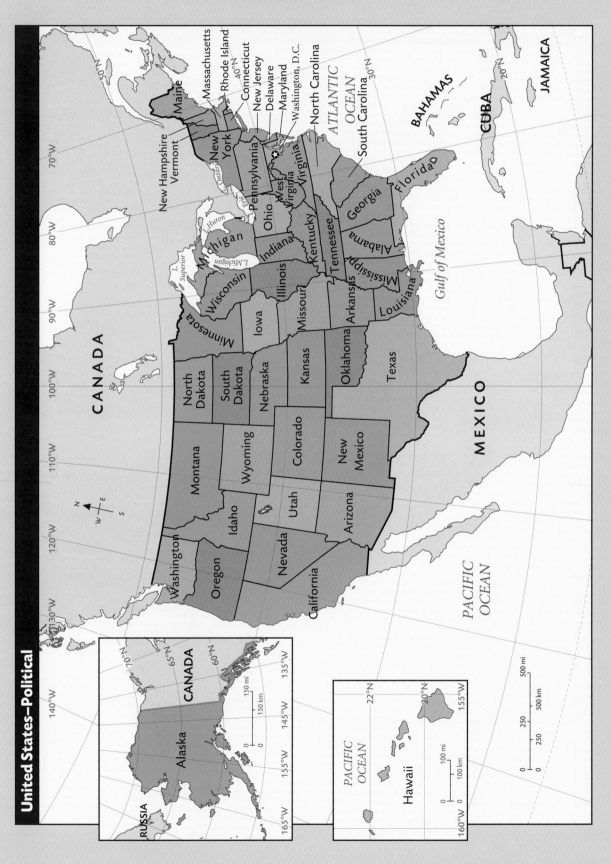

ATLAS

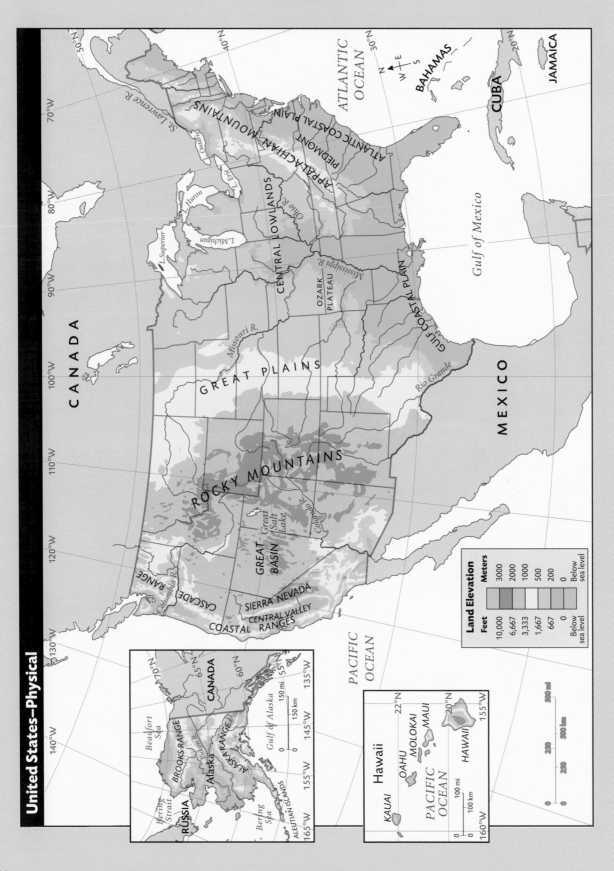

United States—Physical

Land Elevation

Feet	Meters
10,000	3000
6,667	2000
3,333	1000
1,667	500
667	200
0	0
Below sea level	Below sea level

CANADA

RUSSIA

Bering Strait

Beaufort Sea

Brooks Range

Yukon R.

Alaska

ALASKA RANGE

Gulf of Alaska

Bering Sea

ALEUTIAN ISLANDS

70°N
65°N
60°N
55°N

135°W
145°W
155°W
165°W

150 mi
150 km

Hawaii

KAUAI
OAHU
MOLOKAI
MAUI
HAWAII

PACIFIC OCEAN

22°N
20°N

155°W
160°W

100 mi
100 km

PACIFIC OCEAN

500 mi
500 km
250

CANADA

RUSSIA

Bering Strait

Bering Sea

PACIFIC OCEAN

COASTAL RANGES

CENTRAL VALLEY

SIERRA NEVADA

CASCADE RANGE

Columbia R.

GREAT BASIN

Great Salt Lake

ROCKY MOUNTAINS

Colorado R.

GREAT PLAINS

Missouri R.

OZARK PLATEAU

CENTRAL LOWLANDS

L. Superior
L. Michigan
Huron
L. Erie
Ontario

St. Lawrence R.

APPALACHIAN MOUNTAINS

PIEDMONT

ATLANTIC COASTAL PLAIN

Ohio R.

Mississippi R.

GULF COASTAL PLAIN

Rio Grande

Gulf of Mexico

MEXICO

ATLANTIC OCEAN

BAHAMAS

CUBA

JAMAICA

N
W   E
S

50°N
40°N
30°N
20°N

70°W
80°W
90°W
100°W
110°W
120°W
130°W
140°W

Atlas

ATLAS

Europe–Political

Barents Sea

Reykjavík ★ **ICELAND**

Arctic Circle

Norwegian Sea

Gulf of Bothnia

FINLAND

Helsinki ★

ATLANTIC OCEAN

FAROE IS.
(Den.)

SHETLAND IS.
(U.K.)

NORWAY

Oslo ★

SWEDEN

★ Stockholm

Tallinn ★
ESTONIA

RUSSIA

Moscow ★

Scotland

North Sea

Baltic Sea

Riga ★ **LATVIA**

No. Ireland

Dublin ★
IRELAND

**UNITED
KINGDOM**

DENMARK

Copenhagen ★

LITHUANIA
Vilnius ★
RUSSIA

Minsk ★

Celtic
Sea

Wales
England

Amsterdam ★
The Hague ★
NETHERLANDS

Berlin ★

POLAND

Warsaw ★

BELARUS

Kiev ★

London ★

Brussels ★
BELGIUM

GERMANY

Prague ★
CZECH REP.

UKRAINE

Bay of
Biscay

Paris ★

LUXEMBOURG

LIECHTENSTEIN

SLOVAKIA
Bratislava ★
Vienna ★ Budapest ★

MOLDOVA
Chisinau ★

FRANCE

Bern ★
SWITZ.

AUSTRIA
HUNGARY

ROMANIA

MONACO

Ljubljana ★
SLOVENIA

Zagreb ★
CROATIA
Belgrade ★

Bucharest ★

Black
Sea

ANDORRA

SAN MARINO

ITALY

Adriatic Sea

**BOSNIA–
HERZEGOVINA**
Sarajevo ★

SERBIA

BULGARIA

PORTUGAL

Madrid ★

CORSICA
(Fr.)

Rome ★

Podgorica ★
MONTENEGRO

Sofia ★
Skopje ★
MACEDONIA

Lisbon ★

SPAIN

SARDINIA
(It.)

ALBANIA

Tirana ★

Ankara ★

Strait of
Gibraltar

Gibraltar (U.K.)

BALEARIC IS. (Sp.)

Mediterranean Sea

GREECE

Aegean
Sea

TURKEY

SICILY
(It.)

MALTA

Athens ★

CRETE (Gr.)

★ National capital
— International boundary

| | 250 | 500 Miles |
| 0 | 250 | 500 Kilometers |

AFRICA

Europe–Physical

30°W 20°W 70°N 10°W 0° 10°E 20°E 30°E 40°E

N
W + E
S

Barents Sea

ICELAND

Arctic Circle

60°N

Norwegian Sea

FAROE IS.

SHETLAND IS.

KJØLEN MOUNTAINS

SCANDINAVIAN PENINSULA

Gulf of Bothnia

ATLANTIC
OCEAN

Baltic Sea

JUTLAND
PENINSULA

North Sea

BRITISH ISLES

50°N

Thames R.

NORTHERN EUROPEAN PLAIN

Elbe R.

Ruhr
Valley

Oder R.

Vistula R.

English Channel

Seine R.

Rhine R.

Dnepr R.

Bay of
Biscay

Loire R.

CARPATHIAN MTS.

Danube R.

Dniester R.

Garonne R.

ALPS

Rhône R.

Po R.

PYRENEES

Ebro R.

40°N

IBERIAN PENINSULA

Tagus R.

Guadiana R.

CORSICA

APENNINES

ITALIAN PENINSULA

Adriatic Sea

DINARIC ALPS

Danube R.

BALKAN MTS.

*Black
Sea*

Bosporus

BALKAN PENINSULA

Sea of Marmara

BALEARIC
ISLANDS

SARDINIA

*Aegean
Sea*

Dardanelles

Strait of
Gibraltar

M e d i t e r r a n e a n   S e a

SICILY

*Ionian
Sea*

PINDUS MTS.

CRETE

30°N

Land Elevation

Feet		Meters
13,333		4000
6,667		2000
3,333		1000
1,667		500
667		200
0		0

AFRICA

0   250   500 mi.

0   250   500 km

ATLAS

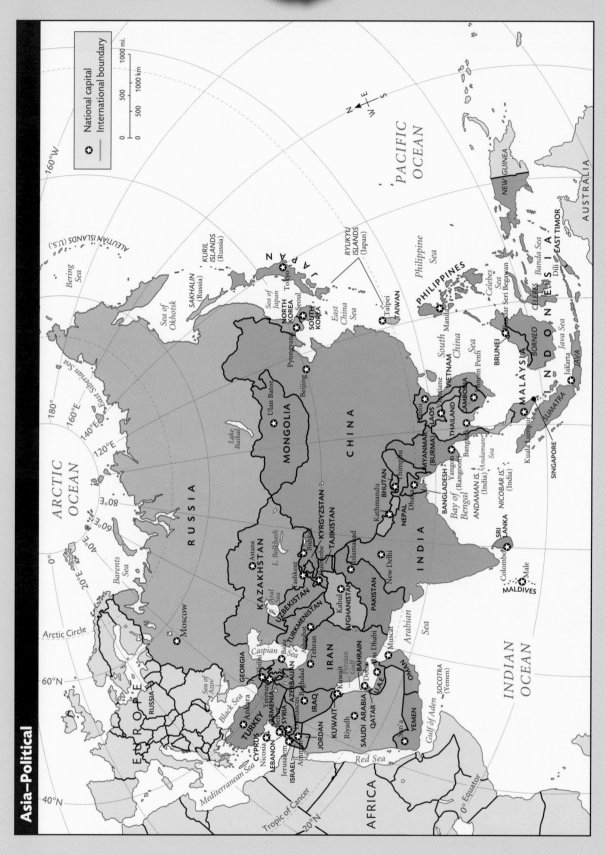

National capital
International boundary

1000 mi.
1000 km
500
500
0
0

PACIFIC
OCEAN

ARCTIC
OCEAN

Barents
Sea

Bering
Sea

Sea of
Okhotsk

ALEUTIAN ISLANDS (U.S.)

SAKHALIN
(Russia)

KURIL
ISLANDS
(Russia)

RYUKYU
ISLANDS
(Japan)

NEW GUINEA

AUSTRALIA

EAST TIMOR
Dili
Banda Sea

CELEBES

Bandar Seri Begawan

BRUNEI

Celebes
Sea

Philippine
Sea

PHILIPPINES

Manila

Taipei
TAIWAN

JAPAN

Tokyo

Sea of
Japan

NORTH
KOREA

Pyongyang

SOUTH
KOREA

Seoul

East
China
Sea

South
China
Sea

BORNEO

Jakarta
JAVA

Java Sea

I N D O N E S I A

SUMATRA

Kuala Lumpur
MALAYSIA

SINGAPORE

Phnom Penh

CAMBODIA

Bangkok

THAILAND

Hanoi
VIETNAM

LAOS
Vientiane

MYANMAR
(BURMA)

Yangon
(Rangoon)

Andaman
Sea

Bay of
Bengal

ANDAMAN IS.
(India)

NICOBAR IS.
(India)

Naypyidaw

BANGLADESH
Dhaka

BHUTAN
Thimphu

NEPAL
Kathmandu

I N D I A

New Delhi

SRI
LANKA
Colombo

Male
MALDIVES

Beijing

C H I N A

MONGOLIA

Ulan Bator

Lake
Baikal

R U S S I A

East Siberian Sea

KAZAKHSTAN

Astana

L. Balkhash

KYRGYZSTAN
Bishkek

TAJIKISTAN
Dushanbe

Islamabad

PAKISTAN

AFGHANISTAN
Kabul

Tashkent
UZBEKISTAN

TURKMENISTAN
Ashgabat

Aral
Sea

Moscow

E U R O P E

RUSSIA

Sea of
Azov

Black Sea

GEORGIA
Tbilisi

Caspian
Sea

Baku
AZERBAIJAN

Yerevan
ARMENIA

Ankara

TURKEY

CYPRUS
Nicosia

LEBANON
Beirut
Damascus
SYRIA

ISRAEL
Jerusalem
Amman
JORDAN

Baghdad
IRAQ

Tehran

I R A N

Kuwait
KUWAIT

Riyadh

SAUDI ARABIA

QATAR
Doha

BAHRAIN
Manama

Abu Dhabi
U.A.E.

Muscat
OMAN

Persian
Gulf

Arabian
Sea

INDIAN
OCEAN

SOCOTRA
(Yemen)

Gulf of Aden

YEMEN
Sana'a

Red Sea

AFRICA

Mediterranean Sea

Arctic Circle

Tropic of Cancer

Equator

160°W
180°
160°E
140°E
120°E
100°E
80°E
60°E
40°E
20°E
0°

80°N
60°N
40°N
20°N
0°

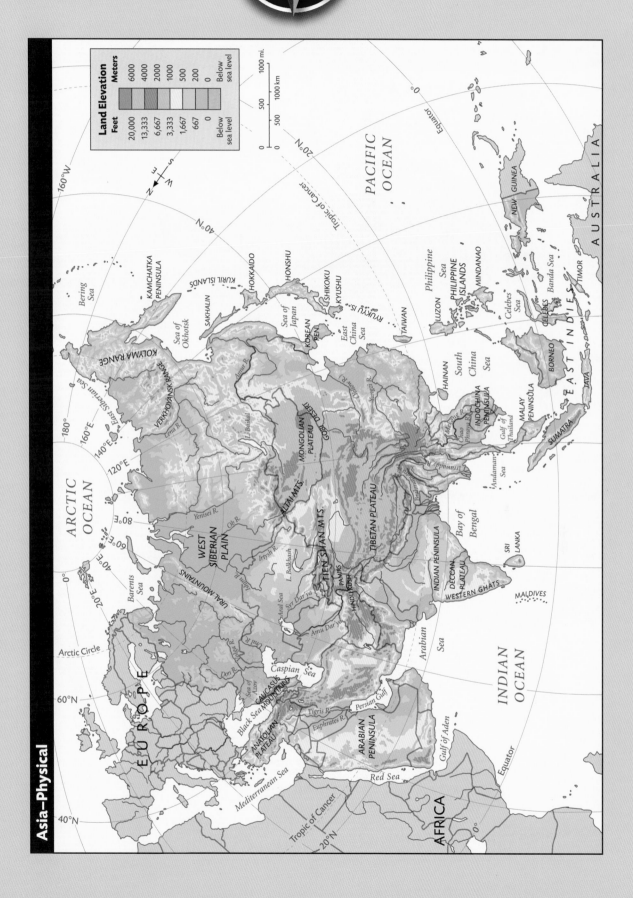

Asia–Physical

Land Elevation

Feet	Meters
20,000	6000
13,333	4000
6,667	2000
3,333	1000
1,667	500
667	200
0	0
Below sea level	Below sea level

1000 mi.
1000 km
500
500
0
0

ARCTIC OCEAN

EUROPE

Arctic Circle

60°N

Barents Sea

Sea of Azov

Black Sea

Mediterranean Sea

AFRICA

40°N

20°N

Tropic of Cancer

Red Sea

Gulf of Aden

Equator

ANATOLIAN PLATEAU

CAUCASUS MOUNTAINS

Tigris R.
Euphrates R.

Persian Gulf

ARABIAN PENINSULA

Arabian Sea

INDIAN OCEAN

MALDIVES

SRI LANKA

WESTERN GHATS

DECCAN PLATEAU

INDIAN PENINSULA

Bay of Bengal

Caspian Sea

Aral Sea

Ural R.

Don R.

Syr Dar'ya
Amu Dar'ya

L. Balkhash

URAL MOUNTAINS

WEST SIBERIAN PLAIN

Yenisei R.
Ob R.
Irtysh R.
Tobol R.

ALTAI MTS.

PAMIRS
HINDU KUSH

TIEN SHAN MTS.

TIBETAN PLATEAU

GOBI DESERT

MONGOLIAN PLATEAU

Brahmaputra R.

Ganges R.

Indus R.

Irrawaddy R.

Andaman Sea

SUMATRA

MALAY PENINSULA

Mekong R.

Chao Phraya R.

Gulf of Thailand

INDOCHINA PENINSULA

HAINAN

South China Sea

Yangzi R.

Huang R.

BORNEO

JAVA

EAST INDIES

CELEBES

Celebes Sea

Banda Sea

TIMOR

NEW GUINEA

AUSTRALIA

MINDANAO

PHILIPPINE ISLANDS

LUZON

Philippine Sea

TAIWAN

RYUKYU IS.

East China Sea

KYUSHU
SHIKOKU
HONSHU

KOREAN PEN.

Sea of Japan

HOKKAIDO

KURIL ISLANDS

SAKHALIN

Sea of Okhotsk

Bering Sea

KAMCHATKA PENINSULA

KOLYMA RANGE

VERKHOYANSK RANGE

Amur R.

Lena R.

L. Baikal

East Siberian Sea

PACIFIC OCEAN

Tropic of Cancer

Equator

20°N
40°N

60°E
80°E
100°E
120°E
140°E
160°E
180°
160°W

0°
20°E
40°E

0°

Africa–Political

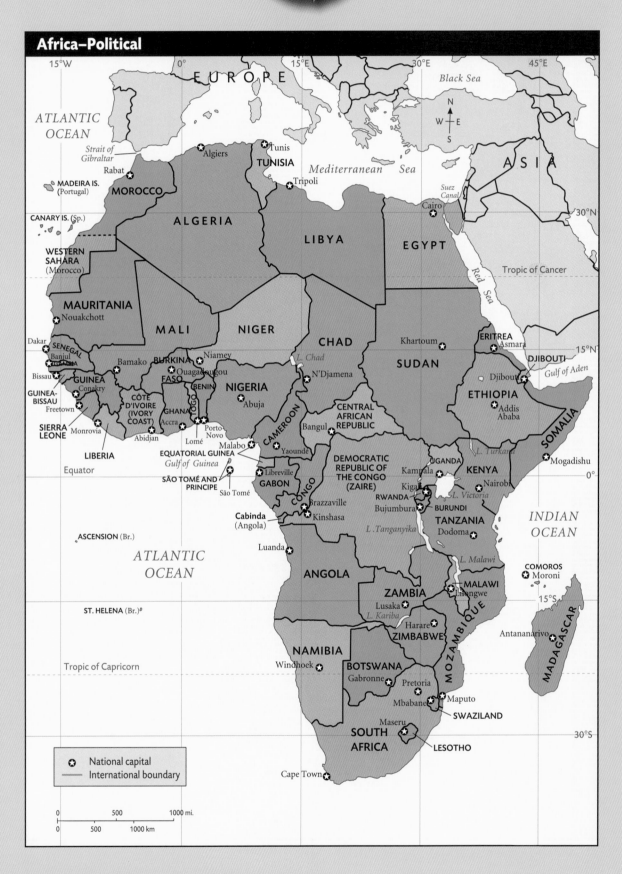

15°W   0°   15°E   30°E   45°E

E U R O P E

Black Sea

**ATLANTIC
OCEAN**

*Strait of
Gibraltar*

A S I A

Algiers

✪ Tunis

TUNISIA

Mediterranean   *Sea*

MADEIRA IS.
(Portugal)

Rabat ✪

MOROCCO

Tripoli ✪

*Suez
Canal*

CANARY IS. (Sp.)

ALGERIA

LIBYA

EGYPT

Cairo ✪

30°N

**WESTERN
SAHARA**
(Morocco)

Red Sea

Tropic of Cancer

MAURITANIA

Nouakchott ✪

MALI

NIGER

CHAD

Khartoum ✪

ERITREA

Asmara ✪

15°N

Dakar ✪

SENEGAL

Banjul ✪

Niamey ✪

DJIBOUTI

Gulf of Aden

Bamako ✪

BURKINA

Ouagadougou ✪

FASO

N'Djamena ✪

SUDAN

Djibouti ✪

Bissau ✪

GUINEA

Conakry ✪

BENIN

NIGERIA

ETHIOPIA

**GUINEA-
BISSAU**

Freetown ✪

**CÔTE
D'IVOIRE
(IVORY
COAST)**

GHANA

Abuja ✪

**CENTRAL
AFRICAN
REPUBLIC**

Addis
Ababa ✪

**SIERRA
LEONE**

Monrovia ✪

Accra ✪

Porto-
Novo ✪

CAMEROON

Bangui ✪

SOMALIA

LIBERIA

Abidjan ✪

Lomé

Malabo ✪

Yaoundé ✪

Mogadishu ✪

Equator

EQUATORIAL GUINEA

Gulf of Guinea

**DEMOCRATIC
REPUBLIC
OF THE
CONGO
(ZAIRE)**

L. Turkana

UGANDA

KENYA

0°

**SÃO TOMÉ AND
PRINCIPE**

São Tomé

Libreville ✪

GABON

Kampala ✪

Nairobi ✪

CONGO

RWANDA

Kigali ✪

L. Victoria

ASCENSION (Br.)

Cabinda
(Angola)

Brazzaville ✪

Kinshasa ✪

Bujumbura ✪

BURUNDI

TANZANIA

Dodoma ✪

**INDIAN
OCEAN**

**ATLANTIC
OCEAN**

Luanda ✪

L. Tanganyika

L. Malawi

COMOROS

Moroni ✪

ANGOLA

ZAMBIA

Lusaka ✪

L. Kariba

MALAWI

Lilongwe ✪

15°S

ST. HELENA (Br.)

Harare ✪

ZIMBABWE

MOZAMBIQUE

Antananarivo ✪

MADAGASCAR

Tropic of Capricorn

NAMIBIA

Windhoek ✪

BOTSWANA

Gabronne ✪

Pretoria ✪

Maputo ✪

Mbabane ✪

SWAZILAND

Maseru ✪

**SOUTH
AFRICA**

LESOTHO

30°S

Cape Town ✪

✪ National capital
— International boundary

0   500   1000 mi.

0   500   1000 km

ATLAS

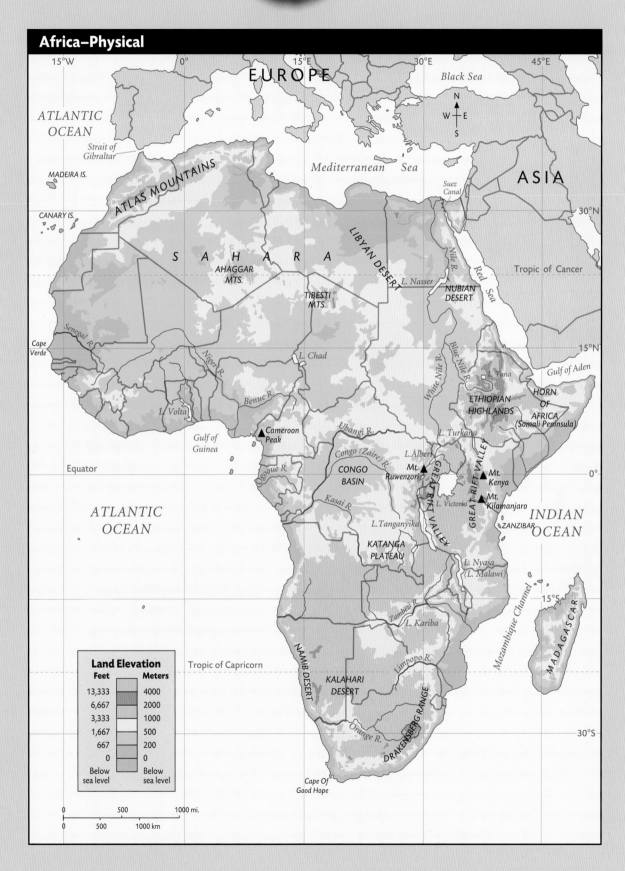

Africa–Physical

EUROPE

Black Sea

ATLANTIC
OCEAN

Strait of
Gibraltar

MADEIRA IS.

Mediterranean   Sea

ASIA

CANARY IS.

ATLAS MOUNTAINS

Suez
Canal

30°N

S   A   H   A   R   A

AHAGGAR
MTS.

L. Nasser

Tropic of Cancer

LIBYAN DESERT

NUBIAN
DESERT

TIBESTI
MTS.

Nile R.

Red Sea

Senegal R.

15°N

Niger R.

L. Chad

White Nile R.

Blue Nile R.

Tana

Gulf of Aden

Cape
Verde

Benue R.

ETHIOPIAN
HIGHLANDS

HORN
OF
AFRICA
(Somali Peninsula)

L. Volta

Gulf of
Guinea

Cameroon
Peak

Ubangi R.

L. Turkana

Equator

Ogooue R.

Congo (Zaire) R.

CONGO
BASIN

Mt.
Ruwenzori

L. Albert

GREAT RIFT VALLEY

Mt.
Kenya

GREAT RIFT VALLEY

Mt.
Kilamanjaro

ZANZIBAR

INDIAN
OCEAN

0°

Kasai R.

L. Victoria

ATLANTIC
OCEAN

L. Tanganyika

KATANGA
PLATEAU

L. Nyasa
(L. Malawi)

Mozambique Channel

15°S

MADAGASCAR

Zambezi R.

L. Kariba

NAMIB DESERT

Tropic of Capricorn

Land Elevation

Feet		Meters
13,333		4000
6,667		2000
3,333		1000
1,667		500
667		200
0		0
Below sea level		Below sea level

KALAHARI
DESERT

Limpopo R.

DRAKENSBERG RANGE

Orange R.

30°S

Cape Of
Good Hope

0   500   1000 mi.

0   500   1000 km

ATLAS

The Pacific Realm–Political/Physical

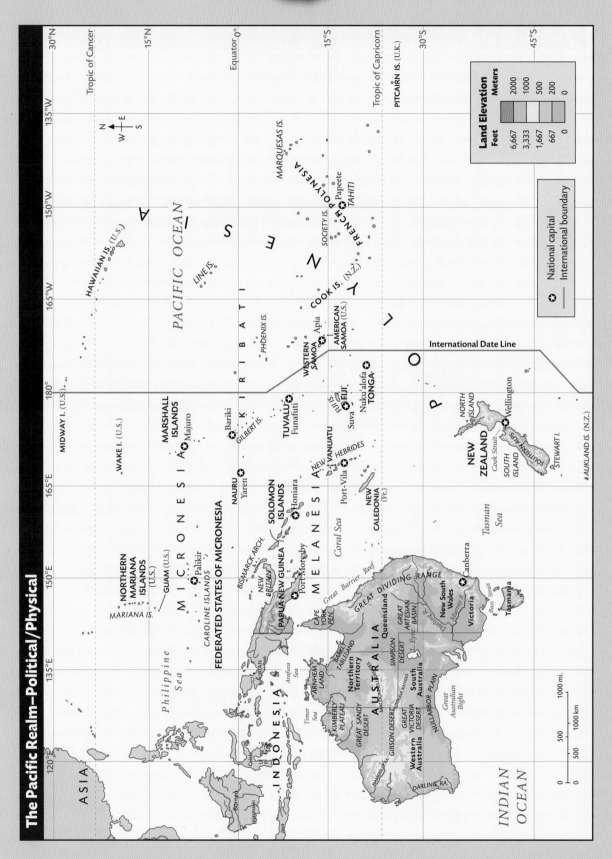

Land Elevation

Feet	Meters
6,667	2000
3,333	1000
1,667	500
667	200
0	0

✪ National capital
— International boundary

North Carolina–Political/Physical

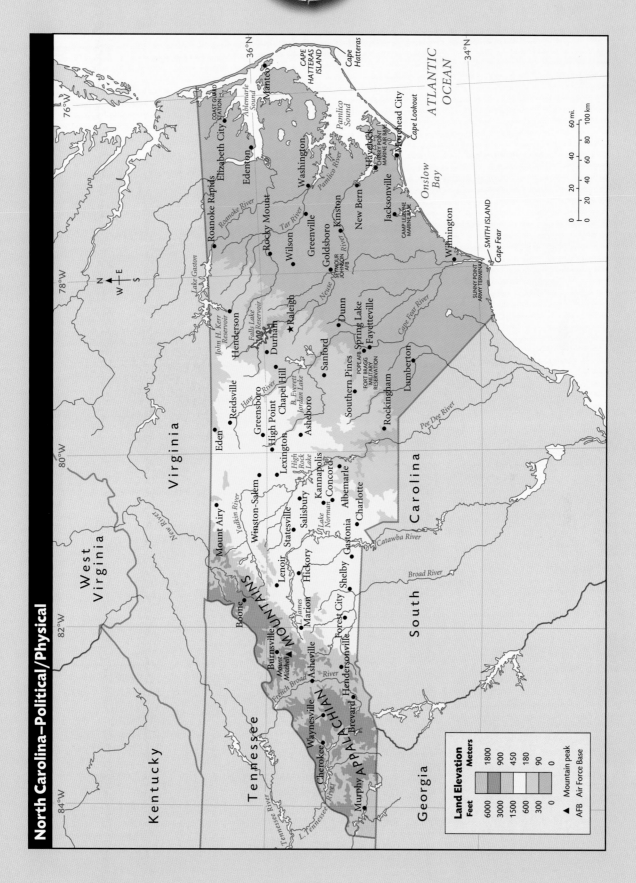

Land Elevation

Feet	Meters
6000	1800
3000	900
1500	450
600	180
300	90
0	0

▲ Mountain peak
AFB Air Force Base

South America—Political/Physical

N
W E
S

Gulf of
Venezuela

Caribbean Sea

Caracas

10° N

Lake
Maracaibo

Orinoco R.

GUYANA

SURINAME

VENEZUELA

Georgetown

Paramaribo

Gulf of
Panama

Medellín

Bogotá

GUIANA HIGHLANDS

FRENCH GUIANA (Fr.)

Cali

COLOMBIA

Cayenne

LLANOS

Equator

Quito

0°

ECUADOR

Manaus

Amazon R.

Guayaquil

**AMAZON
BASIN**

Madeira R.

Xingu R.

PERU

BRAZIL

Recife

10° S

Lima

Araguaia R.

Tocantins R.

São Francisco R.

Lake
Titicaca

BOLIVIA

Brasilia

La Paz

Sucre

BRAZILIAN

Lake
Poopó

Paraguay R.

HIGHLANDS

20° S

PARAGUA

Paraná R.

Rio de Janeiro

Tropic of Capricorn

GRAN
CHACO

São Paulo

Asunción

**PACIFIC
OCEAN**

CHILE

Córdoba

Uruguay R.

**ATLANTIC
OCEAN**

▲ Mt. Aconcagua
(22,835 Ft.)

30° S

Santiago

Rosario

URUGUAY

Buenos Aires

Montevideo

ARGENTINA

Paraná R.

Rio de la Pla

PAMPAS

40° S

Gulf of
San Matías

PATAGONIA

Gulf of
San Jorge

Land Elevations

Feet	Meters
13,333	4000
6,667	2000
3,333	1000
1,667	500
667	200
0	0

⊛ National capital
▲ Mountain peak

TIERRA DEL
FUEGO

FALKLAND ISLANDS (U.K.)

50° S

Strait of
Magellan

Cape Horn

Drake Passage

0   250   500 mi.

0   250   500 km

100° W   90° W   80° W   70° W   60° W   50° W   40° W   30° W   20° W

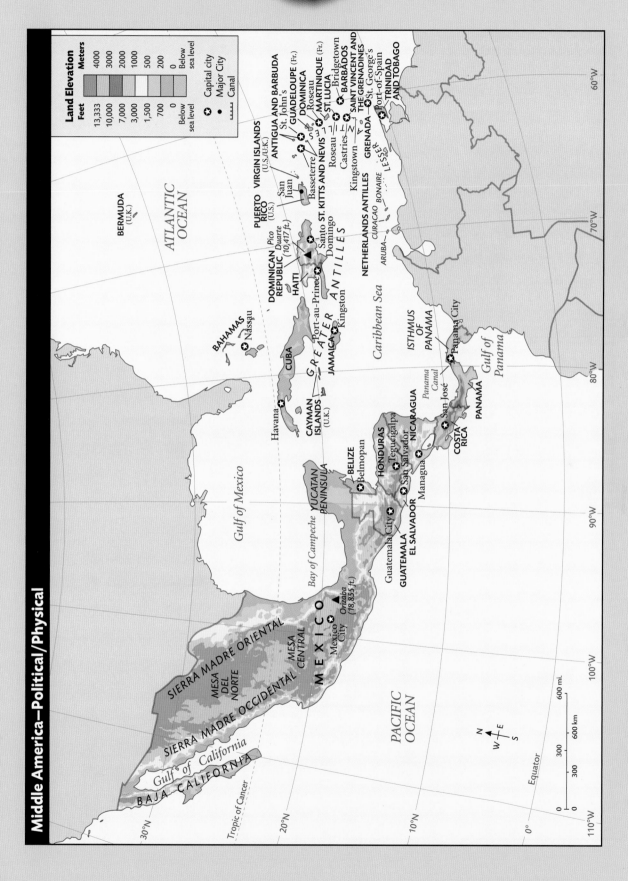

Middle America—Political/Physical

Land Elevation

Feet	Meters
13,333	4000
10,000	3000
7,000	2000
3,000	1000
1,500	500
700	200
0	0
Below sea level	Below sea level

✪ Capital city
• Major City
‒‒‒‒ Canal

BERMUDA (U.K.)

ATLANTIC OCEAN

ANTIGUA AND BARBUDA
St. John's
GUADELOUPE (Fr.)
DOMINICA
Roseau
MARTINIQUE (Fr.)
ST. LUCIA
Castries
Bridgetown
BARBADOS
SAINT VINCENT AND THE GRENADINES
Kingstown
GRENADA
St. George's
Port-of-Spain
TRINIDAD AND TOBAGO

PUERTO RICO (U.S.)
VIRGIN ISLANDS (U.S./U.K.)
San Juan
Basseterre
ST. KITTS AND NEVIS

LESSER ANTILLES

NETHERLANDS ANTILLES
CURAÇAO
BONAIRE
ARUBA

DOMINICAN REPUBLIC
Pico Duarte (10,417 ft.)
Santo Domingo
HAITI
Port-au-Prince

GREATER ANTILLES

BAHAMAS
Nassau

CUBA

JAMAICA
Kingston

Caribbean Sea

ISTHMUS OF PANAMA
Panama City

Havana

CAYMAN ISLANDS (U.K.)

Gulf of Panama

Panama Canal

San José

BELIZE
Belmopan

HONDURAS
Tegucigalpa

NICARAGUA
Managua

COSTA RICA

PANAMA

Gulf of Mexico

YUCATAN PENINSULA

Bay of Campeche

San Salvador
EL SALVADOR
Guatemala City
GUATEMALA

SIERRA MADRE ORIENTAL

MESA DEL NORTE

MESA CENTRAL

M E X I C O

Orizaba (18,835 ft.)
Mexico City

SIERRA MADRE OCCIDENTAL

PACIFIC OCEAN

Gulf of California

BAJA CALIFORNIA

Tropic of Cancer

30°N
20°N
10°N
0°

110°W
100°W
90°W
80°W
70°W
60°W

N
W E
S

Equator

0	300	600 mi.
0	300	600 km

ATLAS

North America–Political

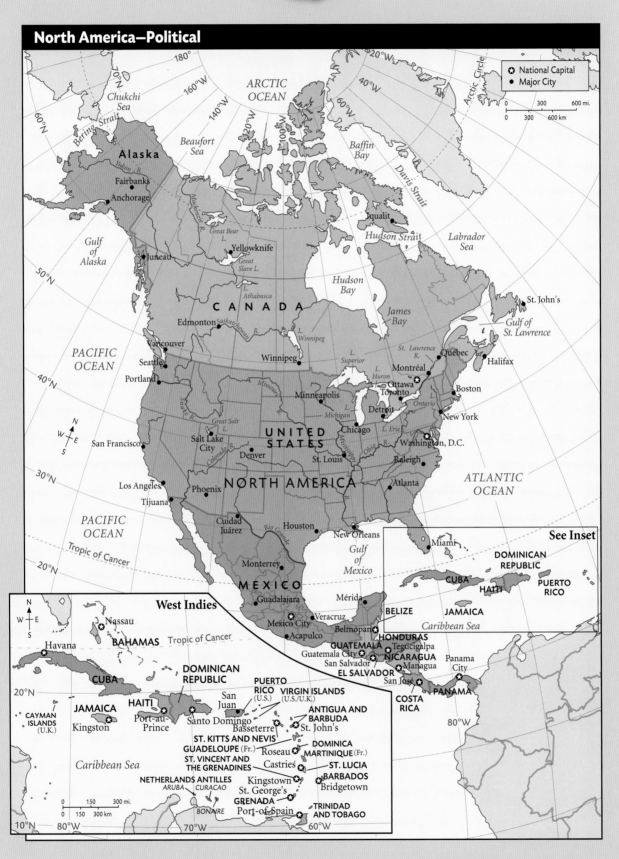

National Capital
Major City

| 0 | 300 | 600 mi. |
| 0 | 300 | 600 km |

ARCTIC OCEAN

Chukchi Sea

Beaufort Sea

Baffin Bay

Arctic Circle

Alaska

Fairbanks

Anchorage

Yukon R.

Mackenzie R.

Great Bear L.

Yellowknife

Great Slave L.

Davis Strait

Labrador Sea

Iqualit

Hudson Strait

Juneau

Gulf of Alaska

L. Athabasca

Hudson Bay

James Bay

St. John's

CANADA

Edmonton

Saskatchewan R.

L. Winnipeg

PACIFIC OCEAN

Vancouver

Seattle

Portland

Winnipeg

L. Superior

St. Lawrence R.

Québec

Gulf of St. Lawrence

Halifax

Montréal

L. Huron

Ottawa

Toronto

Minneapolis

Detroit

L. Michigan

L. Ontario

L. Erie

Boston

New York

San Francisco

Salt Lake City

Snake R.

Great Salt L.

UNITED STATES

Missouri R.

NORTH AMERICA

Chicago

St. Louis

Mississippi R.

Ohio R.

Washington, D.C.

Raleigh

ATLANTIC OCEAN

Denver

Colorado R.

Los Angeles

Phoenix

Atlanta

Tijuana

PACIFIC OCEAN

Tropic of Cancer

Cuidad Juárez

Rio Grande

Houston

New Orleans

Gulf of Mexico

Miami

See Inset

DOMINICAN REPUBLIC

CUBA

PUERTO RICO

HAITI

Monterrey

Mérida

MEXICO

Guadalajara

Veracruz

BELIZE

JAMAICA

Caribbean Sea

Mexico City

Acapulco

Belmopan

HONDURAS

GUATEMALA

Tegucigalpa

NICARAGUA

Guatemala City

San Salvador

EL SALVADOR

Managua

Panama City

San José

PANAMA

COSTA RICA

80°W

West Indies

N
W E
S

Nassau

BAHAMAS

Tropic of Cancer

Havana

CUBA

DOMINICAN REPUBLIC

PUERTO RICO (U.S.)

VIRGIN ISLANDS (U.S./U.K.)

20°N

JAMAICA

HAITI

San Juan

ANTIGUA AND BARBUDA

CAYMAN ISLANDS (U.K.)

Kingston

Port-au-Prince

Santo Domingo

Basseterre

St. John's

ST. KITTS AND NEVIS

GUADELOUPE (Fr.)

DOMINICA

Roseau

MARTINIQUE (Fr.)

ST. VINCENT AND THE GRENADINES

Castries

ST. LUCIA

BARBADOS

Caribbean Sea

NETHERLANDS ANTILLES

ARUBA

CURACAO

Kingstown

St. George's

Bridgetown

GRENADA

BONAIRE

Port-of-Spain

TRINIDAD AND TOBAGO

| 0 | 150 | 300 mi. |
| 0 | 150 | 300 km |

10°N

80°W

70°W

60°W

North Carolina Journeys

North America—Physical

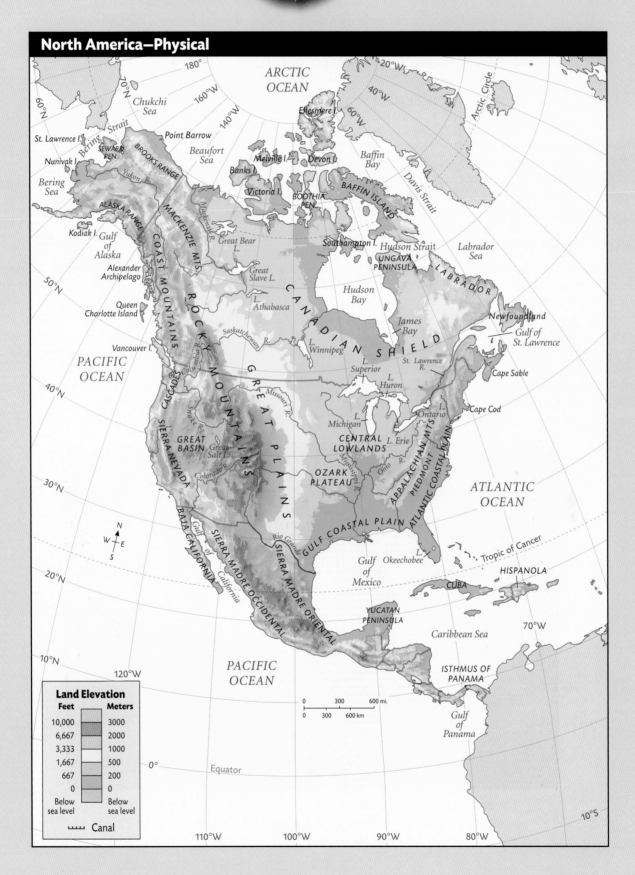

ARCTIC OCEAN

Chukchi Sea

St. Lawrence I.

Bering Strait

Point Barrow

Beaufort Sea

Ellesmere I.

SEWARD PEN.

BROOKS RANGE

Nunivak I.

Yukon R.

Melville I.

Devon I.

Banks I.

Baffin Bay

Bering Sea

Victoria I.

BOOTHIA PEN.

BAFFIN ISLAND

Davis Strait

ALASKA RANGE

Kodiak I. Gulf of Alaska

MACKENZIE MTS

Mackenzie R.

Great Bear L.

Southampton I.

Hudson Strait

UNGAVA PENINSULA

LABRADOR

Labrador Sea

Alexander Archipelago

COAST MOUNTAINS

Great Slave L.

Hudson Bay

Queen Charlotte Island

ROCKY MOUNTAINS

L. Athabasca

CANADIAN SHIELD

James Bay

Newfoundland

Gulf of St. Lawrence

Vancouver I.

Saskatchewan R.

Columbia R.

L. Winnipeg

St. Lawrence R.

Cape Sable

PACIFIC OCEAN

CASCADES

GREAT PLAINS

Missouri R.

L. Superior

L. Huron

L. Ontario

Cape Cod

SIERRA NEVADA

Snake R.

GREAT BASIN

Great Salt L.

L. Michigan

L. Erie

APPALACHIAN MTS

PIEDMONT

ATLANTIC COASTAL PLAIN

Colorado R.

CENTRAL LOWLANDS

Mississippi R.

Ohio R.

OZARK PLATEAU

ATLANTIC OCEAN

BAJA CALIFORNIA

Gulf of California

SIERRA MADRE OCCIDENTAL

SIERRA MADRE ORIENTAL

Rio Grande

GULF COASTAL PLAIN

L. Okeechobee

Tropic of Cancer

HISPANOLA

Gulf of Mexico

CUBA

YUCATAN PENINSULA

Caribbean Sea

70°W

PACIFIC OCEAN

ISTHMUS OF PANAMA

Gulf of Panama

Equator

N
W E
S

Land Elevation

Feet	Meters
10,000	3000
6,667	2000
3,333	1000
1,667	500
667	200
0	0
Below sea level	Below sea level

----- Canal

0   300   600 mi.
0   300   600 km

There are many types of governments in the regions of the world we study. Many governments use similar terms to describe different functions and organizational structures. This guide reviews the basic structures of constitutional governments, including constitutional monarchies and republics. It also reviews non-constitutional governments, including autocratic and totalitarian regimes.

A constitution is a set of fundamental customs, traditions, rules, and laws that set forth the basic way a government is organized and operated. A nation may have a constitution, but that does not mean it has a constitutional government.

Constitutional Governments

A constitutional government is a government whose actions are limited by law and institutions. If a constitution permits unlimited political power held by one person, a few people, or only one political party, then it is not the basis of a constitutional government. If a constitution does not include ways to enforce limits on the power of government, it is also not the basis for a constitutional government. The separation of powers and the checks and balances system set forth in the United States Constitution are examples of limits of the

actions of government. Each branch of the United States government—executive, legislative, and judicial—has the responsibility and the power to "check," or limit, actions taken by the other branches.

In a constitutional government, the constitution is considered a higher law. The constitution, or higher law, provides for the protection of the rights of the individual against unfair and unreasonable infringement by the government and other individuals. This typically includes establishment of a private domain into which the government may not intrude. The individual also typically has "due process of law"—the right to follow the formal procedures written into the law which protect the rights of both innocent and guilty from the arbitrary power of the state. In the United States, these rights are set forth in the Bill of Rights and the due process clause of the Fourteenth Amendment.

President George W. Bush addresses Congress. The United States is a republic with a presidential system of government. The president is not a member of Congress, but is elected by the people through the electoral college.

Power is also limited by informal means. These include such group pressure as lobbying and demonstrations, and publicity given to government actions by the media. Another effective restraint is the awareness of citizens and public officials of the traditional limits of power on the government. When a person knows that they have certain rights they are more likely to both exercise them and protect them.

Nearly all constitutional governments are representative democracies. Most are either constitutional monarchies or republics.

Constitutional Monarchies and Republics

Some governments have a monarch as head of state and are called constitutional monarchies. The United Kingdom, the Netherlands, and Sweden are examples of this form of government. Australia, Botswana, and Canada, as members of the British Commonwealth, accept the British monarch as their own and are considered constitutional monarchies as well.

Constitutional states that have no monarch are called republics. Examples include Germany, the United States, Israel, and Venezuela.

In both constitutional monarchies and republics, the practice and process of governing is by representative democracy. The type of representative democracy is either a parliamentary system or a presidential system.

In a parliamentary system, the chief executive is chosen from among members of the legislative body and is directly responsible to them. Often, this chief executive is called the prime minister. Canada, India, and Japan are examples of parliamentary systems.

In presidential systems, the chief executive is not a member of the legislative body and is independently chosen. The president is not directly responsible to the legislature, and is removable by the legislative body only in extraordinary circumstances. A good example of the presidential system is the United States. France has a modified presidential system, combining a strong presidency with elements of a parliamentary system.

Constitutional governments may operate under either a unitary or federal system. In a unitary system, power is concentrated in a central government. France and Japan are examples of unitary systems. In a federal system, power is divided between a central government and territorial subdivisions. Australia, Canada, and the United States are examples of federal systems. In the United States, the Tenth Amendment reserves the rights not granted to the national government to the states and to the people, thus creating the federal system.

Non-Constitutional Governments

In non-constitutional governments there are no effective means available to the general public for limiting the powers of the rulers. In general, rulers are not effectively restrained by law in the exercise of their powers. Often, the government's rulings, actions, and decisions are made arbitrarily. In the Soviet Union under Joseph Stalin, for example, the fate of whole ethnic groups was decided by the dictator.

Under a non-constitutional government, any rights of the individual may be violated by the ruler or rulers. Typically there is no private domain where the individual is protected from the power of the state. Whatever rights the individual may be considered to possess, rather than being protected by stringent standards of due process of law, are subject to arbitrary deprivation. In Uganda, under Idi Amin, the people were terrorized by the Bureau of State Research, which arrested and tortured people at will.

Autocracies and totalitarian states are forms of non-constitutional governments.

Autocracies, or autocratic regimes, may take various forms. These are characterized by the unlimited power exercised by one person or a small group of people. Some autocracies are military, others are civilian. Many present-day autocracies call themselves republics, but many do not have the characteristics of a true republic. Examples of historic autocratic regimes are Haiti under the Duvaliers, the Philippines under Ferdinand Marcos, and Spain under Franco. Contemporary examples are Cuba under Fidel Castro and Libya under Muammar Qaddafi.

Dictatorships that attempt to exercise absolute control over all spheres of human life are called totalitarian dictatorships. The classical examples of totalitarian dictatorships are the Soviet Union under Josef Stalin, Germany under Adolf Hitler, and China under Mao Zedong. Contemporary examples are North Korea under Kim Il Sung and after his death under Kim Jong Il. Iraq under Saddam Hussein was another example.

Non-constitutional governments may also have constitutions that set forth the basic way they are—or are said to be—organized and operated. They also may be organized as parliamentary or presidential governments and may call themselves federal rather than unitary systems. These names, however, are used only to obscure the true nature of the autocratic or totalitarian state. One must study the actual functioning of a government on a daily basis to determine its true nature.

DICTIONARY OF GEOGRAPHIC TERMS

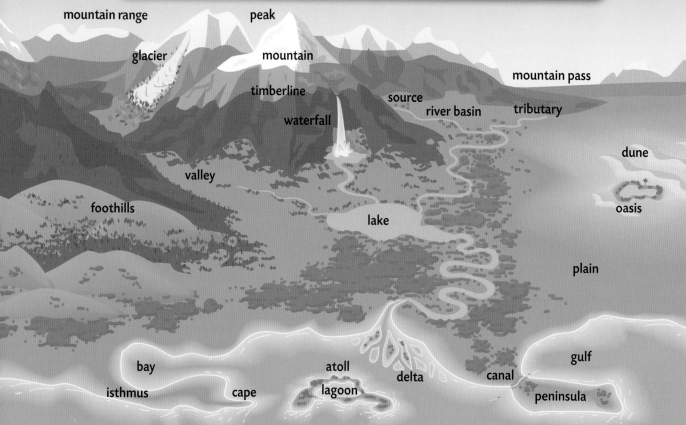

mountain range peak

glacier mountain

mountain pass

timberline source tributary

waterfall river basin

dune

valley

foothills oasis

lake

plain

bay gulf

atoll delta

isthmus lagoon canal

cape peninsula

ocean
(sea)

archipelago (ar·kee·PELL·ah·goh) A large group or chain of islands.

atoll A ring-shaped coral island or string of islands surrounding a lagoon.

basin An area of low-lying land surrounded by higher land. *See also* **river basin**.

bay Part of an ocean, sea, or lake extending into the land. Usually smaller than a gulf.

beach The gently sloping shore of an ocean or other body of water, especially that part covered by sand or pebbles.

butte (beyoot) A small, flat-topped hill. A butte is smaller than a plateau or a mesa.

canal A waterway built to carry water for navigation or irrigation. Navigation canals usually connect two other bodies of water.

canyon A deep, narrow valley with steep sides.

cape A projecting part of a coastline that extends into an ocean, sea, gulf, bay, or lake.

cliff A high, steep face of rock or earth.

coast Land along an ocean or sea.

dam A wall built across a river to hold back the flowing water.

delta Land formed at the mouth of a river by deposits of silt, sand, and pebbles.

desert A very dry area where few plants grow.

dune A mound, hill, or ridge of sand that is heaped up by the wind.

fjord (fyord) A deep, narrow inlet of the sea between high, steep cliffs.

foothills A hilly area at the base of a mountain range.

glacier (GLAY·sher) A large sheet of ice that moves slowly over some land surface or down a valley.

gulf Part of an ocean or sea that extends into the land. A gulf is usually larger than a bay.

harbor A protected place along a shore where ships can safely anchor.

hill A rounded, raised landform, not as high as a mountain.

island A body of land completely surrounded by water.

isthmus (ISS·muss) A narrow strip of land bordered by water that connects two larger bodies of land.

lagoon A shallow body of water partly or completely enclosed within an atoll. Also, a shallow body of sea water partly cut off from the sea by a narrow strip of land.

DICTIONARY OF GEOGRAPHIC TERMS

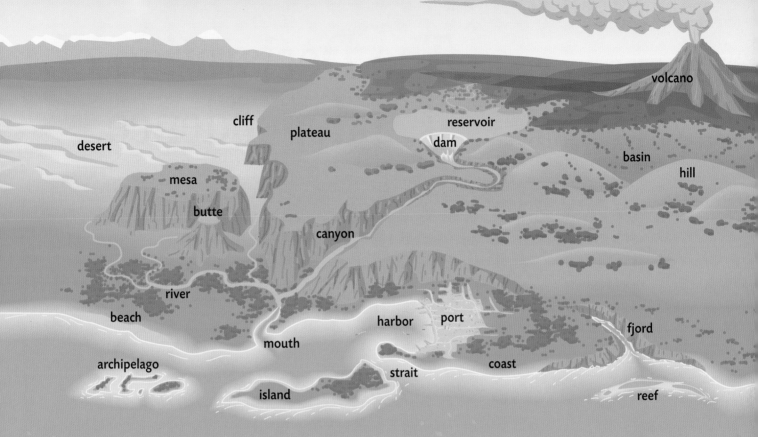

lake A body of water surrounded by land.

mesa A high, flat landform rising steeply above the surrounding land. A mesa is smaller than a plateau and larger than a butte.

mountain A high, rounded or pointed landform with steep sides, higher than a hill.

mountain pass An opening or gap through a mountain range.

mountain range A row or chain of mountains.

mouth The place where a river empties into another body of water.

oasis A place in the desert made fertile by a steady supply of water.

ocean One of the earth's four largest bodies of water. The four oceans are really a single connected body of salt water that covers about three fourths of the earth's surface.

peak The pointed top of a mountain or hill.

peninsula A body of land nearly surrounded by water.

plain A large area of flat or nearly flat land.

plateau A high, flat landform that rises steeply above the surrounding land. A plateau is larger than a mesa or a butte.

port A place where ships load and unload goods.

reef A ridge of sand, rock, or coral that lies at or near the surface of a sea.

reservoir A natural or artificial lake used to store water.

river A large stream of water that flows across the land and usually empties into a lake, ocean, or other river.

river basin All the land drained by a river and its tributaries.

sea A large body of water partly or entirely surrounded by land. Another word for ocean.

source The place where a river or stream begins.

strait A narrow waterway or channel connecting two larger bodies of water.

timberline An imaginary line on mountains above which trees do not grow.

tributary A river or stream that flows into a larger river or stream.

valley An area of low land between hills or mountains.

volcano (vol·KAY·no) An opening in the earth through which lava, rock, gases, and ash are forced out.

waterfall A flow of water falling from a high place to a lower place.

The Declaration of Independence

The printed text of the Declaration of Independence below shows the spelling and punctuation of the actual document. The signers are listed with the names of their states. Most members signed the declaration on August 2, 1776.

In Congress, July 4, 1776. The unanimous Declaration of the thirteen united States of America,

Preamble

When in the Course of human events, it becomes necessary for one people to dissolve the political bands which have connected them with another, and to assume among the powers of the earth, the separate and equal station to which the Laws of Nature and of Nature's God entitle them, a decent respect to the opinions of mankind requires that they should declare the causes which impel them to the separation.

impel to force by moral pressure

Declaration of Natural Rights

We hold these truths to be self evident, that all men are created equal, that they are endowed by their Creator with certain unalienable Rights, that among these are Life, Liberty and the pursuit of Happiness.—

endowed provided

That to secure these rights, Governments are instituted among Men, deriving their just powers from the consent of the governed,—

That whenever any Form of Government becomes destructive of these ends, it is the Right of the People to alter or to abolish it, and to institute new Government, laying its foundation on such principles and organizing its powers in such form, as to them shall seem most likely to effect their Safety and Happiness. Prudence, indeed, will dictate that Governments long established should not be changed for light and transient causes; and accordingly all experience hath shewn, that mankind are more disposed to suffer, while evils are sufferable, than to right themselves by abolishing the forms to which they are accustomed. But when a long train of abuses and usurpations, pursuing invariably the same Object evinces a design to reduce them under absolute Despotism, it is their right, it is their duty, to throw off such Government, and to provide new Guards for their future security.—

Despotism absolute power and control over a people by one person, for example, a ruler.

List of Grievances

Such has been the patient sufferance of these Colonies; and such is now the necessity which constrains them to alter their former Systems of Government. The history of the present King of Great Britain is a history of repeated injuries and usurpations, all having in direct object the establishment of an absolute Tyranny over these States. To prove this, let Facts be submitted to a candid world.

usurpations seizures or possessions by force or without right

He has refused his Assent to Laws, the most wholesome and necessary for the public good.

He has forbidden his Governors to pass Laws of immediate and pressing importance, unless suspended in their operation till his Assent should be obtained; and when so suspended, he has utterly neglected to attend to them.

He has refused to pass other Laws for the accommodation of large districts of people, unless those people would relinquish the right of Representation in the Legislature, a right inestimable to them and formidable to tyrants only.

relinquish to give up, yield
inestimable priceless, too valuable to be measured

He has called together legislative bodies at places unusual, uncomfortable, and distant from the depository of their public Records, for the sole purpose of fatiguing them into compliance with his measures.

He has dissolved Representative Houses repeatedly, for opposing with manly firmness his invasions on the rights of the people.

He has refused for a long time, after such dissolutions, to cause others to be elected; whereby the Legislative powers, incapable of Annihilation, have returned to the People at large for their exercise; the State remaining in the mean time exposed to all the dangers of invasion from without, and convulsions within.

Annihilation destruction

convulsions violent disturbances

He has endeavoured to prevent the population of these States; for that purpose obstructing the Laws for Naturalization of Foreigners; refusing to pass others to encourage their migrations hither, and raising the conditions of new Appropriations of Lands.

Naturalization of Foreigners allowing people from other countries to become citizens

He has obstructed the Administration of Justice, by refusing his Assent to Laws for establishing Judiciary powers.

He has made Judges dependent on his Will alone, for the tenure of their offices, and the amount and payment of their salaries.

tenure term

He has erected a multitude of New Offices, and sent hither swarms of Officers to harrass our people, and eat out their substance.

He has kept among us, in times of peace, Standing Armies without the Consent of our legislatures.

He has affected to render the Military independent of and superior to the Civil power.

quartering providing lodging or shelter

render to make

abdicated give up responsibility for

perfidy treachery

insurrections rebellions or revolts against civil authority

Petitioned for Redress sent formal written requests asking that wrongs be corrected

unwarrantable jurisdiction unjustifiable power or right to exercise authority over someone

consanguinity descended from the same ancestor

He has combined with others to subject us to a jurisdiction foreign to our constitution, and unacknowledged by our laws; giving his Assent to their Acts of pretended Legislation:

For Quartering large bodies of armed troops among us:

For protecting them, by a mock Trial, from punishment for any Murders which they should commit on the Inhabitants of these States:

For cutting off our Trade with all parts of the world:

For imposing Taxes on us without our Consent:

For depriving us in many cases, of the benefits of Trial by Jury:

For transporting us beyond Seas to be tried for pretended offences:

For abolishing the free System of English Laws in a neighbouring Province, establishing therein an Arbitrary government, and enlarging its Boundaries so as to render it at once an example and fit instrument for introducing the same absolute rule into these Colonies:

For taking away our Charters, abolishing our most valuable Laws, and altering fundamentally the Forms of our Governments:

For suspending our own Legislatures, and declaring themselves invested with power to legislate for us in all cases whatsoever.

He has abdicated Government here, by declaring us out of his Protection and waging War against us.

He has plundered our seas, ravaged our Coasts, burnt our towns, and destroyed the lives of our people.

He is at this time transporting large Armies of foreign Mercenaries to compleat the works of death, desolation and tyranny, already begun with circumstances of Cruelty & perfidy scarcely paralleled in the most barbarous ages, and totally unworthy the Head of a civilized nation.

He has constrained our fellow Citizens taken Captive on the high Seas to bear Arms against their Country, to become the executioners of their friends and Brethren, or to fall themselves by their Hands.

He has excited domestic insurrections amongst us, and has endeavoured to bring on the inhabitants of our frontiers, the merciless Indian Savages, whose known rule of warfare, is an undistinguished destruction of all ages, sexes and conditions.

In every stage of these Oppressions We have Petitioned for Redress in the most humble terms: Our repeated Petitions have been answered only by repeated injury. A Prince whose character is thus marked by every act which may define a Tyrant, is unfit to be the ruler of a free people.

Nor have We been wanting in attentions to our Brittish brethren. We have warned them from time to time of attempts by their legislature to extend an unwarrantable jurisdiction over us. We have reminded them of the circumstances of our emigration and settlement here. We have appealed to their native justice and magnanimity, and we have conjured them by the ties of our common kindred to disavow these usurpations, which, would inevitably interrupt our connections and correspondence. They too have been deaf to the voice of justice and of consanguinity. We must, therefore, acquiesce in the necessity, which denounces our Separation, and hold them, as we hold the rest of mankind, Enemies in War, in Peace Friends.

Resolution of Independence by the United States

We, therefore, the Representatives of the united States of America, in General Congress, Assembled, appealing to the Supreme Judge of the world for the rectitude of our intentions, do, in the Name, and by Authority of the good People of these Colonies, solemnly publish and declare, That these United Colonies are, and of Right ought to be Free and Independent States; that they are Absolved from all Allegiance to the British Crown, and that all political connection between them and the State of Great Britain, is and ought to be totally dissolved; and that as Free and Independent States, they have full Power to levy War, conclude Peace, contract Alliances, establish Commerce, and to do all other Acts and Things which Independent States may of right do. And for the support of this Declaration, with a firm reliance on the protection of divine Providence, we mutually pledge to each other our Lives, our Fortunes and our sacred Honor.

rectitude rightness, moral integrity

John Hancock
*President, from
  Massachusetts*

Georgia
Button Gwinnett
Lyman Hall
George Walton

North Carolina
William Hooper
Joseph Hewes
John Penn

South Carolina
Edward Rutledge
Thomas Heyward, Jr.
Thomas Lynch, Jr.
Arthur Middleton

Maryland
Samuel Chase
William Paca
Thomas Stone
Charles Carroll of
  Carrollton

Virginia
George Wythe
Richard Henry Lee
Thomas Jefferson
Benjamin Harrison
Thomas Nelson, Jr.
Francis Lightfoot Lee
Carter Braxton

Pennsylvania
Robert Morris
Benjamin Rush
Benjamin Franklin
John Morton
George Clymer
James Smith
George Taylor
James Wilson
George Ross

Delaware
Caesar Rodney
George Read
Thomas McKean

New York
William Floyd
Philip Livingston
Francis Lewis
Lewis Morris

New Jersey
Richard Stockton
John Witherspoon
Francis Hopkinson
John Hart
Abraham Clark

New Hampshire
Josiah Bartlett
William Whipple
Matthew Thornton

Massachusetts
Samuel Adams
John Adams
Robert Treat Paine
Elbridge Gerry

Rhode Island
Stephen Hopkins
William Ellery

Connecticut
Roger Sherman
Samuel Huntington
William Williams
Oliver Wolcott

Constitution of the United States of America

The following text is a transcription of the Constitution showing the spelling, capitalization, and punctuation of the original. Parts of the Constitution that have been altered by amendment are crossed out.

The **Preamble** sets out the origin, scope, and purpose of the Constitution. It declares that the power of the government comes from the citizens of the United States.

Article I: The Legislative Branch

Section 1: Congress A two-house legislature is established. Powers are granted by the people to their government. Some powers are denied the government.

Section 2: House of Representatives

1. Election and Terms Representatives are elected by the voters every two years.

2. Qualifications of a Representative Representatives must be at least twenty-five years old, United States citizens for at least seven years, and residents of the state they represent.

3. Divisions of Representatives Among the States The number of representatives a state has is based upon population. The total number of representatives was set at 435 in 1929. Each state must have a minimum of one representative. Each state is divided into congressional districts of equal population. States may lose or gain a representative based upon population decreases or increases. This clause was changed by the Fourteenth Amendment. Before it was changed, Native Americans were not counted at all and only three fifths of a state's slave population was counted.

A law enacted in 1967 abolished all "at-large" elections except in those less populous states entitled to only one representative. An "at-large" election is one in which a representative is elected by the voters of the entire state rather than by the voters in a congressional district within the state.

Preamble

We the People of the United States, in Order to form a more perfect Union, establish Justice, insure domestic Tranquility, provide for the common defense, promote the general Welfare, and secure the Blessings of Liberty to ourselves and our Posterity, do ordain and establish this Constitution for the United States of America.

Article I

Section 1

All legislative Powers herein granted shall be vested in a Congress of the United States, which shall consist of a Senate and House of Representatives.

Section 2

1. The House of Representatives shall be composed of Members chosen every second Year by the People of the several States, and the Electors in each State shall have the Qualifications requisite for Electors of the most numerous Branch of the State Legislature.

2. No Person shall be a Representative who shall not have attained to the Age of twenty five Years, and been seven Years a Citizen of the United States, and who shall not, when elected, be an Inhabitant of that State in which he shall be chosen.

3. Representatives and direct Taxes shall be apportioned among the several States which may be included within this Union, according to their respective Numbers, ~~which shall be determined by adding to the whole Number of free Persons, including those bound to Service for a Term of Years, and excluding Indians not taxed, three fifths of all other Persons.~~ The actual Enumeration shall be made within three Years after the first Meeting of the Congress of the United States, and within every subsequent Term of ten Years, in such Manner as they shall by Law direct. The Number of Representatives shall not exceed

one for every thirty Thousand, but each State shall have at Least one Representative; ~~and until such enumeration shall be made, the State of New Hampshire shall be entitled to chuse three,~~ Massachusetts eight, Rhode-Island and Providence Plantations one, Connecticut five, New-York six, New Jersey four, Pennsylvania eight, Delaware one, Maryland six, Virginia ten, North Carolina five, South Carolina five, and Georgia three.

4. When vacancies happen in the Representation from any State, the Executive Authority thereof shall issue Writs of Election to fill such Vacancies.

5. The House of Representatives shall chuse their Speaker and other Officers; and shall have the sole Power of Impeachment.

Section 3

1. The Senate of the United States shall be composed of two Senators from each State, chosen ~~by the Legislature thereof~~ for six Years; and each Senator shall have one Vote.

2. Immediately after they shall be assembled in Consequence of the first Election, they shall be divided as equally as may be into three Classes. The Seats of the Senators of the first Class shall be vacated at the Expiration of the second Year, of the second Class at the Expiration of the fourth Year, and of the third Class at the Expiration of the sixth Year, so that one third may be chosen every second Year; and if Vacancies happen by Resignation, or otherwise, ~~during the Recess of the Legislature of any State, the Executive thereof may make temporary Appointments until the next Meeting of the Legislature, which shall then fill such Vacancies.~~

3. No Person shall be a Senator who shall not have attained to the Age of thirty Years, and been nine Years a Citizen of the United States, and who shall not, when elected, be an Inhabitant of that State for which he shall be chosen.

4. The Vice President of the United States shall be President of the Senate, but shall have no Vote, unless they be equally divided.

5. The Senate shall chuse their other Officers, and also a President pro tempore, in the Absence of the Vice President, or when he shall exercise the Office of President of the United States.

6. The Senate shall have the sole Power to try all Impeachments. When sitting for that Purpose, they shall be on Oath or Affirmation. When the President of the United States is tried, the Chief Justice shall preside: And no Person shall be convicted without the Concurrence of two thirds of the Members present.

7. Judgment in Cases of Impeachment shall not extend further than to removal from Office, and disqualification to hold and enjoy any Office of honor, Trust or Profit under the United States: but the Party convicted shall nevertheless be liable and subject to Indictment, Trial, Judgment and Punishment, according to Law.

Section 4

1. The Times, Places and Manner of holding Elections for Senators and Representatives, shall be prescribed in each State by the Legislature thereof; but the Congress may at any time by Law make or alter such Regulations, except as to the Places of chusing Senators.

Enumeration refers to the census.

The figure of 30,000 people represented by one representative is now irrelevant. Today, each member of the House roughly represents 500,000 people.

4. Vacancies Vacancies are filled through special elections called by the state's governor. Most of the state legislatures have granted their governors the ability to appoint a replacement instead of holding an election.

5. Officers of the House of Representatives The speaker of the House is the leader of the party that holds a majority of seats. He or she is elected by the members of the House. The speaker appoints the heads of the House committees. Impeachment means to bring charges against an official.

Section 3: The Senate

1. Number of Members and Terms of Office The Senate is made up of two senators from each state. Senators were originally elected by their state's legislators, but this has been changed by the Seventeenth Amendment. Today they are elected directly by the people of their state and serve a six-year term.

2. Staggered Elections; Filling Vacancies The authors of the Constitution wanted the senators to serve longer terms than the representatives in the House. They created a system of staggered elections, whereby one third of senators are elected every two years. The first senators were elected for two-, four-, or six-year terms, with subsequent elections for six-year terms. The terms of both senators from a particular state are arranged so that they do not terminate at the same time. Of the two senators from a state serving at the same time the one who was elected first (or if both were elected at the same time, the one elected for a full term) is referred to as the "senior" senator from that state. The other is referred to as the "junior" senator. The Seventeenth Amendment changed the method of filling vacancies in the Senate.

3. Qualifications of a Senator Senators must be at least thirty years old, United States citizens for at least nine years, and residents of the state they represent.

4. President of the Senate The vice president of the United States serves as president of the Senate. He or she only votes in the case of a tie. This is the vice president's only constitutional responsibility.

5. Other Officers of the Senate The Senate selects its officers, including a president pro tempore. When the vice president is absent, or if he or she has become president of the United States, the president pro tempore serves as the presiding officer.

6. Trial of Impeachments While the House impeaches, or bring charges against an official, the Senate tries the impeachments. When it tries an impeachment it convenes as a court. When the president of the United States is tried, the Chief Justice of the Supreme Court presides. A two thirds vote of the senators present at the impeachment trial is necessary to convict the official of the charges brought against him or her.

7. Penalty for Conviction An official found guilty by the Senate may only be removed from office and prevented from holding other federal offices. The convicted official may be tried for the same offense in a regular court of law.

Section 4: Elections and Meetings

1. Holding Elections Congress has authority over the elections of its members. In 1845, Congress established the first Tuesday after the first Monday in November as the day for selecting presidential electors (those who vote in the electoral college).

2. Meetings The Twentieth Amendment changed the date of the opening of the regular session of Congress to January 3.

Section 5: Rules and Procedures

1. Organization The minimum number of members who must be present in order for the House or Senate to hold a session is a quorum. For a regular House session, the quorum is 218 of the 435 members. In order to fulfill this constitutional responsibility, in the absence of a quorum, 15 members may initiate a call of the House to compel the attendance of absent members.

2. Rules Each house sets its own rules. Either can punish members for disorderly behavior and expel a member by a two-thirds vote.

3. Journal Both houses are required to keep Journal of their proceedings. Both the House and the Senate publish a *Journal*. Each lists all bills, resolutions, votes, and messages from the president. This is not the publication known as *The Congressional Record*. *The Congressional Record* is the official record of everything said on the floor and all roll call votes. It is published daily by the Government Printing Office.

4. Adjournment Neither house may adjourn for more than three days or move to another location without the approval the other house.

Section 6: Pay, Privileges, and Restrictions

1. Pay and Privileges Members of Congress are paid by the federal government instead of the state they represent. The current salary for members of Congress is $145,100. A small number of leadership positions, like Speaker of the House, receive a somewhat higher salary. This clause has been changed by the Twenty-seventh Amendment.

Members cannot be sued or prosecuted for anything they say in Congress. They cannot be arrested while Congress is in session except for treason or serious crimes.

2. Restrictions Members of Congress cannot use their authority or pass laws to benefit them personally. They also cannot hold another position in the federal government while they are in office.

Section 7: Method of Passing Laws

1. Revenue Bills All bills for raising revenue, or money coming into the government, must originate in the House of Representatives. The Senate may propose or agree with amendments. Taxes are the main form of raising revenue. By tradition, general appropriation bills, or bills determining how money should be spent, also originate in the House of Representatives.

2. How a Bill Becomes Law A bill may only become a law by passing both the House and the Senate and then be signed by the president. If Congress is in

2. The Congress shall assemble at least once in every Year, ~~and such Meeting shall be on the first Monday in December, unless they shall by Law appoint a different Day.~~

Section 5

1. Each House shall be the Judge of the Elections, Returns and Qualifications of its own Members, and a Majority of each shall constitute a Quorum to do Business; but a smaller Number may adjourn from day to day, and may be authorized to compel the Attendance of absent Members, in such Manner, and under such Penalties as each House may provide.

2. Each House may determine the Rules of its Proceedings, punish its Members for disorderly Behaviour, and, with the Concurrence of two thirds, expel a Member.

3. Each House shall keep a Journal of its Proceedings, and from time to time publish the same, excepting such Parts as may in their Judgment require Secrecy; and the Yeas and Nays of the Members of either House on any question shall, at the Desire of one fifth of those Present, be entered on the Journal.

4. Neither House, during the Session of Congress, shall, without the Consent of the other, adjourn for more than three days, nor to any other Place than that in which the two Houses shall be sitting.

Section 6

1. The Senators and Representatives shall receive a Compensation for their Services, to be ascertained by Law, and paid out of the Treasury of the United States. They shall in all Cases, except Treason, Felony and Breach of the Peace, be privileged from Arrest during their Attendance at the Session of their respective Houses, and in going to and returning from the same; and for any Speech or Debate in either House, they shall not be questioned in anyother Place.

2. No Senator or Representative shall, during the Time for which he was elected, be appointed to any civil Office under the Authority of the United States, which shall have been created, or the Emoluments whereof shall have been encreased during such time; and no Person holding any Office under the United States, shall be a Member of either House during his Continuance in Office.

Section 7

1. All Bills for raising Revenue shall originate in the House of Representatives; but the Senate may propose or concur with Amendments as on other Bills.

2. Every Bill which shall have passed the House of Representatives and the Senate, shall, before it become a Law, be presented to the President of the United States: If he approve he shall sign it, but if not he shall return it, with his Objections to that House in which it shall have originated, who shall enter the Objections at large on their Journal, and proceed to reconsider it. If after such Reconsideration two thirds of that House shall agree to pass the Bill, it shall be sent, together with the Objections, to the other House, by which it shall likewise be reconsidered, and if approved by two thirds of that House, it shall become a Law. But in all such Cases the Votes of both Houses shall be determined by yeas and Nays, and the Names of the

Persons voting for and against the Bill shall be entered on the Journal of each House respectively. If any Bill shall not be returned by the President within ten Days (Sundays excepted) after it shall have been presented to him, the Same shall be a Law, in like Manner as if he had signed it, unless the Congress by their Adjournment prevent its Return, in which Case it shall not be a Law.

3. Every Order, Resolution, or Vote to which the Concurrence of the Senate and House of Representatives may be necessary (except on a question of Adjournment) shall be presented to the President of the United States; and before the Same shall take Effect, shall be approved by him, or being disapproved by him, shall be repassed by two thirds of the Senate and House of Representatives, according to the Rules and Limitations prescribed in the Case of a Bill.

Section 8

The Congress shall have Power

1. To lay and collect Taxes, Duties, Imposts and Excises, to pay the Debts and provide for the common Defence and general Welfare of the United States; but all Duties, Imposts and Excises shall be uniform throughout the United States;
2. To borrow Money on the credit of the United States;
3. To regulate Commerce with foreign Nations, and among the several States, and with the Indian Tribes;
4. To establish an uniform Rule of Naturalization, and uniform Laws on the subject of Bankruptcies throughout the United States;
5. To coin Money, regulate the Value thereof, and of foreign Coin, and fix the Standard of Weights and Measures;
6. To provide for the Punishment of counterfeiting the Securities and current Coin of the United States;
7. To establish Post Offices and post Roads;
8. To promote the Progress of Science and useful Arts, by securing for limited Times to Authors and Inventors the exclusive Right to their respective Writings and Discoveries;
9. To constitute Tribunals inferior to the supreme Court;
10. To define and punish Piracies and Felonies committed on the high Seas, and Offences against the Law of Nations;
11. To declare War, grant Letters of Marque and Reprisal, and make Rules concerning Captures on Land and Water;
12. To raise and support Armies, but no Appropriation of Money to that Use shall be for a longer Term than two Years;
13. To provide and maintain a Navy;
14. To make Rules for the Government and Regulation of the land and naval Forces;
15. To provide for calling forth the Militia to execute the Laws of the Union, suppress Insurrections and repel Invasions;
16. To provide for organizing, arming, and disciplining, the Militia, and for governing such Part of them as may be employed in the Service of the United States, reserving to the States respectively, the Appointment of the Officers, and the Authority of training the Militia according to the discipline prescribed by Congress;
17. To exercise exclusive Legislation in all Cases whatsoever, over such District (not exceeding ten Miles square) as may, by Cession of

session and the president does not sign the legislation within ten days, it becomes law without his signature. Within the ten days, the president may reject the legislation. This is called a veto. A veto returns the bill to the house which originated it. The president must include a message containing the reasons for the veto. The House and Senate then may schedule a vote to override the veto, or make the law over the president's disapproval. To override a veto, a two-thirds vote of those present in each house is necessary. If the vote fails to achieve two thirds in the first chamber, the second never receives the legislation. If a two-thirds vote is achieved in both bodies, the bill becomes law without the signature of the president. If Congress adjourns within ten days of submitting legislation to the president for his or her signature, and the president does not sign it or return it to Congress with objections, the legislation does not become law. This is known as a "pocket veto."

3. Presidential Approval or Veto A bill is a draft of a proposed law. A resolution is the legislature's opinion on an issue.

Section 8: Powers Delegated to Congress

1. Tax, Pay Debts; Provide for the National Defense Congress may raise and spend revenue. Federal taxes must be the same throughout the nation. Congress may do this to provide for the defense and welfare of the United States.

2. Borrowing The federal government may issue bonds to raise funds, which is borrowing on credit.

3. Commerce Congress may regulate national and international commerce, or business.

4. Naturalization and Bankruptcy Congress may set immigration policy, including naturalization, or how an immigrant becomes a citizen, and bankruptcy rules.

5. Currency Congress has the power to create national money, or currency.

6. Counterfeiting Congress protects the currency by preventing or punishing counterfeiters, or those who use illegal copies of money.

7. Postal System The Post Office was a cabinet level department. In 1970, the United States Postal Service replaced the Post Office Department.

8. Patents and Copyrights Congress may pass laws to protect patents of inventions and intellectual property rights, also called copyrights.

9. Court System Congress has the power to create a system of lower courts.

10. Piracy Congress has the right to control and protect citizens and ships when they are out of the country.

11. Declare War Congress has the power to make a declaration of war. However, troops may be sent into combat by the president without a formal declaration.

12. Army Congress may raise and support an Army.

13. Navy Congress may establish a navy.

14. Armed Forces Rules Congress may regulate the armed forces and establish procedures for military discipline.

15. Militia Congress may provide for a militia, now called the National Guard, to be organized by the states.

16. National Guard Congress may pass legislation governing the National Guard.

17. District of Columbia Congress has the right to exercise control over the District of Columbia and other federal property.

18. The "Elastic Clause" This clause gives Congress the right to make any law "necessary and proper" to carry out its powers.

Section 9: Powers Denied to the Federal Government

1. Slavery This is the compromise where slavery was to be prohibited no earlier than 1808.

2. Habeas Corpus Habeas Corpus is a Latin term meaning "you may have the body." In legal terms, it means that when an order of habeas corpus is issued by a judge, a law official must bring a prisoner to court and show why the prisoner must continue to be held. Habeas corpus allows the jailed person to be released
to the control of his or her lawyer before his or her trial. This can only be suspended during wartime.

3. Bills of Attainder and Ex Post Facto Congress may not pass a bill of attainder, a bill that punishes a person without a jury trial. The ex post facto clause means that a person cannot be prosecuted for a crime committed before the law prohibitting it is made.

4. Direct Taxes Congress could not directly tax individuals. This clause has been changed by the Sixteenth Amendment, which allowed an income tax.

5. State Exports Congress may not tax goods that move from one state to another.

6. Uniformity of Treatment Congress may not pass laws that favor one region over another in the regulation of trade.

7. Appropriation No money from the treasury may be spent without the consent of Congress.

8. Title of Nobility No title of nobility will be granted by the United States.

Section 10: Powers Denied to the States

1. Limitations Some powers granted or denied to the federal government are granted or denied to states. States cannot conduct foreign affairs, carry on a war, or control interstate and foreign commerce. This prevents overlapping authority of the federal and state laws. States also cannot pass bills of attainder and ex post facto laws.

2. Export and Import Taxes States may not tax imports and exports because that could interfere with Congress's power to regulate interstate and foreign commerce.

3. Duties, Armed Forces, War States cannot maintain their own army or navy, nor can they wage war. Additionally, states cannot make treaties with other nations or collect duties, or fees, from foreign ships.

Article II: The Executive Branch

---

particular States, and the Acceptance of Congress, become the Seat of the Government of the United States, and to exercise like Authority over all Places purchased by the Consent of the Legislature of the State in which the Same shall be, for the Erection of Forts, Magazines, Arsenals, dock-Yards, and other needful Buildings;—And

18. To make all Laws which shall be necessary and proper for carrying into Execution the foregoing Powers, and all other Powers vested by this Constitution in the Government of the United States, or in any Department or Officer thereof.

Section 9

1. ~~The Migration or Importation of such Persons as any of the States now existing shall think proper to admit, shall not be prohibited by the Congress prior to the Year one thousand eight hundred and eight, but a Tax or duty may be imposed on such Importation, not exceeding ten dollars for each Person.~~

2. The Privilege of the Writ of Habeas Corpus shall not be suspended, unless when in Cases of Rebellion or Invasion the public Safety may require it.

3. No Bill of Attainder or ex post facto Law shall be passed.

4. No Capitation, or other direct, Tax shall be laid, unless in Proportion to the Census or enumeration herein before directed to be taken.

5. No Tax or Duty shall be laid on Articles exported from any State.

6. No Preference shall be given by any Regulation of Commerce or Revenue to the Ports of one State over those of another; nor shall Vessels bound to, or from, one State, be obliged to enter, clear, or pay Duties in another.

7. No Money shall be drawn from the Treasury, but in Consequence of Appropriations made by Law; and a regular Statement and Account of the Receipts and Expenditures of all public Money shall be published from time to time.

8. No Title of Nobility shall be granted by the United States: And no Person holding any Office of Profit or Trust under them, shall, without the Consent of the Congress, accept of any present, Emolument, Office, or Title, of any kind whatever, from any King, Prince, or foreign State.

Section 10

1. No State shall enter into any Treaty, Alliance, or Confederation; grant Letters of Marque and Reprisal; coin Money; emit Bills of Credit; make any Thing but gold and silver Coin a Tender in Payment of Debts; pass any Bill of Attainder, ex post facto Law, or Law impairing the Obligation of Contracts, or grant any Title of Nobility.

2. No State shall, without the Consent of the Congress, lay any Imposts or Duties on Imports or Exports, except what may be absolutely necessary for executing it's inspection Laws: and the net Produce of all Duties and Imposts, laid by any State on Imports or Exports, shall be for the Use of the Treasury of the United States; and all such Laws shall be subject to the Revision and Controul of the Congress.

3. No State shall, without the Consent of Congress, lay any Duty of Tonnage, keep Troops, or Ships of War in time of Peace, enter into any Agreement or Compact with another State, or with a foreign

Power, or engage in War, unless actually invaded, or in such imminent Danger as will not admit of delay.

Article II
Section 1

1. The executive Power shall be vested in a President of the United States of America. He shall hold his Office during the Term of four Years, and, together with the Vice President, chosen for the same Term, be elected, as follows:

2. Each State shall appoint, in such Manner as the Legislature thereof may direct, a Number of Electors, equal to the whole Number of Senators and Representatives to which the State may be entitled in the Congress: but no Senator or Representative, or Person holding an Office of Trust or Profit under the United States, shall be appointed an Elector.

3. ~~The Electors shall meet in their respective States, and vote by Ballot for two Persons, of whom one at least shall not be an Inhabitant of the same State with themselves. And they shall make a List of all the Persons voted for, and of the Number of Votes for each; which List they shall sign and certify, and transmit sealed to the Seat of the Government of the United States, directed to the President of the Senate. The President of the Senate shall, in the Presence of the Senate and House of Representatives, open all the Certificates, and the Votes shall then be counted. The Person having the greatest Number of Votes shall be the President, if such Number be a Majority of the whole Number of Electors appointed; and if there be more than one who have such Majority, and have an equal Number of Votes, then the House of Representatives shall immediately chuse by Ballot one of them for President; and if no Person have a Majority, then from the five highest on the List the said House shall in like Manner chuse the President. But in chusing the President, the Votes shall be taken by States, the Representation from each State having one Vote; A quorum for this purpose shall consist of a Member or Members from two thirds of the States, and a Majority of all the States shall be necessary to a Choice. In every Case, after the Choice of the President, the Person having the greatest Number of Votes of the Electors shall be the Vice-President. But if there should remain two or more who have equal Votes, the Senate shall chuse from them by Ballot the Vice-President.~~

4. The Congress may determine the Time of chusing the Electors, and the Day on which they shall give their Votes; which Day shall be the same throughout the United States.

5. No Person except a natural born Citizen, or a Citizen of the United States, at the time of the Adoption of this Constitution, shall be - eligible to the Office of President; neither shall any Person be eligible to that Office who shall not have attained to the Age of thirty five Years, and been fourteen Years a Resident within the United States.

6. In Case of the Removal of the President from Office, or of his Death, Resignation, or Inability to discharge the Powers and Duties of the said Office, the Same shall devolve on the Vice President, and the Congress may by Law provide for the Case of Removal, Death, Resignation or Inability, both of the President and Vice President,

Section 1: President and Vice President

1. Power and Term Executive power is given to the president to enforce laws passed by Congress. The president and the vice president serve a term of four years. This clause has been changed by the Twenty-second Amendment.

2. Electoral System The electoral college system is a method of indirect popular election of the president. Federal office holders cannot serve as electors. Voters in each state vote for electors who are pledged to vote for a particular candidate. These electors, in turn, vote for the presidential candidate. Each state has a number of electors equal to the total number of their congressional delegation—the total of their senators and representatives.

3. Former Method of Election Under this original system, the House of Representatives elected Thomas Jefferson president in the election of 1800 when the electoral college resulted in a tie vote. This clause has been superseded by the Twelfth Amendment.

4. Time of Elections Congress determines the dates when the electors are chosen and when they vote. All electors must vote on the same day. Electors vote on the Monday after the second Wednesday in December.

5. Qualifications The president must be a citizen of the United States by birth, be at least thirty-five years old, and have been a resident of the United States for 14 years.

6. Filling Vacancies If the president is removed from office (impeached and convicted), dies, resigns, or is unable to function as president, the vice president becomes president. This clause has been changed by the Twenty-fifth Amendment, which deals with presidential disability. The Presidential Succession Act of 1947 mandates that if the president of the United States is incapacitated, dies, resigns, is for any reason unable to hold his or her office, or is removed from office, people in the following offices, in this order, will become president, provided they are qualified (as required by the Constitution): Vice President, Speaker of the House, President Pro Tempore of the Senate, Secretary of State, Secretary of the Treasury, Secretary of Defense, Attorney General, and the Secretaries for the following departments in order: Interior, Agriculture, Commerce, Labor, Health and Human Services, Housing and Urban Development, Transportation, Energy, Education, Veterans Affairs, and Homeland Security.

7. Salary In 2001, the president's salary was raised to $400,000, plus $50,000 for expenses. The president cannot receive any other income from federal or state governments while in office.

8. Oath of Office The oath of office is the promise a president makes to uphold the duties of the office and the Constitution. In a traditional inauguration ceremony, the president-elect places his or her hand on the Bible, raises his or her right hand, and takes the oath as directed by the chief justice.

Section 2: Powers of the President

1. Military, Cabinet, and Pardons The president serves as the commander-in-chief of the armed forces. He or she is the civilian in control of the military. He or she can authorize the use of troops overseas without declaring war. To declare war officially, though, he or she must get the approval of the Congress.

The president receives advice and assistance in executing the laws from what we now call the cabinet. The cabinet is made up of the head of each of the executive departments. Unlike the powers of the president, their responsibilities are not defined in the Constitution. This is the only reference to the cabinet in the Constitution.

The president may pardon, or excuse, people who have committed federal crimes except in cases of impeachment.

2. Treaties and Appointments The president is responsible for foreign policy. He or she may makes treaties with other nations; however, the Senate must approve any treaty before it becomes official. The president nominates officials, including Supreme Court justices and ambassadors, with the agreement of a majority of the Senate.

3. Filling Vacancies When the Senate is not in session, the president may fill vacancies by temporarily appointing officials.

Section 3: Duties of the President

The president presents information on the state of the union to Congress (this has become the annual State of the Union Address) and recommends legislation to Congress. The president cannot write bills. He or she can propose a bill, but a member of Congress must submit it for him or her. The president may call for special sessions of Congress. The president receives ambassadors of other nations and recognizes those lands as official countries.

Section 4: Impeachment of the President and Civil Officers

The president and other executive branch officeholders may be impeached for treason, bribery, and other high crimes and misdemeanors. If found guilty by the Senate he or she may be removed from office. Only Presidents Andrew Johnson and William J. Clinton have been impeached. Neither were found guilty.

declaring what Officer shall then act as President, and such Officer shall act accordingly, until the Disability be removed, or a President shall be elected.

7. The President shall, at stated Times, receive for his Services, a Compensation, which shall neither be increased nor diminished during the Period for which he shall have been elected, and he shall not receive within that Period any other Emolument from the United States, or any of them.

8. Before he enter on the Execution of his Office, he shall take the following Oath or Affirmation:—"I do solemnly swear (or affirm) that I will faithfully execute the Office of President of the United States, and will to the best of my Ability, preserve, protect and defend the Constitution of the United States."

Section 2

1. The President shall be Commander in Chief of the Army and Navy of the United States, and of the Militia of the several States, when called into the actual Service of the United States; he may require the Opinion, in writing, of the principal Officer in each of the executive Departments, upon any Subject relating to the Duties of their respective Offices, and he shall have Power to grant Reprieves and Pardons for Offences against the United States, except in Cases of Impeachment.

2. He shall have Power, by and with the Advice and Consent of the Senate, to make Treaties, provided two thirds of the Senators present concur; and he shall nominate, and by and with the Advice and Consent of the Senate, shall appoint Ambassadors, other public Ministers and Consuls, Judges of the supreme Court, and all other Officers of the United States, whose Appointments are not herein otherwise provided for, and which shall be established by Law: but the Congress may by Law vest the Appointment of such inferior Officers, as they think proper, in the President alone, in the Courts of Law, or in the Heads of Departments.

3. The President shall have Power to fill up all Vacancies that may happen during the Recess of the Senate, by granting Commissions which shall expire at the End of their next Session.

Section 3

He shall from time to time give to the Congress Information of the State of the Union, and recommend to their Consideration such Measures as he shall judge necessary and expedient; he may, on extraordinary Occasions, convene both Houses, or either of them, and in Case of Disagreement between them, with Respect to the Time of Adjournment, he may adjourn them to such Time as he shall think proper; he shall receive Ambassadors and other public Ministers; he shall take Care that the Laws be faithfully executed, and shall Commission all the Officers of the United States.

Section 4

The President, Vice President and all civil Officers of the United States, shall be removed from Office on Impeachment for, and Conviction of, Treason, Bribery, or other high Crimes and Misdemeanors.

Article III

Section 1

The judicial Power of the United States shall be vested in one supreme Court, and in such inferior Courts as the Congress may from time to time ordain and establish. The Judges, both of the supreme and inferior Courts, shall hold their Offices during good Behaviour, and shall, at stated Times, receive for their Services a Compensation, which shall not be diminished during their Continuance in Office.

Section 2

1. The judicial Power shall extend to all Cases, in Law and Equity, arising under this Constitution, the Laws of the United States, and Treaties made, or which shall be made, under their Authority;—to all Cases affecting Ambassadors, other public Ministers and Consuls;— to all Cases of admiralty and maritime Jurisdiction;—to Controversies to which the United States shall be a Party;—to Controversies between two or more States; ~~between a State and Citizens of another State;~~ ~~between~~ Citizens of different States;— between Citizens of the same State claiming Lands under Grants of different States, and between a State, or the Citizens thereof, and foreign States, Citizens or Subjects.

2. In all Cases affecting Ambassadors, other public Ministers and Consuls, and those in which a State shall be Party, the supreme Court shall have original Jurisdiction. In all the other Cases before mentioned, the supreme Court shall have appellate Jurisdiction, both as to Law and Fact, with such Exceptions, and under such Regulations as the Congress shall make.

3. The Trial of all Crimes, except in Cases of Impeachment, shall be by Jury; and such Trial shall be held in the State where the said Crimes shall have been committed; but when not committed within any State, the Trial shall be at such Place or Places as the Congress may by Law have directed.

Section 3

1. Treason against the United States, shall consist only in levying War against them, or in adhering to their Enemies, giving them Aid and Comfort. No Person shall be convicted of Treason unless on the Testimony of two Witnesses to the same overt Act, or on Confession in open Court.

2. The Congress shall have Power to declare the Punishment of Treason, but no Attainder of Treason shall work Corruption of Blood, or Forfeiture except during the Life of the Person attainted.

Article IV

Section 1

Full Faith and Credit shall be given in each State to the public Acts, Records, and judicial Proceedings of every other State. And the Congress may by general Laws prescribe the Manner in which such Acts, Records and Proceedings shall be proved, and the Effect thereof.

Section 2

1. The Citizens of each State shall be entitled to all Privileges and

---

Article III: The Judicial Branch

The judicial branch is the system of courts. Courts interpret the laws made by Congress.

Section 1: Federal Court System

This article establishes the judicial branch of government with the creation of the Supreme Court. This court is the highest court in the country. There are lower federal courts but they were not created by the Constitution. Congress established them using powers granted by the Constitution.

Section 2: Jurisdiction of Federal Courts

1. General Jurisdiction This clause describes the origin of the laws of the United States. Law and equity refers to the types of laws the colonies inherited from the British justice system. Law means common law, which is laws based on five centuries of judicial decisions in Great Britain. Equity refers to the special types of laws created in Britain for handling specific cases. Admiralty and maritime jurisdiction means laws applying to ships and shipping on oceans, lakes, rivers, and canals. This clause has been changed by the Eleventh Amendment.

Courts decide arguments about the meaning of laws and how laws are applied. Courts also determine whether laws violate the Constitution. The power is called judicial review. The power of judicial review provides checks and balances on the legislative and executive branches. Judicial review is not an explicit power given to the courts in the Constitution. It is an implied power. In an important early Supreme Court decision, *Marbury* v. *Madison* (1803), the courts' power of judicial review was determined.

2. Supreme Court Original jurisdiction means the right to try a case before any other court may hear it. Appellate jurisdiction means the right of a court to try cases appealed, or decisions that are protested, from lower courts.

The Supreme Court has authority over the federal courts but has only limited power over state courts. The Supreme Court has the final word on cases heard by lower federal courts (cases that are appealed to the Supreme Court). The Supreme Court writes procedures that federal courts must follow. All federal courts must abide by the Supreme Court's interpretation of laws passed by Congress, regulations issued by the executive branch, and the Constitution. The Supreme Court's interpretations of federal law and the Constitution also apply to the state courts, but the Court cannot interpret state law or issues arising under state constitutions, and it does not supervise state court operations.

3. Trials Persons accused of a crime have a right to a trial by jury, except in cases of impeachment. This right is expanded by the Fifth, Sixth, and Seventh Amendments.

Section 3: Treason

1. Treason Treason is the only crime specifically defined in the Constitution. Treason is to wage war against the United States or to give aid and comfort to its enemies. There must be at least two witnesses to the same act or a confession to convict someone of treason.

2. Punishment of Treason Punishment for treason cannot be extended to the children of a traitor.

Article IV: Relations Among States

Respect and unity among states is established.

Section 1: Official Acts and Records of States

Court decisions and official records of one state (such as birth certificates, wills, corporation charters) are respected in all the other states.

Section 2 Duties of States

1. Privileges Rights and protections for citizens must be equal in all states.

2. Extradition Governors of states have authority over returning a person charged with a crime to the state charging the person with the crime.

3. Fugitive Slaves This clause meant that a slave could not become a free person by escaping to a free state. The Thirteenth Amendment brought an end to slavery in 1865.

Section 3: New States and Territories

1. Admission of New States Congress may admit new states. This outlines the guidelines for applying for statehood.

2. Territories Congress has power over territories and other federal property.

Section 4: Guarantees to the States

The government must protect each state against invasion. The federal government may send troops into a state to maintain law and order.

Article V: Amendments: How to Change the Constitution is Established

Adaptability is one of the most important features of the Constitution. There are two methods of proposing amendments. A two-thirds majority in Congress may submit a proposed amendment to the states, or a national convention called by two thirds of the states' legislatures may propose an amendment. Three fourths of the states must approve, or ratify, an amendment before it may become law. No amendment has yet been proposed by a national convention called by the states.

Article VI: National Supremacy

Covers general provisions and "the law of the land."

1. Public Debts The new government will pay the debts of the colonies from the Revolutionary War and the government under the Articles of Confederation.

2. The Supreme Law Declares that the "supreme law of the land" is the Constitution. The Constitution and federal law have higher authority than state constitutions when they come into conflict.

3. Oaths of Office There are no religious qualifications for holding public office.

Immunities of Citizens in the several States.

2. A Person charged in any State with Treason, Felony, or other Crime, who shall flee from Justice, and be found in another State, shall on Demand of the executive Authority of the State from which he fled, be delivered up, to be removed to the State having Jurisdiction of the Crime.

3. ~~No Person held to Service or Labour in one State, under the Laws thereof, escaping into another, shall, in Consequence of any Law or Regulation therein, be discharged from such Service or Labour, but shall be delivered up on Claim of the Party to whom such Service or Labour may be due.~~

Section 3

1. New States may be admitted by the Congress into this Union; but no new State shall be formed or erected within the Jurisdiction of any other State; nor any State be formed by the Junction of two or more States, or Parts of States, without the Consent of the Legislatures of the States concerned as well as of the Congress.

2. The Congress shall have Power to dispose of and make all needful Rules and Regulations respecting the Territory or other Property belonging to the United States; and nothing in this Constitution shall be so construed as to Prejudice any Claims of the United States, or of any particular State.

Section 4

The United States shall guarantee to every State in this Union a Republican Form of Government, and shall protect each of them against Invasion; and on Application of the Legislature, or of the Executive (when the Legislature cannot be convened), against domestic Violence.

Article V

The Congress, whenever two thirds of both Houses shall deem it necessary, shall propose Amendments to this Constitution, or, on the Application of the Legislatures of two thirds of the several States, shall call a Convention for proposing Amendments, which, in either Case, shall be valid to all Intents and Purposes, as Part of this Constitution, when ratified by the Legislatures of three fourths of the several States, or by Conventions in three fourths thereof, as the one or the other Mode of Ratification may be proposed by the Congress; Provided that no Amendment which may be made prior to the Year One thousand eight hundred and eight shall in any Manner affect the first and fourth Clauses in the Ninth Section of the first Article; and that no State, without its Consent, shall be deprived of its equal Suffrage in the Senate.

Article VI

1. All Debts contracted and Engagements entered into, before the Adoption of this Constitution, shall be as valid against the United States under this Constitution, as under the Confederation.

2. This Constitution, and the Laws of the United States which shall be made in Pursuance thereof; and all Treaties made, or which shall be made, under the Authority of the United States, shall be the supreme Law of the Land; and the Judges in every State shall be bound

thereby, any Thing in the Constitution or Laws of any State to the Contrary notwithstanding.

3. The Senators and Representatives before mentioned, and the Members of the several State Legislatures, and all executive and judicial Officers, both of the United States and of the several States, shall be bound by Oath or Affirmation, to support this Constitution; but no religious Test shall ever be required as a Qualification to any Office or public Trust under the United States.

Article VII

The Ratification of the Conventions of nine States, shall be sufficient for the Establishment of this Constitution between the States so ratifying the Same.

Done in Convention by the Unanimous Consent of the States present the Seventeenth Day of September in the Year of our Lord one thousand seven hundred and Eighty seven and of the Independence of the United States of America the Twelfth. In witness whereof We have hereunto subscribed our Names,

George Washington
President and Deputy from Virginia

Article VII: Ratification
How the proposed and signed Constitution is to be officially adopted by the states.
The Constitution only required ratification by nine of the thirteen states to come into effect.

Delaware
George Read
Gunning Bedford, Jr.
John Dickinson
Richard Bassett
Jacob Broom

Maryland
James McHenry
Daniel of St. Thomas Jenifer
Daniel Carroll

Virginia
John Blair
James Madison, Jr.

North Carolina
William Blount
Richard Dobbs Spaight
Hugh Williamson

South Carolina
John Rutledge
Charles Cotesworth Pinckney
Charles Pinckney
Pierce Butler

Georgia
William Few
Abraham Baldwin

New Hampshire
John Langdon
Nicholas Gilman

Massachusetts
Nathaniel Gorham
Rufus King

Connecticut
William Samuel Johnson
Roger Sherman

New York
Alexander Hamilton

New Jersey
William Livingston
David Brearley
William Paterson
Jonathan Dayton

Pennsylvania
Benjamin Franklin
Thomas Mifflin
Robert Morris
George Clymer
Thomas FitzSimons
Jared Ingersoll
James Wilson
Gouverneur Morris

Witnesses to the Constitution
Names of the delegates agreeing to the provisions of the Constitution.

Attest: William Jackson, *Secretary*

Bill of Rights

At first, some states would not accept the Constitution. North Carolina was one of those states. After Congress passed the first ten amendments to the Constitution, called the Bill of Rights, North Carolina voted for the Constitution.

The Bill of Rights best expresses how the people's rights are protected. It keeps the government from taking away the freedom of individuals. The Bill of Rights limits the power of government by strengthening the rights of individuals. The majority rules in deciding issues of government through voting. But the Constitution makes sure that individual rights are not taken away.

Amendment 1: Freedom of Religion, Speech, Press, Assembly, and Petition

The government cannot tell someone how or how not to worship God. The government cannot stop people from saying or printing what they think. Anyone can criticize the government. A group can gather peacefully to debate what the government does. People can ask the government to correct wrongs.

Amendment 2: Right to Keep Arms

States have the right to form militias and citizens have the right to own guns.

Amendment 3: Quartering of Troops

The government cannot force citizens to house, or quarter, troops in their homes.

Amendment 4: Search and Seizure; Warrants

No soldier or police officer can enter a house or be housed on a person's property without his or her permission. If police do enter, they must have an order from a judge.

Amendment 5: Rights of Accused Persons

No one has to go to trial just because one person accuses another of a crime. A grand jury has to meet and decide if that person should be tried. No one tried and found not guilty can be tried again for the same crime. A person does not have to testify against himself or herself.

Amendment 6: Right to a Speedy Trial

A jury chosen from the people decides cases before a judge. Accused persons have the right to a speedy and fair trial, and they have the right to meet their accusers.

Amendment 7: Jury Trial in Civil Cases

Civil cases, meaning a case where a person sues another person, are entitled to jury trials when suing for more than $20. In practice, people do not go to federal courts unless a substantial sum of money is involved.

Amendment 8: Bail, Fines, Punishments

Guilty people must not be punished in a cruel way. Bail fines must not be excessive.

Amendment I

Congress shall make no law respecting an establishment of religion, or prohibiting the free exercise thereof; or abridging the freedom of speech, or of the press; or the right of the people peaceably to assemble, and to petition the Government for a redress of grievances.

Amendment II

A well regulated Militia, being necessary to the security of a free State, the right of the people to keep and bear Arms, shall not be infringed.

Amendment III

No Soldier shall, in time of peace be quartered in any house, without the consent of the Owner, nor in time of war, but in a manner to be prescribed by law.

Amendment IV

The right of the people to be secure in their persons, houses, papers, and effects, against unreasonable searches and seizures, shall not be violated, and no Warrants shall issue, but upon probable cause, supported by Oath or affirmation, and particularly describing the place to be searched, and the persons or things to be seized.

Amendment V

No person shall be held to answer for a capital, or otherwise infamous crime, unless on a presentment or indictment of a Grand Jury, except in cases arising in the land or naval forces, or in the Militia, when in actual service in time of War or public danger; nor shall any person be subject for the same offence to be twice put in jeopardy of life or limb; nor shall be compelled in any criminal case to be a witness against himself, nor be deprived of life, liberty, or property, without due process of law; nor shall private property be taken for public use, without just compensation.

Amendment VI

In all criminal prosecutions, the accused shall enjoy the right to a speedy and public trial, by an impartial jury of the State and district wherein the crime shall have been committed, which district shall have been previously ascertained by law, and to be informed of the nature and cause of the accusation; to be confronted with the witnesses against him; to have compulsory process for obtaining witnesses in his favor, and to have the Assistance of Counsel for his defence.

Amendment VII

In suits at common law, where the value in controversy shall exceed twenty dollars, the right of trial by jury shall be preserved, and no fact tried by a jury, shall be otherwise reexamined in any Court of the United States, than according to the rules of the common law.

Amendment VIII

Excessive bail shall not be required, nor excessive fines imposed, nor cruel and unusual punishments inflicted.

Amendment IX

The enumeration in the Constitution, of certain rights, shall not be construed to deny or disparage others retained by the people.

Amendment X

The powers not delegated to the United States by the Constitution, nor prohibited by it to the States, are reserved to the States respectively, or to the people.

Amendment XI

The Judicial power of the United States shall not be construed to extend to any suit in law or equity, commenced or prosecuted against one of the United States by Citizens of another State, or by Citizens or Subjects of any Foreign State.

Amendment XII

The Electors shall meet in their respective states and vote by ballot for President and Vice President, one of whom, at least, shall not be an inhabitant of the same state with themselves; they shall name in their ballots the person voted for as President, and in distinct ballots the person voted for as Vice President, and they shall make distinct lists of all persons voted for as President, and of all persons voted for as Vice President, and of the number of votes for each, which lists they shall sign and certify, and transmit sealed to the seat of the government of the United States, directed to the President of the Senate; —the President of the Senate shall, in the presence of the Senate and House of Representatives, open all the certificates and the votes shall then be counted; —The person having the greatest number of votes for President, shall be the President, if such number be a majority of the whole number of Electors appointed; and if no person have such majority, then from the persons having the highest numbers not exceeding three on the list of those voted for as President, the House of Representatives shall choose immediately, by ballot, the President. But in choosing the President, the votes shall be taken by states, the representation from each state having one vote; a quorum for this purpose shall consist of a member or members from two thirds of the states, and a majority of all the states shall be necessary to a choice. And if the House of Representatives shall not choose a President whenever the right of choice shall devolve upon them, before the fourth day of March next following, then the Vice President shall act as President, as in case of the death or other constitutional disability of the President. —* The person having the greatest number of votes as Vice President, shall be the Vice President, if such number be a majority of the whole number of Electors appointed, and if no person have a majority, then from the two highest numbers on the list, the Senate shall choose the Vice President; a quorum for the purpose shall consist of two thirds of the whole number of Senators, and a majority of the whole number shall be necessary to a choice. But no person constitutionally ineligible to the office of President shall be eligible to that of Vice President of the United States.

Amendment 9: Rights Not Listed are Retained by the People

Rights not listed in the Constitution are kept by the people.

Amendment 10: Powers Not Listed are Reserved to the States and People

Any power not given to the national government nor to the states is held by the people.

Amendment 11: Suits Against States

Passed by Congress March 4, 1794. Ratified February 7, 1795. Article III, section 2, of the Constitution was modified by this amendment.

Places limits on judicial power. Lawsuits against a state must be tried in that state's courts.

Amendment 12: Election of President and Vice President

Passed by Congress December 9, 1803. Ratified June 15, 1804. Note: A portion of Article II, section 1 of the Constitution, was superseded by the Twelfth Amendment.

Changed the electoral college. Electors are to use separate ballots for president and vice president.

*Superceded by section 3 of the Twentieth Amendment.

Amendment 13: Slavery Abolished

Passed by Congress January 31, 1865. Ratified December 6, 1865. Note: A portion of Article IV, section 2, of the Constitution was superseded by the Thirteenth Amendment.

Abolishes slavery. The Thirteenth, Fourteenth, and Fifteenth Amendments are sometimes called the "Reconstruction Amendments" because they followed the Civil War and were drafted to abolish slavery and prevent slavery under other names.

Amendment 14: Rights of Citizens

Passed by Congress June 13, 1866. Ratified July 9, 1868. Note: Article I, section 2, of the Constitution was modified by section 2 of the Fourteenth Amendment.

This amendment was designed to prevent state governments from violating the rights of former slaves after the Civil War. It has been used to extend almost all of the rights granted in the Bill of Rights to citizens and prevent state governments from denying those rights.

Section 1: Citizenship Defined

Declares that all persons born or naturalized in the United States are American citizens and citizens of their state of residence. This established the citizenship of former slaves. States cannot violate the rights of citizens, deprive any person of life, liberty, or property without due process of law, or deny any person the equal protection of the laws.

This has been used extensively by the Supreme Court to test the validity of state legislation based upon the due process and the equal protection clauses, which apply to all persons whether or not they are citizens of the United States.

Section 2: Representation in Congress

Representation in the House of Representatives must be made on the basis of the whole state population, excluding Native Americans not taxed. Reduction of a states Congressional representation is allowed if a state forbids male citizens over twenty-one years old the ability to vote.

*Changed by section 1 of the Twenty-sixth Amendment. ### Section 3: Penalty for Rebellion

This excluded leaders of the Confederacy from holding state or federal offices unless Congress agreed to remove the ban by a two-thirds vote of each house. Most former Confederate leaders were allowed to return to public life by the end of Reconstruction.

Section 4: Public Debt

Confirms the public debt from the Civil War. However, the debt of the Confederacy was declared invalid. Former slave owners could not collect compensation for the loss of slaves.

Amendment XIII
Section 1

Neither slavery nor involuntary servitude, except as a punishment for crime whereof the party shall have been duly convicted, shall exist within the United States, or any place subject to their jurisdiction.

Section 2

Congress shall have power to enforce this article by appropriate legislation.

Amendment XIV
Section 1

All persons born or naturalized in the United States, and subject to the jurisdiction thereof, are citizens of the United States and of the State wherein they reside. No State shall make or enforce any law which shall abridge the privileges or immunities of citizens of the United States; nor shall any State deprive any person of life, liberty, or property, without due process of law; nor deny to any person within its jurisdiction the equal protection of the laws.

Section 2

Representatives shall be apportioned among the several States according to their respective numbers, counting the whole number of persons in each State, excluding Indians not taxed. But when the right to vote at any election for the choice of electors for President and VicePresident of the United States, Representatives in Congress, the Executive and Judicial officers of a State, or the members of the Legislature thereof, is denied to any of the male inhabitants of such State, being twenty one years of age,* and citizens of the United States, or in any way abridged, except for participation in rebellion, or other crime, the basis of representation therein shall be reduced in the proportion which the number of such male citizens shall bear to the whole number of male citizens twentyone years of age in such State.

Section 3

No person shall be a Senator or Representative in Congress, or elector of President and Vice President, or hold any office, civil or military, under the United States, or under any State, who, having previously taken an oath, as a member of Congress, or as an officer of the United States, or as a member of any State legislature, or as an executive or judicial officer of any State, to support the Constitution of the United States, shall have engaged in insurrection or rebellion against the same, or given aid or comfort to the enemies thereof. But Congress may by a vote of two thirds of each House, remove such disability.

Section 4

The validity of the public debt of the United States, authorized by law, including debts incurred for payment of pensions and bounties for services in suppressing insurrection or rebellion, shall not be questioned. But neither the United States nor any State shall assume or pay any debt or obligation incurred in aid of insurrection or rebellion against the United States, or any claim for the loss or emancipation of any slave; but all such debts, obligations and claims shall be held illegal and void.

Section 5

The Congress shall have the power to enforce, by appropriate legislation, the provisions of this article.

Amendment XV

Section 1

The right of citizens of the United States to vote shall not be denied or abridged by the United States or by any State on account of race, color, or previous condition of servitude—

Section 2

The Congress shall have the power to enforce this article by appropriate legislation.

Amendment XVI

The Congress shall have power to lay and collect taxes on incomes, from whatever source derived, without apportionment among the several States, and without regard to any census or enumeration.

Amendment XVII

Section 1

The Senate of the United States shall be composed of two Senators from each State, elected by the people thereof, for six years; and each Senator shall have one vote. The electors in each State shall have the qualifications requisite for electors of the most numerous branch of the State legislatures.

Section 2

When vacancies happen in the representation of any State in the Senate, the executive authority of such State shall issue writs of election to fill such vacancies: Provided, That the legislature of any State may empower the executive thereof to make temporary appointments until the people fill the vacancies by election as the legislature may direct.

Section 3

This amendment shall not be so construed as to affect the election or term of any Senator chosen before it becomes valid as part of the Constitution.

Amendment XVIII

Section 1

After one year from the ratification of this article the manufacture, sale, or transportation of intoxicating liquors within, the importation thereof into, or the exportation thereof from the United States and all territory subject to the jurisdiction thereof for beverage purposes is hereby prohibited.

Section 2

The Congress and the several States shall have concurrent power to enforce this article by appropriate legislation.

Section 3

This article shall be inoperative unless it shall have been ratified as an

Section 5: Enforcement

Congress may pass legislation to enforce the amendment. This is the basis upon which the Civil Rights Act of 1964 was passed.

Amendment 15: Right to Vote with No Racial Barriers

Passed by Congress February 26, 1869. Ratified February 3, 1870.

Section 1: African American Suffrage

The right of citizens to vote cannot be based on race, color, or previous condition of servitude (slavery). This did not give the right to vote to African American women. All women were still banned from voting in federal and most state elections.

Section 2: Enforcement

Congress may pass legislation to enforce this amendment. This amendment became the basis for the Voting Rights Act of 1965.**Amendment 16: Income Tax Authorized**

Passed by Congress July 2, 1909. Ratified February 3, 1913. Note: Article I, section 9, of the Constitution was modified by the Sixteenth Amendment.

The power to lay and collect taxes on incomes from whatever source.

Amendment 17: Election of Senators by Direct Popular Vote

Passed by Congress May 13, 1912. Ratified April 8, 1913. Note: Article I, section 3, of the Constitution was modified by the Seventeenth Amendment.

Prior to this amendment, senators were chosen by the state legislatures. This amendment changed the selection process to election by popular vote, giving citizens more control.

Amendment 18: National Prohibition of Intoxicating Liquors

Passed by Congress December 18, 1917. Ratified January 16, 1919. Repealed by the Twenty-first Amendment.

Prohibits manufacture, sale, or transportation of intoxicating liquors.

Amendment 19: Right to Vote for Women

Passed by Congress June 4, 1919. Ratified August 18, 1920.

Political action groups struggled for many years to extend the right to vote to women nationwide in both state and federal elections.

Amendment 20: "Lame Duck" Amendment

Passed by Congress March 2, 1932. Ratified January 23, 1933. Note: Article I, section 4, of the Constitution was modified by section 2 of this amendment. In addition, a portion of the Twelfth Amendment was superseded by section 3.

Section 1: New Term Dates

In the early years of our nation, without modern means of communication and transportation, a longer interval between the date of an election and the beginning of the term of office was necessary. It took time for the results of elections to be known and for public officials to make the sometimes long journey to Washington, D.C., from faraway states.

The session of Congress held immediately after an election still had the Representatives from the prior election. The terms for the newly-elected Representatives did not begin until 13 months after the election. Members who lost the election still served those 13 months until the new Representatives took office. This was a "Lame Duck" session.

"Lame Duck" is used to describe a president or any public officeholder who will not be returning when his or her current term ends. They may not be returning because they are not seeking reelection, or they were defeated in an intervening election, or their office is term-limited, as in the case of the president. The expression is also applied to a Congress which reconvenes after an election. A lame duck Congress continues in session with members known not to be returning still serving in it. The influence of the out-going officeholder is considered crippled, or "lamed," by the fact that he or she will soon be out of power.

To make the starting date of a new Congress and a new member's term coincide, this amendment changed the beginning of a member's term from March 4 to January 3. This amendment also shortens the time between the election of a new president and vice president and the inauguration.

Section 2: Meeting Time for Congress

Moves the date on which a new session of Congress began from the first Monday in December—13 months from the previous November elections—to January 3, just two months after the elections.

Section 3: Presidential Succession

If the president-elect dies before taking office, the vice president-elect becomes president.

Section 4: Filling Presidential Vacancies

If a presidential candidate dies while a presidential election is being decided in the House of Representatives, or a vice presidential candidate dies

---

~~amendment to the Constitution by the legislatures of the several States, as provided in the Constitution, within seven years from the date of the submission hereof to the States by the Congress.~~

Amendment XIX

The right of citizens of the United States to vote shall not be denied or abridged by the United States or by any State on account of sex.

Congress shall have power to enforce this article by appropriate legislation.

Amendment XX

Section 1

The terms of the President and the Vice President shall end at noon on the 20th day of January, and the terms of Senators and Representatives at noon on the 3d day of January, of the years in which such terms would have ended if this article had not been ratified; and the terms of their successors shall then begin.

Section 2

The Congress shall assemble at least once in every year, and such meeting shall begin at noon on the 3d day of January, unless they shall by law appoint a different day.

Section 3

If, at the time fixed for the beginning of the term of the President, the President elect shall have died, the Vice President elect shall become President. If a President shall not have been chosen before the time fixed for the beginning of his term, or if the President elect shall have failed to qualify, then the Vice President elect shall act as President until a President shall have qualified; and the Congress may by law provide for the case wherein neither a President elect nor a Vice President shall have qualified, declaring who shall then act as President, or the manner in which one who is to act shall be selected, and such person shall act accordingly until a President or Vice President shall have qualified.

Section 4

The Congress may by law provide for the case of the death of any of the persons from whom the House of Representatives may choose a President whenever the right of choice shall have devolved upon them, and for the case of the death of any of the persons from whom the Senate may choose a Vice President whenever the right of choice shall have devolved upon them.

Section 5

Sections 1 and 2 shall take effect on the 15th day of October following the ratification of this article.

Section 6

This article shall be inoperative unless it shall have been ratified as an amendment to the Constitution by the legislatures of three fourths of the several States within seven years from the date of its submission.

Amendment XXI

Section 1

The eighteenth article of amendment to the Constitution of the United States is hereby repealed.

Section 2

The transportation or importation into any State, Territory, or Possession of the United States for delivery or use therein of intoxicating liquors, in violation of the laws thereof, is hereby prohibited.

Section 3

This article shall be inoperative unless it shall have been ratified as an amendment to the Constitution by conventions in the several States, as provided in the Constitution, within seven years from the date of the submission hereof to the States by the Congress.

Amendment XXII

Section 1

No person shall be elected to the office of the President more than twice, and no person who has held the office of President, or acted as President, for more than two years of a term to which some other person was elected President shall be elected to the office of President more than once. But this Article shall not apply to any person holding the office of President when this Article was proposed by Congress, and shall not prevent any person who may be holding the office of President, or acting as President, during the term within which this Article becomes operative from holding the office of President or acting as President during the remainder of such term.

Section 2

This article shall be inoperative unless it shall have been ratified as an amendment to the Constitution by the legislatures of three fourths of the several States within seven years from the date of its submission to the States by the Congress.

Amendment XXIII

Section 1

The District constituting the seat of Government of the United States shall appoint in such manner as Congress may direct:

A number of electors of President and Vice President equal to the whole number of Senators and Representatives in Congress to which the District would be entitled if it were a State, but in no event more than the least populous State; they shall be in addition to those appointed by the States, but they shall be considered, for the purposes of the election of President and Vice President, to be electors appointed by a State; and they shall meet in the District and perform such duties as provided by the twelfth article of amendment.

while a vice presidential election is being decided in the Senate, Congress may pass legislation to deal with the situation.

Section 5: Effective Dates

Sections 1 and 2 took effect in the 1934 Congressional elections and the 1936 presidential election.

Section 6: Time Limit for Ratification

The time period for ratification of this amendment by the states was limited to seven years.

Amendment 21: Repeal of National Prohibition

Passed by Congress February 20, 1933. Ratified December 5, 1933.

This amendment cancels the Eighteenth Amendment. This is an example of the adaptability of the Constitution to meet the changing needs of the citizens.

Amendment 22: Two-Term Limit for Presidents

Passed by Congress March 21, 1947. Ratified February 27, 1951.

Before 1951, the president could run for as many terms as he wanted. After serving two terms as president, George Washington chose not to run again. All other presidents followed his example until Franklin D. Roosevelt. Roosevelt successfully ran for office four times. In 1945, early in his fourth term, he died. Six years later, Congress passed this amendment limiting presidents to two terms. This amendment did not apply to President Truman, who held office at the time the amendment was ratified.

Amendment 23: Presidential Vote for District of Columbia

Passed by Congress June 16, 1960. Ratified March 29, 1961.

Enables residents of the District of Columbia to vote for president and vice President. This amendment gives Washington, D.C., three members in the electoral college. Residents of Washington, D.C., still do not have full representation in Congress.

Amendment 24: Poll Tax Banned in Federal Elections

Passed by Congress August 27, 1962. Ratified January 23, 1964.

States cannot require a poll tax for citizens to vote. People who have failed to pay any other taxes may still vote.

Amendment 25: Presidential Disability and Succession

Passed by Congress July 6, 1965. Ratified February 10, 1967. Note: Article II, section 1, of the Constitution was affected by the Twenty-fifth Amendment.

Covers presidential disability, vice presidential vacancies, and order of succession to the office of the president.

Section 1: Presidential Succession

If the president is removed from office, either by death, resignation, or as a result of impeachment, the vice president becomes the president. There had been some uncertainty until this amendment as to whether, upon a president's death, the vice president was actually the president or a vice president acting as president.

Section 2: Filling a Vacancy in the Vice Presidency

If the vice presidency is vacant, the president is to appoint a new vice president with the approval of the Congress. Until this amendment, there was no provision for dealing with a vacancy in the vice presidency. If a president died in office, the vice president then became president. The vice presidency was vacant for the rest of the term. Similarly, if a vice president died in office, the vacancy in the vice presidency existed through the president's term.

Section 3: Presidential Disability

If the president believes that he or she is unable to carry out the duties of the office, the president can send a written declaration to Congress informing them of the disability. The vice president becomes the acting president until the president is able to resume his or her duties. **Section 4**

If the president is unable to carry out the duties of the office, but is unable (as in the case of illness) or unwilling to inform Congress of his or her disability, the vice president and the majority of the president's cabinet can declare a president disabled. The vice president becomes acting president. If there is disagreement between the president and the vice president and the cabinet as to whether or not the president is disabled, then Congress must resolve the disagreement in 21 days. The term disability or inability is not defined in this amendment or in the Constitution, leaving the interpretation of

Section 2

The Congress shall have power to enforce this article by appropriate legislation.

Amendment XXIV
Section 1

The right of citizens of the United States to vote in any primary or other election for President or Vice President, for electors for President or Vice President, or for Senator or Representative in Congress, shall not be denied or abridged by the United States or any State by reason of failure to pay poll tax or other tax.

Section 2

The Congress shall have power to enforce this article by appropriate legislation.

Amendment XXV
Section 1

In case of the removal of the President from office or of his death or resignation, the Vice President shall become President.

Section 2

Whenever there is a vacancy in the office of the Vice President, the President shall nominate a Vice President who shall take office upon confirmation by a majority vote of both Houses of Congress.

Section 3

Whenever the President transmits to the President pro tempore of the Senate and the Speaker of the House of Representatives his written declaration that he is unable to discharge the powers and duties of his office, and until he transmits to them a written declaration to the contrary, such powers and duties shall be discharged by the Vice President as Acting President.

Section 4

Whenever the Vice President and a majority of either the principal officers of the executive departments or of such other body as Congress may by law provide, transmit to the President pro tempore of the Senate and the Speaker of the House of Representatives their written declaration that the President is unable to discharge the powers and duties of his office, the Vice President shall immediately assume the powers and duties of the office as Acting President.

Thereafter, when the President transmits to the President pro tempore of the Senate and the Speaker of the House of Representatives his written declaration that no inability exists, he shall resume the powers and duties of his office unless the Vice President and a majority of either the principal officers of the executive department or of such other body as Congress may by law provide, transmit within four days to the President pro tempore of the Senate and the Speaker of the House of Representatives their written declaration that the President is unable to discharge the powers and duties of his office. Thereupon Congress shall decide the issue, assembling within forty eight hours for that purpose if not in session. If the Congress, within twenty one days after receipt of the latter written declaration, or, if Congress is not in session, within twenty one days after Congress is required to assemble, determines by two thirds vote of both Houses that the President is unable to discharge the powers and duties of his office, the Vice President shall continue to discharge the same as Acting President; otherwise, the President shall resume the powers and duties of his office.

Amendment XXVI

Section 1

The right of citizens of the United States, who are eighteen years of age or older, to vote shall not be denied or abridged by the United States or by any State on account of age.

Section 2

The Congress shall have power to enforce this article by appropriate legislation.

Amendment XXVII

No law, varying the compensation for the services of the Senators and Representatives, shall take effect, until an election of representatives shall have intervened.

presidential disability open to debate.

This amendment was used during the Nixon and Ford administrations. For the first time in our history two men who had not faced the voters in a national election became president and vice president. First, Vice President Spiro Agnew resigned on October 10, 1973. President Nixon nominated Representative Gerald R. Ford of Michigan to succeed him. Both Houses thereafter confirmed the nomination. Vice President Ford took the oath of office on December 6, 1973. Next, President Richard M. Nixon resigned his office August 9, 1974, and Vice President Ford immediately succeeded to the office and took the presidential oath of office at noon of the same day. Finally, President Ford nominated Nelson A. Rockefeller of New York to be vice president, which was confirmed by Congress. Mr. Rockefeller took the oath of office for the vice presidency on December 19, 1974.

Amendment 26: Voting Age Lowered to Eighteen Years

Passed by Congress March 23, 1971. Ratified July 1, 1971. Note: Section 2 of the Fourteenth Amendment was modified by section 1 of the Twenty-sixth Amendment.

Lowered the voting age to eighteen in all federal, state, and local elections. This amendment was the result of the public's belief that citizens who are serving in the military should have the right to vote.

Amendment 27: Congressional Pay

Originally proposed September 25, 1789. Ratified May 7, 1992.

Members of a session of Congress which has approved a pay raise may only receive the increase after the next election.

The Emancipation Proclamation

The Emancipation Proclamation was issued by President Abraham Lincoln in 1863 during the Civil War. It declared that the slaves in the Confederate states were free. This document later became the foundation of the Thirteenth Amendment to the Constitution

JANUARY 1, 1863
BY THE PRESIDENT OF THE UNITED STATES OF AMERICA:

A PROCLAMATION.

Whereas, on the twenty second day of September, in the year of our Lord one thousand eight hundred and sixty two, a proclamation was issued by the President of the United States, containing, among other things, the following, to wit: "That on the first day of January, in the year of our Lord one thousand eight hundred and sixty three, all persons held as slaves within any State or designated part of a State, the people whereof shall then be in rebellion against the United States, shall be then, thenceforward, and forever free; and the Executive Government of the United States, including the military and naval authority thereof, will recognize and maintain the freedom of such persons, and will do no act or acts to repress such persons, or any of them, in any efforts they may make for their actual freedom.

"That the Executive will, on the first day of January aforesaid, by proclamation, designate the States and parts of States, if any, in which the people thereof, respectively, shall then be in rebellion against the United States; and the fact that any State, or the people thereof, shall on that day be, in good faith, represented in the Congress of the United States by members chosen thereto at elections wherein a majority of the qualified voters of such State shall have participated, shall, in the absence of strong countervailing testimony, be deemed conclusive evidence that such State, and the people thereof, are not then in rebellion against the United States."

This document did not free all of the slaves. It protected slavery in the border states that did not join the Confederacy as well as areas of the South under Union control in Louisiana and Virginia.

However, the Emancipation Proclamation had other important effects. The Proclamation clarified for many Northerners the Union's cause and strengthened the war effort. It also freed approximately 500,000 African Americans who had escaped to free states. This allowed them to join—as about 200,000 of them did—the Union Army and Navy and fight their former owners.

Now, therefore I, Abraham Lincoln, President of the United States, by virtue of the power in me vested as Commander in Chief, of the Army and Navy of the United States in time of actual armed rebellion against the authority and government of the United States, and as a fit and necessary war measure for suppressing said rebellion, do, on this first day of January, in the year of our Lord one thousand eight hundred and sixty three, and in accordance with my purpose so to do publicly proclaimed for the full period of one hundred days, from the day first above mentioned, order and designate as the States and parts of States wherein the people thereof respectively, are this day in rebellion against the United States, the following, to wit:

Arkansas, Texas, Louisiana, (except the Parishes of St. Bernard, Plaquemines, Jefferson, St. John, St. Charles, St. James Ascension, Assumption, Terrebonne, Lafourche, St. Mary, St. Martin, and Orleans, including the City of New Orleans) Mississippi, Alabama, Florida, Georgia, South Carolina, North Carolina, and Virginia, (except the forty eight counties designated as West Virginia, and also the counties of Berkley, Accomac, Northampton, Elizabeth City, York, Princess Ann, and Norfolk, including the cities of Norfolk and Portsmouth[)], and which excepted parts, are for the present, left precisely as if this proclamation were not issued.

And by virtue of the power, and for the purpose aforesaid, I do order and declare that all persons held as slaves within said designated States, and parts of States, are, and henceforward shall be free; and that the Executive government of the United States, including the military and naval authorities thereof, will recognize and maintain the freedom of said persons.

And I hereby enjoin upon the people so declared to be free to abstain from all violence, unless in necessary self defence; and I recommend to them that, in all cases when allowed, they labor faithfully for reasonable wages.

And I further declare and make known, that such persons of suitable condition, will be received into the armed service of the United States to garrison forts, positions, stations, and other places, and to man vessels of all sorts in said service.

And upon this act, sincerely believed to be an act of justice, warranted by the Constitution, upon military necessity, I invoke the considerate judgment of mankind, and the gracious favor of Almighty God.

In witness whereof, I have hereunto set my hand and caused the seal of the United States to be affixed.

Done at the City of Washington, this first day of January, in the year of our Lord one thousand eight hundred and sixty three, and of the Independence of the United States of America the eightyseventh.

By the President: ABRAHAM LINCOLN
WILLIAM H. SEWARD, Secretary of State.

George Washington
Term: 1789–1797
Party: Federalist1
Vice President: John Adams
State of Birth: Virginia
Birth Date: Feb 22, 1732
Death Date: Dec 14, 1799

John Adams
Term: 1797–1801
Party: Federalist
Vice President: Thomas Jefferson
State of Birth: Massachusetts
Birth Date: Oct 30, 1735
Death Date: July 4, 1826

Thomas Jefferson
Term: 1801–1809
Party: Demo-Republican
Vice President: Aaron Burr, George Clinton
State of Birth: Virginia
Birth Date: April 13, 1743
Death Date: July 4, 1826

James Madison
Term: 1809–1817
Party: Demo-Republican
Vice President: George Clinton, Elbridge Gerry
State of Birth: Virginia
Birth Date: March 16, 1751
Death Date: June 28, 1836

James Monroe
Term: 1817–1825
Party: Demo-Republican
Vice President: Daniel D. Tompkins
State of Birth: Virginia
Birth Date: April 28, 1758
Death Date: July 4, 1831

John Quincy Adams
Term: 1825–1829
Party: Demo-Republican
Vice President: John C. Calhoun
State of Birth: Massachusetts
Birth Date: July 11, 1767
Death Date: Feb 23, 1848

Andrew Jackson
Term: 1829–1837
Party: Democratic
Vice President: John C. Calhoun
State of Birth: South Carolina
Birth Date: March 15, 1767
Death Date: June 8, 1845

Martin Van Buren
Term: 1837–1841
Party: Democratic
Vice President: Richard M. Johnson
State of Birth: New York
Birth Date: Dec 5, 1782
Death Date: July 24, 1862

Willian Henry Harrison
Term: 1841*
Party: Whig
Vice President: John Tyler
State of Birth: Virginia
Birth Date: Feb 9, 1773
Death Date: April 4, 1841

John Tyler
Term: 1841–1845
Party: Whig
Vice President: None
State of Birth: Virginia
Birth Date: March 29, 1790
Death Date: Jan 18, 1862

James K. Polk
Term: 1845–1849
Party: Democratic
Vice President: George M. Dallas
State of Birth: North Carolina
Birth Date: Nov 2, 1795
Death Date: June 15, 1849

Zachary Taylor
Term: 1849–1850*
Party: Whig
Vice President: Millard Fillmore
State of Birth: Virginia
Birth Date: Nov 24, 1784
Death Date: July 9, 1850

Millard Fillmore
Term: 1850–1853
Party: Whig
Vice President: None
State of Birth: New York
Birth Date: Jan 7, 1800
Death Date: March 8, 1874

Franklin Pierce
Term: 1853–1857
Party: Democratic
Vice President: William King
State of Birth: New Hampshire
Birth Date: Novr 23, 1804
Death Date: Oct 8, 1869

James Buchanan
Term: 1909–1913
Party: Democratic
Vice President: John C. Breckinridge
State of Birth: Pennsylvania
Birth Date: April 23, 1791
Death Date: June 1, 1868

Abraham Lincoln
Term: 1861–1865**
Party: Republican
Vice President: Hannibal Hamlin
State of Birth: Kentucky
Birth Date: Feb 12, 1809
Death Date: April 15, 1865

Andrew Johnson
Term: 1865–1869
Party: Union2
Vice President: None
State of Birth: North Carolina
Birth Date: Dec 29, 1808
Death Date: July 31, 1875

Ulysses S. Grant
Term: 1869–1877
Party: Republican
Vice President: Schuyler Colfax
State of Birth: Ohio
Birth Date: April 27, 1822
Death Date: July 23, 1885

Rutherford B. Hayes
Term: 1877–1881
Party: Republican
Vice President: William Wheeler
State of Birth: Ohio
Birth Date: Oct 4, 1822
Death Date: Jan 17, 1893

James A Garfield
Term: 1881**
Party: Republican
Vice President: Chester A. Arthur
State of Birth: Ohio
Birth Date: Nov 19, 1831
Death Date: Sept 19, 1881

Chester A Arthur
Term: 1881–1885
Party: Republican
Vice President: None
State of Birth: Vermont
Birth Date: Oct 5, 1829
Death Date: Nov 18, 1886

Grover Cleveland
Term: 1893–1897³
Party: Democratic
Vice President: Thomas Hendricks
State of Birth: New Jersey
Birth Date: March 18, 1837
Death Date: June 24, 1908

Benjamin Harrison
Term: 1889–1893
Party: Republican
Vice President: Levi P. Morton
State of Birth: Ohio
Birth Date: Aug 20, 1833
Death Date: June 24, 1908

Grover Cleveland
Term: 1893–1897³
Party: Democratic
Vice President: Adlai E. Stevenson
State of Birth: New Jersey
Birth Date: March 18, 1837
Death Date: June 24, 1908

William McKinley
Term: 1897–1901**
Party: Republican
Vice President: Garret Hobart, Theodore Roosevelt
State of Birth: Ohio
Birth Date: Jan 29, 1843
Death Date: Sept 14, 1901

Theodore Roosevelt
Term: 1901–1909
Party: Republican
Vice President: Charles Fairbanks
State of Birth: New York
Birth Date: Oct 27, 1858
Death Date: Jan 6, 1919

William Howard Taft
Term: 1909–1913
Party: Republican
Vice President: James S. Sherman
State of Birth: Ohio
Birth Date: Sept 15, 1857
Death Date: March 8, 1930

Woodrow Wilson
Term: 1913–1921
Party: Democratic
Vice President: Thomas R. Marshall
State of Birth: Virginia
Birth Date: Dec 28, 1856
Death Date: Feb 3, 1924

Warren G. Harding
Term: 1921–1923*
Party: Republican
Vice President: Calvin Coolidge
State of Birth: Ohio
Birth Date: Nov 2, 1865
Death Date: Aug 2, 1923

Calvin Coolidge
Term: 1923–1929
Party: Republican
Vice President: Charles G. Dawes
State of Birth: Ohio
Birth Date: Nov 2, 1865
Death Date: Jan 5, 1933

Herbert Hoover
Term: 1929–1933
Party: Republican
Vice President: Charles Curtis
State of Birth: Iowa
Birth Date: Aug 10, 1874
Death Date: Oct 20, 1964

Franklin D. Roosevelt
Term: 1933–1945*
Party: Democratic
Vice President: John Nance Garner, Henry A. Wallace, Harry S Truman
State of Birth: New York
Birth Date: Jan 30, 1882
Death Date: April 12, 1945

Harry S. Truman
Term: 1945–1953
Party: Democratic
Vice President: Alben W. Barkley
State of Birth: Missouri
Birth Date: May 5, 1894
Death Date: Dec 26, 1977

Dwight Eisenhower
Term: 1953–1961
Party: Republican
Vice President: Richard M. Nixon
State of Birth: Texas
Birth Date: Oct 14, 1890
Death Date: March 28, 1969

John F. Kennedy
Term: 1961–1963**
Party: Democratic
Vice President: Lyndon B. Johnson
State of Birth: Massachusetts
Birth Date: May 29, 1917
Death Date: Nov 22, 1963

Lyndon B. Johnson
Term: 1963–1969
Party: Democratic
Vice President: Hubert H. Humphrey
State of Birth: Texas
Birth Date: Aug 27, 1908
Death Date: Jan 22, 1973

Richard M. Nixon
Term: 1969–1974[4]
Party: Republican
Vice President: Spiro T. Agnew, Gerald R. Ford
State of Birth: California
Birth Date: Jan 9, 1913
Death Date: April 22, 1994

Gerald R. Ford
Term: 1974–1977[5]
Party: Republican
Vice President: Nelson R. Rockefeller
State of Birth: Nebraska
Birth Date: July 14, 1913
Death Date: Dec 26, 2006

Jimmy Carter
Term: 1977–1981
Party: Democratic
Vice President: Walter F. Mondale
State of Birth: Georgia
Birth Date: Oct 1, 1924
Death Date:

Ronald Reagan
Term: 1981–1989
Party: Republican
Vice President: George H. W. Bush
State of Birth: Illinois
Birth Date: Feb 6, 1911
Death Date: June 5, 2004

George H. W. Bush
Term: 1989–1993
Party: Republican
Vice President: J. Danforth Quayle
State of Birth: Massachusetts
Birth Date: June 12, 1924
Death Date:

William J. Clinton
Term: 1993–2001
Party: Democratic
Vice President: Albert Gore, Jr.
State of Birth: Arkansas
Birth Date: Aug 19, 1946
Death Date:

George W. Bush
Term: 2001–
Party: Republican
Vice President: Richard Cheney
State of Birth: Connecticut
Birth Date: July 6, 1946
Death Date:

---

* Died in office
** Assassinated in office

[1] There were no parties in the first election. The parties formed during Washington's first term.

[2] The Republican National Convention of 1864 adopted the name Union Party and renominated Lincoln for president. The Union Party nominated Johnson, a Democrat, for vice president. Although frequently listed as a Republican vice president and president, Johnson returned to the Democratic Party when the Union Party broke apart after 1868.

[3] Second nonconsecutive term.

[4] Resigned August 9, 1974.

[5] Appointed Vice President in 1973 after Spiro Agnew's resignation; assumed presidency after Nixon's resignation.

A

Acapulco A port city on the Pacific Ocean and a famous tourist spot; in the 1500s an important harbor in the Spanish Empire.

Acadia The French colonial territory in northeastern North America that included parts of today's eastern Quebec, New Brunswick, Nova Scotia, and New England.

Africa The world's second largest continent. Western regions were the homelands of many ancestors of African Americans living today throughout the Americas.

Alaska A state of the United States located in northwestern North America. One of two states that does not touch the other 48.

Alberta A Canadian province located in the west central region. The province contains part of the rich Interior Plains and the Western Mountains.

Appalachian Mountains A mountain chain in eastern North America, reaching from Alabama in the United States into northeastern Canada.

Arctic Plains Canada's most northerly area, stretching almost to the North Pole. Most of the land is frozen nearly all year, so few things are able to grow during the short summer.

Aruba An island in the Caribbean Sea just off the Venezuelan coast (part of the Lesser Antilles) that is a territory of the Netherlands. Aruba's capital is Oranjestad.

Atlantic Ocean One of the world's largest bodies of water, separating North and South America from Europe and Africa.

Atlantic Coastal Plain A flat or sloping plain bordering the Atlantic Ocean and reaching from Maine into Florida.

B

Baffin Island Located northeast of the Canadian mainland. Sparsely inhabited, mostly by Native Americans known as Inuit.

Bahamas A group of islands off the southeastern coast of Florida. One of three island groups of Middle America.

Barbados A small nation occupying an island in the Lesser Antilles of the Caribbean Sea.

Bay of Campeche Southwestern section of the Gulf of Mexico, forming a wide shallow bay extending into southeastern Mexico.

Belize A small nation located on the northeastern coast of Central America in mainland Middle America.

Beringia A land bridge that once connected Asia and northwestern North America. Now covered by the waters of the Bering Strait.

Blue Ridge Mountains Part of the Appalachian Mountains that extend from West Virginia through North Carolina into Georgia.

Bonaire An island in the Caribbean Sea just off the Venezuelan coast (part of the Lesser Antilles) that is a territory of the Netherlands. Bonaire's capital is Kralendijk.

British Columbia Canada's most western province borders the Pacific Ocean.

C

Calgary Located on the western edge of the Interior Plains in southwestern Alberta. Calgary, now a cosmopolitan city, began as a frontier cattle town.

Canada The world's second largest nation, located in northern North America. Made up of ten provinces and two territories.

Canadian Shield A large forested plain extending south of the Arctic Plains and covering most of Canada. Soil that once covered the shield was pushed south by glaciers thousands of years ago, exposing an ancient, hard rock surface.

Canal Zone A 10-mile (16-km)-wide strip in Panama bordering the Panama Canal.

Cancún An island resort in southeastern Mexico off the northeast coast of the Yucatán Peninsula.

Caribbean Sea Part of the southern Atlantic Ocean between North and South America. Enclosed by the Lesser Antilles to the east and the Greater Antilles and Yucatán Peninsula to the west.

Caribbean Islands Located in the sea between North and South America, these lands are part of the Middle American region.

Central America Part of mainland Middle America, located south of Mexico on the land bridge connecting North and South America. Seven nations—Guatemala, Belize, Honduras, El Salvador, Nicaragua, Costa Rica, and Panama—are found there.

Central Lowlands The eastern part of a vast plains area that makes up much of the central part of the United States.

Central Volcanic Zone A major physical region of mainland Middle America that stretches from Guatemala southward to Panama. The zone has many active volcanoes that have caused damage to people and property.

Chesapeake Bay Located on the Atlantic coast, the bay has served as a rich fishing ground and has provided access to Baltimore.

Chiapas A state in southeastern Mexico, home of the modern Highland Maya.

Chichén Itzá A village in the Yucatán state of Mexico; once one of the principal centers of the Maya; extensive ruins, some still well preserved.

Chihuahua A northern state of Mexico; a rich silver-mining district.

Ciudad Juárez A border city in the northern Mexican state of Chihuahua, opposite El Paso, Texas.

Continental Divide An imaginary line twisting through the Rocky Mountains. The streams west of the divide flow toward the Pacific Ocean, and those to the east flow toward the Mississippi River and the Gulf of Mexico.

Costa Rica A nation located in Central America west of Panama, southwest of the Caribbean Sea, and east of the Pacific Ocean.

Cozumel An island off the northeast coast of Quintana Roo territory, in southeastern Mexico.

Cuba A nation occupying the largest island in the Caribbean Sea. One of four islands of the Greater Antilles.

Curaçao An island in the Caribbean Sea just off the Venezuelan coast (part of the Lesser Antilles) that is a territory of the Netherlands. Curaçao's capital is Willemstad.

D

Dominican Republic A nation that occupies two thirds of Hispaniola, a Caribbean Island.

Durango A state in northwestern central Mexico; industrial center known for its large mining operations.

E

El Salvador A nation in Central America on the Pacific Ocean.

England A once independent nation that is now linked with Wales, Scotland, and Northern Ireland to form the United Kingdom. Located on islands off the western coast of Europe. Homeland of the founders of the 13 colonies from which the United States grew. London was for many years the seat of Canada's government.

Europe A small continent located on a peninsula of the Eurasian landmass. The homeland of people who conquered the Americas and settled there.

F

Fort St. George An English colonial settlement in North America founded in 1607 and lasting until 1608. It was located in the present-day town of Phippsburg, Maine near the mouth of the Kennebec River.

Four Corners An informal, but commonly used, name for the place where the states of Arizona, New Mexico, Utah, and Colorado meet.

France Western European nation that competed with England for control of North America. Ancestors of many of today's Canadians emigrated from this nation.

G

Grand Banks Shallow waters lying off the coast of Newfoundland. For centuries one of the world's richest fishing areas but now depleted by overfishing.

Grand Canyon Colorado River gorge in the northwestern corner of Arizona. (p. 324)

Great Lakes Five large lakes—Superior, Michigan, Huron, Erie, and Ontario—located along the border of the United States and Canada in central North America.

Greenland A large, barren island lying off the northeastern coast of North America and mostly within the Arctic Circle.

Great Lakes-St. Lawrence Lowlands The smallest of Canada's regions, but the center of about half of the nation's population. Located east of the Great Lakes and along the St. Lawrence River valley.

Great Plains The western part of a huge flat or rolling area that makes up a large section of central United States and Canada (see Interior Plains).

Greater Antilles A group of the largest islands in the Caribbean—Cuba, Jamaica, Hispaniola, and Puerto Rico.

Grenada An island nation in the Caribbean.

Guadalajara A densely settled city in the state of Jalisco, in western central Mexico; a rich agricultural and industrial area, and an important mining center.

Guanajuato For many centuries the wealthiest city in Mexico because of its silver and gold deposits; on the Mesa Central, north of Mexico City.

Guatemala A nation in Central America south of Mexico and north of the Pacific Ocean.

Gulf of Mexico East of Mexico and south of the United States, connected to the Atlantic Ocean and Caribbean Sea.

H

Haiti Shares the island of Hispaniola with the Dominican Republic.

Hawaiian Islands A large group of islands in the northern Pacific Ocean settled originally by Polynesian people. One of two states of the United States not connected to the other 48.

Hispaniola An island in the Caribbean divided between the Dominican Republic and Haiti. One of four islands of the Greater Antilles.

Honduras A nation in northern Central America on the Caribbean Sea.

Hudson Bay An inland sea in northern Canada.

I

Iberian Peninsula Located in southwestern Europe. A land area shared by Portugal and Spain, the first European countries to explore and settle in the Americas.

Imperial Valley A large agricultural area in southern California where fertile soil and a growing season that lasts nearly all year enable farmers to produce much of our nation's fruit and vegetables.

Interior Plains A vast, gently rolling agricultural region in central Canada connected to the Great Plains and Central Lowlands in the United States.

Iqualuit The capital and the largest city of Nunavut Territory, Canada. It is located on Frobisher Bay, on the southeastern part of Baffin Island.

Ireland A country in northwestern Europe occupying part of an island west of Great Britain. The homeland of many emigrants to the United States.

Isthmus of Tehuantepec Isthmus in southern Mexico, between the Bay of Campeche on the north and the Gulf of Tehuantepec on the south; 137 meters wide.

J

Jamaica An island nation in the Caribbean Sea. One of four islands of the Greater Antilles.

Jamestown Site of the first permanent English settlement in North America. Located on the coast of southeastern Virginia.

L

L'Anse aux Meadows The location where evidence of Norse settlement in North America was found. It is located on the island of Newfoundland, now part fo the Canadian province of Newfoundland and Labrador.

Labrador Located in the Canadian province of Newfoundland. Sparsely populated but contains some of Canada's best sources of wood, iron ore, and other minerals.

León A city in the central Mexican state of Guanajuato; known for its tanneries, flour mills, and leather and woolen goods.

Lesser Antilles A group of islands in the eastern Caribbean Sea.

M

Manitoba Canadian province midway between the east and western boundaries of the nation. Part of the Interior Plains region of Canada.

Matamoros A busy Mexican border town opposite Brownsville, Texas, near the Gulf of Mexico.

Mexico A nation south of the United States in mainland Middle America.

Mazatlán Famous resort and largest Mexican seaport on the Pacific coast.

Mesa Central The middle region of Mexico—the central part of the Mexican Plateau. Mexico City and Puebla are located here.

Mesa del Norte The northernmost section of the Mexican Plateau; lies between the Sierra Madre Oriental and the Sierra Madre Occidental.

Mexico City Capital and largest city in Mexico. Built on the site of the ancient Aztec capital, Tenochtitlán.

Mid-Atlantic A part of the Northeastern Region of the United States. Includes the states of Maryland, Delaware, New Jersey, Pennsylvania, and New York, as well as the District of Columbia, the site of the nation's capital city, Washington.

Midwest Region Includes states of Ohio,

GAZETTEER

Illinois, Indiana, Michigan, Wisconsin, Missouri, Iowa, Kansas, Minnesota, Nebraska, North Dakota, and South Dakota.

Mississippi River The longest river in the United States and North America, located in the central part of the nation. Flows from Minnesota south into the Gulf of Mexico.

Missouri River Flows from Montana to St. Louis, Missouri, where it joins the Mississippi River. Helped move people and freight westward, especially in the 1800s.

Monterrey The third-largest city in Mexico, near the border and Laredo, Texas; a center of international trade and manufacturing.

Montreal Canada's second largest city, located on the St. Lawrence River. The city serves as a transportation hub and financial center.

Mount McKinley Tallest mountain in North America, located in the Alaska Range. Native Americans call it Denali, which means "Great One."

N

New Brunswick Eastern Canadian province bordering the state of Maine. Part of the Appalachian Highlands region.

New England A part of the Northeast Region of the United States. Includes states of Maine, Vermont, New Hampshire, Massachusetts, Connecticut, and Rhode Island.

New France A colony established and held by France from 1609 to 1763. Occupied large areas in what are now Canada and the United States.

Newfoundland Easternmost Canadian province. Part of the Appalachian Highlands region.

New Orleans A city on the Mississippi River in Louisiana settled by France nearly 300 years ago. Has served as a major port for freight using the Mississippi River and the Gulf of Mexico.

New Spain Name often used to identify some of Spain's colonies. In the Western Hemisphere these were chiefly in North America and the Caribbean Sea.

New York City The largest city in the United States. A major port, commercial, and communications center located on the Mid-Atlantic coast.

Nicaragua A nation in Central America

west of the Caribbean Sea and northeast of the Pacific Ocean.

North America The world's third largest continent, occupied by Canada and the United States. Geographers generally agree that the islands of the Caribbean, Mexico, and Central America are physically parts of North America. These latter countries, however, have their own cultural identity and are called Middle America.

Northern Hemisphere The half of the earth lying north of the Equator.

Northern Highlands A major physical region of mainland Middle America located in northern Mexico. Made up of two mountain ranges—the Sierra Madre Occidental and Sierra Madre Oriental—which flank a central plateau.

Northwest Territories Located in north central Canada. One of three territories in Canada.

Nova Scotia A small Canadian province bordered on the north by the Gulf of St. Lawrence and on the east by the Atlantic Ocean. Settled by Loyalists after the American Revolution.

Nuevo Laredo A town in the eastern Mexican state of Tamaulipas, on the Rio Grande, opposite Laredo, Texas.

Nunavut Territory A territory in northern Canada created for the Inuit, a Native American people.

O

Oaxaca A state in southeastern Mexico; conquered by the Spanish in 1521, was the home of Bento Juárez and Porfirio Díaz.

Ontario Canadian province in the east central part of the nation, lying north of the Great Lakes and south of Hudson Bay.

Ottawa Canada's capital city, located in the province of Ontario.

Ohio River A major river flowing from Pittsburgh southwestward to the Mississippi River. Continues to serve transportation needs of the United States.

P

Pacific Coast States A region of the United States that includes California, Oregon, and Washington.

Pacific Ocean A large body of water that stretches from the Arctic to Antarctica along the western boundaries

of North and South America.

Panama A nation in Central America, connected to the continent of South America to the east. Borders the Caribbean Sea to the north and the Pacific Ocean to the South.

Panama Canal An important shipping lane built by the United States early in the 1900s. Links the Pacific Ocean with the Atlantic through the Caribbean Sea.

Pan-American Highway International highway system, extending from the United States-Canada border to Santiago, Chile; Mexico's primary road.

Pátzcuaro a town in the state of Michoacán, southwest Mexico; famous for its festivals.

Piedmont An area of rolling hills lying between the Atlantic Coastal Plain and Appalachian Mountains. Stretches from New Jersey to Alabama.

Plymouth Site of the landing of English colonists called Separatists or Pilgrims seeking religious freedom in 1620. In present-day Massachusetts.

Popocatépetl A volcano, sometimes active, in the Puebla state of southeastern central Mexico; stands almost 18,000 feet tall.

Portugal A nation on the Iberian Peninsula in south-western Europe. Explored, settled, and ruled Brazil as a colony.

Prince Edward Island Canada's smallest province on the eastern edge of the nation. Part of the Appalachian Highlands region.

Puebla A state in southeastern central Mexico; Puebla city is the fourth-largest in Mexico.

Puerto Rico An island commonwealth in the Caribbean Sea, transferred by Spain to the United States in 1898. One of four islands of the Greater Antilles.

Q

Quebec (city) A major Canadian city of French culture. Capital of the province of Quebec.

Quebec (province) The largest province and center of French culture in Canada. Located in eastern Canada.

R

Rio Grande Flows from Colorado southward into the Gulf of Mexico. The river marks the border between Texas and Mexico.

Rocky Mountains A chain of rugged

mountains in western North America. Stretches from Alaska through Canada and the United States into New Mexico.

Rocky Mountain States A region of the United States that includes Colorado, Wyoming, Montana, Idaho, Utah, and Nevada.

S

St. Lawrence River Flows from Lake Ontario and into the Gulf of St. Lawrence. Forms part of the boundary between the United States and Canada.

St. Lawrence Seaway A system of rivers, canals, and lakes that permits oceangoing ships to sail from the Atlantic Ocean to ports on the Great Lakes in central North America.

San Cristóbal de Las Casas A city in the southern Mexican state of Chiapas; today is a center of Highland Mayan culture.

San Francisco A major West Coast port and commercial center linking the United States with nations bordering the Pacific Ocean.

San Luis Potosí A state in central Mexico, northeast of León; a major industrial center, known especially for its silver mines.

San Miguel de Allende A town in the central Mexican state of Guanajuato; known for its large population of American citizens.

Saskatchewan A Canadian province in the central area of the nation. Landscape is occupied by vast Interior Plains.

Seattle Located in Washington in the Pacific Northwest. Serves as a major port linking the United States with the Pacific.

Siberia A vast northern area of Asia extending from the Ural Mountains to the Pacific Ocean. Native Americans, the first settlers in the Americas, crossed a land bridge from Siberia into modern-day Alaska.

Sierra Madre Occidental Range of mountains in Mexico running parallel to the Pacific Ocean coast and bordering the Mesa Central on the west; about 700 miles long.

Sierra Madre Oriental Range of mountains in Mexico running parallel to the Gulf of Mexico coast and bordering the Mesa Central on the east.

Sonora A state in northwestern Mexico on the coast of the Gulf of California; known for its silver mines.

Spain A nation on the Iberian Peninsula in south-western Europe. Explored, settled, conquered, and ruled (from the 1500s to the early 1800s) much of the Americas from the southern borders of the modern-day United States to the southern tip of South America.

Southwest States A region of the United States that includes Arizona, New Mexico, Oklahoma, and Texas.

Sun Belt An informal name for the region stretching from the southern states along the Atlantic coast through the Southwest into California. An area that has enjoyed rapid population and economic growth since the 1960s.

T

Taxco A town in the Mexican state of Guerrero known for the production of beautiful silver jewelry.

Tenochtitlán Capital of the ancient Aztec Empire. Located on the site of modern-day Mexico City.

Teotihuacán A town in the central state of México, 30 minutes northeast of Mexico City; site of famous Toltec ruins, including the Pyramid of the Sun, the Pyramid of the Moon, and of Quetzalcoatl.

Tijuana a town in Baja California Norte, in north-western Mexico; a popular tourist center and point of entry on the United States–Mexico border.

Toronto Capital and largest city of Ontario Province. Located in Canada's most heavily populated region.

Trinidad and Tobago A nation of the Lesser Antilles in the Caribbean Sea located north of South America. Composed of two islands.

U

United States of America A North American nation made up of 48 contiguous states, the District of Columbia, and Alaska and Hawaii.

Uxmal Ancient city in the state of Yucatán, southeast Mexico; capital of the later Mayan Empire.

V

Vancouver A major port city on Canada's southwestern coast. Provides important links between Canada and nations bordering the Pacific.

Vinland Part of North America settled by Leif Eiríksson and his Viking followers, about the year 1000.

W

Washington, D.C. The capital city of the United States, located near the Atlantic coast and on the borders of Virginia and Maryland.

Winnipeg A major midwestern Canadian city in southern Manitoba, near the United States border.

X

Xochimilco A lake in the Valley of Mexico, in central Mexico, only a few inches deep; site of the Floating Gardens of Aztec fame.

Y

Yucatán Peninsula A low, flat peninsula in southeast Mexico.

Yucatán Plain A major physical region of mainland Middle America of fertile flat land that extends south of the Yucatán Peninsula into Belize and Guatemala.

Yukon Territory Located in northwestern Canada along the Alaskan border. One of three territories in Canada.

Z

Zacatecas A state in central Mexico; known for its large mines and smelters.

This glossary will help you understand the Key Terms in this book and other important social studies terms.

A

abolish Do away with slavery.

abolitionists Those who favored doing away with slavery.

absolute location The unique spot on earth where a particular place is located, using coordinates of longitude and latitude.

absolute monarchs Hereditary rulers with life tenure whose powers are unlimited.

acid rain Sulfur and nitrogen released into the air by industries, killing vegetation.

adobe (ah·doh·bee) Native American house made of sun-dried mud and straw packed over wood.

affirmative action A policy or program to ensure equal opportunity in order to make up for past discrimination practices.

alliances Agreements between people or states to help one another.

Allied Powers France, Great Britain, Italy, and Russia, who were united in World War I against the Central Powers—Germany and Austria-Hungary.

allies Partners.

Allies Chiefly the United States, Great Britain, and the Soviet Union, who were united in World War II against the Axis Powers—Germany, Italy, and Japan.

amaranth A tall flowering plant with protein-rich seeds, grown by the Aztecs and used in their religious ceremonies.

amendments Changes to the Constitution.

Anaconda Plan The Union's strategy to divide the Confederacy and end the American Civil War, specifically by using blockades and controlling the Mississippi River.

Anansi Character in popular African folktales brought to the Caribbean.

Appalachian Mountains Eastern North America mountain range extending from Quebec to Alabama.

appeal A review of a lower court's ruling by a higher court.

archaeologists Scientists who study cultures of the past.

arid climate Excessively dry; having insufficient rainfall to support agriculture.

Arctic Attic Popular term referring to the vast spaces of Canada's Nunavut, Northwest, and Yukon Territories.

arms Weapons, including guns, bombs, or other devices.

Articles of Confederation (1781) First written Constitution of the United States, which emphasized the powers of the states.

asphalt Material used to pave roads.

assassinated Deliberately killed openly or secretly, often for political reasons.

assembly Group of elected representatives.

autocratic Kind of government in which one person has unlimited powers.

axis One of the horizontal or vertical lines that make up the grid of a line graph. Also, an imaginary line that runs from the North Pole and the South Pole.

Axis Powers Germany, Italy, and Japan, who were united in World War II against the Allies—chiefly the United States, Great Britain, and the Soviet Union.

Aztecs Native Americans that founded the Mexican empire conquered by Cortés in 1519.

B

barbecue Meat whole or split roasted over an open fire or a fire in a pit. The word is credited to the Taino language, from the Caribbean Island Native American tribe of the same name.

bauxite Mineral ore from which aluminum is refined. A large deposit has been found in Jamaica.

beavers Large, semiaquatic rodents at one time highly prized for their fur.

Beringia (beh·ren·gee·ah) Land bridge that connected Asia and the Western Hemisphere.

bilingual Ability to speak two languages with equal fluency.

Bill of Rights First ten amendments to the Constitution that guarantee the rights of the individual. Also, a document written by the English Parliament in 1689 that gave certain rights to the king's subjects.

Bleeding Kansas The name given the state of Kansas before the Civil War after violent debates between those who wanted Kansas to be a slave state and those who did not. Many people were killed

blockade A string of ships that blocks other ships from entering a harbor.

blues African American–derived songs usually describing loneliness or sadness.

board of county commissioners In the United States, the governing body of a county.

Boston Massacre Five colonists died when British soldiers fired into a crowd protesting British-imposed taxes.

Boston Tea Party Colonial protest where taxed tea was thrown into Boston harbor.

braceros Temporary laborers admitted legally into the United States to help with seasonal crop harvests.

brand A distinguishing mark made by burning with a hot iron—on cattle, for example—to identify ownership.

bribe Money or favor given or promised in order to influence the judgment or conduct of someone in a position of trust.

British Commonwealth of Nations An international group of nations that includes Great Britain and some of its former colonies.

British North America Act (1887) Created Canada's national government and gave Great Britain power to approve Canadian laws.

Brown v. Board of Education of Topeka, Kansas 1954 United States Supreme Court decision declaring school segregation unconstitutional.

bus boycott Organized nonviolent tactic used by African American citizens in Montgomery, Alabama, in 1955. They refused to ride the local buses until the segregated seating policy was changed.

C

cabinet Body of advisors of a head of state or a governor or a mayor.

cacao Beans used in making cocoa, chocolate, and cocoa butter.

Calgary Stampede July celebration in Calgary, Alberta, honoring the western heritage of Canada.

Calypso A type of music invented in the Caribbean. It is distinctive because the lyrics are emphasized rather than the instruments. Some consider it a distant cousin of rap music.

campesinos Rural land dwellers in Middle America.

Canada Day July 1 legal holiday once called Dominion Day.

Canadian Pacific Railway (1885) Stretched from the Atlantic to the Pacific.

capital resources Goods produced and used to produce other goods and services.

cardinal directions The directions north, south, east, and west.

carnival Season or festival of merrymaking before Lent.

carpetbaggers Northerners who moved to the South during Reconstruction for economic or political gain.

cartographer A person who makes maps.

cash crop A product that can be sold for a profit.

caudillo A Spanish or Latin American dictator.

ceiba A tree sacred to the Maya; it has wide, above-ground roots, a huge trunk and branches stretching to 130 feet.

cenotes Limestone sinkholes that collect water runoff from storms.

Central Lowlands Flat and grassy rich farmland in the United States Midwest.

Central Pacific Railroad/Union Pacific Railroad Combined to create first railway across the West, from Nebraska to California.

Central Powers Germany and Austria-Hungary, who were united in World War I against the Allied Powers—France, Great Britain, Italy, and Russia.

Central Valley Valley of Sacramento and San Joaquin Rivers in California.

checks and balances The system in which the three branches of government in the United States limit the powers of one another to balance equally each branch.

Chol Native American language; one of three branches of Maya spoken in the Mexican state of Chiapas.

civil disobedience A strategy for causing social change by means of nonviolent resistence to unfair laws.

civil rights Constitutional guarantee that all citizens will receive equal rights.

Civil Rights Act The law passed by the U.S. Congress in 1964 that ended segregation.

climate Average weather—temperature, wind velocity, precipitation—at a place over time.

Coastal Plain Flat land that reaches from Maine to Florida, in a narrow strip along the Atlantic coast, then widens westward to Texas along the Gulf of Mexico.

Coastal Range Mountains extending along Pacific coast west of the Sierra Nevada and north through British Columbia to Alaska.

Cochineal A insect of the Andes whose brilliant red body was used to produce a dye by Native Americans and then the Europeans.

Cold War The name given to the dangerous rivalry between the United States and the Soviet Union from 1945 to the 1990s.

Columbian Exchange A process of exchanging needed, or wanted, items between the Spanish and the Native Americans; initiated in the sixteenth century. Included plants, animals, ideas, and technologies. Negative exchanges included diseases.

commerce The exchange or buying and selling of commodities on a large scale involving transportation from place to place.

Committees of Correspondence Groups of colonists formed in the 1770s to protest against taxes imposed by the British.

commodities Products of agriculture, such as eggs, grain, and cattle.

commonwealth An association of self-governing autonomous states more or less loosely associated in a common allegiance (as to the British crown).

communism Form of government in which the government alone decides how to use the resources of its country.

Communist Party The political party that was largely responsible for the leadership of the Russian Revolution in 1917, and that continued as the dominating force in the development of the Soviet Union. Even after the break-up of the Soviet Union in the 1990s, the Communist Party is still influential in Russia. Its programs are based upon the general principles set forth by Karl Marx and Friedrich Engles in the Communist Manifesto (1848).

competition The relationship between two or more businesses striving for the same customers.

compromise To reach an agreement to solve a problem that benefits both sides.

Compromise of 1850 Admitted California to the Union as a nonslave state. Utah and New Mexico entered with no decision on slavery.

concentration camps Where war and political prisoners, and refugees are confined.

concessions Favors given by a country to a foreign company to encourage it to do business with that country.

Confederate States of America, Confederacy The name of the independent government formed by the seceding Southern states. South Carolina was the first state to withdraw from the Union, in December 1860. The following year Mississippi, Florida, Alabama, Georgia, Louisiana, and Texas followed. North Carolina, Tennessee, Arkansas, and Virginia seceded shortly after the Battle of Fort Sumter, in April 1861.

confederation An association to further the common interests of its members.

Congress The legislative branch of the United States.

conquistador Those who conquer. The conquistadors were the leaders of the Spanish conquest of the Americas.

consent Agreement by the people.

conserve To protect from loss or harm; to preserve.

Constitution Document written in 1787 to create a strong national government for the United States that shares powers with the states, governs through three branches, and protects the rights of individuals through the Bill of Rights.

Constitutional Convention Meeting of 59 delegates in Philadelphia in May 1787 to debate whether to keep or revise the Articles of Confederation.

Constitution Act of 1982 Revised Constitution

Consumers A buyer of goods or services for personal use.on putting Canadians in charge of their government.

contiguous Being in contact with—touching along a boundary or at a point.

Continental Army The American army during the American Revolution.

continental climate Cold, snowy winters and summers either short and cool or long and hot.

Continental Divide North America's watershed, where waters flow west, north, or east.

continental drift The theory that the

continents slowly and constantly move within the earth. Compare plate tectonics.

continents The major land masses of earth: Africa, Antarctica, Asia, Australia, Europe, North America, and South America.

Convert To change someone's religious or political beliefs.

coral polyps Tiny sea animals, with limestone skeletons, that form coral.

Corn Belt Region of the Midwest where corn is a major crop.

counterfeit Anything made in imitation of something else with the intent to deceive.

countries Geographical areas that are independent political units. Countries have their own governments, laws, and populations.

county seat In the United States, the town where county government is located.

coureurs de bois (coo·ruhr·duh·bwah) French trappers who traded with Native Americans in Canada.

creole (kree·ol) People born in New Spain, today's Mexico, of Spanish parents.

Creole A dialect of French or Spanish.

crown corporations Companies owned and controlled by national and provincial governments in Canada.

cultural diversity Different ways of life practiced by different groups of people.

cultural mosaic The term used in Canada to describe how its different cultures remain unique while forming a whole society.

culture Ways of life and beliefs of a people.

D

Day of the Dead A fall holiday when Mexicans go into cemeteries to honor their dead ancestors.

D-Day Day set for launching a military operation. D-Day in Europe during World War II was June 6, 1944.

death rate The number of deaths per hundred or per thousand persons in a given group within a given time.

deciduous forests Trees that shed their leaves in autumn. Found in temperate climates.

Declaration of Independence July 4, 1776, document explaining why the American colonies should be separate from England.

de facto segregation The separation of races in fact but not supported by law.

Defeat To beat or win victory over, as in war.

deforestation The removal of forests. Deforestation has contributed to erosion and the loss of soil. See reforestation.

degree Unit of measurement indicating distance between lines of latitude and longitude. Also, a unit of temperature expressed in Fahrenheit (F) or Centigrade (C).

Delegates People selected or elected to represent the wishes of others at a meeting or convention. *See* REPRESENTATIVES.

deltas Triangular-shaped plains of sediment where rivers flow into large bodies of water.

demand The quantity of a good or service wanted at a specific price and time. See supply.

Democratic Based upon the principles of democracy or social equality, as in a "democratic government."

democracy System of government in which power is held and exercised by the people.

Democratic Party One of two major political parties in the United States.

density As regards to population, the average number of individuals per space unit (e. g., per square mile). Determined by amount of rainfall, farmland fertility, or availability of natural resources.

deported Legally sent back to one's own country, usually because of illegal entry.

depression (economic) A period of low general economic activity marked especially by rising levels of unemployment.

desalination The process of changing salty seawater into freshwater that can be used for drinking and irrigation, also called desalinization.

desert Very dry, barren land.

desert climate Less than 10 inches (25 cm) of rain a year.

Desert Storm The United States' military operation in 1991 to free Kuwait from the invading Iraqi forces.

desert vegetation Cactus and scrub bush grow here, but little else.

developed (country) One with a high level of industrialization and standard of living.

developing (country) Poor one trying to build an economy and a higher standard of living.

dictator Ruler with absolute power. An example was Adolf Hitler. See totalitarian.

Diplomats Persons, such as ambassadors, who have been appointed to represent a government in its relations with foreign governments.

Diversity Differing from one another. The United States is a land of diversity because many people live there.

distribution map Shows distribution of people, resources, climate, and vegetation.

District of Columbia Federal district that is the seat of the United States government.

Dominion Day Original name for the July 1 legal holiday in Canada celebrating self-governing status in 1867. Now called Canada Day.

Dred Scott v. Sanford 1857 Supreme Court case that ended compromises over slavery. The court said that Congress did not have the right to exclude slavery from the territories or the states.

Drought A shortage of rainfall.

dry climate Found within the temperate latitudes and near the tropical latitudes.

dry temperate grasslands Grasslands well suited for grazing.

due process Legal procedures outlined in the Constitution and amendments to protect an individual's rights.

Dust Bowl United States Southwest made barren by droughts and wind storms in the 1930s.

E

Earth Day April celebration in the United States observed to show concern for the environment.

earthquake A shaking or trembling of the earth that is volcanic or tectonic in origin.

Eastern Hemisphere The half of the earth east of the prime meridian.

ecology Study of the way plants and animals relate to one another and the environment.

ecosystem The complex of a community of organisms and its environment functioning as an ecological unit in nature.

ecotourism Ecological tourism. Entry fees to national preserves pay for the upkeep of the parks.

"El D.F." Mexican shorthand for the capital Mexico City.

El Niño An irregularly occurring flow of

unusually warm surface water along the western coast of South America that is accompanied by abnormally high rainfall in usually arid areas and that prevents upwelling of nutrient-rich cold deep water, causing a decline in the regional fish population. *See* la niña.

electoral college (United States) Delegates that officially elect the president and vice president.

electronic media Computers, radio, television, and movies.

elevation Height above sea level.

Ellis Island New York City port where most people from Europe entered America from 1892 to 1954.

Emancipation Proclamation President Abraham Lincoln's order on New Year's Day, 1863, freeing all slaves living in the Confederate states disloyal to the Union.

embargo A legal prohibition on commerce

emingrated/emigration Moving away from one's country to live elsewhere. See immigration.

environment All the surroundings of a place, such as land, water, weather, plants, and the changes people have made.

Environmental Protection Agency (EPA) Established by the United States government in 1970 to fight pollution.

Entrepreneur A person who starts his or her own business.

Equator Imaginary line circling the earth halfway between the North and South Poles, dividing the earth into two hemispheres.

Erie Canal First United States canal, from Albany, New York, to Buffalo, New York.

erosion Slow wearing away of soil and rocks by glaciers, running water, wind, or waves.

estuary A water passage where the tide meets a river current, especially an arm of the sea at the lower end of a river.

ethanol Ethyl alcohol, fuel made from sugar.

ethnic heritage One's ancestry.

ethnicity Refers to the quality or affiliation of people with the same cultural background, united by language, religion, or ancestry.

evergreen forests Trees with leaves that stay green year-round. Exist throughout the temperate latitudes.

executive (branch) Carries out laws

passed by Congress. Headed by the president.

export To carry or send (as a commodity) to some other place (as another country). See import.

F

Faction A group of people who form a political group, such as a political party.

fall line Line marking the point where rivers descend from upland to lowland.

fault lines Breaks in the earth's crust.

federalism System of government where the national government and the states share power.

federal government The national government, which makes laws for the nation.

fiesta patronal (fee·ess·tah) Saint's day celebration in Spain and Middle and South America.

First Continental Congress Congress of colonial representatives that voted to stop all trade with England until the Intolerable Acts were repealed.

Five Themes of Geography Location, Place, Human-Environmental Interaction, Movement, and Region—the concepts used to describe a place on the earth.

forced migration The act of people involuntarily being moved from one country, place, or locality to another. The Trail of Tears is an example of this.

foreign affairs Relationships between nations.

foreign trade The buying and selling of goods between countries.

forest vegetation Exists in highland, temperate, and tropical climates.

fossil fuels Nonrenewable fuels, such as coal, oil, or natural gas, formed in the earth from plant or animal remains.

fossils Remains of plants or animals that lived long ago, preserved in rock.

Four Corners Where Arizona, New Mexico, Utah, and Colorado meet.

Fourteen Points President Woodrow Wilson's plans for peace, proposed ten months before the end of World War I. Terms called for fair treatment of Germany and redrawn boundaries, especially in Eastern Europe.

free enterprise The foundation of a capitalist economy, where private citizens, not government, make decisions to produce and market goods.

This system in the United States operates with some government regulation to protect workers, customers, and the environment.

Freedmen's Bureau Organization created by President Lincoln and Congress that provided food, shelter, and medical care for freed slaves in the South. The bureau also helped needy whites, and ultimately provided medical care for more than a million people.

French and Indian War War fought in North America between the French and Native Americans and the British colonies, 1754–63.

futbol Throughout Latin America, the name of the game known here as soccer. It is the most popular sport in the world.

G

garifuna People of mixed African and Native American descent who live along the Atlantic coast of Central America, from Belize to Nicaragua.

gauge Distance between railroad tracks.

General Assembly Legislative branch of the government of North Carolina.

Geographical Information Systems (GIS) A computer system that records, stores, displays, and analyzes information about the features making up the earth's surface. GIS can generate two- or three-dimensional images of an area showing such features as hills, rivers, roads, and power lines.

Gettysburg Address President Abraham Lincoln's speech on November 19, 1863, dedicating the famous Pennsylvania battlefield cemetery of the Civil War.

glaciers Great sheets of ice moving slowly down a slope or valley.

Global Positioning System (GPS) Navigational aid that uses satellites to find absolute location.

global interdependence The theory that every country in the world is affected by what happens in other countries; much of the interdependence among nations is economic in nature, based on the production and trading of goods and services.

global warming The scientific theory that the earth is steadily getting hotter because the protective ozone layer is slowly but surely being eroded by man-made pollutants.

globalization The process of increasing the realtionships and interdependence of the world's markets and businesses.

"God Save the Queen" The anthem of Great Britain and Canada's national anthem until 1980.

gold rush A rush to newly discovered gold fields in pursuit of riches.

"Good Neighbor Policy" During Presidents Herbert Hoover's and Franklin Delano Roosevelt's administrations, a determination to cooperate with Latin American nations instead of using military power to bully them. This policy is generally considered to have been a success.

goods Something manufactured or produced for sale.

governor The highest executive in state government.

governor general Canada's official head of state. The queen of England's representative.

Grand Banks Shoal in the Atlantic Ocean southeast of Newfoundland. An area of historically rich fishing until recently.

Grand Canyon Colorado River gorge in the northwestern corner of Arizona. It is more than 1 mile (1.61 km) deep.

grasslands vegetation Exists in highland, temperate, and tropical climates.

Great Basin Low, dry region in the western United States between the Sierra Nevada and Wasatch Range.

Great Compromise An agreement during the Constitutional Convention (1787) in which delegates agreed that there would be two houses in the legislative branch of government. One house would have an equal number of representatives from each state. In the other house, representation would be based on population.

Great Depression The most devastating economic downturn in the nation's history. This depression began in October 1929 and raged throughout the 1930s.

Great Lakes Chain of five lakes—Superior, Michigan, Huron, Erie, and Ontario—in central North America.

Great Plains Plains west of the Central Lowlands in North America. Dry, with almost no trees.

grid A network of uniformly spaced horizontal and perpendicular lines (as for locating points on a map).

gross domestic product The total value of a country's goods and services produced in a given year.

Group of Eight (G-8) Organization of eight major industrial nations who meet periodically to discuss world economics and other issues. Established September 22, 1985. Members are Canada, France, Germany, Italy, Japan, Russia, the United Kingdom, and the United States.

guerrilla wars (guh·rill ·ah) Conflicts between groups of people who want change and dictators.

H

habitat The place or environment where a plant or animal naturally or normally lives and grows.

haciendas (ah·see·en·dahs) Large estates, usually in Spanish-speaking countries.

Harlem A famous Manhattan, New York City, community that was a center of African American culture in the early twentieth century.

harpoons Barbed spears or javelins used to hunt fish or whales.

Harvard College First college in the United States, founded in 1636.

haven A safe place.

hierarchy The classification of a group of people according to ability or to economic, social, or professional standing.

hieroglyphic Writing in picture symbols, not words.

high-tech industry Businesses that require specialized systems to make something.

highlands climate Determined by elevation—the higher a place is, the colder and windier.

Hispanic Latin Americans who speak Spanish or Portuguese. Those who have emigrated to the United States have come mainly from Middle America and South America.

Hispaniola (hiss·pan·nyo·lah) One of the four islands of the Greater Antilles in the Caribbean Sea. Site of the first permanent colony in the Americas (present-day Haiti and the Dominican Republic).

House of Burgesses Virginia's group of elected representatives.

House of Representatives One of two houses of the United States Congress.

hub The connection center of a transportation network. By 1860, Chicago had become a railroad hub for more than ten companies.

Hudson River School Art movement of the early nineteenth century in the United States characterized by landscape paintings of New York's Hudson Valley.

human characteristics of place Cultural and government elements of a place.

human-environmental interaction One of the Five Themes of Geography. Describes a place in terms of the environment's effect on humans who live there and how humans affect that environment.

human resources The workforce; also called human capital.

humid subtropical climate Cool, rainy summers and mild, rainy winters.

humid temperate grasslands Grasslands that grow on flat or rolling plains in fertile areas suitable for growing grain.

hunting and gathering Collection of food by killing game, catching fish, or eating edible wild plants.

hurricanes Tropical storms with winds of 74 miles (119 km) per hour or greater.

hydroelectric (high·drow·ee·leck·trik) The production of electricity by water power.

I

Ice Age A period of time that lasted for millions of years, when glaciers covered most of the earth.

ice hockey National sport of Canada.

igloos Inuit houses made of sod, wood, or stone when permanent or of blocks of snow or ice when temporary.

illiterates People who cannot read or write.

immigrants People who come to a country to take up permanent residence.

immigration The act of entering—and usually becoming established in—a country of which one is not a native for permanent residence. See emigration.

import To bring (as merchandise) into a place or country from another country. See export.

indentured servants English colonists to the Americas who agreed to work without pay in exchange for free passage across the Atlantic Ocean and room and board.

Independence Day The day the Declaration of Independence was adopted, July 4, 1776.

Indians Columbus's mistaken term for Native Americans he found in the

Caribbean. He thought he had landed in the Asian East Indies.

Indigo A deep blue dye made from xiquilite, a Central American plant.

Industrial Revolution Term for sweeping changes in the way goods were produced and the way people lived and worked. Began in England and spread throughout the world.

industrialized Any country with industries that produces goods its people need.

inequality Occurs when a few have more money or political power than others. Discrimination based on ancestry is a big factor.

infant mortality The number of infant deaths in a given time or place.

infrastructure The system of public works of a country, state, or region. Also, the resources—personnel, buildings, equipment—required for an activity.

Institutional Revolutionary Party (PRI) The political party that ruled Mexico from 1921 until 2000, when the National Action Party won the national election.

intermediate directions Directions between the cardinal directions—northeast, southeast, southwest, and northwest.

internal migration Moving from one place to another in the same country.

International Date Line Imaginary line, mainly along the 180°E longitude in the Pacific Ocean, that marks the boundary between one day and the next.

Internet Network of computer users and information.

Intolerable Acts American colonists' term for the laws passed by the British Parliament in response to the Boston Tea Party.

Inuit Native Americans who settled the far North of North America.

Iroquois Large Native American association of the Eastern Woodlands. Included the Cayuga, Mohawk, Oneida, Onondaga, Seneca, and Tuscarora people.

irrigation The watering of dry land by means of streams, canals, or pipes to grow crops.

isolationism A policy of national isolation by abstention from alliances and other international political and economic relations.

isthmus (Any narrow strip of land connecting large mainlands. Also called land bridges.

J

jai alai Court game similar to handball, popular in Cuba.

James Bay Project Hydroelectric power station in northern Quebec.

jazz Music derived from spirituals and blues.

Jim Crow laws Legal enforcement of discrimination against African Americans.

joint stock companies Special partnerships to raise monies for businesses.

judicial (branch) The United States Supreme Court and federal courts, which interpret laws passed by Congress.

Judiciary The branch of government that interprets the law; the court system.

Juries A group of citizens who listens to evidence given at civil and criminal trials and makes decisions as to the guilt or innocence of the accused person on trial.

K

Kansas-Nebraska Act (1854) Overturned the Missouri Compromise.

kayaks Inuit canoes.

Ku Klux Klan A post–Civil War secret society that supported white supremacy. These hate groups intimidated—and killed—African American men, women, and children.

L

land redistribution Division of large land holdings among the poorer citizens in an effort to relieve poverty.

landform A shape on the earth's surface, such as a plain, mountain, or valley.

landlocked Enclosed or nearly enclosed by land.

Landmarks Anything that easily recognizable, such as features of the landscape, monuments, buildings, or other structures.

"last best west" Phrase used in newspaper ads in 1885 urging people to come to Canada.

La Niña An irregularly occurring flow of unusually cold ocean temperatures in the eastern equatorial Pacific that is accompanied by wetter than normal conditions across the Pacific Northwest and dryer and warmer than normal conditions across much of the southern tier; winter temperatures are warmer than normal in the Southeast and cooler than normal in the Northwest. See el niño.

La Raza Cosmica (Cosmic Race) Complimentary term used by Mexicans to refer to the diversity of their population.

latitude Distance north or south of the Equator, expressed in degrees (°).

lava Molten rock under the earth's surface.

League of Nations President Woodrow Wilson's proposed international mediating body that offered provisions for the security of every country. His dream was turned down by the American public in the presidential election of 1920.

leeward Being in or facing the direction toward which the wind is blowing.

legislative (branch) Congress, which passes laws. There are two congressional houses, the Senate and the House of Representatives.

Legislature An elected or appointed body of people (representatives) with the responsibility and power to make laws for a province, state, or nation. See ASSEMBLY.

Lent The 40 days between Ash Wednesday and Easter. A time of penance and prayer.

Lexington and Concord Sites of the first battles of the American Revolution.

Lichen Plant-like growths of fungi and algae that are combined and form a crust-like growth on rocks or tree trunks.

life expectancy The average life span.

Line of Demarcation Drawn by Spain and Portugal dividing the Western Hemisphere. Spain kept lands west of the line, Portugal east of it.

literacy rate The degree to which a group of people can read and write.

literacy tests Used by some states to keep African Americans from voting by requiring people to read before being allowed to register to vote. The practice was outlawed by the Voting Rights Act passed in 1965. See also polls.

Livestock Farm animals, such as beef cattle, dairy cows, sheep, hogs, chickens and turkeys.

location One of the Five Themes of Geography. Describes a place by its nearness to other places (relative location) or by its exact latitude and longitude (absolute location).

loess (less) Fertile, powdery, rockless soil found in North America, Europe, and Asia.

longitude Distance east or west of the prime meridian, expressed in degrees (°).

Lords Proprietors English owners of the colony of Carolina, present-day North Carolina and South Carolina.

loran Long-range navigation system used to find absolute location of a ship or airplane.

Lost Colony English colony attempted on Roanoke Island in modern-day North Carolina. All colonists disappeared before organizers returned. They had been delayed by England's sea battle with the Spanish Armada.

Louisiana Purchase In 1803, the United States acquired territory from France that would later become the states of Louisiana, Arkansas, Missouri, Minnesota, Iowa, Oklahoma, Kansas, Nebraska, North Dakota, South Dakota, Wyoming, Montana, and parts of Colorado.

Loyalists Colonists who sided with Great Britain in the American Revolution.

M

machetes Large, heavy knives used for cutting sugarcane and underbrush and as a weapon.

malnutrition Inadequate nutrition caused by poor diet.

Manifest Destiny The belief common in America in the 1800s that it was the fate of the United States to expand west to the Pacific Ocean; the phrase was coined in 1845 by journalist John L. O'Sullivan.

map key List of map symbols with explanation of what each symbol stands for.

map projection A way of representing a three-dimensional object on a two-dimensional surface.

Maple Leaf Canada's national flag.

maquiladora Mexican factory that assembles parts or raw materials from the United States into finished products; more than 1 million Mexicans work in the maquiladoras.

Mardi Gras Literally, Fat Tuesday, the last day of carnival celebration before Lent begins.

mariachi Mexican street band.

marimba A band of several people playing a xylophone at the same time.

Marine West Coast climate Cool, rainy summers and mild, rainy winters.

Marshall Plan United States aid to Europe after World War II.

mass production The making of goods in large quantities in factories, often using standard designs and assembly lines.

Massachusetts Fifty-fourth Most famous African American regiment of the Civil War.

Maya (migh·yah) Native Americans of Yucatán Peninsula in Mexico, Belize, and Guatemala.

Mayflower Compact (1620) Agreement among Pilgrims for a government of "just and equal laws" made aboard their ship, the Mayflower, before landing in Massachusetts.

mechanized farming Farming dependent on machinery to complete the work.

Mediterranean climate Hot, dry summers and mild, rainy winters.

megalopolis Thickly populated region encompassing more than one city.

mercantilism System of unequal trade established by England at the expense of the colonists.

mercenaries Soldiers who fight for money.

meridian Any line of longitude west or east of the prime meridian.

Mesa Central Middle region of Mexico—the central part of the Mexican Plateau. Mexico City and Puebla are located here.

Mesa del Norte Northernmost section of the Mexican Plateau. It lies between the Sierra Madre Oriental and the Sierra Madre Occidental.

mestizo (meh·stee·zoh) Person of mixed European and Native American ancestry. About half of the Mexican people are mestizo.

metropolitan Cities and the suburbs that surround them.

Mexican-American War (1846–48) Won by the United States. Under terms of the treaty, the United States acquired territory that would become Texas, California, Nevada, Utah, most of Arizona, and parts of New Mexico, Colorado, and Wyoming.

Mexican Revolution Initially, the uprising against Porfirio Díaz and his dictatorship; evolved into fighting between Mexicans with different ideas about Mexico's future.

mezcla Spanish for "mixture"; refers to the Mexican population.

Mid-Atlantic Eastern region of the United States: New York, New Jersey, Pennsylvania, Maryland, and the District of Columbia.

Mid-Atlantic Ridge Longest mountain chain in the world, 2.5 miles (4.03 km) underwater in the Atlantic Ocean.

Middle America Mexico, Central America, and the Caribbean Islands.

Middle Passage Long ocean voyage from Africa to America that brought slaves to the New World.

migrate To move from one region to another.

militia Army of citizens who come together during a crisis.

minerals Natural substances, such as iron, copper, or salt, obtained by digging.

minutemen American colonial citizen soldiers who would show up at a moment's notice when fighting broke out.

missions Self-contained villages built by missionaries to try to convert Native Americans to Christianity.

Missionaries People sent to another place to spread a religion.

Mississippi River Longest river in the United States, flows from north central Minnesota to the Gulf of Mexico.

Missouri Compromise (1820) Agreement in Congress admitting Missouri to the Union as a slave state and Maine as a nonslave state.

Mixtec Primary Native American language spoken in the Mexican state of Oaxaca.

Mojave Desert Desert of the Great Basin in the western United States.

monarchy Undivided rule or absolute sovereignty by a single person.

Monopoly Control by one business over the production or sale of a good or service.

monotheism Belief in one god.

Monroe Doctrine Policy begun by President James Monroe prohibiting European involvement in the affairs of the Western Hemisphere.

Mormons Members of the Church of Jesus Christ of Latter-day Saints.

mosaic Decoration made with small

pieces of variously colored material to form pictures or patterns. Canadiens compare their country to a mosaic.

movement One of the Five Themes of Geography. Describes a place by its movement of people, goods, and ideas.

mulattoes People of mixed European and African ancestry.

multinational Of or relating to more than two nationalities (a multinational society) or more than two nations (a multinational alliance); or having business divisions in more than two countries (a multinational corporation).

municipal Referring to local self-government of towns and cities.

mural A large picture painted directly on the walls and ceilings of buildings.

muskeg Wet and spongy flat lowland areas that are part of the Canadian Shield region of northern North America.

N

NAACP The National Association for the Advancement of Colored Persons, an organization that won a series of court cases that eventually overturned Plessy v. Ferguson.

NAFTA North American Free Trade Agreement between Canada, the United States, and Mexico.

Nahuatl Primary Native American language spoken in east central Mexico.

National Action Party Mexican political party that defeated the Institutional Revolutionary Party in 2000.

National Park System Created by the United States Congress in 1916. There are more than 384 acres in the system for recreation.

National Road Connected Maryland with territory north of the Ohio River. This improvement in transportation encouraged people to settle in the Midwest.

nationalized Ownership of industries taken over by the government.

Native Americans First people in the Western Hemisphere, not including the Inuit.

naturalized Those born in other countries who have been made citizens of the United States.

NATO An Alliance of nations, inlcuding the United States, Canada, and the United Kingdom, as well as other European nations. It was created to counter the Communist threat of the Soviet Union in Europe during the Cold War.

Navigation The process of plotting or directing the course of a vessel, usually a ship or airplane.

neighborhoods Communities moved into by immigrants to America that reminded them of home, where people spoke their language and shared their culture.

neutral Any country not engaged with any other country that is at war.

New Deal The legislative and administrative program of President Franklin D. Roosevelt designed to promote economic recovery and social reform during the 1930s.

New England Region in the northeastern United States: Connecticut, Maine, Massachusetts, Vermont, New Hampshire, and Rhode Island.

New France Possessions of France in North America before 1763.

New Laws of the Indies Spanish laws passed in the early 1500s banning the slavery of Native Americans.

nonrenewable resource Fuel, such as coal, gas, and natural gas, formed in the earth from plant or animal remains. See renewable resource.

NORAD The North American Aerospace Defense Command (NORAD). NORAD is a joint United States and Canadian organization charged with the missions of aerospace warning and aerospace control for North America. Aerospace warning includes the monitoring of man-made objects in space, and the detection and warning of attack against North America whether by aircraft, missiles, or space vehicles.

north arrow On most maps, a small arrow that points to the North Pole.

Northern Hemisphere The half of the earth north of the Equator.

Northwest Passage Rumored link between Atlantic and Pacific Oceans. It was never found.

nuclear weapon A device, such as a bomb or warhead, with great explosive power coming from the release of atomic energy.

Nunavut Newest territory of Canada created for the Inuit people. Also, Inuit word that means "our land."

O

obsidian Dark natural glass formed by cooling of molten lava.

"O Canada" Canada's national anthem.

oligarchy A government in which a small group exercises control, especially for corrupt and selfish purposes.

Oregon Trail The primary westward route across the country used by settlers of the Northwest in the 1840s and 1850s.

Otomi Primary Native American language spoken near Mexico City and in the Mexican states of Puebla and Veracruz.

overfishing When more fish are caught in a fishing ground than are hatched yearly.

override A bill becomes law without the president's signature; an override occurs when, after a president has vetoed a bill, Congress passes the bill with at least two-thirds of the votes in each house.

P

Pacific Rim Countries in or bordering on the Pacific Ocean.

Panama Canal Ship canal across the Isthmus of Panama built by the United States. Opened August 1914.

paracaidistas Rural Mexicans who move to Mexico City in huge numbers each year in search of a better life.

parallels Any lines of latitude north or south of the Equator.

pardon Forgiveness granted by the president to lawbreakers.

Parliament Supreme legislative body in Canada and Great Britain.

parliamentary government A system of government having the real executive power vested in a cabinet composed of members of the legislature who are individually and collectively responsible to the legislature.

party An organized political group.

patents Licenses giving inventors exclusive rights to make, use, or sell their inventions.

Patriots Colonists who wanted to be independent of England.

patron saint Special guardian of a person, place, or activity.

Petroleum A substance that occurs naturally formed from the remains of animals and plants that lived millions of years ago in a marine (water) environment. Over time, heat and pressure from layers of mud and rock helped the remains turn into crude oil . The word "petroleum" means "rock oil" or "oil from the earth." It also refers to crude oil and oil products in all forms. When distilled, it yields gasoline, kerosene, paraffin, and fuel oil, and other products which are used in fuels, lubricating oils, asphalt, and other products.

permafrost Permanently frozen soil below ground level, found in arctic regions.

physical map Shows landforms and elevation.

physical characteristics of place Natural features and landforms of a place.

Piedmont Rolling hills connecting the mountains and the Coastal Plain on the East Coast.

Pilgrims English religious group persecuted for not joining the Church of England. They founded Plymouth Colony.

place One of the Five Themes of Geography. Describes a spot on the earth by its physical (landforms and climate) and human (cultural and government) characteristics.

plank roads Made from wooden boards, built along stretches where heavy wagons traveled regularly. These roads were common in this country during the 1850s.

plantation (plan·tay·shun) Large farming estate where mainly one crop is grown.

plate tectonics Theory that the continents move around on large plates of rock. Compare continental drift.

Plateau A relatively flat highland.

plaza Public square in a city or town.

Plessy v. Ferguson 1896 United States Supreme Court decision making segregation legal.

political map Gives information about nations, states, provinces, counties, or cities.

polls The places where votes are cast or recorded. The Ku Klux Klan tried to keep African Americans away from the polls after the Civil War. See also literacy tests.

poll taxes Payments required of people who wanted to vote. The Voting Rights Act of 1965 made this illegal.

polytheism Belief in more than one god.

popular vote Vote by citizens. In the presidential election in the United States, citizens vote for members of the electoral college.

population distribution The statistical detailing of distinct populations within a certain area, state, or country, usually expressed in map or graph form.

population growth rate The percentage of population increase in a specific place over a specific period of time.

population profile Graph that shows the characteristics of a country's population.

Porfiriato The name for the long rule (1876–1911) in Mexico of the caudillo Porfirio Díaz, a mestizo hero in the fight against the French. He was toppled by the Mexican Revolution.

postindustrial Describes today's society. Technology that produces knowledge and information.

prejudices Negative opinions formed beforehand or without knowledge or examination of the facts; bias.

prairie Land that has deep fertile soil, tall coarse grasses, and few trees.

precedents Standards for others to follow.

precipitation A deposit on the earth of hail, mist, rain, sleet, or snow.

president Head of the executive branch.

presidential government A system of government, as in the United States, in which the president is constitutionally independent of the legislature.

primary industries Those industries that gather and sell natural resources—oil, natural gas, minerals, timber, and farm crops.

prime meridian Line of longitude (0°) from which longitude east and west is measured.

prime minister Chief executive of a parliamentary government.

print media Newspapers, books, and magazines.

provinces Political divisions of a country, as in Canada, similar to states in the United States.

Prosperity Economic growth and high employment rates; an economic boom.

public opinion The views of the people on a topic.

pueblo Dwelling of Native Americans in southwestern United States. Also the name used by the Spanish for the people who lived there.

Puritans English religious group persecuted for their faith. They founded Massachusetts bay Colony.

Q

quaternary economic activities Those activities responsible for collecting, processing, and manipulating information; for example, business management and data processing.

quetzal A bird sacred to the Maya; an endangered species that cannot live in captivity, and is thus a symbol for freedom.

quotas Laws limiting the number of immigrants.

R

racism The belief that one race is superior to another.

radar Navigation system that uses radio waves to detect and locate objects.

rain shadow effect Exists when mountain peaks block rain from the leeward side.

ratify To approve and sanction formally. A majority of a state's votes for an amendment, making it an article of their state constitution or the United States Constitution.

rebelled To have resisted, refused to support, or opposed with force a government or ruler.

Reconstruction President Lincoln's plan to reorganize and rebuild the defeated South after this country's Civil War.

recycling Discarding glass, paper, or metal for reuse.

redistribution of wealth The shifting wealth from a rich minority to a poor majority. Income redistribution has been the focus of some international development efforts.

reforestation The action of renewing forest cover by planting seeds or young trees. See deforestation.

reform To make changes that improves a government or organization.

refugee A person who flees to a foreign country or power to escape danger or persecution.

reggae Jamaican music with chants and a strong, steady beat that is popular throughout the Caribbean.

region One of the Five Themes of Geography. A region is a particular place on earth that contains many similar characteristics, such as landforms, climate, natural resources, language, and politics, among others.

relative location Approximate location found by using nearby references.

religion A personal set or institutionalized system of religious attitudes, beliefs, and practices.

religious persecution Being treated unfairly because of one's religious beliefs.

Religious Toleration Act Colonial Maryland law giving religious freedom to most faiths.

renewable resource One that is capable of being replaced by natural ecological cycles or sound business practices. See nonrenewable resource.

repeal Revoke or undo a law through legislation.

representative democracy That system of government in which the many are represented by persons chosen from among them, usually by election. See republic.

Representatives People selected or elected to stand for and vote for the wishes of others at a meeting or convention. See DELEGATES.

republic Form of government in which people elect their leaders by voting. See representative democracy.

Republican Party One of two major political parties in the United States, formed in 1854 by opponents of slavery.

reservations Tracts of land set aside by the government beginning in 1871. Native Americans were relocated to these reservations, and some of their descendants continue to live there today.

resistance Opposing something that you disapprove of or disagree with.

retirement community Group of retired people living together within a larger society.

retreated Having withdrawn all troops to a new position in order to escape the enemy's forces or after a defeat.

revolution Overthrow of an existing political system and its replacement with another.

Ring of Fire A rim of volcanoes, from Japan to Alaska to Chile, encircling the Pacific Ocean.

ritual Ceremonies or traditions used in a place of worship or for special occasions.

rivalry Competition.

rock 'n' roll Music derived from jazz, rhythm and blues, country, and gospel.

Rocky Mountains Mountain range extending from northern Alaska to New Mexico. Also western region of the United States: Colorado, Wyoming, Montana, Idaho, Utah, and Nevada.

Rough Riders Members of the 1st U. S. Volunteer Cavalry regiment in the Spanish American War commanded by Theodore Roosevelt.

royal proclamation Orders publicly announced by the king or queen in a monarchy.

rural Open land usually used for agriculture.

S

sapodilla Central American tree that produces chicle, which is used to make chewing gum.

sanctions Measures taken by one or more nations to apply pressure on another nation to conform to international law or opinion. Such measures usually include restrictions on or withdrawal of trade, diplomatic ties, and membership in international organizations.

scalawags White Southerners who supported Reconstruction after the American Civil War, often for private gain.

scale Relative size as shown on a map, such as one inch = 100 miles (161 km).

scarcity Limited resources; when society does not have enough resources to produce enough to meet people's wants.

scientific farming Applying the findings of science to farming.

seasons The four quarters into which the year is divided: spring, summer, autumn, winter.

secede To withdraw from an organization. Southern states seceded from the Union in the early 1860s, setting off the Civil War.

Second Continental Congress (1775) Chose George Washington to head the Revolutionary War against the British.

secondary economic activities Those activities in which workers take raw materials and produce something as a finished product; for example, manufacturing.

secondary industries Those industries that make goods from primary products.

secular Not controlled by a religious body or concerned with religious or spiritual matters.

sediment Mud and soil particles small enough for river water to carry.

segregated Practicing the separation or isolation of a race, class, or ethnic group by discriminatory means, as in a segregated society.

Senate One of two houses of the United States Congress.

Separatists Those who wish Quebec to be separate from Canada.

separate but equal The idea, approved by the United States Supreme Court in Plessy v. Ferguson (1896), that the entrenched policies of segregation were legal, that segregation did not violate African American rights under the Constitution.

service industries Productive or profit-making enterprises that help people and businesses, such as restaurants, banks, and schools.

sharecropping Financial arrangement whereby former slaves and poor white farmers rented farmland and shared a portion of the harvest with the landowners. Sharecroppers, however, rarely made a profit, and the system prevented African Americans from getting out of poverty.

Sherman's March Union General William T. Sherman's devastating Civil War campaign from Atlanta to Savannah, Georgia, in 1864.

Silicon Valley California headquarters for computer companies.

slash-and-burn farming Clearing land for planting by cutting and burning vegetation.

slavery Owning people as property.

smelting Using furnaces to separate metal from mined ore.

Smithsonian Institution Collection of many famous museums in Washington, D.C.

smog Fog made heavier and darker by smoke and chemical fumes.

snowshoes Light oval frames strengthened by crosspieces and strung with thongs. Allows someone to walk on soft snow without sinking.

socialist One who advocates or practices socialism: a system or condition of society in which the means of production are owned and controlled by the state.

Social Security A U. S. government program established in 1935 to include old-age and survivor's insurance, contributions to state unemployment insurance, and old-age assistance. This was one of FDR's New Deal programs.

software The entire set of programs, procedures, and related documentation associated with a computer system.

Southeast Eastern region of the United States: Virginia, Tennessee, West

Virginia, Kentucky, North Carolina, South Carolina, Georgia, Florida, Alabama, Mississippi, Louisiana, and Arkansas.

Southern Hemisphere The half of the earth south of the Equator.

Sovereignty A country's power and ability to rule itself and manage its own affairs.

Spanish Armada Fleet of war ships that invaded England and was defeated, beginning Great Britain's domination of the Atlantic Ocean and eventually North America.

spawn Refers to fish laying eggs.

spirituals Emotional religious songs developed by African Americans.

St. Lawrence Seaway Waterway of locks, canals, and the St. Lawrence River that permits passage of deep-draft vessels between the Atlantic Ocean and the Great Lakes.

Stamp Act Passed by the British Parliament in 1765 imposing taxes on the colonists.

standard of living In economics, the measure of consumption and welfare of a country, community, class, or person. Individual standard-of-living expectations are heavily influenced by the income and consumption of other people in similar jobs.

Stanley Cup National Hockey League championship trophy.

state government Makes state laws. Shares power with the federal government.

steelpan Music from the Caribbean played by hammering on oil drum bottoms.

steppe Level and treeless areas in regions of extreme temperature range and loess soil.

steppe climate Not as dry as desert climates. Sometimes called semiarid regions.

stereotype Something conforming to a fixed or general pattern.

stock A share in business ownership.

storm surges Large waves created by hurricane winds that can cause enormous destruction and flooding.

strikes The stoppage of work by a number of workers with the purpose of reaching a certain end.

strip mine An efficient, though controversial, method of extracting coal by stripping soil from veins of coal. Environmentalists say that this

method causes erosion.

subarctic climate Found in northern Canada and most of Alaska. Very cold but warm enough for trees to grow.

subjects People who are under the rule of another or others, such as a king or queen in a monarchy.

subregion A subdivision of a region; one of the primary divisions of a biogeographic region.

subsistence agriculture Farming or a system of farming that produces a minimum and often inadequate return to the farmer.

suburbs Communities on the edge of cities.

suburb Small community that is connected to a large city.

Sun Belt Warm states stretching from California to Florida.

supply The act or process of filling a want or need; the quantities of goods or services offered for sale at a particular time or at one price. See demand.

Supreme Court (United States) Highest judicial court in the land.

surplus More than of what is needed or required. See SCARCITY.

surrendered/surrender When soldiers give up fighting.

sustainable resource A resource harvested or used in such a way that it is not depleted or permanently damaged.

sweatshops A shop or factory in which workers are employed for long hours at low wages and under unhealthy conditions.

symbols Anything that stands for something else, such as a blue line standing for a highway on a map.

T

tariffs Taxes imposed by a government on imported goods.

taro Tropical plant grown for its edible tuber, similar to a potato.

tax A fee charged by a government on goods, services, or income.

telecommuter One who works at home via telephone and computer.

temperate Having a moderate climate.

temperate climate Characterized by a lack of extremes in temperature.

tenement houses Rundown apartment buildings.

tepee (tee·pee) Skin-covered tent once used by Native Americans of the Great Plains.

terraced fields Series of horizontal ridges made in a hillside to increase arable land, conserve moisture, and minimize erosion.

territories Political divisions in Canada with less power than provinces.

terrorism Generally thought to be the use, or threatened use, of violence, including killing or injuring people or taking hostages, to intimidate a government in order to achieve a goal, usually political. Terrorist acts take many forms and occur all over the world. They are not confined to one place, one religion, or one form.

terrorists Individuals or groups, some sponsored by governments, who systematically use violence in an attempt to make nations change their ways of doing things.

tertiary economic activities Those activities promoting, distributing, selling, or using what is made from raw materials; for example, education, finance, office work, and retailing.

textiles Machine-produced cloth.

theocracy A government that claims to rule with divine authority. Iran is an example.

Thirteenth Amendment The legislative change to the Constitution in 1865 that abolished slavery in the United States.

Three-Fifths Compromise An agreement reached by delegates to the Constitutional Convention in which enslaved African Americans would be counted as three fifths of an individual for purposes of population.

Tidewater The area along the coast where waters rise and fall each day from ocean tides.

tiendas Mexican shops.

Tierra Caliente Or Hot Land. Central American elevation zone that extends from sea level up to about 2,500 feet. Temperatures are hot, and the main crops are bananas, sugarcane, and rice.

Tierra Fria Or Cold Land. Central American elevation zone that extends from about 6,000 feet to 12,000 feet above sea level. Main activities here are growing potatoes and grains, and grazing livestock.

Tierra Helada Or Icy Land. Central American elevation zone above 12,000 feet.

Tierra Templada Or Temperate Land. Central American elevation zone that extends from about 2,500 feet to 6,000 feet. Most people in this region live in this zone, where temperatures are mild. Major crops are coffee, corn, wheat, and vegetables.

time zone A geographical region within which the same standard time is used.

toleration Allowing people to follow their own beliefs, especially religious.

toll A fee charged for the use of roads or bridges.

Toltecs The people that dominated central and southern Mexico prior to the Aztecs.

topographic Of, relating to, or concerned with topography.

topography The art or practice of graphic delineation in detail usually on maps or charts of natural and man-made features of a place or region, especially in a way to show their relative positions and elevations.

tornado A violent destructive swirling wind accompanied by a funnel-shaped cloud that progresses in a narrow path over the land.

totalitarian Of or relating to a political regime based on subordination of the individual to the state and strict control of all aspects of the life and productive capacity of the nation, especially by force. See dictator.

trade Dealings between persons, groups, or countries; the business of buying and selling or bartering commodities.

trade deficit When one country buys more goods from other countries than it sells.

trade surplus When one country sells more goods to other countries than it buys.

trade winds Those that blow almost constantly toward the Equator from the northeast.

trading partners Countries that trade closely with each other.

Trail of Tears Forced migration of Cherokee Native Americans from the Southeast to Indian Territory in 1830.

transcontinental railroad The first rail system that connected the east and west coasts of America. The Union Pacific Railroad, laying track westward from Omaha, Nebraska, met the Central Pacific Railroad, laying track eastward from Sacramento, California, on May 10, 1869, at Promontory, Utah.

transnational Extending or going beyond national boundaries. Transnational corporations are those that do business with other countries.

Treaty of Paris 1763 treaty. France ceded most of its North American empire to England.

Treaty of Paris 1783 treaty between the United States of American and Great Britain. Ended the American Revolutionary War.

tribal governments A governing body of a tribe, community, village, or group of Native Americans or Alaska Natives.

tributaries Rivers or brooks feeding larger rivers or brooks or lakes.

Tropic of Cancer Latitude 23.5°N that marks the northern boundary of the Tropics.

Tropic of Capricorn Latitude 23.5°S that marks the southern boundary of the Tropics.

tropical grasslands Grasslands that grow in lowland areas of the Tropics.

tropical rain forests Marked by lofty broad-leafed evergreens forming a continuous canopy.

tropical rain forest climate Annual rainfall of at least 100 inches (254 cm). Alternates between hot and rainy seasons.

tropical savanna climate Alternates between rainy and dry seasons.

Tropics The region lying between the Tropic of Cancer (23.5°N) and the Tropic of Capricorn (23.5°S), where temperatures remain hot all year.

truck farms Farms that produce vegetables for the market.

trust territories Territories supervised by other nations. Guam and American Samoa are territories of the United States.

Tsotsil Native American language; one of three branches of Maya spoken in the Mexican state of Chiapas.

tsunamis (soo·nah·meez) Huge destructive ocean waves caused by earthquakes and volcanic eruptions.

tundra Vast, treeless plain in the northern parts of North America, Asia, and Europe.

tundra vegetation Includes lichens, mosses, algae, and—briefly in the short summers—wild flowers.

tundra climate Arctic or subarctic with a layer of permafrost below ground.

Tzeltal Native American language; one of three branches of Maya spoken in the Mexican state of Chiapas.

U

umiaks Open Inuit boat made of a wooden frame covered with animal hide.

Underground Railroad Escape system by which fugitive slaves were secretly helped to reach the North or Canada.

union A group of workers who are organized for the purpose of gaining better wages, hours, and other benefits.

Union The northern states that fought to preserve the United States during the Civil War.

Union Jack United Kingdom flag.

United Nations An international organization established in October 1945 whose purpose was, and is, to maintain international peace and security.

United States Constitution In 1787, the Articles of Confederation were dropped in favor of this document, which emphasized a stronger national government and the rights of the individual.

urban Of, relating to, characteristic of, or constituting a city.

urbanization Process by which the proportion of a population living in or around towns and cities increases through migration as the agricultural population decreases. A relatively recent phenomenon, dating back only about 150 years to the beginning of the Industrial Revolution.

V

vegetation Plant life.

veto To reject a bill passed by Congress.

vice president Second in command to the president; also serves as president of the Senate.

Virgin of Guadalupe The patron saint of Mexico.

volcano A vent in the crust of the earth from which usually molten or hot rock and steam come forth.

voluntary migration To move from one country, place, or locality to another as an act of free will. See forced migration.

GLOSSARY

W

War Hawks Congressmen who urged President James Madison to wage war against Great Britain prior to the War of 1812.

War of 1812 War between the United States and Great Britain in 1812.

Warsaw Pact A Cold War Alliance between the Societ Uion and Central and Eastern European Communist nations.

Washington, D.C. The capital of the United States.

water pollution The contamination of waters, especially with man-made waste.

watershed A region or area bounded peripherally by a divide and draining ultimately to a particular watercourse or body of water.

wattle and daub A construction method for some Native American homes. Wattle is poles intertwined with twigs, reeds, or branches, used for walls and roofs. Daub is the mud or clay or other substance that is smeared over the wattle to create a solid surface.

weather State of the atmosphere with respect to heat or cold, wetness or dryness, calm or storm, clearness or cloudiness.

Western Hemisphere The half of the earth west of the prime meridian.

wigwams Native American huts in North America having a framework of poles overlaid with tree bark or animal hides.

Wilderness Road Opened up over the Appalachian Mountains into Kentucky by Daniel Boone.

windward Being in or facing the direction from which the wind is blowing.

World Bank An autonomous agency that has a functional relationship with the United nations. Provides loans and technical assistance for economic development projects in developing member countries; encourages co-financing for projects from other public and private sources.

World War I War fought in Europe between the Central Powers and the Allied Powers, 1914–1918.

World War II War fought in Europe, North Africa, Asia, and the Pacific Ocean between the Allies and the Axis, 1939–1945

Y

Yucatec Maya Primary Native American language spoken in the Yucatán Peninsula.

Z

Zapatista National Liberation Army Anti-NAFTA protesters, mainly Mayan farmers from Chiapas, who are concerned with issues of self-government and the survival of Native American cultural identity.

Zapotec Primary Native American language spoken in the Mexican state of Oaxaca.

zero growth No increase in population in a specific area over a given time.

Acknowledgements

52, Excerpt from *Five Letters: 1519-1526* by Hernándo Cortés, translated by J. Bayard Morris, Copyright 8 {196C}. Reprinted by permission of W.W. Norton & Company; **199-200,** Excerpt from *The Promised Land* by Mary Antin, Copyright 8 1912. Reprinted by permission of Houghton Mifflin Company. All rights reserved; **201,** Excerpt from *The Jungle* by Upton Sinclair, Copyright 8 1971. Reprinted by permission of R. Bentley; **300,** Excerpt from *Wooden Ship,* Copyright 8 1978 by Jan Adkins. Reprinted by permission of Houghton Mifflin Company. All rights reserved; **320,** Excerpt from *The Treeless Plains,* Copyright 8 1967 by Glen Rounds. Reprinted by permission of Holiday House; **387,** Taken from *A Prairie Boy's Summer,* Copyright 8 1975 by William Kurelek, published by Tundra Books; **493,** Excerpt from *The Brief and Summary Relation of the Lords of New Spain* by Alonso de Zorita, translated and edited by Benjamin Keen, page 213, Copyright 8 1963. Used by permission of Rutgers University press.

Index

Infodex, Raleigh, North Carolina

Maps

Mapping Specialists Limited

Illustrations

R.W. Cloudt: 458; **DECODE, Inc.:** 14, 36, 40, 56, 76, 86, 91, 112, 113, 117, 141, 146, 178, 196, 213, 222, 237, 243, 257, 276, 277, 306, 311, 312, 314, 325, 345, 365, 390, 427, 445, 468, 487, 505, 515, 541; **Precision Graphics:** 7 (t), 8, 21, 26, 32, 80, 114, 192, 202, 323, 342, 356-7, 357, 380-1, 383, 386, 400, 407, 425, 444-5, 476-7, 498, 564-5.

Photographs

ALCOA Aluminum Company of America; **AP** Associated Press/WideWorld Photos; **DJ/NCSU** Dan Johns/North Carolina State University; **DSG** Doreen Sullivan-Garcia; **JA/NCSU** Jim Alchediak/North Carolina State University; **JG** Jimmy Garcia; **JJ** John Jenkins III; **LC** Library of Congress; **MMA** Mint Museum of Art, Charlotte, North Carolina; **NASA** National Aeronautics and Space Administration; **NCC** North Carolina Collection, UNC-Chapel Hill Library; **NCMH** North Carolina Museum of History; **NCT** North Carolina Division of Travel and Tourism; **NGS** National Geographic Society; **NH/NCSU** Neal Hutcheson/North Carolina State University; **OMCTR** Ontario Ministry of Culture, Tourism and Recreation; **PAM** Provincial Archives of Manitoba; **PRC** Picture Research Consultants; **UNC** University of North Carolina; **UPI** United Press International.

xiv, (t) NH/NCSU, (b) Bob Jordan/AP; **1,** (t) Bob Jordan/AP, (b) Ric Feld/AP; **2,** (t) Jay Sailors/AP; **2-3,** Dave Martin/AP; **3,** (t) Buddy Mays/Corbis, (m) Phil Schermeister/Corbis, (b) Eric Gay/AP; **4,** (t) Annie Griffiths Belt/Corbis, (m) Courtesy of the Panama Empanada Factory; **5,** (t) Kelly-Mooney/Corbis, (m) Ric Vasquez/AP, (bl) Tim Thompson/Corbis, (bm) Little Rock Convention & Visitors Bureau; **6,** (l) Joseph Sohm/Corbis, (m) Seth Perlman/AP, (br) JA/NCSU; **6-7,** Carlos Osorio/AP; **7,** (tr) Richard Cummins/AP; (m) Beth Keiser/AP, (ml)Kevin Fleming/Corbis; **8,** (tr) Valan Photos, (mr) JA/NCSU, (m) Jon Hicks/Corbis, (br) Dallas & John Heaton/Corbis; **9,** (t) Don Heupel/AP, (b) NCMH, (br) David Muench/Corbis; **10,** (t) Richard T. Nowitz/Corbis, (tr) Bettmann/Corbis, (m) Craig Aurness/Corbis, (br) Joel Andrews/AP; **10-11,** James P. Blair/Corbis; **11,** (t) James P. Blair/Corbis, (br) Buddy Mays/Corbis; **12,** Orange County Economic Development Commission; **14-15,** Photo Library International/Corbis; **16,** (b) Peter Fredin/AP, (br) NASA/AP; **18,** NH/NCSU; **24,** (m) Bettmann/Corbis, (bl) Bettmann/Corbis; **24-25,** MMA, Gift of Mr. and Mrs. Maurice R. Smith; **25,** (ml) William Hubbell/Woodfin Camp, (mr) Courtesy of Intergraph Corporation, (bl) NASA; **30,** (bl) Courtesy of Garmin International, Inc., (br) Charles W. Campbell/Corbis; **32,** Gary Braasch/Corbis; **34,** (bl) NGS, (bm) JA/NCSU; **34-35,** NGS; **35,** NGS; **36,** NASA; **37,** (l) Carl Pellegrini Photography, (r) Annie Griffiths Belt/Corbis; **39,** Office du Tourisme de la Martinique; **41,** JJ; **42,** DJ/NCSU; **43,** JA/NCSU; **45,** NH/NCSU; **47,** Scott T. Smith/Corbis; **49,** (t) William Russ/NCT, (m & b) NCT; **52-53,** Tony Morrison/South American Pictures; **54,** (t) Bettmann/Corbis; **54-55,** G. Dagli-Orti (Paris); **58,** DJ/NCSU; **61,** (l) MMA, Gift of Mr. Harold Kaye, (r) Courtesy of Dr. Charles Ewen; **62,** (l) JA/NCSU; **62-63,** Woodfin Camp; **64-66,** NCMH; **67,** Mark C. Burnett/Photo Researchers; **69,** NCT; **72,** (t) Archivo Iconografico/Corbis, (b) "Christopher Columbus," by Sebastiano del Piombo, Metropolitan Museum of Art; **73,** NCT; **76,** (t) Archivo Iconografico/Corbis, (m) Organization of American States Photo Library; **76-77 & 77,** Rare Book Collection, UNC-Chapel Hill Library; **78,** Bettmann/Corbis; **79,** Peter Harholdt/Christie's/Corbis; **80,** Historic New Orleans Collection, Accession No. 1952.3; **81,** NCC; **82,** Association for the Preservation of Virginia Antiquities; **83,** Jerry Cotten/NCC; **84,** Bettmann/Corbis; **85,** Archive Photos; **86,** NCMH; **87,** New Hampshire Historical Society; **90,** (t) "William Penn," by Francis Place/Historical Society of Pennsylvania, (b) Archive Photos; **91,** Art Resource; **93,** (t) Chuck Burton/AP, (m) AP, (b) Ross Taylor/AP; **96-97,** Yale University Art Gallery; **98,** (t) Bettmann/Corbis; **98-99,** Yale University Art Gallery; **99,** (r) Guilford Courthouse National Military Park; **101,** Richard T. Nowitz/Corbis; **102,** (t) Bettmann/Corbis, (b) Pilgrim Society/Pilgrim Hall Museum; **103,** Library of Congress; **104,** Bettmann/Corbis; **107,** Archivo Iconografico/Corbis; **108,** (t) Courtesy of the Massachusetts Historical Society, (b) Bettmann/Corbis; **109,** Courtesy of the Bostonian Society/Old State House; **110,** (t) Courtesy of the Massachusetts Historical Society, (bm) Bettmann/Corbis; **110-111,** Bettmann/Corbis; **111,** (m) Bettmann/Corbis; **111,** Corbis; **114,** Art Resource; **115,** Metropolitan Museum of Art; **116,** (m) Bettmann/Corbis, (bl) Courtesy of the Massachusetts Historical Society, (br) Bettmann/Corbis; **117,** (ml) Yale University Art Gallery, (mr) Corbis, (bl) National Archives and Records Administration, (br) Yale University Art Gallery; **118,** Corbis; **122,** (t) Bettmann/Corbis; **122-123,** Joseph Sohm/Corbis; **123,** (bl) Monticello/Thomas Jefferson Foundation, (r) NCC; **125,** (t) National Archives and Records Administration, (b) Bettmann/Corbis; **126,** Corbis; **127,** Bettmann/Corbis; **128,** Independence National Historical Park; **130,** Archivo Iconografico/Corbis; **131,** (t) Archivo Iconografico/Corbis, (b) Courtesy of the Smithsonian National Numismatic Collection; **132 & 133,** Bettmann/Corbis; **134,** (t) Montana State Capitol, (b) NGS; **135,** (m) Missouri Historical Society, (bl) State Historical Society of South Dakota, (br) Rare Book Collection, UNC-Chapel Hill Library; **136,** "A View of New Orleans taken from the Plantation of Marigny," (1803), by Boqueto de Woieseri, also known as "The American Eagle Over New Orleans," Chicago Historical Society 1932.0018; **137,** Bettmann/Corbis; **138,** David H. Wells/Corbis; **139,** "The Trail of Tears," by Robert Lindneux, Woolaroc Museum, Bartlesville, Okla.; **141,** (t) California State Library, Sacramento, (b) Science Museum/E. T. Archive; **142,** Bettmann/Corbis; **143,** Layne Kennedy/Corbis; **146,** (t) NCMH, (bl) AP, (br) Bettmann/Corbis; **147,** State Archives of North Carolina; **149,** (l) Bettmann/Corbis, (r) Warner Collection, Gulf States Paper Corporation; **150,** (l & inset) Bettmann/Corbis; **151,** New York Public Library; **152,** Sophia Smith Collection, Smith College; **153,** AP; **154,** Southern Historical Collection, UNC-Chapel Hill Library; **155,** Anne S. K. Brown Military Collection, Brown University; **156,** (ml) Museum of the Confederacy, (bl) Southern Historical Collection, UNC-Chapel Hill Library; **156-157,** Corbis; **157,** (ml & br) Bettmann/Corbis; **158,** (m) Bettmann/Corbis, (bl) Corcoran Gallery of Art/Corbis, (br) "Distant Thunder," by Mort Kuntsler, Courtesy of Kuntsler Enterprises, Ltd.; **159,** (ml) Bettmann/Corbis, (mr) Art Resource, (bl) Archive Photos, (br) Bettmann/Corbis; **160 & 161,** Bettmann/Corbis; **162,** (l) Bettmann/Corbis, (r) JA/NCSU, Courtesy of the Nashville Depot; **163,** Bettmann/Corbis; **164,** (tr) NCC, (bl) JA/NCSU; **165 & 166,** State Archives of N. C.; **170,** (t) Rare Book Collection, UNC-Chapel Hill Library, (b) Courtesy of the Mariners' Museum, Newport News, Va.; **172,** NCC; **173,** (l) David Muench/Corbis, (r) NCC; **174-175,** Archive Photos; **176,** Bettmann/Corbis; **177,** State Archives of N. C.; **178,** Albany Institute of History & Art; **179,** NCC; **180,** Bettmann/Corbis; **182,** (t) Corbis, (b) Bob Rowan/Progressive Image/Corbis; **183,** Bettmann/Corbis; **184,** Corbis; **185,** Karen Tweedy-Holmes/Corbis; **186,** (ml) Craig Aurness/Corbis, (bm) SEF/Art Resource, (br) Archives Snark/Art Resource; **187,** (mr) Bettmann/Corbis, (bl) Andrew J. Russell Collection, Oakland Museum of California, (br) Underwood & Underwood/Corbis; **188,** Bettmann/Corbis; **189,** Photography Collection, University of Maryland-Baltimore County; **194,** (t) Stephanie Maze/Corbis; **194-195,** NH/NCSU; **195,** Karen Tam/AP; **196 & 197,** Corbis; **198,** Bettmann/Corbis; **199,** Corbis; **200,** Bettmann/Corbis; **202 & 203,** Ellis Island Immigration Museum; **204,** Lewis W. Hine/Corbis; **205,** Corbis; **206 & 207,** Bettmann/Corbis; **208,** Corbis; **209,** Lewis W. Hine/Corbis; **210 & 211,** Bettmann/Corbis; **212,** Macduff Everton/Corbis; **213,** AP; **214,** Karen Tam/AP; **215,** Library of Congress; **218,** (t) Corbis, **218-219,** Bettmann/Corbis; **219,** Fort Bragg Historical Office; **220,** Bettmann/Corbis; **221,** The Granger Collection; **222,** Hulton-Deutsch/Corbis; **223,** (mr) The Granger Collection, (b) Corbis; **225,** National Portrait Gallery, Smithsonian Institution/Art Resource; **226 & 228,** Bettmann/Corbis; **229,** (t) Bettmann/Corbis, (b) Picture Research Consultants; **230 & 231,** Bettmann/Corbis; **232,** (ml) Oscar White/Corbis, (mr) Paul J. Fair/Corbis, (br) Bettmann/Corbis; **232-233,** Underwood & Underwood/Corbis; **233,** (ml & mr) Bettmann/Corbis; **234,** Corbis; **235,** UPI/Bettmann/Corbis; **236,** (t) AP, (b) Bettmann/Corbis; **237,** Hulton-Deutsch/Corbis; **238,** AP; **240,** (t) NCMH, (b) Rare Book Collection, UNC-Chapel Hill Library; **241,** Japanese American National Museum; **242,** AP; **243,** State Archives of N. C.; **246,** (t) AP; **246-247,** NASA; **247,** (r) NCSU Southeastern Plant Environment Laboratory, Courtesy of Carole Saravitz; **248,** NASA; **249-251,** Bettmann/Corbis; **252,** Sovfoto; **253,** AP; **254,** Beth A. Keiser/AP; **255,** AP; **256,** Courtesy of Alex M. Rivera; **257,** UPI/Bettmann/Corbis; **258,** Bettmann/Corbis; **259,** UPI/Bettmann Newsphotos/Corbis; **260,** Bettmann/Corbis; **261,** Courtesy of Burton F. Beers, Jr.; **262,** (l) Bettmann/Corbis, (r) State Archives of N. C.; **263,** (ml) Corbis, (bl) UPI/Bettmann Newsphotos/Corbis, (br) JA/NCSU; **264,** Kobal Collection; **265,** Jim Stratford/Burlington Industries; **266,** John Hayes/AP; **267,** (l) L. Clarke/Corbis, (r) Courtesy of the Nokia Corporation; **268,** Owen Franken/Corbis; **272-273,** Simon Griffiths Photography, Courtesy of Linda Peterson, E. C. Brooks Elementary School (Raleigh, N. C.); **274,** (t) Bettmann/Corbis; **274-275,** Daniel Laine/Corbis; **275,** (r) North Carolina A & T University; **277,** (t) JA/NCSU, (b) John Cross/AP; **278,** National Weather Service (Raleigh, N. C.); **279,** Tom Bean/Corbis; **281,** Jim McNee/The Photo File; **283,** MCNC, Courtesy of Dr. Tom Krakow; **284,** Pictorial Parade/Archive Photos; **285,** (mr) Bettmann/Corbis, (m) Archive Photos, (bl & b) Earth Observation Satellite Company; **286,** Simon Griffiths Photography; **287,** Nict Ut/AP; **288,** Don McKenzie/UNC Hospitals; **289,** Bettmann/Corbis; **290,** (l) Reuters/Bettmann/Corbis, (r) Bettmann/Corbis; **291,** JA/NCSU, Courtesy of Houghton Mifflin Company; **292,** NH/NCSU, Courtesy of Linda Peterson, E. C. Brooks Elementary School (Raleigh, N. C.); **293,** Ben Margot/AP; **296,** (t) Jason Plotkin/AP; **296-297,** NCT; **298,** George Ranalli/Photo Researchers; **299,** Toby Talbot/AP; **300,** (l) MMA; **300-301,** "New York Harbor," by Fitz Hugh Lane, Bettmann/Corbis; **301,** (t) Peabody Essex Museum, (ml) "Building of the Frigate *Philadelphia*, Bettmann/Corbis, (br) Ships Locked in Ice Off of Ten Pound Island, Gloucester, by Fitz Hugh Lane, Bettmann/Corbis; **302,** Judy Griesedieck/Corbis; **303,** Craig Line/AP; **304,** DJ/NCSU; **305,** Jeff Greenberg/Hulton/Archive/Getty; **306,** Richard T. Nowitz/Corbis; **307,** "In the Catskills" (1836), by Thomas Doughty, Reynolda House Museum of American Art, Gift of Barbara B. Millhouse; **308,** Jeff Greenberg/Archive Photos; **309,** JA/NCSU; **311,** James Blair/NGS; **312,** JA/NCSU; **316,** "Spring Turning" (1936), by Grant Wood, Reynolda House Museum of American Art; **317,** Gerald L. French/The Photo File; **320,** Bettmann/Corbis; **321,** Jeff Christensen/Reuters/Bettmann/Corbis; **323,** John Swart/AP; **324,** Cheyenne Rouse Photography; **326-327,** Bettmann/Corbis; **327,** (ml) Bettmann/Corbis, (mr) Western History Collections, University of Oklahoma Libraries; **328,** U. S. Bureau of Reclamation; **329,** Scott Riggan/NCSU; **330,** JA/NCSU; **332,** Martin Rogers/Woodfin Camp; **333,** Ed

CREDITS